T0211947

Lecture Notes
in Business Information Processing 215

More information about this series at http://www.springer.com/series/7911

Anne Persson · Janis Stirna (Eds.)

Advanced Information Systems Engineering Workshops

CAiSE 2015 International Workshops
Stockholm, Sweden, June 8–9, 2015
Proceedings

 Springer

Editors
Anne Persson
University of Skövde
Skövde
Sweden

Janis Stirna
Stockholm University
Stockholm
Sweden

ISSN 1865-1348   ISSN 1865-1356   (electronic)
Lecture Notes in Business Information Processing
ISBN 978-3-319-19242-0   ISBN 978-3-319-19243-7   (eBook)
DOI 10.1007/978-3-319-19243-7

Library of Congress Control Number: 2015939171

Springer Cham Heidelberg New York Dordrecht London

Printed on acid-free paper

Springer International Publishing AG Switzerland is part of Springer Science+Business Media
(www.springer.com)

Preface

The Conference on Advanced information Systems Engineering (CAiSE) has traditionally been focusing on aspects that intersect our field – technological and human, theoretical and application, organizational and societal. CAiSE 2015 focuses on creativity, ability, and integrity in information systems engineering in order to design, develop, and deploy artifacts that can extend the boundaries of human and organizational capabilities. The 27th CAiSE was held in Stockholm, Sweden, June 8–12, 2015.

It has been an established tradition that each year CAiSE is accompanied by a significant number of high-quality workshops. Their aim is to address specific emerging challenges in the field, to facilitate interaction between stakeholders and researchers, to discuss innovative ideas, as well as to present new approaches and tools. This year, CAiSE had two associated working conferences (BPMDS and EMMSAD) and ten workshops. The accepted workshops were chosen after careful consideration, based on maturity and compliance with our usual quality and consistency criteria.

This volume contains the proceedings of the following seven workshops of CAiSE 2015 (in alphabetical order):

- The Second International Workshop on Advances in Services DEsign based on the Notion of CApabiliy (ASDENCA)
- The Third International Workshop on Cognitive Aspects of Information Systems Engineering (COGNISE)
- The First International Workshop on Digital Business Innovation and the Future Enterprise Information Systems Engineering (DiFenSE)
- The First International Workshop on Enterprise Modeling (EM 2015)
- The First Workshop on the Role of Real-World Objects in Business Process Management Systems (RW-BPMS)
- The 10th International Workshop on Trends in Enterprise Architecture Research (TEAR)
- The Fifth International Workshop on Information Systems Security Engineering (WISSE)

The 11th International Workshop on Enterprise and Organizational Modeling and Simulation (EOMAS) published post-proceedings in a separate LNBIP volume. The First International iStar Teaching Workshop (iStarT) and the First International Workshop on Socio-Technical Perspective in IS development (STPIS) published their proceedings in the CEUR Workshop Proceedings series. Each workshop adhered to the CAiSE 2015 submission and acceptance guidelines. The paper acceptance rate for the workshops included in these proceedings was approximately 43%.

As workshop chairs of CAiSE 2015 we would like to express our gratitude to all workshop organizers and to all corresponding scientific committees of the workshops for their invaluable contribution.

June 2015

Anne Persson
Janis Stirna

The 2nd International Workshop on Advances in Services DEsign based on the Notion of CApabiliy – ASDENCA 2015

Preface

Lately the notion of *capability* is gaining much presence within the field of Information Systems Engineering, due to a number of factors: the notion directs business investment focus, it can be used as a baseline for business planning, and it leads directly to service specification and design. Historically, it has been examined in Economics, Sociology, and Management Science. More recently, it has been considered in the context of business-IT alignment, in the specification and design of services using business planning as the baseline, in Enterprise Architecture, and in Service Oriented Architecture.

Capability is commonly seen as an *ability* or *capacity* for a company to deliver value, either to customers or shareholders, right beneath the business strategy. It consists of three major components: business processes, people, and physical assets.

Thus it is as an abstraction away from the specifics of how (process), who (agent), and why (goals), i.e. with focus on results and benefits. At the same capability should allow fairly straightforward integrations with the mentioned established bodies of knowledge and practices, such as goals (through "goal fulfillment"), processes (through "modeling"), and services (through "servicing").

The idea for the ASDENCA workshop has come from the academic and industrial community gathered in EU/FP7 project – CaaS. The special theme of the 27th edition of CAiSE was Creativity, Ability, and Integrity in IS Engineering. As systems are moving beyond traditional information management and need to organically blend into the environment appealing to large and diverse user bases, capability orientation in IS design with services may play an important role in novel solutions making use of information from different sources that need to be merged and molded to become meaningful and valuable (creativity), capable to deliver business in excellent, competitive and agile way (ability), as well as in ensuring quality in ethical codes – modifications by authorized parties, or only in authorized ways (integrity).

The Program Committee selected five high-quality papers for the presentation on the workshop, which are included in this proceedings volume. Divided in four sessions, the program of the workshop included two paper sessions reflecting important topics of capability-oriented IS design: modeling, and applications; an invited talk, and a discussion panel.

We owe special thanks to the Workshop Chairs of CAiSE 2015 for supporting ASDENCA workshop, as well as for providing us facilities to publicize it. We also thank the Program Committee for providing valuable and timely reviews for the submitted papers.

April 2015

Jelena Zdravkovic
Oscar Pastor
Peri Loucopoulos

ASDENCA 2015 Organization

Organizing Committee

Jelena Zdravkovic	Stockholm University, Sweden
Pericles Loucopoulos	University of Manchester, UK
Oscar Pastor	University of Valencia, Spain

Program Committee

Jaelson Castro	Universidade Federal de Pernambuco, Brazil
Lawrence Chung	The University of Texas at Dallas, USA
Dolors Costal	Universitat Politècnica de Catalunya, Spain
Sergio España	PROS Research Centre, Spain
Jānis Grabis	Riga Technical University, Latvia
Paul Johannesson	KTH Royal Institute of Technology, Sweden
Dimitris Karagiannis	University of Vienna, Austria
Evangelia Kavakli	University of the Aegean, Greece
Marite Kirikova	Riga Technical University, Latvia
Lidia Lopez	Universitat Politècnica de Catalunya, Spain
Kalle Lyytinen	Case Western Reserve University, USA
Selmin Nurcan	Université de Paris 1 Panthéon - Sorbonne, France
Antoni Olivé	Universitat Politècnica de Catalunya, Spain
Andreas Opdahl	University of Bergen, Norway
Ilias Petrounias	University of Manchester, UK
Naveen Prakash	MRCE, India
Jolita Ralyté	University of Geneva, Switzerland
Gil Regev	École Polytechnique Fédérale de Lausanne, Switzerland
Kurt Sandkuhl	The University of Rostock, Germany
Jorge Sanz	IBM Research, USA
Isabel Seruca	Universidade Portucalense, Portugal
Janis Stirna	Stockholm University, Sweden
Victoria Torres	Universidad Politécnica de Valencia, Spain
Francisco Valverde	Universidad Politécnica de Valencia, Spain
Hans Weigand	Tilburg University, The Netherlands
Carson Woo	University of British Columbia, Canada

The 3rd International Workshop on Cognitive Aspects of Information Systems Engineering – COGNISE 2015

Preface

Cognitive aspects of information systems engineering is an area that is gaining interest and importance in industry and research. In recent years, human aspects and specifically cognitive aspects in software engineering and information systems engineering have received increasing attention in the literature and conferences, acknowledging that these aspects are as important as the technical ones, which have traditionally been in the center of attention. This workshop was planned to be a stage for new research and vivid discussions involving both academics and practitioners.

The goal of this workshop is to provide a better understanding and more appropriate support of the cognitive processes and challenges practitioners experience when performing information systems development activities. Understanding the challenges and needs, educational programs as well as development supporting tools and notations may be enhanced for a better fit to our natural cognition, leading to better performance of engineers and higher systems' quality. The workshop aimed to bring together researchers from different communities such as requirements engineering, software architecture, design and programming, and information systems education, who share interest in cognitive aspects, for identifying the cognitive challenges in the diverse development-related activities.

The 3rd edition of this workshop, held in Stockholm on June 9, 2015, was organized in conjunction with the 27th International Conference on Advanced Information Systems Engineering (CAiSE 2015). This edition attracted 15 international submissions, continuing the trend of increasing interest in this workshop. Each paper was reviewed by three members of the Program Committee. Of these submissions, seven papers were accepted for inclusion in the proceedings (45%). The papers presented at the workshop provide a mix of novel research ideas, presenting research in progress or research plans.

We hope that the reader will find this selection of papers useful to be informed and inspired by new ideas in the area of Cognitive Aspects of Information Systems Engineering, and we are looking forward to future editions of the COGNISE workshop following the three editions we had so far.

June 2015

Irit Hadar
Barbara Weber

COGNISE 2015 Organization

Organizing Committee

Irit Hadar	University of Haifa, Israel
Barbara Weber	University of Innsbruck, Austria

Program Committee

Daniel M. Berry	University of Waterloo, Canada
Xavier Franch	Universidad Politecnica de Catalunya, Spain
Stijn Hoppenbrouwers	HAN University of Applied Sciences, Arnhem and Radboud University, Nijmegen, The Netherlands
Marta Indulska	University of Queensland, Australia
Joel Lanir	University of Haifa, Israel
Meira Levy	Shenkar College of Engineering and Design, Israel
Jan Mendling	WU Vienna, Austria
Jeffrey Parsons	Memorial University, Canada
Jakob Pinggera	University of Innsbruck, Austria
Hajo Reijers	VU University of Amsterdam and TU Eindhoven, The Netherlands
Pnina Soffer	University of Haifa, Israel
Irene Vanderfeesten	TU Eindhoven, The Netherlands
Stefan Zugal	University of Innsbruck, Austria

The 1st International Workshop on Digital Business Innovation and the Future Enterprise Information Systems Engineering – DiFenSE 2015

Preface

Disruptive technological change has contributed in the last decade to accelerate the transition from a business-driven culture to a more 'social-oriented' one. Open innovation has become more influential and models of production and value creation are changing. The advent of social media, cloud computing, big data, and the Internet of things outlines a new idea of socioeconomic organization, exemplified by the App Economy, already emerging as a collection of interlocking innovative ecosystems. "New Forms of Enterprises" emerge, driven by constant business model transformation and innovation, acting as multisided platforms built on -as well as emerging from-digital innovations at the global, as well as local level, to produce shared value including that beyond monetization.

The scope of the 1st International Workshop on Digital Business Innovation and the Future Enterprise Information Systems Engineering (DiFenSE 2015) encompasses all aspects of digital business innovation, and the role of information systems engineering and conceptual modeling for design thinking and the discovery and exploitation of digital opportunities. Powered by the FP7 Future Enterprise Project, the workshop aims to promote and exchange ideas on the role and use of information systems engineering for future digital enterprises, digital business innovation, and web entrepreneurship. In particular, the accepted papers cover different disciplinary perspectives on the various DiFenSe topics and challenges.

Darek Haftor's paper presents a summary of ongoing research with regard to the reconfiguration of business models with the help of digital technologies, identifying dimensions such as business model's outputs, activities, actors, transaction mechanism and governance, which may be regarded as a set of heuristics to guide managers' business development efforts. Erdelina Kurti's research in progress aims to explore the challenges and success factors in the transformation from traditional to digital business models. The assumed focus is on cognitive dependencies that hinder and enable such transformation given that this transformation involves a fundamental shift of core cognitive assumptions and beliefs held by the management of organizations in terms of value creation and value network. The paper by Kurt Sandkuhl and Janis Stirna addresses the question how the potential of capability management is related to business model innovation by considering a case study from business process outsourcing as an example. The aim is to apply an established business model conceptualization as a framework for analyzing the case study and to compare the possibility to identify business innovations with and without defined capability characteristics.

Yannick Lew Yaw Fung and Arne-Jørgen Berre present a value development framework, called ServiceMIF, which can contribute to service innovation during service development, thus creating new or improved customer value. Mahsa Hasani Sadi, Jiaying Dai, and Eric Yu consider popular mobile software ecosystems to question how to attract external developers to a platform, and how to establish sustainable collaborative relationships with them. Their point is that eliciting and in-depth analyzing developers' objectives and criteria facilitates the design of sustainable collaborative relationships in a software ecosystem. Scenarios from Apple iOS and Google Android ecosystems are used for illustration. Luca Cremona, Aurelio Ravarini, and Gianluigi Viscusi investigate the role of business models for exploiting digital options within digital clusters (that are clusters where collaboration is IT-dependent). To this aim, this research focuses on digital platforms, a specific IT artifact supporting an inter-organizational system (IOS), which finds a typical application domain in clusters of enterprises. An exploratory case study is then discussed in this paper, meant to represent the early stages of application of the DSR method (building, evaluating). The paper of Carlos Agostinho, Fenareti Lampathaki, Ricardo Jardim-Goncalves, and Oscar Lazaro explores novel forms of technological and digital business innovation putting the full potential of the Future of Internet into Web-based innovation, Web-Entrepreneurship and Internationalization (IEI) of businesses. Accordingly, the paper introduces an approach to extend and complement existing incubation environments, which are no longer sufficient to deal with the dynamicity of the Web-Entrepreneur. Finally, the paper of Iosif Alvertis, Panagiotis Kokkinakos, Sotirios Koussouris, Fenareti Lampathaki, John Psarras, Gianluigi Viscusi, Christopher Tucci discusses a roadmap for future digital enterprises together with potential scenarios for Enterprises of the Future, related a set socio-political, economic, innovation, and technological trends.

We hope the above selection of papers will provide insights and ideas to both academics and practitioners suitable to support further investigation and experimentation with solutions for the challenges of digital business innovation and future enterprise information Systems Engineering.

June 2015

Fenareti Lampathaki
Christopher Tucci
Gianluigi Viscusi

DiFenSE 2015 Organization

Organizing Committee

Fenareti Lampathaki	National Technical University of Athens, Greece
Christopher Tucci	EPFL, Switzerland
Gianluigi Viscusi	EPFL, Switzerland

Program Committee

Sabine Brunswicker	Purdue University, USA
Jonathan Cave	University of Warwick, UK
Yannis Charalabidis	University of Aegean, Greece
John Psarras	National Technical University of Athens, Greece
Sotiris Koussouris	National Technical University of Athens, Greece
Daniel M. Berry	University of Waterloo, Canada

The 1st First International Workshop on Enterprise Modeling – EM 2015

Preface

The upcoming of recent trends such as Enterprise Mobility, Cloud Computing, Internet-of-Things, and Factories-of-the-Future presents profound challenges for today's enterprises. This concerns both technological and organizational aspects that need to be taken into account for realizing innovative, user-centric, and sustainable solutions. Enterprise modeling offers a concept to cope with these challenges by using machine processable languages to facilitate the interaction with complex business and technological scenarios, by engaging in knowledge management, and by supporting organizational engineering. It thus directly contributes to the design, implementation, use, and evaluation of solutions. Thereby it spans from traditional fields such as business process management and business intelligence to more recent areas such as enterprise architecture and semantic information systems.

The aim of the First International Workshop on Enterprise Modeling, which was organized in conjunction with the 27th International Conference on Advanced Information Systems Engineering (CAiSE 2015), was to bring together scientists working on innovative approaches for enterprise modeling. A particular focus was thereby given to engineering approaches that aim for IT-based solutions to advance the current state-of-the-art in enterprise modeling.

For this first time of the workshop we received in total 14 papers. From these papers six were selected based on at least two peer-reviews.

The accepted papers represent the wide spectrum of research that is currently being undertaken in enterprise modeling. In Sandkuhl et al. experiences and recommendations for the construction of ontologies are given, which today often serve as a conceptual base and semantic extension for enterprise models. Svee and Zdravkovic report about the extension of a meta model for enterprise architecture based on a survey of practitioners. Naranjo et al. propose a semi-automatic approach for combining different enterprise models using visualizations. In Corradini et al. an extension of feature models for representing business process variability is proposed and prototypically implemented. Bakhtiyari et al. propose a method for modeling enterprise architectures which focuses on inter-organizational and re-use aspects. Demuth et al. present a cloud-based knowledge-sharing approach for enterprise modeling that has been implemented using a service-driven approach.

March 2015

Hans-Georg Fill
Manfred Jeusfeld
Dimitris Karagiannis
Matti Rossi

EM 2015 Organization

The 1st Workshop on the Role of Real-World Objects in Business Process Management Systems RW-BPMS 2015

Preface

The increased availability of sensors disseminated in the world has led to the possibility to monitor in detail the evolution of several real-world objects of interest. GPS receivers, RFID chips, transponders, detectors, cameras, satellites, etc. concur in the depiction of the current status of monitored things. Therefore, the opportunity arose to connect physical reality to digital information. The screening of real-world objects makes indeed sensors the interface toward real-world information, as they are the originators of machine-readable events. The exploitation of such knowledge is leading to successful applications such as Smart Cities, Flight Monitoring, Pollution Control, Internet of Things, and Dynamic Manufacturing Networks.

The amount of information at hand would consent a fine-grained monitoring, mining, and decision support for business processes, stemming from the joint observation of business-related objects in the real world. However, the main focus of process and data analysis in Business Process Management (BPM) still lies at a high level of abstraction, such as activities' status, and is based on digital-to-digital information, such as information systems' data- and activity-centric logs. Furthermore, a limited investigation from the BPM community has been evinced toward the physical-to-digital bridge so far. Such a bridge would be naturally provided by rethought information systems, where the knowledge extracted from real-world objects would best depict the contingencies and the context in which business processes are carried out. At the same time, awareness of physical reality for undertaken actions would allow for a better control over the interaction that the Business Process Management Systems (BPMSs) have with the real world.

The objective of the 1st Workshop on the Role of Real-World Objects in Business Process Management Systems (RW-BPMS 2015), organized in conjunction with the 27th Conference on Advanced Information Systems Engineering (CAiSE 2015), was therefore to attract novel research and industry approaches investigating the connection of business processes with real-world objects. Conceptual, technical, and application-oriented contributions were pursued within the scope of this theme.

For the first year of the workshop, we received eight high-quality submissions from researchers in different fields of information systems and business process management communities. Each paper was peer-reviewed by three to four members of the Program Committee. Out of these submissions, two contributions were selected as full papers. One position paper and a demonstration-oriented one were also accepted as short papers, due to their promising research plans and preliminary results. The workshop is complemented by a keynote.

The contributions show an increasing interest in the investigation of the impact of real-world facts on various aspects of BPM, ranging from modeling, to monitoring, and mining. In particular, Meyer et al. propose a new element for the existing BPMN standard, namely "PhysicalEntity", to the extent of modeling the concept of "thing" in process models, under the perspective of the Internet of Things. Leotta et al. discuss the possibility to apply methods and approaches from process mining to derive models of human behavior from smart spaces sensor logs. Filtz et al. present an approach for predicting ocean ships arrival times in the context of logistics processes, based on marine weather information and ship traffic data available on-line. Finally, Wong et al. introduce a framework for monitoring batch activities in business processes, along with an implemented prototype. In his keynote, Avigdor Gal addresses the relation of complex event processing and processes through rules.

We would like to express our gratefulness to all the authors and our keynote speaker for their valuable contributions, and the members of the Program Committee for their excellent and timely work during the reviewing phase. We would also like to thank the organizers of CAiSE 2015 for hosting the workshop, and the GET Service European Project (www.getservice-project.eu) for inspiring and promoting the event.

June 2015

Claudio Di Ciccio
Anne Baumgraß
Remco Dijkman

RW-BPMS 2015 Organization

Organizing Committee

Claudio Di Ciccio	Vienna University of Economics and Business, Austria
Anne Baumgraß	Hasso-Plattner-Institut at University of Potsdam, Germany
Remco Dijkman	Eindhoven University of Technology, The Netherlands

Program Committee

Christian Janiesch	Karlsruhe Institute of Technology, Germany
Stefan Krumnow	Signavio GmbH, Germany
André Ludwig	University of Leipzig, Germany
Fabrizio Maria Maggi	University of Tartu, Estonia
Andrea Marrella	Sapienza University of Rome, Italy
Massimo Mecella	Sapienza University of Rome, Italy
Jan Mendling	Vienna University of Economics and Business, Austria
Marco Montali	Free University of Bozen-Bolzano, Italy
Felix Naumann	Hasso-Plattner-Institut at the University of Potsdam, Germany
Frank Puhlmann	Bosch Software Innovations GmbH, Germany
Stefanie Rinderle-Ma	University of Vienna, Austria
Stefan Schulte	Vienna University of Technology, Austria
Pnina Soffer	University of Haifa, Israel
Mark Strembeck	Vienna University of Economics and Business, Austria
Hagen Völzer	IBM Zürich, Switzerland
Barbara Weber	University of Innsbruck, Austria
Matthias Weidlich	Imperial College London, UK
Mathias Weske	Hasso-Plattner-Institut at the University of Potsdam, Germany
Josiane Xavier Parreira	Siemens AG, Austria

RW-BPMS 2015 Keynote by Avigdor Gal

When Processes Rule Event Streams

Abstract. Big Data brings with it new and exciting challenges to complex event processing. Large volumes of simple events that stream in high velocity to our processing stations from a variety of sources call for rethinking traditional methods of processing complex events. In this talk we shall explore the interesting phenomenon of event streams that are produced by processes, e.g., bus data that is governed by bus routes or real-time positioning system tracking patients in an outpatient clinic. The talk shall answer some of the related interesting questions: how do we discover the rules that govern event creation? how do we use such rules to optimize complex event processing? and suggest directions for future research. The talk will be accompanied by examples of urban transportation in Dublin (the INSIGHT European project) and patient visits to Dana-Farber Cancer Institute (DFCI), a large outpatient cancer in the US.

The 10th International Workshop on Trends in Enterprise Architecture Research – TEAR 2015

Preface

Over the past two decades, Enterprise Architecture (EA) has been established as a scientific discipline and a practical tool to manage the increasing complexity of modern enterprises. At the heart of this endeavor is the realization that enterprise decision-makers require not only detailed models of specifics, but also overarching models of the grand scheme of things. As such, EA does not aim to replace IT architecture, software architecture, systems architecture, or business architecture, but rather to complement them and to describe the bigger picture. This is only becoming more important in today's fast-paced business landscape, where enterprises quickly need to adapt to rapid market changes. Managing change, making sure that the introduction of new business processes and technology does not have unforeseen adverse affects throughout the enterprise, is thus a key priority for EA.

The use of models, explicitly including both IS/IT artifacts and business artifacts as well as the relationships between them, is at the heart of the EA discipline. As a consequence, much EA research is devoted to enterprise modeling, to reference models, meta-models, and frameworks, and to modeling tools. However, for models to be useful, they also need to be maintained, populated with accurate data, and properly governed over time, giving rise to other EA research fields. Furthermore, for EA to support decision-making, models must be suitable for analysis of relevant business concerns and informed by subject matter research into these decision-making domains, thus indicating yet further directions in EA research. And the list goes on.

For almost ten years, the international TEAR workshop has brought EA researchers from all over the world together to discuss the latest developments in the field – all the research strands indicated above, and many more. The aim of the workshop has always been to bridge different research communities and provide a forum where EA research results from many disciplines can be presented and discussed from complementary perspectives. Additionally, TEAR should mirror the developments of the field as such, and offer plenty of opportunities to discuss new EA trends and directions.

In 2015, the TEAR workshop, organized in conjunction with the 27th International Conference on Advanced Information Systems Engineering (CAiSE 2015), received 24 submissions. All of them went through a rigorous review process, which involved at least three reviewers per paper. Out of these submissions, 10 high-quality papers were accepted, resulting in an acceptance rate of 42%. The paper presentations were divided into four sessions of two or three presentations each.

In the session on EA modeling and meta-modeling, there were three papers. Heiser et al. study the interplay between the product architecture and the architecture of the organization developing the product. Based on a case study of software and hardware development, they apply EA models to analyze different alternatives for organizational transformation. Cohen et al. apply formal modeling rules to ensure that EA models are correct. They report on a case study where rules expressed in a controlled natural language were applied in two large-scale enterprise architecture projects. Jugel et al. investigate how to adapt EA models to the specific concerns of different stakeholders. They contribute an extended EA meta-model, which links enterprise decisions to architectural elements.

In the session on EA value and benefits, there were three papers. Plessius et al. address the important question of how to measure EA benefits. They report on the development of an EA measurement instrument, tested in a survey with 287 respondents. Aldea et al. investigate how the ArchiMate modeling language can be used to describe value. They suggest several improvements which can help enterprise architects to model and visualize how business value is created. Aier et al. observe that while EA has become well established, its effectiveness beyond IT is still limited. The 'architectural thinking' paradigm aims to extend EA beyond IT, and the authors report on a case study of how this works in practice.

In the session on EA governance and management, there were two papers. Waltl et al. address the issue of data governance on EA information assets. They show how non-monotonic defeasible logic can support data governance by assigning accountability and responsibility roles for architectural data. Aleatrati Khosroshahi et al. study Federated EA Model Management (FEAMM). Based on qualitative interviews with industry experts, they offer success factors for FEAMM from both the technical and social perspectives.

In the session on EA in today's business landscape, there were two papers. Azevedo et al. observe that EA lacks representations of enterprise strategic planning. They discuss how EA could contribute to strategic planning and identify requirements on suitable EA extensions. Babar and Yu examine EA in the context of the ongoing digitalization of business operations. They suggest that as a response to emerging trends, EA models need to be enriched and expanded in scope to remain relevant.

All of these papers are interesting in their own right, but together they also offer an interesting snapshot of current trends in EA research, thus bringing an added value to TEAR 2015.

March 2015

Ulrik Franke
Pontus Johnson
Mathias Ekstedt

TEAR 2015 Organization

Workshop Co-chairs

Ulrik Franke	FOI Swedish Defence Research Agency, Sweden
Pontus Johnson	KTH Royal Institute of Technology, Sweden
Mathias Ekstedt	KTH Royal Institute of Technology, Sweden

Steering Committee

Erik Proper	Radboud University Nijmegen, The Netherlands and Public Research Centre – Henri Tudor, Luxembourg
Florian Matthes	Fakultät für Informatik, Technische Universität München, Germany
James Lapalme	École de technologie supérieure, Canada
João Paulo A. Almeida	Federal University of Espírito Santo, Brazil
Marc M. Lankhorst	BiZZdesign, The Netherlands
Mathias Ekstedt	KTH Royal Institute of Technology, Sweden
Pontus Johnson	KTH Royal Institute of Technology, Sweden
Stephan Aier	University of St. Gallen, Switzerland

Program Committee

Stephan Aier	University of St. Gallen, Switzerland
Antonia Albani	University of St. Gallen, Switzerland
João Paulo A. Almeida	Federal University of Espírito Santo, Brazil
Giuseppe Berio	Université de Bretagne Sud, France
Nacer Boudjlida	Université de Lorraine and LORIA, France
Sabine Buckl	Technische Universität München, Germany
Quang Bui	Bentley University, USA
François Coallier	École de technologie supérieure, Canada
Sybren de Kinderen	University of Luxembourg, Luxembourg
Rebecca Deneckere	Université de Paris 1 Panthéon - Sorbonne, France
Mathias Ekstedt	KTH Royal Institute of Technology, Sweden
Hans-Georg Fill	University of Vienna, Austria
Ulrik Franke	FOI Swedish Defence Research Agency, Sweden
Aurona Gerber	CAIR and Meraka Institute and CSIR, South Africa
Jānis Grabis	Riga Technical University, Latvia
Wilhelm Hasselbring	Kiel University, Germany
Maria-Eugenia Iacob	University of Twente, The Netherlands
Pontus Johnson	KTH Royal Institute of Technology, Sweden
Juergen Jung	DHL Global Mail
Elena Kornyshova	CNAM, France
Robert Lagerström	KTH the Royal Institute of Technology, Sweden

Additional Reviewers

The 5th International Workshop on Information Systems Security Engineering – WISSE 2015

Preface

Information systems security problems are currently a widespread and growing concern that covers most of the areas of society, such as business, domestic, financial, government, healthcare, and so on. The scientific community has realized the importance of aligning information systems engineering and security engineering in order to develop more secure information systems. Nevertheless, there is lack of an appropriate event that will promote information systems security within the context of information systems engineering. The proposed workshop fulfills this gap.

The International Workshop on Information System Security Engineering (WISSE) aims to provide a forum for researchers and practitioners to present, discuss, and debate on one hand the latest research work on methods, models, practices, and tools for secure information systems engineering, and on the other hand relevant industrial applications, recurring challenges, problems, and industrial led solutions at the area of secure information systems engineering.

This fifth edition of the workshop, held in Stockholm (Sweden) on June 8th, 2015, was organized in conjunction with the 27th International Conference on Advanced Information Systems Engineering (CAiSE 2015). In order to ensure a high-quality workshop, following an extensive review process, seven submissions were accepted as full papers addressing a large variety of issues related to Secure Information Systems Engineering.

We wish to thank all the contributors to WISSE 2015, in particular the authors who submitted papers and the members of the Program Committee who carefully reviewed them. We express our gratitude to the CAiSE 2015 Workshop Chairs, for their helpful support in preparing the workshop. Finally, we thank our colleagues from the Steering Committee, Jan Jürjens, Haralambos Mouratidis, Carlos Blanco, and Daniel Mellado, and our colleagues from Publicity Chairs, Shareeful Islam, Luis Enrique Sánchez, and Akram Idani, for initiating the workshop and contributing to its organization.

June 2015

Nadira Lammari
David G. Rosado
Christos Kalloniatis

WISSE 2015 Organization

General Chair

Nadira Lammari   Conservatoire National des Arts et Métiers, France

Program Co-chairs

David G. Rosado   University of Castilla-La Mancha, Spain
Christos Kalloniatis   University of the Aegean, Greece

Steering Committee

Jan Jürjens   Technical University of Dortmund, Germany
Nadira Lammari   Conservatoire National des Arts et Métiers, France
Haralambos Mouratidis   University of Brighton, UK
David G. Rosado   University of Castilla-La Mancha, Spain
Carlos Blanco   University of Cantabria, Spain
Christos Kalloniatis   University of the Aegean, Greece

Publicity Chairs

Shareeful Islam   University of East London, UK
Luis Enrique Sánchez   University of Armed Forces, Ecuador
Akram Idani   University of Grenoble, France

Program Committee

Antonio Maña   University of Malaga, Spain
Akram Idani   University of Grenoble, France
Benjamin Nguyen   SMIS, Inria-Rocquencourt, France
Brajendra Panda   University of Arkansas, USA
Bruno Defude   Télécom SudParis, France
Carlos Blanco   University of Cantabria, Spain
Csilla Farkas   University of South Carolina, USA
Daniel Mellado   Spanish Tax Agency, Spain
Djamel Benslimane   LIRIS, Claude Bernard Lyon I University, France
Eduardo Fernández-Medina   University of Castilla-La Mancha, Spain
Eduardo B. Fernández   Florida Atlantic University, USA
El-Bay Bourennane   University of Bourgogne, Dijon, France
Eric Dubois   CRP Henri Tudor, Luxembourg
Ernesto Damiani   Università degli Studi di Milano, Italy
Frédéric Cuppens   Télécom Bretagne, France
Günther Pernul   University of Regensburg, Germany
Guttorm Sindre   Norwegian University of Science and Technology, Norway

Haris Mouratidis	University of Brighton, UK
Hanifa Boucheneb	École Polytechnique de Montréal, Quebec, Canada
Isabelle Comyn-Wattiau	Cnam Paris, France
Jacky Akoka	Cnam Paris, France
Javier López	University of Málaga, Spain
Jan Jürjens	Technical University of Dortmund, Germany
Ludovic Apvrille	Telecom ParisTech, France
Luis Enrique Sánchez	University of Castilla-La Mancha, Spain
Marc Frappier	University of Sherbrooke, Québec, Canada
Marc Chaumont	University of Montpellier, France
Matt Bishop	University of California, USA
Mohammad Zulkernine	Queen's University, Canada
Oliver Popov	Stockholm University, Sweden
Paolo Giorgini	University of Trento, Italy
Régine Laleau	LACL, Université Paris-Est Créteil, France
Sabrina De Capitani di Vimercati	Università degli Studi di Milano, Italy
Shareeful Islam	University of East London, UK
Stefanos Gritzalis	University of the Aegean, Greece
Steven Furnell	Plymouth University, UK
Tristan Allard	University of Montpellier 2, France
Vincent Nicomette	INSA de Toulouse, France
Yves Ledru	LIG, University of Grenoble, France

Contents

WISSE 2015

ASDENCA 2015

Investigating the Potential of Capability-Driven Design and Delivery in an SME Case Study

Kurt Sandkuhl[1,2](✉)

[1] University of Rostock, Albert-Einstein-Straße 22, Rostock 18059, Germany
kurt.sandkuhl@uni-rostock.de
[2] ITMO University, St. Petersburg, Russia

Abstract. In many business sectors, competitiveness on an international market is closely linked to the ability to quickly adapt business models and company strategies to changes in the market environment or in customer demands. Capability management is among the approaches which have been proposed as contributions to tackle these challenges. One of the key features is to explicitly capture the delivery context of a business services and to provide mechanisms for configuring or generating its deliver. Among the approaches to capability management is the capability-driven design and delivery (CDD) approach proposed in the EU-FP7 project CaaS. The aim of this paper is to contribute to (1) a better understanding of the potential of CDD and (2) the validation of the CDD approach. The paper addresses these aspects by considering the case of a small and medium-sized enterprise (SME) as an example.

Keywords: Capability modelling · Business potential · SME · Capability management

1 Introduction

In many business sectors, competitiveness on an international market is closely linked to the ability to quickly adapt business models and company strategies to changes in the market environment or in customer demands. In this context, enterprises offering IT-based business services to their customers need a way to quickly adapt both, their business services and the IT-infrastructure for delivering them. Capability management is among the approaches which have been proposed as contributions to tackle these challenges. One of the key features is to explicitly capture the delivery context of a business services and to provide mechanisms for configuring or generating its delivery (see Sect. 2).

Among the approaches to capability management is the capability-driven design and delivery (CDD) approach proposed in the EU-FP7 project CaaS (see Sect. 2.2) which is described in our previous work [16, 17]. So far, work on CDD focused to a large extent on the conceptual and technical aspects of capability modelling and delivery. Validation of the CDD approach has largely been done within the CaaS project only by using the CaaS use case. Furthermore, the suitability of CDD for different target groups has not been investigated in much detail.

© Springer International Publishing Switzerland 2015
A. Persson and J. Stirna (Eds.): CAiSE 2015 Workshops, LNBIP 215, pp. 3–14, 2015.
DOI: 10.1007/978-3-319-19243-7_1

The aim of this paper is to contribute to (1) a better understanding of the potential of CDD and (2) the validation of the CDD approach. The paper addresses these aspects by considering the case of a small and medium-sized enterprise (SME) as an example. With the results from this case, we intend to provide the basis for future case studies and to investigate what the potential of CDD for different target groups is, whether there are differences between different target groups and what the reasons for those differences are.

The rest of the paper is structured as follows: Sect. 2 summarizes the background for the work from the area of capability management and presents the main aspects of the CaaS approach to capability design and delivery. Section 3 discusses the case study including interviews and a qualitative content analysis performed in the case. Section 4 discusses threats to validity of our work in Sect. 3. Section 5 summarizes the work and draws conclusions.

2   Background

As a background for the work presented in this paper, this section briefly summarizes work in the area of capability management and the capability design and delivery approach developed in the CaaS project.

2.1   Capability Management

The term capability is used in different areas of business information systems. In the literature there seems to be an agreement about the characteristics of the capability, still there is no generally acceptance of the term. The definitions mainly put the focus on "combination of resources" [5], "capacity to execute an activity" [4], "perform better than competitors" [7] and "possessed ability [12]".

The capabilities must be enablers of competitive advantage; they should help companies to continuously deliver a certain business value in dynamically changing circumstances [8]. They can be perceived from different organizational levels and thus utilized for different purposes. According to [9] performance of an enterprise is the best, when the enterprise maps its capabilities to IT applications. Capabilities as such are directly related to business processes that are affected from the changes in context, such as, regulations, customer preferences and system performance. As companies in rapidly changing environments need to anticipate to these variations and respond to them [6], the affected processes/services need to be adjusted quickly. In other words, adaptations to changes in context can be realized promptly if the required variations to the standard processes have been anticipated and defined in advance and can be instantiated.

In this paper capability is defined as the ability and capacity that enable an enterprise to achieve a business goal in a certain context [15]. Ability refers to the level of available competence, where competence is understood as talent intelligence and disposition, of a subject or enterprise to accomplish a goal; capacity means availability of resources, e.g. money, time, personnel, tools. This definition utilizes the notion of context, thus stresses the need to take variations of the standard processes into consideration. To summarize, capabilities are considered as specific business services delivered to the enterprises in an application context to reach a business goal. In order to facilitate capability management, we propose business service design explicitly considering delivery context by an approach that supports modelling both, the service as such and the application context.

2.2 CaaS Approach to Capability Design and Delivery

Business services are IT-based services which digital enterprises provide for their customers. Business services usually serve specified business goals, they are specified in a model-based way and include service level definitions. In order to ease adaptation of business services to changes in customer processes or other legal environments CDD approach explicitly defines (a) the potential delivery context of a business service (i.e. all contexts in which the business service potentially has to be delivered), (b) the potential variants of the business service for the delivery context and (c) what aspect of the delivery context would require what kind of variation or adaptation of the business service.

The potential delivery context basically consists of a set of parameters or variables, the so called context elements, which characterize the differences in delivery. The combination of all context elements and their possible ranges defines the context set, i.e. the problem space to cover. The potential variants of the business service, which form the solution space, are represented by process variants. Since in many delivery contexts it will be impractical to capture all possible variants, we propose to define patterns for the most frequent variants caused by context elements and to combine and instantiate these patterns to create actual solutions. If no suitable pattern is available, the conventional solution engineering process has to be used. The connection between context elements, patterns and business services has to be captured as transformation or mapping rules. These rules are defined during design time and interpreted during runtime.

The above simplified summary of our approach has been further elaborated by defining meta-model and method components, by specifying a development and delivery environment and by performing feasibility studies. Detailed discussions of meta-model and method components are available in [10] and [16], respectively.

In order to implement the CaaS approach, a capability development and delivery environment was designed, which is currently under development. The main components of the environment are capability design tool, context platform, capability delivery navigation application, as well as capability delivery application. The architecture of the environment is shown in Fig. 1. The main components are illustrated with parallelograms. Functional components are represented in rectangular and they are related to each other as well as to their respective main components. The functional components of the environment are as follows:

- Capability modeling module - provides modeling elements defined in the capability meta-model and models the required capability including business service (e.g. business process model), business goals, context and relations to delivery patterns.
- Pattern composition module - identifies appropriate patterns for capability delivery and composes the patterns together. It supports incorporation of external resources into the composition. If some of the patterns required are not available then the modeling of missing information is supported and new patterns can be proposed and documented.

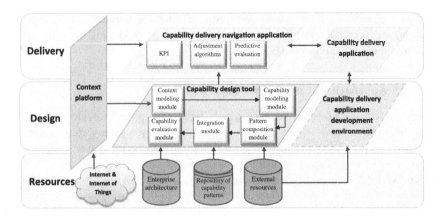

Fig. 1. Components of the capability development environment

- Repository of capability patterns - storage and maintenance of available capability delivery patterns.
- Context platform - captures data from external data sources including sensing hardware and Internet based services such as social networks. It aggregates data and provides these data to subscribers.
- Context modeling module - represents the context data in terms of the capability modeling concepts and provides means for context analysis and amalgamation.
- Capability assessment (evaluation) module - performs assessment of financial and technical feasibility of the proposed capability.
- Capability integration module - generates the capability delivery navigation application, which also incorporates algorithms for capability delivery adjustment.
- Capability delivery navigation application - provides means for monitoring and adjustment of capability delivery. It includes monitoring module for monitoring context and goal KPI, predictive evaluation of capability delivery performance and delivery adjustment algorithms. The capability delivery adjustment algorithms are built-in in the capability delivery navigation application. The algorithms continuously evaluate necessary adjustments and pass capability delivery adjustment commands to the capability delivery application.

Capability delivery application is developed following the process and technologies used by a particular company. The CDD methodology only determines interfaces required for the capability delivery application (CDA) to be able to receive capability delivery adjustment commands from the capability delivery navigation application and to provide the capability delivery performance information.

3   Investigating the Potential of CDD in an SME Case

As a contribution to understanding the potential of capability management and at the same time to validation of the CDD approach, we investigated the case of a small and medium-sized company offering IT-based business services to their customers. More concrete, we considered the case of SOLVIN AG, Hamburg and Berlin. Solvin is a full-service consulting firm with a wide range of tools, own solutions and methods with a focus on the field of project management. The main question considered in the interviews with Solvin was:

From the perspective of a medium-sized company, what is the potential of the CaaS approach for improving business performance?

This question can be broken down into a number of sub-questions:

- What kind of business services does the company offer?
- How is the delivery of each business service affected by the delivery context?
- Is it possible to make explicit, what context elements relevant for the business services?
- How much efforts and what time frame does it require to adapt a business service to a new delivery context?
- What preconditions does the CDD approach need to fulfill to be applicable in the company regarding (a) methodology, (b) technology, (c) qualification, (d) resources?

The main purpose of the interviews was an external validation of the CDD approach from two perspectives: would the approach be applicable in the enterprise under consideration and, if so, what would be the expected benefits? The development of the CDD approach primarily was based on academic literature and the input from three specific use cases of CaaS industrial partners. By selecting experts from another application domain than the CaaS use cases, we aim to balance theory and practice as well as to add another perspective to the validation of the CDD approach. From a methodical perspective, the aim of the interviews was to collect qualitative data relevant for the above questions which would be analyzed with qualitative content analysis techniques. Thus, the requirements of the analysis technique posed to the data had to be taken into account when designing the process. More concrete, we selected Mayring's [1] approach for conducting qualitative content analysis.

As a preparation for the interviews, a list of questions was developed (open questions), which covered the background of the experts interviewed, business services in general and the process of adapting these services to new delivery contexts in particular. Two interviews were conducted on the same afternoon; one interview was with the manager of the business process outsourcing (BPO) unit, the other one the ramp-up manager for project management services. The BPO unit of Solvin is under development and supposed to offer reporting and planning processes within project management as service to Solvin's clients. The ramp-up manager is in charge of setting up project management services for new clients according to their requirements. The interviews were recorded; additionally the interviewer took notes during the interviews.

Mayring's approach includes 6 steps: step 1 is to decide what material to analyze, which obviously consists of the recordings of the two interviews and the notes taken. The BPO and the ramp-up manager both are experienced in the field of project management and served as consultants for many clients in this area, which included projects in IT, manufacturing industries and process industries. Step 2 is to make explicit how the data collection (i.e. in our case the interviews) was arranged and prepared. The purpose of this step is to make all factors transparent which could be relevant for interpreting the data. The company Solvin was selected from existing contacts of the researchers involved. As preparation for the interviews, the interviewees received information about the purpose of the interview, general information about CaaS and the CDD approach. This information was given in a 30 min presentation plus 15 min discussion session, which was followed by the interviews. The interview with the BPO manager was 48 min long. The interview with the second expert lasted 56 min.

Step 3 is to make explicit, how the transcription of the material had to be done. The material was analyzed step by step following rules of procedure devising the material into content analytical units. The rules included what IDs to use for the units of different interviews, how to tag content related to the interviewer and content from the interviewees, how to mark comments, etc. Step 4 concerns the subject-reference of the analysis, i.e. that the connection to the concrete subject of the analysis is made sure. Subject-reference was implemented by (a) defining the research questions and their sub-questions in the interview guidelines and (b) using the subjects of these sub-questions as categories during the analysis.

Step 5 recommends theory-guided analysis of the data, which is supposed to balance fuzziness of qualitative analysis with theoretical stringency. For theory-guidance, we took the state-of-the-art into account during both, formulation of the sub-questions and analysis of the material. Step 6 defines the analysis technique, which in our case was content summary. This attempts to reduce the material in such a way as to preserve the essential content and by abstraction to create a manageable corpus which still reflects the original material. For this the text was paraphrased, afterwards generalized, reduced and assigned to categories mentioned in step 4: a first reduction is achieved by removing paraphrases with the same meaning from the paraphrased text. A second reduction is the result of summarizing similar paraphrases. The categories reflect the aspects needed to answer the research questions. Table 1 illustrates the result of the 2nd reduction step.

For brevity reasons, Table 1 presents only a small part of the result of the 2nd reduction. Out of in total 12 categories represented in the interview questions, we selected "business services", "service delivery" and "context elements" for presentation in this paper. Based on the information collected during the interviews our conclusions regarding the investigated main question are as follows:

(a) What kind of business services does the company offer?

The business services offered by Solvin are supposed to cover typical activities of a project management unit (PMU) for medium-sized and large development or design projects. Examples for the services included are change management (change requests, change tracking, scope change control), plan management (plan documentation, schedule control), cost management (cost planning, cost control, cost reporting), communication management (reporting to stakeholders, documentation platform), quality management (quality planning, documentation of quality control actions) and risk management (risk registers, risk control). Solvin offers to set up the organizational and technical prerequisites for the project management units, to train the staff and to perform the actual management. Future services are supposed to include outsourcing services.

Table 1. Result of the 2nd reduction step (excerpt)

Category #	Category	Statement
C 2	Business services	All a PMU has to do
		Change management and what belongs to it
		Change control, change tracking
		Control schedule, document project plan
		Cost control, cost reporting and planning
		Stakeholder communication
		Reporting, manage documents
		Quality plan and control
		Maintain risk register, document decisions
C 8	Service delivery	Individual solution for every customer
		Platform is configured
		Layout and content of reporting
		Stakeholders
		Periods and time-related constraints
		Work flows
		Integration with enterprise IT
		Resources relevant for project
C 9	Context elements	Checklist for project ramp-up
		Platform configuration partly automatable
		Import from enterprise systems, conversion of format, matching to tables in database
		Supplier changes
		Policy changes
		Some manual adjustments
		Document layouts
		Stakeholder information
		Periods and time frames
		Have to test it

(b) How is the delivery of each business service affected by the delivery context?

Currently, the customer selects the required business services from Solvin's offering and a dedicated technical platform is configured for each customer which makes each PMU solution unique. In addition to the selected services, many possibilities of configuring the solution to the customer demands are offered. These include content and layout of reports, reporting and planning periods, basic work flows (e.g. for reporting), stakeholder involvement, and integration with the enterprise resource planning (e.g. for importing basic information about personnel, cost structures or subcontractors and for exporting information about resource consumption and achieved progress). Furthermore, the deployment environment has to be decided, which currently either is to run the IT-platform and services at the customer's premises or to use Solvin's infrastructure for this purpose.

(c) Is it possible to make explicit, what context elements relevant for the business services?

The interviewees consider it as very useful to think of each new customer as delivery context for their PMU services and to make explicit what defines this context.

They mention an internal check list for ramp-up of solutions for new customers. This check list (which was not available during the interview) would be a source for identifying context elements.

The discussion of potential context elements showed that the interviewees were dividing the elements into (a) context elements affecting the configuration of the PMU solution and requiring manual adjustments, (b) elements affecting the configuration which could be used for automated adjustments and (c) context elements affecting the operations of the PMU solution. Examples for category (a) are document layouts to be adjusted or stakeholder names and addresses. The import of data from existing systems which can be performed as variants of a tool chain belongs to category (b). Category (c) would include supplier information triggering changes in risk register or policy changes leading to changed information supply to stakeholders.

(d) How much efforts and what time frame does it require to adapt a business service to a new delivery context?

For small projects which use the standard configuration of the PMU solution, it requires just one working day to adapt the business service. For complex projects with specific requirements to import and export of information and to work flows and decision rights to be reflected by the system, this can take up to 2 months. Figures about the average size of adaptation are not available.

(e) What preconditions does the CDD approach need to fulfill to be applicable in the company regarding (a) methodology, (b) technology, (c) qualification, (d) resources?

When judging the potential of the CDD approach, the interviewees had different opinions. The ramp-up manager had his doubts that CDD approach of capability modeling, capability delivery and capability navigation would substantially improve the business service currently offered to Solvin's customers. Context modeling would probably help to raise awareness for improvement potential, but the current target group is used to set-up time and efforts involved in this. Thus, the need for automatic configuration of PMU solutions and for adjustments during delivery for this target group is not very high. The efforts to be spent in further automation would probably not generate enough savings or payback in terms of new customer projects. On the other side, the manager of the BPO unit saw a great potential for the CDD approach when implementing business process outsourcing. This segment of the business is supposed to primarily address a new target group acknowledges the need for professional project management services, but does not want to implement a fully-developed PMU. They are interested in a reliable documentation and reporting processes, a high data quality and procedures compliant to industry standards. Processes will be more standardized and delivery of the business services has a much higher automation potential.

From a methodology perspective, CDD should ideally support the modeling of capabilities, the configuration of the delivery platform for a specific delivery context and the management of capability delivery during runtime. If CDD offers this possibility, Solvin would be open to change the own methodology to the CDD approach, even though this requires investments in qualifying the employees. Solvin is Microsoft solution partner and would clearly like to stay with solutions applicable on a Microsoft platform. Regarding the qualification, the interviewees would expect that the consultants who currently analyze customer requirements and implement the customization should be able to do the context modeling and configuration. As the BPO unit is under design, the interviewees did not have a firm opinion about the overall process and the resource requirements.

4 Threats to Validity

Research including empirical studies has threats regarding its validity, and so have the interviews performed for investigating the potential of capability management. However, to early identify such threats and to take actions to mitigate the threats can minimize the effect on the findings. Common threats to empirical studies are discussed, for example in [2, 3]. The threats to validity can be divided into four categories: construct validity, internal validity, external validity and conclusion validity. Construct validity is concerned with obtaining the right indicators and measures for the concept being studied. Internal validity primarily is important for explanatory studies with the objective to identify causal relationships. External validity is addressing the question about to which extent the findings in a study can be generalized. Conclusion validity addresses repetition or replication, i.e. that the same result would be found if performing the study again in the same setting.

With respect to construct validity, the following threats were identified and actions taken:

- Selection of participants: The results are highly dependent on the people being interviewed. Only persons experienced in design and development of business services and the use of IT for delivering them will be able to judge suitability and potential of the proposed CDD approach. To obtain a high quality of the sample, only experts having worked in this area for a long time and hence having the required background were selected.
- Reactive bias: A common risk in studies is that the presence of a researcher influences the outcome. Since the selected participants in the study and the research group performing the study have been collaborating for a while, this is not perceived as a large risk. However, as the researchers performing the interviews were part of the team developing the CDD approach there is the risk that the interviewees are biased towards the CDD approach to find evidence for its innovative character. In order to reduce this threat, the interviewees were informed that the new approach can be configured in different ways and the purpose of the study was to test a certain configuration.
- Correct interview data: There is a risk that the questions of the interviewer may be misunderstood or the data may be misinterpreted. In order to minimize this risk, the interview guidelines were double-checked by another researcher to ensure a correct interpretation of the questions by the interviewees. Furthermore, the interviews were documented and recorded, which allowed the researcher to listen to the interview again if portions seemed unclear.

Regarding the internal validity, confounding factors and the ability to inference are the two most important aspects for our work:

- Confounding factors: In many studies, there is a risk that changes detected by measurements or observations are not solely due to the new approach, but also due to confounding factors. Since we only focused on the step from business service to capability and kept all other elements stable, we made all efforts possible to rule out confounding factors as an influence on the interview outcome.
- Ability to make inferences: Another potential threat to internal validity is that the data collected in the interviews did not completely capture the view of the interviewees regarding the CDD approach. However, this threat was reduced by breaking down the research question in a sub-questions covering the different aspects of CDD potential. Thus, this threat to validity is considered being under control.

A potential threat of the study regarding external validity is of course that the actual interviews have been conducted with only two participants from the field. It will be part of the future work, to conduct a study with more participants and with members from other industry and academic contexts.

With respect to conclusion validity, interpretation of data is most critical, i.e. the outcome of the study potentially could be affected by the interpretation of the researcher. To minimize this threat, the study design includes capturing the relevant aspects by different interview questions, i.e. to conduct triangulation to check the correctness of the findings. Furthermore, another risk could be that the interpretation of the data depends on the researcher and is not traceable. To reduce the risk the data collection and interpretation was performed according to Mayring's approach (see Sect. 3). Furthermore, the results were discussed with other researchers and validated by them.

In summary, actions have been taken to mitigate the risks identified, which from our perspective results in an appropriate confidence level regarding construct and internal validity. Future work (i.e. an extension of the study) will contribute to increasing the confidence level regarding external validity and also conclusion validity.

5   Conclusion and Outlook

In order to investigate the potential of capability-driven design and development, this paper conducted and analysed two interviews with representatives from an SME providing project management services to their clients. The interviews were also expected to contribute to validation of the CDD approach with respect to its suitability and usefulness for enterprises that are not in CaaS project. The overall conclusions to be drawn for the specific case of Solvin are:

- The basic concept of reaching a new productivity level for business services by making their delivery context explicit and designing adaptation possibilities during delivery was considered as very promising.
- For highly individualized business services with a substantial share of manual configuration needs, the CDD approach was considered as less suitable.
- The usefulness of the CDD approach for BPO was confirmed. Solvin would be willing to explore the use of the CDD approach and tools.

- There is an openness to change the own methodology to the CDD approach, even if this requires investments in qualifying the employees.
- Compatibility to technical platforms established in the enterprise is a success criterion.
- It is difficult to calculate the benefits of CDD, as the required figures regarding average project size and distribution of efforts are not available.

As already discussed in Sect. 4, the above findings cannot be generalized for all small and medium-sized enterprises but rather form a starting point for future studies. With the Solvin case, this paper provides a first indication as where the potentials of CDD can be expected and what aspects to take into account when further developing the approach. The implications can be summarized in a hypothesis as follows:

Adoption and successful implementation of the CDD approach in an SME depends on (1) the existence of business services (potentially) offered in different contexts, (2) compatibility to established technical platforms and (3) the willingness to modify the internal methodology for business service design and delivery of the SME under consideration.

Future work will have to consist of more case studies to support or falsify the hypothesis. With respect to their design, these future studies should use the same research questions and to some extent the same study design in order to cater for comparability of the results.

Furthermore, people experienced in IT service management tend to compare the CDD approach with service management approaches, as for example with ITIL [18]. This subject was also raised by Solvin during the 30 min presentation before the interviews (see Sect. 3), but it was not addressed in the interviews as such. Although CDD has a focus on business services of an enterprise and engineering aspects of the services whereas ITIL has a focus on IT-infrastructure services, there seem to be intersections, e.g. when it comes to service design. Future work should investigate the conceptual and process-oriented intersections between CDD and ITIL.

Acknowledgments. This work has been performed as part of the EU-FP7 funded project no: 611351 CaaS – Capability as a Service in Digital Enterprises.

References

1. Mayring, P.: Qualitative content analysis. Forum Qual. Soc. Res. **1**(2), Art. 20 (2000). http://nbn-resolving.de/urn:nbn:de:0114-fqs0002204
2. Wohlin, C., Runeson, P., Host, M., Ohlsson, C., Regnell, B., Wesslén, A.: Experimentation in Software Engineering: an Introduction. Kluver Academic Publishers, Boston (2000)
3. Yin, R.K.: Case Study Research: Design and Methods. Applied Social Research Methods Series, vol. 5, 3rd edn. Sage Publications Inc., Thousand Oaks (2002)
4. Jiang, Y., Zhao, J.: An empirical research of the forming process of firm inter-organizational e-business capability: based on the supply chain processes. In: 2010 2nd International Conference on Information Science and Engineering (ICISE), pp. 2603–2606 (2010)
5. Antunes, G., Barateiro, J., Becker, C., et al.: Modeling contextual concerns in enterprise architecture. In: 2011 15th IEEE International Enterprise Distributed Object Computing Conference Workshops (EDOCW), pp. 3–10 (2011)

6. Eriksson, T.: Processes, antecedents and outcomes of dynamic capabilities. Scandinavian Journal of Management (2013). doi:10.1016/j.scaman.2013.05.001
7. Boonpattarakan, A.: Model of thai Small and medium sized enterprises' organizational capabilities: review and verification. JMR **4**(3), 15 (2012). doi:10.5296/jmr.v4i3.1557
8. Stirna, J., Grabis, J., Henkel, M., Zdravkovic, J.: Capability driven development – an approach to support evolving organizations. In: Sandkuhl, K., Seigerroth, U., Stirna, J. (eds.) PoEM 2012. LNBIP, vol. 134, pp. 117–131. Springer, Heidelberg (2012)
9. Chen, J., Tsou, H.: Performance effects of 5IT6 capability, service process innovation, and the mediating role of customer service. J. Eng. Tech. Manage. **29**(1), 71–94 (2012). doi:10.1016/j.jengtecman.2011.09.007
10. Zdravkovic, J., Stirna, J., Henkel, M., Grabis, J.: Modeling business capabilities and context dependent delivery by cloud services. In: Salinesi, C., Norrie, M.C., Pastor, Ó. (eds.) CAiSE 2013. LNCS, vol. 7908, pp. 369–383. Springer, Heidelberg (2013)
11. Wirtz, B.W.: Business Model Management. Design - Instruments - Success Factors, 1st edn. Gabler, Wiesbaden (2011)
12. Brézillon, P., Cavalcanti, M.: Modeling and using context. Knowl. Eng. Rev. **13**(2), 185–194 (1998). doi:10.1017/S0269888998004044
13. Zott, C., Amit, R.: Designing your future business model: an activity system perspective. Long Range Plan. **43**, 216–226 (2010)
14. Sandkuhl, K., Stirna, J., Persson, A., Wißotzki, M.: Enterprise Modeling: Tackling Business Challenges with the 4EM Method. The Enterprise Engineering Series. Springer, Heidelberg (2014). ISBN 978-3662437247
15. Bērziša, S., Bravos, G., Gonzalez Cardona, T., Czubayko, U., España, S., Grabis, J., Henkel, M., Jokste, L., Kampars, J., Koc, H., Kuhr, J., Llorca, C., Loucopoulos, P., Juanes Pascual, R., Sandkuhl, K., Simic, H., Stirna, J., Zdravkovic, J.: Deliverable 1.4: Requirements specification for CDD, CaaS – Capability as a Service for Digital Enterprises, FP7 project no 611351, Riga Technical University, Latvia (2014)
16. Sandkuhl, K., Koç, H., Stirna, J.: Context-aware business services: technological Support for business and IT-alignment. In: Abramowicz, W., Kokkinaki, A. (eds.) BIS 2014 Workshops. LNBIP, vol. 183, pp. 190–201. Springer, Heidelberg (2014)
17. Bērziša, S., Bravos, G., Gonzalez Cardona, T., Czubayko, U., España, S., Grabis, J., Henkel, M., Jokste, L., Kampars, J., Koç, H., Kuhr, J.-C., Llorca, C., Loucopoulos, P., Juanes Pascual, R., Pastor, O., Sandkuhl, K., Simic, H., Stirna, J., Zdravkovic, J.: Capability driven development: an approach to designing digital enterprises. Bus. Info. Syst. Eng. (BISE) **57**(1), 15–25 (2015). doi:10.1007/s12599-014-0362-0
18. Office of Government Commerce: The Official Introduction to the ITIL Service Lifecycle, 2007th edn. The Stationery Office, London (2007)

Advanced Context Processing for Business Process Execution Adjustment

Jānis Grabis[1(⊠)] and Janis Stirna[2]

[1] Information Technology Institute, Riga Technical University,
Kalku 1, Riga, Latvia
grabis@rtu.lv
[2] Department of Computer and Systems Sciences, Stockholm University,
Postbox 7003, 16407 Kista, Sweden
js@dsv.su.se

Abstract. Business process execution is affected by various contextual factors. Context-aware business processes consider the contextual factors during process design and execution. There is a large variety of possible context situations and their impact on the business process is difficult to know in advance. To this end an advanced context processing to adjust business process execution is proposed. It allows flexible definition of meaningful context categories using measurable properties of the context and run-time adjustment of the categories. The adjustment is performed depending on the progress towards achieving business goals. The proposal is demonstrated by a travel management example.

Keywords: Business process · Context · Adjustment · Performance indicators

1 Introduction

Adaptation of business process (BP) execution to changes in the real world emerges as a challenge. Context is any information that can be used to characterize the situation of an entity [1]. An information system (IS) is context-aware if it uses context to provide relevant information and/or services to the user. Business services and processes are among areas significantly affected by context [2]. To address the need to adjust businesses and IS, the Capability Driven Development (CDD) approach [3, 4] has been proposed. CDD supports business service provisioning by ensuring that business capabilities are delivered in accordance to goals in various contexts. CDD relies on Enterprise Modeling, context processing, as well as knowledge and variability management to design capabilities. The capability delivery is dynamically adjusted to improve delivery performance depending on the context.

The major issues of *designing and running* context aware BP are: (1) diversity of process execution circumstances causes excessive variability in BP designs; (2) not all context situations can be foreseen at design time; and (3) relationships among context and BP performance are not well-understood. Issues (1) and (2) are addressed by categorizing context values into a set of meaningful values, for which process design and execution is differentiated. Issue (3) is addressed by adjusting context definitions at run-time using a search procedure.

A. Persson and J. Stirna (Eds.): CAiSE 2015 Workshops, LNBIP 215, pp. 15–26, 2015.
DOI: 10.1007/978-3-319-19243-7_2

The objective of this paper is *to elaborate a method for advanced context processing based on using context definition run-time adjustments to improve performance of BP execution.*

A running example of a travel management process of a university is used. BPMN [5] is used for BP modeling and to indicate context dependencies. The context is modeled with the approach proposed in [6]. It is refined by elaborating a method for advanced context processing that includes context representation and specification of context processing expressions during design of the context aware IS and context processing adjustment during run-time of the context aware IS. The context processing adjustment is performed to optimize process execution performance as prescribed by BP goals. The context processing is evaluated using a simulation study. The contributions of the paper are (1) a flexible approach for defining meaningful context categories and (2) a search method for redefining the categories if sufficient information was unavailable at design time.

The rest of the paper is organized as follows. Section 2 summarizes related work on BP contextualization. The research framework and the running example are introduced in Sect. 3. Section 4 presents BP contextualization and Sect. 5 presents the advanced context processing is presented. Section 6 reports evaluation results and Sect. 7 presents concluding remarks.

2   Related Work

BP variants is currently one of the most frequently used approaches for supporting adjustment of BP for specific conditions and requirements. Process variants can be constructed either by configuration or adaptation [7]. In the case of adaptation, the variants are designed by applying BP change operations such as insertion, deletion of tasks or other process flow elements. In the execution phase, Switching between the process variants is possible also during the process execution phase to deal with dynamic context changes [8]. Principles of autonomic computing are used for process management to maintain the process execution performance within certain bounds [9] by selecting appropriate operational variants depending on the current execution performance and context. Reference [10] proposes a dynamic adaption of service composition and can be seen as opposite to static adaptation that requires shutting down the IS for manual modification. The key issues of dynamic adaptation are context awareness, adaptation policies, supporting infrastructure and verification.

The adaptive and context aware workflows [11, 12] are used to provide process-oriented services tailored to the current operating circumstances using either context data to alter workflow execution sequence without changing the underlying schema or running workflow instance or adapt the workflow schema or running instances. Majority of the surveyed solutions deal with workflow instance adaption [12].

Various techniques ranging from judgmental to data mining [13] can be used to identify relevant context factors. Contextual analysis is applied to develop process execution variants depending on the process execution context in [14]. A method for dynamic configuration of BP according to the context at run-time is elaborated in [15].

These works primarily address the identification of the context factors; context processing and interpretation is rarely considered.

BP exception handling patterns provide possible solutions for dealing with various exceptional circumstances during the process execution [16]. A method for using context-based configuration rules for post-design adaptation of case management processes has been elaborated in [17]. It demonstrates that context information is important for driving BP adaption.

3   Research Framework

This research is part of an EC FP7 project CaaS – Capability as a Service for Digital Enterprises (no. 611351). Its objective is to develop an approach and an environment for context dependent design and delivery of business services, including adjustments at run-time. CaaS has of three industrial cases at Everis (Spain), FreshT (UK), and SIV (Germany). The validation at each company started with requirements analysis [18] followed by capability design [19, 20]. The next step is development of the connections between the capability designs and the supporting IS, executing the capabilities as well as adjusting them at run-time. The travel case presents the initial elaboration and validation by the means of simulation of the CDD method components for context processing based on using context definition run-time adjustments. The overall ethos of the research approach taken is that of Design Science [21]. The travel case is used in the project as initial design-evaluation cycle that is followed by separate design-evaluation cycles at each use case company.

3.1   Running Example

The travel management process consists of four main activities (Fig. 1). The travel planning specifies purpose, destination and time of the business trip. The travel budgeting specifies the planned travel expenses in compliance with internal and external regulatory requirements. During the trip, the travel objectives are achieved and expenses are accumulated. The travel results and expenses are reported upon returning.

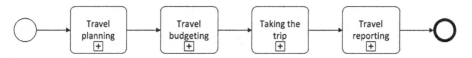

Fig. 1. Overall travel management process

Table 1 lists some of the business goals for this process and performance indicators that are deemed important for the case. In the CaaS use cases the goals and indicators are represented by a goal model. The business trip needs to contribute university's academic outcomes (goal G1) and the travel costs need to be optimized (G2). Trips are affected by uncertainties such as weather conditions and unexpected events causing delays, leading to extra costs and scheduling conflicts, in spite of which trips need to be completed on time (G3). Trips take time away from other academic activities; hence scheduling conflicts should be minimal (G4). The paperwork for reporting the trip should be minimized (G5).

Table 1. The travel management goals and associated performance indicators

Goal	Performance indicator
G1. To maximize traveling outcomes	I_1. Number of resulting publications I_2. Number of contacts established
G2. To optimize travel costs	I_3. Average travel costs per trip
G3. To complete trip on time	I_4. Number of trips not completed on time I_5. Sum of days late
G4. To minimize scheduling conflicts	I_6. Average severity of scheduling conflicts
G5. To minimize travel management paperwork	I_7. Percentage of trips requiring additional evaluation/approvals

Goals achievement depends on the environmental factors and circumstances. E.g. travel costs might increase due to a major event at the planned destination, or a trip is delayed due to weather or unexpected important events are added to the organizational calendar. The process execution context can capture some of these circumstances. Therefore, contextualization of the travel management process is highly desirable.

4 Context Aware Business Process

BP contextualization is performed in three steps: (1) association of BP activities with business goals and appropriate performance measures; (2) identification of process elements affected by the context; (3) reasoning about relationships among the business goals and the context.

BP have specific goals to be achieved. The goals will be used to adjust context processing. The process execution is measured for individual process instances using selected process indicators. The indicators are defined following guidelines provided in [22]. The indicators can be graphically represented in the process model as data objects. The context dependence can be represented as: (a) context dependent script tasks; (b) decision-making at the complex gateway; (c) throwing a regular event; and (d) throwing an attached event (Fig. 2). The elements are chosen because they allow evaluation of context depend expressions although other process flow elements could also take context as input data. The context is represented as data objects attached to relevant flow elements. Relations between context and the process elements are indicated without further elaboration of context processing.

To represent context dependent branching decisions using complex gateways we assume that context values can be categorized in a meaningful categories and every outgoing branch of the context dependent complex gateway corresponds to treatment

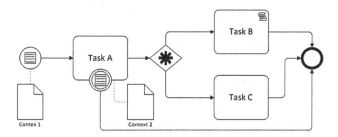

Fig. 2. BPMN elements used for representing context dependence

of one of these categories. The task is to establish these categories and if necessary to adjust the categories to better comply with the BP goals.

Advanced context processing takes place at both design time and run-time. The BP is designed and its context dependent features are specified at the design time. If the BP is developed using executable BPMN, it can be readily deployed and executed in the run-time environment. Execution of BP instances also includes capturing the context data and feeding them to the running BP and monitoring the process performance. The context processing is adjusted during the run-time using the context data and the process performance measures. The adjustment is done without redeploying the BP.

The travel planning activity is contextualized (Fig. 3). The goals relevant to this activity are G1, G3, G4 and G5. The tasks are affected by context factors - *travel conditions*, *calendar* and *weather*. The travel conditions are general conditions at the planned destination, e.g., the US Department of State issuing warnings and alerts for visiting certain countries. The calendar is a university-wide calendar of events to evaluate significance of overlapping between planned travel dates and other events. The calendar contains both general events of varying importance and events assigned to specific employees. The weather context affects ability to complete trips on time.

The process has variability to deal with the context. If travel conditions are hazardous the trip is canceled. Procedures for addressing calendar and weather concerns are also proposed. Depending of perceived severity of the calendar conflicts, their resolution is performed or warning suggesting optional conflict resolution is generated.

5 Context Processing

Context processing is done in three stages: (1) context representation; (2) design-time processing including specifying expressions for context categorization; and (3) run-time processing, i.e. adjusting the context categorization according to situation.

5.1 Context Representation

The context factors affecting the process execution are referred as to context elements [6]. The context categories are defined using the context element range (Fig. 4).

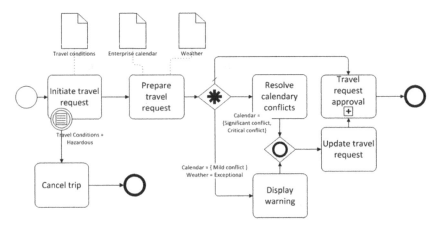

Fig. 3. The expanded travel planning activity

Contextual circumstances are captured using measurable properties (MP) that measure the actual phenomena affecting the process. Context elements are an interpretation of the measurements in the business sense. The context element range is identified during the process design. If a context element is associated with a complex gateway then the process model should have a branch for processing every category in the range.

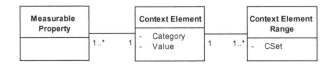

Fig. 4. Concepts used for context representation

MP give flexibility for changing context processing without changing the BP. E.g., if additional of MP become available they can be used to evaluate the context element category more precisely.

Figure 3 shows the contextualized travel planning activity Travel conditions, Calendar and Weather are the context elements. The Travel conditions context element has Context Element Range (Normal, Hazardous). The context element is measured using the US Department of State warnings and alerts for visiting certain countries. It there is a warning or an alert issued for the planned destination then the travel conditions are Hazardous (in this case category and value are the same since the measure is already categorical) otherwise Travel conditions are Normal. These kinds of warnings can be seen as rather coarse data and other MP from different context data providers can be added later to evaluate travel conditions more precisely.

5.2   Design-Time Processing

Transformation of MP into context element values is defined during process design. Given the ith context element and MP $P_i = (p_{i1}, \ldots, p_{iM})$, the context element value V_i is calculated as

$$V_i = f(P_i) \tag{1}$$

Every context element has its range of context elements defined as $R_i = (r_{i1}, \ldots, r_{iN})$.

The relationship between the context element value and range is expressed as

$$C_i = \begin{cases} r_{ij}, b_{ij}^L \leq V_i < b_{ij}^U \\ r_{iN}, V_i \geq b_{iN-1}^U \end{cases} \tag{2}$$

where $b_{ij}^L = \phi((j-1)\Delta V_i)$ is the lower bound for jth range and $b_{ij}^U = \phi(j \times \Delta V_i)$ is the upper bound for the jth range. $\Delta V_i = N_i^{-1}(\max(V_i) - \min(V_i))$ and ϕ is a function to be specified.

The categorization of the context depends upon decisions made by business analysis and process owners. Some of the categories occur naturally in the business environment while others are derived as a result of expert judgment. In the case of limited information, the categories ought to be reevaluated as more data become available. The way categories are defined can be used as an instrument to manage achievement of the process goals. E.g., in the travel management case there are two conflicting goals: (1) minimizing the calendar conflicts among the travel dates and other events; and (2) minimizing travel management paperwork.

5.3   Run-Time Adjustment

Relationships between context categories and goals are implemented as run-time adjustments. The process of run-time adjustment is as follows:

- instances of context aware BP are executed
- performance measurements are accumulated and goals are evaluated
- if performance targets are not met, perform adjustment of the context categorization expression (Eq. 3)
- apply the new categorization expression to newly created process instances.

The adjustment can be made automatically using formalized adjustment rules although a human approval might often be needed. The adjustments are implemented at run-time without redeploying the BP execution solution. They are implemented by redefining Eqs. 2 and 3. The expressions depend on functional form of f and its parameters referred as to ω. The values of ω are changed according to observed values of indicators. An exact relationship between context categories and indicators is unknown, hence a search approach is used to identify proper categories.

$$\omega_i = \begin{cases} \omega_i + \Delta\omega_i, I_j < I_j^{Target} \\ \omega_i - \Delta\omega_i, I_j \gg I_j^{Target} \end{cases} \tag{3}$$

The dependency implies that greater values of ω contribute to improving indicator I_j (depending on indicator, the opposite may be true and the sign is reversed). The much more relation $\gg$ is used to indicate that reduction should be made only in regards to other conflicting indicators, for which impact of ω is different.

In the travel management case, larger ω is preferred to reduce calendar conflicts because more cases are classified as having significant or severe conflict and the resolution activity should take place. However, that might also cause an increasing amount of paperwork and indicator I_7 prefers smaller values of ω.

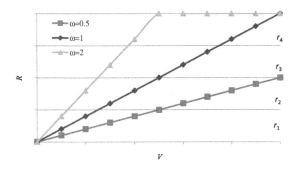

Fig. 5. Impact of ω on categorization results

If ϕ is a linear function, the impact of ω on categorization is illustrated in Fig. 5, where context element category is shown depending on the context element value. $\omega = 1$ gives evenly distributed ranges of context values. If ω is increased more context values are categorized to belonging to the upper category. If ω is decreased majority of context values fall into the lower categories.

If the BP execution environment is relatively steady then a categorization steady-state can be achieved. In that case, the adjustment is used to deal with the initial lack of information during the process design. However, if the environment is not stable, then the adjustment allows for continuous updating of the categories.

6 Evaluation

The proposed advanced context processing is evaluated using the travel management case. The evaluation objective is to demonstrate the impact of run-time adjustment of context processing on BP performance. The evaluation is performed by simulating multiple travel requests and contextual data and using these to adjust context processing. The simulation focuses only on the travel planning activity and, more specifically, on relations between the calendar context element and goals G4 and G5.

The calendar context element is defined in Table 2. The calendar context element relies on the university-wide calendar of events to evaluate the significance of overlapping between planned travel dates and other events. The calendar contains both general events of varying importance and events assigned to specific employees.

Table 2. Definition of the Calendar context element

Context element	Measurable properties	Context Element Range
Calendar	p_1 is the count of the scheduled hours of regular importance overlapping with travel dates	No conflict, Mild conflict,
	p_2 is the count of the scheduled hours assigned to the employee and overlapping with the travel dates p_3 is the count of the scheduled hours overlapping with the travel dates and marked as high importance	Significant conflict, Critical Conflict

The context element value is calculated as

$$V_c = \frac{w_1 p_1 + w_2 p_2 + w_3 p_3}{w_3 H}, \tag{4}$$

where c refers to the calendar context element, H is the total duration of the trip in hours, p_1 is the count of the scheduled hours of regular importance overlapping with travel dates, p_2 is the count of the scheduled hours assigned to the employee and overlapping with the travel dates, p_3 is the count of the scheduled hours overlapping with the travel dates and marked as high importance, and w_j are appropriate weight coefficients indicating importance of every measurable property in calculating the measure.

The context element category is evaluated following Eq. 2 and using a linear adjustment function, i.e., the lower and upper bounds are reformulated as $b_{cj}^L = \omega(j-1)\Delta V_c$ and $b_{ij}^U = \omega \times j \times \Delta V_c$, respectively.

Performance indicators I_6 and I_7 reference to goals G4 and G5, measure the travel planning activity and the target values are set as 0.1 and 20 %, respectively. I_6 is evaluated using expression Eq. 4 and I_7 is measured as a percentage of trips categorized as having significant of critical conflict and thus requiring additional conflict resolution (rescheduling, finding replacement etc.). It is reasoned that:

1. More trips categorized as having a high level of conflict results into increasing amount of paperwork, thus, negatively affecting goal G5;
2. More trips categorized as having a low level of conflict results into increasing level of scheduling conflicts, thus, negatively affecting goal G4.

The goals are mutually contradicting. Achieving G5 would favor adjustment by decreasing ω while achieving G4 would favor adjustment by increasing ω.

The process is simulated as follows: (1) generate trip data including starting date, duration and destination; (2) generate the measurable properties; (3) evaluate context category; (4) simulate scheduling conflict resolution; (5) evaluate process performance; and (6) update ω using Eq. 3.

The trip duration is distributed as N(4,1), where N denotes normal distribution with mean 4 and standard deviation 1. Similarly, MP p_1, p_2 and p_3 are generated using N(1,1), N(2,1) and N(0.8, 0.5), respectively. The conflict resolution is simulated using the following rules. If R_c = "No conflict" no adjustment is performed. If R_c = "Mild conflict" then a non-binding warning is displayed to an employee about presence of the scheduling conflict and the employee voluntary resolves some of the scheduling conflicts. The reduction is done by h percent where $h_1 \sim$ N(10,5) (it is applied to all MP). If $R_c \in$ (Significant conflict, Critical conflict) an employee enters the conflict resolution task resulting in conflict reduction by h percent, where h is distributed N (30,10) and N(75,25) for respective categories. These values imply that all conflicts are not necessarily resolved, though the percentage of conflicts resolved correlates with the severity of scheduling conflicts as identified by the calendar context element.

The context processing adjustment is performed according to both I_6 and I_7. ω is increased if the I_6 target is not met and is decreased if I_7 target is not met. The starting value of ω is one. 500 trips are simulated and ω is updated after every 10 trips with $\Delta\omega = 0.1$.

Figure 6a shows the convergence of ω values according to a number of adjustments, suggesting that the search procedure quickly identifies an improved categorization of the Calendar context element. Settling on $\omega < 1$ indicates that the process goals can be better achieved if fewer cases have high level of conflict. ω fluctuates between 0.5 and 0.6 because G4 and G5 are contradicting each other and an equilibrium satisfying both goals cannot be found (Fig. 6b). At $\omega = 0.5$, the paperwork reduction is achieved but the severity of scheduling conflicts target is not satisfied. Increasing of ω leads to deterioration of I_7. The figure also shows evaluation results for two other selected values of ω. The results highlight that for this case the adjustment alone cannot ensure achieving all business goals and other process improvement options are needed.

Obviously, the evaluation results depend upon the way I_6 is calculated and other parameters. These parameters are set up during the context aware process design and can be updated during the process execution if necessary.

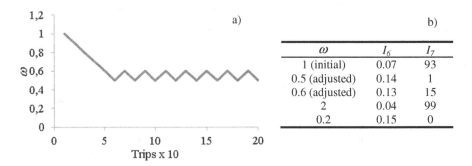

Fig. 6. Evaluation results: (a) convergence of ω; and (b) BP performance

7 Concluding Remarks and Future Work

The paper investigated the advanced context processing as a part of research on the CDD of context aware IS. The advanced context processing allows defining the context in a way of minimizing BP variability and maximizing achievement of the business goals. The process variations are developed only for the context categories meaningful to the business and run-time adjustments allow realigning these categories to improve BP execution performance.

More complex functional relationships between the context value and the context category can be defined. E.g., a rule can be added that if $p_1 > 0$ then R_c ="Critical conflict". This requires additional design and convergence of the search procedure would be slower (i.e., it would be harder to identify appropriate categories). The search procedure could be improved in various ways. E.g., variable $\Delta\omega$ could be used to find an optimal value of ω though that would be possible only in the stable environment.

The run-time adjustment of context categories is not applicable for all types of business decisions. In many situations any changes in categories would require additional validation and approval. If that is a case, then the run-time adjustment provides suggestions for changing the way context is processed in the BP, and proposed changes are not implemented automatically.

The next step of this research is validation of the advanced context processing using the CaaS use cases. This research will also serve as input for developing an application visualizing changes in the context and adjustments performed.

References

1. Abowd, G.D.: Software engineering issues for ubiquitous computing. In: Proceedings of the International Conference on Software Engineering, pp.75–84 (1999)
2. Rosemann, M., Recker, J., Flender, C.: Contextualisation of business processes. Int. J. Bus. Process Integr. Manag. **3**, 47–60 (2008)
3. Stirna, J., Grabis, J., Henkel, M., Zdravkovic, J.: Capability driven development – an approach to support evolving organizations. In: Sandkuhl, K., Seigerroth, U., Stirna, J. (eds.) PoEM 2012. LNBIP, vol. 134, pp. 117–131. Springer, Heidelberg (2012)
4. Bērziša, S., Bravos, G., González, T., Czubayko, U., España, S., Grabis, J., Henkel, M., Jokste, L., Kampars, J., Koç, H., Kuhr, J., Llorca, C., Loucopoulos, P., Pascual, R.J., Pastor, O., Sandkuhl, K., Simic, H., Stirna, J., Giromé, F.V., Zdravkovic, J.: Capability driven development: an approach to designing digital enterprises. Bus. Inf. Syst. Eng. **57**, 15–25 (2015)
5. OMG: Business Process Model and Notation. http://www.omg.org/spec/BPMN/2.0/. (2011)
6. Zdravkovic, J., Stirna, J., Henkel, M., Grabis, J.: Modeling business capabilities and context dependent delivery by cloud services. In: Salinesi, C., Norrie, M.C., Pastor, Ó. (eds.) CAiSE 2013. LNCS, vol. 7908, pp. 369–383. Springer, Heidelberg (2013)
7. Döhring, M., Reijers, H.A., Smirnov, S.: Configuration vs. adaptation for business process variant maintenance: an empirical study. Inf. Syst. **39**, 108–133 (2014)
8. Hallerbach, A., Bauer, T., Reichert, M.: Capturing variability in business process models: the Provop approach. J. Softw. Maintenance Evol. **22**, 519–546 (2010)

9. Oliveira, K., Castro, J., España, S., Pastor, O.: Multi-level autonomic business process management. In: Nurcan, S., Proper, H.A., Soffer, P., Krogstie, J., Schmidt, R., Halpin, T., Bider, I. (eds.) BPMDS 2013 and EMMSAD 2013. LNBIP, vol. 147, pp. 184–198. Springer, Heidelberg (2013)

10. Alférez, G.H., Pelechano, V., Mazo, R., Salinesi, C., Diaz, D.: Dynamic adaptation of service compositions with variability models. J. Syst. Softw. **91**, 24–47 (2014)

11. Muller, R., Greiner, U., Rahm, E.: AGENT WORK: a workflow system supporting rule-based workflow adaptation. Data Knowl. Eng. **51**, 223–256 (2004)

12. Smanchat, S., Ling, S., Indrawan, M.: A survey on context-aware workflow adaptations. In: Proceedings of the MoMM 2008, pp. 414–417 (2008)

13. Ramos, E.C., Santoro, F.M., Baião, F.: A method for discovering the relevance of external context variables to business processes. In: proceedings of KMIS 2011, pp. 399–408 (2011)

14. De la Vara, J.L., Ali, R., Dalpiaz, F., Sánchez, J., Giorgini, P.: Business processes contextualisation via context analysis. In: Parsons, J., Saeki, M., Shoval, P., Woo, C., Wand, Y. (eds.) ER 2010. LNCS, vol. 6412, pp. 471–476. Springer, Heidelberg (2010)

15. Santos, E., Pimentel, J., Castro, J., Finkelstein, A.: On the dynamic configuration of business process models. In: Bider, I., Halpin, T., Krogstie, J., Nurcan, S., Proper, E., Schmidt, R., Soffer, P., Wrycza, S. (eds.) EMMSAD 2012 and BPMDS 2012. LNBIP, vol. 113, pp. 331–346. Springer, Heidelberg (2012)

16. Russell, N., van der Aalst, W.M., ter Hofstede, A.H.: Workflow exception patterns. In: Martinez, F.H., Pohl, K. (eds.) CAiSE 2006. LNCS, vol. 4001, pp. 288–302. Springer, Heidelberg (2006)

17. Rychkova, I.: Towards automated support for case management processes with declarative configurable specifications. In: La Rosa, M., Soffer, P. (eds.) BPM Workshops 2012. LNBIP, vol. 132, pp. 65–76. Springer, Heidelberg (2013)

18. Bravos, G., González, T., Grabis, J., Henkel, M., Jokste, L., Koc, H., Stirna, J.: Capability modeling: initial experiences. In: Johansson, B., Andersson, B., Holmberg, N. (eds.) BIR 2014. LNBIP, vol. 194, pp. 1–14. Springer, Heidelberg (2014)

19. Zdravkovic, J., Stirna, J., Kuhr, J.-C., Koç, H.: Requirements engineering for capability driven development. In: Frank, U., Loucopoulos, P., Pastor, Ó., Petrounias, I. (eds.) PoEM 2014. LNBIP, vol. 197, pp. 193–207. Springer, Heidelberg (2014)

20. España, S., González, T., Grabis, J., Jokste, L., Juanes, R., Valverde, F.: Capability-driven development of a soa platform: a case study. In: Iliadis, L., Papazoglou, M., Pohl, K. (eds.) CAiSE Workshops 2014. LNBIP, vol. 178, pp. 100–111. Springer, Heidelberg (2014)

21. Hevner, A.R., March, T.S., Park, J., Sudha, R.: Design science in information systems research. MIS Q. **28**, 75–105 (2004)

22. Strecker, S., Frank, U., Heise, D., Kattenstroth, H.: MetricM: a modeling method in support of the reflective design and use of performance measurement systems. IseB **10**, 241–276 (2012)

Towards Systemic Risk Management in the Frame of Business Service Ecosystem

Christophe Feltus[(✉)], François-Xavier Fontaine, and Eric Grandry

Luxembourg Institute of Science and Technology,
5 Avenue des Hauts-Fourneaux, 4362 Esch-sur-Alzette, Luxembourg
{Christophe.Feltus,Francois-Xavier.Fontaine,
Eric.Grandry}@list.lu

Abstract. Ecosystems gather enterprises which collaborate to achieve a common systemic goal like guaranteeing the national healthcare, the telecommunication, or the financial stability. These systems are governed by regulators that supervise the services provided at the ecosystem level using systemic capabilities and resources. In the same way at the enterprise level, risk management at the ecosystem level is a paramount activity for the stability of the targeted sector. This paper proposes a metamodel for modelling the ecosystem capabilities and resources, a risk management approach based on this metamodel, and an ArchiMate extension language to sustain the systemic risk management. The approach is illustrated with a real case study from the Luxembourgish financial market.

Keywords: Capability · Systemic risk · Resource · Business service · Regulation

1 Introduction

Today's enterprises are interconnected and form an ecosystem of interdependent entities delivering value-added products to their customers. As a service economy, Luxembourg is hosting many business service ecosystems, which are interconnected and constitute a constellation of entities delivering services: let's consider the financial ecosystem formed of financial service providers (PFS) and support service providers (Support-PFS), connected to infrastructure and telecommunication ecosystem formed of data centres and telecommunication service providers. Since the Luxembourgish environment is characterised by high-level of costs in terms of HR, buildings and infrastructure, Luxembourg-based service providers can only differentiate their service offering in terms of qualities such as performance, compliance and security rather than their price. The global IT strategy of Luxembourg (Digital Lëtzebuerg) is aligned with this view and aims at positioning Luxembourg as a safe data hub, where compliance and information security are core enabling properties.

In order to increase trust in the business service ecosystems, national regulators are appointed to supervise and control the compliance of the participating actors with the regulation. As such, the regulator is part of the business service ecosystems, as it is responsible for the compliance of the delivered services. The added-value of the

© Springer International Publishing Switzerland 2015
A. Persson and J. Stirna (Eds.): CAiSE 2015 Workshops, LNBIP 215, pp. 27–39, 2015.
DOI: 10.1007/978-3-319-19243-7_3

regulator in the ecosystem is therefore to transform business services into regulated business services, through additional services and controls. As an ecosystem is usually a complex system (many elements and many interactions), risk management is a mean exploited by the regulator to control specific aspects of the ecosystem: the *Institut Luxembourgeois de Régulation* (http://www.ilr.lu), regulating the telecommunication ecosystem, imposes that each telecommunication service provider performs a security risk analysis to guarantee the availability of their networks. To date, regulators require that appropriate risk management activities are performed by each organisation. In the future, the regulator will also focus their attention on the risks at the level of the ecosystem, the systemic risk. In this paper we investigate how the concept of capability can be leveraged to drive risk analysis at the ecosystem level.

After a review of the concept of capability, in the next section, we present our metamodel of a Business Service Ecosystem (BSE) in Sect. 3, and we demonstrate how this metamodel perfectly supports systemic risk analysis in Sect. 4. We propose a systemic risk management language for expressing the BSE metamodel at the enterprise and at the systemic level, based on an ArchiMate extension, in Sect. 5, and we conclude the paper in Sect. 6. Our approach is illustrated with a use case that has been run in a project with the national regulator of the financial System.

2   State of the Art

Strategic sourcing is the essence of the capability theory. It requires the right capability to be delivered at the right cost from the right source and right shore [10].

The CaaS project has defined a Capability metamodel [1, 2, 6, 7]. This metamodel gathers elements from three domains: the context, the enterprise modelling, and the reuse and variability dimension [2]. At the CaaS metamodel level, the Capability is defined as *the ability of an organization to manage its resources to accomplish a task* [4] and *as the ability and capacity that enables an enterprise to achieve a business goal in a certain context* [7]. This context represents the *characterisation of a solution in which the capability should be provided* [1]. Consequently, the context is used to evaluate and adjust the pattern that must be applied to deliver capabilities and represents a reusable solution in terms of business process, roles, supporting IT and resources. The definition of the capability from CaaS covers both the organisation capability (enabling a firm to make a living in the present [3]) and the dynamic capability (enabling a firm adaption to rapidly and discontinuously changing external environments [5]). [3] addresses this distinction between dynamic and operational (or ordinary) capability. The latter represents what is used and what enables a firm to extend or modify what brings it to live. The organizational capability implies that the organization has the capacity to perform a particular activity in a reliable and at least minimal satisfactory manner. This organizational capability is equivalent to the main capability as expressed by [4]. The goal (that requires capabilities), as defined in CaaS, may be of five types according to [1]: *Strategic, Business, Technical, Design time and Run-time,* and therefore they may be achieved by dynamic or organizational capabilities. [14] considers that a capability is composed of *capacity*: resources (e.g. money, time, staff, tools) for delivering the capability, and *ability*: competence (e.g. talent, intelligence and disposition), skills, processes. For [14], capabilities are of three types: *strategic, value-added, commodity*. According to [13], the capability is an *ability to perform* that requires *investment of time and effort*. [13] also considers the resources as an element which *can be bought* or *easily acquired*. An explanation of resource is proposed by [10] which consider it as the *assets that organization has or can call upon*. In order to procure competitive advantage to the enterprise, it must be - as far as possible - Rare, Valuable, Inimitable, and Non-substitutable (VRIN) [11].

Reference [4] proposed an approach to support business transformations based on capability. It assumes that an enterprise consists in any organization that generates operation activities funded by stakeholders that do not work for the enterprise. This organization has the capability to produce value for external entities (like customers in case of private organizations or citizens in the case of public ones) in exchange of money. In this context, [4] suggests structuring the organizations as a recursive structure of capability and resources, and using a set of transformation patterns. The (main) capability that produces value for which external stakeholders are ready to pay are supported by resources, themselves supported by supporting capabilities, and are called sub-capabilities. To uncover the structure of an organization regarding these capability-resource patterns, [4] has introduced the capability resource type that helps identifying the resources which constitute a particular capability and the capability sub-type to explore the capability that is needed by the resources which constitute the (main) capability. The recurring repetition of patterns constitutes a fractal organization which supports the achievement of organizational and dynamic goals from the business layer of the organization down to the supporting layers. According to [6], this pattern also aggregates process variants, which are themselves specialisations of processes. The variability in capability modelling allows facing the rapidly changing environment in companies. Therefore [6] suggests to introduce the variation aspects as the cause of a variation and the variation points as the locations of variation in the elements that compose the business service.

3 Towards a Business Service Ecosystem Metamodel

The ecosystem services aim to achieve ecosystem goals (like defining the required level of security of the information in the financial sector) and represent a high value for the beneficiaries of the ecosystem (state or private companies) that are generally willing to pay for it.

In [4], the authors explain that *any organization where the operational activities of which are financed by external stakeholder* may be considered as an enterprise. Based on this statement, we assume that an ecosystem may be perceived as a specialization of an enterprise too, provided that this ecosystem has a specific and well dedicated goal (for instance, the goals of a financial ecosystem is to guarantee the delivery of highly secured financial products). To achieve its goals, the ecosystem gets money from external stakeholders (e.g. the customers paying for the financial products, the state injecting money to stabilize the financial). In exchange, the ecosystem produces high value for its beneficiaries (guarantee the performance of the financial activities at the national level). To deliver this value, the ecosystem uses capabilities at the ecosystem level. These capabilities are amongst others, the capability to regulate the system, the capability to support core activities (archiving, control, etc.)

Given the similarity between the enterprise structure and the ecosystem structure, we propose to extend the fractal organization approach proposed by [4] and raising the capability-resource pattern from the enterprise level (pattern B of Fig. 1) up to the eco-system level (pattern A). This allows elaborating what we have named the Business Service Ecosystem (BSE) metamodel where the (main) capability of the entire system is the ecosystem capability and where the resources of the ecosystem are derived from the ecosystem enterprises capability.

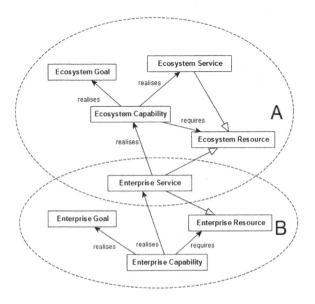

Fig. 1. Business Service Ecosystem metamodel

The Systemic Capability metamodel relies on three concepts: resource, capability and goal. These elements have already been defined in the CaaS metamodel and we have decided to keep their definitions unchanged, namely: the Capability is *the ability and capacity that enable an enterprise to achieve a business goal in a certain context* [7]. Given patterns A and B, we distinguish the ecosystem capability from the enter-prise capability. The ecosystem capability in the financial sector is for instance the ability to regulate the system, at the national level. At the enterprise level, for instance, it is the capacity to provide financial advice to the customers. The resource *is an asset that an organization has or can call upon* [10]. At the ecosystem level, a resource may consist of a set of employees that manage the ecosystem (like the regulators) and at the enterprise level, it could consist, e.g. in a financial asset management software. The goal *is a desired state of affairs that needs to be obtained* [1]. At the ecosystem level, a goal could be to guarantee the delivery of secure financial services to customers, although it could be to make profits for a private financial institution. A specialization of the resource has been represented in Fig. 1 and consists in the enterprise service.

The enterprise services have been defined as *acts performed for others, including the provision of resources that others will use* [18]. As a result, it is a type of behaviour that allows an enterprise's goal to be realized and that requires enterprise capability to exist. For instance, the analysis of the level of risk regarding certain financial assets is a service provided by a unit of the bank which also constitutes a resource for analysing the customer risk profile by the customer service unit.

Postulated that the capabilities consist in elements that require a set of resources (enterprise human resources, software, material, processes, etc.) from the enterprise [13], they may hardly be directly exploited by the ecosystem. For instance, the financial asset management software is resource owned by a company and it may not be directly exploited without agreement for delivering ecosystem capabilities. As a consequence, to be friendly offered outside the perimeter of the enterprise, the resources are organised in services. As a result, the latter constitutes a hyphen between the enterprise capability and the ecosystem resource and hence, a common element to both patterns A and B. At the ecosystem level, this enterprise service may be considered as a type of resource that is required by an ecosystem capability or by another capability of the same institution. For instance, the service of risk analysis associated to certain financial assets may be sold outside the institution to analyse, e.g. the risk associated to the ecosystem assets, or required by the institution to analyse, e.g. the average risk associated to all the assets managed by this institution.

4   Systemic Risk Management

The capability-driven approach for modelling enterprise ecosystems paves the way to an innovative method for managing the risks of the ecosystem, aka systemic risks. To present our approach, we exploit the information system security risk management reference model (ISSRM) and apply it at both levels (A and B) of the BSE metamodel of Fig. 1. This alignment between the metamodels is illustrated with the following case:

Since mid-2014, the LIST is mandated by the *Commission de Surveillance du Secteur Financier* (CSSF - regulator - http://www.cssf.lu) to structure and model systemic risk management approaches for the Luxembourgish financial sector. The ecosystem related to this collaboration is partially represented in Fig. 3 which models two specific actors of the sector (CSSF and Lab Group) following the BSE metamodel. The CSSF is a specific type of enterprise with a regulator goal to regulate the ecosystem. Hence, it is a public institution which supervises the professionals and products for the financial sector. To reach this goal, the CSSF regulates the enterprises that compose this ecosystem and offers services that generate systemic capabilities. It is also in charge of promoting transparency, simplicity and fairness in the financial products and services market, and is responsible for the law enforcement on financial consumer protection, on the fight against money laundering, and terrorist financing [15]. As part of its mission, the CSSF has several objectives: promoting a considered and prudent business policy in compliance with the regulatory requirements; protecting the financial stability and of the financial sector; supervising the quality of the organisation and internal control systems; and strengthening the quality of risk management.

Lab Group (http://www.labgroup.com) is a financial sector professional that supports the financial sector. One characteristic of the Support-PFS (like Lab group) is that they do not exercise a financial activity themselves, but act as subcontractors of operational functions on behalf of other financial professionals. Lab Group is a CSSF certified document and data management company, with offices in Luxembourg, Dublin and Gibraltar. On 18 July 2012, the CSSF published the circular 12/544 [15], which imposes the Support-PFS's to perform risk self-assessments and provide the CSSF with the risk analysis reports. Because of the low quality in risk reports, the CSSF has decided to produce a risk reference model to be used in the self-assessment exercise. The LIST has been charged with designing this reference model.

4.1   ISSRM

In the ISSRM [12], a risk is composed of event and impact and it occurs when the first leads to the second. The event is in itself composed of threat and vulnerability and equally exists when the first leads to the second. The impact harms an asset of the enterprise which may be of a resource type or business asset. The resource is the target of the threat and is characterized by vulnerability. We have voluntarily simplified the ISSRM in order to focus on the most significant concepts and relationships among concepts. The cardinalities have also been removed, for the same reasons. Fig. 2 shows the mapping between the ISSRM and BSE metamodel at the systemic level and at the enterprise level.

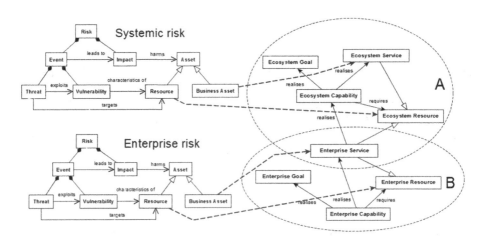

Fig. 2. Mapping ISSRM – BSE metamodel

4.2   Mapping ISSRM-Business Service Ecosystem Metamodel

This section explains the mapping between the ISSRM and the BSE metamodel illustrated by the financial system (Fig. 3). The ecosystem goals are to *professionalise the financial system* and to *stabilise the financial system*.

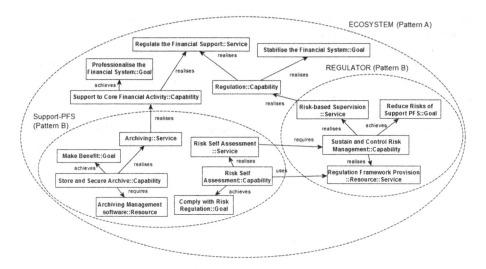

Fig. 3. Business Service Ecosystem metamodel instantiated to the financial system

At the enterprise level, the risk analysis is achieved by depicting the resource's vulnerability, the threat that exploits this vulnerability and the assets that are impacted by the risk occurrence. For instance, the *archiving management software* (resource) of the Support-PFS does not use the security module (vulnerability) and the heap buffer overflow attack (threat) risks to be led. This even makes a hacker able to corrupt (impact) the archiving service (business asset).

This structured and "classical" way of managing the IS risk may be investigated following the capability-resource pattern approach. The concept of resource is defined in ISSRM as a component of the IS which supports business assets. It is also named an IS asset and corresponds, for instance, to the a*rchiving management software*. The concept of capability from the BSE model (pattern B of Fig. 1) is composed of resources and corresponds to the concept of resource from the ISSRM model presented in Fig. 2. According to the above financial case, we argue that the enterprise capability to *store and secure archives* is composed of the *archiving management software* (resource) and that this enterprise capability is required for the *archiving service* which is an enterprise service (business asset). This correspondence between the ISSRM and the capability-resource pattern model highlights how using the capability-resource pattern at the sectorial level helps identifying the resources and capabilities that achieve business services. These resources and capabilities are thus the ones to be considered during the risk management activity.

At the ecosystem level, in [8, 9], we have observed that a structured way does not yet exist for managing the risks and that, on the spot, sectorial risk analysts often make the amalgam between the enterprise resources and capabilities, and the sectorial resources and capabilities. In the following, we argue and explain how using the capability-resource pattern approach contributes in structuring the analyst's approach. Therefore, we consider the correspondence between the ISSRM and the capability-resource pattern model but, this time, at the ecosystem level. The concept of business asset, at the ecosystem level, represents a service provided by the ecosystem. To realise this ecosystem service, the ecosystem requires ecosystem capabilities. According to the pattern based fractal structure of the ecosystem proposed in Fig. 1, the latter aggregates ecosystem resources and enterprise's services, i.e. the enterprise service from pattern B corresponds to a type of ecosystem resource at pattern A. For instance, in a financial sector, at the ecosystem level, the ecosystem must *regulate the financial support*. To justify this ecosystem service to the government, the ecosystem must have the *regulation capability* and the *support to core financial activity capability*. These capabilities are realized respectively by the *risk-based regulation service* and by the *archiving service*. Both of these services are also types of ecosystem resource.

To analyze the risk of not being able to *Professionalize the financial system* and to *Stabilize the financial system* (ecosystem goal) as well as, not being able to deliver (impact) the *regulation of the financial support* ecosystem service (business asset), the risk analysis assesses the threats that might exploit vulnerabilities of the ecosystem capabilities (types of resource at the ISSRM level). This means, in the financial system case, that the Support-PFS does no longer provide the archiving or that the CSSF does no longer provide the regulation.

This correspondence between the ecosystem capability-resource pattern model and the ISSRM shows that, at the ecosystem level, the right abstraction for risk management is the enterprise service (regulator or support-PFS services). This implies that the main focus of the risk analysis, at the sectorial regulation level, is the ecosystem services and ecosystem capabilities, including the ecosystem resources and enterprises services. Thereby, the risk management at the enterprise level in not an activity to be handled and performed by the ecosystem, but an activity that is enforced by the latter. In practice, this risk management activity is sub-contracted from the ecosystem (represented, e.g. by the state) to the ecosystem regulator (often a publicly financed body). In that sense, the regulator may impose rules to be followed by the enterprise such as the legal obligation to make risk analysis and to report annually, and may control rules which are applied and sanction accordingly.

A second consequence of this abstraction of the risk analysis, at the ecosystem level, is related to the counter-measures to be put in place to mitigate the risk. Given that the risk mitigation is at the enterprise service level, the vulnerability and the threat must also be considered at this ecosystem level. For instance, a service vulnerability could be that the enterprise is not able to deliver the service anymore in case of workload increase and a threat could be a sudden workload increase. Practically, an insurance cannot reimburse all the insured (vulnerability) in case of a major disaster due to exceptional conditions (threat). This involves, at the ecosystem level, that the ecosystem service to assure all inhabitants of a country (business asset) is no longer possible.

5   Risk Management Language

In [16], we have highlighted that, in general, risk analysis approach lacks from formal notation and representation, and that the traceability between the different elements of the risk model is also difficult to manage. To overcome these difficulties, we have proposed to extend the enterprise architecture model in the ArchiMate modelling language [17] with the ISSRM. Therefore, we have considered the business motivation model from ArchiMate, which we use through the ArchiMate motivation extension, for expressing the specific risk analysis related motivations for architecture principles and decisions. At the systemic level, in the previous sections of this paper, we have explained how, at the metamodel level, it is possible to integrate the enterprise capability and resource with the systemic capability and resource, using the fractal approach from [4]. Than we have explained how to manage the risk at both levels using the ISSRM. At this level, no language exist yet for managing the risk. Given the mapping between the ISSRM and the BSE, the risk management language defined in [16] may be extended at the systemic level.

Next sections illustrate how the ArchiMate risk extension language is usable for managing the risk at the enterprise and at ecosystem levels. In both cases, our approach is carried out in two stages. First we design the domain model (Sect. 4.1, Fig. 3). Second, we model the risk based on the domain model. The models represented with the ArchiMate Language are illustrated in Figs. 4 and 5. Practically, since the concept of business capability is not supported by ArchiMate we opted for the Business Function to represent the Capabilities. A business function is indeed defined by

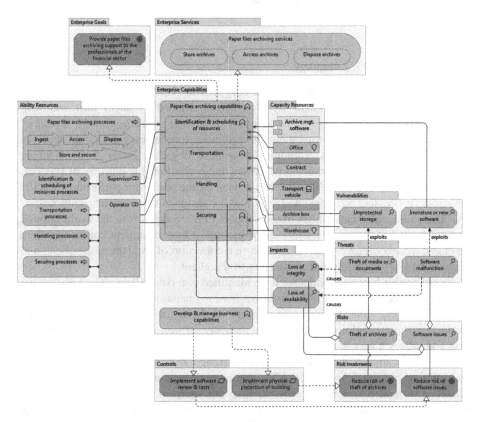

Fig. 4. Use case: Paper files archiving services

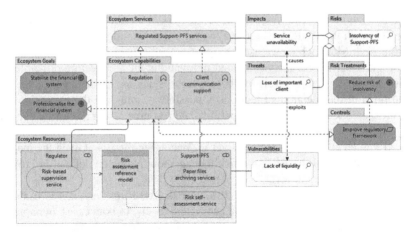

Fig. 5. Use case: Regulation Regulated Support PFS services

ArchiMate as *a behavior element that groups behavior based on a chosen set of criteria (typically required business resources and/or competences)*. The language will probably integrate the concept of Capability in the future, according to current works at The Open Group.

5.1   Enterprise Risk Language

In Fig. 4, the business model starts with a goal *provide paper file archiving support to the professionals of the financial sector* which is realised by *paper files archiving capabilities: identification & scheduling of resources, transportation, handling, securing*. Each capability groups a bunch of abilities (processes, roles) and capacities (applications, infrastructures, equipment, business objects). *Paper files archiving processes* are high-level operational processes that orchestrate the delivery of services. The roles of *Supervisor* and *Operator* are defined by the ability for performing specific behaviour (processes, activities) and they may be assigned to actors (capacity resources). The value-added capabilities of the Support-PFS are exposed to the world through *paper files archiving services: Store archives:* ingest new document collections from the client; *Access archives*: deliver and return a collection of archives to the client; and *Dispose archive*: definitely return archives to the client.

Based on this business model we have identified two risks. Risk1: *Theft of archives* (information security) and Risk2: *Software issues* (operational). Since a risk is composed of threats, vulnerabilities and impacts we have for Risk1: *theft of media or documents* (threat) exploits vulnerability of *unprotected storage* (warehouse and archive box) and causes a *loss of integrity* (impact) on the *securing* and *handling* capabilities. The chosen treatment is to reduce the risk through *the implementation of physical protection of building*. And for Risk2: *software malfunction* (threat) exploits vulnerabilities of *immature or new software* (archive management software component) and causes a *loss of availability* (impact) of the *paper files archiving* capabilities, thus the *paper files archiving* services and consequently impacts all the clients of the Support-PFS. The chosen treatment is to *reduce the risk through the implementation of software review and tests*. Both risk treatment requirements are realised through the capability *Develop & manage business capabilities*.

5.2   Systemic Risk Language

In Fig. 5 we define two business goals at the ecosystem level: *Stabilise the financial system*, which is realised by the *regulation* capability; and *Professionalise the financial system*, which is realised by *the client communication support* capability. Put together both capabilities realise high-level regulated Support-PFS services. The regulation capability requires a *risk self-assessment service* provided by the *Support-PFS* and a *risk-based supervision service* provided by the *regulator*. The latter uses the *risk assessment reference model* produced by the LIST and used by all the *Support-PFS* during their *risk self-assessment* service. The *client communication support* requires, among others, *paper file archiving services* provided by the *Support-PFS*.

In the risk model we identify a risk of *insolvency of the Support-PFS* that comes with the threat *loss of an important client*. That threat exploits the vulnerability of *lack of liquidity*. The impact is *service unavailability* of the regulated service for all the Support-PFS clients. The chosen risk treatment is to reduce the risk through an improved regulatory framework, applicable to the ecosystem regulation capability.

6   Conclusions and Future Works

In this paper, we have investigated how the capability may contribute in sustaining the risk management at the system level. To that end, our first contribution is a BES metamodel built from the capability-resource pattern from [4] that we have reproduced at the systemic level and associated to the enterprise capability through the service. Secondly, the ISSRM has been mapped with the BSE metamodel. This mapping has been illustrated on the basis of a case study for the Luxembourgish financial sector. Finally, we have exploited the security risk management extension of the ArchiMate language to represent and sustain the risk management at the ecosystem level.

This preliminary research paves the way to many interesting and new perspectives. Firstly the BSE metamodel may gather in the same model (1) all the actors of a system (e.g. enterprise, regulator) and (2) systemic information (e.g. systemic goal, capability and services). Secondly, this approach has been exploited in the frame of risk management but it could be extended to other purposes, e.g. better alignment between the services offered by the enterprises and the resources needed by the system. Thirdly, it has been illustrated in a system with one regulator but it could be extended to system with many regulators and hence, acts as a facilitator for information sharing between these regulators. Fourthly, the BSE metamodel has been limited to the ecosystem level. It could also be extended outside the boundaries of the ecosystem to model how the ecosystem services is required by other (higher) system resources.

The first future work consists in more accurately aligning the BSE and the ISSRM. This will be performed using appropriate methods like those proposed by [18] or [19]. The second future work aims at deepening the role of the service as a hyphen between both levels. We consider that some systemic resources are the services provided by the entities of the ecosystem, while others might be actual shared resources. The question is to know if in a service ecosystem, all ecosystem resources are services provided by some entities: a shared network considered as a common resource for the ecosystem, is operated by some entity, whether public or private, and therefore can be seen from the service provision perspective as well. An alignment with service system theories will be considered in order to address this question.

References

1. España, S., González, T., Grabis, J., Jokste, L., Juanes, R., Valverde, F.: Capability-Driven Development of a SOA Platform: A Case Study. In: Iliadis, L., Papazoglou, M., Pohl, K. (eds.) CAiSE Workshops 2014. LNBIP, vol. 178, pp. 100–111. Springer, Heidelberg (2014)
2. Stirna, J.: Capability as a Service in digital enterprises, position presentation at "Digital Business Innovation Paths" Event - How to take Digital Business Innovation to the next level? Belgium, 8 July 2014
3. Helfat, C.E., Winter, S.G.: Untangling dynamic and operational capabilities: strategy for the (n)ever-changing world. Strat. Mgmt. J. 32(11), 1243–1250 (2011)
4. Henkel, M., Bider, I., Perjons, E.: Capability-Based Business Model Transformation. In: Iliadis, L., Papazoglou, M., Pohl, K. (eds.) CAiSE Workshops 2014. LNBIP, vol. 178, pp. 88–99. Springer, Heidelberg (2014)
5. Teece, D.J., Pisano, G., Shuen, A.: Dynamic capabilities and strategic management. Strateg. Manage. J. 18(7), 509–533 (1997)
6. Sandkuhl, K., Koc, H.: On the Applicability of Concepts from Variability Modelling in Capability Modelling: Experiences from a Case in Business Process Outsourcing. In: Iliadis, L., Papazoglou, M., Pohl, K. (eds.) CAiSE Workshops 2014. LNBIP, vol. 178, pp. 65–76. Springer, Heidelberg (2014)
7. Stirna, J., Sandkuhl, K.: An Outlook on Patterns as an Aid for Business and IT Alignment with Capabilities. In: Iliadis, L., Papazoglou, M., Pohl, K. (eds.) CAiSE Workshops 2014. LNBIP, vol. 178, pp. 148–158. Springer, Heidelberg (2014)
8. Mayer, N., Aubert, J., Cholez, H., Grandry, E.: Sector-based improvement of the information security risk management process in the context of telecommunications regulation. In: McCaffery, F., O'Connor, R.V., Messnarz, R. (eds.) EuroSPI 2013. CCIS, vol. 364, pp. 13–24. Springer, Heidelberg (2013)
9. Cholez, H., Feltus, C.: Towards an innovative systemic approach of risk management. In: SIN 2014, 61 p. ACM, New York
10. Rafati, L., Poels, G.: Capability Sourcing Modeling. In: Iliadis, L., Papazoglou, M., Pohl, K. (eds.) CAiSE Workshops 2014. LNBIP, vol. 178, pp. 77–87. Springer, Heidelberg (2014)
11. Barney, J.B.: Gaining and Sustaining Competitive Advantage. Prentice-Hall, Upper Saddle River (2002)
12. Mayer, N., Heymans, P., Matulevicius, R.: Design of a Modelling Language for Information System Security Risk Management. In: RCIS. (2007)
13. Taking Service Forward. http://takingserviceforward.org

14. Rosen, M.: Are Capabilities Architecture? BPTrends (2013). http://www.bptrends.com/ publicationfiles/02-05-2013-COL-BA-Are%20Capabilities%20Arch.pdf
15. CSSF, Circulaire CSSF 12/544, Optimisation of the supervision exercised on the "support PFS" by a risk-based approach (2012)
16. Grandry, E., Feltus, C., Dubois, E.: Conceptual integration of enterprise architecture management and security risk management. In: SOEA4EE, EDOC WS (2013)
17. The Open Group: ArchiMate 2.1 Specification. Van Haren Publishing (2012)
18. Parent, C., Spaccapietra, S.: Database integration: the key to data interoperability. In: Papazoglou, M., Spaccapietra, S., Tari, Z. (eds.) Advances in Object-Oriented Data Modeling, pp. 221–253. Springer, Heidelberg (2000)
19. Zivkovic, S., Kühn, H., Karagiannis, D.: Facilitate modelling using method integration: an approach using mappings and integration rules. In: ECIS (2007)

Strategies for Capability Modelling: Analysis Based on Initial Experiences

Sergio España[1], Jānis Grabis[2], Martin Henkel[3(✉)], Hasan Koç[4],
Kurt Sandkuhl[4], Janis Stirna[3], and Jelena Zdravkovic[3]

[1] Universitat Politècnica de València, Valencia, Spain
sergio.espana@pros.upv.es
[2] Riga Technical University, Riga, Latvia
grabis@rtu.lv
[3] Stockholm University, Stockholm, Sweden
{martinh,js,jelenaz}@dsv.su.se
[4] University of Rostock, Rostock, Germany
{hasan.koc,kurt.sandkuhl}@uni.rostock.de

Abstract. Competitiveness and growth on an international market is for many businesses tightly coupled to their ability of quickly implementing new company strategies, business services and products or market entries. Capability management is among the approaches proposed to tackle these challenges. A feature is capturing the context of capability delivery and providing mechanisms for configuring the delivery. Among the work on capability management is the capability-driven design and delivery (CDD) approach that has been proposed by the EU-FP7 project CaaS. The aim of this paper is to contribute to CDD by (i) introducing different strategies for capability modelling, (ii) elaborating on the differences between these strategies, and (iii) contributing to an understanding of what strategy should be used under what preconditions. The paper addresses these aspects by describing the strategies and initial experiences gathered with them.

Keywords: Capability modelling · Capability management · Goal-first strategy · Process-first strategy · Concept-first strategy

1 Introduction

Competitiveness and growth on an international market is for many businesses tightly coupled to their ability to quickly implement new company strategies, business services and products or market entries. Businesses that offering products and services based on information technology (IT) require a way to efficiently adapt their services together with the IT infrastructure for delivering them. Capability management is among the approaches that have been proposed to tackle these challenges. One of the key features is capturing the delivery context of customer services and providing mechanisms for configuring or generating its delivery.

Authors are ordered alphabetically to reflect equal contributions to this work.

© Springer International Publishing Switzerland 2015
A. Persson and J. Stirna (Eds.): CAiSE 2015 Workshops, LNBIP 215, pp. 40–52, 2015.
DOI: 10.1007/978-3-319-19243-7_4

Among the approaches to capability management the capability-driven design and delivery (CDD) approach has been proposed by the EU-FP7 project CaaS [14, 15]. Recently, work on CDD has focused on development strategies for capability management that so far have been designed and applied independently of each other. There is not enough knowledge about the differences among the strategies and their suitability for different enterprise contexts.

The contributions of the paper are: (i) description of different strategies for capability modelling, (ii) discussion of the differences of the strategies and (iii) analysis of the preconditions of each strategy and its fit for different organisational situations. The initial experiences of using the strategies are also presented.

The rest of the paper is structured as follows. Section 2 summarises the background for the work from the area of capability management and presents the main aspects of the CaaS approach to capability design and delivery. Section 3 discusses the strategies for capability modelling and initial experiences. Section 4 presents a comparative analysis of the approaches. Section 5 summarises the work and draws conclusions.

2   Background

This section briefly summarises the existing work in the area of capability management and the CDD approach developed in the CaaS project.

2.1   Capability Management

The term capability is used in different areas of business information systems. In the literature there seems to be an agreement about the characteristics of the term capability, but still there is no wide acceptance of the term. The definitions mainly put focus on "combination of resources" [2], "capacity to execute an activity" [1], "perform better than competitors" [4] and "possessed ability [8]".

The capabilities are enablers of competitive advantage; they should help companies to continuously deliver a certain business value in dynamically changing circumstances [5]. They can be perceived from different organisational levels and thus utilised for different purposes. According to [6] the performance of an enterprise is the best, when the enterprise maps its capabilities to IT applications. Capabilities are directly related to business processes that are affected from the changes in context, e.g., regulations, customer preferences and system performance. As companies in rapidly changing environments need to foresee the variations and respond to them [3], the affected processes and services need to be adjusted quickly. I.e., adaptations to changes in context can be realised promptly if the required variations to the standard processes have been anticipated and defined in advance and can be instantiated.

In the CaaS project capability is defined as *the ability and capacity that enable an enterprise to achieve a business goal in a certain context* [15]. Ability refers to the level of available competence, where competence is understood as talent intelligence and disposition, of a subject or enterprise to accomplish a goal; capacity means availability of resources, e.g. money, time, personnel, tools. This definition uses the notion of context, thus stresses the need to take variations of the standard processes into consideration. To summarise, capabilities are considered as specific business services delivered to the enterprises in an application context to reach a business goal. To facilitate capability management, we propose business service design explicitly considering delivery context by an approach that supports modelling both the service as such and the application context.

2.2 The CaaS Approach to Capability Design and Delivery

The main goal of the CaaS project is to facilitate a shift from the service-oriented paradigm to a capability delivery paradigm. This paradigm shift requires development a new methodical framework supporting capability-driven design and development in general and it also requires changes in the development processes and engineering methods used. The CDD approach is supported by a set of method components.

The CaaS methodology for capability-driven design and development consists of the following top-level method components; Capability design, Enterprise modelling (EM), Context Modelling, support for Reuse of capability design, and Run-time delivery adjustment. The *Capability design* method component contains three approaches to start with capability design (goal, process and concepts). The *EM* component is required for identifying business goals related to the capability under consideration. EM includes for example business process modelling and goal modelling. The *Context modelling* component is used to specify the potential context situations of the capability. The component for supporting *Reuse* specifies how the concept of patterns can be used to elicit, elaborate and store enterprise models. The component *for Run-time capability adjustment* concerns the specification of adjustments needed in order to cater to changes in capability context.

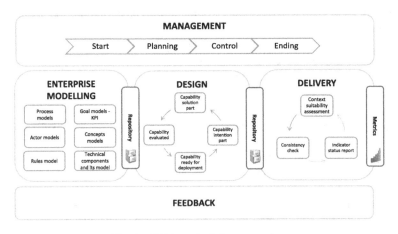

Fig. 1. CDD methodology overview

The CDD methodology is structured according to three phases (Fig. 1). The *EM phase* represents the traditional approach to business design and development of information systems. Existing EM approaches (e.g. EKD [7, 8] and 4EM [9]) will be applied to give input for the capability design. Other EM methods are also potentially applicable. The capability *design phase* concerns the design of capabilities (see next section.) The *delivery* phase entails the execution and monitoring of the capability.

3 Strategies for Capability Modelling

Different strategies for capability modelling and design have been explored and so far three strategies have been elaborated for use by the industrial partners. The strategies consist of three steps. As the different strategies are basically proposing different ways to identify and design capabilities, only step 1 is different for the strategies whereas steps 2 and 3 are the same for all strategies:

Step 1, capability design: there are three alternative pathways of proceeding with capability design – starting with goals, starting with business service processes, or starting with business concepts. Each pathway is described in the Sects. 3.1 to 3.3.

Step 2, capability evaluation: Capability evaluation checks whether the result of capability design is feasible from the business and technical perspective before committing to capability implementation. The capability feasibility can be assessed using simulation and cost/benefit analysis. A failed evaluation may trigger a new cycle of the capability design phase.

Step 3, development of capability delivery application: The capability development activity prepares the capability for the deployment. The indicators for monitoring and algorithms for runtime adjustments are packaged as a runtime-support application. The capability design also serves as a basis for modifying or implementing the IT components used for capability delivery.

Furthermore, all three strategies are based on the CaaS meta-model [15]. Relevant terms are shown in Table 1. They will be used in Sects. 3.1 to 3.3.

Table 1. Concepts used in capability design strategies

Concept/term	Explanation
Capability	Capability is the ability and capacity that enable an enterprise to achieve a business goal in a certain context
KPI	Key Performance Indicators (KPIs) are measurable properties that can be seen as targets for achievement of Goals
Context Element	A Context Element is representing any information that can be used to characterise the situation of an entity
Context Set	Context Set describes the set of Context Elements that are relevant for design and delivery of a specific Capability
Context Element Range	Context Element Range is used to specify boundaries of permitted values for a specific Context Element and for a specific Context Set
Goal	Goal is a desired state of affairs that needs to be attained. Goals can be refined into sub-goals and expressed in measurable terms such as KPIs
Process	Process is series of actions that are performed in order to achieve particular result. A Process supports Goals and has input and produces output in terms of information and/or material
Process Variant	Process variant is a part of the Process, which uses the same input and delivers the same outcome as the process in a different way
Pattern	Patterns are reusable solutions for reaching business Goals under specific contexts. The context defined for the Capability (Context Set) should match the context in which the Pattern is applicable

3.1 Goals-First Capability Design

Goals are used to model the intentional perspective of organisational design. Hence, capability design can start with analysing the existing goal hierarchy and/or setting new goals and then shifting to analysing how they should be reached in terms of capabilities, business processes and which context properties should be considered. The modelling process includes steps as outlined below. It is also worth mentioning that the modelling process is not entirely sequential. Instead it is rather iterative and incremental, i.e. the modeller has to develop all parts of the capability design (e.g. goals, capability, context, process) in balance and consistent with each other.

Activity G1: Analyse the overall business vision and goals. The existing business goals need to be analysed with respect to identifying which goals are required to be supported by capabilities. Goals are typically organised in a goal hierarchy with more strategic goals on the top and more operational goals below. The goals that require capability support typically are on a more operational level because capabilities are concerned with explicit business designs and concrete actions. But in principle, some top-level goals could also be supported by capabilities. The goals that are the likely candidates for capability design should have elaborated KPIs for monitoring. If the existing goals do not have an explicit design that connects the KPIs and goals, then this needs to be established. A goals model is central for this activity.

Activity G2: Identify specific capabilities required by goals. The goals are analysed, relevant capabilities are defined and relationship between the capabilities and the goals established to indicate how the capabilities support the goals. The contribution of a capability to a goal should also be analysed with respect to the whole goal hierarchy, e.g. if a capability is deemed to support several sub-goals in the same goal hierarchy, then it might be more appropriate to associate it with their top-goal.

Activity G3: Analyse the existing business processes. The relationship to existing business processes is to be established. If the business processes documentation exists and processes are linked to goals, then the capability should be associated with the same business processes that its goals are. This is sufficient at this stage because the process variants will be designed later, once the application context is modelled.

Activity G4: Identify and model the context affecting the identified capabilities. For each capability the context set in which it is applicable should be defined, including the relevant context element and the ranges within which the capability is applicable.

Activity G5: Analyse and define process variants. A capability is realised by a set of business processes. In many cases there are some adjustments to capability delivery according to changes in context. To produce a more complete capability design, the overall business process is analysed and potential context changes are assessed to identify variations in capability delivery. This leads to defining process variants.

Activity G6: Model delivery adjustments. The needed capability delivery adjustments and links them to the capability design are specified. The adjustments are defined by analysing the context changes and associated process variants.

Activity G7: Review and/or incorporate relevant patterns. Capability design is based on the existing best practices. Hence we foresee that at any stage of this process the capability designer should be able to review the existing patterns that present relevant best practices in the form of process variants, concept models, algorithms and include them in the capability design.

Our initial experiences with the goal-first strategy to capability design come from two cases within the CaaS project. Both cases are in a public organisation offering on-line services for citizens. The gathered experience concerns the *starting point for goal modelling*, and reflections on the way *goals, KPI and capabilities are interlinked*.

Regarding the first experience, *the starting point for goal modelling*, it was clear from both cases that the threshold for starting the goal modelling was low. This was due to two factors: either the organisation had top-level goals clearly defined or the organisation had a sense of what changes that were needed (this was the case for the two cases at the public organisation). E.g., in one case the public organisation had existing problems with their SOA platform and therefore defined several goals intended to improve the platform. Thus, the starting point could be either goals/visions or existing issues.

While working with the goal-first capability design strategy it was clear that the ways that the *goals were interlinked with KPIs and capabilities* was non-trivial. E.g., in the public organisation it was difficult to identify KPIs that could be used to monitor the capability delivery. While it is natural to define KPIs that are related to high-level business goals, such as the goal "To provide incident resolution", it was more difficult to express KPIs to provide valuable information during monitoring of capability delivery. A conclusion here is that a set of guidelines for KPI definition based on capability goals are needed. E.g., asking questions such as "What would be a lead indicator to show when there is a high risk that my capabilities will not fulfil the goals?" can guide this part of the goal-first strategy.

3.2   Process-First Capability Design

The process-first capability modelling pathway proposes that the starting point of the capability design is a process underlying a business service. The business service is further refined and extended by adding context awareness and adaptability, so as to establish a capability that can deliver this service in varying circumstances.

Many organisations at this level have already defined and modelled business processes that are implemented to offer business services. Hence, the process-first capability design assumes that services are modelled and implemented as business process models. The modelling process includes the following activities:

Activity P1: Define scope. The organisation offers services based on business processes that are already modelled. To design the capabilities by means of business processes the capability designer first selects the service and sets the scope of the capability design depending on various factors, such as optimising the services with high process costs or managing services that frequently change and require the adjustment of business processes.

Activity P2: Define level of granularity. This step defines the abstraction level, at which the processes supporting the business service to be improved are identified and analysed. An option to describe different levels of granularity could be applying the decomposition method proposed by [12]. This method differentiates between a *main process*, which does not belong to a larger process and is decomposed into sub-processes. Regarding the business goals and offered capabilities needed to reach them, the method user most probably models at *main process* level. Nevertheless, the main processes might be refined by sub-processes in Activity P3.

Activity P3: Identify processes/activities/tasks. This identifies the processes modelled and used by the enterprise that are relevant for capability delivery. For this purpose 5-policies approach proposed by [11] can be applied, which describes a general strategy for identifying processes. It should be emphasised that capturing possible variations of the processes are not included in these activities.

Activity P4: Analyse existing BPM and refine if necessary. The activity assures that selected business process models are up-to-date and applies changes if required.

Activity P5: Identify or name the capability to be delivered. The capability designer has a view on selected business service and supported processes. The information that the capability designer acquired during the execution of prior steps can be used as an input to establish a capability definition. The level of granularity is to be considered when identifying capabilities since overly refined capabilities could lead to complex models. If the capabilities are unclearly defined or cannot be established at this level yet, then the modeller should execute the upcoming activities to identify the context elements via observing the variations. In that case the capability is refined or established in Activity P9, where the method user has an enhanced view on the goals, processes and context elements as of in Activity P5.

Activity P6: Update goals model and KPIs. The capability designed should be aligned with the goals that an enterprise aims to achieve. To check if business goals are satisfied during the capability delivery, KPIs are used to measure the achievement of goals. This steps analyses and updates the goal models as well as KPIs, if any exist. If no goals model is available, then the designer continues to activity P7.

Activity P7: Develop goals model and KPIs. Goals define the requirements to be fulfilled during the delivery of a capability. If the enterprise has no goals model, then it is created in alignment with the scope of the business service. To check if business goals are satisfied during the capability delivery, KPIs are used to measure the achievement of goals. The modeller develops KPIs required by the goals developed in this activity or updated in the aforementioned activity.

Activity P8: Relate goals, capabilities and processes. This activity establishes the connection between the developed/identified/analysed components. The behaviour of the components under varying situations should be studied in the following step.

Activity P9: Identify and model context. A capability is defined by specific business services, a defined application context for these business services and goals of the enterprise to be reached. The context of the capability delivery, is modeled i.e. the potential application context where the offering is supposed to be deployed. Four method components are used, namely, find variations, capture context element, design context, and prepare for operational use.

Activity P10: Model delivery adjustments. This activity outlines the components needed to adjust capability adjustment at runtime and refers to the method component.

Activity P11: Link components. This activity finalises the capability model with interlinking the outputs that have been previously developed.

Our initial experiences with the process-first strategy to capability design are based on two cases of the CaaS project. The first case is from a software vendor in the utilities industry, which owns a business service provider (BSP) executing a complete business process for a business function outside of an organisation. The second case is from a public organisation providing electronic services to municipalities, which are then used by citizens. The gathered experience concerns the eliciting of context elements, modelling goals and process variants, and identification of patterns.

In both use cases the business processes required for capability delivery were modelled. Regarding the first experience, *context element eliciting*, we became aware of the need to differentiate between process variables and context elements, since both types of parameters originate during the execution of the process but have different design and runtime implications. For this purpose, we provided guidelines on what constitutes a context element and which parameters should be treated as process variables. Moreover, a framework was proposed to classify the parameters causing variability in the business processes. The parameters were analysed in detail to decide whether they qualify as context elements or process variables. Concerning the *modelling of process variants*, the use cases have also proven that the values of such parameters have an influence on the decision logic and it is sometimes confusing to distinguish variability from business processes decisions. To solve this problem the term variation point and an initial set of guidelines were introduced, Particularly in the second use case we identified services that share the same parts of the business process models, which only to some extent differ from one another. Here we proposed a new primitive "variability refinement" to eliminate redundancy.

The process-first capability design strategy requires an analysis of business process models. This allowed us to investigate whether there were processes representing the best practices in the company, which can be captured as *patterns*. In both use cases *goals model* did not exist and had to be developed from the scratch. Here, the methods and guidelines in [12] were applied for goals modelling. Moreover the involvement of the domain experts and product owners to modelling sessions was required.

3.3   Concept-First Capability Design

Concepts are used for modelling the static aspects of the business, such as product structures, organisational structures, customer profiles, material, as well as information used and produced by the business processes. The concept models can be seen as knowledge models of the organisation. Capabilities may be designed by starting with analysing the existing knowledge structures and their relationships with the application context. The following activities illustrate such a way of working:

Activity C1: Analyse the existing concepts. This step aims to identify concepts describing relevant products and/or services that are realised in the company. They may be modelled as a whole or as aggregate concepts; in some cases the concepts associated with the supporting information structure is also modelled.

Activity C2: Elicit candidate capabilities. The purpose of this step is to identify products or services (modelled as concepts) that need to be realised by capabilities taking into account the findings from analysing the dependencies in the previous step.

Activity C3: Analyse dependencies between the identified capabilities and existing business processes and business goals. This activity aims to identify which business goals are relevant and what are the KPIs that monitor their achievement, as well as what business processes are used to realise the concepts, e.g. products have development, production, sales and support processes. In some cases these processes might not be fully defined and/or modelled and if so, the necessary models may need to be defined later if they are influenced by the context and subjects to variability. New or additional business goals and KPIs might also be defined at this step.

Activity C4: Identify the context affecting the identified capabilities. For each capability the context set in which it is applicable should be defined. Note that this activity is the same as G4 in the goal-first strategy.

Activity C5: Analyse and define process variants. A capability is realised by a set of business processes, there might be different process variants needed for different product versions, or some variations of the manufacturing process need to be introduced because of different material or customer requirements. This activity corresponds to G5 in the goal-first strategy.

Activity C6: Model delivery adjustments. This step specifies the needed capability delivery adjustments and links them to the overall capability design. This activity corresponds to G6 in the goal-first strategy.

Activity C7: Review and/or incorporate relevant patterns. This activity corresponds to G7 in the goal-first strategy.

Our experiences with the concepts-first approach come from one case in the CaaS project. The case is within an organisation operating in the maritime business. The scope of the case was to apply the CDD approach to analyse the capabilities of the organisation, with a focus on its compliance with maritime regulations. The organisation already had a well-defined organisational structure, with well-defined areas of responsibilities, thus the concept-first strategy was deemed suitable. Our initial experiences with the concept-first strategy concerns the *drivers for capability definition* and the *complexity of mapping capabilities to goals and processes.*

The *drivers for capability definition* are slightly more complex when using a concept-first strategy, compared to a process or goal-first strategy. The reason is that process and goal models often have an inherent hierarchical structure, and it is thus possible to identify a certain level that correspond to, or easily maps to, capabilities. For the concept-first approach it is instead necessary to look at groups of concepts that are related (cohesion within the concepts) and how they relate to other groups (coupling between groups). For the maritime case, the basis for the analysis became the management structure. This resulted in capabilities such as "Maritime management", "Ship financial management" and "Ship technical management".

From the maritime case, we also experienced *the complexity of mapping capabilities to goals and processes*. For the goal-first and processes-first strategies, one of the mappings to goals or process are done as an integral part of the capability identification process, sometimes leading to a 1:1 mapping between goals/processes and capabilities. However, when applying the concept-first strategy, we discovered that it was common that one identified capability was mapped to several goals. To handle this, the mapping was visualised in matrices, linking capabilities to goals.

4   A Comparative Analysis of the Modelling Strategies

The goal-first strategy, naturally, has the primary view that capabilities exists as a way to fulfil long-term business objectives of an organisation. To get *started* with the goal-first strategy it is therefore beneficial, i.e. to capture the intentional aspect of a business and to merit it through well-defined KPIs. Since the strategy is focused on the elaboration of goals and KPIs, it provides at the same time the basis for run-time monitoring of the quality of capability delivery in respect to the established KPIs.

The primary view of the process-first strategy is that capabilities are delivered through enacting the business processes. This strategy assumes that specifications of the current business processes exist or, at least, that the organisational culture is oriented towards processes. Domain experts and product owners are required to identify context influences on the processes, and to (re)design process variants and adaptation business rules accordingly. Strategic management staff should be involved during goal model creation or update. Representative workers may also provide valuable input concerning current problems and operational needs. The process-first strategy suits organisations with well-conceived and stable processes, since any non-trivial reengineering of processes requires revising the capability designs. The advantage is that the resulting capability delivery fosters context awareness within the organisation and enables flexible variability management in the running processes.

The concept-first strategy views concepts as the primary means for capability identification and is assumed to be based on well-defined products or organisational structures. The concept-first strategy are likely to fit organisations that have a stable product or organisation structure, while not necessarily having well defined goals or strong process orientation.

Following the above discussion, we identified different aspects suitable for comparing the developed strategies. These aspects are:

- Primary view on capabilities. What are the bases for capability identification?
- Preconditions with respect to models. What kind of preconditions with respect to existing models or specification is needed for using the strategy?
- Stakeholders required. Besides the actual capability "modeller", the strategies have different requirements regarding what stakeholders (domain experts, capability owners, product owners, etc.) need to be involved during the strategy.
- Effects on the succeeding steps. What are the next modelling or development steps followed by the strategy?

Table 2. Comparison of capability modelling strategies

Aspect of comparison	Strategy		
	Goal-first	Process-first	Concept-first
Primary view on capabilities	A capability fulfils key organisational goals	A capability is operationalised as a set of processes	A capability encompass the management of key concepts
Preconditions with respect to models	Ideally, top-level organisational goals should be defined	Pre-existing business process specifications or process-oriented culture	Pre-defined management structures, product structures or other conceptual models
Stakeholders required	Different levels of management personnel	Domain experts, product owners, strategic management	Product managers/owners
Effects on the succeeding steps	Provides a comprehensive base for capability monitoring by the use of KPIs	Provides a detailed specification for context-aware variability management	Provides a base for having the concept of capabilities as the main subject for organisational analysis and change management
Characteristics of enterprise	Organisations with a high degree of adaptable/non-routine work	Mature organisations with well-established processes	Organisations with a well-defined and stable organisational or product structure
Degree of flexibility of the strategy	Can also start with visions or existing issues. Highly iterative and incremental modelling process	The strategy can cope with ill specified goal or concept models. Process reengineering requires thorough revision of capability designs	Can cope with different levels of concept granularity. The drivers for capability definition are slightly more complex. Is flexible with regard to the degree of specification of business processes
Impact on the organisational culture	Reinforces strategic vision and clarifies the IT-business alignment	Improves the perspective of the enterprise (or service) context	It brings perspective over the organisational concepts by identifying (highly-cohesive and lowly-coupled) groups of concepts

- Characteristics of enterprise. What are the characteristics of an enterprise (regarding size, domain or type) the strategy is expected to be useful for?
- Degree of flexibility of the strategy. To what extent does the strategy allow for adapting the flow of activities to project contingencies? (e.g. changes in the order of activities, dealing with missing or unreliable input, etc.)
- Impact on the organisational culture. What is the impact that the strategy is expected to have on the way the organisation conceives their services? The fact of introducing novel perspectives on the enterprise strategy, structure and work practice may alter how the own organisation views their current capabilities.

Table 2 summarizes how the three strategies relate to the above aspects.

5   Summary and Future Work

Based on the capability design and delivery approach developed in the CaaS project this paper has proposed three different strategies for capability modelling, presented initial application experiences and compared them.

During the application of the three strategies, several areas for improvement have been identified. For the goal-first strategy, it is evident that there is a need for guidelines when it comes to the identification of KPIs that can be used for the monitoring of capability delivery. The concept-first strategy, being intuitively easy to follow, also needs stricter guidelines for capability identification. The process-first strategy has shown that the guidelines and activities for analysing the inputs influencing the business processes are needed to (i) identify context elements accurately, (ii) distinguish variation points from decision logic and (iii) model process variants efficiently. Moreover, we observed that the tasks in the business process models reflect the knowledge of domain experts and exhibit insights to best practices of the organisations, which constitute a good starting point for pattern analysis.

Future work entails merging parts of the three approaches, to build on their respective strengths.

Acknowledgments.   This work has been performed as part of the EU-FP7 funded project no: 611351 CaaS – Capability as a Service in Digital Enterprises.

References

1. Jiang, Y., Zhao, J.: An empirical research of the forming process of firm inter-organizational e-business capability: based on the supply chain processes. In: 2010 2nd International Conference on Information Science and Engineering (ICISE), pp 2603–2606 (2010)
2. Antunes, G., Barateiro, J., Becker, C., et al.: Modeling contextual concerns in enterprise architecture. In: 2011 15th IEEE International Enterprise Distributed Object Computing Conference Workshops (EDOCW), pp 3–10 (2011)
3. Eriksson, T.: Processes, antecedents and outcomes of dynamic capabilities. Scand. J. Manage. **15**(2), 142–155 (2013). doi:10.1016/j.scaman.2013.05.001

4. Boonpattarakan, A.: Model of Thai small and medium sized enterprises' organizational capabilities: review and verification. JMR **4**(3), 1–28 (2012). doi:10.5296/jmr.v4i3.1557

5. Stirna, J., Grabis, J., Henkel, M., Zdravkovic, J.: Capability driven development – an approach to support evolving organizations. In: Sandkuhl, K., Seigerroth, U., Stirna, J. (eds.) PoEM 2012. LNBIP, vol. 134, pp. 117–131. Springer, Heidelberg (2012)

6. Chen, J., Tsou, H.: Performance effects of 5IT6 capability, service process innovation, and the mediating role of customer service. J. Eng. Tech. Manage. **29**(1), 71–94 (2012). doi:10.1016/j.jengtecman.2011.09.007

7. Loucopoulos, P., Kavakli, V., Prekas, N., Rolland, C., Grosz, G., Nurcan, S.: Using the EKD approach: the modelling component (1997)

8. Bubenko, J.A.J., Persson, A. Stirna, J.: User Guide of the Knowledge Management Approach Using Enterprise Knowledge Patterns. Deliverable D3 IST Programme project Hypermedia and Pattern Based Knowledge Management for Smart Organisations, Project no. IST-2000-28401 (2001). ftp://ftp.dsv.su.se/users/js/d3_km_using_ekp.pdf. Accessed February 2015

9. Sandkuhl, K., Stirna, J., Persson, A., Wißotzki, M.: Enterprise Modeling – Tackling Business Challenges with the 4EM Method. The Enterprise Engineering Series. Springer, Heidelberg (2014). ISBN 978-3-662-43724-7

10. Brézillon, P., Cavalcanti, M.: Modeling and using context. Knowl. Eng. Rev. **13**(2), 185–194 (1998)

11. Hallerbach, A., Bauer, T., Reichert, M.: Capturing variability in business process models: The Provop approach. Journal of Software Maintenance and Evolution **22**(6–7), 519–546 (2010)

12. Milani, F., Dumas, M., Ahmed, N., Matulevicius, R.: Modelling Families of Business Process Variants: A Decomposition Driven Method, CoRR abs/1311.1322 (2013)

13. Bērziša, S., Bravos, G., Gonzalez Cardona, T., Czubayko, U., España, S., Grabis, J., Henkel, M., Jokste, L., Kampars, J., Koc, H., Kuhr, J., Llorca, C., Loucopoulos, P., Juanes Pascual, R., Sandkuhl, K., Simic, H., Stirna, J., Zdravkovic, J.: Deliverable 1.4: Requirements specification for CDD, CaaS – Capability as a Service for Digital Enterprises, FP7 project no 611351, Riga Technical University, Latvia (2014)

14. Sandkuhl, K., Koç, H., Stirna, J.: Context-aware business services: technological support for business and IT-alignment. In: Abramowicz, W., Kokkinaki, A. (eds.) BIS 2014 Workshops. LNBIP, vol. 183, pp. 190–201. Springer, Heidelberg (2014)

15. Bērziša, S., Bravos, G., Gonzalez Cardona, T., Czubayko, U., España, S., Grabis, J., Henkel, M., Jokste, L., Kampars, J., Koç, H., Kuhr, J.-C., Llorca, C., Loucopoulos, P., Juanes Pascual, R., Pastor, O., Sandkuhl, K., Simic, H., Stirna, J., Zdravkovic, J.: Capability Driven Development: An Approach to Designing Digital Enterprises. Business and Information Systems Engineering (BISE), February 2015. doi:10.1007/s12599-014-0362-0

Analyzing IT Flexibility to Enable Dynamic Capabilities

Mohammad Hossein Danesh[1(✉)] and Eric Yu[1,2]

[1] Department of Computer Science, University of Toronto, Toronto, Canada
{danesh, eric}@cs.toronto.edu
[2] Faculty of Information, University of Toronto, Toronto, Canada

Abstract. The ability to respond to change is an ongoing concern in information systems engineering. Designing flexible and adaptable information technology (IT) solutions is challenging due to difficulties in identifying and predicting adaptation needs influenced by environmental changes and enterprise competitive positioning. In this paper, we draw upon theories in strategic management, particularly conceptions of dynamic capabilities that deal with sustainable advantage, to identify and represent enterprise requirements. This research enables analysis of enterprise transformation by modeling coupling and alignment between IT and organizational capabilities using the i* framework. Potential inflexibilities and impact of changes are studied with analysis of dependency propagations. A hypothetical case using experiences from SOA and BPM implementations demonstrates use of the proposed modeling constructs.

Keywords: Capability modeling · Dynamic capability · i* · Flexibility analysis

1 Introduction

Success of information system (IS) deployment in enterprises relies on proper understanding and analysis of the requirements of the organization [1–3]. Models of business process and services and other business-level artifacts are increasingly used to model and analyze requirements during IS development. Today, as enterprises face highly dynamic environments, information systems must be able to meet requirements that are dynamic and uncertain. When making decisions regarding IT-enabled enterprise transformation and evolution, it becomes important to understand and analyze the strategic objectives behind processes and services [2, 4, 5].

To represent strategic and investment objectives, IS researchers have used the notion of capabilities as an ideal abstract layer [1, 2, 5]. Capability modeling has been used in IS to express investment profile [5], facilitate business-IT alignment [2], plan and design service oriented implementations [4, 5], identify IT capabilities requisites [5, 6] and facilitate runtime adjustment to changing context [4]. Capabilities in enterprise modeling are often associated with goals to represent strategic investment intentions [1, 2, 6]. However the mentioned IS Engineering approaches have used capabilities in the design process without considering their dynamic and evolutionary nature and do not reason on capability development, orchestration and deployment choices.

© Springer International Publishing Switzerland 2015
A. Persson and J. Stirna (Eds.): CAiSE 2015 Workshops, LNBIP 215, pp. 53–65, 2015.
DOI: 10.1007/978-3-319-19243-7_5

Dynamic capability, the ability to intentionally alter capabilities and resources to transform an enterprise to a desirable state, is a source of sustainable advantage in high-turbulent environments [7]. Flexibility of capabilities relates to how manageable they are and enables dynamic capabilities by providing more choices for resource management [8, 9]. Therefore the ability to analyze capabilities characteristics and qualities has a substantial role in the success of capability modeling.

The challenge of facing dynamic and evolving requirements of enterprise software systems is twofold, (1) adaptable and reconfigurable services/systems that can adjust to changes and (2) flexible capabilities and organizational setting that can create and support them. The challenge cannot be addressed with bounded analysis of system context or variability in the technical solutions; because of the dynamic complexities and emergent behaviors that arise from interactions of different entities at the enterprise level [10]. Hence, designers should represent and analyze the socio-technical characteristics of enterprises to capture what kinds of flexibilities are needed when studying the coupling of business and technical architectures.

In this paper we posit using the notions of capability and dynamic capability from the strategic management literature [7], as the integrative concepts that can represent organizational portfolio and analyze its evolution. A modeling approach that enables representation of capabilities requisites, alternatives, complementarities and transformation states is introduced. The approach uses the Strategic Alignment Model (SAM) [11] to extend the i* framework and enable analysis of potential inflexibilities in a particular organizational setting.

2 Related Work in Analysis of Enterprise and IT Flexibility

Research on scenario based architectural tradeoffs [12], design patterns and principles [13] and change impact analysis [14] are examples of studies in IS engineering that facilitate design for changeability. Assessment of the effort required for a change and its rippling effect is a fundamental step in these approaches [12, 14]. However, analysis of flexibility at the enterprise level is different from software flexibility due to the complexities that arise from dynamic relations of entities in the organizational context [10]. Research propositions enable management of enterprise wide implementations of changes. In this section we review approaches that facilitate (1) service-oriented adjustment to changing context, (2) enterprise level modifiability analysis, and (3) quantitative approaches that measure enterprise-level qualities.

Researchers in IS that adopt the notion of capability have not considered social identities, complementarities and alternative development paths of capabilities. They have rather focused on using them to design business aligned services. For example, Zdravkovic et al. [4] propose identification of contextual information for capabilities to enable automated adjustment of services in response to changes in context variables. Therefore the services are only flexible towards a predefined context and one cannot analyze how the enterprise as a whole would react to unanticipated changes.

Modifiability of modeled enterprise solutions has been studied. De Boer et al. [14] facilitate change impact analysis in ArchiMate to trace changes triggered at the business-level. The research takes advantage of semantic relations in ArchiMate and proposes heuristic rules to identify direct and indirect impacts. The analysis is used to signal necessary adjustments to architects. The approach can analyze what-if scenarios regarding changes but cannot identify potential inflexibilities to guide the design and decision making process. In a different approach, Lagerstrom et al. [15] present a meta-model and a PRM quantitative analysis to estimate cost and effort of changes in enterprise software while considering uncertainties. However the approach is more suitable for managing and planning implementation of changes as gathering the required information for the analysis at early stages of decision making is difficult.

A number of approaches offer quantitative analysis of architectural qualities at the enterprise level. Johnson et al. [16] use and extend influence diagrams to depict and trace causality among entities in architectural models. The approach takes advantage of scenario development to represent and compare alternatives. In a slightly different method, Langermeier et al. [17] propose a meta-model and a data-flow based analysis to evaluate organization specific measures. The quantitative information required to perform such analysis is often not available at early stages of decision making. Furthermore the approaches perform analysis on a given architecture and do not capture socio-technical alternatives that influence enterprise level flexibility.

3 Towards Modeling Capabilities and Their Flexibility

Capabilities embed social and technical characteristics attained in their lifecycle which can accommodate or restrain their development choices [6, 18]. Decision makers require the ability to analyze such characteristics such as autonomy [7], complementarities [7] and flexibility [8, 18]. Particularly when designing IT capabilities, alignment to organizational capabilities and strategies plays a major role [3].

The Dynamic Capability View (DCV), first introduced by Teece [7], deals with enterprise evolution using conceptions of capabilities, positions and paths. However DCV only provides implicit guidelines for analysis and decision making. A decision maker should be able to answer questions such as (1) where are the boundaries of a capability and how does it relate to organizational actors, to understand capability identity and autonomy; (2) How does the capability relate to other capabilities, to understand complementarities; (3) what are the alternative design choices; (4) how can one identify causes of inflexibilities; (5) what are the intents behind relations among heterogeneous capabilities such as IT and organizational capabilities?

In this section we first review concepts from DCV and examine the suitability of the i* modeling framework for representing them. We then study flexibility in the context of strategic management as well software architecture, and consider how i* might be extended to represent the alignment intents of IT capabilities.

3.1 Modeling Capabilities from a Strategic Management Perspective

Capability is defined as a set of differentiated skills, complementary assets and organizational routines that provide basis for competitiveness [18]. Capabilities are intentionally developed to realize strategic goals, they are autonomous so as to facilitate decentralization, yet depend on each other to achieve synergy [7]. By modeling capabilities as specialized i* actors, one can depict intentions of capabilities using i* goals and softgoals, point to necessary skillsets and assets as i* resources and describe employed routines as i* tasks within the actor's boundary. The i* framework uses *Actors, Roles, Positions* and *Agents* to depict the social aspects of enterprises. By modeling a capability as a specialized actor, we are able to treat it as a social actor which has an ongoing identity, with responsibilities and (social) dependency relationships with organizational actors and other capabilities. This is motivated by findings in DCV that emphasize the role of collaborative learning process that agents with individual skills participate in and employ their expertise in a particular organizational setting [19]. If capabilities are represented as static properties of agents or roles, it would be difficult to model and reason about the collaborative aspects.

In IS engineering, it is common to consider transitions from an "as-is" to a "to-be" state. However according to DCV the possible paths of transition are constrained by current state of the enterprise (referred to as "position" in DCV) [7]. For example a SOA software infrastructure built on a Microsoft platform would need a software development capability with ".NET" skillsets (a capability development constraint) and a deployment team that can configure and run Windows servers (a deployment constraint). If the solution is adopted at the enterprise level it will impose constraints on the kinds of software-as-a-service solutions that the human resource department can adopt (orchestration constraint). In a previous work [6], the representation of social and technical considerations of capability development, orchestration and deployment alternatives using the i* framework has been discussed.

We use i* dependencies to capture the kinds of complementary relations among capabilities and organizational entities, i.e. capabilities complement one another by fulfilling goals, satisfying softgoals, providing resources, or performing tasks. i* diagrams that depict the overall capability configurations and relationships are called Strategic Dependency (SD) models. The Strategic Rational (SR) models express alternative means of achieving capability intentions and their contribution to quality attributes represented as softgoals while specifying required tasks and resources. Hence the future state of an organization is articulated by a series of choices regarding potential alternatives that shape a transition path from the current state.

3.2   Analyzing Inflexibilities Using Dependency and Alignment Propagation

Our approach draws on conceptions of flexibility from strategic management and IT systems architecture. We identify potential inflexibilities in terms of (1) how tightly they are coupled to other capabilities and organizational entities; (2) how and what kinds of impacts (strategic intent) to expect from a change in a capability throughout the organization. To address the first aspect, we enable analysis regarding the effect of dependencies and their propagation across the organization. Therefore one could answer questions regarding how capability couplings influences value creation and how a change would affect their complementary relations. To address the second aspect, we allow analysis of (1) which dependencies and of what kinds are influenced by a change and (2) propagation of alignment intents of IT and organizational capabilities, to understand what kinds of strategic consequences to expect from a change.

The strategic management literature identifies flexible capabilities that enable enterprise transformation as a necessity to achieve dynamism [8, 9]. Flexibility in strategic management refers to how manageable a capability is; in other words "the ability to deploy and use a capability in multiple settings and conditions without adjusting its nature" [8]. In a study of new development projects, Leonard-Barton recognized that the more enterprises invest in a core capability, the higher the probability of causing rigidities towards new and innovative evolutionary alternatives [18].

In IS engineering, flexibility refers to how easy it is to change a system. Studies identify architectural design principles to enable flexibility such as simplicity, coupling, modularity, interoperability and compatibility, autonomy, scalability and redundancy [13]. Quantifications of flexibility are proposed in software architecture research [12, 20]. Bekkers [21], studies flexibility in e-government and identifies the technical aspect that deals with linkages among variety of systems and networks and the social aspect which deals with participants autonomy and strategic interest.

In order to capture the strategic intent of effective coupling between IT capabilities on one hand and organizational capabilities on the other, we assign an "alignment intent" to each of these dependencies in i* model. By analyzing how these alignment intents propagate across the network of dependencies, we are able to determine the impact of change on the achievement of strategic objectives.

To classify alignment intents, we adopt the well-known Strategic Alignment Model (SAM) by Henderson and Venkatraman [11]. Although the original model was conceived for alignment at the enterprise level, subsequent research has applied it at a finer-grained level, e.g., at the level of alignment between projects [22]. We apply SAM at the level of alignment between capabilities. SAM distinguishes four "perspectives" in strategic alignment depending on the domain in which the alignment is triggered and the path it follows. (1) The *Strategy Execution* perspective is triggered by business strategy, influencing organizational infrastructure, and then IT infrastructure. (2) In the *Technology Transformation* perspective the objective is set by business strategy, but then IT strategy articulates the requirements, with IT infrastructure implementing the strategy. (3) The *Competitive Potential* perspective indicates the ability of IT capabilities to influence enterprise competitiveness. The objective is set by IT strategy, articulated by business strategy, and then adopted by organizational infrastructure. (4) The *Service Level* alignment perspective deals with IT services directly generating value, hence dominating the strategy making process. The objectives are set by IT strategy, appear in IT infrastructure, and then implemented by organizational infrastructure. The mnemonic symbols in Fig. 5 signify the path across the familiar two-by-two grid of the SAM model for each of the four perspectives.

4   Applying Capability Modeling to an SOA Implementation

In this section a hypothetical case of SOA implementation in an educational institute is presented. The models presented in this section give a visual representation of the current state of capabilities and will answer questions such as (1) what are the capabilities? (2) What are their intents and associated routines and resources? (3) How do they collaborate to generate value? In Sect. 5, we build on these models to answer (4) whether the current state of IT capabilities can address changing requirements? (5) What inflexibilities can appear in the future state? Current state of enterprise IT capabilities and immediate organizational capabilities are presented in Fig. 1.

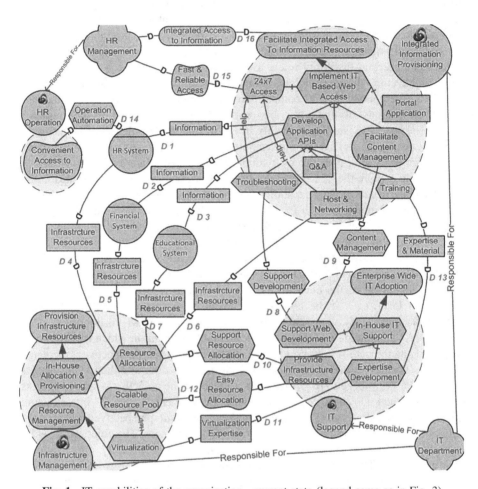

Fig. 1. IT capabilities of the organization - current state (legend same as in Fig. 3)

First the context of the organization and its i* representation is discussed. The enterprise relies on three major IS for its day-to-day operation, *Human Resource (HR) management System*, *Educational System* and *Financial System* represented as i* agents in Fig. 1. These systems are developed and maintained by partner organizations and hosted in-house, hence dependent on the capability of *Infrastructure Management*. The *Infrastructure Management* consists of people, processes, and resources (hard goods and operational budget) within the organization and therefore modeled as a capability. It intends to enable server administration and resource allocation. The *IT* *support* capability intends to facilitate *Enterprise Wide IT Adoption* which is currently achieved by in-house staff and processes. Doing this in-house is only one deployment option among others, as indicated by the use of the i* means-ends relationship. The *Integrated Information Provisioning (IIP)* capability (at the top right corner of Fig. 1) enables personalized access to information. The *IT department* is responsible for decision making regarding mentioned IT capabilities.

We focus our attention on the dependencies that *HR System* has on *HR Operation* and *HR Management*. Similar dependencies exist among *Educational* and *Financial systems* to their corresponding entities but are not shown in Fig. 1 for brevity. Likewise the details of the *HR Operation* capability are not presented as it is not the subject of analysis and decision making. However if the capability models are used for strategic planning one would expect expression of the big picture [5].

In the second step, a dependency propagation graph is introduced in Fig. 2 to allow change impact analysis and determine capabilities role in value creation. The principle used in constructing the graph is based on impact analysis approaches in software architecture [20]. The identifiers in the circles of Fig. 2 correspond to dependency labels of Fig. 1 and the links represent causalities among dependencies. For example, *Virtualization Expertise (D11)* is needed to perform *Virtualization* (in *Infrastructure Management capability)* that enables *Scalable Resource Pool* which in turn will provide *Easy Resource Allocation (D12)*. The link between the two dependencies entails the propagation effect of a change from *"D11"* to *"D12"* as shown in the cloud.

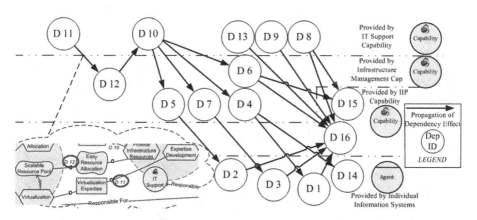

Fig. 2. Dependency propagation graph – showing propagation effect of capabilities dependencies – the closer to the right, the more direct contribution to value creation

Analyzing and tracing the capabilities role in value creation has significant influence in decision making [7]. The requirement is amplified when facing capabilities that are not directly associated with revenue generation such as most IT capabilities [3]. To track capabilities offerings, the nodes in Fig. 2 are presented in vertical segmentations that represent IT capabilities of Fig. 1. For example, *"D15"* and *"D16"* in the third row are provided by the *IIP* capability. The first, second and the fourth row respectively present dependencies provided by *IT Support* capability, *Infrastructure Management* capability, and information systems such as *HR System*.

5   Analyzing Inflexibilities Arising from an SOA Implementation

In this section we first analyze whether the current state of IT capabilities can address changing requirements to enable Business Process Management (BPM) and Business Intelligence (BI). We then study how the expansion of the *Integrated Information Provisioning (IIP)* capability can cause inflexibilities; and point to design requirements for the evolution with the intent to preserve flexibility. Our study, particularly points out requirements for (1) virtualization expertise development and training to overcome potential inflexibilities of the *Infrastructure Management* capability and (2) careful engineering of the *IIP* capability to balance competing requirements of application autonomy and flexible resource orchestration.

In Fig. 3, change requirements for *BPM*, *BI* and *Enterprise Management* capabilities are presented. The *BI* capability relies on *IIP* to facilitate *Access to Business Aligned Data Objects*. The *BPM* capability depends on *IIP* to facilitate *Application Autonomy* while providing *Flexible Access to Information*.

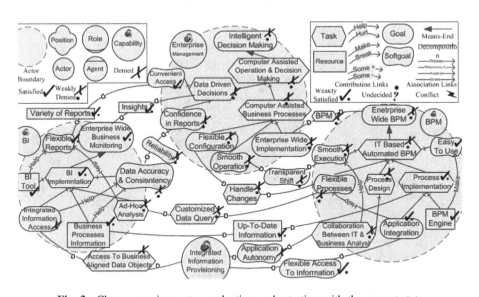

Fig. 3. Change requirement – evaluating orchestration with the current state

A qualitative reasoning approach [23] is adopted to enable analysis of whether *IIP* can satisfy *BPM* and *BI* requirements or not. The current status of the *IIP* capability presented in Fig. 1, i.e. its *Portal Application* and *Content Management* processes, cannot produce *Business Aligned Data Objects*. Furthermore the required *Flexibility* in accessing information and making changes to applications are weakly satisfied.

Therefore the analysis motivates expansion of *IIP* with Service Oriented Architecture (SOA) solutions. In Fig. 4 the future state is presented with the proposed expansion. The decomposition of *IIP* to *Content Management* and *SOA* infrastructure is not shown for brevity. SOA is modeled as a capability because it is more than a software solution and introduces a new architectural paradigm [24]. Introduction of the SOA capability will impact the orchestration of *BI* and *BPM* capabilities.

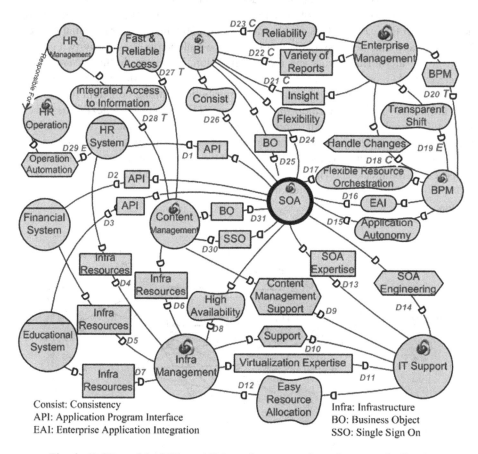

Fig. 4. i* SD model of IT capabilities – future state (legend same as in Fig. 3)

The letters "E", "T" and "C" are assigned to dependencies among IT and organizational capabilities to indicate alignment intent. The letters represent alignment perspectives of SAM [11] as discussed in Sect. 3.2. The *HR Operation Automation* dependency (*D29*) between *HR Operation* and *HR system* is an example of an executive alignment intent presented with an "E" in Fig. 4. Similar to Avison et al. [22], the alignment intent is determined based on the domain that triggers alignment and the path it follows through as described by SAM. For example, "*D27*" and "*D28*" are assigned with a "T" representing technology transformation alignment as the IT department (IT Infrastructure domain) implements systems to provide real-time access to information

(IT strategy domain). However the IT strategy itself is derived by business requirement of *HR Management* (business strategy domain). In contrast *"D18"* and *"D21"* make fundamental changes to the decision making process; thereby indicating a competitive potential alignment and represented with a "C".

The dependency propagation graph in Fig. 5 corresponds to the state presented in the i* SD model of Fig. 4. The number on the bottom of the circles is calculated by counting the propagation effect of the dependencies, meaning the rank for *"D11"* equals to the sum of the ranks of dependees (in this case 10 + 10) plus the number of dependees (in this case 2). This enables ranking the elements by their potential impact. The colors and mnemonic symbols that signify the path across the two-by-two grid of SAM depict alignment intents and their propagation. For example the *Virtualization Expertise (D11)* provided by *IT Support* to *Infrastructure Management* provides executive, transformational and competitive contributions through different routes. The high influential ranking of *Virtualization Expertise (D11)* can cause inflexibilities when scaling IT capabilities without careful planning. In this example, if the necessary training and engineering effort on virtual servers hosting information systems is not provided in advance, adding the *SOA Solution* to the mix can cause resource deficits for support and maintenance. The propagation graph not only points to causes of such inflexibilities but also depicts the kinds of consequences to expect using alignment intents.

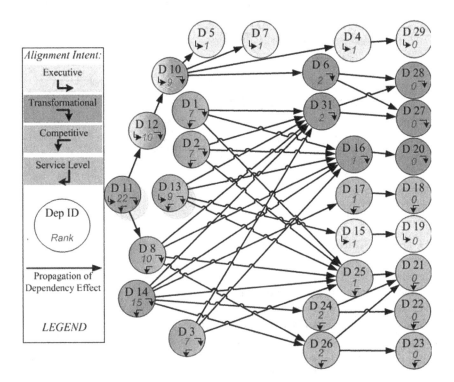

Fig. 5. Dependency propagation graph showing propagation of alignment Intent – potential for causing inflexibilities increase when moving from the right to the left

The *SOA* capability which enables *Flexibility in Resources Orchestration (D17)* and provides *Business Objects (D24* and *D25)*, can raise inflexibilities due to its highly engineered design *(D14)*. The commitment to *SOA Engineering (D14)* requires heavy investments and limits future choices of the enterprise. The propagation graph facilitates identification of such sensitive elements so the enterprise can mitigate the risk by monitoring and planning before they become rigidities.

6 Discussion and Conclusion

Designing information systems that can adapt and accommodate highly dynamic environments is an ongoing challenge. In this paper, we examined the use of the i* framework to depict capability complementarities and relations to organizational entities. The i* framework was extended to facilitate modeling alignment intents of IT and organizational capabilities. Furthermore by analyzing propagation effects of dependencies, the approach facilitates analysis of value creation, potential inflexibilities and change impacts. Such analysis assists decision makers and designers to identify flexibility requirements for IT capabilities and architecture, therefore enable easier enterprise transformations.

The use of the proposed modeling constructs were demonstrated in a BPM and SOA implementation for a hypothetical case. The analysis revealed the need for careful planning when (1) scaling the institute's infrastructure management and (2) engineering SOA implementation, before deploying new IT capabilities as they both can pose rigidities. Moreover the analysis of dependencies suggest a more gradual and nuanced flow of intent among organizational and IT capabilities in contrast to the clear-cut architectural levels or domains typically adopted in enterprise architecture frameworks, such as business, application and technology. The analysis will enable design of complementary capabilities and allow planning for changes with different intents and consequences whether business or technical.

The analysis in this paper was limited to IT capabilities of the organization. Further investigation and validation of the findings with real case studies and complete capability portfolios is required. Tool support for reading and interpreting the dependency propagation graph is essential as the models grow in size. The use of the dependency propagation graph accompanied with quantification methodologies can enable economic analysis of value creation. However the proposed propagation graph cannot reason on how different quality attributes influence one another. Further investigation on approaches that allow identification of cause and effects of capabilities and their quality attributes to evaluate future behavior of alternatives is required.

References

1. Stirna, J., Grabis, J., Henkel, M., Zdravkovic, J.: Capability driven development – an approach to support evolving organizations. In: Sandkuhl, K., Seigerroth, U., Stirna, J. (eds.) PoEM 2012. LNBIP, vol. 134, pp. 117–131. Springer, Heidelberg (2012)

2. Iacob, M.-E., Quartel, D., Jonkers, H.: Capturing business strategy and value in enterprise architecture to support portfolio valuation. In: 16th International Enterprise Distributed Object Computing Conference (EDOC 2012), pp. 11–20 (2012)

3. Nevo, S., Wade, M.: The formation and value of IT-enabled resources: antecedents and consequences. Manage. Inf. Syst. Q. **34**, 163–183 (2010)

4. Zdravkovic, J., Stirna, J., Henkel, M., Grabis, J.: Modeling business capabilities and context dependent delivery by cloud services. In: Salinesi, C., Norrie, M.C., Pastor, Ó. (eds.) CAiSE 2013. LNCS, vol. 7908, pp. 369–383. Springer, Heidelberg (2013)

5. Ulrich, W., Rosen, M.: The Business Capability Map: The "Rosetta Stone" of Business/IT Alignment (2011). http://www.cutter.com/content-and-analysis/resource-centers/enterprise-architecture/sample-our-research/ear1102.html

6. Danesh, M.H., Yu, E.: Modeling enterprise capabilities with i*: reasoning on alternatives. In: Iliadis, L., Papazoglou, M., Pohl, K. (eds.) CAiSE Workshops 2014. LNBIP, vol. 178, pp. 112–123. Springer, Heidelberg (2014)

7. Teece, D.J., Pisano, G., Shuen, A.: Dynamic capability and strategic management. Strateg. Manag. J. **18**, 509–533 (1997)

8. Combs, J.G., Ketchen Jr., D.J., Ireland, R.D., Webb, J.W.: The role of resource flexibility in leveraging strategic resources. J. Manage. Stud. **48**, 1098–1125 (2011)

9. Sirmon, D.G., Hitt, M.A.: Contingencies within dynamic managerial capabilities: interdependent effects of resource investment and deployment on firm performance. Strateg. Manag. J. **30**, 1375–1394 (2009)

10. Dreyfus, D., Iyer, B.: Managing architectural emergence: a conceptual model and simulation. Decis. Support Syst. **46**, 115–127 (2008)

11. Henderson, J.C., Venkatraman, N.: Strategic alignment: leveraging information technology for transforming organizations. IBM Syst. J. **38**(2–3), 472–484 (1999)

12. Bengtsson, P., Lassing, N., Bosch, J., van Vliet, H.: Architecture-level modifiability analysis (ALMA). J. Syst. Softw. **69**, 129–147 (2004)

13. Fricke, E., Schulz, A.P.: Design for changeability (DfC): principles to enable changes in systems throughout their entire lifecycle. J. Syst. Eng. **8**(4), 342–359 (2005)

14. De Boer, F.S., Bonsangue, M.M., Groenewegen, L.P.J., Stam, A.W., Stevens, S., van der Torre, L.: Change impact analysis of enterprise architectures. In: Proceedings of IEEE International Conference on Information Reuse and Integration, pp. 177–181 (2005)

15. Lagerström, R., Johnson, P., Höök, D.: Architecture analysis of enterprise systems modifiability – models, analysis, and validation. J. Syst. Softw. **83**, 1387–1403 (2010)

16. Johnson, P., Lagerström, R., Närman, P., Simonsson, M.: Enterprise architecture analysis with extended influence diagrams. Inf. Syst. Front. **9**, 163–180 (2007)

17. Langermeier, M., Saad, C., Bauer, B.: A unified framework for enterprise architecture analysis. In: Proceedings of the Enterprise Model Analysis Workshop in the Context of the 18th EDOCW, pp. 227–236 (2014)

18. Leonard-Barton, D.: Core capabilities and core rigidities: a paradox in managing new product development. Strateg. Manag. J. **13**, 111–125 (1992)

19. Zollo, M., Winter, S.G.: Deliberate learning and the evolution of dynamic capabilities. Organ. Sci. **13**(3), 339–351 (2002)

20. Bohner, S.A.: Software change impacts-an evolving perspective. In: Proceeding of International conference on Software Maintenance, (ICSM 2002), pp. 263–272 (2002)

21. Bekkers, V.: Flexible information infrastructures in Dutch E-Government collaboration arrangements: experiences and policy implications. Gov. Inf. Q. **26**, 60–68 (2009)

22. Avison, D., Jones, J., Powell, P., Wilson, D.: Using and validating the strategic alignment model. J. Strateg. Inf. Syst. **13**(3), 223–246 (2004)

23. Horkoff, J., Yu, E.: Evaluating goal achievement in enterprise modeling – an interactive procedure and experiences. In: Persson, A., Stirna, J. (eds.) PoEM 2009. LNBIP, vol. 39, pp. 145–160. Springer, Heidelberg (2009)
24. Fiammante, M.: Dynamic SOA and BPM: Best Practices for Business Process Management and SOA Agility. IBM Press/Pearson, Upper Saddle River NJ (2010)

COGNISE 2015

Towards Guiding Process Modelers Depending upon Their Expertise Levels

Jonas Bulegon Gassen[1]([⊠]), Jan Mendling[1], Lucineía Heloisa Thom[2], and José Palazzo M. de Oliveira[2]

[1] Wirtschaftsuniversität Wien, Vienna, Austria
{jonas.gassen,jan.mendling}@wu.ac.at
[2] Universidade Federal do Rio Grande do Sul, UFRGS - PPGC, Porto Alegre, Brazil
{lucineia,palazzo}@inf.ufrgs.br

Abstract. Business process modeling is an important task for supporting business process management. One challenge of process modeling is the diversity of expertise from novice modelers to expert designers, which defines the need to provide different sorts of guidance during modeling. In this paper, we discuss these expertise differences based on the cognitive load theory and present an experiment that tested how people with different levels of expertise work with different instructional material presented as automatic feedback of a tool. Our conclusions suggest that guidance on reworking models needs to take different levels of expertise into account.

Keywords: Business process · Process modeling · Cognitive load theory · Process of process modeling

1 Introduction

The quality of business process modeling is of crucial importance for business process management. Various works discuss techniques and concepts for improving the quality of process models covering modeling guidelines [1,2], labeling guidelines [3,4], and pitfalls of process modeling [5]. Also the importance of the way of how a model is created, which is called the process of process modeling (PPM), is discussed in this context [6,7]. However, many challenges are still open [8], a.o. to take the diverse levels of modeling expertise into account.

It is generally agreed that suitable feedback and guidance during PPM (e.g. by means of a tool) can help to raise the quality of process models, in particular for *novices*. These are modelers with little experience that do not yet fully understand how correct and meaningful models can be created. The problem in this context is that *experts* will likely be annoyed by seeing basic hints, which distract them from the actual modeling task. Indeed, it has been found in experiments that what helps novices to increase performance can actually decrease performance of experts [9].

© Springer International Publishing Switzerland 2015
A. Persson and J. Stirna (Eds.): CAiSE 2015 Workshops, LNBIP 215, pp. 69–80, 2015.
DOI: 10.1007/978-3-319-19243-7_6

The objective of this paper is to investigate this trade-off in more detail. We formulate the idea that guidance has to be adapted to the level of expertise in order to be fully effective. To substantiate the benefits of such an strategy, an experimental research approach is required. We describe the cognitive foundations of such an experiment in terms of cognitive load theory [10]. We complement our argument with initial insights from a pre-study.

Against this background, this paper is structured as follows. Section 2 presents the background of effective guidance in terms of cognitive research. Section 3 describes our overall research design and the way how the experiment was conducted. Section 4 presents the study results along with a discussion of the findings. Section 5 concludes the paper.

2   Background

The central difference between novices and experts is that the latter will find tasks easy that the former find difficult. Cognitive load theory [10] helps to discuss this matter in more detail by distinguishing intrinsic and extraneous cognitive load. In essence, the intrinsic source of effort is related to the information itself and the extraneous load is related to the presentation of the information. Both can vary due to many factors: such as knowledge of the modeler, instructional procedures, or complexity of information.

Both types of cognitive load are related to differences between novices and experts while solving problems, such as the use of means-ends analysis versus domain-specific knowledge, respectively. Means-ends analysis, which is natural for humans, requires considering the current state and the goal state. While moving from the current state in the direction of the goal-state, humans verify differences between them and try to apply problem-solving strategies to change the state. Another difference according to cognitive load theory is that novices need more effort, since they use thinking, different from experts, which use knowledge. Instructional data may help novices. This bigger effort spent by a novice is clarified by recent research with functional magnetic resonance imaging, which demonstrates that the cerebral adaptation modifies the brain of an established professional such that energy consumption is reduced [11]. Confirmatory experiments have been conducted with different conceptual tasks such as translation or interpretation [12].

These findings have implications for guidance in process modeling, specifically the so-called worked example effect, the expertise reversal effect, or the guidance fading effect. These effects imply that guidance for novices should present more detailed instructional information and fill the knowledge gaps on novice's knowledge. Designers with higher level of expertise should work with problem-solving based on prior knowledge. Thus, the instructional information should follow the level of expertise of the designer; otherwise it may compromise the PPM.

These observations are complementary to recent research on process modeling that identify user characteristics as factors of performance. Recker and Dreiling [13] analyzed the comprehension of models and find that prior knowledge of a modeling grammar and of business process management showed to be significant factors. Process modeling of novices is investigated in [14], suggesting that a hybrid representation of text plus abstract graphical shapes lead to better semantic quality. Theoretical arguments in this direction had been provided before by Moody [15]. The observation that users approach a modeling task differently is described by Pinggera et al. [16]. The cognitive phases of comprehension, modeling and reconciliation are identified in the record of their modeling experiment. Similar observations are made by Soffer et al. [17].

In summary, the need for differentiating guidance for novices and experts can be deducted from the literature. In the following, we describe a research design to clarify the benefits of such an approach.

3 Research Design

This section presents our idea of guidance concerning different expertise levels, our experiment and its threats to validity.

3.1 Guidance

We divide guidance in two types: (i) to help the modeler immediately during the process modeling and (ii) after the modeling task is completed in order to enhance learning, for instance regarding the complexity and the compliance with formal guidelines [18] and number of errors per model. For this paper we focus on (i).

Considering a situation of immediate feedback in terms of instructional material such as diagrams with detailed textual explanations. According to Sweller, regarding the expertise reversal effect, [10], each of these materials would be suitable for novices, as they are new knowledge for them. However, the same instruction presented to experts may require additional cognitive resources to process redundant material, compared to the same material without detailed text. An example in the context of PPM occurs after the detection of a deadlock. If the designer has a low expertise level, a worked example is shown, describing why the deadlock may occur. A worked example exposes a step-by-step solution, which provides the person with the problem-solving schemas that need to be stored in long-term memory [10]. This may fill the gap of knowledge of the user, because he may not know why deadlocks occur in process models. If the user has a higher level of expertise, the elements causing the error may be marked, allowing the designer to fix it. However, since the user knows why the deadlock happens, the detailed explanation and even the worked example could create an extraneous cognitive load and should not be shown.

Figure 1 presents an example for that case. A novice could be shown a red marking in case of a deadlock. The image shows a simplified case, because the situation where it occurred in the user's modeling environment could be more complicated, causing extraneous cognitive load. Besides the figure, a text explaining why it occurs would be shown, such as: "The XOR Split, by its semantic, will execute only ONE outgoing flow. The AND Join will wait for ALL incoming flows before continuing the execution. Thus, the presented use will never

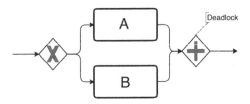

Fig. 1. Worked example for a deadlock

complete, generating a deadlock". This would help the novice designer to learn during the modeling. If the user has a mid-low expertise level, the same image with the short text "deadlock" could be shown. For users with a higher expertise level the markers could be done in the current model and a short text "deadlock" could be shown. For experts, only the markers in the current model could be more suitable. Empirical tests should be done in order to understand the threshold and level of instructional material to use for each case. Besides guidance during process modeling, based on data regarding modeler's actions during PPM, a personalized plan of study could be drawn for each modeler. Thus, the modelers could follow the plan to learn about their mistakes outside of the modeling activity.

In psychology the act of following common norms for a group, such as: staying in line or stopping before a red signal is called conformity. Asch [19] and other works present experiments that show the conformity behavior in humans and discuss how this is important for life in society. We assume the process modeling community to be a society. Thus, an operationalization for conformity could be done by means of guidelines and best practices used by modelers. Data in this context is used to measure conformity of the user within the society.

3.2 Experiment Description

In this work we tested, through an online experiment, how designers react to some instructional material. The experiment was performed as within-subjects, all participants received the same treatment. However, there are possible differentiation amongst the participants regarding expertise level on process modeling. The purpose of the experiment was to analyze the influence of different levels of instructional material during the PPM. First of all, we asked the designers to answer demographics (based on [6]), in order to try to assess their knowledge on business process modeling and Business Process Modeling and Notation (BPMN). The demographics are presented later on. Secondly, we inserted errors intentionally in three process models - mortgage application, company resupplying and travel booking (based on models from an online collection[1]). The designers had to describe which changes they would suggest to each model to improve or fix them, nothing could be added to or removed from the models, only changed. The problems applied were: for Model A, a deadlock, for Model B

---

[1] http://bpmai.org.

a livelock and for Model C, verb-object style misuse. Assuming that a tool would show instructional information about the detected problems, we organized the same procedure. Models A and C have instructions, in two different levels. They were presented in the following order:

1. **Model A1:** no instruction.
2. **Model B1:** no instruction.
3. **Model A2:** worked example (Fig. 1).
4. **Model B2:** no instruction.
5. **Model A3:** worked example plus textual description on the problem.
6. **Model B3:** no instruction.
7. **Model C1:** no instruction.
8. **Model C2:** red marks in the model to spot the problem, only.
9. **Model C3:** red marks plus examples and textual description on the problem.

Each of these steps was composed by a set of elements, some of them allowing the participant to enter information (inputs). They are presented on Table 1.

Table 1. Elements of each step of the experiment, after demographics

Element	Type	Occurence	Input
Model name plus description	Text	All	No
Image of the process model	BPMN model	All	No
Instruction level 1	Example	A2	No
Instruction level 2	Example plus text	A3, C3	No
Marks in the model	Red marks	C2, C3	No
Question for changes in the model	Free text	All	Yes
Why the change should be made	Free text	All	Yes
Mental effort for answering	Likert 1–5	After each	Yes
Confidence on the answer	Likert 1–5	After each	Yes
Wheter the participant knew VO	Yes-No	After C3	Yes

The subjective labels of the Likert scales varied from very low to very high mental effort/confidence on checking the model quality, which were transformed to 1 to 5, as presented on Table 1. To support this approach we consider the work of Paas [20] that pointed out self-evaluation as valuable asset for mental effort evaluation. The questions answered as free text require human evaluation, which will be explained further on in this paper. Showing the same model could cause a control problem. One could look different for the model because it is showed repeatedly. We defined three variants (one per step) of models A and B. The structure was kept the same, but we applied changes in domain, layout and used synonyms where terms repeated amongst models. In this way, the models look different but are actually the same regarding flow and mistakes presented. We did not create variants of Model C because we spot the problem in the second and third times that it was shown. Model B does not have an instruction in order to test if the instruction of Model A will help a similar problem.

In the steps where instruction was provided, the participant had to at least open the instruction, only then the questions (the same for other steps) were made available. Thus, he keeps the instruction open as much as was needed. Based on answers of two questions for the same model we can infer the following about guidance:

- **Wrong and Wrong:** necessary and not sufficient;
- **Wrong and Correct:** necessary and sufficient;
- **Correct and Correct:** not necessary and sufficient.

The reason why experts may find necessary to have marks showing the problems could be explained by the Anchoring & Adjustment phenomenon [21]. Besides the questions presented above, we also stored the overall time to perform the experiment, time that each instruction remained open and amount of times that each instruction was opened. We conjectured that experts will keep the instructions open by much less time than novices.

3.3 Threats to Validity

Regarding the experiment, a possible drawback is the evaluation of experts vs. novices. In addition, some measurements might not be possible, such as additional effort of experts caused by detailed instructional material. Our current sample do not allow to perform statistical significance tests, a bigger and more balanced sample is required. Lastly, the evaluation of answers is performed by humans and thus it has to be done carefully to avoid causing bias.

4   Experiment Execution

This section presents the execution of the experiment altogether with analysis and results.

4.1 Data Cleansing

A total of 33 persons participated of the experiment, from which 2 participants have answered in Portuguese and were removed even before the evaluation of answers. A translation could lead to bias and then was avoided. Another criteria applied was to remove participants that applied less than 10 min in the experiment, four participants were removed. Lastly, participants who stated having more than 6 days of self-education or formal training were removed, as they could have misunderstood the question, this happened to 5 participants. The questionnaire presented that one semester of classes would result in 3 days of training, as the questions referred to self-education or training within the last 12 months, is unlikely to have more than 6 days within 12 months. The possibility of having two courses at the same time was not considered for our sample. Therefore, 22 participants out of 33 stand after data cleansing.

4.2 Demographics

The participants are from academy (undergraduate, master and Ph.D. students) and were chosen intentionally and not statistically at random. We sent invitation for a known sample, some of them answered and some did not. In order to have information about the participants we asked demographic questions based on Pinggera (2012), which resulted 10 variables. They are presented, altogether with a normalization, in Table 2:

Table 2. Descriptive for demographics variables and normalization

Variable	Mean	SD	Scale	Normalization	New scale
Years of modeling	1.05	2.17	0–inf	value * 2	0–inf.
Models analyzed	3.36	10.68	0–inf	0;25;50;75;100, +1 per level	0–5
Models Created	1.59	4.28	0–inf	0;25;50;75;100, +1 per level	0–5
Activities average	4.50	7.36	0–inf	0;5;10;15;20, +0.3 per level	0–1.5
Formal training	1.14	1.86	0–inf	Value / 2	0–3
Self-education	0.59	0.80	0–inf	Value / 2	0–3
Self-evaluation	1.86	1.39	1–7	IF (Value>2; Value-2; 0)	0–5
BPMN familiarity	1.95	1.50	1–7	IF (Value>2; Value-2; 0)	0–5
BPMN competence	1.86	1.39	1–7	IF (Value>2; Value-2; 0)	0–5
BPMN months	3.05	8.96	0-inf	Value /12 * 2	0–inf.

The proper categorization of expert and novice users requires a deeper evaluation and we do not discuss this specific point here. In order to analyze our data we performed a categorization based on years of modeling, transforming the other variables to a value related to a year of modeling. For the variables normalized by means of levels (i.e. models analyzed), for each level a certain value was add, for example, reading 40 models gives the participant 2 points. For variables arising from Likert scales (i.e. self-evaluation), points were given only to participants that have value greater than 2. The first two options of the scale were "strongly disagree" and "disagree" on questions such as "Are you an experienced business process modeler?". In this sense, selecting any of these questions gives 0 points for the participant. After the normalization, we sum each variable and participants with a score higher than 10 were considered experts, the remainder novices. Based on that, 5 participants were selected as experts and 17 as novices. This sample has an imbalance, which difficult the realization of statistics and should be solved by having more participants.

To achieve 10 points the user needs at least almost one point in each variable. It is not possible to achieve 10 points with only one variable, besides years of modeling or BPMN months, which would give a certain degree of expertise in case they are high. Also, it is very unlikely to have some variable and to not have another, as some of them are connected.

4.3 Answers Evaluation

The experiment required free text answers in some points and an evaluation of those answers is necessary. We performed a peer review evaluation. Each reviewer gave a score to each of the questions of all participants. The reviewer had three options: wrong, somewhat correct and correct. After the subjective answers, they were transformed to 0, 1 and 2, respectively. The mean was performed for the scores and was used as score for each participants answer.

4.4 Results

The experiment allows us to compare many different aspects. First, we compared the means of scores for each questions. A t-test would be suitable to test the significance of the differences between the means of each group, however due to the imbalance of our sample, novices group with 17 participants and experts group with 5 participants, we did not perform significance tests. Table 3 show the means for each question, comparing novices and experts.

Table 3. Means of scores based on answers evaluation (0–2)

	A1	A2	A3	B1	B2	B3	C1	C2	C3
Novices	0.00	0.29	1.21	0.12	0.47	0.56	0.00	0.00	0.59
Experts	0.80	0.80	0.80	1.20	0.80	0.80	0.20	0.60	0.80

It is possible to see in Table 3 that only in question 3 of model A the group of novices achieved better scores than experts. Novices having higher scores than experts on A3 may be due to issues such as incorrect categorization of groups (novice vs. expert), novices applying more attention and effort than experts or that some experts did not detected the problems due to anchoring and adjustment phenomena. Also, it is possible to note that aside of Models A and B for experts, all groups increased scores, as the questionnaire evolves. In addition, another interesting point here is that model B did not present an instruction, it was expected that the instructions of model A, being similar, would help the participants in questions of model B. They were showed in a paired fashion with questions from model A, as presented on Sect. 3.2. Table 3 shows the means increasing as instructions of model A were shown, for novices group, this may suggest retention and transfer [22]. Table 4 show the means for model C using as group the participants that did not know and that knew the guideline.

Table 4. Scores separated by knowledge about verb-object style (0–2)

	C1	C2	C3
Did not know	0.06	0.06	0.59
Knew	0.00	0.40	0.80

For all cases besides the first question, which did not have any help to spot the problem, the group that knew the guideline achieved better scores. The second question had marks in the activities containing the problematic labels, but only the last question (instruction 3) presented knowledge about the verb-object style. It is possible to note how complete knowledge elevates score for novices. Suggesting that proper material is fundamental as feedback during modeling. Besides the scores, we also analyzed time, Table 5 exposes the means of time and count of instruction access for our experiment.

Table 5. Time and access means

	Novices	Experts
Total time for experiment	1343.6	977.4
Time for Instruction 1	48.7	9.4
Time for Instruction 2	70.6	43.6
Time for Instruction 3	78.1	50.6
Access count for Instruction 1	3.1	1.2
Access count for Instruction 2	2.4	1.4
Access count for Instruction 3	1.65	1.4

The novices group needed a greater amount of time to complete the whole experiment. We used simple measurements of time, thus it is not possible to have a great precision in this regard. Some participants did not go through all the experiment at once. Thus, participants that used more than 50 min to perform the experiment were set as missing values (2 participants). Also, participants that used more than 5 min in any of the instructions were set as missing values (1 participant). Novices had greater means for all instructions, both for time spent and counting times opening each instruction, as conjectured.

As presented on Sect. 3.2, based on wrong and correct answers we infer whether instructions were necessary and sufficient for participants. We performed a percentage for each conclusion. It is important to note that we used only full scores. For example, necessary and not sufficient (N&NS) means Q(N) and Q(N+1) as wrong or score 0 for both. Necessary and sufficient (N&S) means wrong (score = 0) and correct (score = 2). Finally, unnecessary and sufficient (UN&S) means both correct (score = 2). Figure 2 shows the percentages for each inference to all instructions, separated by novices and experts.

Figure 2 allows to verify that instructional material is necessary and should be well studied as an improvement for process modeling tools. All instructions on their first apparition (A1, B1 and C1) were at least 40 % necessary and not sufficient for experts and at least 71 % necessary and not sufficient for novices. Second apparitions had smaller percentages, thus the previous material or the second material completeness might have helped.

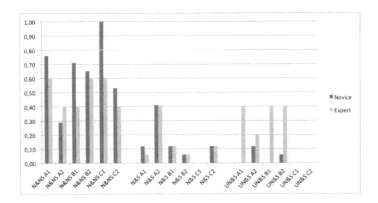

Fig. 2. Necessary and sufficient conditions

4.5 Discussion

Due the imbalance of the current sample, we are not able to perform statistical tests regarding significance, in this sense we cannot accept or reject our hypotheses. However, the results allows us to have an idea on differences between experts and novices and their interaction with instructional material regarding process modeling. The classification of one as expert or novice is an important point. Referring to instructional material presented by tools, in order to improve process modeling, the use of the term experienced instead of expert might provide a better semantics. Which means that the person in question has a wider range of knowledge about process modeling. Yet, to provide better instruction to the user, it would be interesting to gather data about a variety of different aspects concerning the process of process modeling. It is possible to see the difference on results between questions concerning a problem occurring in process models, such as deadlock, and a guideline, such as verb-object style. Thus conformity should also be considered. An expert modeler might not know specific guidelines, what does not make of him a novice. Hence a fine-grained approach, might be more suitable than only classifying users as experts vs. novices. Web services could be made available to tools that are willing to present this personalization. They would have to call the web services in modeling time, based on modelers' actions, and send the related data. Then the web services could provide suitable feedback accordingly. In addition, improvement plans could be generated to the modeler, describing aspects that should be studied by each modeler.

5   Conclusions

We presented discussions about expertise and conformity level of business models designers and reactions based on that. Complementary empirical research has to be done in order to test which specific aspects should be considered to suggest the expertise level of users. Also, the instructional material for different levels of expertise has to be calibrated. However, defending the expertise level of modelers is a very complex task. In this sense, gathering a wide range of data in a fine-grained fashion might be a better solution. The feedback can be focused in each fine-grained aspect. For example, an expert modeler might not know about the verb-object style and it does not make of him a novice.

Other experiments in many directions should be performed. Companies may have their own guidelines and best practices, which would create a local society. The conformity is measured based on the global society, which refers to the process modeling community in general. Thus it is possible to match the designer with the local and global societies. Also, the conformity of the local society (company) can be matched against the global society (BPM community).

Acknowledgments. This work has been partially supported by Conselho Nacional de Desenvolvimento Científico e Tecnológico (CNPq) and Coordenação de Aperfeiçoamento de Pessoal (CAPES), Brazil.

References

1. Becker, J., Rosemann, M., von Uthmann, C.: Guidelines of business process modeling. In: van der Aalst, W., Desel, J., Oberweis, A. (eds.) Business Process Management. LNCS, vol. 1806, pp. 30–49. Springer, Heidelberg (2000)
2. Mendling, J., Reijers, H.A., Cardoso, J.: What makes process models understandable? In: Alonso, G., Dadam, P., Rosemann, M. (eds.) BPM 2007. LNCS, vol. 4714, pp. 48–63. Springer, Heidelberg (2007)
3. Mendling, J., Reijers, H.A., Recker, J.: Activity labeling in process modeling: empirical insights and recommendations. Inf. Syst. **35**(4), 467–482 (2010)
4. Leopold, H., Smirnov, S., Mendling, J.: On the refactoring of activity labels in business process models. Inf. Syst. **37**(5), 443–459 (2012). Best papers from DOLAP 2010
5. Rosemann, M.: Potential pitfalls of process modeling: part a. Bus. Proc. Manage. J. **12**(2), 249–254 (2006)
6. Pinggera, J., Zugal, S., Weber, B.: Investigating the process of process modeling with cheetah experimental platform. EMISA Forum **30**(2), 25–31 (2010)
7. Claes, J., Vanderfeesten, I., Reijers, H.A., Pinggera, J., Weidlich, M., Zugal, S., Fahland, D., Weber, B., Mendling, J., Poels, G.: Tying process model quality to the modeling process: the impact of structuring, movement, and speed. In: Barros, A., Gal, A., Kindler, E. (eds.) BPM 2012. LNCS, vol. 7481, pp. 33–48. Springer, Heidelberg (2012)
8. Indulska, M., Recker, J., Rosemann, M., Green, P.: Business process modeling: current issues and future challenges. In: van Eck, P., Gordijn, J., Wieringa, R. (eds.) CAiSE 2009. LNCS, vol. 5565, pp. 501–514. Springer, Heidelberg (2009)
9. Schweppe, J., Rummer, R.: Attention, working memory, and long-term memory in multimedia learning: an integrated perspective based on process models of working memory. Educ. Psychol. Rev. **26**(2), 285–306 (2014)
10. Sweller, J., Ayres, P., Kalyuga, S.: Cognitive Load Theory. Explorations in the Learning Sciences, Instructional Systems and Performance Technologies. Springer, New York (2011)

11. Nigmatullina, Y., Hellyer, P.J., Nachev, P., Sharp, D.J., Seemungal, B.M.: The Neuroanatomical Correlates of Training-Related Perceptuo-Reflex Uncoupling in Dancers. Cerebral Cortex, New York (2013)
12. Moser-Mercer, B.: The search for neuro-physiological correlates of expertise in interpreting. Translation and Cognition, pp. 263–287 (2010)
13. Recker, J.C., Dreiling, A.: The effects of content presentation format and user characteristics on novice developers' understanding of process models. Commun. Assoc. Inf. Syst. **28**(6), 65–84 (2011)
14. Recker, J., Safrudin, N., Rosemann, M.: How novices design business processes. Inf. Syst. **37**(6), 557–573 (2012)
15. Moody, D.: The physics of notations: toward a scientific basis for constructing visual notations in software engineering. IEEE Trans. Softw. Eng. **35**(6), 756–779 (2009)
16. Pinggera, J., Zugal, S., Weber, B., Fahland, D., Weidlich, M., Mendling, J., Reijers, H.A.: How the structuring of domain knowledge helps casual process modelers. In: Parsons, J., Saeki, M., Shoval, P., Woo, C., Wand, Y. (eds.) ER 2010. LNCS, pp. 445–451. Springer, Heidelberg (2010)
17. Soffer, P., Kaner, M., Wand, Y.: Towards understanding the process of process modeling: theoretical and empirical considerations. In: Daniel, F., Barkaoui, K., Dustdar, S. (eds.) BPM Workshops 2011, Part I. LNBIP, vol. 99, pp. 357–369. Springer, Heidelberg (2012)
18. Mendling, J., Reijers, H.A., van der Aalst, W.M.P.: Seven process modeling guidelines (7pmg). Inf. Softw. Technol. **52**(2), 127–136 (2010)
19. Asch, S.: Opinions and social pressure. Sci. Am. **193**(5), 31–35 (1955)
20. Paas, F.: Training strategies for attaining transfer of problem-solving skill in statistics: a cognitive-load approach. J. Educ. Psychol. **84**, 429–434 (1992)
21. Tversky, A., Kahneman, D.: Judgment under uncertainty: heuristics and biases. Science **185**(4157), 1124–1131 (1974)
22. Mayer, R.: Multimedia Learning. Cambridge University Press, Cambridge (2001)

How Does It Look? Exploring Meaningful Layout Features of Process Models

Vered Bernstein[✉] and Pnina Soffer

University of Haifa, Mount Carmel, 3498838 Haifa, Israel
vbernste@campus.haifa.ac.il, spnina@is.haifa.ac.il

Abstract. The layout of business process models has a substantial effect on their understandability. However, currently only few layout properties are well defined, thus appropriate support for creating well-laid-out models is limited. This position paper indicates the importance of developing a collection of layout features which will correspond to meaningful layout properties perceived by human. It reports an exploratory study for obtaining such a collection.

Keywords: Model layout · Understandability · Exploratory study · Cognitive load

1 Introduction

Business process models have been the subject of extensive research in the past decade. They serve different purposes and may have different forms along the life cycle of a business process. This paper focuses on business process models as conceptual models, facilitating understanding and communication among people.

For this purpose, model understandability is of crucial importance. Much research has been conducted in recent years on factors that impact the understandability of conceptual models in general (e.g., [4]) and process models in particular. Attention has mostly been given to visual properties of the modeling language [9], but some research also addressed properties of individual models. Examples include the influence of model complexity [7, 14], modularity [19], grammatical styles of labeling activities [8], and secondary notation [5, 15]. Obtained insights led to the development of empirically grounded guidelines for business process modeling [8], and for avoiding process model smells [18], such as unnecessarily complex process fragments [14] or edge crossings [8]. Yet, as far as we know, a systematic investigation of the effect of the layout of a model on its understandability has not been conducted.

Specific layout features have been discussed (e.g., line-crossing [8]). However, layout can be characterized by a variety of features. Currently, only a few are accurately defined [13]. Furthermore, there is no evidence that these features are the most relevant layout features in terms of human perception. We argue that a basic collection of well-defined layout features is essential for investigating the effect of model layout on its understandability. Moreover, a collection of well-defined and meaningful layout features can also be beneficial for gaining a better understanding of how individuals construct process models.

© Springer International Publishing Switzerland 2015
A. Persson and J. Stirna (Eds.): CAiSE 2015 Workshops, LNBIP 215, pp. 81–86, 2015.
DOI: 10.1007/978-3-319-19243-7_7

This paper explores the layout features of a process model with the aim of identifying the features that are dominant in forming the human perception of the visual appearance of a process model. We report an exploratory study extracting a collection of layout features through questionnaires and interviews.

The remainder of the paper is organized as follows: following a motivating example, Sect. 3 discusses cognitive implications of model layout for model understanding and construction. The exploratory study and its findings are reported in Sect. 4. Finally, a concluding discussion and future directions are in Sect. 5.

2 Motivating Example

As a motivating example, consider the models in Fig. 1, both depicting the same process. The difference in their appearance is clear to the eye, but it is hard to clearly indicate what makes this difference. We currently lack precise concepts to verbalize or measure the appearance of the models and their differences. Our aim is to take a step towards filling this gap.

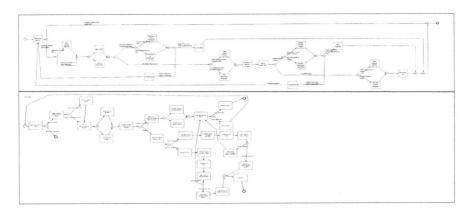

Fig. 1. Two models of the same process

3 Cognitive Considerations

This section discusses cognitive implication of layout features for model understanding and for model construction.

3.1 Implications for Process Model Understanding

When reading a process model for the purpose of performing a certain task, the individual uses the limited capacity of her short-term memory. According to the cognitive load theory [16], three types of cognitive load are involved: intrinsic load, which stems from the task, extraneous load, which relates to the information representation (in our context, the visual appearance of the model), and germane load, relating to the integration of the current information with long-term memory knowledge. Many researches (e.g., [1]) indicate that effective task performance can be achieved when extraneous load is minimized, releasing more capacity for intrinsic load. Indeed, based on cognitive load considerations, Mayer [6] has indicated that even a small representation manipulation can yield significant differences in task performance results. A recent study that used eye-tracking technology [3] has measured eye movements between different parts of the display, reflecting an effort devoted to integrating information that was scattered in different places. It was found that for display configurations which required less integration effort (thus less extraneous cognitive load), higher learning performance was achieved. Considering process models, the layout of a model determines the extent to which information integration efforts would be required. If elements that closely relate to each other are located separately in the model, the reader spends more effort integrating this information, thus extraneous cognitive load increases. Note that some layout constraints can be imposed by the modeling language. As an example, consider the swimlanes that denote roles in BPMN. Using these constructs, activities performed by one role are visually located in one lane, making their integration easier. On the other hand, tracking the sequence of activities might be challenging if it moves among different roles, since information from different lanes needs to be integrated.

It follows that further investigation of the impact of different layout configurations on model understandability is needed. We believe that identifying a meaningful set of layout features would allow targeted investigation of their effect on process model understandability and advance the construction of more understandable models.

3.2   Implications for Process Model Construction

When constructing a process model, the modeler determines its layout. In addition to affecting the understandability of the resulting models, recent studies indicate that extensive dealing with the layout during model creation can result in a long and unfocused model construction process [10]. Reference [11] suggested that the modeling style is affected by four groups of factors – individual interface preferences, cognitive properties of the modeler, intrinsic and extraneous task properties. In particular, individual preferences are reflected in the layout of the resulting model. Consider, for example, the two models given in Fig. 2. These are models of different processes, constructed by the same modeler. While some visual similarity is clear to the eye, we currently lack an appropriate set of concepts for expressing this similarity.

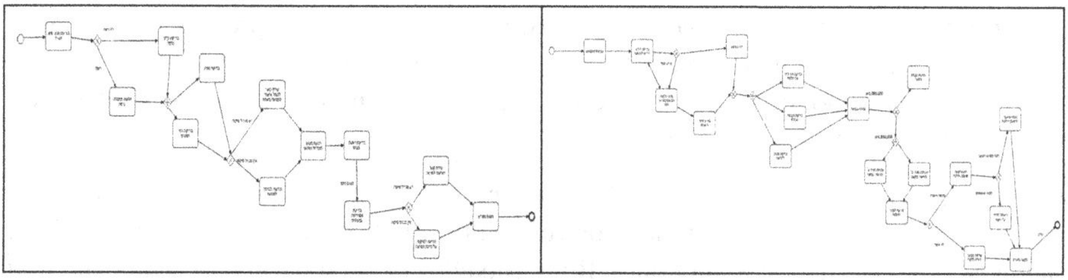

Fig. 2. Two models of different processes constructed by the same modeler

4 Exploratory Study

4.1 Setting and Data Analysis

This section reports an exploratory study aimed at extracting a set of visual layout features that are meaningful to the human perception. The study used questionnaires and interviews with the participation of 22 Information Systems students. 15 undergraduate students answered the questionnaire and 7 graduate students were interviewed, using the questionnaire as a basis for the interview. The questionnaires included 5 pairs of process models, to prompt the indication of features through comparison of models. The models were made small to fit a single page, yet their structure was clear visually. Any label in the model elements or on the edges was blurred in order to have participants address only the visual aspect of the model. Examples of such pairs can be seen in Figs. 1 and 2. Considering each pair, participants were asked to rate the similarity of the models using a 7 points Likert scale and to indicate three different aspects and three similar aspects in the models. In the interviews more detailed information was prompted using additional questions. In particular, the questions related to features that support or hamper the understandability of the models in order to encourage participants to engage in the specific appearance features. All participants had basic knowledge of process modeling. Participation in the study was voluntary.

The data analysis considered the text of the written questionnaires and the interviews text. Using qualitative methods [17], textual segments were first coded by the model(s) they referred to and classified to categories of features. Saturation of the categories was reached by the 4th interview. Second, the identified categories were aggregated to higher-level categories of layout features.

4.2 Findings

The identified layout feature categories relate to the general structure of the model, its direction, its ending points, properties of the edges and the angles between them, alignment of the elements, and symmetry of blocks. Below we explain each category and list the lower-level categories it includes.

Model structure – this includes the model's general *shape* (e.g., horizontally or vertically rectangular, square) and the model *size* – the space used on the canvas. This category relates to a coarse-grained view of the model and its boundaries, indicated in statements like "the size of the models is different".

Ending points – the *number of ending points*, while reflecting the process itself, affects the flow viewed by the model reader. The ending points form an anchor while reading the model, thus a model with multiple ending points is more difficult to read than a model with a single ending point.

Direction – includes several features. The *general direction* of the model, which can be horizontal (left to right or right to left) or vertical (top-bottom or bottom-top). A typical statement concerning the direction: "Both models are vertical". The *placement of ending point(s)* – in case of a single ending point it clearly marks the direction of the model; otherwise if ending points are placed apart from each other the direction might be unclear. *Branching off* is a situation where different branches of the model go in opposite directions (without forming a loop), blurring the direction of the model, as said "It then goes in many directions". *Change in direction* – when the general flow of the model changes its direction, usually in attempt to fit a large model into one page. This feature was highly indicated, e.g., "this model looks like a stair case".

Edges – many sub-categories relate to the edges of the model. The *length of the edges* may vary, creating a "messy" model. Alternatively, very short edges form a dense model, while long ones result in a widely spread one. *"Broken" edges* that include bending points bothered some of the participants ("Need to straighten all the broken edges"). *Crossing edges* are a long recognized feature whose avoidance was recommended [6]. Our participants indicated "…there are edges here that just go one on top of the other". *Text on edges* – annotations that are not necessarily related to branching conditions were also indicated as reducing the readability of the model.

Angles – the angles between edges can affect the general look of the model and how "neat" it appears. Specifically, 90° angles, sometimes referred to as "Manhattan layout", result in an easy to read model (as said: "90° angles gives a cleaner look").

Alignment – when the elements of the model are aligned, forming a straight line, the impression is of a tidy and clear model. A typical statement: "This model is clearer and very aesthetic"

Symmetry – symmetry of the placed elements in the structured blocks appears aesthetic and makes the model easy to read.

5   Concluding Discussion

The collection of layout features identified in the exploratory study provides an initial terminology with which the layout of a model can be characterized. Yet, these are qualitative terms rather than measurable properties. To this end, their quantification to a set of metrics is in process.

We note that quantitative layout metrics already exist [12] and are used as a basis for automatic layout functionality, which is available in process modeling tools (e.g., [2]). Nevertheless, these metrics are not anchored in any theory or evidence of what humans perceive as meaningful. Rather, they include properties which seemed important enough and possible to implement. The most comprehensive set of metrics we are aware of has been suggested by [13], relating to graphs in general. It includes metrics for the following features: edge crossing, bends ("broken" edges), symmetry, minimum angle between edges, orthogonality of edges and of nodes (alignment), upward flow (consistent direction of edges), and width of layout. All these features are included in the collection obtained in our study, which includes 7 additional ones.

We consider a set of layout metrics to be important for several purposes. First, they can be used in future studies for gaining a deep understanding of the effect of model layout on its understandability. Second, they can serve in future studies of individual preferences and layout decisions in the construction process of a model. Third, they can serve for modeling guidelines and for enhancing the automatic layout functionality in modeling tools. Thus, eventually, the understandability of the created process models will be promoted.

References

1. Ginns, P.: Integrating information: A meta-analysis of the spatial contiguity and temporal contiguity effects. Learn. Instr. **16**(6), 511–525 (2006)
2. Gschwind, T., et al.: A linear time layout algorithm for business process models. J. Vis. Lang. Comput. **25**(2), 117–132 (2014)
3. Johnson, C.I., Mayer, R.E.: An eye movement analysis of the spatial contiguity effect in multimedia learning. J. Exp. Psychol.: Appl. **18**(2), 178 (2012)
4. Khatri, V., Vessey, I., Ramesh, P.C.V., Park, S.J.: Understanding Conceptual Schemas: Exploring the Role of Application and IS Domain Knowledge. Inf. Syst. Res. **17**, 81–99 (2006)
5. La Rosa, M., ter Hofstede, A., Wohed, P., Reijers, H., Mendling, J., van der Aalst, W.M.P.: Managing process model complexity via concrete syntax modifications. IEEE Trans. Ind. Inf. **7**, 255–265 (2011)
6. Mayer, R.E.: Multimedia Learning. Cambridge University Press, New York (2014)
7. Mendling, J.: Metrics for Process Models: Empirical Foundations of Verification, Error Prediction, and Guidelines for Correctness, vol. 6. Springer, Heidelberg (2008)
8. Mendling, J., Reijers, H.A., van der Aalst, W.M.P.: Seven process modeling guidelines (7pmg). Inf. Softw. Technol. **52**, 127–136 (2010)
9. Moody, Daniel L.: The "physics" of notations: toward a scientific basis for constructing visual notations in software engineering. IEEE Trans. Softw. Eng. **35**(6), 756–779 (2009)
10. Pinggera, J., Soffer, P., Zugal, S., Weber, B., Weidlich, M., Fahland, D., Reijers, H.A., Mendling, J.: Modeling Styles in Business Process Modeling. In: Bider, I., Halpin, T., Krogstie, J., Nurcan, S., Proper, E., Schmidt, R., Soffer, P., Wrycza, S. (eds.) EMMSAD 2012 and BPMDS 2012. LNBIP, vol. 113, pp. 151–166. Springer, Heidelberg (2012)
11. Pinggera, J., Soffer, P., Fahland, D., Weidlich, M., Zugal, S., Weber, B., Mendling, J.: Styles in business process modeling: an exploration and a model. Softw. Syst. Model. 1–26 (2013)
12. Purchase, H.: Which aesthetic has the greatest effect on human understanding? In: DiBattista, G. (ed.) GD 1997. LNCS, vol. 1353, pp. 248–261. Springer, Heidelberg (1997)
13. Purchase, Helen C.: Metrics for graph drawing aesthetics. J. Vis. Lang. Comput. **13**(5), 501–516 (2002)
14. Reijers, H.A., Mendling, J.: A Study into the Factors that Influence the Understandability of Business Process Models. IEEE Trans. Syst. Man Cybern. Part A **41**, 449–462 (2011)
15. Schrepfer, Matthias, Wolf, Johannes, Mendling, Jan, Reijers, Hajo A.: The Impact of Secondary Notation on Process Model Understanding. In: Persson, Anne, Stirna, Janis (eds.) PoEM 2009. LNBIP, vol. 39, pp. 161–175. Springer, Heidelberg (2009)
16. Sweller, J., Van Merriënboer, J., Paas, F.: Cognitive architecture and instructional design. Educ. Psychol. Rev. **10**(3), 251–296 (1998)
17. Taylor-Powell, E., and M. Renner. "Analyzing qualitative data. University of Wisconsin-Extension Program Development & Evaluation." (2003)
18. Weber, B., Reichert, M., Mendling, J., Reijers, H.A.: Refactoring large process model repositories. Comput. Ind. **62**(5), 467–486 (2011)
19. Zugal, S., Soffer, P., Haisjackl, C., Pinggera, J., Reichert, M., & Weber, B.: Investigating expressiveness and understandability of hierarchy in declarative business process models. Softw. Syst. Model. 1–23 (2013)

Advanced Dynamic Role Resolution
in Business Processes

Irene Vanderfeesten$^{(\boxtimes)}$ and Paul Grefen

School of Industrial Engineering,
Eindhoven University of Technology, Eindhoven, The Netherlands
{i.t.p.vanderfeesten,p.w.p.j.grefen}@tue.nl

Abstract. In business processes tasks are often executed by humans. Dynamic role resolution is the (run time) selection of the optimal resource to execute a task for a certain process instance based on conditions and requirements that are specified at design time. For this purpose a classification of resources is made, usually based on their organizational position (department, role). This is, however, a very simple way of modeling resources. In this position paper, we propose conceptual extensions to the current approach to role resolution that focus on a more detailed and extended characterization of resources, cases and process objectives in order to improve human and cognitive aspects of the system such as motivation, learning and training of employees.

Keywords: Role resolution · Resource assignment · Task allocation · Human and cognitive aspects

1 Introduction

Business processes are often supported by Business Process Management Systems (BPMSs), a type of Information System that manages and coordinates the execution of the business process and the allocation of tasks to resources in the process. Based on a design time specification of the tasks and their order, and the organizational structure, the BPMS selects at run time the optimal resource for the execution of a task for a certain process instance. This allocation mechanism is often termed *(dynamic) role resolution*, as the allocation of a resource is based on the role and position the resource has in the organization (e.g. clerk of the financial department).

Current resource models and role resolution mechanisms are rather basic and limited in their specification [1]. They focus on single human actors per activity, only take into account basic organizational features of a resource (e.g. role, position, department), and do not consider case information in the allocation of tasks to resources. In this position paper we propose ideas to extend and advance the resource modeling and role resolution capabilities of BPM technology specifically to enhance human and cognitive aspects of the system. We propose a.o. to extend the resource model with a resource's characteristics such as its capabilities, experience and expertise and to use this information in role resolution in order to improve e.g. the quality of work, satisfaction, motivation, learning and training of employees.

© Springer International Publishing Switzerland 2015
A. Persson and J. Stirna (Eds.): CAiSE 2015 Workshops, LNBIP 215, pp. 87–93, 2015.
DOI: 10.1007/978-3-319-19243-7_8

The structure of this position paper is as follows. First, the current state-of-the-art in role resolution is discussed in Sect. 2. Next, extensions towards human and cognitive aspects are discussed and examples illustrating the opportunities and advanced requirements for role resolution are presented. Finally, Sect. 4 presents a brief research agenda and Sect. 5 concludes this paper.

2   Dynamic Role Resolution

BPMSs support and automate business processes by leading *process instances* (also called *cases*) through the tasks of the process in the right order and by coordinating the resources that execute these tasks. A *resource* is an entity that is assigned to a task and is requested at runtime to perform a *work item* for a specific process instance in order to complete the objective of the task for that case [1].

At the basis for this type of process support are two models: the *process model* specifies which tasks have to be executed in which order, and the *resource model* specifies the resources that are involved in the execution of tasks in the process, their mutual relationships (who can replace who) and the organizational structure. These models are specified at design time. In the process model it is indicated per task which type of resource is allowed to execute the task, linking to the organizational structure defined in the resource model. For instance, in Fig. 1 task B has to be executed by an employee of role R1 and department G2. The specific resources that may execute task A are employees Clare and Jody. At run time, when specific process instances are executed, one of these specific resources is allocated to the work item.

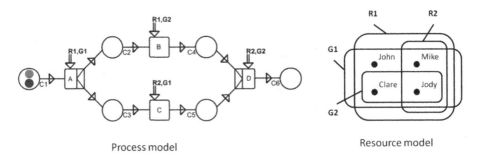

Process model   Resource model

Fig. 1. A process model and accompanying resource model (taken from [2])

Mostly, the resource models used in contemporary BPM technology and theory are rather simple: resources belong to an organizational structure (group or department) and execute a certain role (e.g. clerk, expert, manager). Role resolution mechanisms are limited to this 2-dimensional organizational view. This paper proposes a number of (conceptual) extensions to this limited view in order to improve the match between the case and the resource and to enhance human aspects of work allocation.

Some researchers, however, have focused on further describing the allocation of work items to resources from a technical perspective. [1] elaborates on assignment and synchronization policies that determine in which way the work items from a case are distributed and assigned to employees. They distinguish for instance between push (the system forces the resource to start working on a certain item) and pull (the resource requests the next work item from the system) patterns, individual or group work item inboxes, whether or not delegation to another resource after assignment is possible, and whether the queuing of work items is done in a queue (fixed order) or pool (free selection). Also, [3] presents a number of resource patterns that describe the technical features in BPMSs mainly driven by the lifecycle of a work item. They evaluate which of these theoretical patterns are actually supported by commercially available BPMSs. And they also discuss a number of standard *allocation rules* such as round robin, shortest work queue, selection of the same resource as for the previous activity for the case, and the 'four eyes principle'. Finally, some more recent work focuses on the optimization of work item/resource allocation with respect to *process performance* indicators such as waiting time, throughput time and resource utilization, e.g. [4], and on most optimal work-handovers [5]. Neither of these prior works, however, focus on a more advanced specification of work item allocation to resources with respect to cognitive and human aspects.

3 Proposed Advancements

In order to advance role resolution mechanisms, we propose extensions to the current state-of-the-art, being inspired by a number of practical BPM research projects [7, 8]. Figure 2 graphically depicts these extensions that are discussed one by one here.

Resource Characteristics - The current practice often considers a resource to be an individual human being with a certain organizational position that allows him or her to execute certain tasks in a process. In practice, especially in application domains outside the administrative domain such as manufacturing and healthcare, also different *types of resources* exist: teams consisting of several experts (e.g. surgery teams with a surgeon, anesthesiologist, and nurses), non-human resources (e.g. robots, web services), etc. In order to be suitable candidates for the execution of a task, these resources have to satisfy a number of criteria (*task requirements*) that are not included in the organizational model. The different resource types may be interchangeable (e.g. a robot and a human may both execute the same task). Furthermore, human resources are currently selected based on their organizational position only. However, humans in the same position are never exactly the same. They have e.g. different *backgrounds*, *capabilities*, *experience*, *preferences* and *personal goals*. These additional characteristics may be taken into account when allocating a resource: for instance, a clerk with many years of experience executing a task may be more suitable to handle a difficult case than a clerk who has just started. Or the allocation of work items may be matched with personal learning goals of the employees.

Case Characteristics - In none of the existing allocation approaches the characteristics of the cases that run through the process are taken into account. Of course, these cases all have something in common – they have to be handled by the same process – but still many specific characteristics such as *history*, *personal details of the client*, and *details*

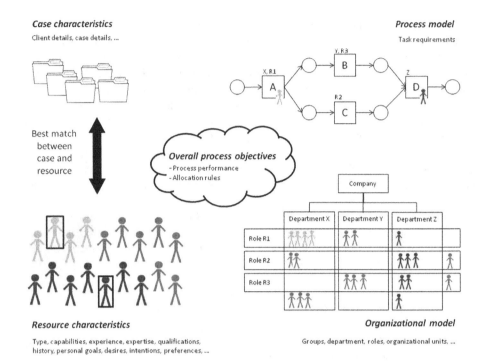

Fig. 2. Overview of ingredients for advanced role resolution.

of the case (e.g. the amount of a loan, credibility category of the applicant, etc.) can be taken into account to match the case with the best resource to execute a task. This may also improve human and cognitive aspects of the system. For instance, a request for a high amount of loan may be assigned to an expert employee to avoid mistakes (good for both satisfaction and external quality), or a case may be assigned to the employee that has communicated with the client before (in the context of another case or process) leading to higher familiarity and less set-up time.

Process Objectives - The current role resolution mechanisms, including the proposed extensions above, focus on the *operational* allocation of resources. On top of that, one may also consider the goals of the process on the *tactical* level to improve the overall process. Apart from the already researched *process performance* (e.g. shortest waiting time) [5, 6], there may also be other objectives for the overall management of the process. For instance, by using the detailed case characteristics and resource capabilities, one may be able to match cases based on training purposes for the human resources (once in a while the resource gets a more difficult case to execute), or improve work variety for the human resource (the activities to be executed and the cases to be executed differ enough such that the resource doesn't feel bored). In addition to that, the set of general *allocation rules,* such as the 'four-eyes principle', may be extended with rules based on historical information and case and resource specific information (e.g. a task that is disapproved always should be sent back to the resource that originally handled it such that this resource can learn from mistakes).

These proposed extensions to the current state-of-the-art in role resolution are illustrated with a few examples from practice that show the possibilities of improving cognitive and human aspects in the process by advancing work item allocation.

Example 1 (inspired by [6]) – The invoicing department of a telecommunications company has to process many invoices received from national and international suppliers. These invoices can be of several types (from a preferred supplier or not, based on a purchase order or not, etc.). All invoices are handled by the same process and are therefore considered the same, but after an analysis of the process performance, it turns out that many mistakes are made. The reason for this is that not all employees are well-trained and experienced for all types of invoices. The inexperienced workers for instance make many mistakes with the VAT of international invoices. When the characteristics of the invoices and the capabilities of the resources are better mapped, the matching between the resource and the invoice could be improved. First of all, one could think of only assigning invoices to resources that are known to handle these correctly, but in a later stage one could also try to improve the work variety of the employees by offering alternating types of invoices and prevent workers from boredom, or train and help the resources build new skills by assigning more difficult invoices once in a while.

Example 2 (inspired by [7]) – a financial company offers personal loans to clients via the internet. In order to request a loan the (prospected) client has to fill an online form and add details about himself, his financial situation and the requested loan. When this online form is received, some automatic checks are performed and a call agent calls back the requestor to discuss the request, complete the information and to explain the procedure that will follow. This call agent appears to have a large impact on the success rate of eventually getting the loan offer accepted. Therefore, a good match between the request/requestor and the call agent is essential. For instance, historical data showed that a male applicant best could be called by a female agent, that the client should preferably be addressed in his native language, that call agents with a lot of experience were more successful with borderline cases, and that the time of calling back related to the time of the online request also made a difference (the business rule of calling back within an hour from the request was abandoned).

4 Research Challenges

In the previous section, we have explained our proposed conceptual advancements of the current practice in role resolution in order to create better matches between cases and resources, focusing on human aspects in the allocation. This section briefly discusses the research challenges to implement the above ideas in BPM technology.

At design time, the process, organizational model, but also the case characteristics, resource capabilities, experience, goals, etc., and the allocation rules and process objectives have to be modeled. Therefore, current process modeling languages have to be extended in order to include this information. In some cases this may be a simple information element added to an existing modeling language, but especially for modeling case characteristics and resource characteristics new models have to be created. We may build on recent developments in the area of resource modeling [8] experience and skill modeling [9, 10] and plan to investigate insights from the field of work- and organizational psychology.

Secondly, at run time, the process execution engine also has to interpret the additional information that was stored in the extended models (i.e., resource and case characteristics, allocation rules, and performance) and select the optimal resource. This requires a more advanced decision algorithm that can deal with the operational as well as the tactical process objectives. Also, the process execution engine has to deal with possible exceptions, such as sudden unavailability of a resource, and re-assign to another resource on the fly in a more advanced way.

5   Conclusion

In this paper, we have proposed a number of extensions to the current state-of-the-art in role resolution in BPMSs. The main goal of these proposals is to make a better match between the case and the resources executing tasks for the case and by that improve the process performance and process outcome (external quality), but also human and cognitive aspects of the system such as work motivation, satisfaction (internal work quality) and training. The ideas presented are mainly conceptual and still have to be elaborated upon and implemented in a (prototype) BPMS.

References

1. Zur Muehlen, M.: Organizational management in workflow applications – issues and perspectives. Inf. Technol. Manag. **5**, 271–291 (2004)
2. van der Aalst, W.M.P., van Hee, K.M.: *Workflow Management: Models, Methods, and Systems.* MIT Press, Cambridge (2004)
3. Russell, N., van der Aalst, W.M., ter Hofstede, A.H., Edmond, D.: Workflow resource patterns: identification, representation and tool support. In: Pastor, Ó., Falcãoe Cunha, J. (eds.) CAiSE 2005. LNCS, vol. 3520, pp. 216–232. Springer, Heidelberg (2005)
4. Kumar, A., van der Aalst, W.M.P., Verbeek, E.M.W.: Dynamic work distribution in workflow management systems: how to balance quality and performance. J. Manag. Inf. Syst. **18**(3), 157–194 (2002)
5. Kumar, A., Dijkman, R., Song, M.: Optimal resource assignment in workflows for maximizing cooperation. In: Daniel, F., Wang, J., Weber, B. (eds.) BPM 2013. LNCS, vol. 8094, pp. 235–250. Springer, Heidelberg (2013)
6. Ariaans, B.:Task allocation within teams - A Socio-Technical and Workflow Resource Pattern Perspective, Master thesis, Eindhoven University of Technology (2014)
7. van Bussel, M.: The RecLog2 method for process improvement - using historical data to improve work-item assignment, Master thesis, Eindhoven University Technology (2012)
8. Cabanillas, C., Resinas, M., Ruiz-Cortés, A.: RAL: A high-level user-oriented resource assignment language for business processes. In: Daniel, F., Barkaoui, K., Dustdar, S. (eds.) BPM Workshops 2011, Part I. LNBIP, vol. 99, pp. 50–61. Springer, Heidelberg (2012)

9. Koschmider, A., Yingbo, L., Schuster, T.: Role assignment in business process models. In: Daniel, F., Barkaoui, K., Dustdar, S. (eds.) BPM Workshops 2011, Part I. LNBIP, vol. 99, pp. 37–49. Springer, Heidelberg (2012)
10. Kabicher-Fuchs, S., Mangler, J., Rinderle-Ma, S.: Experience breeding in process-aware information systems. In: Salinesi, C., Norrie, M.C., Pastor, Ó. (eds.) CAiSE 2013. LNCS, vol. 7908, pp. 594–609. Springer, Heidelberg (2013)

A Position Paper Proposing Behavioral Solutions to Challenges in Software Development Projects

Ofira Shmueli[(✉)], Nava Pliskin, and Lior Fink

Ben-Gurion University of the Negev, Beer-Sheva, Israel
ofirash@post.bgu.ac.il, {pliskinn, finkl}@bgu.ac.il

Abstract. Based on empirical evidence, acquired in two experiments, we argue in this position paper that cognitive biases play a role in software engineering. Our research has targeted mainly the problem of over-requirement, which refers to specifying a system beyond the actual needs of the customer. The results of our experiments have demonstrated the impact of four cognitive biases in the context of software development, showing their connection to over-requirement, as well as over-scoping and time-underestimation. We further argue that accounting for cognitive biases in the software development context is not enough and that it is important, in both the practice and research arenas, to investigate solutions that already proved effective in reducing cognitive biases in other contexts. This paper contributes to a better understanding of some of the cognitive processes underlying software engineering, focusing on improvement of software development activities toward better performance and higher quality.

Keywords: Over-requirement · Endowment effect · IKEA effect · I-designed-it-myself effect · Planning-fallacy

1 Introduction

Software development projects have always had considerable failure rates. Charette [1] has reported about more than 30 software development mega projects that failed between 1992 and 2005, noting that more than half of them were actually abandoned. To overcome this unfortunate lack of success, new software development techniques have been introduced over the years. Thus, software development approaches evolved from the code-and-fix techniques, through traditional waterfall techniques, to rapid prototyping as well as spiral incremental techniques and agile techniques [2]. Despite these technical approaches hoped to increase success, the 2009 Standish Group Report [http://www.standishgroup.com/newsroom/chaos_2009.php, cited by Boehm & Lane [3]], reported the highest failure rate in the first decade of the 21st century in software development projects. Specifically, only 32 % of 9,000 projects delivered full capability within budget and on schedule, 44 % were significantly over budget, over schedule and/ or incompletely delivered, and 24 % were completely abandoned before completion.

© Springer International Publishing Switzerland 2015
A. Persson and J. Stirna (Eds.): CAiSE 2015 Workshops, LNBIP 215, pp. 94–99, 2015.
DOI: 10.1007/978-3-319-19243-7_9

Within the list of challenges associated with software development failures, the primary focus of this position paper is on over-requirement, also termed gold-plating [4] and over-specification [5]. Over-requirement refers to the problem of specifying a product or a system beyond the actual needs of the customer or the market, overloading it with excessive unnecessary features, sometimes called "bells and whistles". Some reports assert that at least 30% of developed features in software projects are over-required [6]. The vastly negative consequences of over-requirement in software development projects include project resource overruns, excessive system complexity, decreased user satisfaction, and demise of the entire project [7–10].

Yet, the phenomenon of over-requirement has barely been explored. A search in 20 highly-rated Information Systems and Project Management journals rarely found references to the over-requirement problem. Expanding the search to other closely-related problems revealed only 13 papers to match this search.

The other problems closely related to over-requirement have similar overload characteristics and consequences. Over-scoping, which refers to setting a scope that is too large and includes more functionality than can be implemented within available resources [11], is one example of a problem associated with the overload challenge. Another example is the set of creep phenomena (scope creep, requirements creep, and feature creep), which refer to expanding the project scope by changing and adding requirements and features once the project is already under way [12]. A somewhat different problem related to the overload challenge is time-underestimation, which refers to overly optimistic schedules and completion time [13] that might result with the commitment to doing more than can be accomplished.

Technical approaches to system development have solved neither over-requirement nor the other related problems plaguing software development projects. Thus, since the overload challenge has persisted despite technical progress in software development methods and techniques, one is motivated to look elsewhere for solutions.

According to the literature, the paths leading to the problems we consider in this paper are mostly rooted in human nature and behavior. Over-requirement, for instance, is mainly attributed to the tendency of developers and users to overload the project. On one hand, users follow their desire to ask for as much as possible [9, 14, 15]. Developers, on the other hand, follow their professional interest to work at the forefront of technology and often strive like users for the best possible solution [5, 10, 16], adding just-in-case functionality to fulfill all potential future needs [8, 9].

Research on the behavioral aspects of the above problems associated with the overload challenge in software development projects is thus needed, in line with the call by Goes [17] for the consideration of behavioral economics in the context of information systems (IS). The position we present next is mostly to raise awareness for the cognitive biases that might be at the root of project overloading. In addition, we call for studying solutions recommended by behavioral economists as means towards coping with the overload challenge, presenting empirical evidence in support of our position.

Four behavioral biases are addressed next. The first bias is the endowment effect, which refers to the tendency of people to overvalue their possessions [18]. The second bias is the IKEA effect, which refers to the tendency of people to overvalue their self-constructed products [19]. The third bias is the I-designed-it-myself effect, which refers to the tendency of people to overvalue their self-designed products [20]. The fourth bias is the planning fallacy, which refers to the tendency of people to underestimate the time needed to perform a task and to overestimate its benefits [21].

2 Argumentation

We argue first that the over-requirement problem in software development projects is partially due to the emotional involvement of developers with the software features that they deal with. Similar involvement has been demonstrated for physical items due to the endowment effect, the IKEA effect, and the I-designed-it-myself effect because people come to overvalue items they possess, create or design [18–20, 22]. We also posit that the problems of over-requirement, over-scoping and time-underestimation are partially the result of too optimistic assessments about the number of required and over-required functions that can be delivered on time and the importance of these functions. This behavior involving benefit overestimation and schedule underestimation is recognized as a cognitive bias termed the planning-fallacy [21, 23], and has been demonstrated for a wide variety of tasks, including origami folding, school work, tax-form completion, and computer programming [24].

To test our arguments, we conducted four experiments in which the behavioral effects were manipulated in the context of software development. All the experiments were based on factorial designs, with advanced undergraduate students majoring in IS as participants. For the sake of brevity, and since the results of all the experiments were similar, we describe next two of the four experiments. The first experiment involved specification of one feature and evaluation of feature importance. The second experiment involved estimation task of feature development time and the proper project scope.

The first experiment [25] involved 212 participants assigned with a specification task. For each effect, i.e., the endowment, IKEA, and I-designed-it-myself effects, we respectively manipulated and measured time, difficulty and freedom. Each of these factors is known to impact the specific effect. All participants were presented with a fictitious to-be-developed software system along with 16 potential features, diverse in terms of importance toward achieving the goal of the system, and were asked to evaluate the importance of each (on a 1 to 100 scale). After we randomly assigned them to four experimental groups that differed by task duration (10 or 30 minutes) and task freedom (low or high), they were asked to complete a specification task for one of the features, deliberately chosen to be unnecessary but nice to have. Finally, after completing the specification task, they were asked to help management decide about scope reduction, evaluate once again the importance of the over-required feature that they specified, and assess the difficulty they experienced in performing the task.

The results of the first experiment demonstrate the presence of the endowment, IKEA, and I-designed-it-myself effects in behavior of those charged with software development tasks and their potential impact on over-requirement. Supporting this conclusion is the finding that the overall valuations participants provided after completing the specification task (M = 78.11) were significantly above the valuations they provided before the specification task began (M = 70.77; $t_{203} = 4.113$, $p < 0.001$). The experiment provided additional interesting results in support of previous research.

Measuring the perceived difficulty of the specification task, for example, the results confirmed the argument of Norton et al. [19] that for higher valuation to hold, the task should be difficult enough but not too difficult. This experiment thus highlights the overload challenge and demonstrates that people involved in a specification of a software feature, even an unnecessary one, overvalue it and are unwilling to exclude it from project scope.

The second experiment involved 85 participants assigned with an estimation task. It focused on the planning fallacy and tested whether the outside-view approach, shown to mitigate problems related to the planning-fallacy, can also help overcome over-requirement, over-scoping, and time-underestimation in planning software development projects. In four experimental groups, we manipulated two outside-view mechanisms: reference-information about past completion times (present/absent) and role-perspective (developer/consultant). Participants in the second experiment were first presented with a fictitious to-be-developed software system along with 16 potential features, diverse in terms of their importance toward achieving the goal of the system. They were then asked to estimate feature development times and to recommend which of the features to include within scope given a pre-determined project duration.

The results of the second experiment confirm the presence of over-requirement, over-scoping, and time-underestimation in software development projects. Moreover, the results show that these problems are mitigated, yet not eliminated, by presenting reference-information about past completion times and by holding a consultant role. On average, while participants without reference-information estimated it would take 17.73 h to develop all features and included 12.00 features within scope, of which 2.54 were over-required, participants with reference-information estimated it would take 28.18 h to develop all features and included 9.82 features within scope, of which 1.74 were over-required. Similarly, on average, developers were more inclined towards time-underestimation, over-scoping, and over-requirement (with 21.64 h, 12.22 features within scope, and 2.97 over-required features, respectively) than consultants (with 24.37 h, 9.61 features within scope, and 1.32 over-required features, respectively). This experiment thus highlights the overload challenge, demonstrating not only the manifestation of the planning-fallacy in software development projects, but also the effectiveness of solutions recommended by behavioral economists.

3   Conclusion

This position paper calls for the exploration of the underlying behavioral mechanisms that drive biased requirement definition problems in software development projects, including the over-requirement, over-scoping, and time-underestimation problems associated with the overload challenge. The results of the two experiments presented above provide empirical evidence in support of our argument that cognitive biases do play a role and, therefore, it makes sense to look for solutions found effective in solving problems related to behavioral effects in contexts other than software engineering. Once such solutions would prove effective, costs of over-requirement and other problems as well as budget and schedule overruns would diminish while system quality and integrity would increase.

Along different phases of a software project lifecycle, cognitive biases seem to interfere with and sabotage the quality of decisions [25, 26]. Indeed, we empirically demonstrated that the endowment, IKEA, and I-designed-it-myself effects are related to over-requirement. We also showed that the planning-fallacy is related to over-requirement, over-scoping, and time-underestimation.

Our search for solutions focused on remedies that behavioral economists recommend for overcoming problems related to the planning fallacy. Indeed, our results show that over-requirement, over-scoping, and time-underestimation problems are mitigated, yet not eliminated, by the presence of reference-information about past completion times and by holding a consultant role. Mitigation, yet not elimination, of problems related to the planning fallacy already proved effective when outside-view solutions are applied in contexts other than software development.

The exploration we thus recommend should assess the problems associated with the overload challenge, their relationship to cognitive biases, and the relevant solutions proved effective in overcoming problems emanating from the respective biases. A comprehensive exploration would not only enhance our knowledge and awareness of such problems but also identify effective remedies for their mitigation.

Among other goals, the move away from plan-base development methods toward agile ones aimed to improve requirement definition. Yet agile software development did not eliminate the persisting overload challenges [11]. In addition to the experiments conducted by us, we call for empirical research to explore the consequences of the cognitive biases we investigated, as well as of other cognitive biases reported in the behavioral economics literature, in software development projects that employ agile methods.

References

1. Charette, R.N.: Why software fails. IEEE Spectr. **42**(9), 42–49 (2005)
2. Boehm, B.: A view of 20th and 21st century software engineering. In: Proceedings of the 28th International Conference on Software Engineering, Shanghai (2006)
3. Boehm, B., Lane, J.A.: Evidence-Based software processes. In: Münch, J., Yang, Y., Schäfer, W. (eds.) ICSP 2010. LNCS, vol. 6195, pp. 62–73. Springer, Heidelberg (2010)
4. Boehm, B., Papaccio, P.: Understanding and controlling software costs. IEEE Trans. Softw. Eng. **14**(10), 1462–1477 (1988)
5. Ronen, B., Pass, S.: Focused Operations Management: Achieving More with Existing Resources. John Wiley and Sons, Hoboken (2008)
6. Coman, A., Ronen, B.: Overdosed management: how excess of excellence begets failure. Hum. Syst. Manage. **28**(3), 93–99 (2009)
7. Buschmann, F.: Learning from failure, part 1: scoping and requirements woes. IEEE Softw. **26**(6), 68–69 (2009)
8. Buschmann, F.: Learning from failure, part 2: featuritis, performitis, and other diseases. IEEE Softw. **27**(1), 10–11 (2010)
9. Coman, A., Ronen, B.: Icarus' predicament: managing the pathologies of overspecification and overdesign. Int. J. Project Manage. **28**(3), 237–244 (2010)
10. Rust, R.T., Thompson, D.V., Hamilton, R.W.: Defeating feature fatigue. Harv. Bus. Rev. **84** (2), 98–107 (2006)

11. Bjarnason, E., Wnuk, K., Regnell, B.: Are you biting off more than you can chew? a case study on causes and effects of overscoping in large-scale software engineering. Inf. Softw. Technol. **54**(10), 1107–1124 (2012)
12. Elliott, B.: Anything is possible: managing feature creep in an innovation rich environment. In: Proceedings of the IEEE International Engineering Management Conference, Piscataway (2007)
13. Nelson, R.: IT project management: infamous failures, classic mistakes, and best practices. MIS Quart. Executive. **6**(2), 67–78 (2007)
14. Cule, P., Schmidt, R., Lyytinen, K., Keil, M.: Strategies for heading off is project failure. Inf. Syst. Manage. **17**(2), 65–73 (2000)
15. Ropponen, J., Lyytinen, K.: Components of software development risk: how to address them? a project manager survey. IEEE Trans. Softw. Eng. **26**(2), 98–112 (2000)
16. Westfall, L.: The what, why, who, when and how of software requirements. In: Proceedings of the ASQ World Conference on Quality and Improvement. Seattle (2005)
17. Goes, P.B.: Editor's Comments: Information Systems Research and Behavioral Economics. MIS Quart. **37**(3), iii–viii (2013)
18. Kahneman, D., Knetsch, J.L., Thaler, R.: Anomalies the endowment effect, loss aversion, and status quo bias. J. Econ. Perspect. **5**, 193–206 (1991)
19. Norton, M.I., Mochon, D., Ariely, D.: IKEA effect: when labor leads to love. J. Consum. Psychol. **22**(3), 453–460 (2012)
20. Franke, N., Schreier, M., Kaiser, U.: The "I Designed It Myself" effect in mass customization. Manage. Sci. **56**(1), 125–140 (2010)
21. Kahneman, D., Tversky, A.: Intuitive prediction: biases and corrective procedures. TIMS Stud. Manage. Sci. **12**, 313–327 (1979)
22. Ariely, D., Jones, S.: Predictably Irrational: The Hidden Forces that Shape our Decisions. Harper Collins, New York (2008)
23. Lovallo, D., Kahneman, D.: Delusions of success: how optimism undermines executives' decisions. Harv. Bus. Rev. **81**(7), 56–63 (2003)
24. Buehler, R., Griffin, D., Peetz, J.: The planning fallacy: cognitive, motivational, and social origins. Adv. Exp. Soc. Psychol. **43**, 1–62 (2010)
25. Shmueli, O., Pliskin, N., Fink, L.: Explaining over-requirement in software development projects: an experimental investigation of behavioral effects. Int. J. Project Manage. **33**(2), 380–394 (2015)
26. Parsons, J., Saunders, C.: Cognitive heuristics in software engineering: applying and extending anchoring and adjustment to artifact reuse. IEEE Trans. Softw. Eng. **30**(12), 873–888 (2004)

To Document or Not to Document?
An Exploratory Study on Developers'
Motivation to Document Code

Yulia Shmerlin[1(⊠)], Irit Hadar[1], Doron Kliger[2], and Hayim Makabee[3]

[1] Information Systems Department, University of Haifa, Haifa, Israel
{yshmerlin,hadari}@is.haifa.ac.il
[2] Economics Department, University of Haifa, Haifa, Israel
kliger@econ.haifa.ac.il
[3] Yahoo! Research Labs, Haifa, Israel
makabee@yahoo-inc.com

Abstract. Technical debt represents the situation in a project where developers accept compromises in one dimension of a system in order to meet urgent demands in other dimensions. These compromises incur a "debt", on which "interest" has to be paid to maintain the long-term health of the project. One of the elements of technical debt is documentation debt due to under-documentation of the evolving system. In this exploratory study, our goal is to examine the different aspects of developers' motivation to document code. Specifically, we aim to identify the motivating and hindering aspects of documentation as perceived by the developers. The motivating aspects of code documenting we find include improving code comprehensibility, order, and quality. The hindering aspects include developers' perception of documenting as a tedious, difficult, and time consuming task that interrupts the coding process. These findings may serve as a basis for developing guidelines toward improving documentation practices and encouraging developers to document their code thus reducing documentation debt.

Keywords: Documentation · Technical debt · Motivation

1 Introduction

Technical debt is a metaphor describing a situation where long-term code quality is traded for short-term gain, creating future pressure to remediate the expedient [2]. Some technical-debt inducing elements are code-related and some are not. Documentation debt [15] is one of the elements of technical debt; this form of debt occurs when software products lack the necessary internal documentation. A detailed review of technical debt and documentation debt can be found at [11].

Documentation contributes to understanding of [4], and communicating about, the software system, thus making it more maintainable. Maintenance is known to be a substantial, as well as the most expensive, part in the software lifecycle [9]. Lacking and outdated documentation is one of the main causes of the high cost of software

© Springer International Publishing Switzerland 2015
A. Persson and J. Stirna (Eds.): CAiSE 2015 Workshops, LNBIP 215, pp. 100–106, 2015.
DOI: 10.1007/978-3-319-19243-7_10

maintenance [8]; in other words, inappropriate documentation creates a technical debt to be redeemed, with interest, in the maintenance phase.

Despite the importance of code documentation, studies show that code comments are often neglected relatively to code development [6]. There may be several reasons for this phenomenon: external, referring to the work environment, and internal, referring to the programmers themselves. For instance, an external reason could be that practitioners often work under very strict deadlines and therefore choose to leave the documentation behind, and an internal reason, that documenting is not perceived a creative activity, thus developers prefer solving algorithmic problems over writing documentation [2]. An additional internal reason related to developers' lack of motivation to document is that not documenting behavior in some cases may promote job security [5].

The internal explanations may indicate that there are additional motivation-related factors that cause developers' reluctance to document their code. Therefore, we believe that it is important to investigate these factors further, as it will allow proposing effective solutions for encouraging documentation. This research aims to explore and better understand developers' motivation for code documenting. Specifically, our research question is: "What are the motivating and the hindering aspects that can influence developers' code documenting behavior?"

The rest of the paper is organized as follows: Sect. 2 presents related works with regard to different aspects of documentation; Sect. 3 focuses on the research method of our ongoing research, with the preliminary findings presented in Sect. 4. We discuss these findings and our future research directions in Sect. 5.

2 Related Work

Software documentation refers to several types of documents, which accompany the development process; for example, documents describing requirements, design, marketing demands, end-user manuals, and technical documentation. The latter is documentation of code, algorithms, and interfaces, which is very important for understanding software programs [14].

Code is not documented enough in practice, despite the high, agreed upon, importance of code documentation, and specifically software engineers' understanding of its importance [14]. Moreover, the growth rate of code tends to be much higher than the growth rate of comments, because developers' tendency to neglect documenting newly added code [6].

In agile development, face-to-face conversations are considered the most efficient and effective method of conveying information and documentation is often paid less attention. However, over half of the developers in agile development teams find documentation to be important or even very important while, at the same time, too little documentation is available in their projects [12].

One of the reasons for the scarcity of documentation seems to be the lack of developers' motivation to document their code. The Fogg Behavior Model (FBM) [7] suggests that behavior depends on the following three factors: motivation, ability, and triggers, each of which has several subcomponents. The motivation factor consists of three core motivators, each of which having two sides: pleasure vs. pain, hope vs. fear and social acceptance vs. rejection. In our ongoing research, we aim to address the three factors of FBM. The current paper is a starting point, in which we focus on the motivation factor. To encourage documentation, a triggering environment has to be devised, in which developers' motivation will be channeled toward enhanced documentation. In addition, the devised environment should also boost developers' ability to document in an efficient and informative manner.

Several research works have focused on investigating motivating and de-motivating aspects in software engineering in general. Two of the main models that refer to software developers' motivation are the job characteristics model, and the model of task design [10]. These models examine the motivation for the software development profession as a whole [1]. However, as far as we know, no such model was proposed in the context of code documentation, despite the evidence for its importance on the one hand, and the relatively little attention it receives in practice on the other hand.

3   Method

The goal of this study is to explore and better understand what influences developers' motivation for code documenting. Data collection and analysis were performed using qualitative research methods based on the grounded theory research principles [13].

The research consists of three stages, planned according to its exploratory nature. First, in order to gain an initial understanding of the problem, we conducted five in-depth interviews. Second, based on the results of the interviews, we developed a pilot questionnaire and distributed it among ten additional participants. Third, yet to be accomplished, stage, is a refinement of the questionnaire toward large-scale distribution. The results reported here are based on the preliminary findings obtained in the first two stages.

The participants of the study were software developers with various seniority levels, with at least two years of development experience, employed in different software firms. We interviewed five software developers (three women and two men). We used semi-structured interviews, which consisted of predefined open questions, and also allowed time for free discussion. The interviews, as well as the later constructed questionnaire, consisted of two types of questions: open-ended questions regarding motivation to document and background questions. Ten developers (two women and eight men), with an average experience of about 7 years, filled in the pilot questionnaire. The data elicited were inductively analyzed, classifying answers to emergent categories in the investigated topics: motivating and hindering aspects of documentation.

4   Findings

Table 1 describes categories that emerged from the analysis of the answers regarding the motivating aspects of code documenting. Specifically, we asked: "What do you enjoy when documenting your code?"

Table 1. Categories of motivating aspects of documentation

Category	Example
Increases code comprehensibility	"Documenting the code helps me to better understand my own work." "Makes it [the code] more readable, easier to understand later on for me and for other people that look at the code." "It's useful when the code is complex and there is no good refactoring. When going over the code, it [documentation] helps to remember."
Increases order	"It helps to keep things in order." "Adds more structure to the code."
Increases code quality	"It [Documenting] helps to organize my thoughts. I find that this [practice] is directly related to TDD- if you write comments prior to the coding [instead of the tests as in TDD] before the code, it helps to develop better code". "Good documentation shows that your work was done perfectly."

Three participants did not provide any motivating aspects of documentation. One jokingly answered: "the suffering," another asked with wonder: "enjoy?" and the third replied: "Odd question... nothing. It's part of the job."

In order to identify the hindering aspects of documenting, we asked the participants: "What don't you enjoy when documenting your code?" The categories that emerged from the analysis of the answers are presented in Table 2.

Table 2. Categories of hindering aspects of documentation

Category	Example
Tedious task	"To explain complicated issues - why this was done in a particular way." "To explain what each parameter does." "This [documentation] is no fun, because I solved the problem already."
Difficult task	" To be formal", "Sometimes it [documenting] is difficult, because I do not know how to explain the change. For example, I entered a fix reusing a feature that worked in a different place in the code."
Interruption of coding	"Breaks the continuity of coding;" "Documenting is difficult to do retroactively, after you had written the method, because you think it is self-explanatory and that it is quite obvious how it works."
Time constraints	"It [documentation] takes time." "When I have a tight deadline, documenting is left behind."

In addition, we wanted to check whether peer or management feedback and company policy play a role in developers' motivation to document. For this purpose, we asked the participants whether they recalled receiving positive or negative feedbacks regarding documentation on code they had developed, or general instructions regarding documentation.

Four out of the ten questionnaire respondents replied that they had never received any feedback on their documentation when participating in code reviews. The other six participants recalled receiving positive feedbacks to documentation on the code they had developed. For example: *"Yes, [I was told] that it helped them [the colleagues] to understand my code."* Only two participants recalled receiving negative feedbacks on their documentation, for example, that the documentation was not detailed enough.

All ten participants answered that that their company does not have a strict policy regarding documentation, and one respondent mentioned an informal policy: *"We [the developers] are advised to document our code and our manager reminds us about it."* One of the developers stated that in his opinion, "being forced" to document by company policy would not be effective. *"Most of the developers are creative people and do not like being told how to do their job".* These results further emphasize the need to focus on internal motivation of developers in order to encourage them to document, which may be more effective than external ones.

5   Discussion and Future Work

Our study aimed to identify the aspects that influence developers' motivation to document, as a first step toward meeting the objective of our ongoing research to increase developers' motivation and performance of documentation activities. The results of this study indicate that developers are often aware of the importance of documentation, which corresponds with previous findings [14]. However, commensurate with other previous studies, code documentation is often overlooked in practice [6].

We found that developers' reluctance to document is related to their perception of the task of documenting as tedious, difficult and distracting from the main task of coding as well as being time consuming; however, most of them could find motivating aspects as well. Accordingly, we contend that emphasizing the motivating aspects of documentation tasks, for example the documentation contribution of the developers' understanding and promoting the quality of their own code, and masking the hindering aspects thereof, for example by making this a less tedious task, would allow devising a solution that would increase developers' motivation to document.

These findings should be carefully considered, given the limitations of the study. For example, our findings indicate that a motivating aspect of code documentation is improving code comprehensibility. In this context, it is worth mentioning that the fact that documentation promotes code understanding may also serve as a de-motivator to documentation, for example, when producing unclear code promotes job security [5]. Noteworthy, this de-motivating reason did not appear in our findings. The absence of evidence regarding such de-motivating reasons could indicate either that our participants do not subscribe to these reasons, or it could possibly reflect responders' strategy to withhold such 'selfish' reasons, a limitation rooted in our use of self-reporting methods for data collection.

As for hindering aspects of documenting, the participants stated that they do not enjoy the writing process itself, and that code documenting breaks the continuity of coding. Moreover, code documenting requires time, which is often a scarce resource in developers' daily work. Time constraints were mentioned as a hindering aspect of documentation; however, the presence of this aspect in the interviews and questionnaires was not as dominant as we had expected. This may indicate that the lack of documentation in practice is mainly a result of developers' perception of this task as not enjoyable, rather than it being time consuming, as perhaps is commonly believed.

The results confirm that currently there is a lack of motivation among developers to document. Recall that motivation is a key factor upon which behavior is dependent according to the FBM model [7]. Thus, we believe that our findings are an important step in order to develop a solution that will encourage developers to document their code.

This study has several limitations. First, our sample consists of Israeli participants only. It is possible that cultural factors are related to motivational issues, and this study has to be replicated on populations from different cultures. The full-scale survey will focus on recruiting a large number of participants from different parts of the globe and from different cultures. Second, our data gathering tools were interviews and questionnaires, and relied on self-reports of the participants; the data may therefore reflect self-serving bias, to some extent.

In the next step of the research, we plan to distribute a survey for further validation and extension of our findings. Subsequently, a solution will be sought using motivations theories for increasing developers' motivation to document their code.

References

1. Beecham, S., Baddoo, N., Hall, T., Robinson, H., Sharp, H.: Motivation in software engineering: a systematic literature review. Inf. Softw. Technol. **50**(9), 860–878 (2008)
2. Clear, T.: Documentation and agile methods: striking a balance. ACM SIGCSE Bull. **35**(2), 12–13 (2003)
3. Cunningham, W.: The WyCash portfolio management system. ACM SIGPLAN OOPS Messenger **4**(2), 29–30 (1992)
4. De Souza, S.C.B., Anquetil, N., De Oliveira, K.M.: A study of the documentation essential to software maintenance. In: Proceedings of the 23rd Annual International Conference on Design of Communication: Documenting and Designing for Pervasive Information, pp. 68–75. ACM (2005)
5. Drevik, S.: How to comment code. Embedded Syst. Prog. **9**, 58–65 (1996)
6. Fluri, B., Wursch, M., Gall, H.C.: Do code and comments co-evolve? on the relation between source code and comment changes. In: Reverse Engineering 14th Working Conference, pp. 70–79. IEEE (2007)
7. Fogg, B.J.: A behavior model for persuasive design. In: Proceedings of the 4th ACM International Conference on Persuasive Technology (2009)
8. Martin, J., McClure, C.: Software Maintenance: The Problem and the Solutions. Prentice Hall, New York (1983)
9. Seacord, R.C., Plakosh, D.A.: Modernizing Legacy Systems: Software Technologies, Engineering Processes, and Business Practices. Addison-Wesley Professional, Boston (2003)
10. Sharp, H., Baddoo, N., Beecham, S., Hall, T., Robinson, H.: Models of motivation in software engineering. Inf. Softw. Tech **51**(1), 219–233 (2009)

11. Shmerlin, Y., Kliger, D., Makabee, H.: Reducing technical debt: using persuasive technology for encouraging software developers to document Code. In: Iliadis, L., Papazoglou, M., Pohl, K. (eds.) CAiSE Workshops 2014. LNBIP, vol. 178, pp. 207–212. Springer, Heidelberg (2014)
12. Stettina, C.J., Heijstek, W.: Necessary and neglected? An empirical study of internal documentation in agile software development teams. In: Proceedings of the 29th ACM International Conference on Design of Communication, pp. 159–166. ACM (2011)
13. Strauss, A., Corbin, J.M.: Basics of Qualitative Research: Grounded Theory Procedures and Techniques. Sage Publications, London (1990)
14. Tenny, T.: Program readability: procedures versus comments. IEEE Trans. Softw. Eng. **14** (9), 1271–1279 (1988)
15. Tom, E., Aurum, A., Vidgen, R.: An exploration of technical debt. J. Syst. Softw. **86**, 1498–1516 (2013)

When a Paradigm is Inconsistent with Intuition: The Case of Inconsistency Management

Irit Hadar and Anna Zamansky[(✉)]

Information Systems Department, University of Haifa,
A. Hushi 199, 3498838 Haifa, Israel
{hadari,annazam}@is.haifa.ac.il

Abstract. The acceptance and correct use of new paradigms in information systems engineering is highly affected by cognitive dispositions of the individual engineers. In particular, the engineers' intuition – based on their vast experience – may come in the way of accepting the rationale of a new paradigm. Analyzing engineers' reaction to a newly introduced paradigm through the lens of cognitive psychology may highlight potential barriers to the paradigms' successful adoption and use. In this position paper we demonstrate the potential benefit of the above-proposed approach via a case study focusing on the paradigm of inconsistency management. We present our findings, based on in-depth interviews with 20 practitioners, and analyze them using the dual-process theory, highlighting a clear clash between their intuition and the paradigm's rationale.

Keywords: Cognitive processes · Paradigm acceptance · Dual-process theory · Inconsistency management

1 Introduction

New paradigms for information systems engineering are constantly introduced. Organizational processes and related aspects, such as organizational climate and culture, play an important role in new paradigms' acceptance and adoption, and are vastly discussed in literature. However, a necessary condition for a successful adoption is the individual engineers' acceptance of the paradigm and their ability to correctly use it, which highly depends on their cognitive disposition. This aspect of paradigm acceptance has received far less attention thus far. Analyzing paradigms through the lens of cognitive psychology may provide new insights into the cognitive aspects that may hinder the paradigms' successful adoption and use. In order to demonstrate the potential benefit of this approach, in this position paper we discuss, as an example, the paradigm of inconsistency management, which has been gaining attention in recent years in the field of information systems.

Handling inconsistencies is a key challenge in the process of information systems (IS) development. Inconsistency may occur, for example, when requirements or specifications contain conflicting or contradictory descriptions of the expected behavior

© Springer International Publishing Switzerland 2015
A. Persson and J. Stirna (Eds.): CAiSE 2015 Workshops, LNBIP 215, pp. 107–113, 2015.
DOI: 10.1007/978-3-319-19243-7_11

of the system or of its domain. Such conflicting descriptions may come, for example, as a result of conflicting goals between different stakeholders, changes introduced during the evolution of the requirements, etc. [11].

Until recently, inconsistencies in IS development were viewed as a problem that needs to be eliminated before further activities can take place. Over the last two decades, however, a more tolerant approach toward inconsistency has evolved (e.g., [2, 3, 11, 13]. In "Leveraging inconsistency in software development" Nuseibeh et al. [11] argue: "Maintaining consistency at all times is counterproductive. In many cases, it may be desirable to tolerate or even encourage inconsistency to facilitate distributed teamwork and prevent premature commitment to design decisions" (p. 24). Finkelstein [3] further advocates this paradigm shift, proposing that rather than removing inconsistency, we need to manage it by "preserving inconsistency where it is desirable to do so, identifying inconsistency at the point where decisions are required and removing (or otherwise remedying) inconsistency prior to taking action. This requires a major change in the way we think" (p. 2).

But changing the way we think is not always simple. In our ongoing research on practitioners' perceptions regarding a paradigm of inconsistency management, we found that practitioners strongly reject the very idea of not immediately eliminating inconsistency, many times even when they admit that it makes sense. Cognitive psychology theories provide a possible explanation for this phenomenon: Our thinking processes rely many times on automatic responses based on our vast past experience, roughly corresponding to what is commonly called intuition, rather than on analytical reasoning [9, 14]. This intuition may hinder integrating new ideas, as reasonable as they may be, into our thinking processes. Therefore, an in-depth understanding of this cognitive phenomenon is a necessary step toward 'changing the way we think.' In this paper we demonstrate this cognitive analysis on the case of inconsistency management based on empirical evidence, reflect on its implications, and propose directions for future research.

2   Preliminary Observations

2.1   Data Collection

The original objective of the empirical study was to understand practitioners' perceptions regarding the paradigm of inconsistency management. Due to the exploratory nature of our study, we took a qualitative research approach [10]. More specifically, we used the grounded theory methodology, which is appropriate in order to generate descriptive or explanatory theory [15]. When applying grounded theory, consideration of literature is allowed for guiding data analysis [16].

Twenty participants were carefully selected and interviewed in our study. Participants' sampling was performed according to the theoretical sampling principles [15]. The sampling criteria we defined were as follows: Only participants with academic background in IS or computer science, and professional experience in industry and/or in research in IS, were selected. In order to reflect variations within our data, we also aimed to achieve a diverse sample of participants, with different levels of experience and from different domains. The participants' sample included software developers of different seniorities and different roles, including: software architects, requirements analysts and project managers. The participants' professional experience was 13 years in average, varying from three to 35 years.

The main tool of data collection was semi-structured in-depth interviews, which were conducted by the authors. The interview questions focused on the notion of inconsistency in the context of IS. We asked the interviewees to explain what inconsistency is and how it is manifested in IS, and scrutinized their perceptions and attitudes toward its different manifestations. The full result set obtained in this study is beyond the scope of this paper. Here we focus on the data related to the strong rejection of the ideas of inconsistency management demonstrated by the study participants, and its interplay with their own analytical reasoning about this topic.

2.2   Cognitive Analysis of the Empirical Results

Already during the first interviews, we found that participants react very strongly toward inconsistency, and specifically could not accept the possibility of tolerating it. When asked how inconsistency should be handled, in the context of examples brought up by the participants, their answers were typically uncompromising. Examples of answers we received from different participants include: *"We must eliminate [the inconsistency] on sight.";* *"[The inconsistency] must always be resolved. ASAP.";* *"It [the inconsistency] must be fixed. It must be clean.";* *"As soon as we find it [the inconsistency] it needs to be investigated and solved."*

Witnessing this strong uncompromised reaction, we decided to present to the participants a case in which it makes sense to tolerate inconsistency, based on the inconsistency management literature [11]: "The observation that some inconsistencies never get fixed seems counterintuitive at first. [...] Many local factors affect how you handle an inconsistency, including the cost of resolution, the cost of updating the documentation, and the developers' level of shared understanding. Ultimately, the decision to repair an inconsistency is risk-based. If the cost of fixing it outweighs the risk of ignoring it, then it makes no sense to fix it" (p. 27). Accordingly, we asked the following question: Imagine there is a case in which there is an inconsistency in requirements relevant only to rare cases, however resolving this situation would be of high cost. What would you do?

Following this question, we observed different reactions; while answering, the participants expressed their thoughts out loud, reflecting the thinking process that took place. We observed two patterns of response:

1. Immediate acceptance of the rationale of tolerating inconsistency, despite having rejected it until that point of the interview. For example:

– *"The fact that there are two contradictory requirements doesn't mean that they are important. Perhaps they refer to situations most users won't encounter, and then perhaps they do not even have to be fixed."(Developer, three years of experience)*
– *"I guess that in such situations one can consider leaving it [the inconsistency] as is, and of course document [its existence]."* Notably, a far less tolerant attitude toward

inconsistency was reflected in this participant's' answers to previous questions, e.g.: *"One has to think ahead and not get into these situations [of inconsistency]. But, it's not always possible, therefore it has to be resolved on sight."* (Developer, six years of experience)

- *"In this case, the inconsistency may be tolerated. If it has no legal meaning, it's possible to leave it."* Here, too, a less tolerant attitude toward inconsistency was reflected previously, e.g.: *"Immediately when it [an inconsistency] is detected, the problem must be investigated; its source must be found and resolved."* (Project manager, 17 years of experience)

2. Transitioning from strong rejection to reluctant acceptance.

- *"No one would ever agree to live with it [the inconsistency]. I, for sure, wouldn't be able to live with it. [Pause] It's all about cost verses benefit. It it's a minor problem, it would ignored."* (Senior developer, 10 years of experience)
- *"I can't see how that's possible. In my case, there are no situations like this. If it's a primary issue, I don't see how it can be ignored regardless the cost. If it's something small, it may be possible. The final answer depends on the type of inconsistency."* (Senior architect, 16 years of experience)
- *"There is no such thing! It shows a severe failure. [Pause] It's all about matching expectations. It's about the contract between you and the customer."* (Chief architect, 20 years of experience).

In both patterns we see that the participants changed their minds from their previous general disposition of intolerance toward inconsistency to a more tolerant attitude. Moreover, in the second pattern we observe a significant change of view during the participants' thinking processes, without any external interaction. What are the cognitive mechanisms that may account for this change? One of the mainstream theories in cognitive psychology that may explain this phenomenon is the *dual- process theory* [9, 14].[1] According to this theory, our cognition operates in two different modes, called System 1 (S1) and System 2 (S2), roughly corresponding to the notions of intuitive and analytical thinking respectively. S1 processes are characterized as being fast, automatic, effortless, unconscious, and inflexible (difficult to change or overcome). In contrast, S2 processes are slow, conscious, effortful and relatively flexible, and serves as monitor and critic of the fast automatic responses of S1. There are situations in which S1 produces quick automatic non-normative responses, while S2 may or may not intervene in its role as monitor and critic [9].

Analyzing the data through the lens of the dual-process theory, we can explain the change in the participants' attitude toward the presented case of inconsistency tolerance as the intervention of S2, namely the analytic reasoning, in the thinking process, overriding the initial S1 response made based on the participants' intuition that inconsistency is an evil to be eliminated on sight.

The data further indicate that while the participants typically understood the rationale of tolerating inconsistency in certain cases and agreed with it, employing S2,

---

[1] There are many theories about the dual process of the human mind. We rely here on the research program of 30 years by Kahneman and Tversky, summarized in [9].

in terms of the dual-process theory, they struggled to reconcile the conflict between the two systems. This struggle was reflected, for example, in the following quotes:

- *"If I have a way to confirm, that this [the inconsistency] is indeed very esoteric, and that it would indeed cost a lot to fix it, then it may be tolerated. It's a decision of the higher management. But it seems to me very individual. I would for sure fix it. But it can be a strategic decision [to tolerate the inconsistency]. Ideally, clearly it should be fixed. In reality there are additional considerations, mainly economic ones."*
- *"It [the inconsistency] can be tolerated. I, personally, would fix it in any case, because things need to be consistent. Consistency is important for software."*

This tension between S1 and S2 is a known phenomenon, as vividly described by Gould [5], referring the normative decision in the famous Linda problem[2]: "yet a little homunculus in my head continues to jump up and down, shouting at me [that the normative decision cannot be correct]" (p. 469). Our participants explain that although they understand the rationale of tolerating inconsistency, they would not have felt comfortable following it.

3 Discussion and Future Research

'Changing the way we think', as suggested by [8], is not always simple. It is not enough to rationally accept an idea that contradicts one's intuition; people consistently make non-normative decisions that contradict knowledge they evidently hold [9]. This was also found specifically in the field of software development [6, 7]. Moreover, the stronger S1 is, the more difficult it is for S2 to override it. In our case, S1 was based on the participants' vast experience of software development, which led them to believe that *"Consistency is important for software"* to an extent that does not allow compromise under any circumstances. This is usually not a bad heuristic, and the reason that this heuristic exists lies in the vast experience that formulated it. For this reason, S1 decision-making is generally more often than not the correct one [4, 17]. However, there are cases, such as the one we witness here, where a heuristic that is usually useful, needs to be set aside.

Our impression was that the participants' years of experience and their role might affect their pattern of behavior. More specifically, we saw that developers with many years of experience were more reluctant to tolerate inconsistency, while product managers and less experienced developers found it easier to accept this rationale. A quantitative research is required to confirm these hypotheses. Based on the explanation above such a finding would make sense; the more experience participants have in software development, the stronger their S1 influence is in this matter.

Our findings highlight the importance of exploring practitioners' intuition when introducing a new paradigm. Importantly, the identification of potentially counter-intuitive principles of a paradigm is only the first step, the next being exploring means for reconciling these principles (as understood by S2) with intuition (S1). Therefore,

---

[2] A frequently cited example in this field: http://en.wikipedia.org/wiki/Conjunction_fallacy.

another important direction for future research is exploring means for overcoming the conflict between S1 and S2, toward an acceptance of new paradigms that may cause this conflict. An approach that could be beneficial to this end is the one proposed in the context of mathematical education: To help students bridge the gap between S1 and S2 thinking, one needs to bridge down the analytical solution to the students' intuition by devising and presenting a bridging task which would be logically (roughly) equivalent to the original analytical task, but psychologically much easier to accept (i.e. closer to intuition) [1]. In the information systems field, constructing bridging means for overcoming a paradigm's conflict with intuition may go a long way toward wider acceptance of the paradigm in practice.

It is our hope that this position paper will initiate a discourse on the cognitive concerns that are involved in new paradigms' adoption. We intend to continue the research presented in this paper, for further validation and generalization of its results in the context of inconsistency management.

References

1. Ejersbo, R.L., Leron, U., Arcavi, A.: Bridging intuitive and analytical thinking: four looks at the 2-glass puzzle. Learn. Math. **34**(5), 2–7 (2014)
2. Ernst, N.A., Borgida, A., Mylopoulos, J., Jureta, I.J.: Agile requirements evolution via paraconsistent reasoning. In: Ralyté, J., Franch, X., Brinkkemper, S., Wrycza, S. (eds.) CAiSE 2012. LNCS, vol. 7328, pp. 382–397. Springer, Heidelberg (2012)
3. Finkelstein, A.: A foolish consistency: technical challenges in consistency management. In: Ibrahim, M., Küng, J., Revell, N. (eds.) DEXA 2000. LNCS, vol. 1873, pp. 1–5. Springer, Heidelberg (2000)
4. Gigerenzer, G., Todd, P.M.: The ABC Research Group: Simple Heuristics that Make us Smart. Oxford University Press, New York (1990)
5. Gould, S.J.: Bully for Brontosaurus: Reflections in Natural History. Norton, New York (1992)
6. Hadar, I., Leron, U.: How intuitive is object oriented design? Commun. ACM **51**(5), 41–46 (2008)
7. Hadar, I.: When intuition and logic clash: the case of the object oriented paradigm. Sci. Comput. Program. **78**, 1407–1426 (2013)
8. Finkelstein, A.C., Gabbay, D., Hunter, A., Kramer, J., Nuseibeh, B.: Inconsistency handling in multiperspective specifications. IEEE Trans. Software Eng. 208569578 (1994)
9. Kahneman, D. (Nobel Prize Lecture): Maps of bounded rationality: a perspective on intuitive judgment and choice. In: Les Prix Nobel, Frangsmyr, T. (eds.) 416–499 (2002). www.nobel.se/economics/laureates/2002/kahnemann-lecture.pdf
10. Myers, M.D., Avison, D.: Qualitative research in information systems. Manag. Inf. Syst. Q. **21**, 241–242 (1997)
11. Nuseibeh, B., Easterbrook, S., Russo, A.: Leveraging inconsistency in software development. Computer **33**(4), 24–29 (2000)
12. Nuseibeh, B., Easterbrook, S., Russo, A.: Making inconsistency respectable in software development. J. Syst. Softw. **58**(2), 171–180 (2001)
13. Spanoudakis, G., Zisman, A.: Inconsistency management in software engineering Survey and open research issues. In: Chang, S.K. (ed.) Handbook of Software Engineering and Knowledge Engineering, pp. 329–380. World Scientific Publishing Co., Singapore (2001)

14. Stanovich, K.E., West, R.F.: Individual differences in reasoning: implications for the rationality debate. Behav. Brain Sci. **23**, 645–726 (2000)
15. Strauss, A., Corbin, J.M.: Basics of Qualitative Research: Grounded Theory Procedures and Techniques. Sage Publications Inc., New Delhi (1990)
16. Suddaby, R.: From the editors: what grounded theory is not. Acad. Manag. J. **49**(4), 633–642 (2006)
17. Todd, P.M., Gigerenzer, G.: Ecological Rationality: Intelligence in the World. Oxford University Press, Oxford (2012)

An Argument for More User-Centric Analysis of Modeling Languages' Visual Notation Quality

Dirk van der Linden[1,2(✉)]

[1] Luxembourg Institute of Science and Technology, Luxembourg, Luxembourg
[2] EE-Team, Luxembourg, Luxembourg
`dirk.vanderlinden@list.lu`

Abstract. In this position paper we argue against the application of universal quality criteria for the visual notation of modeling languages. Instead, we make a point that (1) the cognitive capabilities that modelers have, and (2) the different cognitive requirements placed on them while modeling specific aspects (e.g., processes, goals, regulations) mean that a visual notation should be optimal for a specific modeling effort, and not a best-for-everyone solution. We clarify this point by giving an example of a modeling effort where this comes into play, and propose a research agenda that can set out to deal with these issues.

Keywords: Modeling language · Visual notation · Cognitive requirements

1 Introduction

Many modeling language notations are not as suitable for their users as they can be. One major component of that is the fit, or lack thereof, with their users' cognitive properties. As a result, elements of modeling languages may be difficult or outright counterintuitive for their (intended) users. On the one hand, sometimes a visual notation is too sparse in what it offers, causing its users to improvise and make up their own additional symbols and structures. On the other hand, sometimes a notation will offer so many different elements that it becomes difficult to still easily comprehend the models created with them – let alone knowing which notational elements to choose while modeling.

There is a large body of research focused on the comprehensibility of modeling language notations, analyzing and critiquing their quality from a variety of perspectives. This research is generally based on theories and frameworks that synthesize existing literature, best practices, and insights from other fields like cognitive science, semiotics, and interface design in order to arrive at a well-informed best practice for how a visual notation ought to be (re)designed. Earlier frameworks used for such improvements, like the Cognitive Dimensions of Notations [3], although widely used at some time, have been critiqued to lack scientific rigor [4], and were further developed into more well founded set of principles constituting a design theory for visual notations: Moody's "Physics of

© Springer International Publishing Switzerland 2015
A. Persson and J. Stirna (Eds.): CAiSE 2015 Workshops, LNBIP 215, pp. 114–120, 2015.
DOI: 10.1007/978-3-319-19243-7_12

Notations" [4]. Moody's work has been actively used to analyze, critique and propose improvements to the visual notations of a number of modeling languages, including for example UML [6], i* [5], UCM [1], and BPMN [2].

2   The Modeler-Notation Mismatch

The systematic way in which this single, 'universal' theory for improving a visual notation has been applied to such a diverse amount of modeling language notations is problematic. Applying the same standards of quality to languages that are used for different purposes, capturing different aspects[1] is a practice that should be critically reflected on. By applying one theory and one set of quality criteria to the notations of all our modeling languages we essentially say that there is little difference in the quality criteria important for these modeling languages. But is that really the case? Should the quality of the notation used for, say, a UML class diagram giving a quick overview of the component structure of a web service be judged in the same way as the notation for a complex overview of an organization's total process structure in BPMN?

While there is ample work on model quality, also performed on specific languages [8,11] (albeit having much less interest on the notational quality), the focus on the person doing the modeling remains under researched. We see two points here that deserve more attention to determine whether a single theory to critique visual notations by is optimal:

1. Modeling efforts have different purposes and cognitive requirements

The creation of conceptual models is done to facilitate communication between stakeholders, capture (current) knowledge of a domain, to reason with those models about the domain, and so on [7]. While there are many other purposes as well such as the more practical modeling of (IT) solutions and their impact [12], creating a model that represents (some part of) a domain remains the major focus for most modeling efforts. If the purpose of a model is to communicate with other non-technical stakeholders (e.g., 'the business'), such models – if shown to them at all – should be as simple and understandable as possible. But when these models are used between experts to create a systematic mapping of all elements in a domain, or to create a comprehensive overview of the dynamics and interconnections between, for example, processes of a business, it stands to reason that the model can be more complicated. In this case the purpose of the models are clearly different. The *cognitive requirements*, that is, the mental skills and properties expected of their users to work with them correctly and easily is likely different, with the latter model demanding more abstraction capabilities. The requirements and quality criteria that we set for the visual notation used for these two modeling purposes should thus not automatically be the same, as the former model has to be much more forgiving than the latter.

---

[1] By different aspects of we mean different areas of modeling like process modeling, goal modeling, software architecture modeling, and so on.

2. Differences between (groups of) modelers themselves

Determining the quality criteria for how understandable a visual notation is purely on basis of the elements of the model and its notation (e.g., enforcing upper limits on shapes and colors, limiting complexity via the amount of elements shown) foregoes a major aspect of the modeling process: the people doing the modeling. Earlier research has shown that for model understandability personal factors have a stronger positive correlation than the properties of the model itself [10]. This means that even when a model is unclear, for instance the notation used for it is too vague or ambiguous, the model can still be understood fine depending on the person interpreting it. Indeed, Petre found that: "experts are capable of understanding even complex and poorly laid out diagrams" [9]. It has also been shown that people have different abstraction levels, which impacts their ability to model complicated domains or aspects (cf. [13,14]). Focusing purely on the intrinsic quality of the notation without involving the (cognitive differences) of their users then forfeits a major, perhaps primary component of understandability. Thus, not only the properties of a model and its notation, but also those of the users of the model should be taken into account when making claims about how understandable a notation is. As modeling different aspects and using them for different purposes likely place different *cognitive requirements* on their users, it stands to reason that being aware of their differences and cognitive capabilities becomes important.

Based on these arguments, it does not seem to make sense that the analysis and critiquing of the quality of a modeling language's visual notation should be performed on a one-size-fits-all basis using one 'optimal' theory. Instead, a clearer understanding of the cognitive requirements placed upon modelers engaged in modeling different kinds of aspects, combined with an understanding of what (quality) aspects of a notation are most important to them should be achieved before anything else. After achieving such understandings, (re)designing optimal visual notations for modeling languages can then be done more in line with the actual cognitive requirements placed on their users.

3   An Example Modeling Effort

To motivate our idea we will give a fictional example of a modeling effort where we belief the quality criteria for the visual notations used should not be judged by the same standards.

A rather large, internationally operating business wants to stay up to date with the ever-changing business environment, new regulations placed upon it by local and international regulating bodies, in doing so optimizing how it works. Hopefully by doing so also maximizing its profits. The main product they offer to consumers is a complicated package of services and products say, of a pharmaceutical nature. Not wanting to simply experiment with how they do business by trial and error, their first step is to create a comprehensive Enterprise Model that captures all the important aspects of their organization, hopefully being able to use this model to make well informed business decisions with. They contract a company to do so, which sets out to map these different aspects. They model all their business processes (i.e., what they do) in BPMN, the exchanges between company and consumer where value is generated in e3Value, the strategic and tactical goals of the enterprise in i*, a number of other specialized aspects in equally as specialized modeling languages, and finally, a comprehensive integration in an EM language, say, ArchiMate.

The enterprise modelers start creating an overview of all the aspects, and quickly run into the point that some aspects of the business are more complicated than others. The process structure is complicated, but manageable as the main issue is simply the sheer number of processes to capture and interrelate, nonetheless managing to do so without to many inconsistencies. They then move on to capture the regulations the business needs to adhere to, for example in how many pharmaceutical objects they are allowed to sell to intermediaries per time unit, and so on. These models become quickly very complicated as they run into inconsistencies between national and international regulations, and as the legal advisors of the business inform them of ways to work around certain regulations but not others. Another team of modelers sets out to capture the value exchanges, which for this business were fairly straight forward, clearly generating value at points of sales, and generating value at points of exclusivity contracts, and so on. The different levels (and kinds of) complexities of these models made it so that for some aspects the modelers wanted to be able to use a great amount of visual elements, shapes, colors, and so on to clearly denote all the different elements in the domain, and to use even more visual markers for conflicting information in the regulation models.

Being experts in their field, the modelers who captured all the regulation information chose to extend the notation they used with additional symbols, just to be able to more accurately capture all the different elements. While this decreased the ease of reading of these models for non-experts, they quickly realized the business stakeholders preferred to be told *about* the models, instead of being shown them and asked to work with them. Thus, in the end the modelers decided to adapt the modeling languages they used to (perhaps) the limit of their cognitive abilities where it was necessary to do so, using some other languages as-is because the domain was not too demanding, and finally always communicated with the business using PowerPoint and pen and paper sketches[2]. When the business asked the enterprise modelers to translate their ideas and strategies for changes in the business into the model environment, the modelers did so, and convened the outcomes to them in more simplified models and natural language.

In this example, due to the different requirements placed upon modelers by the aspect they worked on (e.g., the complexity of regulations, the great amount of processes), they decided to adapt the notations they used to deal with them.

---

[2] While this is a fictional example, it is be backed up by the real-world practice of modeling. As evidenced by a quote from an ongoing series of interviews we are performing among Enterprise Architects: "The primary tool for communicating [with business people] is PowerPoint".

The models whose purpose was to capture the information about a domain were accepted to be more complicated, because the modelers themselves could deal with it and translate it to more understandable explanations for business stakeholders. Thus, we strongly believe that efforts to optimize a modeling language's visual notation should be done in line with the requirements placed upon it by the specific *purpose of the modeling effort*, and by the *cognitive requirements* placed upon its users.

4   Research Agenda

We propose the following research agenda to deal with the issue we have presented and exemplified in this paper. The major aims are to have a stronger understanding of the personal differences between people in regards to how well they can still understand a model and use it, and whether such differences can perhaps be said to be specific to particular modeling efforts and domains. These tie into two hypotheses to be tested by investigating some research questions.

Hypothesis 1. *The quality criteria for the visual notations of different modeling efforts and aspects are not universal.*

We see the following questions contribute towards the testing of this hypothesis.

1. What quality criteria for the visual notation of a modeling language are most important to its users?
2. Does the creation and use of models of different aspects place different (levels of) cognitive requirements on its users?

The first would be investigated by using factor elicitation (i.e., Repertory Grid) and structured interviews with users of multiple modeling domains and efforts. The second question can be explored by using the Think-Aloud-Protocol for a number of modeling tasks of different aspects. In such a study participants would be asked to model a textual description, and to verbalize all their thoughts. Analysis of the recording of such sessions together with coding schema to determine the difficulty users verbalized would give a good approximation of the different levels of cognitive skill that users experienced.

Hypothesis 2. *The visual notation of a modeling language can be optimized for the modeling of a specific aspect with a specific purpose.*

The following question here contributes towards the testing of this hypothesis.

3. Given prior cognitive requirements for specific aspects, what is the optimal trade-off between complexity and usability for modeling a given aspect?

Investigating this research question relies on data elicited from the earlier research questions. If quality criteria are important to users, and different cognitive requirements from aspects are known, a design science approach with a strong focus on evaluation can then be taken. Several 'dialects' of the visual notation for a specific modeling language can be made and evaluated with users in to find a balance between how well the notation accommodates the modelers in their work, and how difficult the created models become to work with. This can be done through experiments, again using Think-Aloud-Protocol, where modelers are asked to capture the same domain in a number of different dialects, and coding of the recorded verbalizations are used to determine which dialect is most successful. As a result, a notation optimal for the specific aspect(s) and modelers involved should be found.

5   Concluding Outlook

We have argued that analyzing and critiquing the visual notation of modeling languages should not be done to a universal standard. We made a point that different aspects of a domain might place different (cognitive) requirements upon its users, and that users have different cognitive abilities in themselves. Visual notations should thus optimized for such specific modeling efforts. The research agenda we proposed can lead to changes in the way modeling languages are developed, as it could lead to guidelines for adapting the visual notations more closely to the needs of the domain and aspect the language is used for, as well as the people (envisioned) using the modeling language.

References

1. Genon, N., Amyot, D., Heymans, P.: Analysing the cognitive effectiveness of the UCM visual notation. In: Kraemer, F.A., Herrmann, P. (eds.) SAM 2010. LNCS, vol. 6598, pp. 221–240. Springer, Heidelberg (2011)
2. Genon, N., Heymans, P., Amyot, D.: Analysing the cognitive effectiveness of the BPMN 2.0 visual notation. In: Malloy, B., Staab, S., van den Brand, M. (eds.) SLE 2010. LNCS, vol. 6563, pp. 377–396. Springer, Heidelberg (2011)
3. Green, T., Blandford, A., Church, L., Roast, C., Clarke, S.: Cognitive dimensions: achievements, new directions, and open questions. J. Visual Lang. Comput. **17**(4), 328–365 (2006)
4. Moody, D.: Theory development in visual language research: Beyond the cognitive dimensions of notations. In: 2009 IEEE Symposium on Visual Languages and Human-Centric Computing, VL/HCC 2009, pp. 151–154, September 2009
5. Moody, D.L., Heymans, P., Matuleviaius, R.: Visual syntax does matter: improving the cognitive effectiveness of the i* visual notation. Requirements Eng. **15**(2), 141–175 (2010)
6. Moody, D., van Hillegersberg, J.: Evaluating the visual syntax of UML: an analysis of the cognitive effectiveness of the UML family of diagrams. In: Gašević, D., Lämmel, R., Van Wyk, E. (eds.) SLE 2008. LNCS, vol. 5452, pp. 16–34. Springer, Heidelberg (2009)
7. Mylopoulos, J., Borgida, A., Jarke, M., Koubarakis, M.: Telos: representing knowledge about information systems. ACM Trans. Inf. Syst. **8**(4), 325–362 (1990)
8. Nelson, M.G.H.J., Piattini, M.: A systematic literature review on the quality of uml models. In: Innovations in Database Design, Web Applications, and Information Systems Management, p. 310 (2012)

9. Petre, M.: Why looking isn't always seeing: readership skills and graphical programming. Commun. ACM **38**(6), 33–44 (1995)
10. Reijers, H., Mendling, J.: A study into the factors that influence the understandability of business process models. IEEE Trans. Syst. Man Cybern. Part A Syst. Hum. **41**(3), 449–462 (2011)
11. Rittgen, P.: Quality and perceived usefulness of process models. In: Proceedings of the 2010 ACM Symposium on Applied Computing, pp. 65–72. ACM (2010)
12. Wieringa, R.: Real-world semantics of conceptual models. In: Kaschek, R., Delcambre, L. (eds.) The Evolution of Conceptual Modeling. LNCS, vol. 6520, pp. 1–20. Springer, Heidelberg (2011)
13. Wilmont, I., Barendsen, E., Hoppenbrouwers, S.J.B.A., Hengeveld, S.: Abstract reasoning in collaborative modeling. In: Sprague, R. (ed.) HICCS 2012. pp. 170–179. IEEE Computer Society (2012)
14. Wilmont, I., Hengeveld, S., Barendsen, E., Hoppenbrouwers, S.: Cognitive mechanisms of conceptual modelling. In: Ng, W., Storey, V.C., Trujillo, J.C. (eds.) ER 2013. LNCS, vol. 8217, pp. 74–87. Springer, Heidelberg (2013)

DiFenSE 2015

Some Heuristics for Digital
Business Model Configuration

Darek M. Haftor[(⊠)]

Linnaeus University, Växjö, Sweden
darek.haftor@lnu.se

Abstract. This paper presents a summary of ongoing research with regard to the reconfiguration of business models with the help of digital technologies. Based in Amit and Zott's seminal notion of a business model, studies of a large set of digital business models have uncovered a set of *dimensions* that when reconfigured with the help of digital technologies may produce successful digital businesses. These dimensions are a business model's *outputs*, *activities*, *actors*, *transaction mechanism* and *governance*, and may be regarded as a set of heuristics to guide managers' business development efforts into the digital world.

Keywords: Digitalization · Economic value · Unbundling · Decoupling · Sharing

1 Introduction

The renewed American firm *Kodak* was a hugely successful market leader in the camera and film industry, at its peak employing more than 120 thousand people. In 2012 it filed for reconstruction as it was on the brink of bankruptcy. Despite being early in developing digital options to its main analogue products, *Kodak* failed to align its business model to this new technology and died from relying on an outdated business model that had lost market relevance [1]. In the same year, the tiny start-up firm *Instagram* employing only a dozen people was acquired by *Facebook* for $1 billion, after having been in the marketplace for less than a year! [1] Today's market capitalization of *Facebook* is greater than $ 200 billion (e.g. *ychart.com*) and all these three firms are operational in the same fundamental business, namely information logistics. This is also valid for many other digital companies such as *Google*, *Spotify*, *Netflix*, *UberTaxi* and *AirB2B* and also for traditionally non-digital firms that are now pursuing digitalization efforts, such as *General Electric's* digitalization of electric power generators and related equipment [2].

One question that emerges is why some firms succeed with their digital efforts while others fail. This is of course a complex question that resists simplistic answers. Our research efforts address the structure, content, governance and dynamics of digital business models [3], where *a digital business* is understood broadly as a business that employs contemporary information and communication technologies for its business activities. This includes such aspects as the actual configuration of the content of a digital business model, the managerial processes needed for their development and

© Springer International Publishing Switzerland 2015
A. Persson and J. Stirna (Eds.): CAiSE 2015 Workshops, LNBIP 215, pp. 123–130, 2015.
DOI: 10.1007/978-3-319-19243-7_13

adaptation, their revenue models, and their sources of value creation and appropriation. This paper presents a summary of the preliminary findings of ongoing research that addresses configuration of the content of a digital business model.

The paper is organized as follows; the next section summarizes some key challenges, both empirical and theoretical, to the comprehension of a digital business. Thereafter, the assumed notion of a Digital Business Model, with its theoretical underpinnings, is briefly accounted for. The next part represents the main contribution of this paper, being a summary of our current research findings with regard to the configuration dimensions of the content of a digital business models. These dimensions may be utilized by managers as heuristics, or rules of thumb, for challenging existing business models and guiding their transformation into digital business models. The paper ends with a brief description of areas for future research.

2   The Digital Challenges of Conventional Notions of a Business

The desire to acquire a comprehensive understanding of a firm, including its nature, success and failure has been around at least since Adam Smith's The Wealth of Nations. To that end, a number of qualified candidates have been advanced. Such a list may include at least the following intellectual contributions: Schumpeterian innovation [4], value chain analysis [5], competitive strategies [5], corporate strategies [5], strategic capabilities [6], dynamic capabilities [7], game theory [8], strategic network theory [9], transaction cost economics [10], and more recently organization economics as such [11]. When faced with an empirical phenomenon such as *Instagram*, *Facebook* or *Spotify*, a practitioner may ask how to make sense of the theoretical bodies provided by decades of research and their studies.

Indeed, one limitation of current comprehension attempts of any business is that the conventional theoretical bodies currently available provide a *partial* understanding at best – sometimes complementary while other times contradictory [12]. Another key limitation inherent in those theoretical bodies, which is particularly pertinent to our context of digital businesses, is that those theoretical constructions have largely been developed from empirical studies conducted several decades ago, prior to the advent and adoption of contemporary information and communication technologies (ICT), as well as other key changes of marketplaces, for instance massive deregulations. This means that potentially, most current theoretical bodies addressing the notion of a business cannot fully account for the phenomenon of a digital business and its context of contemporary marketplaces.

3   The Notion of a Digital Business Model

Given the assumed position that current theoretical bodies are not equipped to offer a comprehensive conception of digital businesses, various attempts have emerged with the aspiration to overcome the mentioned theoretical partiality and to account for the digital reality of businesses. These attempts are sometimes rather unfortunately labelled '*business models*'. This is not the place to provide a comprehensive review of business model literature, including its various strands of thought; rather we rely on one such recent and excellent review [13]. The research findings reported here rely on one particular notion of a business model, as advanced by Amit and Zott [1, 3, 14–16]. This notion is by far the most advanced in terms of theoretical groundings and empirical support, and offers some unique abilities to account for the realities of digital business models.

In summary, Amit and Zott's elaboration understands a business model as the *structure*, *content* and *governance* of a specific actor network, linked by transaction mechanisms that jointly execute value chain activities so as to create and appropriate value in a marketplace [1]. In this conception, the *structure* accounts for the actors involved, how they are related and the transaction mechanisms involved in their interactions as well as the order of actors' interaction. The *content* of a business model accounts for the inputs received and outputs generated, so as to provide products to their recipients in the network; the content also accounts for the capabilities inherent in the actor network conducting the transformation of inputs into outputs. Finally, the *governance* of a business model refers to the present design of command and control set-ups that govern the mentioned transformation of inputs to outputs (both informational and material) and the actor-network conducting it; this also includes the legal content of the *contracts* that govern both each actor and the actor network, as well as their *incentive* set-ups. Both early and recent contributions emphasize that a business model should be regarded as a *system*, hence featuring and accounting for its *systemic* characteristics [14, 17, 18], even though some challenges to this have been observed [19].

This business model notion focuses on how economic value is created and appropriated and who generates it, and is thereby not limited to a single firm only or an industry – indeed it is truly boundary spanning of firms and even industry [14], thereby being able to account for such firms as Apple, whose business model spans several industries and is highly dependent upon a successful interaction with a large set of actors.

By integrating several existing theoretical bodies, this conception of a business model enables us to articulate several sources of economic value creation and appropriation. The Schumpeterian foundation accounts for business models that offer *novel* designs and generate value from creative destruction. The resource-based view of business focuses on the importance of *complementarity* of capabilities, and products that a business model can account for. The strategic network theory accounts for the frequent situations when the locus of value creation is not a single firm but a network of firms, and thereby brings in the *lock-in* mechanism as value appropriator. Transaction cost economics account for the governance *efficiency* of alternative governance mechanisms that mediate transactions between actors.

Given the above conception of a digital business model, with its constituents and functions that generate economic value creation and appropriation, the core question of our concern here is: how can the content of a business model be configured by means of digitalization. The remaining part of this paper addresses that question.

4   Heuristics for the Configuration of a Digital Business Model

The starting point here is how conventional, not digitalized, business models can be transformed into digital business models. At least five dimensions of a business model may be regarded as areas for modification, which have shown capability of producing novel digital business models. These are *Output, Activity, Actors, Transaction Mechanisms,* and *Governance*.

4.1   Reconfiguring Outputs

Reconfiguration of the products that are present in a marketplace was one of the first effects of novel digital business models in the market places. Often referred to as unbundling [20] this kind of reconfiguration focuses on the content of given information products, such as books or newspapers. As such products are typically composed of several subcomponents that are bound into one offering, the reconfiguration or unbounding of such a package aims to provide the customer with some of its parts only or another configuration or bundling of the product. For example in the case of a book constituted by a dozen chapters, the customer may acquire one or two chapters only if so desired and is not forced to acquire the whole book due to its bounding. In this manner, the customer acquires only what represents value to her while the business model differentiates itself from the conventional by offering that freedom to acquire only those parts of a given book that are needed.

It is difficult for conventional business models to defend themselves against such reconfigurations. One defence is to block the technical opportunities to unbound and rebound bound products, which is rather difficult both technologically and also from a market opportunity viewpoint – i.e. if a chosen album of music is not provided digitally song by song, then customers will take their money elsewhere. Another defence of business models that unbundle products of conventional business models is to reconfigure the products in novel manners aimed at various customer segments with different pricing models. For example; music, songs, films, and books or magazines may be bundled into packages with a single monthly fee, and where a specific bundling is provided to a given customer segment with distinct needs. This approach realizes transaction efficiency in so far as it reduces the cognitive burden for customers' search and also offers significant discounts for the consumption of the given products during a given time period, while at the same time securing a certain volume of revenues per customer.

4.2   Reconfiguring Activities

As the notion of reconfiguration of a business model into a digital one, as such, was introduced above, together with the output reconfiguration, the focus here is on the reconfiguration of activities present in the actor network that constitutes a business model. Starting with non-digital reconfigurations, a notable example is the Swedish furniture maker IKEA, who reconfigured the notion of furniture production, distribution and consumption. One key change to the old business model of furniture was to sell them disassembled accompanied with instructions so that consumers who bought them could assemble their new kitchen table at home from the parts provided – in this, the assembling activity was relocated from the producer to the consumer. This solution together with IKEA's sales via very large outlets positioned in the suburbs of major cities realized both on innovation and transaction efficacy and complementarity as their product range with regard to home furniture is almost endless.

Innovative digital business models frequently disentangle, or decouple, an existing activity chain [21]. One such reconfiguration is manifested by IP telephony providers, such as *Skype*. In the conventional business model the calling activity is coupled with paying-per-each-call activity, where the latter offers revenue stream for the telephone service provider. IP telephony, on the other hand, succeeded with a decoupling of those two activities – the first value creating and the second value appropriation – and cut a large part of long distance calls from the conventional telecom industry. As a response, these companies must look to change their business model both with regard to outputs and activities and also revenue sources. In the case of telecom firms, one such attempt is to rebalance the revenue streams from being dominated by telephone calls into data traffic. At the same time, IP telephony is associated with another value appropriation activity, namely advertising. *Skype's* main value creation came from its disruptive innovation, hence novelty, and also the efficiency offered – the first faded as other players with similar offerings arrived in the market place while the second is still present. It also shows the power of the lock-in mechanism, as by being first in the marketplace *Skype* realized network effects, as the more subscribers this free service acquired the harder it was for them to move to another supplier.

4.3   Reconfiguring Actors

Yet another form of business model reconfiguration targets the actual resources that execute the activities present in a business model. A recent and somewhat sensational example of this is the *UberTaxi* firm that offers a new business model for taxi rides [22]. Conventional taxi firms acquire their key resource, the taxi car, and typically use it for that purpose only while also employing car drivers; they also offer a taxi calling function and a payment transaction service. *UberTaxi*, on the other hand, does not acquire cars nor employ drivers; rather it connects people with a car to those in need of transportation at a given point of time and place by offering dedicated digital services for calling and payment. Clearly, the key resources of the conventional taxi business model – the car and the driver – are here replaced with other resources. As this business model assumes a significantly lower cost mass than any given taxi drive, it is able to ask a much lower ride-fee and thus attract a large customer segment out of the conventional business model. This business model also realizes novelty and effectivity as sources of economic value creation.

4.4   Reconfiguring Transaction Mechanisms

Yet another reconfiguration of the digital business model addresses the way a transaction mechanism is designed. A transaction *"occurs when a good or service is transferred across a technologically separable interface. One stage of processing or assembly activity terminates, and another begins"*, says Williamson [10:104]. Indeed, the advent of internet has shown a large array of transaction mechanism reconfigurations, enabling for example the so-called outsourcing of some business model activities to other suppliers, often operating at distance, geographically, temporally and culturally. Procurement of digital books from *Amazon.com* capitalizes on its transaction mechanism being radically different from the conventional book store, with regard to how information about products is exchanged, how the actual products are exchanged and also how payment is conducted. One of the more radical transaction mechanism reconfigurations is represented by the case of *Priceline.com* with so-called reversed auctions (that received a US patent!). In this case, a potential customer provides information about travel and the fee that she or he is willing to pay for such travel, while travel providers can bid for that customer by offering as favourable offerings as possible. Besides the obvious innovation, this transaction mechanism also offers significant transaction efficiencies for both parties: the buyers and the sellers.

4.5   Reconfiguring Governance Set-ups

The last reconfiguration area of a business model to be articulated here is that of the actual governance of a business model, which addresses the set-up of command and control of the actors, the activities and the transaction being conducted. This includes the legal content of contracts, business norms, and incentive structures. The obvious digitalization of the governance of some activities and actors is that of automation that has been pursued since the advent of the computer. However, it is particularly the effects of the dimensions of the business model being digitized as detailed above that gives rise to a reconfiguration of the governance set-ups of a business model. One example is peer-to-peer lending, where money is lent to unrelated individuals, or peers, without going through the conventional banking activities of risk assessment and so on. In this governance reconfiguration, the lending and risk assessment (i.e. activities) is not allocated to a central bank but to a peer (i.e. actors), who decides on whether to lend money or not, how much and with what conditions. In addition, music streaming services, such as *Spotify*, reconfigure the legal content of the music, by offering the right to listen to a song and not to download a file, where the latter is also a legal reformulation compared with the DVD-based music distribution.

5   Further Research

The above-listed dimensions of a business model articulate characteristics that can be re-configured with the help of digital technologies. While these dimensions are presented one-by-one, as the various accompanying illustrations suggest, they are in practice often reconfigured jointly in a specific and unique manner to produce a digital business model that aims to realize some of the four sources of the economic values creation and appropriation. With regard to this kind of business model re-configuration, much research is still necessary if we are to discover which digitized configurations succeed and why. Do some particular underlying patterns of reconfigurations give rise to particular patterns of value creation and appropriation? Another crucial area, mentioned above briefly only, is that of the revenue models utilized by a specific business model configuration. Do some specific business model configurations depend more on certain revenue model set-ups, and if so which? These and similar questions deserve further attention if we are to develop a firm understanding of our future digital businesses.

References

1. Economist: Coming to an office near you. The Economist, 18 January 2014
2. Iansiti, M., Lakhani, K.R.: Digital ubiquity: how connections, sensors, and data are revolutionizing business. Harvard Bus. Rev. **92**, 91–99 (2014)
3. Amit, R., Zott, C.: Value creation in e-business. Strateg. Manag. J. **22**, 493–520 (2001)
4. Schumpeter, J.A.: The Theory of Economic Development: An Inquiry into Profits, Capital, Credit, Interest, and the Business Cycle. Harvard University Press, Cambridge (1934)
5. Porter, M.E.: Competitive Advantage: Creating and Sustaining Superior Performance. Free Press, New York (1985)
6. Barney, J.B.: Firm resources and sustained competitive advantage. J. Manag. **17**, 99–120 (1991)
7. Teece, D., Pisano, G., Shuen, A.: Dynamic capabilities and strategic management. Strateg. Manag. J. **18**(7), 509–533 (1997)
8. Brandenburger, A.M., Nalebuff, B.J.: The right game: use game theory to shape strategy. Harvard Bus. Rev. **73**(4), 57–71 (1995)
9. Dyer, J., Singh, H.: The relational view: cooperative strategy and sources of inter-organizational competitive advantage. Acad. Manag. Rev. **23**, 660–679 (1998)
10. Williamson, O.E.: Markets and Hierarchies, Analysis and Antitrust Implications: A Study in the Economics of Internal Organization. Free Press, New York (1975)
11. Gibbons, R., Roberts, J. (eds.): The Handbook of Organizational Economics. Princeton UP, Princeton (2012)
12. Roberts, J.: Modern Firm: Organizational Design for Performance and Growth. OUP, Oxford (2007)
13. Zott, C., Amit, R., Massa, L.: The business model: recent developments and future research. J. Manag. **37**(4), 1019–1040 (2011)
14. Amit, R., Zott, C.: Creating value through business model innovation. Sloan Manag. Rev. **53**(3), 41–49 (2012)
15. Zott, C., Amit, R.: Business model design and the performance of entrepreneurial firms. Organ. Sci. **18**(2), 181–199 (2007)
16. Zott, C., Amit, R.: The fit between product market strategy and business model: implications for firm performance. Strateg. Manag. J. **29**(1), 1–26 (2008)
17. Osterwalder, A., Tucci, C.L., Pigneur, Y.: Clarifying business models: origins, present, and future of the concept. Commun. Assoc. Inf. Syst. **16**, 1–40 (2005)
18. Berglund, H., Sandström, C.: Business model innovation from an open systems perspective: structural challenges and managerial solution. Int. J. Prod. Dev. **18**(3–4), 171–184 (2013)

19. Haftor, D.M., Koczkas, A.: Two limitations of the systemic conception of a business model. In: Presented at the 3rd Business Systems Laboratory International Symposium Advances in Business Management. Towards Systemic Approach, Perugia, 20 November 2015

20. Koukova, T., Kannan, P.K., Ratchford, B.T.: Bundling and unbundling of electronic content. In: Shaw, M.J. (ed.) E-Commerce and the Digital Economy. Advances in Management Information Systems, vol. 4. M.E. Sharpe, Armonk (2006)

21. Teixeira, T.S., Jamieson, P.: The Decoupling of Digital Disruptors. Working Paper 15-031, 28 October 2014, Harvard Business School (2014)

22. Economist: Peer-to-Peer Rental: The Rise of the Sharing Economy: On the Internet, Everything is for Hire. The Economist, 9 March 2013

Inherent Cognitive Dependencies
in the Transformation of Business Models
from Non-digital to Digital

Erdelina Kurti[✉]

Linnaeus University, Växjö, Sweden
erdelina.kurti@lnu.se

Abstract. Digital technologies persuasively are changing business landscape thus disrupting traditional business models of many sectors, particularly those that engage with information-based products. Organizations struggle to change their business models. Overtime business models become deeply ingrained and represent the dominant logic. This research in progress aims to explore the challenges and success factors in the transformation from traditional to digital business models. The assumed focus is on cognitive dependencies that hinder and enable such transformation given that this transformation involves a fundamental shift of core cognitive assumptions and beliefs held by the management of organizations in terms of value creation and value network.

Keywords: Digital business models · Cognitive dependencies

1 Introduction

Rapid developments of Information and Communication Technologies (ICTs) and digitalization are creating numerous opportunities for organizations. Many new ventures (EBay, Spotify, Netflix etc.) have taken advantage of these developments, creating novel business models and at the same time disrupting business models of incumbent organizations [1, 4]. The impact of digital innovation has been prevalent particularly for business models of organizations that deal with information-based products due to their potential to be fully digitized [13]. In order to succeed incumbents must innovate their business models. Nevertheless literature and practice indicates that business model change is multifaceted and only few such transformations succeed [6, 15]. The question is, why is business model change difficult for incumbent organizations? Why some organizations are actually able to adapt while others fail? A recurring explanation in the business model literature is that overtime business models become path-dependent and represent the management dominant logic of value creation. Managers become cognitively bounded by this logic and these cognitive schemas or as often called knowledge structures act as a funnel that filters information, with an attention directed only on the data that conform to the dominant logic while discharging others. For example, Polaroid's failure to adapt to digital imaging is predominantly attributed to the inability of altering managerial strong beliefs in the analogue model [18]. Similar explanations are found in the shift of newspapers from print to online [9].

© Springer International Publishing Switzerland 2015
A. Persson and J. Stirna (Eds.): CAiSE 2015 Workshops, LNBIP 215, pp. 131–136, 2015.
DOI: 10.1007/978-3-319-19243-7_14

The purpose of this study is to explore the challenges and success factors in the transformation from traditional to digital business models. The assumed focus is on cognitive dependencies that hinder and enable such transformation. We argue that focusing on cognitive dependencies is important for two reasons. First, transformation from traditional business models to digital business models imposes certain cognitive dependencies due to the significantly distinct nature of these logics. Non-digital businesses function in terms of conventional economic wisdom while digital business models function within the economics of digital information, e.g. negligible marginal costs, significance of network effects, new revenue models, information asymmetry shrinking, transaction cost reduction etc. Second, the boundary-spanning nature of the business model imposes a multi-actor thinking. This feature becomes more evident in the digital word, which challenges the traditional view that value is created within boundaries of the firm only [7]. Consequently, transforming a business model from traditional to digital requires coordination between several actors, each operating on their own dominant logics thus requiring a synchronization of multiple logics. This transformation involves a fundamental shift of core cognitive assumptions and beliefs held by the management of organizations in terms of value creation and value network.

The rest of the paper is structured as follows. We begin by providing a review of digital business models and the economics of digital information. Next, we proceed to explain the relation between cognitive dependencies and business models. We then discuss the theoretical and managerial implications of the study.

2 Digital Business Models and the Underlying Economics of Digital Information

Business models emerged as a term during the dot-com hype, a period that was characterized with emergence of many new ventures that began to conduct business online. The trend, however, fainted quickly with most of these ventures failing. This failure was mostly attributed to the firms adopting flawed business models. Later, a renewed interest was marked, stemming from several fields, using the business model construct to explain the phenomena such as e-business and use of IT in organizations, strategic issues such as value creation, firm performance and innovation and technology management [23].

Digital business models or IT-enabled business models [14] represent one instance of digital innovation alongside product and process innovation [8]. Digital innovation refers to any innovation that is ICT enabled that results in creation of new forms of digitalization [21]. Amit and Zott [2] explored the theoretical foundations of the business model construct by investigating the sources of value creation in e-businesses. Their results show that no single strategy and entrepreneurship theory of value creation such as transaction cost economics, strategic networks, resource bases view, value chain, Schumpeterian innovation can fully account and explain the value creation in the digital world. Value creation in the digital world requires an integration of these theories, enabled by the business model construct itself. In this context a business model is defined as a *'system of interdependent activities that transcend the focal firm and spans its boundaries'* [22]. This conceptualization is inherently comprehensive since it accounts for the mutual interdependence between a firm and its business environment.

Weill and Woerner [20] elegantly illustrate this with a simple example of Wall Street Journal. In the traditional newspaper industry, Wall Street Journal was responsible in producing its own content of the newspaper articles and related photos. This content was then placed in printed newspaper with all the cosmetics and details that newspapers like any other publication needs. Thousands of copies needed to be print and delivered through established infrastructure (e.g. people, trucks). Carefully planned integration and management of these components produced customer value. In the digital world these components have changed. Content of newspaper is no longer as proprietary and has expanded, with Wall Street Journal obtaining content from other sources and engaging other partners to deliver the content to customers. Wall Street does not control infrastructure in the digital world anymore. Infrastructure involves a combination of internal and external digital platforms that can be accessed anytime and everywhere.

As we see from the illustration, traditional business world is product focused, tangible and customer transaction oriented, that operates according to the conventional economic wisdom, while digital realm is concerned with customers' experience and with focus on digital information-based products [20] that challenge the conventional economic rules. Instead they function according to the economics of digital information that involves some inherent unique features such importance of network effects, negligible marginal costs, different pricing mechanisms, reduction of transaction costs, shrinking of information asymmetry and different revenue models [2, 19]. These features make digital information difficult to translate and address in economic terms [10] and require a new set of assumptions, because the production, distribution and consumption of digital information products encompasses a distinct inherent logic [3, 19]. Adaption to the new logic that digital context brings to the forefront, requires a shift of managerial cognitive frames that are ingrained with the old traditional logic.

3 Cognitive Dependencies as a Barrier to Business Model Change

The role of cognition in organizations can be traced back to [11] who claimed that managers are embedded in certain cognitive structures and when faced with uncertain environment that fall outside these structures, managers draw upon these frames to create simplified representations of the information environment. Cognitive perspective is argued to have a great potential to offer insights into any type of organizational renewal. Despite the importance, the way cognitions shape innovation processes have not been empirically examined [17].

Several authors [5, 6, 16, 18] have explored the role of cognitive dependencies in business model change. Cognitive structures or as referred in the business model context as business model schemas are conceptualized as involving *concepts and relations that organize managerial understandings about the design of activities and exchanges that reflect the critical interdependencies and value creation relations in their firms' exchange networks* [12]. There is a common agreement that cognitive frames represent the main driver of path dependence of business models and are crucial in shaping business model change [5, 16]. Although these studies are very insightful and provide a solid foundation, there are some noted limitations. None of the studies particularly address the transformation of the business model from traditional to digital. Sandström and Osborne [15] argue that previous explanations on challenges that incumbents face when changing their business models are not specific for business models but instead they draw on previous arguments deriving from the product innovation and technology management literature and moreover apply to any type of organizational change. The role of managerial cognition occupies a central place in the literature of technology innovation management [6, 18]. While these studies provide deep insights about the role of cognitive dependencies in business model change they approach technology as a black box. Opening the black box is crucial for digital technologies due to the unique properties that are not inherent in any type of other technologies. Moreover [15] argue that challenges that are specific to business model should be intertwined to its network of multi actors, which means that business model is not controlled by the firm itself. This perspective however is often overlooked in previous studies, particularly in those that investigate the role of dominant logic in business model change.

4 Discussion

This paper presents a research in progress that aims to explore the key challenges and success factors involved in the transformation of the business model from traditional to digital. The assumed focus in on cognitive dependencies that hinder and enable such transformation. A central argument around which this study revolves is on the fundamental distinctions between non-digital and digital business models. We argue that traditional business models are guided by conventional economic wisdom whereas digital business models by the economics of digital information. We derive this argument on explanations drawing on the fundamental properties of digital technology and economics of digital information that involve negligible marginal costs, significance of network effects, new revenue models, information asymmetry shrinking, transaction cost reduction etc. Moreover, we argue that exploration of cognitive dependencies and success factors in the transformation of business model should account for boundary-spanning nature of the business model as the most unique feature that differentiates it from other constructs. Digital transformations profoundly change the whole notion of value creation and capture and as such cannot be conceived without the value network, like eBay, Facebook, YouTube who cannot be comprehended without their networks.

The study will contribute to the rather nascent literature on the dynamics of business models. While previous scholarly contributions have given insights about the role of cognitive dependencies and path dependence in general [5, 6, 16] digital context exposes organizations to novel forms of value creation and capture that are quite distinct from the conventional ones, thus requiring a fundamental shift of dominant logic. Given that digital businesses represent the most dynamic and a crucial segment of the new economy, this study will unleash significant implications to the practice.

It will inform managers of information intensive organizations engaged in business model change endeavors by providing s set of structured processes and guidelines that firms can use systematically about cognitive hindrances and success factors to overcome these challenges.

References

1. Al-Debei, M.M., El-Haddadeh, R., Avison, D.: Defining the busines model in the new world of digital business. In: Proceedings of the 14th Americas Conference on Information Systems (AMCIS 2008), Toronto, Canada, pp. 1–11 (2008)
2. Amit, R., Zott, C.: Value creation in e-business. Strateg. Manag. J. **22**(6–7), 493–520 (2001)
3. Benkler, J.: The Wealth of Networks: How Social Production Transforms Markets and Freedom. Yale University Press, New Haven (2006)
4. Bharadwaj, A., El Sawy, O.A., Pavlou, P.A., Venkatraman, N.: Digital business strategy: toward a new generation of insights. MIS Q. **33**(1), 204–208 (2013)
5. Bohnsack, R., Pinkse, J., Kolk, A.: Business models for sustainable technologies: exploring business model evolution in the case of electric vehicles. Res. Policy **43**(2), 284–300 (2014)
6. Chesbrough, H., Rosenbloom, R.S.: The role of the business model in capturing value from innovation: evidence from xerox corporation's technology spin-off companies. Ind. Corp. Change **11**(3), 529–555 (2002)
7. El Sawy, O.A., Pereira, F.: Digital business models: review and synthesis. In: Business Modelling in the Dynamic Digital Space. Springer, Heidelberg (2013)
8. Fichman, R.G., Dos Santos, B., Zheng, Z.: Digital Innovation as a fundamental and powerful concept in the information systems curriculum. MIS Q. **38**(2), 329–353 (2014)
9. Gilbert, C.G.: Unbundling the structure of inertia: resource versus routine rigidity. Acad. Manag. J. **48**, 741–763 (2005)
10. Lester, J., Koehler, W.: Fundamentals of Information Studies: Understanding Information and Its Environment, 2nd edn. Neal-Schuman, New York (2007)
11. March, J.G., Simon, H.A.: Organizations. Wiley, New York (1958)
12. Martins, L., Rindova, V.P., Greenbaum, B.: Unlocking the hidden value of concepts: a cognitive approach to business model innovation. Strateg. Entrepreneurship J. **9**(1), 99–117 (2015)
13. Nylén, D., Holmström, J.: Digital innovation strategy: a framework for diagnosing and improving digital product and service innovation. Bus. Horiz. **58**, 57–67 (2015)
14. Rai, A., Tang, X.: Research commentary—information technology-enabled business models: a conceptual framework and a coevolution perspective for future research. Inf. Syst. Res. **25**(1), 1–14 (2013)
15. Sandstrom, C., Osborne, R.G.: Managing business model renewal. Int. J. Bus. Syst. Res. **5**(5), 461–474 (2011)
16. Sosna, M., Trevinyo-Rodríguez, R.N., Velamuri, S.R.: Business model innovation through trial-and-error learning: the naturhouse case. Long Range Plan. **43**(2–3), 383–407 (2010)
17. Thrane, S., Blaabjerg, S., Hannemann Møller, R.: Innovative path dependence: making sense of product and service innovation in path dependent innovation processes. Res. Policy **39**, 932–944 (2010)
18. Tripsas, M., Gavetti, G.: Capabilities, cognition, and inertia: evidence from digital imaging. Strateg. Manag. J. **21**(10/11), 1147–1161 (2000)
19. Varian, H.R.: Markets for Information Goods. University of California, Berkeley (1998)

20. Weill, P., Woerner, S.L.: Optimizing your digital business model. MIT Sloan Manage. Rev. **54**(3), 71–78 (2013)
21. Yoo, Y., Lyytinen, K., Boland, R., Berente, N., Gaskin, J., Schutz, D., Srinivasan, N.: The Next Wave of Digital Innovation: Opportunities and Challenges: A Report on the Research Workshop Digital Challenges in Innovation Research, Fox School of Business, Temple University, PA, USA. (2010)
22. Zott, C., Amit, R.: Designing your future business model: an activity system perspective. Long Range Plan. **43**, 216–226 (2010)
23. Zott, C., Amit, R., Massa, L.: The business model: recent developments and future research. J. Manag. **37**(4), 1019–1104 (2011)

Capability-as-a-Service: Investigating the Innovation Potential from a Business Model Perspective

Kurt Sandkuhl[1,3]([⊠]) and Janis Stirna[2]

[1] Institute of Computer Science, University of Rostock,
Albert-Einstein-Str. 22, 18059 Rostock, Germany
`kurt.sandkuhl@uni-rostock.de`
[2] Department of Computer and Systems Sciences,
Stockholm University, Forum 100, SE-16440 Kista, Sweden
`js@dsv.su.se`
[3] ITMO University, 49 Kronverkskiy pr., 197101 St. Petersburg, Russia

Abstract. Capability management is expected to contribute to a new level of productivity in developing and deploying IT-based business services offered by digital enterprises to their customers. Work on capability management so far emphasizes the technology perspective of capability design and delivery. The paper addresses the question of what is the potential of capability management with respect to business model innovation by considering a case study from business process outsourcing as an example. The aim is to apply an established business model conceptualization as a framework for analyzing the case study and to compare the possibility of identifying business innovations with and without defined capability characteristics.

Keywords: Capability management · Business model · Innovation potential · Business process outsourcing

1 Introduction

Capability management is expected to contribute to a new level of productivity in developing and deploying IT-based business services offered by digital enterprises to their customers. One of the key features in capability management is to explicitly capture the delivery context of business services and to provide mechanisms for configuring an existing information system (IS) or generating its delivery according to a capability design (see Sect. 3). Work on capability management so far emphasizes the technology perspective of capability design and delivery, for example as designed in the Capability Driven Development (CDD) approach of the EU-FP7-project Capability-as-a-Service (CaaS) (see Sect. 3).

The initial application of capability as a construct for supporting context dependent design and delivery of business has been promising (c.f. for instance [1]). As the next step of making the CDD approach practicable, this paper ponders on the question of *what is the potential of capability management in general and the CDD approach in particular when it comes to business model innovation?* The paper addresses this question

A. Persson and J. Stirna (Eds.): CAiSE 2015 Workshops, LNBIP 215, pp. 137–148, 2015.
DOI: 10.1007/978-3-319-19243-7_15

by considering a case study from business process outsourcing as an example. The aim of the paper is to apply an established business model conceptualization as a framework for analyzing the case study and to compare the possibility to identify business innovations with and without defined capability characteristics. The business model conceptualization provides a number of partial business models that represent perspectives on the business model (see Sect. 2.1). Based on the comparison, we will identify the most promising partial business model for assessing the business innovation potential.

The remainder of the paper is structured as follows: Sect. 2 summarizes the background for the work from the areas of business models and capability management. Section 3 presents the main aspect of the CaaS approach to capability design and delivery which includes essential aspects of capability management. Section 4 introduces the case study including a selected business service. Section 5 analyzes the case study from Sect. 4 using the business model conceptualization from Sect. 2 and the capability design and delivery approach from Sect. 3. Section 6 summarizes the work and draws conclusions.

2 Background

As a background for the work presented in this paper, this section briefly summarizes work in the areas of business models and capability management.

2.1 Business Models

Business models have been an essential element of economic behavior since decades, but received significantly growing attention in research with the advent of the Internet [4] and expanding industries dependent on post-industrial technologies [3]. In general, the business model of an enterprise describes the essential elements that create and deliver a value proposition for the customers, including the economic model and underlying logic, the key resources and key processes.

Zott and Amit identified three major lines of work in their analysis of recent academic work in business model developments [14]:

- Business models for e-business scenarios and the use of IT in organizations
- The strategic role of business models in competitive advantage, value creation and organizational performance
- Business models in innovation and technology management.

For analyzing the business innovation potential of capabilities, we consider both value creation based business models for the service industry and approaches from e-business as promising [2, 12]. For the purpose of this paper, the proposal by Wirtz seems to be most suitable due to the explicit identification of six partial models: *capital model, procurement model, manufacturing model, market model, service offer model*, and *distribution model*. In this way the essential parts of value creation are covered. The *capital model* is subdivided into financing model and revenue model. The *financing model* describes the sources of the capital that is necessary for business activity. The revenue model provides means to generally systemize business models by four dimensions: direct or indirect generation of revenue, as well as the transaction-dependent and the transaction-independent generation of revenue. The *procurement model* describes production factors and their sources. Here the distribution of power between suppliers and demanders is an important aspect. The *manufacturing model* covers the combination of input factors to new goods and services. Demand structures as well as the competitive situation are described by the respective sub-models of the *market model*. The *service offer model* defines which IT services are provided to the customers, while the *distribution model* focuses on the channels that are used to make the IT services available to the specific customer groups. Wirtz has proposed a categorization of e-business models by the kind of IT service offered (see Fig. 1).

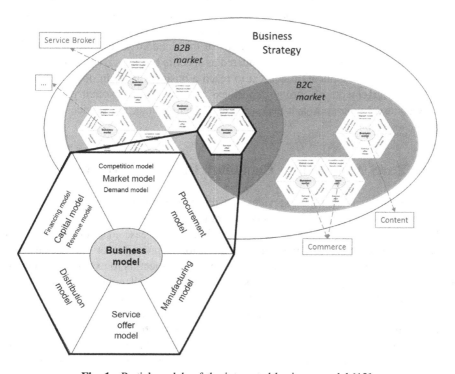

Fig. 1. Partial models of the integrated business model [12]

2.2   Capability Management

The term capability is used in different areas of business IS. In the literature there seems to be an agreement about the characteristics of the capability, yet there is no generally accepted definition of the term. The definitions mainly put the focus on "combination of resources" [6], "capacity to execute an activity" [5], "perform better than competitors" [8] and "possessed ability [13]".

The capabilities must be enablers of competitive advantage; they should help companies to continuously deliver a certain business value in dynamically changing circumstances [9]. They can be perceived from different organizational levels and thus utilized for different purposes. According to [10], performance of an enterprise is the best, when the enterprise maps its capabilities to IT applications. Capabilities as such are directly related to business processes that are affected from the changes in context, such as, regulations, customer preferences and system performance. As companies in rapidly changing environments need to anticipate variations and respond to them [7], the affected processes/services need to be adjusted quickly. i.e., adaptations to changes in context can be realized promptly if the required variations to the standard processes have been anticipated and defined in advance and can be instantiated.

In this paper capability is defined as *the ability and capacity that enable an enterprise to achieve a business goal in a certain context* [16]. Ability refers to the level of available competence, where competence is understood as talent, intelligence and disposition, of a subject or enterprise to accomplish a goal; capacity means availability of resources, e.g. money, time, personnel, tools. This definition utilizes the notion of context, thus stresses the variations of the standard processes.

To summarize, capabilities are considered as specific business services delivered to the enterprises in an application context to reach a business goal. In order to facilitate capability management, we propose business service design explicitly considering delivery context by an approach that supports modeling both, the service as such and the application context.

3   The CaaS Approach to Capability Design and Delivery

Business services are IT-based services that digital enterprises provide for their customers. Business services usually serve specified business goals, are specified in a model-based way, and include service level definitions. To ease adaptation of business services to new delivery contexts, changes in customer processes or other legal environments, the CDD approach, developed in the CaaS project, is to explicitly define (a) the potential delivery context of a business service (i.e. all contexts in which the business service has to be potentially delivered), (b) the potential variants of the business service for the delivery context, and (c) what aspect of the delivery context would require what kind of variation or adaptation of the business service.

The potential delivery context basically consists of a set of parameters or variables, the, so called, context elements, which characterize the differences in delivery. The combination of all context elements and their possible ranges defines the context set, i.e. the problem space to cover. The potential variants of the business service, which form the solution space, are represented by process variants. Since in many delivery contexts it will be impractical to capture all possible variants, we propose to define patterns for the most frequent variants caused by context elements and to combine and instantiate these patterns to create actual solutions. If no suitable pattern is available, the conventional solution engineering process has to be used. The connection between context elements, patterns and business services has to be captured as transformation or mapping rules. These rules are defined during design time and interpreted during runtime.

The above simplified summary of the CDD approach has been further elaborated by defining meta-model and method components (available in [11, 17], respectively), by specifying a development and delivery environment, and by performing feasibility studies.

In order to implement the CaaS approach, a capability development and delivery environment was designed and currently is under development. The main components of the environment are capability design tool, context platform, capability delivery navigation application, as well as capability delivery application. The architecture of the environment is shown in Fig. 2. The main functional components of the environment are as follows:

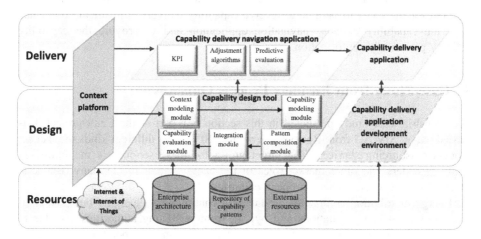

Fig. 2. Components of the capability development environment

- Capability modeling module - provides modeling elements defined in the capability meta-model and models the required capability including business service (e.g. business process model), business goals, context and relations to delivery patterns.
- Pattern composition module - identifies appropriate patterns for capability delivery and composes the patterns together. It supports incorporation of external resources into the composition. If some of the patterns required are not available then the modeling of missing information is supported and new patterns can be proposed and documented.
- Repository of capability patterns - storage and maintenance of available capability delivery patterns.
- Context platform - captures data from external data sources including sensing hardware and Internet based services such as social networks. It aggregates data and provides these data to subscribers.
- Context modeling module - represents the context data in terms of the capability modeling concepts and provides means for context analysis and amalgamation.
- Capability assessment (evaluation) module - performs assessment of financial and technical feasibility of the proposed capability.
- Capability integration module - generates the capability delivery navigation application, which also incorporates algorithms for capability delivery adjustment.
- Capability delivery navigation application - provides means for monitoring and adjustment of capability delivery. It includes monitoring module for monitoring

context and goal KPI, predictive evaluation of capability delivery performance and delivery adjustment algorithms. The capability delivery adjustment algorithms are built-in in the capability delivery navigation application. The algorithms continuously evaluate necessary adjustments and pass capability delivery adjustment commands to the capability delivery application.

Capability delivery application is developed following the process and technologies used by a particular company. The CDD methodology only determines interfaces required for the CDA to be able to receive capability delivery adjustment commands from the capability delivery navigation application and to provide the capability delivery performance information.

4   Case Study from Business Process Outsourcing

The industrial case study presented in this section is a part of the CaaS project. It is carried out at. SIV.AG from Rostock (Germany). SIV offers different kinds of business process outsourcing services. The target group for these services is medium-sized utility providers and other market roles of the energy sector in Germany, Bulgaria, Macedonia and several other European countries.

Energy distribution companies are facing a continuously changing business environment due to new regulations and bylaws from regulating authorities and due to competitors implementing innovative technical solutions in grid operations or metering services, like intelligent metering or grid utilization management. In this context, both the business processes in organizations and IS supporting these processes need to be adaptive to changing organizational needs. Examples for typical business functions are assets accounting, processing and examination of invoices, meter readings, meter data evaluation, automatic billing, customer relationship management, maintenance management, inventory management, order management, and project management.

A key service area of SIV.AG is business process outsourcing (BPO), i.e. the performance of a complete business process for a business function by a service provider outside an organization. This service has to implement potential variations of the clients' way of performing business. One variation is inherent in the business process as such. Even though core processes can be defined and implemented in standard software systems, configurations and adjustments for the organization in question are needed. The second cause of variation is the configuration for the country of use, i.e. the implementation of the actual regulations and bylaws. The third variation is related to the resource use for implementing the actual business process for the customer, i.e. the provision of technical and organizational capacities. Basis for these services is SIV's software product kVASy4. Integrated with the business process environment, the "native" kVASy4 services providing business logic for the energy sector are implemented using a database-centric approach.

As an example for a BPO service offered by SIV, we will in the following describe the MSCONS business service. MSCONS is offered by SIV due to defined business goals. A business goal is defined as desired state of affairs to be attained [16]. The goals in this case are modeled using the 4EM-Approach [15]. Due to the relationships between the SIV.AG and its customers, a distinction was made between customer goals and SIV goals, i.e. customer goals are more operational whereas SIV follows strategic business goals. This can be considered as a support relationship. Respectively the main goal of SIV is to deliver constant business value to its customers, which supports to efficiently control business processes goal of the customer. Goals can be refined into sub-goals, thereby forming a goal hierarchy. To efficiently control business processes, customers aim to optimize case throughput and to achieve a high process quality. Both can be considered as subordinate goals in the use case.

According to the CaaS approach, business goals require capabilities to be successfully fulfilled. Enabling the SIV's customers to optimize their case throughput requires SIV to deliver capabilities for them to route their processes in accordance with the workload. For this case, this capability is called "Dynamic Business Service Provider (BSP) Support".

The high level business process "message validation" is required by the capability "Dynamic BSP Support". In particular, the industrial case implements the MSCONS (Metered Services Consumption Report Message) validation processes from a global view. The purpose of the global process in MSCONS use case is the transmission of energy consumption data from one market role to another role. By regulatory requirement, all data must be sent by e-mail and its format must comply with the international UN/EDIFACT standard. In addition to this requirement, national variants of the EDIFACT standard may exist that add further constraints to the syntactical structure of exchanged messages. Thus, messages must not only comply with the international but also with the national EDIFACT standard, which are subject to periodical change by the regulatory authorities, with usually two releases per year.

An invalid message causes an exception to be thrown. Currently, all of these exceptions are treated manually, involving a knowledge worker; dynamic aspects, such as the handling of exception by customer under certain conditions, are not taken into account. Offering dynamic capabilities to route the exception handling process requires recognizing the application context, in which the exception is thrown. e.g., the customer might prefer to outsource his processes to SIV.AG if there are huge numbers of errors when validating the MSCONS message. The process outsourcing might depend on the backlog size, exception type and available resources at SIV, which are arranged with a service contract between SIV and the customer. As a result, two process variants are of use – the handling of the exception by customer or by SIV. The CaaS approach applies patterns for the implementation of the respective process variants that react to the anticipated changes in context and adjust the capability delivery process properly.

5   Business Model Analysis and Innovation Potential

To illustrate business model analysis and identification of innovation potential, we selected the MSCONS business service discussed in Sect. 4. Starting from an analysis of the partial business models according to Wirtz's approach we will discuss innovation potential in Sect. 5.1. In Sect. 5.2 we will extend the MSCONS business service to a capability using the CaaS approach and, discuss business innovation for this capability as well as compare it to the findings from Sect. 5.1.

5.1   Analysis of MSCONS Business Model

When analyzing the business model of the "MSCONS" service in Table 1, we assume that the IT-infrastructure for providing the service and the software platform (kVASy ERP system, EDIFACT messaging, document management, etc.) already have been installed, i.e. the focus is on the service as such. The actual analysis consists of describing the different partial business models in order to expose the different aspects of the business model.

Table 1. Business model of "MSCONS"

Partial models of business model		Business model of MSCONS
Market model	Demand model	Main target group are medium-sized enterprises from utility industries. Within this group, different segments are distinguished, e.g. energy provides, water providers, gas providers or grid operators
	Competition model	For the MSCONS service, several other software vendors provide platforms which can be used as software-as-a-service, but only two of them offer business process outsourcing. These two BPO providers can be considered as competitors
Procurement model		A few elements of the service are contracted to other service providers: • Transaction printing services, if requested by the client, are outsourced to a printing center • if the client requires post-processing of the transactions and export to specific information system, data conversion services are used from external providers
Manufacturing model		The processing of meter data, business process monitoring and handling of exceptions by knowledge workers all are provided from the own back-office of SIV. SIV offers using IT hardware and software systems, but the client may select to host the actual application in its own data center
Service offer model		The MSCONS BPO service is offered as stand-alone service or as "accounting bundle" with other services within accounting and billing
Distribution model		Distribution is based on VPN connections and dedicated communication lines. Service delivery also depends on the customer's ability to provide an appropriate operating environment for the back office applications needed
Capital model	Financing model	Operating costs are financed by internal funds of the enterprise.
	Revenue model	The pricing for the service includes a basic fee for each client depending on the size of the customer base. An additional fee is charged for exception cases to be handled manually by knowledge workers If the service is bundled within the accounting bundle, the basic fee is the same as for a single service, but the customer-based fee is higher

Business model innovations can be identified by going through each and every partial model, analyzing each model for potential alterations in the current status and examining the effects on the other partial models. e.g., if for the demand model a new target group is identified, this might have immediate effects on procurement and manufacturing model. One of the traditional ways to identify innovations potential is, however, to take a value chain perspective and analyze whether business should be extended to neighboring parts of the value chain. A change in the procurement model to no longer outsource account printing but to do it in-house would be such an example, which again has the effects on most other partial models.

5.2   Capability Analysis Regarding Business Innovation Potential

Following the CaaS approach for capability design and delivery, capability modeling includes as an initial step to capture the delivery context of a business service in a context model with specified relationships to business goals of the enterprise [18]. When doing this for the MSCONS business service, three main business drivers are identified, which cause variations and thus provide stimulus for changes. The first business driver is the contractual aspect, which specifies parameters such as backlog threshold as well as the process variant to be implemented regarding the backlog size, such as "if the backlog size exceeds the agreed threshold, then the case is routed to customer". The second business driver, payload aspect, includes information of the service call such as the market role, the faulty message and the exception type etc. The last driver, the operational aspect, is related to both SIV Services personnel deployment plan and the kVASy-operating environment. These are captured as variation aspects, which are further elaborated to identify context elements. Table 2 illustrates the context elements, their properties and allowed ranges.

Using the context model with the above context elements, the business service MSCONS can be extended to a capability by providing adaptations of MSCONS for all desired delivery contexts, e.g. by using patterns, and by controlling and configuring MSCONS for these different delivery contexts using the capability navigation application.

From a business model perspective, the extension from a business service to a capability will not make the business model described in Sect. 5.1 invalid or obsolete. The initial MSCONS business service still can be offered. However, as the context elements identify potential variations in the business service caused by a change in delivery context, these variation points form starting points for identifying changes in partial business models which eventually will lead to changes in MSCONS and the overall business model.

The variation aspect "operation" with its context element "operating platform" can serve as an example. The three different context element values are "data center", "cloud" and "customer". Each of these values can be considered as representing variants of the existing business model: MSCONS operated in the own data center, in the cloud, in the customer's data center, or as a mixture between own data center, cloud and customer's data center. If it would make sense to actually distinguish the business

Table 2. Context elements as causes of variability

Variation aspect	Context element	Measurable property	Context element range
Operation	Operating platform	kVASy deployment	{data center, cloud, customer}
	BSP human resources	Schedule	{low, average, high}
Payload	Market role	Role segment	{grid access provider, balance supplier, MDC, MOp, consumer}
	Message exchange format	Format segment	{MSCONS, UTILMD}
	Process subtype	Subtype segment	{VL, LG}
	Message version	Version segment	{2.2a, 2.2b, 5.0, 5.1}
Contract	Backlog threshold	Backlog size	[0–5]
	Exception type	BAM notification	{list of exception types}
	Business Service	Process type	{list of business services}

model for these variations depends on the effects on the other partial models. However, the investigation of potential innovations can start from the context elements.

6   Summary and Concluding Remarks

Based on an example of a business service from BPO in energy industries, the paper showed how to decompose the underlying business model into different partial models according to Wirtz's approach. When extending the business service into a capability by – as a first step - modelling the context for service delivery, the context model proved to be useful for identifying potential variants of the existing business model and thus potential business innovations, as the context elements represent starting points for changes in the partial business models.

The main limitation of our work is that we have analysed only the business model for one business service. More services will have to follow to develop our observations into clear implications. Furthermore, the business model analysis was done by a researcher from the field, not by a practitioner from the company. Future work will have to include a validation of the results by a practitioner.

The business model analysis resulted in a so far unrecognized option for capability modelling. We had a strong impression during analysis that the different partial business models could actually help identifying context elements in capability modelling and thus help defining more complete and precise capability definitions. For example, the use of a different supplier for accounting printing was identified as part of the procurement model. This indicates that there probably is one more variation aspect which should be part of the capability definition.

Acknowledgment. This work has been performed as part of the EU-FP7 funded project no: 611351 CaaS – Capability as a Service in Digital Enterprises.

References

1. Bravos, G., González, T., Grabis, J., Henkel, M., Jokste, L., Koc, H., Stirna, J.: Capability modeling: initial experiences. In: Johansson, B., Andersson, B., Holmberg, N. (eds.) BIR 2014. LNBIP, vol. 194, pp. 1–14. Springer, Heidelberg (2014)
2. Rappa, M.: Business Models on the Web: Managing the digital enterprise (2001). www.digitalenterprise.org/models/models.html. Accessed December 2011
3. Perkman, M., Spicer, A.: What are business models? Developing a theory of performative representation. In: Lounsbury, M. (ed.) Technology and Organization Essays in Honour of Joan Woodward (Research in the Sociology of Organizations), pp. 265–275. Emerald Group Publishing, United Kingdom (2010)
4. Tapscott, D., Lowy, A., Ticoll, D.: Digital Capital: Harnessing the Power of Business Webs. Harvard Business School Press, Cambridge (2000)
5. Jiang, Y., Zhao, J.: An empirical research of the forming process of firm inter-organizational e-business capability: based on the supply chain processes. In: 2010 2nd International Conference on Information Science and Engineering (ICISE), pp 2603–2606 (2010)
6. Antunes, G., Barateiro, J., Becker, C., et al.: Modeling contextual concerns in enterprise architecture. In: 2011 15th IEEE International Enterprise Distributed Object Computing Conference Workshops (EDOCW), pp 3–10 (2011)
7. Eriksson, T.: Processes, antecedents and outcomes of dynamic capabilities. Scand. J. Manage. **15**(2), 142–155 (2013). 10.1016/j.scaman.2013.05.001
8. Boonpattarakan, A.: Model of Thai small and medium sized enterprises' organizational capabilities: review and verification. JMR **4**(3), 1–28 (2012). 10.5296/jmr.v4i3.1557
9. Stirna, J., Grabis, J., Henkel, M., Zdravkovic, J.: Capability driven development – an approach to support evolving organizations. In: Sandkuhl, K., Seigerroth, U., Stirna, J. (eds.) PoEM 2012. LNBIP, vol. 134, pp. 117–131. Springer, Heidelberg (2012)
10. Chen, J., Tsou, H.: Performance effects of 5IT6 capability, service process innovation, and the mediating role of customer service. J. Eng. Tech. Manage. **29**(1), 71–94 (2012)
11. Zdravkovic, J., Stirna, J., Henkel, M., Grabis, J.: Modeling business capabilities and context dependent delivery by cloud services. In: Salinesi, C., Norrie, M.C., Pastor, Ó. (eds.) CAiSE 2013. LNCS, vol. 7908, pp. 369–383. Springer, Heidelberg (2013)
12. Wirtz, B.W.: Business Model Management. Design - Instruments - Success Factors, 1st edn. Gabler, Wiesbaden (2011)
13. Brézillon, P., Cavalcanti, M.: Modeling and using context. Knowl. Eng. Rev. **13**(2), 185–194 (1998). doi:10.1017/S0269888998004044
14. Zott, C., Amit, R.: Designing your future business model: an activity system perspective. Long Range Plan. **43**, 216–226 (2010)
15. Sandkuhl, K., Stirna, J., Persson, A., Wißotzki, M.: Enterprise Modeling: Tackling Business Challenges with the 4EM Method. The Enterprise Engineering Series. Springer, Heidelberg (2014). ISBN 978-3662437247

16. Bērziša, S., Bravos, G., Gonzalez Cardona, T., Czubayko, U., España, S., Grabis, J., Henkel, M., Jokste, L., Kampars, J., Koc, H., Kuhr, J., Llorca, C., Loucopoulos, P., Juanes Pascual, R., Sandkuhl, K., Simic, H., Stirna, J., Zdravkovic, J.: Deliverable 1.4: Requirements specification for CDD, CaaS – Capability as a Service for Digital Enterprises, FP7 project no 611351, Riga Technical University, Latvia (2014)
17. Sandkuhl, K., Koç, H., Stirna, J.: Context-aware business services: technological support for business and IT-alignment. In: Abramowicz, W., Kokkinaki, A. (eds.) BIS 2014 Workshops. LNBIP, vol. 183, pp. 190–201. Springer, Heidelberg (2014)
18. Koc, H., Sandkuhl, K.: Task Report 5.2: CaaS Method Component for Context Modelling. CaaS – Capability as a Service for Digital Enterprises, FP7 project no 611351, Rostock University, Germany (2014)

Supporting Service Innovation Through a Value Development Framework

Yannick Lew Yaw Fung[1](✉) and Arne J. Berre[2]

[1] Department of Informatics, University of Oslo, Oslo, Norway
yannickl@ifi.uio.no
[2] Networked Systems and Services, SINTEF ICT, Oslo, Norway
arne.j.berre@sintef.no

Abstract. Services have become a vital catalyst for economic growth worldwide. From a business perspective, innovation in services is regarded as being a key pillar in order to sustain the growth momentum of the service sector. The capability to create innovative services constitutes a complex problem for service providers. A major problem identified through a review of the literature concerns the lack of a service innovation framework that puts emphasis on the development of customer value or value being proposed by a service to customers. This paper presents a value development framework, called ServiceMIF, which can contribute to creating service innovation opportunities during service development through the creation of new or improved customer value. Ongoing preliminary trial results show that ServiceMIF can effectively help businesses to propose new or improved customer value while enhancing the quality of their service offerings.

Keywords: Service innovation · Value development · Service design · Service quality · Service experience

1 Introduction and Motivation

It is an undeniable fact that services have become a vital catalyst for economic growth worldwide. Service innovation is regarded as being a key pillar in order to sustain the growth momentum of the service sector. Despite considerable research efforts to understand and support innovation in services, organisations still face many difficulties in offering new service offerings to their customers.

In order to better understand the service aspects which can have an impact on service innovation, researchers and practitioners have been surveying various service innovation research streams such as New Service Development (NSD) [9] and Service Design [8]. While these research efforts are continuously reshaping the service innovation landscape in positive ways, a major problem identified through a review of the literature concerns the lack of a service innovation framework that puts emphasis on the development of customer value or value being proposed by a service to customers. The creation of new or improved customer

© Springer International Publishing Switzerland 2015
A. Persson and J. Stirna (Eds.): CAiSE 2015 Workshops, LNBIP 215, pp. 149–160, 2015.
DOI: 10.1007/978-3-319-19243-7_16

value is an essential goal of service innovation and is well recognised as being the next source of competitive advantage for service organisations [11]. This value that customers perceive and create through their service usage is linked to the set of individual benefits that a service proposes to its users [7]. The need for a framework to develop new or improved customer benefits is put forward based on a number of identified research gaps. A review of the service innovation literature over the past ten years, performed using Thomson Reuters' Web of Science[1] based on search terms and keywords including "service innovation", "value", and "benefits", indicates an absence of a value development framework to create new or improved customer value at the level of the individual benefits for customers. This is confirmed through extensive and critical reviews of the service innovation literature carried out by Droege et al. [5] and Carlborg et al. [3].

Service design techniques and tools [10], such as the service blueprint and the customer journey map, do not *explicitly* treat value as customer benefits that need to be managed and improved as part of service development. Moreover, popular service innovation methodologies based on a service marketing perspective, such as the outcome-driven innovation [2] and the FORTH methodology[2], concentrate their efforts *only* on the initial *ideation* phase of a service innovation process whereby new service ideas are produced. As a result, these do not consider the potential for innovation during the development of a service throughout its various phases of conception, production, consumption and feedback. The authors argue that ServiceMIF, the value development framework presented in this paper, helps in creating service innovation opportunities during service development.

2   The Value Benefit Template

ServiceMIF refers to the individual benefits that form part of the value proposed by a service as *value benefits*. Each value benefit is represented using a *value benefit template* which adopts a similar structure to that of a user story used to capture software requirements. Each value benefit describes the *service context* in which a service stakeholder performs a *service action* in order to trigger a *customer benefit*.

The service context describes the factors, in terms of 'Who' is interacting with the customer, 'Where' a service encounter is taking place, and 'When' a service encounter is happening, which typically involve some form of physical and/or virtual interactions between a customer and one or more actors from either the service provider's or the network partner's side.

A *service action* or activity refers to one or more operations that a service stakeholder, such as a customer, a service provider's employee, and a service network partner, *performs or would like to perform* as part of a service encounter. Such operations are the ones which will trigger the benefits for the customer. For the latter, a service action can be linked to the use of one or more senses of

---

[1] Web of Science: https://webofknowledge.com.

[2] FORTH Innovation Method: http://www.forth-innovation.com.

a human being such as hearing, sight, taste, smelling, and touch. For example, a customer who calls an after-sales service requires the use of hearing and voice so as to respectively hear and communicate with the called party.

A *customer benefit* is part of a set of benefits that customers expect to perceive through usage of a service. The latter provides benefits, both in terms of functional (what are the tasks a service accomplishes) and non-functional (how the tasks are being provided), to the customer.

3   The DISSECT Approach and Service Models

DISSECT is the value development approach of ServiceMIF and is comprised of five value development stages known as DIScovery, Solicitation, Evaluation, Capture, and Translation.

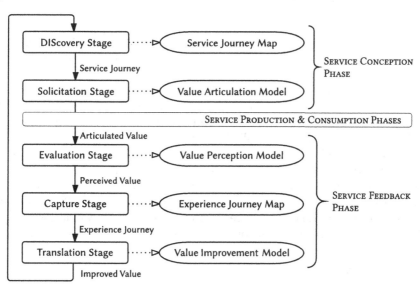

Fig. 1. The DISSECT stages and corresponding Service Models

As shown in Fig. 1, each stage is performed during a specific service development life cycle phase and produces a corresponding service model to process customer value as the latter flows from one stage to the next. The *end* of the Translation stage signifies that a "version" of a service has been developed. The DISSECT approach can then be re-executed for improving this service version.

3.1   First DISSECT Stage: DIScovery

The first stage of the DISSECT approach, called DIScovery, focuses on the discovery of two main aspects of a service, namely: (1) the identification of the points of service interaction in the form of touchpoints through which value

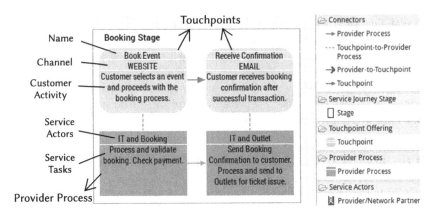

Fig. 2. The Service Journey Map of the DIScovery stage

benefits can be proposed to customers, and (2) the identification of provider processes that are necessary to support the proper execution of touchpoints. In effect, these two service aspects respectively define 'where' and 'how' value benefits can be proposed to customers of a service. The DIScovery stage makes use of a *Service Journey Map* whose model editor support, developed using the Eclipse Graphiti framework [6], is shown in Fig. 2 based on a small example of an online event booking service called *Concierge*.

A service stage along with two touchpoints and two provider processes are shown on the diagram. The 'Booking Stage' is being performed by two touchpoints, namely 'Book Event' and 'Receive Confirmation', which are supported by two respective provider processes. For instance, *Concierge's* 'IT and Booking' departments are the ones involved in the processing and validation of every booking transaction made by customers via the 'Book Event' touchpoint.

3.2   Second DISSECT Stage: Solicitation

The Solicitation stage of DISSECT involves soliciting the feedback of all the service stakeholders to articulate the right set of value benefits for the right customers using the value benefit template described in Sect. 2. This stage is concerned with *what* value benefits to offer and *why* these need to be provided according to three factors, namely: (1) customer needs, (2) value propositions, and (3) business capabilities.

Customer needs imply that value benefits must be connected to the latent needs and quality expectations of customers during each service encounter in the form of touchpoints and service stages. The articulation of value benefits based on customers' needs ensures that a service's "essential" offerings are covered. In addition, service providers must offer *value propositions* which contain *unique* value benefits aimed at the differentiation of a service from others. A service provider needs to ensure that it has the right *business capabilities* such as infrastructure, manpower, and expertise in order to support the provision

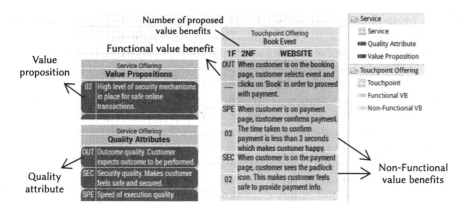

Fig. 3. The Value Articulation Model of the Solicitation stage

of value benefits through tasks performed by provider processes. Value benefits may need to be modified or removed if a service provider and its partners cannot guarantee their provision due to business constraints. For each articulated value benefit in a touchpoint, service employees need to confirm if all the tasks required to be performed by a provider process can reliably be provided based on the provider's business capabilities. If many value offerings are competing for the same set of business capabilities, service providers may have to prioritise their value offerings based on their current business capabilities that they have.

The Solicitation stage makes use of a *Value Articulation Model* whose model editor support is shown in Fig. 3 based on a continuation of the *Concierge* example. Using the Service Journey Map produced during the DIScovery stage, one functional and two non-functional value benefits have been identified for the 'Book Event' touchpoint. Each value benefit can be assigned a quality attribute and one or more value propositions. Some of the service quality attribute tags shown in Fig. 3 include 'OUT' for outcome, 'SPE' for speed of execution, and 'SEC' for security. The value proposition numbered '02' is thus assigned to the non-functional value benefit, 'When customer is on the payment page, customer sees the padlock...', which adheres to the security quality attribute.

3.3   Third DISSECT Stage: Evaluation

The Evaluation stage is aimed towards obtaining feedback from customers about their service experiences at the basic *value benefit level*. Later, the Capture stage will look at their experiences at the touchpoint and overall service levels. Each value benefit can be evaluated by customers according to three possible perception scenarios, namely: (1) fully perceived, (2) not or partially perceived ("lost"), and (3) perceived but not proposed ("extra").

A value benefit is termed as *fully perceived* when its enclosed customer benefit has been perceived or created by customers based on its service context and service action. A fully perceived value benefit for a service provider is a sign that both its business processes and service personnel are effective at providing that particular value benefit to customers. Thus, a service provider should ensure that all its proposed value benefits are being fully perceived by customers.

A value benefit that has *not or has only been partially perceived* by customers is referred to as "lost". This situation may arise from two possible cases. The first case, *not perceived,* involves customers not being able to perceive or create the benefit promised by the value benefit due'to *quantitative* or *qualitative discrepancies* assuming that the service context and service action are unchanged. Therefore, the actual benefit perceived is different than the one described in a value benefit. For example, a quantitative discrepancy may be due to customers perceiving webpage loading times of more than five seconds whereas a value benefit promises a period of less than three seconds. An example of a qualitative discrepancy may arise when customers perceive a 'Low' level of satisfaction from the outcome of a booking transaction instead of the 'High' satisfaction level originally proposed and advertised by the service provider.

The second case, *partially perceived,* occurs when the proposed benefit has been perceived in a different service context or using a service action that was not described in the value benefit. Any deviations which affect the predefined service context or service action need to be investigated as this implies that the provision of the benefit is no longer predictable.

The third value perception scenario relates to a value benefit that is *perceived by customers despite not being proposed* by a service provider and is called an "extra" value benefit. The latter is one that has had *a genuine impact on the service experience of customers and is articulated from their viewpoints*. The causes for an "extra" value benefit may be due to the following reasons, namely: (1) the service provider overlooked the actual value benefit and considered the latter to be not important in the eyes of the customer, (2) the value benefit is the unintentional outcome of the tasks performed within one or more provider processes, and (3) the value benefit has been *indirectly* and *unexpectedly* produced by one or more proposed value benefits.

The Evaluation stage makes use of a *Value Perception Model* whose model editor support is shown in Fig. 4 based on a continuation of the *Concierge* example. Using the Value Articulation Model produced during the Solicitation stage, the functional value benefit, 'When customer is on the. . . ', is marked as fully perceived as is the case with the non-functional value benefit 'When customer is on the payment page, customer sees the padlock. . . '. However, the other non-functional value benefit has been partially perceived with customers perceiving a time of more than five seconds (shown as the red dotted arrow) to confirm payment transactions as compared to the three seconds promised by *Concierge*. Thus, this value benefit is regarded as being "lost". Furthermore, there is an "extra" value benefit that was perceived by customers, namely 'When customer is on payment page, customer sees that payment info. . . '.

3.4   Fourth DISSECT Stage: Capture

The fourth DISSECT stage, *Capture*, aims to capture the service experience of customers by analysing their levels of satisfaction or *emotional attachments*

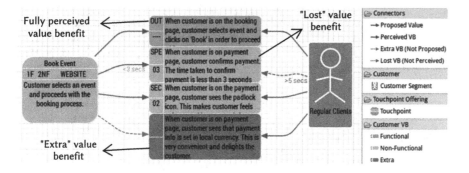

Fig. 4. The Value Perception Model of the Evaluation stage

towards the overall value perceived at both the touchpoint and service levels. To achieve this, two experience indices, known as Single Touchpoint Experience Index (STEI) and Cumulative Touchpoint Experience Index (CTEI), are measured.

The *single touchpoint experience index* measures customers' experiences or levels of satisfaction of the value perceived *from individual touchpoints.* If some customers have had bad service encounters through a particular touchpoint, then the latter may receive a poor STEI rating. Based on the feedback provided by customers during the Evaluation stage, all the "lost" value benefits that they have effectively not been able to perceive from a touchpoint can cause them to give this touchpoint a negative rating. On the other hand, touchpoints with few "lost" value benefits and additional "extra" ones can gain positive ratings from customers. A Value Perception Model can thus come in handy to investigate the root causes of poorly rated touchpoints.

The concept of a *cumulative touchpoint experience index* is different to that of a STEI. Instead of measuring customers' experiences of a single touchpoint, a cumulative touchpoint experience index captures customers' experiences of a touchpoint based on the *accumulated experiences of other touchpoints that are part of the service journey encountered so far.* Based on the CTEI ratings, poorly rated parts of a customer's service journey, which can consist of a collection of consecutive touchpoints, can be clearly identified. The CTEI is based on the notion that while each touchpoint should provide maximum satisfaction to customers, the focus of attention should be on the customer's end-to-end journey by taking into account the experiences of one or more touchpoints together. A cumulative touchpoint experience index can help in the identification of provider processes which need to be optimised or improved since the latter are responsible for supporting customer interactions across touchpoints.

The Capture stage makes use of an *Experience Journey Map* whose model editor support is shown in Fig. 5 based on a continuation of *Concierge.* An Experience Journey Map contains three experience bands for representing possible 'BAD', 'GOOD', and 'GREAT' service experiences. Using the feedback obtained during the previous DISSECT stages, the 'Visit Website' touchpoint was awarded

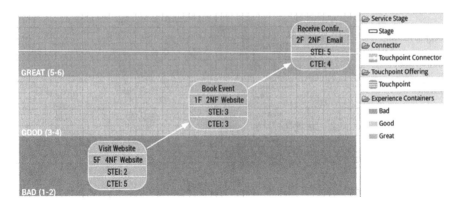

Fig. 5. The Experience Journey Map of the Capture stage

a STEI rating of two while its CTEI rating is five. This indicates that customers did not like the experience proposed by the 'Visit Website' touchpoint – possibly due to problems they faced while browsing *Concierge's* website. On the other hand, a CTEI rating of five might be due to customers' great experiences hearing about *Concierge*, for instance, from friends prior to visiting the website. Due in part to the bad experience perceived from the 'Visit Website' touchpoint, customers awarded the next touchpoint with a lower CTEI rating of three which indicates how customers' cumulative experiences *may change* over time along a service journey. For instance, the last touchpoint, 'Receive Confirmation', illustrates how customers' CTEI rating was upgraded as they perceived a better cumulative touchpoint experience from both 'Book Event' and 'Receive Confirmation'.

3.5   Fifth DISSECT Stage: Translation

The *Translation* stage targets the improvement of a service at three interaction levels, namely: the (1) value benefit, (2) touchpoint, and (3) overall service. Each improvement objective consists in analysing responses gathered from customers during the Evaluation and Capture stages and translating them into improvement opportunities with the renewed participation of customers. The identification of these improvement opportunities is important so as to help service developers align customer needs with service offerings during the next executions of the DIScovery and Solicitation stages for developing the next version of the service.

Value Benefit Improvement Objective. The *value benefit improvement* objective consists in identifying opportunities for proposing improved value benefits in the next version of a service. Three such improvement opportunities have been identified and termed as follows:

- Value Benefit *Addition*: refers to an "extra" value benefit that customers would like to be officially proposed.
- Value Benefit *Modification*: refers to an existing value benefit which has one or more of its components, including the service context or service action or customer benefit, modified.
- Value Benefit *Removal*: refers to an existing value benefit that customers would like to be removed and *not* officially proposed anymore.

Additionally, there is a *fourth* value benefit improvement opportunity which consists in basically taking no action on a value benefit. This implies that the latter can be considered to be proposed again in its current form in the next version of the service. Each type of value benefit discussed in Subsect. 3.3 can be improved based on the above improvement opportunities.

A *fully perceived value benefit* can be improved according to three improvement opportunities: value benefit modification, value benefit removal, and taking no action on it. The *modification* of a fully perceived value benefit occurs when customers are not fully satisfied with one or more components of the value benefit and would like to bring changes to them. For example, the service context component may not accurately capture the state in which customers perceive the benefits. Another reason can be due to an issue faced with the service action component that does not describe the right set of operations involved. Lastly, customers may wish that the benefit perceived is different to the current one. The *removal* of a fully perceived value benefit is due to customers finding it unnecessary to be offered because of its limited significance to their service experiences. This statement implies that the removal of such a value benefit should not have an impact on touchpoints' STEI and CTEI ratings. The fourth and last improvement opportunity for a fully perceived value benefit is concerned with leaving it as it is without any modification. If customers do not require any modifications or removal operations to be made on the value benefit, then the latter is a good candidate to be offered again in the next version of the service.

A *not or partially perceived ("lost")* value benefit presents itself as a warning sign for which the service provider should provide remedial actions. Two improvement opportunities are possible, namely value benefit modification and value benefit removal. The *modification* of a not or partially perceived value benefit is performed because customers have not fully perceived it. Consequently, customers have to point out the changes to be made either to the service or to the description of the value benefit such that they would then be able to fully perceive it. The *removal* of a not or partially perceived value benefit follows the same principle adopted for a fully perceived value benefit as discussed before.

A *perceived but not proposed ("extra")* value benefit is one that has had a genuine impact on customers' service experiences and can become a potential source of innovation for the service provider. To leverage the beneficial aspects of an "extra" value benefit, two improvement opportunities have been identified: value benefit addition and value benefit modification. The *addition* of an "extra" value benefit signifies that customers are satisfied with the benefit perceived and want the value benefit to be officially recognised and proposed. From a service provider's perspective, the addition of an "extra" value benefit involves treating it as an officially proposed value benefit and thus making sure that business resources are properly allocated to ensure the value benefit can be offered. The *modification* of an "extra" value benefit follows the same logic used for a fully perceived value benefit since, by definition, an "extra" value benefit can be regarded as a value benefit that is fully perceived by customers. Thus, an "extra" value benefit is modified because customers are not fully satisfied with one or more of its components. After the "extra" value benefit has been modified, it can be added to the list of officially proposed value benefits.

Touchpoint Improvement Objective. The touchpoint improvement objective involves having an overview of the value perceived from each touchpoint and identifying touchpoint modification opportunities in terms of making *additional changes* to value benefits. Based on customers' assistance, service developers must investigate opportunities to upgrade the STEI rating of each touchpoint as depicted in the Experience Journey Map produced during the Capture stage. For example, if a touchpoint is given a STEI rating of two, customers must be asked about the changes that could be implemented on the touchpoint's value offerings in order for them to award a better experience rating of 'GOOD' and 'GREAT'. Apart from the addition, modification, and removal of value benefits, some customers can also propose to articulate *new value benefits* which they would like to perceive or create during their service experiences. These new value benefits can serve to fulfil *missing* customer needs that can improve customers' satisfaction of touchpoints present in a Service Journey Map.

Service Improvement Objective. The third improvement objective of the Translation stage takes place at the overall service interaction level and focuses on the improvement of customers' service experiences across touchpoints for the entire service journey or parts of it. Based on the CTEI ratings of touchpoints in the Experience Journey Map created during the Capture stage, customers can express their concerns about gaps or problems they have encountered with the service delivery or with the proposed value benefits. Using a similar approach as that adopted for the touchpoint improvement objective, service developers must investigate opportunities to upgrade each touchpoint's CTEI rating along a service journey or parts of it with the help of customers. These service improvement opportunities consist in the creation of new touchpoints as well as the modification and removal of existing ones.

The *creation of new touchpoints* can be attributed to customers willing to have additional service encounters that better connect touchpoints together and enhance their end-to-end service experiences. A Service Journey Map can be used to redesign the service journey based on customers' inputs. The *modification of existing touchpoints* is concerned with the identification of additional touchpoint modification opportunities, based on the articulation, addition, modification, and removal of value benefits, which were previously not identified during the previous value benefit and touchpoint improvement tasks. The *removal*

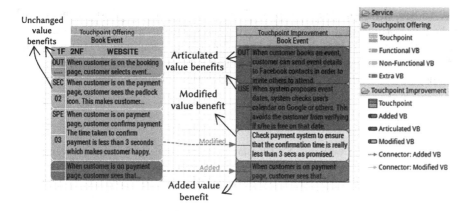

Fig. 6. The Value Improvement Model of the Translation stage

of existing touchpoints can occur if customers feel that one or more touchpoints are not necessary and can thus be safely removed without impacting the STEI and CTEI ratings of other touchpoints.

The Translation stage makes use of a *Value Improvement Model* whose model editor support is shown in Fig. 6 based on a continuation of the *Concierge* example. The four value benefits which were evaluated during the Evaluation stage are now shown in a 'Touchpoint Offering'. No action will be taken on the first two value benefits since they are left unchanged – probably due to customers having fully perceived them and having not identified ways to further improve them. The third value benefit, 'When customer is on payment page, customer confirms payment...', however, was not fully perceived by customers. Thus, this "lost" value benefit needs to be *modified* (e.g., by identifying the cause(s) of the non-perceived benefit) for customers to perceive the promised payment confirmation time of less than three seconds.

The "extra" value benefit now becomes an 'added' value benefit in 'Touchpoint Improvement' indicating that customers would like this value benefit to be officially proposed in the next version of *Concierge*. In addition to the 'modified' and 'added' value benefits, two new value benefits have been articulated for the 'Book Event' touchpoint. These new 'articulated' value benefits can contribute to the outcome and usability quality of *Concierge*.

4 Conclusion

This paper has presented a value development framework that can contribute to creating service innovation opportunities during service development. This framework relies on a practical approach that comprehensively examines how to create innovative service offerings by taking into account key service factors affecting both businesses and customers. Current research is being carried out to validate the five-stage process of the DISSECT approach based on real-world case studies, involving the European CITI-SENSE project [4] and others, with the help of both academic and industry partners. Furthermore, the integration of ServiceMIF with OMG's Value Delivery Modelling Language [1] for modelling both customer value and a service provider's business-focused value, such as revenue, market share, and employee satisfaction, is being envisaged.

References

1. Berre, A.J., Lew Yaw Fung, Y., Elvesæter, B., de Man, H.: Service innovation and service realisation with VDML and ServiceML. In: 2013 17th IEEE International Enterprise Distributed Object Computing Conference Workshops (EDOCW), pp. 104–113 (2013)
2. Bettencourt, L.A.: Service Innovation: How to Go from Customer Needs to Breakthrough Services. McGraw-Hill, New York (2010)
3. Carlborg, P., Kindström, D., Kowalkowski, C.: The evolution of service innovation research: a critical review and synthesis. Serv. Ind. J. **34**(5), 373–398 (2013)
4. CITI-SENSE: Development of sensor-based citizens' observatory community for improving quality of life in cities. http://www.citi-sense.eu
5. Droege, H., Hildebrand, D., Forcada, M.A.H.: Innovation in services: present findings, and future pathways. J. Serv. Manage. **20**(2), 131–155 (2009)
6. Eclipse: Eclipse graphiti framework - a graphical tooling infrastructure. http://www.eclipse.org/graphiti
7. Hoffman, K., Bateson, J.: Services marketing: concepts, strategies, and cases. Cengage Learning, Mason (2010)
8. Miles, I.: Service innovation. In: Maglio, P.P., Kieliszewski, C.A., Spohrer, J.C. (eds.) Handbook of Service Science. Service Science: Research and Innovations in the Service Economy, pp. 511–533. Springer, London (2010)
9. Posselt, T., Förstl, K.: Success factors in new service development: a literature review. Productivity of Services Next Gen-Beyond Output/Input. Fraunhofer Center for Applied Research and Supply Chain Service, Germany (2011)
10. Stickdorn, M., Schneider, J.: This is Service Design Thinking: Basics, Tools, Cases. Wiley, Chichester (2011)
11. Woodruff, R.B.: Customer value: the next source for competitive advantage. J. Acad. Mark. Sci. **25**(2), 139–153 (1997)

Designing Software Ecosystems: How to Develop Sustainable Collaborations?

Scenarios from Apple iOS and Google Android

Mahsa H. Sadi[1(✉)], Jiaying Dai[2], and Eric Yu[1,2]

[1] Department of Computer Science, University of Toronto, Toronto, Canada
{mhsadi, eric}@cs.toronto.edu
[2] Faculty of Information, University of Toronto, Toronto, Canada

Abstract. It has become an increasingly common practice that software companies collaborate with external developers to develop a software platform for a shared market, constituting software ecosystems. One main concern in adopting the practice of software ecosystem is how to attract external developers to a platform, and how to establish sustainable collaborative relationships with them. We discuss that explicating and in-depth analysis of developers' objectives and decision criteria can facilitate the design of sustainable collaborations in software ecosystems. Scenarios from Apple iOS and Google Android ecosystems are used for illustration.

Keywords: Software ecosystems · Analysis · Google Android · Apple iOS · Mobile operating system ecosystem · Design · Modeling · Decision making

1 Introduction

It has become an increasingly common practice for software development companies to collaborate with external developers in order to develop a software platform for a shared market, founding software ecosystems [1, 2]. In a software ecosystem, a key software platform developer (referred to as the keystone) engages external developers in the promotion of its software platform in various ways such as developing or extending the platform, or providing complementary applications and services for the platform [3].

Various forces lead to the adoption of software ecosystem practice among software companies, including sharing the cost of production, dealing with the diverse and numerous demands of end users, using the domain expertise of external stakeholders to develop domain-specific applications, co-innovating, and fighting against competitors. Moreover, the success of software platforms heavily depends on the number of supporting applications and services [4, 5]. To benefit from the above advantages, it is crucial for a keystone software company to expand its collaboration network in software development and service provision, and to attract and retain as many external developers and collaborators as possible.

© Springer International Publishing Switzerland 2015
A. Persson and J. Stirna (Eds.): CAiSE 2015 Workshops, LNBIP 215, pp. 161–173, 2015.
DOI: 10.1007/978-3-319-19243-7_17

The pivotal role that collaboration plays in the success of modern-day software development and provision demands concentrated effort to support the elaborate design and configuration of healthy and sustainable relationships in software ecosystems. Establishing collaborative relationships is a multifaceted problem for a keystone platform developer, spanning various technical, business, organizational, and social concerns that must be addressed simultaneously. A successful software ecosystem needs to have a viable business model, a well-organized inter-organizational interaction model, a well-designed collaborative software development process, and a software platform that enables the collaboration [3, 6–8].

However, despite the widespread adoption of the Software Ecosystem practice among software companies, there is still no rigorous systematic approach for establishing sustainable collaborative relationships in a software ecosystem. Current approaches (e.g. [3, 9]) mostly propose several general rules of thumb to develop software ecosystems. It has been neglected that each software platform and keystone software company has a specific set of characteristics which attracts external developers, and with each software ecosystem specific groups of developers collaborate pursuing a diverse set of business, social, and technical objectives [10]. Moreover, little attention has been given to the systematic structuring and design of collaborations in software ecosystems.

To address the above issue, in this paper, we take two steps:

1. We discuss that in order to create a healthy and sustainable software ecosystem, a keystone platform developer needs to elicit and analyze the objectives and decision criteria of both its organization and external developers for participation.
2. Using real-world scenarios from the smartphone software ecosystem (extracted from [10]), we illustrate how to use the objectives and decision criteria of the collaborators in configuring a sustainable software ecosystem. To model and analyze the objectives of collaborators, we use the i* goal-oriented social modeling technique [11].

2   Motivating Scenario: The Smartphone Software Ecosystem

To make our discussion concrete, we use common scenarios from the smartphone software ecosystem. The scenarios are extracted from a recent study [10] investigating what motivates application developers to join mobile software ecosystems such as Apple iOS and Google Android.

Scenario. In the smartphone software ecosystem, the key platform is mobile operating system, mainly developed by keystone software companies such as Google, Apple, or Microsoft. Complementary software applications and services play a crucial role in the success of a mobile operating system in the market. Hence, it is essential for mobile platform developers to establish a large network of external collaborators. External collaborators are mostly engaged in the development of complementary application and software services for the operating system. For this purpose, the keystone software companies usually provide a software development toolkit (SDK) for the platform.

This toolkit provides necessary infrastructure for the external developers to develop software applications [10].

Question. One main concern for a keystone mobile platform developer is "How to attract and retain a large network of application developers?" or "How to establish sustainable collaborative relationships with application developers?"

3   The Proposed Method

Generic Approach. Intuitively, to answer the above question, the mobile platform developer needs to do the following:

1. *Identify different types of application developers that collaborate with the mobile platform developer, and categorize them according to their behavior by understanding their motivations, expectations, and criteria for deciding to join an ecosystem.* Application developers may contribute to a mobile platform for various reasons. These objectives can be technical (i.e. related to the features and quality attributes of the software platform) or non-technical (related to personal, social, or business motivations). For example, some developers join a software ecosystem based on their business motives of selling applications to the end-users of the mobile platform to achieve financial gain, while others join to improve their programming or technical skills. Knowing these expectations and objectives enables the mobile platform developer to seek for alternatives to fulfill them. Moreover, obtaining information about the objectives of application developers and analyzing these objectives avoids premature commitment to some rules of thumb for attracting external developers in a software ecosystem. Clarifying the objectives and decision criteria of developers can be used as a source of information to derive the specific requirements that adequately fulfills the expectations of each group of application developers.

2. *Explicate and analyze the technical and non-technical requirements for designing a sustainable collaboration.* Having gained overall insight into the main groups of external collaborators and their motivations and expectations, the next step will be to refine and analyze the obtained information about each group of application developers as a source for deriving the requirements of an appropriate collaborative environment.

3. *Derive alternative solutions for designing an appropriate collaborative environment that fulfills the elicited requirements.* After identifying the specific requirements of the software ecosystem, the final step is to decide what courses of action should be taken to design or improve the configuration of the collaborations among the keystone software company and the application developers.

Modeling and Analysis Guidelines. Although the above steps outline the main activities that address the mobile platform developer's concerns, they do not provide specific guidance on how these activities can be performed. To perform the above steps, we adopt a model-based approach. We develop a set of guidelines for how to model and analyze application developers' objectives and criteria in order to establish sustainable collaborative relationships with them. The following steps identify what should be modeled and what analyses are needed to be performed on the models.

1. *Explicate and model the objectives and decision criteria of the developers who contribute to the software platform.* In this model, the developers, the activities and tasks that these developers perform in the software ecosystem, the factors that influence their decision for choosing a specific platform, and their relationships with the keystone software company should be identified and explicated. This information can be obtained through various ways such as surveying (as used in [10]) or interviewing application developers.

2. *Clarify and refine the objectives and decision criteria to the extent that they can be translated into design requirements for a software ecosystem.* To find concrete design solutions, the objectives and decision criteria of developers need to be refined to the extent that they can be translated into alternative design solutions.

3. *Investigate the degree of the fulfillment of the objectives and decision criteria.* From developers' perspective, their expectations and objectives may be fulfilled to various degrees in a software ecosystem. Therefore, it is required to identify and evaluate the fulfillment of the objectives and decision criteria through gathering data about the perception of the developers from the software ecosystem.

4. *Identify the importance of the objectives and decision criteria and prioritize them.* Having gained insight into the requirements of the software ecosystem, the next step is to identify the importance of these requirements and prioritize them in the software ecosystem. The elicited requirements in previous step may be of different degree of importance and influence both from the perspective of keystone platform developer and the external software developers. Therefore, before coming up with alternative design solutions, the priority and influence of the requirements should be explicated. This type of information can be elicited through various sources or approaches such as interviewing application developers.

4   Analyzing and Designing the Smartphone Software Ecosystem

Now, we return to the motivating scenario. We aim to help a mobile platform developer to come up with alternative solutions for structuring sustainable collaborative relationships with application developers, following the proposed method.

In the following, we first explain how to model collaborators' objectives and decision criteria using the i* goal-oriented social modeling technique [11] (Sect. 4.1). Then, we apply the proposed method in Sect. 3 to analyze the objectives and decision criteria of collaborators in the smartphone software ecosystem in order to find out appropriate solutions for developing collaborative relationships. Since we need information about the objectives and decisions of collaborators, in Sects. 4.1 and 4.2, we use available scenarios from the Apple iOS and Google Android ecosystems.

4.1   Guidelines for Model Construction Using the i* Technique

In Fig. 1, based on the content of the scenario described in Sect. 2, we have developed a generic model of collaboration between mobile platform developer and application developer in the smartphone software ecosystem. Figure 1 explicates two main collaborators in the mobile operating system ecosystem, the activities and operations of each collaborator, the objectives and motivations of the collaborators, and the dependencies between them. In the following, we explain how this model is developed from the content of scenario:

(a) Collaborators (modeled as "Roles" or "Actors"): In Fig. 1, "Mobile Platform Developer" and "Application Developer" are modeled as Roles. Each role can be occupied by specific mobile platform developers such as Google and Apple or the specific application developers who collaborate with each of these two companies.

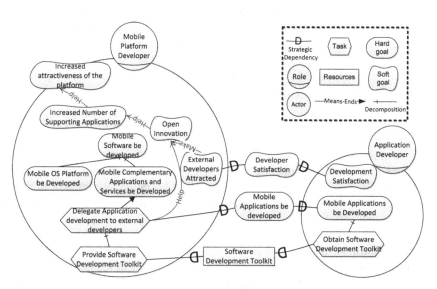

Fig. 1. Generic model of collaboration between keystone software company and software application developers in mobile operating system ecosystem

(b) Operations and Activities (modeled as "Goals" and "Tasks"): The main operation of "Mobile Platform Developer" is to develop the mobile software (expressed in the goal of "Mobile Software be Developed"). Modeling this operation as goal means that it can be achieved via various alternative activities and tasks. Developing mobile software include two finer-grained activities of developing mobile operating system platform and developing complementary applications and services. In the mobile software ecosystem, the common strategy is to delegate the development of complementary applications to external developers. This approach is demonstrated through "Means-Ends" relationship between the hard goal of "Mobile Complementary

Applications and Services be Developed" and the task of "Delegate Application Development to External Developers". On the other side, the main activity of "Application Developer" is to develop complementary mobile applications, which requires to obtain the software development kit for the platform. These activities are depicted in the decomposition relationship between "Mobile Application be Developed" goal and "Obtain software development kit".

(c) Objectives and Decision Criteria of Collaborators (modeled as soft-goals): Capturing motivations and initiatives in soft goals conveys that there is no clear-cut criteria for assessing whether these objectives have been achieved or not. In the mobile software ecosystem, collaborators pursue specific objectives for collaboration. The main objective of "Mobile Platform Developer" is to increase the attractiveness of the platform. To achieve this objective, "Mobile platform developer" pursues open innovation initiatives, explicated as "Open Innovation" soft goal. For Open initiatives to be successful, external developers should be attracted to the mobile platform. This relationship is shown as "Make" relationship between "Open Innovation" and "External Developers Attracted" soft goals. On the other side, application developers would continue to collaborate with the keystone software company if their expectations are satisfied. Although feeling satisfied means differently among various developers, it can be considered as a common objective among all the application developers. This objective is captured in terms of "Development Satisfaction" soft goal in "Application Developer" role.

(d) Reasoning behind the adoption of specific approaches and tasks by each collaborator: In mobile software ecosystem, collaborators adopt specific activities for specific reasons. For example, the reason for delegating development of complementary applications to external developers is that it helps the open innovation initiative which in turn helps promote the attractiveness of mobile operating system as a high-level business objective. These relationships are shown as "Help" relationship between the related tasks and soft goals.

(e) The relationships among collaborators (modeled as "strategic dependencies"): Delegating the development of complementary applications to application developers creates specific relationships between the collaborators: "Mobile Platform Developer" depends on the "Application Developer" for the goal of "Complementary applications be developed" to be achieved. On the other side, "Mobile Platform Developer" depends on "Application Developer" for his/her satisfaction from development.

As Fig. 1 illustrates, for the mobile operating ecosystem to be successful, a "Mobile Platform Developer" needs to fulfill "Development satisfaction" in the "Application Developer". Hence, the mobile platform developer needs to know the different groups of application developers who collaborate with it, understand why they collaborate, and create an environment that motivates them to collaborate.

To explicate and analyze developers' objectives and motivations, in the following, we build upon scenarios from the mobile platform developer of Apple iOS and Google Android the application developers who develop applications for these two platforms.

4.2 The Apple iOS Software Ecosystem

Scenario. *Mobile Platform Developer:* iOS is the Apple operating system for mobile phones and tablets, having been developed since 2007. iOS is exclusively used for smartphones and tablets produced by Apple, its license is proprietary and its source code is not publicly available. To develop applications for iOS, external developers must register in the fee-based "iOS Developers Program", which enables them to download iOS SDK. Third-party applications are extensively reviewed by Apple to check their compliance with the guidelines set in the iPhone SDK agreement, before becoming visible to the end users via App Store. Apple charges developers for 30 % share of the application sale, but no fee is received for free applications [10].

Application Developers: According to the study [10], Apple third-party developers are mainly driven by financial gains. Intellectual stimulation is also an important factor for the developers who join Apple iOS ecosystem. These developers often prefer to charge fee for their application being used by Apple iPhone/iPad end users. The main characteristics of the iOS platform that motivate this group to join Apple iOS ecosystem are as follows: (a) Large network size of the platform (composed of the number of users, the market size, and the number of applications), and (b) the tight integration of the platform. A tightly integrated platform makes the complementary application development process easier for developers with strong motivations in financial gains by optimizing development efforts and facilitating the targeting of the applications.

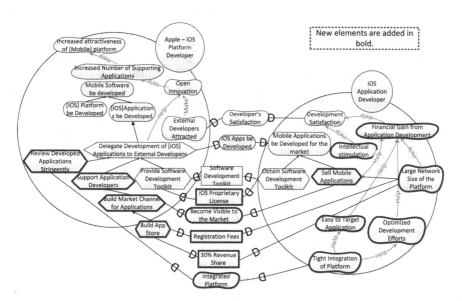

Fig. 2. Collaboration model between keystone software company and software application developers in Apple iOS software ecosystem

Applying the Method. *(1) Explicating the objectives of the developers.* As conveyed in the scenario, one major group of developers who contribute to iOS platform are driven by business and financial motivations. In the scenario, "Financial gain from application development" and "Intellectual stimulation" hint to the main motivations of iOS developers (explicated as two soft goals contributing to "Development Satisfaction" soft goal in Fig. 2). Efforts to improve the satisfaction of these social and business soft goals would help enhance development satisfactions of iOS developers'. Moreover, "Tight integration of software platform" soft goal elicits one technical characteristic of iOS platform which is of importance to external developers. A tightly integrated platform contribute to "Optimized development effort" and "Easy to target application" decision criteria of iOS developers. Therefore, finding solutions to improve the integration of the software platform would also increase the development satisfaction of iOS third-party developers.

(2) Deriving design requirements. (a) Clarifying developers' objectives. "Financial gain from application development", "Intellectual Stimulation", and "Tight Integration of Software Platform" hint to some requirements of Apple iOS software ecosystem. However, to reach to specific design solutions, these requirements need to be further refined and elaborated. For this purpose, questions such as the following should be answered: *"What factors influence or increase intellectual stimulation in Apple application developers?"*, or *"To what factors tight integration of platform refer to?"* Elaborating on these questions requires information which are not provided in the above scenario. Therefore, more information needs to be gathered about Apple iOS software ecosystem to elaborate the requirements. *(b) Investigating the fulfillment of the elicited requirements.* The objectives and decision criteria of the iOS developers may be fulfilled to various extent. For example, it is possible that "Tight integration of platform" is fulfilled to a good extent, but "Being intellectually stimulated" could be not satisfactory enough. Therefore, before focusing the design attempts, it is required to gather information about the fulfillment of the elicited requirements. (c) *Prioritize the requirements:* We assume that from among the two non-technical requirements of "Intellectual Stimulation" and "Financial gain from application development", the latter is probably more important for Apple application developers. Hence, it will be more effective to focus the design efforts to improve the satisfaction of this non-technical requirement among iOS developers.

(3) Concluding the requirements and reaching to design solutions: Since Apple iOS developers are mainly motivated by financial gain, "Sell Mobile Applications" is one activity that these developers perform in the software ecosystem. For performing this task, developers become dependent on iOS platform developer, for the goal of "Applications become visible to the market place" (see Fig. 2). Explicating these requirements enables the Apple iOS platform developer to find out appropriate solutions to support the application developers. One solution for supporting external developers is to "Build market channels for applications" which is currently realized by the development of App Store.

Conclusions from Modeling and Analysis. As identified in the above study, financial gain is one main requirement to sustain a collaborative relationship between iOS application developers and Apple. Therefore, building a market channel for software applications is one appropriate solution to support iOS external developers. We illustrated that this solution can be concluded by elaborate analysis and investigation of the case of third-party developers who collaborate with iOS.

However, depending on the specific situation of a software ecosystem, solutions for supporting external developers differ. To demonstrate this difference, in the next section, we walk through scenarios from Google Android Software Ecosystem.

4.3   Google Android Software Ecosystem

Scenario. *Mobile Platform Developer:* Android OS is developed by Open Handset Alliance − an alliance of 84 companies specialized in software, hardware, and telecommunication led by Google, since 2008 − as an open-source project based on Linux kernel. The open-source strategy aids to increase the adoption of Android OS platform among various mobile device manufactures. A set of software development tool kits are available for Android. External developers can download many of these SDK's for free and without registration. The developed applications undergo a short checking process by Google Employees and are then made available to the market (via Google Play Store). Developers are charged for a non-recurring registration fee to access Google Play. However, there are also other Android app stores besides Google Play store, some of which do not charge developers with fees. The ease of use and high accessibility of free Android SDKs enables Google to attract a wide and diverse range of application developers. Similar to Apple, Google charges the application developers for 30 % of unit sales, but do not charge fees for free applications [10].

Application Developers: According to the study [10], low entry barriers (including low monetary and low technical requirements) and platform openness are the major characteristics of Google Android platform that motivates external developers to join this ecosystem. Low monetary barrier refers to the point that Android SDK is free to download. Low technical barrier refers to the point that Android OS is open-source, various SDKs are available for Android, and there is no specific technical requirements or restrictions for using Android SDKs. As a result, one major group of Android application developers are motivated by intrinsic reasons such as improving their programming skills, and having fun during development. Other social reasons, such as gaining reputation in the Android community also motivates this group of developers to choose Google Android ecosystem. Moreover, the majority of Android application developers publish their application for free on Google Play Store.

Applying the Method. *(1) Explicating the motivations of developers*. As described in the scenario, one major group who contribute to Google Android platform are driven by intrinsic and social motivations, and they mostly develop Android applications for free. In the scenario, "Experiencing fun during software development", gaining "Reputation" among Android developers and end users, and "Low entry barriers" refer to the factors motivating Android application developers.

(2) Deriving design requirements. (a) Clarifying developers' objectives. The above explicated objectives need to be further clarified and elaborated to derive the design requirements in Android ecosystem. Similar to the analysis of Apple iOS, questions such as "*What factors influence or increase the experience of fun in Android developers*", or "*To what factors Low entry barriers refer to?*" should be answered. As described in the scenario, "Low entry barriers" consists of sub factors of "Low technical barriers" and "Low monetary barriers". One factor which contributes to "Low technical barrier" in Android is "Platform Openness". The refinement of the developers' objectives is explicated in decomposing soft goals via "Help" links in Fig. 3. (b) *Prioritize the requirements:* From among the explicated requirements, we assume that "Reputation" is more critical than the others. Consequently, attempts to improve the feeling of being recognized in Android developers would contribute to the sustainability of Android software ecosystem.

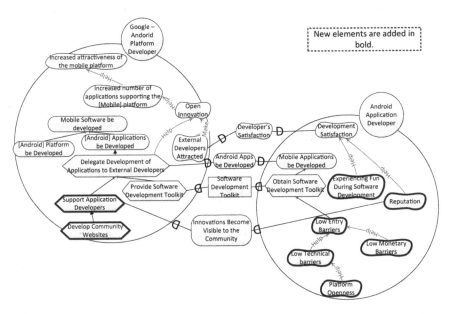

Fig. 3. Collaboration model between Keystone software company and software application developers in Google Android software ecosystem

(3) Concluding the requirements and reaching to design solutions: As reasoned about, to sustain collaborative relationships with Android developers, improving the sense of being recognized in the users and developers community ("Reputation" soft goal) is one main requirement. For the "Reputation" soft goal to be satisfied, Android Developers are dependent on Android platform developer" for the goal of "Innovations become visible to the community". Android platform developer should find out

appropriate solutions to support the application developers. One solution for supporting external developers could be to "Develop Community Websites" to publicize the information about the innovations to the end user and developer community [10].

Conclusions from Modeling and Analysis. As identified above, in contrary to Apple iOS, Android application developers choose the open-source platform to cultivate their intrinsic motivations such as skills development and reputation enhancement. Assuming the reputation enhancement as the main requirement for designing sustainable collaborative relationships with Android developers, it was concluded that different approaches should be adopted to support Android developers, such as developing community websites to publicize developers' innovations.

5 Related Research

In this study, building upon our previous attempts [8, 12], we explained how to systematically explicate and analyze the objectives of the members in order to design sustainable and healthy collaborative relationships in software ecosystems. To the best of our knowledge, no similar approach has been proposed in the literature related to software ecosystems. However, there are two main groups of research efforts that are closely related to this study:

Analysis and Design of Software Ecosystems in General. Analyzing and designing software ecosystems is a recent and multi-faceted issue. To reduce the complexity of the problems raised in the design of software ecosystems, existing efforts mostly advise to separate business, organizational, social, and technical concerns, and address each of these concerns independently (e.g. [13]). While few efforts (e.g. [13, 14]) analyze a set of these aspects simultaneously but separately, the majority of existing research efforts merely focus on one dimension (e.g. [15] focusing on the technical dimension). Very little attention has been given to *(a)* analyzing the interrelationships between technical, business, social and organizational factors in the design of software ecosystems; and *(b)* aligning these dimensions with each other. Herein, we illustrated how to model and analyze the interrelationships among various socio-technical factors in the design of software ecosystems.

Designing Collaborative Relationships in Software Ecosystems in Particular. One specific issue in the design of software ecosystems is structuring collaborative relationships with external stakeholders (i.e. other software companies and individual application developers). Only a few systematic approaches and techniques have been proposed to address this issue (e.g. [14, 16, 17]). However, these efforts mainly focus on the business and inter-organizational relationships between the members of a software ecosystem. There are also few studies, (e.g. [18]) that focus on designing technical collaborations among the members. In this study, we illustrated how to model and analyze the overall perception of the collaborators from the socio-technical environment of a software ecosystem to identify appropriate solutions for developing sustainable collaborations.

6   Conclusions

One main step in transition into a software ecosystem approach is to attract external software developers to a software platform, and to establish sustainable collaborative relationships with them. Using scenarios from Apple iOS and Google Android software ecosystems, we illustrated how modeling and analyzing developers' objectives help find appropriate solutions for designing sustainable collaborative relationships with external developers.

Limitations of this study. (1) This study is performed by post-mortem modeling and analysis of available scenarios on existing software ecosystems. To demonstrate the viability of the developed modeling and analysis guidelines, experimentation in the context of real case studies is required. (2) The developed guidelines outline some analyses that are needed to be performed on collaborators' objectives and decision criteria. These prototype analyses need to be elaborated with specific techniques for eliciting, evaluating, and prioritizing collaborators' objectives and decision criteria.

Acknowledgements. Financial support from the Natural Sciences and Engineering Research Council of Canada (NSERC) and the Ontario Research Foundation (ORF) are gratefully acknowledged.

References

1. Jansen, S., Finkelstein, A., Brinkkemper, S.: A sense of community: a research agenda for software ecosystems. In: 31st International Conference on Software Engineering-Companion Volume, ICSE-Companion 2009, pp. 187–190 (2009)
2. Bosch, J.: From software product lines to software ecosystems. In: Proceedings of the 13th International Software Product Line Conference, Carnegie Mellon University, pp. 111–119 (2009)
3. Jansen, S., Brinkkemper, S., Souer, J., Luinenburg, L.: Shades of gray: opening up a software producing organization with the open software enterprise model. J. Syst. Softw. **85** (7), 1495–1510 (2012)
4. Iansiti, M., Levien, R.: Strategy as ecology. Harv. Bus. Rev. **82**(3), 68–81 (2004)
5. Bosch, J.: Software ecosystems: taking software development beyond the boundaries of the organization. J. Syst. Softw. **85**(7), 1453–1454 (2012)
6. Jarke, M., Loucopoulos, P., Lyytinen, K., Mylopoulos, J., Robinson, W.: The brave new world of design requirements. Inf. Syst. **36**(7), 992–1008 (2011)
7. Sadi, M. H., Yu, E.: Designing software ecosystems: how can modeling techniques help? In: Proceedings of 20th Conference on Exploring Modelling Methods for Systems Analysis and Design (EMMSAD), LNBIP **214**, pp. 360–375 (2015). doi:10.1007/978-3-319-19237-6_23
8. Sadi, M. H., Yu, E.: Analyzing the evolution of software development: from creative chaos to software ecosystems. In: IEEE 8th International Conference on Research Challenges in Information Science (RCIS), pp. 1–11. IEEE (2014)
9. Popp, K., Meyer, R.: Profit from Software Ecosystems: Business Models Ecosystems and Partnerships in the Software Industry. BoD–Books on Demand, Norderstedt (2010)
10. Koch, S., Kerschbaum, M.: Joining a smartphone ecosystem: application developers' motivations and decision criteria. Inf. Softw. Technol. **56**(11), 1423–1435 (2014)

11. Yu, E., Giorgini, P., Maiden, N. (eds.): Social Modeling for Requirements Engineering. MIT Press, Cambridge (2011)
12. Yu, E., Deng, S.: Understanding software ecosystems: a strategic modeling approach. In: Proceedings of 3rd IWSECO, pp. 65–76 (2011)
13. Christensen, H.B., Hansen, K.M., Kyng, M., Manikas, K.: Analysis and design of software ecosystem architectures–towards the 4S telemedicine ecosystem. Inf. Softw. Technol. **56** (11), 1476–1492 (2014)
14. Boucharas, V., Jansen, S., and Brinkkemper, S.: Formalizing software ecosystem modeling. In: Proceedings of the 1st International Workshop on Open Component Ecosystems (2009)
15. Cataldo, M., Herbsleb, J.D.: Architecting in software ecosystems: interface translucence as an enabler for scalable collaboration. In: Proceedings of the Fourth European Conference on Software Architecture: Companion Volume, pp. 65–72. ACM (2010)
16. Baars, A., Jansen, S.: A framework for software ecosystem governance. In: Cusumano, M. A., Iyer, B., Venkatraman, N. (eds.) ICSOB 2012. LNBIP, vol. 114, pp. 168–180. Springer, Heidelberg (2012)
17. Van Angeren, J., Kabbedijk, J., Jansen, S., Popp, K. M.: A Survey of associate models used within large software ecosystems. In: IWSECO@ ICSOB, pp. 27-39 (2011)
18. Pettersson, O., Svensson, M., Gil, D., Andersson, J., Milrad, M.: On the role of software process modeling in software ecosystem design. In: Proceedings of the Fourth European Conference on Software Architecture: Companion Volume, pp. 103–110. ACM (2010)

Fitness of Business Models for Digital Collaborative Platforms in Clusters: A Case Study

Luca Cremona[1(✉)], Aurelio Ravarini[2], and Gianluigi Viscusi[3]

[1] SmartUp and Lab#ID, Università Carlo Cattaneo – LIUC,
Castellanza, VA, Italy
lcremona@liuc.it
[2] CETIC, Università Carlo Cattaneo – LIUC, Castellanza, VA, Italy
aravarini@liuc.it
[3] Ecole Polytechnique Fédérale de Lausanne - College of Management
of Technology, EPFL-CDM, ODY 1 16 (Odyssea) Station 5,
CH-1015 Lausanne, Switzerland
gianluigi.viscusi@epfl.ch

Abstract. This paper investigates the role of business models for exploiting digital options within digital clusters (that are clusters where collaboration is IT-dependent). To this aim, this research focuses on digital platforms, a specific IT artifact supporting an inter-organizational system (IOS), which finds a typical application domain in clusters of enterprises. Thus, the paper first discusses the theoretical background and presents a literature review that has been used to set up a framework for analyzing the factors influencing the exploitation of digital platforms at cluster level. The framework is developed through a Design Science Research (DSR) methodology whose empirical ground will be represented by a cluster of more than a hundred of manufacturing small-medium enterprises. An exploratory case study is then discussed in this paper, meant to represent the early stages of application of the DSR method.

Keywords: Digital platforms · Business models · Clusters of enterprises

1 Introduction

This paper presents a research in progress focusing on the adoption of digital platforms in a cluster of enterprises in the manufacturing sector. Digital platforms for online collaboration (in the following: *Digital collaborative platforms - DCP*) can potentially improve the coordination between different actors (e.g., trading partners) and activities (e.g., joint activities), information diffusion, communication within different groups or communities, and the generation of knowledge [6]. The growth in adoption and relevance of DCPs at societal as well as at business level has raised questions about their value, especially when dealing with participation and knowledge sharing spanning beyond the enterprise boundaries [4, 5]. As argued by [13], IT can act as either an *operand resource* (often tangible and static) "*that an actor acts on to obtain support for executing a task*", or as an *operant resource* "(often intangible and dynamic)" "*that act*

© Springer International Publishing Switzerland 2015
A. Persson and J. Stirna (Eds.): CAiSE 2015 Workshops, LNBIP 215, pp. 174–182, 2015.
DOI: 10.1007/978-3-319-19243-7_18

on other resources to produce effects". Thus, in a case a DCP can be considered an enabler of innovation process and outcomes; whereas, in the other case, it acts as a trigger, informing rather than being informed by the users. At the state of the art, the literature on DCPs and innovation has focused mainly on the role of the single enterprises participating to the platform rather than the inter-organizational network of experts as a whole that a DCP enables [4, 5]. Little consideration has been devoted to the use of DCPs to support clusters of enterprises and the related supplier-customer relationships. Maybe also because of the variety of organizations involved (large incumbent corporations and small and medium enterprises) as well as business models.

Taking these issues into account, in this paper we aim to understand the factors impacting on the use - within clusters - of digital collaborative platforms as an operand resource, and the diverse trajectories that they can trigger as an operant resource. In particular, we are going to investigate the role of business models for exploiting digital options [19] by the use of the platforms adopted for knowledge sharing within what we call *digital clusters*, that are clusters where collaboration is IT-dependent, i.e. dependent on the participation to a DCP. Therefore, the following explorative research questions (RQ) arise:

RQ1: What's the role of business models, among other factors, for the use of DCPs and their digital options exploitation?

RQ2: Consequently, is there a business model for an enterprise that better fits the needs - as well as allows to better exploit the benefits - of using a DCP to support the activities in a being part in a digital cluster?

The paper is structured as follows. First we present the research method and introduce the analysis of the theoretical background as well as the main concepts emerging from the literature review. Then, we propose an analytic framework and we use it to preliminarily discuss the outcomes of a case study about an industrial cluster. The conclusive section outlines limitations and future work.

2 Research Method

This research follows a Design Science Research (DSR) approach [10]. According to [10] scholars applying DSR should carry out a sequence of research activities that are *building, evaluating, theorizing on* and *justifying* artifacts. The work presented in this paper concerns the reconstruction of the theoretical background underpinning the two research questions mentioned above (*building*), the discussion of the outcomes of a case study (*evaluating*) and the proposal of an analytic framework (*theorizing on*). In particular, the case study presented in this paper and the subsequent discussion are meant to represent the early stages of application of the DSR method. The case study is exploratory [24] and based on an interpretive approach to research in information systems [11, 23], involving both researchers and practitioners. The case study aims to produce an understanding of the context of a DCP adoption in a cluster, and how the business model of a company may bind or else enforcing it. As sources of evidence we have considered memoranda and formal reports (documentation and archival records:) as well as interviews [3]. Details on data collection and analysis follow.

2.1 Data Collection

A questionnaire, originally designed in English and later translated in Italian (with the contribution of a native English speaker), was used to carry out interviews. The questionnaire was distributed to two small and medium-sized enterprises (SMEs): one can be considered an innovator given the digital proactivity of its representatives; on the opposite, the other firm can be considered conservative given its digital aversion. To get a higher data reliability the interviews were carried out in two different timings: at the beginning of the project (October 2012) and after almost one year the firms were using the platform (July 2013). The CEO or its representative and/or the marketing and sales manager were interviewed. To increase the validity of our coding and data analysis procedure, we aggregated multiple sources of evidence [24]: artifacts (i.e. extracts from the platform), documents from each firm (about performances and financial situations) and information from websites. All data were collected from primary sources and secondary sources: documentation, archival records, interviews, direct observations, participant observations and physical artifacts [24]. Information coming from websites or from the sections of the platform dedicated to each firm of the cluster was useful in order to triangulate the data: the presentation of the firms, their activities, the representatives, their presence in foreign countries, information regarding international projects (agents, branches or at least a contract). Other data regarded the participation and the presence at the social and business meetings happening inside the cluster and organized with the aim to explain, through practical sessions, how to use the platform.

2.2 Data Analysis

All interviews have been tape-recorded and transcribed: the transcripts from the interviews were aggregated into a case protocol helping the researchers in organizing data. The projects were encoded and structured using the software NVIVO 10 following a grounded theory approach [9, 20] that aims at finding properties or links between data. The coding procedure was done as follows: first, in order to mitigate potential bias, the junior researcher (first coder) who had not taken part in the interviews read and coded the interview transcripts by identifying text passages that included information about the constructs of the theoretical framework. Following the coding of the first coder the senior researcher (second coder), likewise, coded the transcripts. The comparison of the two coding resulted in an average inter-coder reliability of 85%. The two coders then examined the mismatched coding and agreed on a final coding matrix that was used for the data analysis. The reasons for mismatches were always very obvious (e.g. one coder had simply overseen an issue within a statement). Only in two cases the professor (third coder) was called in as a referee.

3 Related Work

Business model emerged as a relevant research topic as well as a business's strategic concern with the advent of the internet, literally exploding between 1995-2010 [1]. Notwithstanding the vast literature actually available, the definition for what is a business model is still subject of debate [25]. Among others, we adopt the perspective by Zott & Amit [26], who conceptualize a business model as *"a system of interdependent activities that transcends the focal firm and spans its boundaries. The activity system enables the firm, in concert with its partners, to create value and also to appropriate a share of that value"* [26]. Furthermore, Zott & Amit [26] identify for an activity system architecture a set of design elements (i.e. content, structure and governance) and design themes (novelty, lock-in, complementarities and efficiency) for the sources of the activity system's value creation.

Business model representations as result of business modeling have been developed to provide a tactical and strategic perspective to requirements engineering, consequently aligning traditional conceptual modeling areas such as business process modeling [2, 8, 14, 15]. Thus, considering business models representations as a way to provide high-level requirements to, e.g., Chief Information Officers to design a company IS, the gap seems to be actually a matter of alignment between different representations of *as-is, as-whished*, or *to-be* IS [18].

However, being the focal firm the traditional focus of the business model's literature, the question about the difference between its application to industrial ecosystems [21] and clusters (as a specific type of such ecosystems) instead of a single organization deserve further attention and seems worth to require further investigation, focusing on the boundary spanning characteristics of business model as a system-level concept [25]. The possibility itself to name with the term "cluster" a set of firms is related to the presence of structural linkages, i.e. systematic - although eventually weak - interactions. As argued by Porter [17], *"clusters are geographic concentrations of interconnected companies and institutions in a particular field. Clusters encompass an array of linked industries and other entities important to competition"*, such as, e.g., suppliers, manufacturers of complementary products, governmental institutions or universities. While it can be debated whether interactions in a cluster can lead to cooperation, coordination or collaboration, there is no doubt they could not occur without the (systematic) exchange of information. Contrary to single organizations alone, firms in a cluster show geographical distances, cultural differences and divergences of strategic aims that shall be bridged through inter-organizational information systems (IOS) such as, e.g., DCPs for coordination, cooperation, and knowledge sharing [16].

Considering now platforms, the state of the art literature provides a clear definition of platform [12] as *"a set of technological building blocks and complementary assets that companies and individuals can use and consume to develop complementary products, technologies and services"*. Furthermore, [7] provides a classification of technological platforms, while [8] has investigated how externally focused so-called "industry platforms" affect innovation. The growth in adoption and relevance of DCPs at societal as well as at business level has raised questions about their value, especially when dealing with participation and knowledge sharing often spanning the enterprise boundaries [4, 5].

At the state of the art, the literature on DCPs and innovation has focused mainly on the role of the single enterprises participating to the platform rather than the inter-organizational network of experts as a whole that a DCP enables [4, 5]. Little consideration has been devoted to the use of DCPs to support activities within clusters of enterprises and their supplier-customer relationships. Clusters are complex organizations, often involving large incumbent corporations and diverse small and medium enterprises, and where different business models as well as aim for entrepreneurial action coexist [2]. In principle, complexity could be smoothed by improving the knowledge sharing among enterprises (as actually digital collaborative platforms are claimed to do [16, 22]). Thus, our work stands from previous research with the aim to study if and how the usage of a DCP in a cluster can lead to improving mutual knowledge and creating joint activities.

4   Case Study

Following Zott & Amit's [26], the business model of a firm can be seen as an activity system that is characterized by a set of important design parameters: activity system content; activity system structure; activity system governance. Within this paper, these parameters are used to map two firms, two SMEs belonging to the Lombardy Energy Cluster (LEC, a cluster of firms in the thermo-mechanical industry located in the Lombardy Region, Italy). It is worth noting that in this paper we added the value proposition perspective to what proposed by [26] and we explicitly described how firms build activities to get to customers. The first firm under study, given its young top management and its proactivity in using the DCP tool, may be considered an "*innovator*". This firm is active on the DCP and posts commercial opportunities and market information that can be exploited by other firms in the cluster. The value proposition of this firm is to become a central firm in the cluster by providing value added activities for other firms in the cluster. The activity system of this firm is based on the following selected activities: treatments and coatings, both for aesthetical and protective purposes on a wide variety of materials.

Other firms in the cluster, which are manufacturer and producers of mechanic component for the oil and gas industry (such as valves, vessels, tubes and pipes), could send them to this firm in order to have executed those specific activities. The activity system, with the usage of the DCP is changed given that the firms is using the new IT tool as a way to improve visibility inside the cluster. Therefore the opportunity to have a personal webpage, where the firm is presenting its relevant activities and competences, is a way to strengthen relations with other firms. With regard to the activity system structure, the firm posted opportunities for collaboration online and organized to make them happen offline. Considering the activity system governance, the son of the CEO plays a pivotal role and acts both as Head of Innovative Projects and formal representative in cluster and institutional meetings (he is, for example, the President of the Italian Delegation of Young Entrepreneurs at G20). This person, proactive and passionate of new digital technologies, acts as a digital champion among other entrepreneurs and helps pushing the growth and usage of the DCP.

A totally different management characterizes the second firm. Both the CEO, (i.e. the entrepreneur) - a baby boomer - and his son, the Head of the Technical Department, are not familiar with and generally reluctant to use digital technologies. Oppositely to the first firm, this one can be labeled as "*conservative*". They access the DCPs few times only and with the attitude of lurkers: they do not share any information about commercial or market opportunities; rather, they try to exploit opportunities posted from other firs participating to the platform.

The value proposition of this firm is to support other firms by providing highly specialization in design of ecologic plants, thermals, handling and stocking ones. From an activity system perspective [26], this firm is specialized on activities of design of specific plants that put the firm in an outlier position in relation to other firms of the cluster. In fact, while the majority of firms are producers and manufacturers of specific components, this firm's activities are peculiar and its needs, therefore, are alike. Referring to the activity system structure, the usage of the DCP impacted at different levels on current firms activities. During the development and first usage of the DCP the representatives of the firm participated in several offline meetings and were pro-active in sharing their needs and objectives. After this positive start, the CEO and his son were not active on the DCP and showed a sense of mistrust towards the DCP because they feared opportunistic behaviors from the other participants. As a result, their interactions with the other firms of the clusters remained limited to traditional media, such as phone calls and offline meetings, to start new projects and make new customers.

Activity system governance is referred to who performs the activities. Within the second firm of the study the design department plays a pivotal role: since all the firm activities are orchestrated from here. The person in charge of this is the son of the CEO and has a complete visibility among all activities performed. The CEO, on the other hand, plays an important role as formal representative during institutional and cluster meetings.

5 Discussion of the Results

The analysis of the case study focused, on the one hand, on the relationship between business models and clusters - seen as business ecosystems -, to explore the possibility to represent a cluster as a "business model ecosystem", i.e. a set of specific, interrelated business models characterizing the firms of a cluster. In doing so, we were interested in the emerging variables able to explain the implications of the different business models on the adoption and usage of DCPs. Figure 1 shows the main constructs of the framework.

A cluster of firms can be abstracted as a configuration of business models, where we recognize two main types: business models describing the firms affiliated to the clusters, and the business model of the organization in charge of formally managing the clusters (the "cluster head"). The business models of the affiliated firms can vary significantly, as the two firms of the case study show rather stereotypically. Such diversity allows highlighting three main factors influencing the fit between the DCP and a certain business model of a cluster affiliated firm. In fact, different business models:

- imply different information needs and IT infrastructures; thus, a firm affiliated to a cluster, when opting to participate into a DCP, would require to verify the *IS/IT alignment* at firm level;

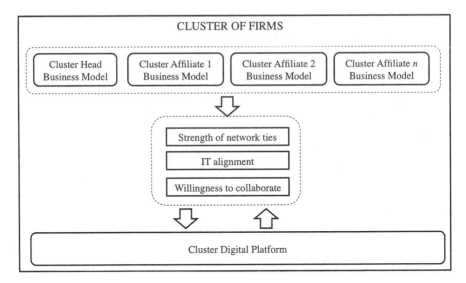

Fig. 1. An analytic framework for understanding the dynamics adoption and exploitation of DCPs at cluster level and the role of business models.

- deal with different types and topologies of networks of social relationships due to different clients and channels; thus eliciting the *strength of network ties* among the actors in the cluster is relevant to anticipate the usefulness of the DCP as a support to such ties;
- incorporate different organizational cultures and in particular different attitudes towards competitive vs. collaborative behaviors, within the firm and with its partners; thus, assessing the *willingness to collaborate* characterizing a business model is key to assess the effectiveness of the DCP as a medium for sharing firms contributions.

The case study reported above provide evidence of two different business models that actually lead to opposite usages of the platform. It is evident that a lurker behavior contradicts the principle of collaboration and - if spread among the firms participating to the DCP – would quickly lead to the ceasing of any contribution on the platform, i.e. the abandoning of the DCP. Nevertheless, the presence of only pure "innovators", like the first firm in our case study, may generate conflicts to achieve a leadership role within the community hosted by the DCP, which, in turn, could lead to disaffection and abandonment of the DCP from the firms. We can anticipate – therefore – that the ideal cluster should include a composition of several business models to exploit at best the potential of a DCP.

Due to the complex and multidisciplinary nature of the subject, we acknowledge the limitations of the state of the art analysis presented above. We can identify two possible directions for further research. First, it would be relevant to identify several business models (beyond the two presented in this case study), to describe a comprehensive business model ecosystem. Second, it would be interesting to address the three variables as dynamic properties of the business models, evolving along time as the cluster evolves and as the usage of the DCP evolves. To do so, we will follow the DSR approach and will run another iteration of the building-evaluating-theorizing cycle using case studies and a further systematic survey to support and improve the analytic framework introduced in this work.

6 Conclusion

The subsequent steps of application of the DSR method will involve the application of the theoretical framework presented above to a specific cluster of firms. The cluster object of the study is the Lombardy Energy Cluster, a cluster of thermo-electro mechanic firms located in Lombardy, a region in Northern Italy. More than 100 firms, mainly SMEs, belong to the LEC and offer a variety of products (e.g., pipes, tubes, valves) and services (e.g., coating, thermal treatments, painting). Since 2012, LEC had adopted a DCP, social-networking like, to foster knowledge sharing and collaboration among cluster members. The research study is based on a qualitative multiple case studies approach that takes into consideration a selected pool of firms, 6 firms, that can be considered representative (in terms of size, turnover, age of top management, relationships with other firms in the cluster, etc.) of the cluster itself. Further extension of the research would be on different directions: first, extending the pool of firms analyzed in order to grant multiple and extended insights on different DCP adoptions; second, combining different research approaches (such as survey-based plus case studies) in order to exploit benefits deriving from multiple perspectives; third, comparing the study carried out within this specific cluster with other clusters that could either have adopted DCPs or willing to do it.

References

1. Amit, R., Zott, C.: Value creation in E-business. Strateg. Manag. J. **22**(6–7), 493–520 (2001)
2. Andersson, B., Bergholtz, M., Edirisuriya, A., Ilayperuma, T., Johannesson, P., Gordijn, J., Grégoire, B., Schmitt, M., Martinez, F.H., Abels, S., Hahn, A., Wangler, B., Weigand, H.: Towards a reference ontology for business models. In: Embley, D.W., Olivé, A., Ram, S. (eds.) ER 2006. LNCS, vol. 4215, pp. 482–496. Springer, Heidelberg (2006)
3. Benbasat, I., Goldstein, D.K., Mead, M.: The case research strategy in studies of information-systems. MIS Q. **11**, 369–386 (1987)
4. Ceccagnoli, M., et al.: Cocreation of value in a platform ecosystem: the case of enterpreise software. MIS Q. **36**, 263–290 (2012)
5. Ceccagnoli, M., et al.: Digital platforms: when is participation valuable? Commun. ACM. **57**(2), 38–39 (2014)
6. Cremona, L., Ravarini, A.: Collective intelligence and social computing: a literature review. In: De Marco, M., Te'eni, D., Albano, V., Za, S. (eds.) Information Systems: Crossroads for Organization, Management, Accounting and Engineering: ItAIS: the Italian Association for Information Systems, pp. 35–41. Physica-Verlag, Heidelberg (2012)
7. Gawer, A.: Bridging differing perspectives on technological platforms: Toward an integrative framework. Resour. Policy. **43**(7), 1239–1249 (2014)

8. Gawer, A., Cusumano, M.A.: Industry Platforms and Ecosystem Innovation. J. Prod. Innov. Manag. **31**(3), 417–433 (2014)
9. Glaser, B.G.: Basics of Grounded Theory Analysis. Sociology Press. Mill Valley, CA (1992)
10. Hevner, A.R., March, S.T., Park, J., Ram, S.: Design Science in Information System Research. MIS Q. **28**, 75–105 (2004)
11. Klein, H.K., Myers, M.D.: A set of principles for conducting and evaluating interpretive field studies in information systems. MIS Q. **23**(1), 67–93 (1999)
12. Muegge, S.: Platforms, Communities, and Business Ecosystems: Lessons Learned about Technology Entrepreneurship in an Interconnected World. Technology Innovation Management Review (2013)
13. Nambisan, S.: Information Technology and Product/Service Innovation: A Brief Assessment and Some Suggestions for Future Research. J. Assoc. Inf. Syst. **14**(4), 215–226 (2013)
14. Osterwalder, A., et al.: Setting up an Ontology of Business Models. In: Grundspenkis, J., Kirikova, M. (eds.) CAiSE'04 Workshops in connection with The 16th Conference on Advanced Information Systems Engineering, Riga, Latvia, 7-11 June, 2004, Knowledge and Model Driven Information Systems Engineering for Networked Organisations, Proceedings, vol. 3, pp. 319–324. Riga Technical University, Riga, Latvia, Faculty of Computer Science and Information Technology (2004)
15. Pigneur, Y.: An ontology for m-Business models. In: Spaccapietra, S., March, S.T., Kambayashi, Y. (eds.) ER 2002. LNCS, vol. 2503, p. 3. Springer, Heidelberg (2002)
16. Pigni, F., Ravarini, A., Saglietto, L.: An explorative analysis of the effects of information and communication technologies and inter-organizational relationships on supply chain management. Supply Chain Forum: An Int. J. **11**, 4 (2010)
17. Porter, M.E.: Clusters and the New Economics of Competition. Harvard Business Review, November-December (1998)
18. Salinesi, C., Rolland, C.: Fitting business models to systems functionality exploring the fitness relationship. In: Eder, J., Missikoff, M. (eds.) CAiSE 2003. LNCS, vol. 2681. Springer, Heidelberg (2003)
19. Sambamurthy, V., Bharadwaj, A., Grover, V.: Shaping agility through digital options: reconceptualizing the role of information technology in contemporary firms. MIS Q. **27**(2), 237–263 (2003)
20. Strauss, A.: Qualitative Analysis for Social Scientists. Cambridge University Press, Cambridge, England (1987)
21. Tsvetkova, A., Gustafsson, M.: Business models for industrial ecosystems: a modular approach. J. Clean. Prod. **29–30**, 246–254 (2012)
22. Venkatraman, N., El Sawy, O.A., Pavlou P.A., Bharadwaj A.: Theorizing Digital Business Innovation: Platforms and Capabilities in Ecosystems. Available at SSRN: http://ssrn.com/abstract=2510111 or http://dx.doi.org/10.2139/ssrn.2510111 (2014)
23. Walsham, G.: Interpretive case studies in is research: nature and method. Eur. J. Inf. Syst. **4**, 74–81 (1995)
24. Yin, R.K.: Case Study Research: Design and Methods, 4th edn. Sage Publications, Thousand Oaks (2009)
25. Zott, C., Amit, R., Massa, L.: The business model: recent developments and future research. J. Manag. **37**(4), 1019–1042 (2011)
26. Zott, C., Amit, R.: Business model design: an activity system perspective. Long Range Plan. **43**(2–3), 216–226 (2010)

Accelerating Web-Entrepreneurship in Local Incubation Environments

Carlos Agostinho[1]([⊠]), Fenareti Lampathaki[2],
Ricardo Jardim-Goncalves[1,3], and Oscar Lazaro[4]

[1] Centre of Technology and Systems, CTS, UNINOVA,
2829-516 Caparica, Portugal
{ca, rg}@uninova.pt
[2] National Technical University of Athens,
15780 Athens, Greece
flamp@epu.ntua.gr
[3] FCT, Universidade NOVA de Lisboa,
2829-516 Caparica, Portugal
[4] Innovalia Association,
48008 Bilbao, Spain
olazaro@innovalia.org

Abstract. This paper explores novel forms of technological and digital societal innovation putting the full potential of the Future of Internet into Web-based innovation, web-Entrepreneurship and Internationalization (IEI) of businesses. It introduces an approach to extend and complement existing incubation environments, which are no longer sufficient to deal with the dynamicity of the Web-Entrepreneur. Based on personal and professional relations, and new business models empowered by social media and the Web 2.0, together with a set of interoperable ICT services supporting virtual or agile enterprises, the authors propose a federation of open-source platforms for the to-be born and existing enterprise life-cycle management, instantiating the Unified Digital Enterprise concept. The novel approach ensures full reuse of existing solutions, developing targeted research to support web-entrepreneurship with cooperation between people, businesses, and assets, namely focusing on innovative methods and architectures for competitive intelligence; crowd-based market sensing; idea incubation and simulation; knowledge intensive team building; as well as interoperability to enable internal federation and external platform integration.

Keywords: Web-Entrepreneurship · Open innovation platforms and services · Unified Digital Enterprise · Future Internet

1 Introduction

Innovation, Entrepreneurship and Internationalization (IEI) are essential processes of an interlinked chain to fight-off an economic and financial crisis that has been considered the World's worst since the U.S. depression in the 1930's. As our world becomes increasingly interconnected, Future Internet (FI) technologies are the tools for change [1, 2] since they enable cultures, industries, and people to collaborate and

© Springer International Publishing Switzerland 2015
A. Persson and J. Stirna (Eds.): CAiSE 2015 Workshops, LNBIP 215, pp. 183–194, 2015.
DOI: 10.1007/978-3-319-19243-7_19

partner in new ways, stimulating businesses, and capitalizing existing assets, such as individuals, technology, data, knowledge, or physical resources. Entrepreneurship, with its emphasis on Web-based innovation and growth, can provide the spark that's needed to ignite new economic and societal vibrancy [3–5].

Jerome Engel [6], claims there is no better timing to kick-start innovative projects of what in periods of decline. However, to be entrepreneur in recessions is not easy, nor can derive only from a logic of survival. He defends it is important to invest in new business models and innovative technology-based ideas that can create an imprint in the digital society of the future. Also, the potential entrepreneur must be prepared for the fact that the capital investment will be much harder to find and the filters for evaluating ideas will become tighter. New forms of business models supporting extended, virtual or agile enterprises in the FI will have the advantage. Thus to maximize that creativity, relationships with universities and research are requested.

For startups that are part of global networks of clusters of innovation, opportunities are increasingly not only a competitive challenge but also a business imperative. Indeed, building upon the ideas of Engel in global clusters of innovation, the emergence of new technology and digital enterprise innovation can be achieved and attributed to the leverage of multi-national, multi-cultural knowledge, people, and other resources around the world. Whereas in the past, this collaboration phenomenon could be related to human physical migrations and the consequent "brain circulation", nowadays it is expected that the FI and the Social-Web can provide new forms of business relations and enhance cooperative networking in the innovative entrepreneurship process.

However, European entrepreneurs fear the possibility of bankruptcy, and the risk of irregular income and unemployment still remains an issue. Among the young, numbers are even more disturbing. In February 2014, 5.392M (under 25 years) were unemployed in the EU-28[1]. Hence, to face these issues, the EC Entrepreneurship 2020 Action Plan ([5]) defines three main actions to encourage the appearance of new entrepreneurs: (1) Entrepreneurial education and training to support growth and business creation; (2) Creating the right business environment and; (3) Role models and reaching out to specific groups.

This paper proposes an approach to extend and complement existing incubation environments for the needs of the Web-Entrepreneur. It specifies an ICT open innovation platform to be deployed at local entrepreneurship clusters, to support an agile enterprise IEI. Section 2 analyses the UDE concept in face of to the to-be born enterprise. Together with advanced modelling and engineering strategies it supports of not only the start-up creation but also its entire lifecycle. Section 3 specifies WEnOIP, a Web-Entrepreneur Open Innovation Platform and its services, while Sect. 4 depicts a possible scenario that highlights the platform's advantages. Finally Sect. 5 concludes the paper, drawing some considerations on the work developed and to-be developed.

1.1   Future Internet and Business Innovation: The Gap to Cover

It is widely acknowledged that the advantage of one company over another stems from the way it manages its process of innovation. However, if the enterprise information systems used are not efficient experiencing communication and automation issues, innovation might not be realized [7]. Hence, Future Internet Enterprise Information Systems (FInES) has been in the past an important area of research to ensure the competitiveness and growth of enterprises [8, 9]. Specific solutions and research is being developed and supported by the EC, and the 2025 Research Roadmap ([10]) has so far addressed existing enterprises, indicating the socio-economic spaces where they prosper, the qualities of being they aim to achieve, the enterprise applications they need to innovate, and the basic FI technologies for a Universal Business System.

In summary, a Web-Entrepreneur is capable of using the social media and the apps "world" for creating concepts for web start-ups and stimulating web-based innovation in existing businesses.

Nevertheless, considering the economical perspective and entrepreneurship vision addressed before, the roadmap attends some issues related to innovation of existing enterprises into digital enterprises, but others remain unattended, e.g.:

- How to accelerate innovation of the to-be-born enterprise?
- How can Internationalization of businesses be better achieved?

To cover the gap, it is required to provide support for web entrepreneurship and Internet businesses, engaging new stakeholders in visions of web-based innovation, enabling and demonstrating innovative services for businesses and citizens which build upon the most advanced technologies.

2   The Unified Digital Enterprise (UDE)

The UDE, as defined in the 2025 FInES Roadmap consists in a full digital image of the enterprise, representing various aspects, such as conceptual and factual (data), behavioural and structural aspects, at various levels of detail. A Unified Digital Enterprise is a complex structure that emerges from the collection of several knowledge resources logically and geographically distributed, inside and outside of the enterprise, e.g. products, clients, human resources, tools, etc. [11]. Figure 1 illustrates a view on the UDE, which addresses enterprise related knowledge in a holistic way, contributing to overcome the current fragmentation, where data of the same enterprise entity is frequently stored in different databases, managed by different departments, and using different tools without interoperability concerns [12].

In the context of UDE, no satisfactory techniques and modelling languages have been developed that can adequately describe in a holistic form all enterprise knowledge components and their inherently complex interactions, including human behaviour. Similar concepts are being explored commercially with management platforms that gather both business and IT information in a common single platform. Nevertheless this is neither a solution focused to starting entrepreneurs nor it is interoperable with many of the legacy system applications in use by a large majority of organizations.

In this work, the authors propose to use and instantiate the UDE components envisaging a holistic view over existing applications to enable innovation, as well as to implement these components in the web-entrepreneur eco-system in which they must be delivered. The idea is to proceed towards a totally integrated approach from the functional point of view, providing a sustainable model constantly aligned with the reality, along the to-be born and innovative enterprise life cycle, supporting the IEI processes. This poses a research challenge that requires significant progress beyond state of the art in highly dynamic scenarios that require constant monitoring of the internal and external events, and quick responses to changes, maintaining the UDE model aligned [13]. Along this line, the notion of Enterprise Architecture (EA) and Enterprise Modelling (EM), as well as methodologies, such as Model-Driven Architecture (MDA - www.omg.org/mda/) are important.

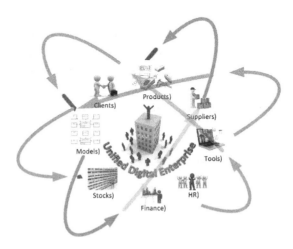

Fig. 1. View on the Unified Digital Enterprise Concept

Following some of the most relevant works in these domains (e.g. [14–18]), methodologies such as MDA/MDI or semantic annotation can provide a valuable addition to more traditional EA/EM frameworks, allowing complementary technologies to be identified and put together, while enabling the recompilation of a full digital representation of the enterprise assets and components at any point in time of the UDE lifecycle.

3   Novel Approach to Supporting Local Clusters of Innovation

So far, the Future Internet (FI) research has provided a plethora of technical solutions addressing the development of better products, services and devices that can improve significantly the enterprises' and industries' performance, but there is a need for complementary support, linking potential web entrepreneurs with key actors at international level. In fact, organizations and institutions from all three major institutional sectors that make up a society (i.e. civil, state, and businesses) are working constantly to resolve the challenges ahead. Facing our common wisdom, they reveal promising new perspectives that meet and need to be met by ICT developments.

Traditionally, local innovation clusters facilitate the connection of entrepreneurs with talent networks, investors and mentors regionally. However, many times they lack the technological support for the web-entrepreneur, and the internationalization potential. Indeed, major difficulties are frequently posed, whether it is in the creation of something new or the innovation of the existing, there is the need to strengthen the environment for web entrepreneurs to grasp the new opportunities offered by the web and the app economy.

Apart from the classic financial difficulties and risk associated with any entrepreneurship project, there is a panoply of other issues that need to be attended, such as:

- The e-conceptualization of the idea;
- The elaboration of e-business/expansion plans;
- The analysis of e-market requirements and e-market monitoring;
- Finding the right team for the job;
- Product support;
- E-Branding, e-marketing and finding customers;

Hence, the authors propose an ICT platform to support local innovation clusters overcome their problems. The proposal is based on a federated concept of innovation platforms interlinked among each other via interoperable services. Together, they create a network capable to capitalize on all the FI technology being developed to provide the above services, and facilitate internationalization. Besides enabling the innovation ecosystem itself through capacity building and stakeholder engagement activities, it has the ability to connect with existing platforms for funding or mentoring.

3.1 Web-Entrepreneur Open Innovation Platform (WEnOIP) Specification

WEnOIP complements that need, setting the ICT framework conditions for web-entrepreneurs to start-up and develop business ideas, bringing them to a worldwide market. It introduces a federation of open source platforms to support the web-innovation, web-entrepreneurship and web-internationalization, as well as the integrated to-be born enterprise life-cycle management, covering the issues identified and enabling the instantiation of the Unified Digital Enterprise (UDE) challenge, as well as establishing synergies and building up existing innovation frameworks.

To realize the vision, the proposed platform explores and pioneers novel forms of technological and digital business innovation, progressing beyond the state of the art by using the full potential of the network effect to support the IEI processes. As illustrated in Fig. 2, the platform to support the web entrepreneur open innovation cluster relies on a next generation model for the web-based digital enterprise set-up, and a set of interoperable ICT services supporting extended, virtual or agile enterprises in the Future Internet. Making an analogy with the Human incubation process, it envisages at modelling the 9-months gestation of the new idea, including tests and ultrasound scans, i.e. identifying what phases to go through, which methods-tools-ICT support are needed in each of the phases, and providing intelligent interconnected services, crowd-mining ideas, crowd-funding or competitive intelligence to deliver the best web-based incubation environment for the UDE.

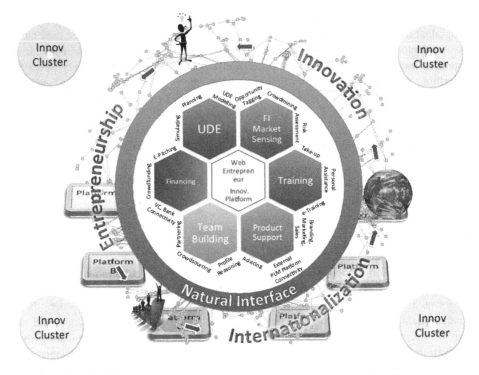

Fig. 2. Platform to support the web entrepreneur open innovation cluster

In detail, six modules are envisaged and accessible through natural-style user interfaces, reflecting advances in conceptual foundations, new models and methodologies, and aggregating services for the web-entrepreneur: (1) "FI Market Sensing" with services made available for the analysis of market requirements and market monitoring, where the proposed crowd mining concept (based on social media and the Web) leads to the identification of short or long term business opportunities; (2) "UDE", with ICT support to planning and conceptualization of the idea (e.g. business plan elaboration), applying modelling technologies to support UDE and build a digital image of the enterprise, overcoming the current fragmentation of concepts and achieving a holistic vision of the enterprise (to-be born or not) which is dynamically aligned with the business reality along its entire lifecycle; (3) "Financing", enabling interconnectivity with traditional systems such as banking platforms (including financial simulators), but envisaging at novel strategies (e.g. crowdfunding and web-based pitch presentations); (4) "Team Building", fostering dynamic alliances/partnering among enterprises with complementary objectives, and intelligent selection of human resources (e.g. semantic capabilities for profile reasoning through the social web); (5) "Product Support", enabling interoperability with existing ICT platforms that can complement the design/development of the Enterprise product/prototype; (6) "Mentoring", providing digital support to the IEI chain, while enabling remote personal assistance.

Ensuring generalization and full reuse/take-up of existing methods and tools, WEnOIP is specified and described exploiting existing frameworks (e.g. OpenIdeo) as well as the Enterprise Interoperability (EI) Science Base (EISB) [9], thus supporting that initiative and sustaining external future developments.

3.2   Open Innovation & Business Innovation Platforms

There are various platforms on open innovation that can be connected and allow companies to use crowd wisdom and diverse capabilities around the world in order to speed up innovations and open the innovation funnel. In that direction OpenIDEO (openideo.com), IdeaConnection (www.ideaconnection.com) and InnoCentive (www.innocentive.com) open the innovation process and assign tasks to teams that get awards to solve specific problems, coming from really industrial needs. Moreover, various platforms try to cultivate a community and ecosystem around their products or services, exporting APIs and SDKs to the community; Facebook and Twitter APIs are some of the most successful examples in that direction, but the FIWARE catalogue (catalogue.fi-ware.org/), DARPA open catalog (www.darpa.mil/opencatalog/) move a step further and try to allow companies use code and services coming from research. There are also many platforms running idea competitions, like IDEA (www.ideacompetition.org), IDSA Idea (www.idsa.org/idea) and Big Ideas @Berkeley (bigideas.berkeley.edu). Other platforms create a network of people and teams, trying to bring them together in order to solve specific problems; P&G was one of the first companies to open its R&D labs, exporting knowledge while trying to boost innovation as never imagined before, with the P&G Connect+Develop platform (www.pgconnectdevelop.com).

There are platforms that support finding a co-founder to run a startup, like FounderDating (founderdating.com), and CoFoundersLab (www.cofounderslab.com). Groups that support team building and startup launching, like Meetup (www.meetup.com), Women 2.0 (women2.com) and Lean Startup Machine (www.leanstartupmachine.com), or platforms that facilitate hiring for Startups, like F6S (www.f6s.com). Additionally, there are many tools that can support business modelling and visual collaboration, like Mural.ly (mural.ly) and Business Model Canvas (www.businessmodelgeneration.com/canvas), or can support customer development process and business model validation, like Business Model Alchemist [19], or FounderSuite (www.foundersuite.com). As entrepreneurs start validating their business model and look funding to expand, there are platforms that enable pitching and advising from distance, e.g. Startup pitching night (www.startuppitchnight.com/startuppitchnight).

Finally, there are also many early-stage networking and idea-sharing platforms, without focusing on the business planning, market fit and business development of an innovative idea or solution. Proven methodologies such as Lean Startup or Customer Development Methodology, and various individual software solutions and visual tools support them [20, 21]. What is really missing is the real online support, the experienced contribution of advisors and investors who will support and drive entrepreneurs out of the "valley of death" of an entrepreneurial idea. The proposed approach meets this need with a platform (i.e. of software and networking solutions) that allows web entrepreneurs to combine existing tools, methodologies and networks coming from successful platforms, with a network of investors and advisors who will support them across Europe through newly developed e-Advising and e-Pitching platforms and events.

4   Scenario

Actors Involved: (1) A web-entrepreneur (John) wishes to set-up a new business and (2) A Capital fund agency (Cap) is willing to support the development of an innovative product in the creative industry market at the start-up stage.

Baseline: John has just finished his engineering studies at university and is a programmer fond of building innovative mobile games. He is willing to sell them to the public so he plans to set-up a company of mobile games. He now has his idea in mind and wants to materialize it into a real product. In order to set-up his own start-up John has to think about the different problems that he will face:

1. It is necessary to explore who are going to be the potential customers and which are their problems and needs. A major reason why start-ups are unable to succeed is that there is little or no market for the product or service that they want to build. Many start-ups find it really difficult to know exactly the size of the market accessible for them;
2. It is essential to develop a game that fits the market needs. Too many start-ups begin with an idea of a product that they think people want and spend months, even years, optimizing it without ever showing the product to the prospective customer. When they fail to reach broad uptake from customers, it is often because they never spoke to them and determined whether the product was interesting for them. This normally ends up in the start-up failing, which is a failure to achieve Product/Market fit.
3. Lack of funding. John will need to demonstrate as soon as possible that his idea is feasible to materialize so as to being able to obtain funding.
4. It is essential to incorporate social media into the marketing strategy. It is essential to know how to monitor the impact on the target audience. Monitoring the customers' questions is a great way to understand what is on their mind, their problems and how we could help.
5. Look for an experienced team, with technical and management skills.

All these issues should be solved in a reduced period of time while spending the least possible amount of money, as it is really important to create a product as soon as possible that provides added value to the customer. However, John, who has no previous experience in business making and has no sustainable cash-flow yet, finds really difficult to deal with all these problems without external help (external business consultant) and of course, he does not have the economic capacity to enjoy the full-time support of external consultants.

4.1   How WEnOIP Will Help This Creative IT Industry Start-up to Succeed?

From the Start-up Point of View: WEnOIP provides John different services that will help him cover all the aspects needed to set up his own start-up. First, in order to find the potential customers for John's product, WEnOIP will gather data from social media correlating them with gender, age, education, demographic or seasonal information so as to identify temporary or constant trends in consumers' behaviour, thus detecting short or long term business opportunities.

WEnOIP supports the lean start-up methodology and its "build-measure-learn feedback loop". The first step is figuring out the problem that needs to be solved and then developing a minimum viable product (MVP) to begin the process of learning as quickly as possible. Once the MVP is established, a start-up can work on adapting it to the target public needs. This will involve measurement and learning and must include actionable metrics that can demonstrate cause and effect question. In our use case, and by means of WEnOIP platform the process will be as follows:

1. John selects one of his game ideas as an innovative initiative.
2. Some key indicators are chosen so as to check that the product can work (number of downloads, number of requests for information, number of positive and negative comments in Social Networks, number of likes, number of recommendations to friends, etc.).
3. A prototype or minimum viable product of the game is developed (just a local game with no capabilities to play online yet with friends).
4. Based on users' feedback (e.g. users want to play online with their Facebook friends) and the key indicators chosen, the result of this first launch is analysed.
5. Based on these results, John may decide whether to opt for a different game or to begin again the cycle so as to improve and adapt the game to users' needs. (e.g. John may want to introduce the capability of playing online with online friends).

Enabling this Lean Start-Up methodology, WEnOIP will find it easier to get funding as the feasibility of the product will be demonstrated in a short period of time. As the product will be evolved progressively according to user needs, the funding agency (Cap) may be interested in providing even more funding to the creative start-up. Moreover, WEnOIP will serve also as a human-resources support system as it will help John to find the right team for the job, by looking for CVs in appropriate web locations (such as LinkedIn) and by selecting the best candidates by means of reasoning services. WEnOIP will also help John to find alliances and partnerships with other companies with complementary interests that may be interested in working in a project together. During the whole process, remote assistance will also be facilitated. As it can be seen, the WEnOIP environment will help to set up a digital start-up from the beginning covering all the aspects that should be taken into account so as to be a successful start-up. It will afterwards cover the whole cycle of product optimization, collaboration and even internationalization.

4.2   How WEnOIP Will Help the Funding Company?

From the Funding Company Point of View: Cap is looking for innovative business ideas and projects so as to provide funding and promote the creation of new start-ups in the creative industry. Cap is contacted by WEnOIP so as to provide funding to John and help him develop his idea. After a quick and first market analysis, WEnOIP demonstrates to Cap the business opportunity that has been identified. It decides to provide a certain quantity of money to John so that he can start developing his idea.

As a first prototype of the mobile game is soon in the market, Cap is able to see the results of its investment and as they notice the success of this project, they decide to increase the funding so that John can follow optimizing and adapting his product according to customers' demands.

5 Conclusions and Future Work

As the Flash Eurobarometer 354 reflects in the report "Entrepreneurship in the EU and beyond" [22], entrepreneurs and start-ups are often faced with important barriers to their flourishing and market access. The lack of capital is seen as a barrier to self-employment by a relatively high number of citizens. However, in the case of Europe, people see the current economic climate not being suitable for starting a new business as an important obstacle. Apart from that, not having enough skills to be self-employed and having little or no business ideas are significant restrictions, which discourage potential entrepreneurs to set up new enterprises. Thus, the generation of favourable business ecosystem conditions are critical to both scale and success of start-ups, and is essential to create the right framework to foster entrepreneurs.

The motivation for the presented work is to promote web-entrepreneurship along the IEI chain of processes, while enhancing the full potential of the Future of the Internet and Web 2.0 into Web-based Innovation. The WEnOIP platform and the proposed approach empowers cooperative networking, supporting entrepreneurs to develop their innovative ideas into real business while also supporting funding agencies and business angels to find new potential innovative business to whom provide funding always being based on evidence-based funding policies. This work is targeted to convince SMEs and entrepreneurs willing to set-up their start-ups that innovation is the key in order to be competitive, not just in their set-up but also in their later lifecycle. Indeed, as about 50 % of companies fail in their first five years, it is fundamental to support the whole cycle of product optimization, collaboration and networking with peers, R&D coaching and mentoring, and even internationalization.

Based on the federation of localized innovation clusters, it is possible to maintain proximity with the entrepreneurs, and at the same time, promote interaction between entrepreneurs across countries and support crosslinks that might develop complementary business between start-ups and SME's. Also, besides the advantages for the web-entrepreneur, nowadays, companies such as funding agencies find difficult, if not impossible, to set-up evidence based funding policies. This is particularly true for the implementation of micro-credit allocations. WEnOIP could help to increase their impact, which is a very useful instrument in the start-up phase. It would also allow a more intelligent, dynamic and evidence-based use of the funding resources and will leverage the implementation of incremental funding schemes based on various iterations of MVP development.

For future work the authors intend to validate the proposed approach in a set of local innovation clusters, providing WEnOIP services for market sensing, UDE modelling, financing, team building and interoperability among the platforms, as the MVP to demonstrate the concept in a real life scenario. It is absolutely necessary to delineate at an early stage of its development: the appropriate methodology for intelligent team crowd-building, indicating the information necessary, the decision-making steps, the criteria for a successful team building process and the mitigation plan for possible risks; and the appropriate methodology for social media consulting in each cluster. UDE modelling, trend analysis and market sensing are already developed [23–25] as separate tools, so the remaining services are to-be tested in longer-term perspective.

References

1. Pan, J., Paul, S., Jain, R.: A survey of the research on future internet architectures. IEEE Commun. Mag. **49**(7), 26–36 (2011)
2. Moreno-Vozmediano, R., Montero, R.S., Llorente, I.M.: Key challenges in cloud computing: enabling the future internet of services. IEEE Internet Comput. **17**, 18–25 (2013)
3. Spiegel, O., Abbassi, P.: Going it all alone in web entrepreneurship?: a comparison of single founders vs. co-founders. In: Proceedings of the 2013 Annual Conference on Computers and People Research, pp. 21–31 (2013)
4. Harada, H., Yagi, R., Sashida, N.: Machibata.net — innovation hub for community development. FUJITSU sci. Tech. J. **49**, 440–447 (2013)
5. European Commission: Startup Europe. ec.europa.eu/digital-agenda/en/startup-europe
6. Engel, J.S., Del-Palacio, I.: Global networks of clusters of innovation: accelerating the innovation process. Bus. Horiz. **52**, 493–503 (2009)
7. Jardim-Goncalves, R., Agostinho, C., Malo, P., Steiger-garcao, A.: Harmonising technologies in conceptual models representation. Int. J. Prod. Lifecycle Manag. **2**, 187–205 (2007)
8. FInES Cluster: Future Internet Enterprise Systems (FInES) Position Paper on Orientations for FP8 "A European Innovation Partnership" for European Enterprises: V3.0 (2011)
9. Lampathaki, F., Koussouris, S., Agostinho, C., Jardim-Goncalves, R., Charalabidis, Y., Psarras, J.: Infusing scientific foundations into enterprise interoperability. Comput. Ind. **63**, 858–866 (2012)
10. FInES Research Roadmap Task Force: FInESResearch Roadmap 2025: version 3.0 (2012)
11. Missikoff, M.: The future of enterprise systems in a fully networked society. In: Ralyté, J., Franch, X., Brinkkemper, S., Wrycza, S. (eds.) CAiSE 2012. LNCS, vol. 7328, pp. 1–18. Springer, Heidelberg (2012)
12. Münch, T., Hladik, J., Salmen, A., Altmann, W., Buchmann, R., Karagiannis, D., Ziegler, J., Pfeffer, J., Urbas, L., Lazaro, O., Ortiz, P., Lopez, O., Sanchez, E., Haferkorn, F.: Collaboration and interoperability within a virtual enterprise applied in a mobile maintenance scenario. In: Charalabidis, Y., Lampathaki, F., and Jardim-Goncalves, R. (eds.) Revolutionizing Enterprise Interoperability through Scientific Foundations, vol. 7 (2014)
13. Jardim-Goncalves, R., Agostinho, C., Steiger-Garcao, A.: A reference model for sustainable interoperability in networked enterprises: towards the foundation of EI science base. Int. J. Comput. Integr. Manuf. **25**, 855–873 (2012)
14. Chalmeta, R., Campos, C., Grangel, R.: References architectures for enterprise integration. J. Syst. Softw. **57**, 175–191 (2001)
15. Boudjlida, N., Panetto, H.: Enterprise semantic modelling for interoperability. In: Proceedings of 12th IEEE Conference on Emerging Technologies and Factory Automation (ETFA 2007), pp. 847–854, Patras, Greece (2007)
16. Chen, D., Doumeingts, G., Vernadat, F.: Architectures for enterprise integration and interoperability: past, present and future. Comput. Ind. **59**, 647–659 (2008)

17. Agostinho, C., Černý, J., Jardim-Goncalves, R.: MDA-based interoperability establishment using language independent information models. In: van Sinderen, M., Johnson, P., Xu, X., Doumeingts, G. (eds.) IWEI 2012. LNBIP, vol. 122, pp. 146–160. Springer, Heidelberg (2012)

18. Frankel, D.: Model Driven Architecture – Applying MDA to Enterprise Computing. OMG Press, Wheat Ridge (2003)

19. Osterwalder, A.: Test your value proposition: superchargeable lean startup and custdev principles. http://businessmodelalchemist.com/2012/09/test-your-value-proposition-supercharge-lean-startup-and-custdev-principles.html

20. Blank, S.: The Four Steps to the Epiphany: Successful Strategies for Products that Win. Lulu Enterprises, Pascadero (2006)

21. Blank, S.: Why the lean start-up changes everything. enterprisersproject.com/article/hbr-article-why-lean-start-changes-everything(2014)

22. TNS Opinion & Social: Flash Eurobarometer 354: Entrepreneurship in the EU and beyond (2012)

23. Agostinho, C., Sesana, M., Jardim-Goncalves, R., Gusmeroli, S.: Model-driven service engineering towards the manufacturing liquid-sensing enterprise. In: Proceedings of the 3rd International Conference on Model-Driven Engineering and Software Development (ModelsWard 2015)., Angers, France (2015)

24. Marques-Lucena, C., Sarraipa, J., Fonseca, J., Grilo, A., Jardim-Gonçalves, R.: Framework for customers' sentiment analysis. In: Angelov, P., Atanassov, K.T., Doukovska, L., Hadjiski, M., Jotsov, V., Kacprzyk, J., Kasabov, N., Sotirov, S., Szmidt, E., Zadrożny, S. (eds.) Proceedings of the 7th IEEE International Conference Intelligent Systems IS'2014. AISC, vol. 322, pp. 849–860. Springer, Heidelberg (2015)

25. Biliri, E., Petychakis, M., Alvertis, I., Lampathaki, F., Koussouris, S., Askounis, D.: Infusing social data analytics into future internet applications for manufacturing. In: Proceedings of the 11th ACS/IEEE International Conference on Computer Systems and Applications (AICCSA 2014)

Challenges Laying Ahead for Future Digital Enterprises: A Research Perspective

Iosif Alvertis[1(✉)], Panagiotis Kokkinakos[1], Sotirios Koussouris[1],
Fenareti Lampathaki[1], John Psarras[1], Gianluigi Viscusi[2],
and Christopher Tucci[2]

[1] National Technical University of Athens,
Heroon Polytechniou 9, 15780 Zografou, Greece
{alvertisjo,pkokkinakos,skous,flamp,john}@epu.ntua.gr
[2] College of Management of Technology,
Ecole Polytechnique Fédérale de Lausanne, EPFL-CDM, ODY 1 16 (Odyssea)
Station 5, 1015 Lausanne, Switzerland
{gianluigi.viscusi,christopher.tucci}@epfl.ch

Abstract. Nowadays, digital enterprises are confronted with disruptive technological advancements in their constant quest for innovation and creativity. In order to evolve towards new forms of enterprises, driven by constant business model transformation, a number of challenges need to be addressed from a research and practice perspective. In this paper, a glimpse of the technological trends and visionary scenarios for Enterprises of the Future is provided, leading to the elaboration of the research challenges along the following dimensions: (a) Collaborative, Real-time, Proactive Business Analytics-as-a-Service, (b) Innovative, Web-based Business Models for New Kinds of Economies, (c) Federated, Innovation-driven Enterprise Collaboration Platforms, (d) Dynamic Discovery and Negotiation of the Intellectual Property Rights' Flow.

Keywords: Digital enterprise · New forms of enterprises · Technological trends · Scenarios · Research roadmapping · Research challenges

1 Introduction

The world is experiencing one of the most extraordinary periods in history. Returning to growth and higher levels of employment, combating climate change, and moving towards a low-carbon society require urgent and coordinated action. A convergence of forces is reshaping the global economy: emerging regions, such as Africa, Brazil, China, and India, have overtaken economies in the West as engines of global growth; the pace of innovation is increasing exponentially; new technologies have created new industries, disrupted old ones, and spawned communication networks of astonishing speed; and global emergencies seem to erupt at ever-shorter intervals. Any one of these developments would have profound implications for organizations and the people who lead them. Taken together, these forces create many challenges and opportunities, thus, a new context for entrepreneurship [1]. Entrepreneurship has never been more important than it is today in this time of financial crisis [2]. Innovation and entrepreneurship are

A. Persson and J. Stirna (Eds.): CAiSE 2015 Workshops, LNBIP 215, pp. 195–206, 2015.
DOI: 10.1007/978-3-319-19243-7_20

generally viewed as an engine of technological progress and economic growth and provide a way forward for solving the global challenges of the 21st century, building sustainable development, creating jobs and advancing human welfare [3, 4].

Today, we are living through moments of disruptive technological change accelerating the transition from a business-driven culture to a more 'social-oriented' one. Open innovation has become more influential and models of production and value creation are changing. The advent of big data, social media, cloud computing and the Internet of Everything that will eventually pervade business, government and society heralds a new motif of socioeconomic organization, exemplified by the App Economy that is already emerging as a collection of interlocking innovative ecosystems [5]. In this context, Business Innovation in the Future Internet has already taken new impetus according to analysts across the world. Enterprises of the future thus need to leverage Future Internet-based technologies to define their own paths to competitiveness and generate hybrid value constellations (combining business and social innovation networks).

Digital Enterprise is considered as a long-standing concept that has gained traction over the last decade: initially, intertwined with mere digitalisation of the traditional processes of an enterprise and eventually, encapsulating its digital transformation and digital value creation. Throughout the years, a number of relevant concepts, like Social Enterprise, Sensing Enterprise and Enterprise 2.0, have emerged and transpire similar directions for enterprises who want to thrive and prevail in the Digital era. In the context of our work in the EC-funded FutureEnterprise project, the term "new forms of enterprises" has been adopted to reflect the next evolutionary step of a Digital Enterprise, along the following definition: *New forms of enterprises are "Enterprises of the Future, driven by constant business model transformation and innovation, acting as multi-sided platforms built on -as well as emerging from- digital innovations at the global, as well as local level, to produce shared value including that beyond monetisation".*

Along these lines, the present paper aims at discussing a number of instrumental research challenges that need to be tackled by researchers and practitioners in order for new forms of enterprises to evolve and flourish. In Sect. 2, the methodological approach is presented, leading to Sects. 3 and 4 that summarize the trend analysis and the visionary scenarios for Enterprises. Section 5 outlines the identified research challenges. Section 6 concludes this work and presents next steps along this approach.

2 Methodology

The methodological approach followed towards identifying research directions for future digital enterprises consisted of 5 main phases: (a) identification and analysis of "trends", accompanied by the formulation of "mega-trends"; (b) extraction of "key uncertainties"; (c) conduction of an open crowdsourcing exercise; (d) elaboration of the different socioeconomic factors and of the role of enterprise; (e) elaboration of "future scenarios"; (f) identification of grand challenges and research challenges.

An initial identification of basic technological trends - together with macro-trends concerning Politics, Economy, Society as well as the ones related to Business,

Entrepreneurship, and Innovation - has been carried out to document in a structured way the trends that may affect the future of enterprises. The analysis has been carried out on: (i) the normative visions of the FutureEnterprise Expert's panel, comprising from high-calibre experts in the domain, (ii) the results from an online crowdsourcing exercise carried out between January and March 2014, (iii) comments and notes from a focus group of entrepreneurs held on March 2014, and (iv) a sample of 50 selected secondary sources (from an initial set of 300 documents), made up of:

- Reports and data sets from the European Union and international institutions such as the OECD, United Nations, World Bank;
- Organisational reports working every year on Global Entrepreneurship Monitor or the Global innovation Index;
- Articles and studies from academic research on the considered domains.

Identified trends have been then merged into "Mega Trends", describing at higher level the way that the aforementioned domains are affected. A Mega Trend can be linked with more than one domains of study, as it is a combination of underlying trends. Based on the "Trends" and "Mega Trends", various "Key Uncertainties" have been extracted, handpicked based on their influence to the creation of "New Forms of Enterprises". Then the "Key Uncertainties" have then been placed on open consultation in order to filter out the unrealistic and improbable combinations of these "Key Uncertainties" and the final results have driven the consortium to a set of "Probable" and "Desirable" futures as envisioned by the community. These futures constituted the finalisation of the scenario building exercise, whose purpose is to explore different probable alternatives for the future of society and economy, and elaborate on possible impacts (in terms of both opportunities and risks) that the future of research on New Forms of Enterprises may hold. The starting point for the scenario generation activities was (as described above) the trend analysis, as it allowed the identification of the main impact dimensions that are likely to influence research directions in the area of Digital Business Innovation in the future.

A number of Business Models Innovations [6] (i.e. Closed-Loop Production; Physical to Virtual; Produce on Demand; Rematerialiasation; Sell One, Give One; Cooperative Ownership; Crowd funding; Freemium; Innovative Product Financing; Pay for Success; Bait & Hook; Differential Pricing & Customisation; Microfinance; Micro-Franchise; Open Innovation; Multisided platform) have been studied along the following aspects: Existing enabling technologies, Dependency with innovation diffusion / acceptance factors (analysed under both the current situation in Europe and the future desirable scenario), Changes brought to existing business models (in accordance with the business model canvas elements), Key research directions needed to enable or boost every business model innovation, characterised with the expected impact on enterprises, SMEs and web entrepreneurs. Such an analysis has led to the identification of 25 research challenges, along with the projected timeline for their realization, and to their grouping into Grand Challenges, which represent significant research paths to be followed in the years to come, based on their relevance.

3   Trends

In order to understand the forces that drive enterprises to be born digital (digital native enterprises) or digitise their activities and seek innovation - regardless if it refers to a specific subset of their activities or to their organisation as a whole - it is of the utmost importance to study the underlying technological trends. It can be taken also for granted that, besides technological trends and advancements, additional factors exist that can affect the strategic decisions of both new and existing enterprises and degree of transformations of existing organisations; thus, trends of non-technological nature have to be taken into consideration too. Towards this direction, an extensive state-of-the art analysis was realized and various differentiated sources were studied (e.g. OECD, United Nations, World Bank, private companies mostly of consulting nature) in order to identify, categorise and report key trends that can accelerate digital entrepreneurship and digital transformation of existing enterprises.

The analysis led to the identification of 7 categories of trends, covering a wide spectrum of areas, namely Political, Economic, Societal, Business, Entrepreneurship, Innovation and Technological. Putting more focus on the technological trends, every recognized trend has been classified on the basis of its strength and horizon.

Figure 1 visually depicts the complete list of technology trends accompanied by information on their strength and implementation horizon. The possibility itself to name with the term "cluster" a setof firms is related to thepresence of structural linkages, i.e. systematic - although eventually weak - interactions.

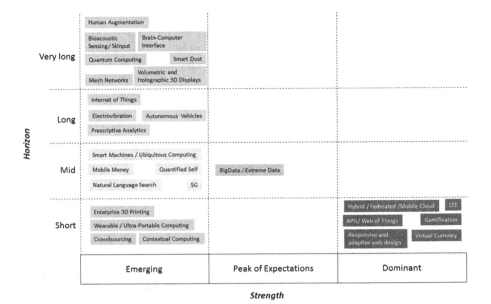

Fig. 1. Technology trends

With regard to its strength, a trend may be considered as:

- Emerging, when its diffusion is limited to a certain territory, and there is a small population with a consequent limited number of mainstream publications or reports discussing it as relevant.
- Peak of expectations, when its diffusion and acknowledgment are mainstream, overcoming a limited set of specialists. However, the trend's impact is still difficult to clearly evaluate, whether it is positive, negative, or else neutral (no effect on business or entrepreneurship), thus, pointing out or leading to a potential failure.
- Dominant, when its diffusion and acknowledgment are mainstream and the impact is clearly evaluated as it is evident in many different cases.

Finally, as far as a trend horizon is concerned, it can be Short (less than two years to be fully deployed), Medium (between two and five years to be fully deployed), Long (between five and ten years to be fully deployed) and Very Long (more than ten years to be fully deployed).

4 Scenarios

A visionary scenario analysis was then conducted based on a foresight exercise, including the analysis of the key areas coming from these trends, placing them in the context of various different future scenarios and envisioning, for each scenario, the future landscape and its implications in an enterprise. Following the classification of Popper [7], a distinction can be made between a methods' orientation (normative or exploratory), its nature (quantitative or qualitative) and its essence (expert-based, creativity-based, interaction-based or evidence-based). The objectives of a foresight exercise and the degree of uncertainty and complexity involved, guide the selection of methods for a particular exercise. A scenario is to be intended as a systematic vision of future possibilities [8]. In foresight research this usually means plausible possibilities and ones that do not rely on too extreme wild cards. They are used as tools for political or strategic decision-making and to explore the impact of particular decisions or developments in the future. More specifically, scenario-building aims to identify uncertain developments in the future and take those uncertainties as elements of the scenario narrative.

The aim of the scenario-design exercise developed as part of Future Enterprise is to explore different possible alternative futures in the context of the enterprises of the future, rather than predicting the future; then elaborate on possible impacts that the future mainstream on society of ICT tools in this domain may have. Both the time horizon of this exercise (i.e. 2030) and the interdependency of various developments affecting it (e.g. rapid developments in specific domains of ICTs) make the future of this domain of research dynamic, complex and uncertain. It is therefore difficult to use quantitative and evidence-based methods. Courtney et al. [9] describe this amount and type of uncertainty as a 'level 3', at which a range of different possible futures can be identified. They describe three types of foresight methods that can be used at this level: scenario writing back casting and early warnings systems. As the latter two approaches are often incorporated into scenario writing, the method of scenario design has been used for this exercise [10].

Having in mind the limitations in current scenario building exercises (like the limitations imposed by the extreme 2-dimensions axes), a differentiated approach has been adopted, where a larger set of Key Uncertainties exists and the different **Probable and Desirable scenarios**, as voted by the experts. This way, not every possible combination of the aforementioned Key Uncertainties is examined (as this would generate a huge number of scenarios) but focus is laid on what is most likely to happen (Probable Scenarios), and also on what seems like an ideal future (Desirable Scenario). The different scenarios that are created are in this way based on the majority of the votes of the public and in this way provide a more realistic, unbiased and collective representation of insights on how our world would look like in some years from now, but also provide the collective perception of people of how an ideal world should look like in the future.

The **Key Uncertainties** for the purpose of the FutureEnterprise roadmap approach that have been selected for building the above discussed scenarios and which correspond with the trends and the megatrends identified in this deliverable and follow the PESTEL (Political, Economic, Sociological, Technological, Legal, Environmental) pattern are presented in the table below. Each column in the following table is independent from the others and presents the three values of each Key Uncertainty (the header row). In this context, a future scenario can be derived as a combination that includes only one value from each column of that table (Table 1).

Table 1. Key Uncertainties and Possible Values

Wealth & Well-Being	Legal Framework	Value Creation and Capture	Operations & Decision Making	Markets
Prosperity	Global Legislation	Corporate Social Responsibility	Machine Intelligence	Global Markets
Stability	Fragmented Legislation	Shared Value	Knowledge based	Glocal Markets
Scarcity	Self-Regulation	Shareholders Value	Crowd Wisdom	Local Markets

It needs to be noted, that all uncertainties and scenarios developed have as a central point of focus the "Enterprise", as the interest of the roadmap would be the recommendations of activities that will help enterprises to evolve and shape into the entities that will drive business innovation and production in the future.

The Key Uncertainties previously discussed have been announced to the public in order to engage it towards providing its feedback by pointing out which they consider more likely to realise (Probable Scenario) and which they would like to happen (Desirable Scenario). Upon collecting a total of 102 responses, the authors analysed the various responses and set some threshold points order to distinguish the different combinations that prevail and that lead to scenarios that are quite different from each other. Based on a qualitative analysis of the patterns received, the threshold was set to

33% of votes for the probable scenario in order to derive 2 probable scenarios which are different from each other in at least 3 dimensions (key uncertainties), while as long as it concerned the desirable scenario, the threshold was set to 50% of votes, which clearly pointed out one scenario. The different votes and the threshold points set by the consortium are visible in the following two figures (Fig. 2).

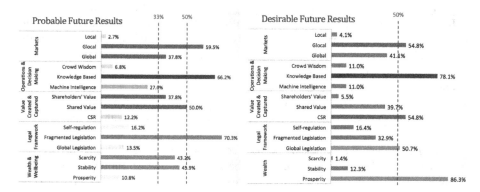

Fig. 2. Answers to Key Uncertainties regarding the Probable and Desirable Scenario

The three scenarios derived, which are also discussed in the next section are the following.

- **Probable Scenario #1** - A global, federated network of self-organised communities (*Disruptive Communitarianism*), which includes the following values of the Key Uncertainties: Stability, Fragmented Legislation, Shared Value, Knowledge-based, Global Markets
- **Probable Scenario #2** - Distributed Islands of Capitalism (*Elysium*), which includes the following values of the Key Uncertainties: Scarcity, Fragmented Legislation, Shareholders Value, Knowledge-based, Glocal Markets
- **Desirable Scenario** – Prosperity, Social Caring and Equal Opportunities (*Garden of Eden*), which includes the following values of the Key Uncertainties: Prosperity, Global Legislation, Corporate Social Responsibility, Knowledge based, Glocal Markets

5   Roadmap

The research challenges that have been eventually identified in a collaborative way have been bundled in the following four grand challenges which represent significant research paths to be followed in the years to come:

Grand Challenge 1: Collaborative, Real-time, Proactive Business Analytics-as-a-Service, dealing with a radically different context for business analytics for the enterprise personnel, either high-level executives or shop floor workers. It encompasses the following research challenges:

- RC1.1 - Multi-source Data Analytics Services for Real-Time Production Critical Decisions. Analysis of data coming from widely deployed IoT and smart dust networks in the production lines of enterprises to constantly monitor information and data towards providing proactive notifications and decision support to the business personnel, regarding the optimum and uninterrupted operation of the enterprise and the maximisation of its goals.
- RC1.2 - Predictive and Prescriptive Crowd-based Analytics powering Business Innovations. Analytics and value added information generation shall be delivered to enterprises through real-time monitoring and analysis of internal and mostly external information sources (such as social networking systems) and of behaviours of targeted stakeholders, towards revealing potential innovation and market-related business opportunities.
- RC1.3 - Business Transformation Platforms combining Human Knowledge with Information Flows. Combining enterprise critical data flows with human derived ideas, knowledge and experience, artificial intelligence enterprise agents transporting knowledge, experience and data across all enterprise divisions (as well as beyond its borders in some cases), will be deployed to grasp on emerging opportunities and automatically transform business realities and processes in a flexible and agile manner.
- RC1.4 - Enterprise-wide smart, personalised intelligence and delivery systems. Next generation analytics, combining raw sensor data, historical logs and business knowledge and best practices, coupled together with smart and personalised recommendation systems to provide intelligence-rich services beyond plain information mining and visualization to various stakeholders over different access channels.
- RC1.5 – Generation and Exposure of SMEs Analytics over federated cloud-based platforms. Deployment of federated cloud-based platforms that interface with hundreds of proprietary and open source business solutions and data repositories, to transform SME data and expose them through meaningful and value-added cloud-based analytics, without compromising their classified business intelligence.
- RC1.6 - Smart and Collaborative APIs for cognisant business processes. Next generation APIs integrated to all business-related systems to allow the controlled exposure of information at real-time, turning every machine and IT platform into IoT elements, and being able to retrieve data as well, acting as cognisant objects collaborating together for a common goal, realising in that way the highest degree of objects and platforms interoperation.
- RC1.7 - Responsive and Dynamic Visualisation and Augmented Reality Services for Business Functions. Intuitive and responsive visualisations and augmented reality methods applied to all business related functions and processes, to combine physical, digital and virtual characteristics of products and services and enterprise knowledge, for demonstrating spherical and inclusive information surrounding products, services and business processes as well towards offering a homogeneous experience to their users.
- RC1.8 - Proactive ICT-powered preventive workforce safety and security systems. Exploitation of sensor data, from the business environment and from wearable gadgets, and extraction of early detection signs on threating conditions for the safety

and the security of employees, resulting in the provision of smart recommendations for active or passive prevention measures.

Grand Challenge 2: Innovative, web-based business models for new kinds of economies, exploring the definition, experimentation and constant evolution of novel business models that challenge traditional operating models, follow the paradigms of the Sharing Economy and the Circular Economy, and capitalize on novel technologies and Future Internet assets in business environments in order to introduce unique innovation propositions at multiple levels, ranging from the innermost configuration and the core offerings of an enterprise, to the customer-facing, networking elements of its business system (user experience). It encompasses the following research challenges:

- RC2.1 – Circular Supply Chain Management. Novel methods and platforms to bi-directionally manage the supply circle operations, to optimize a cycle of disassembly and reuse, to explore efficient recovery and treatment techniques and to create secondary marketplaces need to be developed in order to translate potentially circular products to attractive value propositions for enterprises and end-users.
- RC2.2 - Collaborative Prosumption Models. Applications of next generation technologies (from 3D printing to Wearable technologies and from Social Computing to Internet of Things) and the exploration of intersections between traditionally separate ways of working makes everyone an enterprise in a "peer-to-peer" fashion that eventually not only empowers multi-sided platform thinking, but also disrupts existing industries and creates new markets.
- RC2.3 – Collective Ideas Flow on ever-evolving and interactive Business Plan Lifecycles. Advanced modelling and simulation techniques to understand and simulate how the flow of ideas, that have been expressed internally or beyond the enterprise boundaries, affect the underlying business reality and performance in order to embed collective intelligence in business settings and to proceed with the necessary, ever-evolving adaptations of the adopted business model.
- RC2.4 – Instant, crowd market validation of Business Innovations. Through advanced enterprise gamification and social networking techniques, instant collaboration channels across the supply chain, involving users, suppliers and employees, shall be established, serving the purpose of instant validation of any potential business innovation on which an enterprise plans to invest.
- RC2.5 – Reverse engineering of innovation. With the help of next generation business modelling and simulation techniques, reverse engineering of a business model from its parts shall become feasible, assisting any stakeholder understand the business plan which is recommended to pursue for their offerings when they are trying to "copy" external innovations.
- RC2.6 –Innovation Diffusion & Adaptation Patterns and Techniques. Novel techniques to investigate the innovation patterns across markets in systemic ways, diffuse and adapt innovations beyond the geographic and organizational boundaries still need to be explored in order to assist a company or an entrepreneur to apply inverted /reverse innovation.

Grand Challenge 3: Distributed, Innovation-driven Enterprise Platforms, embodying a radically different context for business innovation and collaboration among organisations, where platforms promote collaboration among enterprises and web entrepreneurs, boost productivity and enable business innovation in consistent lifecycles; from invention to production, from supply chain management to ERP systems, and from customers' adoption to collaboration with internal business functions or external partners. It encompasses the following research challenges:

- RC3.1 - New forms of Enterprise Marketplaces. New forms of marketplaces allowing collaboration among organisations to develop solutions that meet business problems in better, more efficient ways using novel transaction methods and allowing community-driven validation and authentication in decentralised, distributed manners.
- RC3.2 - Real-time, Interoperability and Openness in Enterprise Platforms. Rendering existing enterprise systems available and connectable through common, secure, real-time enabled APIs, enabling trustful transactions among different organisations and offering standardised analytics, protecting at the same time the privacy of all sensitive data of the transaction parties.
- RC3.3 – Subscription Mechanisms to Real-time, Anonymised Business Analytics. Subscription mechanisms and interfaces to infuse real-time, anonymised analytics making them available to third parties, taking advantage of on the spot sensors, wearable devices, logging data and close-communication protocols in combination with mesh networking technologies, to collect and process data.
- RC3.4 – Innovative Project Management Platforms driven by Lean Paradigms and allowing Experimentation. Platforms providing tools, methodologies and management techniques in order to build experimenting frameworks and increase innovation rate, promote internal and external collaboration, and make use of interfaces with crowdsourcing platforms and linked-data to facilitate knowledge management and market research.
- RC3.5 – Independent Platforms for Inter-organisation Relationships and Trust in doing Business. Unstructured data analysis and KPIs evaluating the situation of an organisation, allowing financial situation identification, and building trustful relationships among different organisations, all powered by analytics to evaluate prospective markets, identify consumer patterns, and facilitate decision-making towards stronger synergies and business networks.
- RC3.6 – Recommendation systems in B2B transactions and partnerships deals. New generation recommendation systems, powered by real-time data, to provide useful recommendations to organisations about new B2B offerings, capable of improving their performance, facilitate operations and solve existing problems.

Grand Challenge 4: Dynamic discovery and negotiation of the intellectual property rights' flow, addressing effective management, monitoring, identification and creation of IPRs and knowledge generation and handling, through the use of innovative ICT tools and platforms that will exploit the collaborative features of existing platforms and the power of analytics. It encompasses the following challenges:

- **RC4.1 - Open Repositories and Marketplaces for IPRs.** Implementation of repositories that will accommodate the storage of and effective search amongst the various intangible assets, as well as of intangible assets' marketplaces incorporating specific models for access to enable innovation acceleration and defining novel IPR modelling methods.
- **RC4.2 - IPR Recommendation and Governance Platforms.** Next generation smart platforms for the efficient and effective recommendation and governance of IPRs, allowing discovery of IPR, relevant to a specific issue of interest, relevant recommendation mechanisms and automated reasoning of specific conflicts based on existing IPR schemes.
- **RC4.3 – Traceability of IPR Licences across their derivatives.** Coping with patent schemes and IPRs when developing a new product/service in the one side of the coin. An equally challenging task is to locate and identify the various patents and IPR contained in derivatives of products/services. This research challenge refers to the design and implementation of methods and mechanisms that will allow clear and effective recognition and traceability of all active patents and IPR contained in specific (series for) products/services in order to facilitate all stakeholders aiming either to use or exploit in entrepreneurial activities the aforementioned products/services.
- **RC4.4 - Smart Platforms for Real-Time IPR Negotiation Real time.** The structured ways of describing IPRs and the detailed modelling of them (see RC.3.1) is expected to not only facilitate the quick discovery and use of them, but constitutes a prerequisite for supporting negotiation activities between interested organisations that would like to access and use IPRs for any imaginable reason. Smart platforms should handle the negotiation of such IPRs in real-time, at execution time of transactions, cutting down negotiation costs and time, proposing alternative IPR schemes and pre-defined agreement contracts in order to satisfy the interest of all involved parties to the best possible extent.
- **RC4.5 - Community-based Platforms for Shared IPR and Patents' Generation.** Tapping the power, the dynamics and the wisdom of the crowd to achieve IPR and Patents' generation through open platforms allowing collaboratively conceptualising, describing, modelling and formalising new IPRs and Patents and offering them back to the community for adoption, standardisation and exploitation.

6   Conclusions and Next Steps

In the aftermath of the recent financial crisis and in light of the emergence of disruptive technological paradigms, how to conduct business in an ever-changing environment appears more challenging than ever. The surging app economy, manifested within a platform-oriented, mobile-driven and collaboration-rooted era, has already paved new paths for digital business innovation. Stimulating break-through innovation for added value products and services is in fact well acknowledged at research and policy level and embedded in the mind-sets of leading enterprises, successful entrepreneurs, and forward-looking researchers, yet recognised philosophies of doing business 'better' (e.g. "Think Fast, Move Fast, Fail Fast, Learn Fast, Succeed Fast" [11]) are still not integrated in the strategies and approaches of many companies, especially in Europe.

In the present paper, a number of research challenges to be tackled in the years to come in order for enterprises to evolve towards new forms of enterprises have been elaborated. Next, iterative steps along our approach include: (a) further elaboration of the research challenges based on case studies along the Digital Business Innovation aspects and (b) recommendations on how to maintain a "live" roadmap, with contributions by any interested stakeholder.

Acknowledgments. This work has been partly funded by the European Commission through the Project FutureEnterprise: Road mapping, Research Coordination and Policy activities supporting Future Internet-based Enterprise Innovation (Grant Agreement No. 611948).

References

1. Barton, D., Grant, A., Horn, M. Leading in the 21st century. McKinsey Quarterly (2012)
2. World Economic Forum Educating the Next Wave of Entrepreneurs: Unlocking entrepreneurial capabilities to meet the global challenges of the 21st Century (2009)
3. Gates, Susan M., Leuschner, Kristin J.: In the Name of Entrepreneurship?. WAR Corporation, The Logic and Effects of Special Regulatory Treatment for Small Business (2007)
4. EC (2013) Entrepreneurship 2020 Action Plan. COM(2012) 795 final. http://ec.europa.eu/digital-agenda/en/news/sizing-eu-app-economy
5. Mulligan, M., Card, D.: Sizing the EU app economy. Accessed on 27 March 2014. http://ec.europa.eu/digital-agenda/en/news/sizing-eu-app-economy
6. Model Behavior: 20 Business model innovations for sustainability. February 2014. http://www.sustainability.com/library/model-behavior#.U6duho2SzJE
7. Popper, R.: Foresight methodology. In: Georghiou, L., Cassingena, J., Keenan, M., Miles, I., Popper, R. (eds.) The handbook of technology foresight. Edward Elgar Publishing, Cheltenham (2008)
8. Janssen, M., Duin, van der, P., Wagenaar, R., Blicking, M., Wimmer, M.: Scenario building for e-government in 2020. In: ACM Proceedings of the 8th Annual International Conference on Digital Government Research: Bridging Disciplines and Domains (2007) pp 296 – 297
9. Courtney, H., Kirkland, J., Viguerie, P.: Strategy under uncertainty. Harvard Bus. Rev. **75** (6), 67–79 (1997)
10. Scenario writing is a method that is commonly used in research regarding public services and eGovernment (van der Duin and Huijboom, 2008; Janssen et. al. 2007; Aicholzer, 2005)
11. Stein, A.: Sense of urgency – think fast, move fast, fail fast, learn fast, succeed fast (2012). http://steinvox.com/blog/2012/04/04/sense-of-urgency-think-fast-move-fast-fail-fast-learn-fast-succeed-fast/#ixzz2EMgETBI8

EM 2015

Ontology-Driven Enterprise Modelling in Practice: Experiences from Industrial Cases

Kurt Sandkuhl[1,3], Alexander Smirnov[2,3], Nikolay Shilov[2], and Hasan Koç[1(✉)]

[1] Institute of Computer Science, University of Rostock,
18051 Rostock, Germany
{Kurt.Sandkuhl,Hasan.Koc}@uni-rostock.de
[2] St.Petersburg Institute for Informatics and Automation of the Russian
Academy of Sciences, 39, 14 Line, 199178 St.Petersburg, Russia
{smir,nick}@iias.spb.su
[3] ITMO University, 49, Kronverkskiy pr., 197101 St. Petersburg, Russia

Abstract. Significant progress in ontology engineering during the last decade resulted in a growing interest in using ontologies for industrial applications. This paper presents lessons learned and recommendations for ontology engineering projects with focus on industrial applications. The research is based on the analysis of a number of case studies in different industrial domains. Based on the case studies the paper presents experiences from ontology development and gives recommendations for industrial ontology construction projects. The recommendations concern (1) selection of development methods, (2) perspectives on generalisation/specialisation strategy, (3) aspects of user participation in ontology construction and (4) effects on knowledge management in organizations.

Keywords: Ontology construction · Ontology engineering · Experience report

1 Introduction

During the last decade, significant progress was made in development methods, engineering tools and application environments of ontologies, which resulted in a growing interest from industry in applying ontologies for solving various industrial problems. Research and development in ontology engineering during the last years focused on techniques for reusing ontologies or parts of them, automation of laborious tasks like ontology population or conversion of texts to ontologies, matching between ontologies or the standardization of knowledge representation and its interlinkage with data. Integration with other technology areas, like knowledge management, enterprise knowledge modelling, or information systems is another reason for the increasing use of semantic technologies in industry.

This paper presents experiences and recommendations for ontology construction projects with focus on industrial application contexts. Our aim is to contribute to the body of knowledge in the field of ontology construction by taking a focus on practices. The research is based on a number of case studies that were carried out in industrial

© Springer International Publishing Switzerland 2015
A. Persson and J. Stirna (Eds.): CAiSE 2015 Workshops, LNBIP 215, pp. 209–220, 2015.
DOI: 10.1007/978-3-319-19243-7_21

enterprises from different domains. Two of these cases were caused by the fact that modern market opportunities require companies to introduce new strategic objectives and tools. They have to build strategies that provide maximum flexibility and can optimally respond to changes in their environment [3, 7] In order to cope with these requirements, companies need to deeply transform both their product development structure and the structure of their business processes. Enterprise modelling can significantly contribute into this transformation since in this respect models are often used as a supportive means that are able to capture and represent different aspects and constructs of an enterprise [14]. Usually, enterprise models consider different enterprise aspects and rise to different meta-levels. In this regard, application of ontologies as conceptual bases that can clarify relations within and between different abstraction levels is believed to be helpful. Ontologies have shown their usability for this type of tasks. They provide a way of knowledge representation, which is widely used today for intelligent analysis of knowledge. As a consequence of this, ontologies will also have the power to clarify the relations between focal areas and the constructs within a focal area [18]. Ontologies are content theories about the sorts of objects, properties of objects and relations between objects that are possible in a specified knowledge domain. They provide potential terms for describing the knowledge about the domain [2].

The remainder of the paper is structured as follows: After a brief description of important concepts and methods for ontology construction (Sect. 2) and the research approach taken (Sect. 3), three industrial cases of ontology development from different application domains are introduced (Sect. 4). Experiences and recommendations are presented and discussed (Sect. 5) related to development strategy, development methodologies and user participation. Conclusions and future work are presented in Sect. 6.

2 Background

The background for this work primarily comes from the field of ontology construction. From the many different definitions of the term "ontology" in computer science related research, Gruber's proposal will be used in this paper: "An Ontology is a formal, explicit specification of shared conceptualization." [6].

Ontology Representation: For case 1 and 3 presented in Sect. 4, Protégé frames or the W3C recommendation ontology language OWL (Web Ontology language) are used to represent the ontology. An OWL ontology consists of Individuals, Properties and Classes. In case 2 an object-oriented constraint network paradigm [15] is applied, which supports capturing of constraints in a more sophisticated way. The OOCN-based ontology consists of Classes, Class Attributes (Values), Value Domains and Constraints. The Class Instances (Individuals) are stored separately from the ontology. The OOCN representation can be transformed to OWL and vice versa.

Ontology Development Methods: Ontology construction is a challenging task and ontology engineers are in need of methods and guidelines to increase the possibility of the project success. There has been a series of approaches proposed for developing ontologies. Despite the fact that the methodologies for ontology development have been subject to research during a number of years, there is no one 'correct' way or methodology for developing ontologies. Previous analysis of ontology development methodologies [12] showed differences in the guidelines provided for the user of the ontology and in the coverage of the ontology lifecycle, i.e. is the ontology construction covered or also evaluation, use and supporting activities? Table 1 shows a (non-exhaustive) list of existing methodologies with selected features.

Table 1. Selected ontology development methodologies

Method	Life-cycle coverage	Detailed definition
Enterprise Ontology	incl. whole life-cycle	no detailed guidelines
TOVE	incl. whole life-cycle	no detailed guidelines
METHONTOLOGY	incl. whole life-cycle	fairly detailed
Sugumaran and Storey	Focus on construction	building phase, very detailed
Ontology Development 101	lacks parts (e.g. eval.)	building phase, very detailed
Sure et al.	incl. whole life-cycle	fairly detailed
OntoSME	incl. whole life-cycle	fairly detailed

Experience Reports in Ontology Engineering: There is only a small number of articles that reflect on experiences and practices from ontology engineering and provide the results of applying a development method, most of the work reports experiences with ontology development methods in the conclusion sections, if at all. Reference [5] discusses strong points and weakness of the Systematic Approach for Building Ontologies (SABiO) ontology development approach and proposes improvement opportunities. Reference [8] develops an ontology based on the guidelines provided by METHONTOLOGY, examines the method utility and addresses the drawbacks. Reference [10] presents results of the practice of ontological engineering without addressing any specific method. Reference [1] reflects experiences from merging different ontology development methods and best practices in software engineering. Finally, our previous work in [9] reports on experiences from ontology construction in practice, which is substantially extended and revised in this paper by including many more cases.

3 Research Approach

From a research methodology perspective, we performed a qualitative analytical survey. Since our objective is to derive experiences for ontology engineering in practice our focus has to be on data sources containing very detailed experience reports and rich case descriptions. As this type of report is quite sparse in scientific literature on ontology engineering (see Sect. 2) we decided to base our analytical survey only on ontology development projects performed in our own research groups. For these projects, the original project documentation and the personnel involved in the project are available. The projects analysed originated from three research contexts, (i) Rostock University (Germany), research group business information systems, (ii) St. Petersburg

Institute for Informatics and Automation (Russia), Computer-aided Systems lab and (iii) School of Engineering at Jönköping University (Sweden), research group information engineering who in some projects jointly worked on the tasks.

The analysis of the projects was done in distributed teams using a joint list of aspects to be investigated. Table 2 shows the list of projects analysed.

Table 2. Ontology construction projects analysed in this paper

Project	Main purpose	Methodology	Performed at
BaSeWeP	Integration of knowledge sources in web portals	Ontology Development 101	Fraunhofer ISST, Berlin[a]
SCM-PLM Integration	Interoperability of SCM and PLM	OOCN development	SPIIRAS
SPIDER	Modeling of enterprise competences	Ontology Development 101	Jönköping University
SEMCO (Autoliv)	Product engineering for airbag systems	METHONTOLOGY	Jönköping University
Media-ILOG	Semantic search in newspaper articles	METHONTOLOGY	Jönköping University
Festo	Product knowledge for configuration purposes	OOCN development	SPIIRAS
ExpertFinder	Competence Modeling/ Matching	Ontology Development 101	Jönköping University
IMSK	Knowledge fusion for civil security applications	eXtreme Design (XD)	Jönköping University
Intelligent ILOG	Trailer Surveillance in transport industries	Ontology Development 101	Rostock University

The project was performed by the same staff members who now work at Rostock University or Jönköping University

4 Industrial Cases of Ontology Construction

This chapter introduces the industrial cases forming the basis for discussion of experiences in Sect. 5. When selecting these cases, the objective was to achieve a wide heterogeneity regarding the type of project (research project, applied research, contract development), the application domain and the purpose of the ontology developed (information structuring, model integration, product codification).

4.1 Autoliv Electronics

The first industrial case was taken from automotive industries. Automotive manufacturers and suppliers have to manage a large number of product variations and their integration into a specific car model. In order to manage and control variety, manufacturers and suppliers increasingly recognize the need to manage project entities like models, documents, metadata, and classification taxonomies in such a manner that the integrative usage of these entities is supported.

The application scenario for the ontology developed is integration of different kinds of structures reflecting the artefacts and their interrelations. On the one hand, model hierarchies have to be captured, indicated and implemented by different modelling levels (system, software, hardware, etc.), which furthermore will have model instances (artefacts) to be managed. On the other hand, term networks and taxonomies have to be considered as equally important. These networks represent organizational structures, product structures or taxonomies originating from customers that are closely related to artefacts. Explicit denotation of these relationships is considered beneficial for identification of reuse potential of components or artefacts.

The ontology construction was performed in a Swedish automotive supplier of software-intensive systems. The development process applied is an enhanced version of the METHONTOLOGY process as described in 2.2. Most important knowledge sources were (1) a description of the suppliers internal software development process with defined procedures for all major aspects of software development and software project management and (2) documentation of two example cases for requirement handling, including original customer requirements, system and functional requirements, and (3) interviews and working sessions with members of the software development department were conducted including project manager, software developers and engineers. The resulting ontology consisted of 379 concepts and with an average depth of inheritance of 3.5 [20].

4.2 Festo

The second industrial case originates from long-term joint work with Festo AG&Co KG, an industrial company that has more than 300 000 customers in 176 countries supported by more than 52 companies worldwide with more than 250 branch offices and authorised agencies in further 36 countries [13]. In this case the goal was to build a problem-oriented ontology for the given, specific purpose. Some early steps of this collaboration related to implementation of the product codification system have been reported in [17]. As a result it was more reasonable to build a new ontology using the formalism that met the requirements than to try to adapt other existing ontology models like CYC or SENSUS.

The complete approach used in this case relies on the ontological knowledge representation for its sharing. The ontology describes common entities of the company's knowledge and relationships between them. Besides, the dynamic nature of the company requires considering the current situation in order to provide for actual knowledge or information. For this purpose, the idea of contexts is used. Context represents additional information that helps to identify specifics of the current transaction. It defines a narrow domain that the user of the knowledge management platform works with. One more important aspect covered by the approach is the competence profiling. Profiles contain such information as the network member's capabilities and capacities, terminological specifics, preferred ways of interaction, etc.

The approach is based on the idea that knowledge of the company can be represented by two levels for the modelling purposes. The knowledge of the first level (structural knowledge) is described by a common ontology. In order for the ontology to be of reasonable size it includes only most generic common entities. The common ontology is used to solve the problem of knowledge heterogeneity and enables inter-operability between heterogeneous information sources due to provision of their common semantics and terminology. It describes all the products (produced and to be produced), their features (existing and possible), production processes and production equipment. This ontology is used in a number of different workflows. The tools are interoperable due to the usage of the common ontology and database. Knowledge map connects the ontology with different knowledge sources of the company. Knowledge represented by the second level is an instantiation of the first level knowledge.

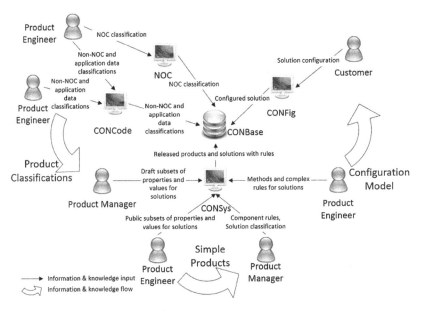

Fig. 1. Product development and configuration process for the Festo case

The ontology creation operation was done automatically based on existing docu-ments and defined rules of the model building. The resulting ontology consists of more than 1000 classes organized into a four level taxonomy, which is based on the VDMA (Verband Deutscher Maschinen – und Anlagenbau, German Engineering Federation) classification [19]. Taxonomical relationships support inheritance that makes it possible to define more common attributes for higher level classes and inherit them for lower level subclasses. The same taxonomy is used in the company's PDM and ERP systems. For each product family (class) a set of properties (attributes) is defined, and for each property its possible values and their codes are defined as well. The lexicon of prop-erties is multilingual and ontology-wide, and as a result the values can be reused for different families. Application of the central single ontology provides for the consis-tency of the product codes and makes it possible to instantly reflect incorporated changes in the codes. The place of the developed ontology in the product development and configuration process is shown in Fig. 1 (the detailed description of the process can be found in [16]).

4.3   Trailer Surveillance Ontology

The third case is based on an industrial research and development project from transport and logistics industries. One of the world's largest truck manufacturers is developing new transport related services based on integration and orchestrated interpretation of different information sources, like on-board vehicle information systems, traffic control systems and fleet management systems. The case aims at using wireless sensor networks in trailers for innovative applications. The wireless sensor network is installed in the position lights of a trailer and could be used for protecting the goods loaded on the trailer against theft, offering additional assistance to the driver of the truck or for surveillance of the goods. The wireless sensor network in the position lights is controlled by a gateway in the trailer, which communicates with the back-office of the owner of the trailer or the owner of the goods, and – for some application cases – with the on-board computer of the truck.

In order to implement the above services, various kinds of knowledge need to be available and combined, which is one of the main purposes of the ontology development performed in the case. Observations acquired through the different sensors in the trailer have to be combined with information coming from other sources, like an authentication service for the driver's identity. Furthermore, we have to detect potential critical events, according to what is specified by the IT services. For this purpose, the ontology had to accommodate transportation domain knowledge, the sensors and their observation possibilities, and a conceptual model for situations.

The ontology development followed an extended version of "ontology development 101" [4]. The resulting ontology for transport surveillance (OTS) was developed in several iterations. OTS adopts the Semantic Web Rules Language (SWRL) for modeling rules which provides the ability to add Horn-like rules expressed in terms of OWL concepts. Observing the relations between objects or entities, *situation awareness* (or assessment) aims at providing a projection based on situations, which describe a state of affairs adhering to a partial view of the world. A subject is aware, if he is capable of observing some objects and making inferences from these observations.

5   Experiences

Experiences and recommendations presented in this section were based on the industrial cases introduced in Sect. 4 and findings from other research and development projects applying ontologies (see Table 2 in Sect. 3). The experiences regarding user participation (5.3) are to a large extent already reported in earlier work (see [9]). They are included in this paper as they were confirmed by the later cases and additional recommendations were added.

5.1   Development Methods

Concerning the ontology construction methodologies, we applied ontology development 101, METHONTOLOGY, XD and OntoSME, as already shown in Table 2. As the individual experiences with these methods have been reported in detail in previous publications (see Table 2), we will focus in this section on the general view.

Although ontology development 101 is considered as rather limited method due to its focus on ontology construction only and the closeness to Protégé as a tool, we find it still one of the most useful approaches when focusing of the core content of its seven development steps and adapting it to contemporary tool support. As in all modelling and development projects, domain and scope of a project should be clearly defined and reuse of proven solutions should be considered, which make the first two steps important. Competency questions from our view are a valuable way to express scope and focus. In case 3 after iteratively listing the competency questions, we searched for the existing ontologies that might be refined or extended. Unfortunately neither transport domain ontologies nor information models for the truck-trailer surveillance domain were identified. Nevertheless the reviewed models were to some extent reusable and beneficial, e.g. through the models, ontologies and approaches, it was practicable to identify important terms & controlled vocabularies, to define the classes, class hierarchies as well as the relationships between them. Hence, it is possible to reuse existing ontologies or even models as an instrument to identify semantic specifications in the domain. The way of defining attributes and value ranges of the concepts and of capturing instances (steps 5 to 7) is affected by the selected tool. Nevertheless, the activities as such remain important and required.

5.2   Concept Identification During the Development Process

Additional experiences contributed by this paper concern the identification of relevant concepts, relation and properties or constraints. One aspect to discuss is whether to work top-down, bottom-up or middle-out. Our impression from ontology development projects indicates that experience from enterprise modelling concerning these strategies can be applied as rule of thumb for ontology projects.

Top-down approaches should be used in application domain well-known to the project team where the complexity in terms of required level of detail and the scope of the development is clearly defined. An example from our background would be the Festo case, where the existing codification system, number of products and potential variation limited the complexity of problem at hand. In cases with unclear or unknown complexity, there is the danger of consuming the resources allocated to the project before reaching the goal of having developed an ontology. Bottom-up approaches can result in a number of thoroughly defined parts of an ontology, which are not very well interlinked and do not cover the intended scope of the ontology. These "solution islands" often contain more details than required for the purpose of the ontology. Our recommendation is to always test suitability of the bottom-up approach by using it in a pre-study with limited scope and clearly defined evaluation criteria. Finally the middle-out approach is from our experience suitable to explore both, complexity of the problem at hand and required level of detail, in application fields unknown to the ontology expert. The approach was used in the trailer surveillance case in order to capture sensor related concepts in combination with situations to be detected. What level of detail of situation information was needed in order to describe the sensor information in sufficient detail became only clear during the ontology development process.

In addition to this generalisation/specialisation strategy, we recommend to also have different lifecycle phases of an ontology in mind during the development process, such as the conceptual, implementation and application stage. In the first stage the main elements, structures, relations and constraints of an ontology are identified based on the knowledge of the domain experts and other knowledge sources. This stage should be independent from the actual ontology representation or ontology engineering tool to be used in order to avoid unnecessary dependencies from implementation technology. The implementation stage codes the result from the conceptual stage in appropriate representation with a suitable tool, which allows for selection of the implementation technology based on the lessons learned from the conceptual stage. The last stage optimizes the implementation for application purposes, which for example can include additional instances or axioms for consistency purposes. To distinguish between these different phases is part of several methods, such as METHONTOLOGY. However, many other methods do not make this strict distinction, which is why this paper emphasizes the importance of clear separation.

5.3   User Participation

Since more than a decade, participative modelling is recognized as valuable and practicable instrument contributing to solving design problems in particular in organizational contexts (see e.g. [11]). As opposed to the traditional approach of gathering facts by interviewing stakeholders in an organization and afterwards developing a solution without stakeholder involvement, the participative way of working includes development of the intended solution with direct involvement and contribution of the future users, like modelling in facilitated group sessions.

Experiences from ontology development projects like the cases presented in Sect. 4 indicate the value of user participation even for ontology development projects. The main recommendations are to thoroughly prepare participation and to concentrate on the conceptual stage of development.

The preparation of user participation should start with the key persons at the industrial company, who should be introduced to the potentials and limits of ontology use. However, this introduction should not include representation techniques or technical details of ontologies, since this usually is not relevant for decision makers and could create distraction from the modelling task. By clearly defining purpose of the project, intended use of ontologies and known limits, the expectation of the industrial partner can reflect the realistic possibilities. This should preferably happen before the ontology development starts.

After sufficient management information and attention, the intended participative steps of the ontology development should be prepared by individual discussions with the participants. Each participant should be informed about the purpose of the ontology development project and the intended way of working. However, main purpose of these individual discussions is to start identifying existing knowledge sources in the organization relevant for the ontology development, to build up trust to the participating users, and to increase their commitment to the project.

During the participative parts of the ontology construction, focus should be on the conceptual stage of the ontology development and on use of techniques like card sorting or pencil and paper sketches. Main reason for this is to not put the burden of learning and understanding the formalities of an ontology language on the domain experts and end users participating. A notation that everyone understands should be used, otherwise to too much attention is lost when the participants try to understand the notation used.

5.4   Organizational Changes Triggered by Ontology Development

In the Festo case we observed that ontology development was part of an organizational change process towards a more knowledge-aware organisation. Implementation of complex changes in large companies faces many difficulties: business process cannot be stopped to switch between old and new workflows; old and new software systems have to be supported at the same time; the range of products, which are already in the markets, has to be maintained in parallel with new products, etc. Another problem is that it is difficult to estimate in advance which solutions and workflow would be efficient and convenient for the employees. Hence, just following existing knowledge management implementation guidelines is not possible and this process has to be and iterative and interactive.

During the work on the mentioned case studies the following observations related to knowledge management implementation in companies have been made:

- Engineers and managers are concentrated on their work and cannot pay enough attention to additional tasks related to trying new knowledge-based workflows. This was in a higher degree applicable to the product managers and product engineers. At the levels of production engineers and production managers, this issue was less obvious, because the "experimental" knowledge-based production planning could be done in parallel with the actual one.

- A target knowledge management consisting of people volunteering to assist in implementing knowledge management in the company group has to be formed. These people have to be experts in their roles and in several other roles, which would re-use some of the knowledge of this role. They will be involved into the processes of building the initial common ontology and implementing knowledge-based workflows, thus slowly involving other roles into the process of knowledge management implementation.

- Role-based approach makes it possible to implement knowledge management incrementally, with initiative coming from employees. E.g., an experimental knowledge-based support of one workflow could be implemented for one user role letting the users estimate its efficiency and convenience. Then, workflows reusing some of the knowledge of the experimental workflow can be added, etc. Representatives of other roles seeing the improvements of the implemented knowledge-based workflows also wish to join and actively participate in the identification of the knowledge needed for their workflows and further turning their workflows into the knowledge-based ones.

6 Conclusions

Based on the analysis of a number of ontology development projects performed in three different research groups and on the discussion of three industrial cases in detail this paper presented a number of experiences and recommendations for ontology construction in an industrial context, which can be summarized as follows:

- Consider using "simple" methods, like ontology development 101, for the construction phase of ontologies; adapt the methodology to the situation at hand, e.g. regarding tool use and iteration of phases
- Use top-down development for well-known domains with clearly defined scope; use middle out development for unknown application fields; always perform a pre-study before deciding to use bottom-up development; clearly separate between conceptual, implementation and application stage
- Create realistic expectations on company management side; use participative work mainly in the conceptual stage, i.e. avoid details of ontology representation
- Prepare for accompanying organizational change projects triggered by ontology development; investigate the role structures in the organization "neighbouring" the ontology development project

Although the work presented in this paper is based on quite a few industrial cases, the main limitation of the research is that the empirical grounding should be improved by an increased number of cases. The recommendations presented are considered useful, but they cannot be expected accurate for all industrial cases. Future work will include further elaboration on the recommendations. The above list of recommendations should be extended in more detailed guidance or good practices for ontology developers. Furthermore, there are a number of experiences from industrial projects not discussed in this paper because they were just based on a single case, like the use of ontology design patterns, the reuse of existing ontologies, or the integration of ontologies with existing IT-systems in the companies under consideration.

Acknowledgements. Some parts of the research presented here were done in collaboration between Festo and SPIIRAS. The research was supported partly by grants # 13-07-13159, # 13–07–12095, # 14–07–00345, # 12–07–00298, and # 12–07–00302 of the Russian Foundation for Basic Research, project 213 (program 15) of the Presidium of the Russian Academy of Sciences, and project #2.2 of the basic research program. This work was also partially supported by Government of Russian Federation, Grant 074-U01. Other parts of this work were financed by the Swedish Knowledge Foundation.

References

1. Brusa, G., Caliusco, M.L., Chiotti, O: A process for building a domain ontology: an experience in developing a government budgetary ontology. In: Proceedings of the Second Australasian Workshop on Advances in Ontologies, vol. 72, pp. 7-15 (2006)
2. Chandrasekaran, B., Josephson, J.R., Benjamins, V.R.: What are ontologies and why do we need them? IEEE Intell. Syst. **14**(1), 20–26 (1999)

3. Christopher, M., Towill, D.: An integrated model for the design of agile supply chains. Int. J. Phys. Distrib. Oper. Manage. **31**, 235–244 (2001)
4. Noy, N.F., McGuinness, L.D.: Ontology development 101: A guide to creating your first ontology. Development **32**(1), 1–25 (2000)
5. Falbo, R.A.: Experiences in using a method for building domain ontologies. In: 16th International Conference on Software Engineering and Knowledge Engineering (SEKE 2004), Workshop on Ontology in Action (OIA 2004), Alberta, Canada, pp. 474-477 (2004)
6. Gruber, T.: A translation approach to portable ontology specifications. Knowl. Acquis. **5**, 199–220 (1993)
7. Gunasekaran, A., Lai, K., Cheng, T.: Responsive supply chain: a competitive strategy in a networked economy. Omega **36**, 549–564 (2008)
8. Park, J., Sung, K., Moon, S.: Developing graduation screen ontology based on the METHONTOLOGY approach. In: Networked Computing and Advanced Information Management, NCM 2008, pp. 375–380 (2008)
9. Sandkuhl, K., Öhgren, A., Smirnov, A., Shilov, N., Kashevnik, A.: Ontology construction in practice - experiences and recommendations from industrial cases. In: 9th ICEIS, 12-16 June 2007, Funchal, Madeira – Portugal (2007)
10. Mizoguchi, R.: Ontological engineering: foundation of the next generation knowledge processing. In: Zhong, N., Yao, Y., Ohsuga, S., Liu, J. (eds.) WI 2001. LNCS (LNAI), vol. 2198, pp. 44–57. Springer, Heidelberg (2001)
11. Nilsson, A., Tolis, C., Nellborn, C. (eds.): Perspectives on Business Modelling: Understanding and Changing Organisations. Springer, Heidelberg (1999)
12. Öhgren, A. Sandkuhl, K.: Towards a methodology for ontology development in small and medium-sized enterprises. In: IADIS Conference on Applied Computing, Algarve, Portugal (2005)
13. Oroszi, A., Jung, T., Smirnov, A., Shilov, N., Kashevnik, A.: Ontology-driven codification for discrete and modular products. Int. J. Prod. Dev. **8**(2), 162–177 (2009). Inderscience
14. Seigerroth, U., Kaidalova, J., Shilov, N., Kaczmarek, T.: Semantic web technologies in business and IT alignment: multi-model algorithm of ontology matching. In: The Fifth International Conference on Advances in Future Internet (AFIN 2013), August 25-31, 2013, Barcelona, Spain, pp. 50-56 (2013). ISBN: 978-1-61208-300-1
15. Smirnov, A., Pashkin, M., Levashova, T., Chilov, N.: Ontology-based support for semantic interoperability between SCM and PLM. Int. J. Pro. Lifecycle Manage. **1**(3), 289–302 (2006). Inderscience Enterprises Ltd
16. Smirnov, A., Sandkuhl, K., Shilov, N., Kashevnik, A.: "Product-Process-Machine" System Modeling: Approach and Industrial Case Studies. In: Grabis, J., Kirikova, M., Zdravkovic, J., Stirna, J. (eds.) PoEM 2013. LNBIP, vol. 165, pp. 251–265. Springer, Heidelberg (2013)
17. Smirnov, A., Shilov, N., Kashevnik, A., Jung, T., Sinko, M., Oroszi, A.: Ontology-driven product configuration. In: International Conference on Knowledge Management and Information Sharing (KMIS 2011), Paris, France, October 26-29, 2011, pp. 38-47 (2011)
18. Kaczmarek, T., Seigerroth, U., Shilov, N.: Multi-layered enterprise modeling and its challenges in business and IT alignment. In: Proceedings of the ICEIS 2012, Wroclaw, Poland, June 28 – July 01, 2012, pp. 257-260 (2012)
19. VDMA, German Engineering Federation (2014). http://www.vdma.org/en_GB/
20. Sandkuhl, K., Billig, A.: Ontology-based artefact management in automotive electronics. Int. J. Comput. Integr. Manufact. (IJCIM) **20**(7), 627–638 (2007)

Extending Enterprise Architectures to Capture Consumer Values: The Case of TOGAF

Eric-Oluf Svee[✉] and Jelena Zdravkovic

Department of Computer and Systems Sciences, Stockholm University,
Box 7003, 16407 Kista, Sweden
{eric-sve, jelenaz}@dsv.su.se

Abstract. This paper explores how to make Enterprise Architecture (EA) aware of consumer values. Current proposals in enterprise modeling recognize the need for user needs, although often without taking explicit account of the consumer values that are at the root of the exchange process. Enterprise architecture provides a roadmap for the development of systems that can support the creation and delivery of products of interest. First, a survey of enterprise architecture practitioners highlights the importance and significance of integrating consumer values into enterprise architecture through. Next, the survey results are used to enhance a consumer value meta-model for better integration with enterprise architecture, specifically The Open Group Architecture Framework (TOGAF).

Keywords: Value · Consumer value · Enterprise modeling · Enterprise architecture

1 Introduction

Consumer values are the interactive, preferential experiences that power commerce: the catalysts leading to the value exchanges between consumers and businesses. A priori to the exchange itself, consumer values are foundational to the well being of enterprises because without them, the reason for that business would not exist.

However, for all of their importance, consumer values are little studied within the realm of information science and are most often left to research communities in marketing and psychology. It is the contention of this paper, however, that their inclusion in the design of information technology (IT) is crucial for its ultimate success; without taking the values of consumers into account from the earliest stages of their design, IT artifacts risk irrelevance and purposelessness.

Indeed, as consumers are requiring more qualitative experiences than ever before, the future of successful information systems (IS) design requires greater alignment between business and its supporting IT infrastructure. These in turn lead to the need for new and novel means and methods to capture real values of consumers and then relate such values to requirements for information technology.

Concurrent to this shift towards a more consumer focus is the need for complex software to coordinate the activities of modern enterprises. This has become a necessity for their success, with the competitive conditions of today, where business sectors are

© Springer International Publishing Switzerland 2015
A. Persson and J. Stirna (Eds.): CAiSE 2015 Workshops, LNBIP 215, pp. 221–232, 2015.
DOI: 10.1007/978-3-319-19243-7_22

rapidly reshaping, organizations are becoming global, and consumers have seemingly endless choices, requiring software engineers to incorporate consumer values—personal judgments based on comparative, preferential experiences—into the design of such supporting software.

This research addresses the problem of the lack of consumer values awareness within enterprise architecture by first establishing a conceptual link between the values of consumers and system requirements. It accomplishes this by engaging directly with the enterprise architecture framework TOGAF [21]. A survey of practicing enterprise architects demonstrates the need for consumer values to be included into enterprise architecture, while also evaluating an initial attempt at integrating consumer values into EA. Next, a known meta-model for working with consumer values—the Consumer Preference Meta-Model [19, 20, 24]—is utilized to capture consumer values and provide them to TOGAF.

This paper is structured accordingly: Sect. 2 introduces information relevant to this research from two areas: consumer values as understood through the Consumer Preference MetaModel; and enterprise architecture through TOGAF framework. Section 3 details the process involved in this research's primary contributions, first by presenting a survey of practicing enterprise architects, and then utilizing its results to restructure an existing consumer values model for integration with TOGAF. Section 4 demonstrates the contributions of this research through a case example of an online education system, and Sect. 5 concludes the paper with a discussion and preview to future work.

2 Background

2.1 Values, Consumer Values, and Value Frameworks

At the highest level, value is viewed as the relative status of a thing, or the esteem in which it is held, according to its real or supposed worth, usefulness, or importance. As evidenced in the previous section, this is very different from the business view of values (e.g., value transfers of resources) and, for Holbrook, a value is simply a preference judgment represented by distinct types within the consumption experience [8]. Value is also the perception of a need-satisfying capability in an object. In this guise, value has a "parasitical" existence; it depends on an object as its value carrier.

To clarify the concept of value, frameworks for its description and discussion, as well as means to measure it, are utilized throughout this research. There are a number of possibilities, from various fields such as psychology and organizational theory, including the three needs theory [13] and retailing, including Servqual [15], among others. For illustrative purposes, this report relies on three: Maslow's Hierarchy of Needs [11], Schwartz's Value Theory [16], and the Typology of Consumer Values [8]. These were selected because of their wide acceptance, application across a variety of industries, and robust conceptual frameworks.

In [24] the Consumer Preference-aware Meta-Model (CPMM) is proposed to explicitly address consumer preferences as an important requirement for information systems development. It accomplishes this by addressing preferences—for example, the Needs of Maslow and Basic Values of Schwartz are seen as generic drivers of human actions, while Holbrook's value framework (Consumer Value) concerns preferences on consumption, i.e. Value Objects. In Sect. 3.3 the CPMM, and its relationship to EA is presented.

2.2 Enterprise Architecture

Architecture is defined as the fundamental organization of a system, embodied in its components, their relationships to each other and the environment, and the principles governing its design and evolution [21]. As the master plan for the whole enterprise, one that takes into account the business in its totality, enterprise architecture enable communication among different stakeholders and promotes a shared terminology. Its primary goal is to align the IT-related activities within the enterprise [21].

TOGAF. The Open Group Architecture Framework (TOGAF) is a framework—a detailed method and a set of supporting tools — for developing an enterprise architecture.

In TOGAF, "architecture" has two meanings depending upon the context:

- A formal description of a system, or a detailed plan of the system at component level to guide its implementation
- The structure of components, their inter-relationships, and the principles and guidelines governing their design and evolution over time.

TOGAF's Architecture Development Method (ADM). TOGAF's Architecture Development Method (ADM) contains nine iterative phases, and is the formalized process of populating the elements of an enterprise's architecture. Key to this research is Phase B: Business Architecture, whose pertinent tasks are: to describe the product and/or service strategy, and the organizational, functional, process, information, and geographic aspects of the business environment, based on the business principles, business goals, and strategic drivers; to select and develop the relevant architecture viewpoints that will enable demonstration of how the stakeholder concerns are addressed in the Business Architecture; and, to select the relevant tools and techniques to be used in association with the selected viewpoints.

TOGAF's Motivation Extension. TOGAF's Content Meta Model (CMM) provides a basic enterprise architecture model with a minimum feature set, one that supports the inclusion of optional extensions during engagement tailoring. One of these is the Motivation Extension, which supports linking drivers, goals, and objectives to organizations and services [21].

Drivers are an external or internal condition that motivates the organization to define its goals. Goals are high-level statements of intent or direction for an organization, typically used to measure success. Objectives are time-bounded milestone for an organization used to demonstrate progress towards a goal. A service is a logical representation of a repeatable business activity that has a specified outcome.

3 Contribution

The values of an individual have an effect on their behavior as consumers through their attitudes, which in turn impact on their choices within the value exchange [1, 10, 17, 23]. Additionally, it has been shown that values relate to real-life choice, and may also influence behavior through different manifestations, such as habits [18].

Many authors have pointed out that cultural and psychological dimensions of consumer behavior should be seen as the core of retail strategy [4, 24] as such data could allow marketers to create new consumer experiences [2, 3].

Consumer values within enterprise architecture are an area that has been discussed but never completely addressed. This is borne out by several facts: first it is known that consumer values are the a priori ingredient necessary for a value exchange to occur. Additionally consumer values are covered tangentially within the Motivation Extension of TOGAF's Content MetaModel, and as well consumer values having been explicitly included in the latest version of Archimate [9], the enterprise architecture modeling language designed around TOGAF. Finally the survey of enterprise architecture practitioners conducted as part of this research indicated a strong belief in the importance of including consumer values into TOGAF (see Sect. 3.2).

Accordingly, the solutions presented in this work focus on capturing consumer values and introducing them into the development of enterprise architectures that support businesses intent on providing goods, services, and experiences to satisfy consumers' needs, on the basis of their values.

Section 3 discusses the creation of the artifacts that are the main contributions of this research study. Section 3.1 provides theoretical and practical justifications for the importance of including consumer values in enterprise architectures. Section 3.2 details a survey of practicing enterprise architects that justifies the inclusion of consumer values within enterprise architecture. The section is concluded Sect. 3.3 in which the results from this survey are used to restructure an existing model—the Consumer Preference Meta-Model—for integration with TOGAF as the CPMM-EA.

3.1 Consumer Values in Enterprise Architecture

The process closest to consumer values that TOGAF provides can be considered the completion of the two viewpoints necessary to complete the Core Content Metamodel's Motivation Extension: the Driver/Goal/Objective Catalog and the Goal/Objective Service Diagram.

Created within Phase B, Business Architecture, of the ADM, the Driver/Goal/Objective catalog provides a cross-organizational reference of how an organization meets its drivers in practical terms through goals, objectives, and (optionally) measures.

The Driver/Goal/Objective catalog contains the following metamodel entities: Organization Unit, Driver, Goal, Objective, Measure (optional) [21].

Also found in Phase B, Business Architecture, the Goal/Objective/Service diagram defines the ways in which a service contributes to the achievement of a business vision or strategy.

Services are associated with the drivers, goals, objectives, and measures that they support, and the Goal/Objective/Service diagram allows the enterprise to understand which services contribute to similar aspects of business performance. It also provides qualitative input on what constitutes high performance for a particular service [21].

TOGAF's ADM is self-admittedly agnostic to the methods employed to fulfill its stepwise and cyclic approach to architecture development. The single process steps are described very generically and hence are not easy to implement without consulting. This flexibility becomes problematic when a topic is considered sufficiently important to include in the framework but concrete methods for fulfilling it are under-researched or are simply not extant.

The purpose of the Motivation Extension is to influence the company's products and services. A problem similar to the ADM is that the Motivation Extension contains no guidelines for how customer values should be captured and classified in order to influence the company's products and services, but is rather a set of to-be-completed entities with no guidance on how to capture them, let alone make them consumer values aware.

3.2 Empirical Study: Consumer Values Potential in TOGAF

In April 2014, a survey of 18 career enterprise architects who are employed by Tieto, the largest IT services company in Scandinavia, was conducted. Founded in 1968, Tieto employs approximately 15 000 people in twenty countries with headquarters in Helsinki, Finland, and through those employees offers IT services that include consulting, operation and maintenance services, system integration, and industry solutions. Tieto uses TOGAF as its primary enterprise architecture framework, both for itself and for its clients. As a large IT consultancy that supports TOGAF internally and externally, the survey respondents were ideal candidates based on their work as practitioners.

Survey Structure. The survey consisted of 12 questions, five covering basic demographic information, five assessing the proposed artifact, and two assessing the inclusion of consumer values within TOGAF. The survey, along with a complete data set, can be downloaded from http://svee.blogs.dsv.su.se/CAME-2014.zip.

Demographic Information. Table 1 summarizes the demographic information collected by the survey: gender, age, job title, education, and experience using TOGAF, for the survey cohort.

Consumer Values Within Enterprise Architecture: Questions 8, 12. These answers highlight the potential benefit of including consumer values within enterprise architectures as seen by experienced practitioners (Table 2).

Artifact Assessment: Questions 6−7,9−11. The artifact that was developed for the survey was named the Consumer Aware Motivation Extension (CAME). It was designed to work within TOGAF's Motivation Extension and was proposed as a way to introduce the concept of consumer values within enterprise architectures that also

Table 1. Summary of survey demographic information

Gender of participants	22.2 % Female
	78.8 % Male
Participants' ages	Avg.: 46.1 years
	Max.: 65 years
Participants' job titles	
Architect (Systems/Software)	44.4 %
Enterprise architect/Enterprise consultant	16.7 %
Technician/Manager/Consultant	38.9 %

Table 2. Summary of consumer values within enterprise architecture

Consumer values should be included in TOGAF	22.2 % Female
	78.8 % Male
Level of expertise	44.5 % Experienced/ Expert

would elicit feedback from TOGAF experts: they would be familiar with TOGAF's vocabulary, but the method was completely new.

CAME was developed by mapping concepts from the value frameworks of Schwartz [16] and Holbrook [8], as used in the CPMM, to the Motivation Extension of TOGAF's Content Meta Model. This allowed for a structure based on TOGAF, but that included a known mechanism for both capturing and describing consumer values. The goals of comprehensibility and ease of use for the survey participants were accomplished by designing CAME using terms from TOGAF, along with a notation similar to what was contained within its standards documentation (Table 3).

Table 3. Summary of artifact assessment

Is CAME understandable?	88.8 % Partly/fully
Is CAME appropriate to use for capturing CV?	83.3 % Yes
Would you use CAME?	66.7 % Probably/definitely

Summary of Results. Analysis of the results leads to the following conclusions: consumer values do and should affect the company's Drivers, Goals and Objectives; CAME is understandable; CAME is informative/instructive; CAME is partly a good model for capturing consumer value and further affect the company Drivers, Goals, and Objectives; it is not clear how CAME can be used in practice; CAME needs to be tested in practice.

The outcomes of the survey were sufficient to conclude that proceeding with integrating consumer values into enterprise architecture was a useful goal, and that using a tested tool for accomplishing the integration would be the preferred means to accomplish this. Additionally, the survey supports the primary contention of this research: that consumer values should be included in the design of enterprise architectures.

3.3   Consumer Preference Meta-Model for Enterprise Architecture

CPMM was then adapted to the findings of the survey and to the vocabulary of TOGAF, becoming CPMM-EA. Its foundational concept is Holbrook's view consumer values as interactive, preferential experiences. Several entities were renamed, and complete definitions can be found in Table 4.

In the original CPMM, following business value modeling studies [6, 7, 14], the exchange of a product, a good, or a service is a transaction involving two primary actors: a provider and a consumer, economically independent entities. The exchange assumes transfer of the value object—the product's ownership or rights for its use—from the provider to the consumer, in return for direct or indirect compensation.

Consumer is a role representing a group of people in the consideration for the evaluation of the value object, based on individual preferences. Any value framework can be taken into consideration, and can categorize its values as a measure; these can be quantitative and/or qualitative. For example, REA could be applied in its standard form [12], or through the use of an enterprise architecture ontology [6].

A segment encompasses the information characterizing a subclass of consumer, further distinguishing it from demographics and context of use properties. A segment is used to refine the measures to elicit a variety of subclasses of consumers. Demographics encompass consumer characteristics, such as age, ethnicity, education, and similar. Context of use reflects an individual's context [5, 9], where the main attributes for context of use are location, where the consumer will use a value object and environment, and which objects, devices, services, and regulations and under which weather conditions the value object will be used. Finally, identity is covered by demographics, i.e., who the consumer is.

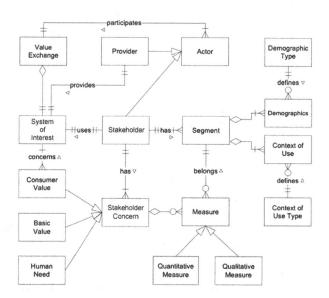

Fig. 1. Consumer preference MetaModel for enterprise architecture [CPMM-EA]

In the transition from CPMM to CPMM-EA, *Consumer* became *Stakeholder*, and because there is no *Value Object* per se in enterprise architecture, TOGAF's term *System of Interest* was adopted. *Value Exchange* is still utilized, though only for the

Table 4. Summary of CPMM-EA classes, with descriptions

Class	Description
Actor	Contains the independent entities that are the primary participants within the exchange of goods, money, rights, or services
Consumer value	Examples of value types that CPMM-EA is capable of utilizing, in this case Holbrook. Basic Values [] and Human Needs [] are also instances in this particular example
Context of use	Information based used to classify the segment sub-class of stakeholder
Context of use Type	Information specifically tailored to suit the needs identified in Context of Use
Demographics	Information based on aggregated data used to classify the segment sub-class of stakeholder
Demographic type	Information based on aggregated data, specifically tailored to suit the needs identified in demographics
Measure	Quantifies and conceptualizes values, with sub-classes of means contained within each of the various frameworks that can be used for conceptualization and quantification
Provider	An independent entity that participates in the value exchange by providing the goods, money, rights, or services in exchange for compensation
Quantitative measure	Information that measures the stakeholder's preferences that is quantitative in nature and supports the stakeholder's concerns
Qualitative measure	Information that measures the stakeholder's preferences that is qualitative in nature and supports the stakeholder's concerns
Segment	Encompasses the information characterizing a subclass of stakeholder, refining the measures used to elicit a variety of subclasses of consumers
Stakeholder	An independent entity that participates in the value exchange by consuming the goods, money, rights, or services in exchange for compensation
Stakeholder Concern	Captures the preferences that drive a stakeholder's evaluative process as they seek fulfillment. Key interests that are crucially important to the stakeholders in the system-of-interest, and determine the acceptability of the system. Concerns may pertain to any aspect of the system's functioning, development, or operation, including considerations such as performance, reliability, security, distribution, and ability to evolve. Used in place of the more commonly known Value Driver
System-of-Interest	Constitutes the focus of the process wherein the stakeholder evaluates whether the system-of-interest satisfies the motivation, value, or need driving their desire to participate in the exchange process. Generally a collection of components organized to accomplish a specific function or set of functions
Value Exchange	Captures the transaction between two parties (a stakeholder and a provider) where ownership is exchanged

appraisal of the *System-of-Interest/Value Object*, as per the interactive, preferential experience derived from Holbrook.

Constraints Within CPMM-EA. Apart from the cardinality constraints included in the meta-model, a set of constraints is also introduced to capture the permissible instantiations of concepts found in the frameworks.

At least one instance of both *Stakeholder* and *Provider* must belong to the same context. Moreover, an instance of *SystemOfInterest* provided by an instance of *Provider* which is an instance of *Actor* which belongs to an instance of *Context* is the same instance of *ValueObject* obtained by an instance of *Stakeholder* which is an instance of actor that belongs to the same instance of *Context*.

Additional constraints include that at least one instance of both *Stakeholder* and *Provider* classes must belong to the same *ValueExchange*. Moreover, Provider provides an instance of *SystemOfInterest* that is part of *ValueExchange*, that is the same instance of *SystemOfInterest* that a *Stakeholder* uses.

An example of the differences between the two populations can be seen in their understanding of the value Universalism/Ethics. Not only was the value prioritized differently (the non-master's students consider it their most important value, whereas for master's students it is their third), but also the ways they choose to express it are quite different. Master's students are more inclined to see ethical lapses as something that the university should manage.

4 Discussion

Enterprise architecture frameworks such as TOGAF [21], etc. are aligned with the concepts of the ISO/IEC 42010 architecture description model. Because of this close relationship TOGAF carries forward concepts from that standard; for example, its definition of stakeholder is nearly identical— "people who have key roles in, or concerns about, the system" [21]. They also share a problem: both lack an explicit consumer value-aware orientation. Certain EA standards do address this issue, though not explicitly, containing concepts which can contain consumer values but which do not explicitly call for them. Prior work has been done to align the ISO standard with consumer preferences [19].

TOGAF is an excellent exemplar of an awareness of consumer values without a concrete implementation; several TOGAF concepts relevant to this research are *Motivation Extension* which contains *Drivers*, or external or internal conditions that motivate an organization to define its goals; *Goals*, or high-level statements of intent or direction for an organization that are typically used to measure success; and *Objectives*, which are time-bounded milestones for an organization used to demonstrate progress towards a goal. The logical progression is that the *Organization* is motivated by the *Driver*, which creates the *Goal*, which is realized through the *Objective*. These benefits can only be accrued when the values are properly elicited and captured, a critical advantage provided by the use of CPMM-EA.

One additional benefit of CPMM-EA is that it both provides means to model those consumer values that are discovered. Archimate, the enterprise architecture modeling language for TOGAF, recognizes the importance of CV: it adds the consumer values concepts that TOGAF is missing: it models *TOGAF:Concern* as *Archimate:Driver*, which leads to *Archimate:BusinessGoal*. These goals are realized by *Archimate: Principle*, which are in turn sharpened as specific *Archimate:Requirement* [9]. However, because it is used for representation, it also does not contain a method of capturing consumer values, something that CPMM-EA does.

5   Conclusions and Future Work

This work proposed to assist in the development of enterprise architectures by modeling values of consumers as a starting point. The presented consumer values-aware requirements framework consists of a value-based Consumer Preference Meta-Model for Enterprise Architecture (CPMM-EA), and a method for its use to capture preferences of stakeholders.

A survey of practicing enterprise architects designed around a simplified version of CPMM-EA (CAME) lead to the following conclusions: consumer values do and should affect the company's Drivers, Goals and Objectives; CAME is understandable; CAME is informative/instructive; CAME is partly a good model for capturing consumer value and further affect the company Drivers, Goals, and Objectives; it is not clear how CAME can be used in practice; CAME needs to be tested in practice.

Future work in the area of enterprise architecture will focus on further developing CPMM-EA into a tool that will address needs indicated by the practitioners in the survey: although it addresses their desire to have consumer values introduced to enterprise architecture, the tool itself must be straightforward as well as lightweight and easy to use in the field. Such a tool would necessarily need to be evaluated on a conceptual level, as well as its usefulness in practice.

The outcomes of the survey were sufficient to conclude that proceeding with integrating consumer values into enterprise architecture was a useful goal, and that using a tested tool for accomplishing the integration would be the preferred means to accomplish this. Additionally, the survey supports the primary contention of this research: that consumer values should be included in the design of enterprise architectures. Future work in these areas is already being planned.

Additionally, the survey of experienced enterprise architects is unique in the literature: any explicit inquiry about the incorporation of consumer values into enterprise architectures in general, and TOGAF specifically, is not extant in the literature. This supports the novelty these initial explorations in the area of enterprise architecture, first from the ISO 42010 standard, next to its framework as expressed in TOGAF, and furthermore with its modeling language Archimate. CPMM-EA is the next vital step in bringing consumer value awareness to enterprise architectures by both providing such values into a conceptual model, but also by having that model be useful for populating the artifacts of the larger enterprise framework.

Future work in the larger subject of consumer values includes their further introduction, integration, and development into areas such as requirements engineering and software engineering, among others.

References

1. Cai, Y., Shannon, R.: Personal values and mall shopping behaviour: the mediating role of intention among chinese consumers. Int. J. Retail Distrib. Manage. **40**(4), 290–318 (2012)
2. Carpenter, J.M., Fairhurst, A.: Consumer shopping value, satisfaction, and loyalty for retail apparel brands. J. Fashion Mark. Manage. **9**(3), 256–269 (2005)
3. Carpenter, J.M., Moore, M., Fairhurst, A.E.: Consumer shopping value for retail brands. J. Fashion Mark. Manage. **9**(1), 43–53 (2005)
4. Cox, R., Brittain, P.: Retailing: An Introduction. Financal Times Management, Dorchester, UK (2004)
5. Dey, A.K.: Understanding and using context. Pers. Ubiquit. Comput. **5**(1), 4–7 (2001)
6. Geerts, G.L., McCarthy, W.E.: An ontological analysis of the economic primitives of the extended-REA enterprise information architecture. Int. J. Acc. Inf. Syst. **3**(1), 1–16 (2002)
7. Gordijn, J., van Eck, P., Wieringa, R.: Requirements Engineering Techniques for e-Services, pp. 331–352. Cooperative Information Systems Series, Service-Oriented Computing (2009)
8. Holbrook, M.: Consumer Value: a Framework for Analysis and Research. Routledge, London (1991)
9. Jonkers, H., Quartel, D., van Gils, B., Franken, H.: Enterprise architecture with TOGAF 9.1 and Archimate 2.0. BizzDesign (2012)
10. Kahle, L.R.: Social values and consumer behavior: research from the list of values. In: Seligman, C., Olson, J.M., Zanna, M.P. (eds.) The Psychology of Values: The Ontario Symposium, vol. 8, pp. 135–151. Lawrence Erlbaum Associates Mahwah, NJ USA (1996)
11. Maslow, A.H.: A theory of human motivation. Psychol. Rev. **50**(4), 370 (1943)
12. McCarthy, W.E.: The REA accounting model: A generalized framework for accounting systems in a shared data environment. Acc. Rev. **57**(3), 554–578 (1982)
13. McClelland, D.C.: Human motivation. Cambridge University Press, Cambridge (1988)
14. Osterwalder, A., Pigneur, Y.: Business model generation: a handbook for visionaries, game changers, and challengers. Wiley, NJ, Canada (2010)
15. Parasuraman, A., Zeithaml, V.A., Berry, L.L.: Servqual. J. Retail. **64**(1), 12–40 (1988)
16. Schwartz, S.H.: Universals in the content and structure of values: theoretical advances and empirical tests in 20 countries. Adv. Exp. Soc. Psychol. **25**(1), 1–65 (1992)
17. Schwartz, S.H., Melech, G., Lehmann, A., Burgess, S., Harris, M., Owens, V.: Extending the cross-cultural validity of the theory of basic human values with a different method of measurement. J. Cross Cult. Psychol. **32**(5), 519–542 (2001)
18. Schwartz, S.H., Bardi, A.: Value hierarchies across cultures. J. Cross Cult. Psychol. **32**(3), 268–290 (2001)
19. Svee, E.-O., Giannoulis, C., Zdravkovic, J.: towards consumer preference-aware requirements. In: Bajec, M., Eder, J. (eds.) CAiSE Workshops 2012. LNBIP, vol. 112, pp. 531–542. Springer, Heidelberg (2012)
20. Svee, E.-O., Zdravkovic, J., Giannoulis, C.: Consumer value-aware enterprise architecture. In: Cusumano, M.A., Iyer, B., Venkatraman, N. (eds.) ICSOB 2012. LNBIP, vol. 114, pp. 55–69. Springer, Heidelberg (2012)
21. The Open Group. TOGAF version 9.1, vol. G116 (2011). The Open Group Accessed on http://pubs.opengroup.org/architecture/togaf9-doc/arch
22. Weeks, W.A., Kahle, L.R.: Social values and salespeople's effort: Entrepreneurial versus routine selling. J. Bus. Res. **20**(2), 183–190 (1990)

23. Weigand, H., Johannesson, P., Andersson, B., Bergholtz, M., Edirisuriya, A., Ilayperuma, T.: Strategic analysis using value modeling–the c3-value approach. In: 40th Annual Hawaii International Conference on System Sciences, HICSS 2007, p. 175c–175c. IEEE (2007)
24. Zdravkovic, J., Svee, E.-O., Giannoulis, C.: Capturing consumer preferences as requirements for software product lines. Requirements Eng. **20**(1), 71–90 (2013). doi:10. 1007/s00766-013-0187-2

The Devil in the Details: Fine-Grained Enterprise Model Weaving

David Naranjo[✉], Mario Sánchez, and Jorge Villalobos

Department of Systems and Computing Engineering,
Universidad de Los Andes, Bogotá, Colombia
{da-naran,mar-san1,jvillalo}@uniandes.edu.co

Abstract. When developing Enterprise Models, it is common to aggregate information from several partial models that describe a fragment of the enterprise. This integration is made by connecting elements from different domain models, and is usually a manual task for two reasons: (1) the criteria for connecting pairs of elements is mostly subjective and requires specialized domain knowledge, and (2) any error may impact the coherency of the whole model. However, manual weaving is a difficult and tedious task, with limited support both from methodologies and tools alike. In this paper, we describe a visual approach for weaving domain models, connecting model elements by using adjacency matrices, and visualizing changes at the moment they are made.

Keywords: Enterprise Architecture · Enterprise Models · Business Models · Composition

1 Introduction

Enterprise Models are the cornerstone of model-based Enterprise Architecture and its related fields. These models cover different dimensions that come across an organization, such as the Business, Application and Technology dimensions. In turn, each dimension can be subdivided into several knowledge domains, at varying levels of abstraction: For instance, we can identify domains such as Strategy, Processes, Value Stream, Products, Organization Structure, among several others, as part of the Business Dimension.

However, with more widespread use and more powerful modeling tools available, we now have two contradictory needs: On one hand, we need small, manageable artifacts to **model** the organization with a reduced set of concerns at the time. On the other hand, in order to answer complex questions through their **analysis**, we need really big and detailed models that give the sense of wholeness to the organization, and enable the examination of cross-cutting properties, such as alignment and change impact.

Under this light, we can identify two tendencies: (1) Heavyweight, established EA Frameworks such as Zachman, TOGAF, and EBMM, that propose a fixed (tough in some cases extensible with profiles) metamodel, and (2) More

© Springer International Publishing Switzerland 2015
A. Persson and J. Stirna (Eds.): CAiSE 2015 Workshops, LNBIP 215, pp. 233–244, 2015.
DOI: 10.1007/978-3-319-19243-7_23

recent, customizable approaches, such as Multi-perspective Enterprise Modeling [7], which aim to incrementally construct the Enterprise Model with multiple extensible domain-specific metamodels.

The former are the product of a group of experts that suggest a modeling method, as well as relevant concepts and their relationships, and aim for a general, one-size-fits-all description of the enterprise. Heavyweight metamodels manage the complexity of modeling by using multiple Views of the model (which are models by their own rights), and offer a limited set of analysis techniques. On the other hand, Multi-perspective approaches argue that there is no easy way to describe every organization by using the same criteria, given their different business needs and maturity. Their flexibility translates into more freedom for designing and analyzing their respective models, but their development can be more expensive, and require more experience and knowledge to accurately describe an organization.

Independent of the approach, we can suggest that Enterprise Models are just a snapshot of the state of an organization in a given instant of time, so it is always subject to change, and it can happen at the instance level or at the meta-level. For example, we can add a new Process at the instance (model) level, or we can enhance the definition of what a Process is, –e.g. to now include an ownership relationship to an OrganizationalArea (see Fig. 1)– at the metamodel level.

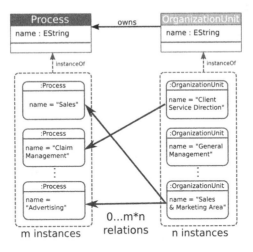

Fig. 1. A single mapping of two concepts at the meta-level can result in m*n relationships at the instance level.

Instance-level modifications are trivial, as it just means that we create, delete, or update an instance or relation of the model. Meta-level change is more troublesome, as we need to consider that changes in the metamodel affect the models that are produced with it. Again, this issue has been approached by several authors, and nowadays we have several languages and tools to perform automated (or semi-automated) weaving of models. However, we have to consider that these approaches are not totally accurate, as they rely on techniques –such as textual comparison of instance attributes– that can miss several matches, for instance, the link between the *Sales and Marketing Area* and the *Advertising Process* in Fig. 1, or make incorrect mappings, like adding a relationship from the *General Management Unit* and the *Claim Management* Process.

Thus, the responsibility of discovering and correcting mistakes in the weaving process falls entirely in the modeler and his ability to grasp the whole model inside his head. This can be a complex and daunting task, even for the smallest of the cases: relating two concepts from different domains at the meta-level can result in a considerable number of relationships (see Fig. 1). This problem is more evident in situations when we must be careful with the details, e.g. when composing multiple domain models that describe different (but related) aspects of the enterprise, without affecting the semantics of individual metamodels.

In this paper, we will argue that current modeling and weaving tools do not work so well under these circumstances, as they do not offer enough information for the modeler to assess if the weaving is being done correctly at any stage of the process. In order to give immediate feedback when modeling, we consider that Visual Analysis techniques can provide a better support for this task, as well as reduce the effort of the modeler. With this in mind, we propose the use of a set of coordinated views to visualize this weaving process and the elements involved, complemented with the use of an adjacency matrix that facilitates the insertion and removal of relationships at the instance level.

In order to explain our approach, Sect. 2 will deepen on the characterization of Fine-grained model weaving, and introduce a concrete use case, the integration of Business Domains. Section 3 will describe similar approaches, both with general purpose modeling tools, as well as specialized weaving approaches. Then, Sect. 4 will describe our proposed approach, as well as the tool that implements it. Finally, Sect. 5 will illustrate the use of the tool for combining five Business Domains of a Social Networking service.

2 Fine-Grained Weaving of Multiple Domains: The Case of Business Models

In order to design, implement, and manage software and technological artifacts, as well as to integrate them to the existing organization structure and infrastructure, we make use of several domain methods that encapsulate domain knowledge. For instance, it is common for us to use Business Process Model and Notation (BPMN) diagrams to describe the Roles, Processes, Tasks, and control flows of a given Core Process, or ArchiMate models to describe the Business, Information, and Technological domains from a high level of abstraction, as well as how they are interconnected.

Each of these models are, of course, limited in scope, and usually describe -in varying levels of detail- a small dimension of a real-world system. In fact, *we want* these models and their metamodels to remain small, as it allows us to break the enterprise into manageable parts. After all, modeling is a human activity, and we have problems visualizing –grasping– hundreds of components of the model in the same view.

Not only we make use of multiple languages; we create new ones, that can be based on existing languages that are too complex, or even brand-new languages for domains that haven't been formalized yet. The development of these tailored metamodels has been gaining traction, as it allows flexibility, modularity, and reuse, and contrasts with one-size-fits-all perspective of early business and enterprise metamodels.

2.1   Business Models

Recently, there has been a lot of interest around the integration of Business Models (BMs) and Enterprise Models [8,14], in order to add coherency to the business dimension of the latter. Ultimately, BMs are a description of the value creation dynamics of an enterprise, describing phenomena that cannot be explained with just its operation, thus becoming a valuable knowledge asset.

Literature on Business Models [16] usually starts by acknowledging that we cannot express how an organization creates value from an individual viewpoint, and several authors have attempted to formalize the term by describing the different components of a Business Model.

For instance, Osterwalder et al. [13] propose a group of nine subject areas that are critical for the proposition of a Business Model, and are the building blocks of the Business Model Canvas –BMC– [12]. They also underscore the need to formalize concepts and provide a common language through *"Rigorously defined meta-models of business models in the form of formal reference models or ontologies"*.

Fig. 2. General purpose views for editing models. **Left:** A visual editor showing a BMC model. **Right:** A tree editor of a Business Model.

However, existing Business Model ontologies, such as the BMC, are mainly descriptive in nature, which means they can be valuable brainstorming tools, but they are not helpful when it comes to implementing BMs [15], as well as to promote experimentation and innovation with those models [2], e.g. by extending their metamodels with other domains. Moreover, constructs such as Strategy, Ecosystem, Business Processes, and Partnership Network are outside of the scope of the BMC, but have a strong relation to Business Models.

With the purpose of exemplifying the need of fine-grained model weaving, we will consider the case of Business Models, which will be our concern for the rest of this paper.

2.2 *Fine-grained* Weaving

We can assert that BMs embed several **domains** (or perspectives) that are of our interest in the context of Enterprise Modeling. Moreover, depending on their context, some aspects can be given more of less detail; for instance, a manufacture company may require Product and Provisioning Models to describe its intent, while a banking company may require detailed information of its financial model, to provide an accurate description of its business.

Our approach for integrating and analyzing these separate domains consists in providing several visual aids that lower the cognitive burden of the addition and deletion of inter-domain relationships, as well as offering a way for diagnosing the quality of this weaving. Please note that this is a particular method that makes sense only when we have multiple domain models that we wish to integrate into an Enterprise Model. We associate elements from different domains because, from the perspective of the modeler, they are related in some way, even when there is no explicit connection by comparing their attributes (see Fig. 1).

In summary, we will use the term *Fine-grained Model Weaving* to refer to the lightweight **integration of different models** under these conditions:

1. This is a sensible task that requires an expert, as errors or missing relationships affect the quality of the integrated model.
2. The weaving at the instance level is considerably complex (i.e. the possible number of inter-domain relations is large).
3. It is mostly manual, but can be assisted by automatic and semi-automatic weaving tools.
4. The modeler requires mechanisms for discovering and correcting errors, as well as providing a feedback of the weaving progress.

3   Related Work

Model Weaving, a discipline of Model Engineering, addresses the different types of changes in models, and is commonly used "to unify two complementary, but potentially overlapping, models that describe different views on the same system" [9]. More formally, weaving is a special case of *model transformation*, and it can be expressed in terms of two input models that are operated by a series of steps, and its output is a single new model. Since the first experiments with model weavers made by Bézivin et al. [1], we have seen excellent methods and tools that support this task. We can identify three categories of approximations to model weaving:

3.1   General Purpose Modeling Editors

Recent modeling environments and editors of specialized Enterprise Architecture Management tools provide the most simple way of relating model instances through relationships. They provide textual, form-based, and graphical views of the model, which can be used simultaneously for better results. However, these views do not scale when the model is of a considerable size (See Fig. 2), resulting in overlapping relationships, or incomplete views: For instance, Tree editors display relationships as properties of a given element (see Fig. 2), so the modeler has to maintain in his head the current state of the weaving. Also, being a manual task, it is error prone, and the only way of validating the quality of the weaving is by exhaustively looking at each element and relationship.

3.2   Specialized Weaving Languages

Considering the pitfalls presented by manual, unconstrained edition of models, several authors have proposed interesting approaches that automate model evolution. Following the Model Driven Paradigm of 'Everything is a model', these approaches are supported by an underlying weaving metamodel that provides the syntax for describing concrete weavings between two models.

The ATLAS Model Weaver [4], as well as other approaches such as Epsilon Merging Language [9], offer a textual method using a language for automated matching and merging of changes. These approaches match model elements by using multiple techniques that compute patterns of similarities using different criteria. In particular, element-to-element similarity is often calculated comparing the source and target instance attributes by string comparison and dictionaries of synonyms [4]. As an automated, unsupervised process, this similarity is a coefficient that indicates the level of confidence in the matching.

This means that there is always the possibility of having false positives and false negatives in this matching process (see Fig. 1). For this reason, Del Fabro and Valduriez [3] suggest an additional verification stage, thus parametrizing the Weaving Engine to consider cases where none of the pattern matching techniques available could find a high degree of similarity. This requires an exhaustive and manual inspection of both models, as well as validating each proposed match.

3.3   Visual Approaches

Fill examines in [5] different methods for the visualization of semantic IS models, and introduces the *business ontology* as a form of integrating multiple metamodels, as it 'structures the terms and relates the concepts that are used within a business', and introduces a framework for visualization in IT-based Management. Fil also provides in [6] a method for annotating Visual Modeling languages, thus allowing traceability in the decisions made in the conceptualization phase of modeling.

3.4   Outlook

While with these approximations we can perform the weaving of any type of input models, we argue that when dealing with multi-domain models, the burden of guaranteeing coherence is mostly in the head of the modeler. This is an issue caused by their large scale, the high number of possible matches for each inter-domain relationship, and the lack of methods for automatically matching elements with absolute confidence. For this reason, but without seeking to replace these approaches, we propose an additional layer on top of the facilities that these approaches suggest, in order to overcome the cognitive burden and complexity of this task, as well as offering the possibility of inspecting the correctness of this weaving at the same time that it is performed.

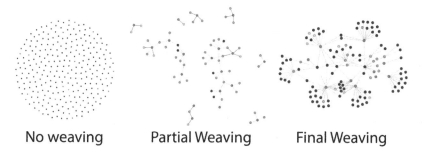

| No weaving | Partial Weaving | Final Weaving |

Fig. 3. Overview of the visual weaving process for an individual relationship type.

4   *Sigourney:* a Visual, Fine-Grained Weaver

Fine-grained Weaving is a goal-oriented and incremental process (see Fig. 3), where the modeler matches pairs of instances for each inter-domain relation type, one pair at the time, and with a refinement and validation stage at the end of each iteration.

We relate this composition to the activity of assembling a jigsaw puzzle. As with real-world puzzles, a good strategy is to first connect pairs of pieces, and when a pattern arises, we can start assembling larger chunks, in order to provide a total view of a fragmented picture. Additional pieces (domains) can be connected to the puzzle (the BM), given that their shapes connect (i.e. concepts between domains are connected by inter-domain relations). A visual approach can be a more effective vehicle for this task, as it does not rely on the memory of the modeler (or his endurance) when adding hundreds (or thousands) of relationships between domains.

4.1   Tool Overview

Sigourney, our tool for Fine-grained Model Weaving, is supported by PRIM-ROSe, a Visual Analysis platform for Enterprise Models [10]. The workbench of

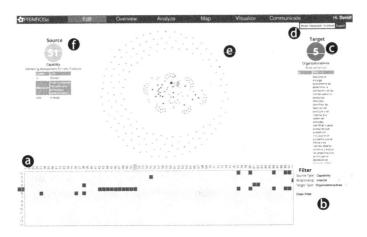

Fig. 4. Workbench of the tool, comprised of multiple sections, which are labeled counter-clockwise: (a) Adjacency matrix for a relation type. (b) Filter panel. (c) Target instance attributes. (d) Visualization technique selection. (e) Visualization panel. (f) Source instance attributes.

Sigourney (see Fig. 4) is comprised of two main parts: an Edition Section –at the bottom of the workbench–, and a View Section, displaying a Visualization of the model, as well as detailed information on source and target instances.

4.2   Edition

In order to filter the model and show only relevant instances and relationships, this panel contains an adjacency matrix that permits their insertion or removal for given Source and Target metatypes. This matrix is a cross product of all the instances of a Source Type S versus all the instances of the Target Type T, so each position in the matrix represents a relationship from an instance of type S to an instance of type T.

Each modification in the matrix is updated immediately in the Visualization Panel, and hovering on each position of the matrix updates the Source and Target Panels. In order to generate the adjacency matrix, the user must select a Source Type, a relationship name, and a Target Type on the Filter Panel. This selection also updates the Visualization, filtering unrelated elements and relationships.

4.3   Visualization

The process of weaving instances of a given pair of metatypes usually starts with an empty adjacency matrix, which translates to a set of unconnected elements (see Fig. 3). As the modeler updates the matrix and connects instances, the visualization is updated with the respective links. The process ends when the modeler deems necessary, and validating the correctness of relationships is easily done, as the visualization contains only the relevant elements.

Visualization Techniques. Currently, the tool provides two interactive visualizations for Fine-grained weaving. The user can switch between them at any time, and both favor different purposes. The first technique, displayed in Fig. 4, is a Force-directed Graph, where each color represents a metatype. Unconnected nodes roam freely, while interconnected nodes pull their neighbors a distance proportional to the number of incoming and outgoing links of each node. At any time, the user can switch between an overview of the whole woven model and a filtered model containing relevant instances.

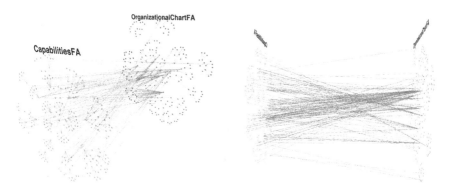

Fig. 5. 3D Layered visualization technique. Each point in the plane represents an instance of a concept, and each line parallel to the plane is a domain relationship. The lines between planes are inter-domain relationships.

The second visualization technique is what we call a Layered Visualization (see Fig. 5). While the graph visualization is constrained to a 2-dimensional space, this one allows the user to roam freely and navigate the model as he pleases. This technique consists of two planes, each one containing the force-directed graph of a domain, and inter-domain relationships appear in the midst of both planes, and are relative to the position of the source and target elements. This visualization is useful for assessing the completeness of the weaving between two metatypes, and also allows individual selection of elements and relationships, both intra-domain (in the domain plane) and inter-domain.

5   Illustration

Forever Alone (FA) is an *'Elite'* social networking service for people with similar interests to meet, communicate, and if both persons agree, plan encounters on the real world. These encounters usually are in establishments that have an agreement with Forever Alone, and are recommended by the platform based on the shared interests of both persons. The service is location-aware, and has a recommendation engine for meeting new people near the user.

The target audience of the service is single males and females, with high income margins, over 27 years old, and in general, that are not interested in

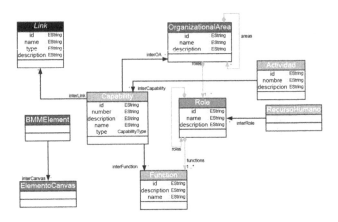

Fig. 6. Fragment of the weaving of Forever Alone at the metamodel level.

having a long-term relationship with anyone. Their high profile usually means that they require additional security and privacy considerations. Being an elite service, Forever Alone is strict with the application process, where potential new users are screened and profiled, in order to determine if they meet the above requirements.

From its inception, the Business Model of Forever Alone was designed using the **Business Model Canvas**, which describes the aspects described above. Its strategy has been described in terms of the **Business Motivation Model** [11], and its high-level **Business Process Architecture** is defined in terms of the Value Chain of the enterprise, using a custom metamodel, where processes are divided into Value-Add (Core), Strategic, and Support Processes. In addition, in order to support decision making and provide a link between the different Business Domains, FA has constructed a *Capability Model*, where high level capacities of the enterprise are formulated, and are realized in the Business Model as Value Chain Links, Organizational Units, and Role Functions. Finally, we have a tailored **Organizational Structure Model** that describes the Areas, Roles, and Functions of employees of the company. The consolidated model contains 798 elements and 1460 relations.

Conscious of the potential gain in knowledge of having an Enterprise Model, for instance, through its analysis, Forever Alone has decided to integrate the Business Domains described above. Each domain model is a detailed description of some aspect of the Business, and it can be considered complex enough.

As a first step, the Enterprise Architecture Committee of FA has integrated five metamodels into one Business Domain Metamodel by connecting concrete concepts of each domain with inter-domain relationships (see Fig. 6). We started by connecting *Capabilities* -from the Capability Model- with *Organizational Areas* of the company. Then, after this weaving is done, we proceeded to connect *Capabilities* with *Value Chain Links*. Later, we matched *Capabilities* with *Functions* that are assigned to Roles of the Organization Structure.

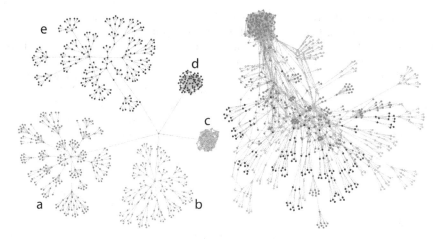

Fig. 7. Graph representations of the model before and after the weaving. Circles are model elements, and arcs are relationships between these elements. **Left:** Initial Business Model of Forever Alone, with five different domain models: (a) Capabilities, (b) Business Process Architecture, (c) Business Model Canvas, (d) Business Motivation Model, and (e) Organization Structure. **Right:** Woven Business Model.

Then, we connected **Activities** of the BMC with Capabilities, *Human Resources*, also of the BMC, with *Roles* from the Organization Structure. Finally, we connected Business Motivation Model elements with Canvas Elements. The final result can be seen in Fig. 7, and consists of 798 elements and 2015 relations.

6   Conclusion

We have described in this paper a novel way for combining Business Models, by using a special case of Model Weaving, which we call Fine-grained Weaving, and consists of interconnecting these domains with optional relationships at the metamodel, and using a tool of our own, Sigourney, for weaving model instances.

The reasons behind creating this tool, instead of using existing approaches, lie in non-functional aspects of modeling and weaving. We consider that the scale of the task has a negative impact on the modeler, and brings the uncertainty with respect to the coherence of created relationships. In our experience, this integration is difficult to attain, and demands new methods for this case of weaving.

Another benefit of this approach, while not shown on this paper, is that we can have it on top of existing weaving methods, thus serving as a validation and diagnosis tool, something that existing approaches lack.

References

1. Bézivin, J., Jouault, F., Valduriez, P.: First experiments with a modelweaver. In: Proceedings of the OOPSLA/GPCE: Best Practices for Model-Driven Software

Development Workshop, 19th Annual ACM Conference on Object-Oriented Programming, Systems, Languages, and Applications (2004)

2. Chesbrough, H.: Business model innovation: opportunities and barriers. Long Range Plan. Bus. Models. **43**(23), 354–363 (2010)

3. Del Fabro, M.D., Valduriez, P.: Semi-automatic model integration using matching transformations and weaving models. In: Proceedings of the 2007 ACM Symposium on Applied Computing, SAC 2007, pp. 963–970. ACM, New York (2007)

4. Didonet Del Fabro, M., Valduriez, P.: Towards the efficient development of model transformations using model weaving and matching transformations. Softw. Syst. Model. **8**(3), 305–324 (2009)

5. Fill, H.G.: Visualisation for Semantic Information Systems. Business and Economics. Gabler Verlag, Wiesbaden (2009)

6. Fill, H.-G.: On the conceptualization of a modeling language for semantic model annotations. In: Salinesi, C., Pastor, O. (eds.) CAiSE Workshops 2011. LNBIP, vol. 83, pp. 134–148. Springer, Heidelberg (2011)

7. Frank, U.: Multi-perspective enterprise modeling: foundational concepts, prospects and future research challenges. Softw. Syst. Model. **13**(3), 941–962 (2014)

8. Iacob, M., Meertens, L., Jonkers, H., Quartel, D., Nieuwenhuis, L., van Sinderen, M.: From enterprise architecture to business models and back. Softw. Syst. Model. **13**(3), 1059–1083 (2014)

9. Kolovos, D., Rose, L., Paige, R., Garcia-Dominguez, A.: The epsilon book. Structure **178**, 1–10 (2010)

10. Naranjo, D., Sánchez, M.E., Villalobos, J.: Primrose - a tool for enterprise architecture analysis and diagnosis. In: ICEIS 2014 - Proceedings of the 16th International Conference on Enterprise Information Systems, Lisbon, Portugal, 27–30 April, 2014, vol. 3, pp. 201–213. SciTePress (2014)

11. OMG: Business motivation model (2008)

12. Osterwalder, A., Pigneur, Y.: Business Model Generation: A Handbook For Visionaries, Game Changers. Wiley, Hoboken (2010)

13. Osterwalder, A., Pigneur, Y., Tucci, C.L.: Clarifying business models: origins, present, and future of the concept. Commun. Assoc. Inf. Syst. **16**(1), 1 (2005)

14. Petrikina, J., Drews, P., Schirmer, I., Zimmermann, K.: Integrating business models and enterprise architecture. In: 18th IEEE International Enterprise Distributed Object Computing Conference Workshops and Demonstrations, EDOC Workshops 2014, Ulm, Germany, September 1–2, pp. 47–56. IEEE (2014)

15. Solaimani, S.: The alignment of business model and business operations within networked enterprise environments. Ph.D. thesis, Delft University of Technology (2014)

16. Zott, C., Amit, R., Massa, L.: The business model recent developments and future research. J. Manage. **37**, 1019–1042 (2011)

Extending Feature Models to Express Variability in Business Process Models

Riccardo Cognini, Flavio Corradini, Andrea Polini, and Barbara Re[✉]

Computer Science Division,
University of Camerino, Camerino, Italy
{riccardo.cognini,flavio.corradini,
andrea.polini,barbara.re}@unicam.it

Abstract. In complex organizations Business Processes tends to exist in different variants that typically share objectives and part of their structure. In recent years it has been recognized that the explicit modeling of variability can brings important benefits to organizations that can more easily reflect on their behavior and more efficiently structure their activities and processes. Particularly interesting in this respect is the situation of the Public Administration that delivers the same service using many different and replicated processes. The management of such complexity ask for methods explicitly supporting the modeling of variability aspects for Business Processes. In this paper we present a novel notation to describe variability of Business Processes and an approach to successively derive process variants. The notation takes inspiration from feature modeling approaches and has been implemented in a real tool using the ADOxx platform. The notation, and the corresponding approach, seems particularly suitable for the Public Administration context, and it has been actually experimented in a complex real scenario.

1 Introduction

In complex organizations Business Processes (BP) tends to exist in different variants that typically share objectives and part of their structure. In recent years it has been recognized that the explicit modeling of variability can brings important benefits to organizations that can more easily reflect on their behavior and more efficiently structure their work.

The delivery of services to citizens by Public Administrations (PAs) can certainly be re-conducted to such a situation. In this case the PA as a whole can be considered as a single organization in which the same BP could be declined in many different forms. So for instance, a residence move service will be supported by a BP that at a certain level of abstraction is described by a specific law also with reference to specific activities that have to be performed. Successively the possible many departments constituting the PA will independently implement their services, and supporting process, taking into account specific constraints related to the specific characteristic of the department itself. All this BP models share many characteristics but without a suitable support to represent such variability it will be difficult to share knowledge among the different part of the organization.

© Springer International Publishing Switzerland 2015
A. Persson and J. Stirna (Eds.): CAiSE 2015 Workshops, LNBIP 215, pp. 245–256, 2015.
DOI: 10.1007/978-3-319-19243-7_24

The case of PA is particularly interesting in reference to the possibility of representing variability for BP. In fact at a certain level of abstraction, and with respect to a specific process, all the departments will share the same abstract process. Nevertheless when detailed activities have to be introduced in order to make the service concrete the process models start to differentiate in order to include specific department characteristics [5]. For instance it is possible that in a big municipality different activities related to residence move will be carried on by different offices, while in a small municipality they will be carried on within the same office.

To solve this gap it is necessary to introduce a modeling approach that is able to represent law constraints and variability according different PA organizational structures.

To do that, we presents the Business Process Feature Model (BPFM) notation that combines in a new notation concepts coming both from feature modeling and from BP modeling. The notation permits to represent activities, their partial execution order, and involved data objects. A BPFM model collects all the possible BP variants, and via a configuration step it is possible derive the most suitable one for the specific organization. From a PA point of view, a BP manager configures the BPFM model according to the PA organizational structure. Then using a set of mapping rules we defined, BP manager can derive BP fragments. These fragments can be further enriched with control flow information considering specific characteristics of the PA. This two stages process to variant definition seems particularly suitable in a context in which all variability dimensions cannot be fully defined a priori. This is the case for instance of organizational aspects that can impact on the structure of a BP to be deployed, and for which variability aspects cannot be easily enumerated a priori.

The approach has been applied, with encouraging results, in the SUAP case study with reference to the *Start-up Certified Notification* scenario. The service refers to the activities that the Italian PAs have to put in place in order to permit to entrepreneurs to set up a new company or more in general to organize a business activity. SUAP includes more than 110 BPs, that are different considering the request target, nevertheless all of them are quite similar and overall they could be considered a single process family. Using the ADOxx development platform we also implemented a modeling environment supporting the usage of the BPFM notation.

The paper is organized as follow. Section 2 reports some background material, while Sect. 3 reports relevant related works. Successively, Sect. 4 gives an overview of the approach, and Sect. 5 shows the proposed notation. Section 6 presents the developed tool. Validation activities are discussed in Sect. 7. Finally Sect. 8 reports conclusions and opportunities for further research.

2   Feature Modeling

Feature modeling is an approach emerged in the context of Software Product Lines to support the development of a variety of products from a common platform. The approach aims at lowering both production costs and time in the development of individual products sharing an overall reference model, while allowing them to differ with respect to specific scenarios to serve, e.g. different markets [15]. In the last years feature modelling have been used also to represent commonality and variability in *Business Information Systems*, introducing the concept of family of BP.

A FM is a graphical model that, using a tree representation where the root represents the general product to develop, permits to express different relationships among the possible features that can be included in a specific variant of the product. In particular, in the first feature modeling approach proposed, named Feature-oriented Domain Analysis (FODA), *mandatory*, *optional* or *alternative* constraints on features have been introduced [9]. A *Mandatory* feature represent a characteristic that each product variant must have. For instance considering the production of different mobile device types we could define a constraint requiring that any mobile device variant have to include a screen. An *Optional* feature is used to represent characteristics that a product can have but a fully functional product can also be derived without including such a feature. For instance this could be the case of mechanisms supporting connection to 4G networks that could be included only in high-profile products. An *Alternative* feature represents characteristics that cannot be present together in a product. For instance a mobile device can have a standard screen or a touch screen, but not both. Researchers have proven that basic FM models are too restrictive to represent all the relationships between features which are useful to characterize a family of products [1]. As a result the FM notation has been extended to permit the definition of feature cardinality, permitting to define how many features in a set are needed to have a working product. It is possible then to express relationships such as *"at least one feature in a set of features is needed in each product"*. This is done via *OR features* constraints. Additionally, *include relationship* constraints are used to express that a feature selection implies the selection of another feature that is on a different part of the tree, and *exclude relationship* constraints are used to express that a feature selection requires to discard another one that is on a different part of the tree.

Once a feature model has been defined it is possible to derive a specific product defining a *configuration* that express explicit features selection, and according to the constraints defined in the feature model.

3   Related Works

BP modeling has been identified as a fundamental phase in order to better understand how to behave and organize activities within a complex organization. Different classes of languages to express BP models have been proposed in the last years such as BPMN 2.0 [12], EPC [18] or YAWL [20]. These notations permits to specify BPs even if they do not have mechanisms to represent classes of similar BP that can be represented as a family. Indeed this has emerged as an important characteristics since in similar contexts processes can share several characteristics which are difficult to reuse with standard notation. As a result in recent years the interest towards techniques for modeling such variability has clearly raised [2].

Modeling variable BP is the ability to represent in a single model many alternative BPs sharing the same goal [16]. In order to describe variable BPs several approaches have been proposed, in some case extending already available notations. Relevant examples are certainly languages such as C-EPC [17], Configurable integrated EPC (C-iEPC) [11], vBPMN [4] or C-YAWL [7]. Also language independent approaches have been proposed. Among the others PROVOP [8] and PESOA [19] are probably the most used.

Differently from our proposal such modeling languages permits to derive variants for which the control flow is fully determined. The configurable model includes all the possible control flow relations and a subset of them are included in a derived variant. This approach cannot be applicable when the characteristics to consider to derive the variant are not enumerable. Our approach instead permits to derive variants for which the control flow have to be successively refined considering information available only at configuration time.

Alternative approaches are those based on the declarative paradigm such as CMMN [13] and Declare [14]. Nevertheless differently from our proposal such approaches do not intend to provide variants with a fully specified control flow and typically defer the definition of a precise order between the activities till their execution.

4   Overview of the Approach

The proposed approach is organized in four main steps (Fig. 1) and it results to be particularly suitable in situations in which an abstract definition of a process needs to be successively refined to consider specific aspects of the deployment context, such as the specific characteristics of the organization supporting the process itself. This is a quite common situation for processes supporting PA services to citizens. In such a case objectives and activities constituting the process are general and independent from the specific characteristics of the offices delivering the service itself. Nevertheless the precise definition of the process, in terms of roles and ordering of the activities, depends from deployment related aspects such as for instance the organizational model.

Input of the proposed approach are the laws regulating the provisioning of a service, while the final output will be a BP variant that can be deployed according to the characteristics of the service under analysis, and the organizational model of the Public Administration which delivers the service to the citizen. In particular the approach is organized in 4 successive steps:

- The first step aims at defining a general model that can be successively constitute the basis for the definition of a process variant for the specific deployment context. The model will be codified using the BPFM notation presented in the next section. This step include knowledge acquisition through the study of legal and regulatory frameworks governing the delivery of the PA service

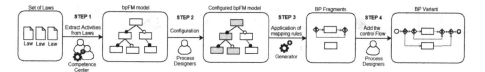

Fig. 1. Steps of the approach.

under study. This step should be carried on only once for each service delivered by the PAs. The activity performed by a focus group or a competence centre, will permit to derive a model that will include only the activities that have to be carried on, the relations among them, and the data structure they possibly get in input or produce in output (as said this information are codified in a BPFM model as illustrated in the following).

- The second step foresees the refinement of the previously defined model taking into account the specific needs of the service that has to be delivered and of its deployment context. Similarly to what it is done in feature modeling this step foresees the definition of a *configuration* on the BPFM model which will permit to define a specific variant from the BP family.
- The third step takes in input activities and data objects resulting from the configuration defined in the previous step. Through the application of mapping rules we define it is possible then to automatically derive BP fragments representing portions of the behaviour that has to be completed to reach the goal of the service to be delivered.
- The last step concerns the derivation of the fully specified BP variant starting from the generated BP fragments. At this stage process designers add control flow relationships among the generated BP fragments, also taking into account the specific characteristics of the PA organization that needs to deliver the service to citizens. It is worth mentioning that the same activity could be associated to different roles in different BP variants, as a result of possible different organizational models for different PA offices.

For the sake of space in this paper we mainly focus on the notation we introduced to perform the first step described above, and we will not report the mapping rules needed to perform step 3 that can be retrieved here [3].

5   Modeling Variability with BPFM

The BPFM notation intends to provide a tool to model a family of BPs that is identified by the root element of a model. In a BPFM model feature elements represent activities that can be included or not in a BP variant successively derived. Activities are decomposed going up-to-down in a tree model giving the opportunity to introduce variability aspects thanks the possibility of using a superset of the connectors used in the standard FM notation (see Fig. 2).

Activities can be atomic in case they are leafs of the BPFM tree, or composed in case they are parents of other activities. Data objects are also included in

Fig. 2. BPFM constraints.

BPFM permitting to include information that will be successfully helpful for the definition of correct BP variants.

Feature constraints express if an activity must or can be inserted in a BP variant, and if it must or can be included within any execution path at the instance level (i.e. real execution of the process). Feature (activity) constraints can be 1-to-1 or 1-to-n depending on how many features they refer to. Moreover each feature can be involved in many binary relations playing the role of the parent. Nevertheless an activity can also be the parent in just one 1-to-n relation.

Feature constraints can be binary or multiple depending on how many child activities are connected to a parent activity. With respect to the binary constraints we consider the following. A *Mandatory Constraint* requires that the connected child activity must be inserted in each BP variant, and it has also to be included in all execution paths (Fig. 2-A). A *Optional Constraint* requires that the connected child activity can be inserted (or not) in each BP variant and it could be included (or not) in each execution path (Fig. 2-B). A *Domain Constraint* requires that the connected child activity must be inserted in each BP variant but it could be included (or not) in each execution path (Fig. 2-C). A *Special Case Constraint* requires that the connected child activity can be inserted (or not) in each BP variant. When it is inserted it has to be included in each execution path (Fig. 2-D).

With respect to multiple constraints we consider the following. An *Inclusive Constraint* requires that at least one of the connected child activities must be inserted in each BP variant, and at least one of them have to be included in each execution path (Fig. 2-E). A *One Optional Constraint* requires that exactly one of the connected child activities has to be inserted in each BP variant, and it could be included (or not) in each execution path (Fig. 2-F). A *One Selection Constraint* requires that exactly one of the connected child activities has to be inserted in each BP variant, and it has to be included in each execution path (Fig. 2-G). A *XOR Constraint* requires that all the connected child activities must be inserted in each BP variant, and exactly one of them has to be included in each execution path (Fig. 2-H). A *XOR Selection Constraint* requires that at least one of the connected child activities has to be inserted in each BP variant, and exactly one of them has to be included in each execution path (Fig. 2-I). Finally, *Include* and *Exclude* relationships between activities are also considered according to the base definition of FM (Fig. 2-J and Fig. 2-K).

In BPFM the modeling of Data Objects plays also an important role. BPFM includes all types of BPMN 2.0 Data Objects and it uses the same symbols (Fig. 3-A). As well as in BPMN 2.0 Data Object elements can be connected as inputs and outputs to activities (features). In particular child features inherit Data Objects from the parent node, and if a Data Object is connected as input (or output) to a feature, all the child activities will need such Data Object. It is worth noting that given that different correct configurations could include or not some node, it is possible that different BP variants will include different sets of Data Objects.

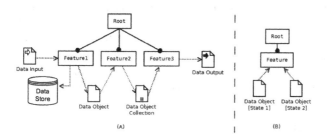

Fig. 3. Data Object in BPFM.

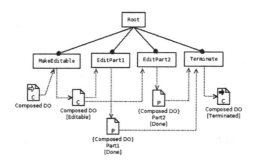

Fig. 4. Composed Data Object in BPFM.

In BPFM a status can be associated to a data. An activity can require or can generate a Data Object in a specific state and consequently can change its state. If the state is not explicitly reported the activity is state independent. A Data Object cannot be in two different states at the same time (Fig. 3-B). The state of a Data Object is represented with square brackets under the Data Object name. Moreover in BPFM, differently from BPMN 2.0, we introduced the possibility to represent composite and *part-of* Data Objects that can be extended for each type of BPMN 2.0 Data Object (see for example Fig. 4).

- A composed Data Object indicates that the Data Object is composed by a set of specific block of data, and it is marked with the letter *C*.
- *Part-of* Data Object indicates that the Data Object is contained in a specific block of data, and it is marked with the letter *P*. It also explicitly refers to the Data Object of which it is part reporting the name of it inside curly brackets.

The increased expressiveness of BPFM in modeling data related information results to be particularly useful in modeling processes within the PA context where complex data structures and relations (forms, documents etc.) typically drive the execution of a BP.

Once a BPFM model have been derived a variant can be obtained thanks to the definition of a configuration. A configuration selects some of the features according to the constraints included in the model. This step is absolutely similar to what it is done with traditional FM models. Nevertheless thanks to the mapping defined in [3] a set of BP fragments will be immediately derived from a configuration. Successively fragments have to be composed by the modeler to finally derive a fully functional BP variant for the specific PA organization.

6   BPFM ADOxx Prototype

The modeling approach illustrated in this article is supported by a modeling environment that can be freely downloaded at the BPFM web page (http://www.omilab.org/web/bpfm). It has been developed thanks to the functionality made available by the ADOxx platform[1]. ADOxx is a set of tools developed in order to make easy the implementation of modeling environments based on meta-models [6,10].

To derive a modelling environment we designed the BPFM meta-model according to what it is shown in Fig. 5. Therefore *Activity* represents atomic or composed tasks. *Constraint* expresses the relationships between activities. Constraints can be *Binary Constraint* or *Multiple Constraint*. Then *Binary Constraint* is further specialized in four sub-classes that are *Mandatory*, *Optional*, *Domain* and *Special Case*. *Multiple Constraint* is specialized in five sub-classes that are *XOR Selection*, *XOR*, *Inclusive*, *Alternative* and *One Optional*. *Data Object* introduces input output data for activities they can be specialized in three sub-classes, they are *Data Input*, *Data Output* and *Data Store*. *Data Object Connector* representing the relationships between activity and Data Object that can be *Input Data Object Connector* or *Output Data Object Connector*.

Focusing on the *Activitiy*, they can be specified using the attribute *type* that can assume the following values: standard, service, send, receive, manual, user, script or business rules. Relationship between an *Activity* and *Constraint*, and vice-versa, are exclusively characterized as binary or multiple. For what concern constraints each activity can take in input zero or one binary constraint or one multiple constraint. There is one special activity, named root, that has zero input constraints. In output the activity can have zero or more binary constraint or one multiple constraint. Relationship between activities can also be expressed via *Include* or *Exclude* relationship. Each *Activity* can include/exclude zero or more *Activities*. From the other side, each *Activity* can be included/excluded by zero or more *Activity*.

Regarding *Data Object* the attribute *Collection* specifies if the *Data Object* is a collection or not. *Data Object* has a self-relationship to represent the notion of

---

[1] http://www.adoxx.org.

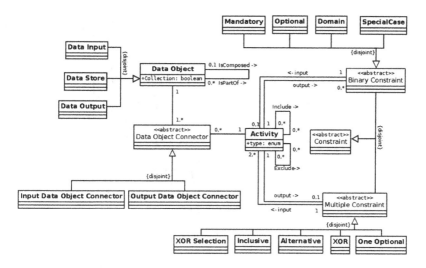

Fig. 5. BPFM meta-model

composition. Each *Data Object* can be part of zero or one Data Object. On the other side each *Data Object* can be composed by zero or more parts. Focusing on the *Data Object* relationship with *Data Object Connector*, each *Data Object* must be connected to at least one *Data Object Connector*. For each *Data Object Connector* there is just one connected *Data Object*. Finally, *Data Object Connector* must be connected to an *Activity*, and an *Activity* can be in relationship to zero or more *Data Object Connector*.

Then according to the described meta-model BPFM ADOxx prototype has been developed. We first created all the elements, constraints and graphical representations discussed in Sect. 5 and then we include them in the BPFM model-type. Therefore using the resulting Modeling Toolkit, it is possible then to define BPFM models using a graphical editor.

7   The SUAP Case: Start-Up Certified Notification

The described approach has been applied to model processes related to the Italian "Sportello Unico per le attività produttive" (SUAP). This is a service that the Italian Public Administrations have to put in place in order to permit to entrepreneurs to set up a new company. Among the many processes composing the service we refer here to the *Start-up Certified Notification* (SCIA). From the point of view of entrepreneurs this is just a notification. Instead if the point of view of the PA is considered, this is a quite complex process that ask to check the correctness and good faith of the application, mainly composed by self-certifications. Therefore it requires to involve, when needed, all the appointed offices in the same or different Public Administrations.

Starting from the law BPFM can be generated representing the SCIA service (Fig. 6). This is a quite simple BPFM that at the same time seems sufficiently

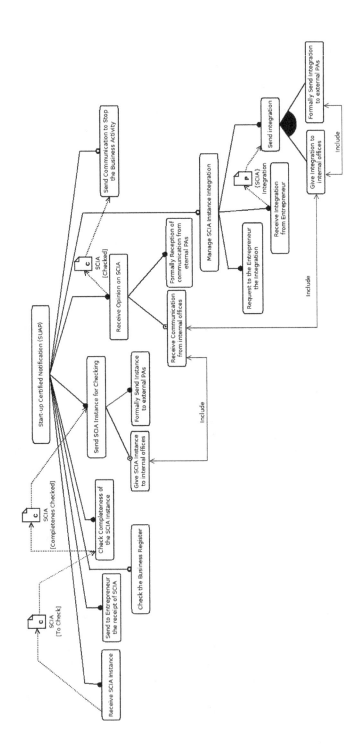

Fig. 6. Start-up certified notification BPFM model in ADOxx

complex to show the potentialities of the notation. The root of the BPFM model represents the SCIA service, and as it can be observed also Data Objects are included. They are input/output for activities in the SCIA BP. For the sake of space we discuss here some interesting detail about the model.

Receive SCIA Instance activity is connected using a *Mandatory Constraint*, it is available in any SCIA variant as well as in any execution path since in any configuration it will obviously necessary to receive the application from the entrepreneur. The entrepreneur self-certification is sent to the PA offices and third parties administrations involved in the verification activity. They check the correctness of the self-certifications and give back feedback in order to clarify if the self-certifications are valid or not. These activities are represented by *Give SCIA instance to internal office* and *Formally send instance to external PAs* connected to *Send SCIA Instance to other PAs* via a *Special Case Constraint* and a *Mandatory Constraint* respectively. *Manage SCIA Instance Integration* is connected to the root using two *Domain Constraints*, so they have to be available in each BP variant and it is not always available in each execution path. Integration is asked to the entrepreneur to complete the self-declaration. *Send Communication to stop the Business Activities* is connected using two *Domain Constraints*, so they have to be available in each BP variant and it is not always available in each execution path. It could be that incomplete self-certification and some legal issues observed during check asks for the termination of the business activity.

Notwithstanding the complexity of the process modeling of the scenario has revealed that the notation permits to focus at different stage to different aspects. In particular the derivation of the BPFM model asks to the modeler to mainly focus on the function and data perspective, while the behavioral perspective is considered in step 4. This separation of concerns results to be particularly fruitful when complex scenario are considered.

8   Conclusion and Future Work

In this paper we presented a notation and a modeling environment to represent variability in business processes. The approach seems particularly suitable to derive process variants for services delivered by the PA. The first experiments made with the notation provided encouraging results and permitted to model quite easily a complex scenario and to derive the corresponding processes.

In the future we plan to continue the experimental work and to continue the implementation of the tool to support all the steps foreseen by the approach. Another important aspect we plan to investigate refers to the definition and introduction of mechanisms to verify that derived BP variants are valid with respect to the BPFM model constraints.

References

1. Capilla, R., Bosch, J., Kang, K.C. (eds.): Systems and Software Variability Management, Concepts, Tools and Experiences. Springer, Heidelberg (2013)

2. Cognini, R., Corradini, F., Gnesi, S., Polini, A., Re, B.: Research challenges in business process adaptability. In: Proceedings of the 29th Annual ACM Symposium on Applied Computing, pp. 1049–1054. ACM (2014)
3. Cognini, R., Corradini, F., Polini, A., Re, B.: Using data-object flow relations to derive control flow variants in configurable business processes. In: Fournier, F., Mendling, J. (eds.) BPM 2014 Workshops. LNBIP, vol. 202, pp. 210–221. Springer, Heidelberg (2015)
4. Döhring, M., Zimmermann, B.: vBPMN: event-aware workflow variants by weaving BPMN2 and business rules. In: Halpin, T., Nurcan, S., Krogstie, J., Soffer, P., Proper, E., Schmidt, R., Bider, I. (eds.) BPMDS 2011 and EMMSAD 2011. LNBIP, vol. 81, pp. 332–341. Springer, Heidelberg (2011)
5. Erkoçak, E., Açıkalın, Ş.N.: Complexity theory in public administration and metagovernance. In: Erçetin, Ş.Ş., Banerjee, S. (eds.) Chaos, Complexity and Leadership 2013. Springer Proceedings in Complexity, pp. 73–84. Springer, Heidelberg (2015)
6. Fill, H.-G., Karagiannis, D.: On the conceptualisation of modelling methods using the ADOxx meta modelling platform. Enterp. Model. Inf. Syst. Architect.-Int. J. 8(1), 2013
7. Gottschalk, F., Van Der Aalst, W.M., Jansen-Vullers, M.H., La Rosa, M.: Configurable workflow models. In. J. Coop. Inf. Syst. 17(02), 177–221 (2008)
8. Hallerbach, A., Bauer, T., Reichert, M.: Capturing variability in business process models: the provop approach. J. Softw. Maintenance Evol. Res. Pract. 22(6–7), 519–546 (2010)
9. Kang, K.C., Cohen, S.G., Hess, J.A., Novak, W.E., Peterson, A.S.: Feature-oriented domain analysis feasibility study. Technical report, DTIC Document (1990)
10. Kühn, H.: The ADOxx® Metamodelling Platform. In: Workshop on Methods as Plug-Ins for Meta-Modelling, Klagenfurt, Austria (2010)
11. La Rosa, M., Dumas, M., ter Hofstede, A.H.M., Mendling, J., Gottschalk, F.: Beyond Control-Flow: extending business process configuration to roles and objects. In: Li, Q., Spaccapietra, S., Yu, E., Olivé, A. (eds.) ER 2008. LNCS, vol. 5231, pp. 199–215. Springer, Heidelberg (2008)
12. OMG. Business process model and notation version 2.0. Technical report (2011)
13. OMG. Case Management Model and Notation, Version 1.0, May 2014
14. Pesic, M., Schonenberg, H., van der Aalst, W.M.: Declare: full support for loosely-structured processes. In: 11th IEEE International Enterprise Distributed Object Computing Conference, EDOC 2007, pp. 287–287. IEEE (2007)
15. Pohl, K., Böckle, G., van der Linden, F.J.: Software Product Line Engineering: Foundations, Principles and Techniques. Springer, Heidelberg (2005)
16. Reichert, M., Weber, B.: Enabling flexibility in process-aware information systems: challenges, methods, technologies. Springer Science & Business Media, (2012)
17. Rosemann, M., van der Aalst, W.M.: A configurable reference modelling language. Inf. Syst. 32(1), 1–23 (2007)
18. Scheer, A.W., Thomas, O., Adam, O.: Process modeling using event-driven process chains. In: Dumas, M., van der Aalst, W., ter Hofstede, A. (eds.) Process-Aware, Information Systems, pp. 119–146. Wiley, Hoboken (2005)
19. Schnieders, A., Puhlmann, F.: Variability mechanisms in e-business process families. In: Abramowicz, W., Mayr, H.C. (eds) BIS, vol. 85, pp. 583–601. GI (2006)
20. Van der Aalst, W.M., Ter Hofstede, A.H.: Yawl: yet another workflow language. Inf. Syst. 30(4), 245–275 (2005)

Enterprise Architecture for Business Network Planning: A Capability-Based Approach

Adel R. Bakhtiyari[✉], Alistair Barros, and Nick Russell

School of Information Systems, Queensland University of Technology,
2 George St., Brisbane, QLD 4000, Australia
{m1.rostamzadehbakhtiyari,alistair.barros,n.russell}@qut.edu.au

Abstract. Enterprise Architecture (EA) has been used for planning business and IT systems capturing different aspects, including services, processes, resources, and data. To date, it has mostly been coordinated by single organisations, even if external interactions with outside organizations play an important role in developing an EA. This paper provides insights about the role of EA in business network planning through the development of a method to conceptualize a multi-partner network, which reflects new affordances opened by a digitally connected world, where shared interactions and dependencies across organizations, through business networks, are converging into *cohesive network businesses*. We present a five stage approach to adopt EA for business network planning by illustrating how *novation requirements* can be defined in integrated scenario models specifying how local roles and their set of skills (capabilities) can be substituted, extended etc. at the level of the network, such that models retain their compact form. Our method benefits from extensive insights observed through the eGovernment One-Stop Shop adopted by Australian governments (Department of Human Services and MyGov at the federal level, Service NSW and One-Stop Shop Implementation Office in Queensland Government) and also from the upstream petroleum oil and natural gas industry. This approach establishes important correspondences between the (internal) operation planning of an organization and (external) business network planning.

Keywords: Business networks · Enterprise architecture · Resource definition · Capabilities · ArchiMate

1 Introduction

IS modeling and architecture methods have become indispensable for the systematic planning, analysis, design and implementation of IT systems. While the focus of systems modeling, at a detailed level, has been on single organisations, many proposals have developed higher-level, contextual modeling for the cross-organisational perspective. Prominent examples include business process choreography modeling [1], service networks [2] and virtual organisational modeling [3]. Enterprise architecture (EA) methods [4] are of particular interest

© Springer International Publishing Switzerland 2015
A. Persson and J. Stirna (Eds.): CAiSE 2015 Workshops, LNBIP 215, pp. 257–269, 2015.
DOI: 10.1007/978-3-319-19243-7_25

because they combine a variety of available modeling concepts and techniques, encompassing several types of organisational artefacts, which are integrated through a core meta-model and layered to support business and IT viewpoints.

Despite the plethora of EA methods and specialized techniques for cross-organisational modeling, a major uncertainty remains about the adequacy of modeling and analysis for dedicated business network planning. Much of the focus is on the modeling of interactions across organisations through coordinative artefacts such as processes, services and resources. As an example, in process choreography modeling [5], a cross business process perspective is modeled based on message (data) exchanges between processes. Thus, an analysis of how artefacts are shifted, as a whole, across partners, to leverage the improvements and opportunities opened up through participation in networks, is only available in a limited range of interaction contexts. Thus, an understanding of the full impact of artefacts deployed through new arrangements introduced by networks, such as understanding the feasibility of offsetting existing artefacts through third-parties for efficiency gains and new innovations, and the creation of virtual enterprise structures out of existing artefacts, remains limited. This paper sheds light on extensions for enterprise architecture to support conceptual business network planning. It is structured as follows. Section 2 develops the use of novation requirements in business networks. Section 3 contains a description of the two case studies including the eGovernment OneStop Shop adopted by Australian governments (Department of Human Services and MyGov at the federal level, Service NSW and One-Stop Shop Implementation Office in Queensland Government) and the upstream petroleum oil and natural gas industry. Given space limitations main focus is on the One-Stop Shop including business architecture and interactions between government agencies. The second case study is discussed in less detail, focusing only on aspects of the integration scenario. Section 4 discusses the related work in EA domain. Finally, Sect. 5 summaries the paper and future work for EA adaptation for business networks.

2 Novation Requirements and their Use in Characterising Business Network Partner Correspondences

Current enterprise modelling techniques provide coarse modelling primitives for the capture of inter-organisation correspondences in regard to business processes but have difficulty in expressing relationships between the artefacts within partner organisations that underpin overall business network composition and operation. Such artefacts may include services, resources and data repositories maintained within a specific organisation which may have broader potential for use by partners in the context of the business network. As a remedy to this shortcoming, we propose the use of *novation requirements* as a means of capturing these correspondences. Novation requirements operate at a business network level as a means of identifying correspondences between artefacts within distinct partner organisations. Such correspondences can relate to obligations, dependencies or affordances

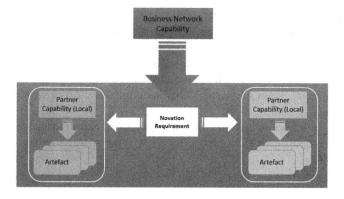

Fig. 1. Illustrative format of a novation requirement

that may exist between then two partners. The general form of a novation requirement is illustrated in Fig. 1.

A novation requirement is indexed from a specific capability in the global
capability map of the business network. This immediately gives its application overall context within the business network in a general format that is
not anchored to any specific partner in the network or their associated business
vocabulary. They are deliberately designed to be easy to capture, ensuring that
service providers can rapidly assemble the range of novation requirements that
define their participation in a business network. The configuration and utilisation
of novation requirements is illustrated in Fig. 2.

There are five distinct steps in preparing to leverage the potential opportunities that they offer:

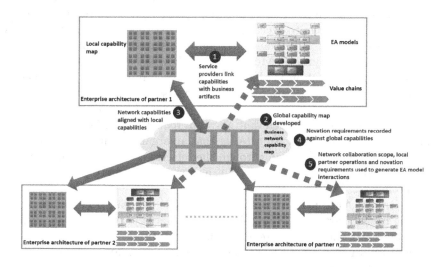

Fig. 2. Configuration and leveraging of novation requirements

1. Local service providers work to delineate their local capabilities and establish mappings from these capabilities to the various artefacts within their enterprise.
2. A global capability map is established that characterises the range of capabilities supported across the business network.
3. Local service providers align their local capabilities with those defined in the global capability map.
4. Novation requirements are specified against global capabilities identifying the novation opportunities that exist between artefacts in distinct business partners enterprises.
5. In conjunction with the network collaboration scope, local partner operations and novation requirements are used to generate new configurations of EA model interactions in terms of their constituent artefacts.

A novation requirement expresses a specific correspondence between artefacts in the context of two specific business network participants. The range of potential correspondence relationships they support is identified in Table 1.

As indicated earlier, the use of these novation requirements provides the opportunity for specifying a range of utilisation scenarios for artefacts at the business network level. This is something that current enterprise architecture techniques do not provide support for. The range of potential use cases pertaining to novation requirements includes:

In-sourcing an Artefact. An organisation participating in a business network can utilise an artefact maintained by another participant in the network in order to access capabilities that it does not possess locally. (relevant novation requirements: R/MS)

Out-sourcing an Artefact. An organisation participating in a business network can provide an artefact that it maintains to other participants in the network allowing them to access capabilities that they otherwise do not possess or have access to. (relevant novation requirements: R/MS)

Migrating the Deployment Model or Availability of an Artefact. In this scenario, an organisation is able to change the way in which an artefact is facilitated or deployed. Part of it may be out-sourced or in-sourced subject particular circumstances or the range of partners to whom the artefact is offered may be changed. (relevant novation requirements: E/R/I/MS/CS)

Augmenting an Artefact. An artefact that an organisation maintains has its capabilities further extended through the selective acquisition and inclusion of other capabilities available in the business network. (relevant novation requirements: E/R/I)

Composing an Artefact. An organisation is able to create an artefact purely on the basis of artefacts offered by other business partners in the business network. (relevant novation requirements: E/R/I)

Constraining an Artefact. An artefact offered by an organisation is restricted in terms of how it can be utilised or accessed. These limitations and constraints are specified in the context of the capabilities and artefacts of other

Table 1. Business network novation requirement alternatives

Novation Requirement	Description	Service	Resource	Data
Dependency (*R*EQUIRES)	A business artefact of a partner REQUIRES that of another partner with DIFFER-ENT capabilities to that partner. E.g. a goods ordering service of a provider REQUIRES a track-and-trace service for improved tracking of customer orders	Y	Y	Y
Anchoring (*I*NCLUDES)	A business artefact of a partner INCLUDES that of another partner with DIFFER-ENT capabilities to that partner. E.g. a goods ordering service of a provider INCLUDES a track-and-trace service for improved tracking of customer order	Y	Y	Y
Extension (*E*XTENDs)	A business artefact of a partner EXTENDS that of another partner with further capa-bilities to that partner. E.g. a firm is restructured so that its domestic shipping service EXTENDS into an international shipping service by another partner with cross-border transportation capabilities	Y	Y	Y
Strict substitution (*M*UST *S*UBSTITUTE)	A business artefact of a partner MUST SUB-STITUTE that of another partner with SIMILAR capabilities to that partner. E.g. a firm is restructured so that its mortgage sales fleet can include indepen-dent mortgage brokers.	Y	Y	Y
Optional substitution (*C*AN *S*UBSTITUTE)	A business artefact of a partner CAN SUB-STITUTE that of another partner with SIMILAR capabilities to that partner. E.g. a firm is restructured so that its mortgage sales fleet can include indepen-dent mortgage brokers	Y	Y	Y
Incompatibility (*C*ONFLICTS)	A business artefact of a partner CONFLICTS with that of another business partner that has similar or different capabilities for legal or other reasons. E.g. a firm is restructured so that it can outsource legal services to agencies without conflict of interest such as competitors being their customers	Y	Y	Y

partners in the business network and may include redirections to other arte-facts in the event that the capabilities of the artefact are not available. (relevant novation requirements: C/MS)

In the following sections we will focus on two illustrative case studies and the use of EA in their planning. The main focus is on One-Stop Shop and its detailed architecture, followed by a selective example from the oil and gas industry to demonstrate the approach in a distinct domain.

3   Case Description

3.1   Case 1: EGovernment One-Stop Shop

In Australia, the federal, state and several local governments have embarked on whole-of-government service delivery transformation initiatives, generally referred to as *One-Stop Shop* (OSS). As the name suggests, OSS strives to provide a uniform and customer-centric approach for the full lifecycle of service delivery, across all of government, as though it were *one* agency. Significant international examples include UK Direct Gov (UKOnline), Hong Kong Online, and Service Canada. They highlight the similarity of vision and strategy across different jurisdictions, and the complex operational and technical frameworks necessary to materialise an OSS. The OSS concept extends upon the call centre or service centre approach, with standard service delivery operations linked across customer-facing staff and back-office processes. The difference is that it involves a diverse range of customer channels, diverse agencies, diverse services and varying complexity of service delivery life-cycles, as exemplified, for instance, by the difference between obtaining a free document and obtaining a business licence. The OSS is governed and operated through multiple agencies with distinct charters, not all of which come under the regime of that business. Through a range of different initiatives at federal and state levels in Australia, we provide insights on how an OSS can be developed as whole-of-government network business - with a common strategy, network business map and business capabilities, shared and virtual network operations, partner alignment and novation of operations. In one stop shop, government agencies register services for central, multi-channel access. Once registered with its processes, business rules and application forms exposed to the wider government, other agencies can aggregate services into value-added offers, e.g. a business formation service can be aggregated out of individual business license provision services, a business opportunity locator, and a variety of supply chain interfaces. Customers can discover services across standard channels for the government, e.g. different web site, mobile devices, call centre or service centres. They can discover services, access and pay for them. To improve access and integration to services across different agencies in the government, a central broker can be used as a connector between front-end channels and backend agencies. The broker can mediate interactions to operations and systems in different agencies, and return responses in a presentable way to the channel being used. The broker can even be involved in collecting service payments and distributing these to the different providers involved. The OSS requires the integration of loose-coupled processes across channels, broker and agencies, ensuring that data and systems are invoked with the right format and protocols. Figure 3 provides a depiction of the OSS framework, generally applicable across the different OSS initiatives. It illustrates a high-level network business map. The use of novation in the context of the OSS framework supports the delineation of a variety of sourcing and delivery arrangements that exist at the network level between the various agencies, call centres and service centres that make up the overall OSS infrastructure. Figure 4 presents an

ArchiMate model of the OSS operational architecture. ArchiMate provides an integrated formalism for describing the design, implementation and operation of business processes, organisational structures, information resources, systems and technical infrastructure associated with an enterprise architecture. In Fig. 4, the processes associated with handling assisted OSS service delivery are illustrated. These involve business capabilities offered by both the OSS service and call centre as well as a range of government agencies. All customer contacts are initiated via the OSS call/service centre, which implements four main processes to handle these requests such that they can be dealt with fully in-channel or handed off to the relevant agency for specialist attention and fulfillment. In overview, these processes are:

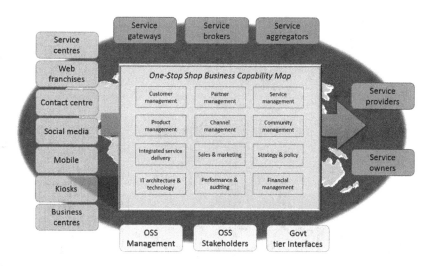

Fig. 3. One stop shop framework overview

Customer Contact. Which involves the initial handling of the incoming customer request to the OSS. This may occur via the call centre channel or in-person at the OSS/service centre front desk. In either case, it is handled by an OSS concierge who seeks to determine the most appropriate call handling pathway and hand on the request for subsequent fulfillment or, where the specifics of the request are unclear, trigger a more detailed service discovery process.

Service Delivery. Which centres on the determination of the required service via local and/or global service discovery tools and then the initiation of the required service. These activities are facilitated via an OSS customer service contact.

Channel Service Delivery. Which involves the in-channel delivery of the required service by suitably qualified OSS or Agency service delivery agents.

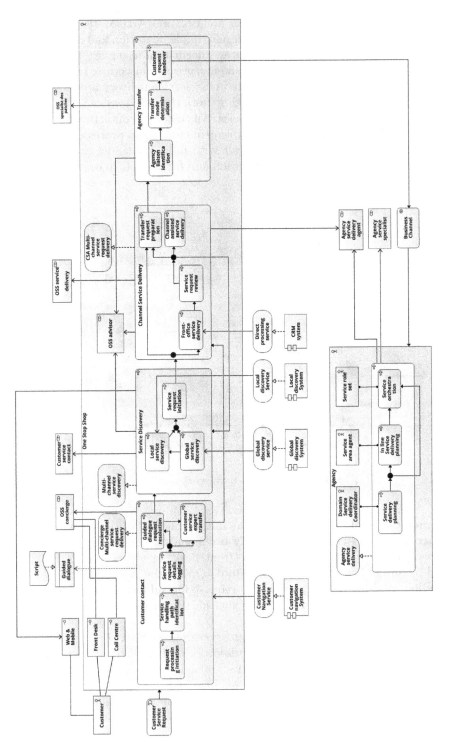

Fig. 4. One-Stop Shop: illustrative ArchiMate model

Agency Transfer. Which centres on the handling of complex or specialist requests that need to be transferred to the relevant supporting agency for resolution, a process handled by an OSS specialist despatcher.

Where a request is transferred to an agency for resolution, there are typically three distinct processes in handling the customer request: *Service delivery planning* which focuses on determining how the incoming request will be dealt with, *In-line service delivery planning* which involves more specialised staff determination of the most suitable service delivery approach for complex or unusual requests and *Service orchestration* which involves the actual delivery of the identified service in order to fulfill the customer request. Within an agency, two distinct roles are identified: *Agency service delivery agent* and *Agency service specialist*. In contrast to the OSS call/service centre, within an agency, the determination of the most suitable resource to undertake a process, depends on the specifics of the customer service request received. The OSS operational environment involves a number of independent parties – OSS call centres, service centres and supporting agencies – all of whom need to collaborate to ensure that each incoming customer request is effectively and efficiently handled. Novation provides a range of facilities for dealing with specific issues that arise in a business network context. These novation arrangements provide the basis for a range of potential sourcing arrangements in the context of organisational entities making up the OSS framework including:

Substitute Sourcing. Where a particular business operation within a partner organisation is instead supported using a business operation from another business partner with similar capabilities (i.e. out-sourcing/in-sourcing).

Alternative Sourcing. Where a particular business operation within a partner organisation could potentially be supported using a business operation from another business partner with similar capabilities (e.g. during periods of peak demand or outage).

Extended Sourcing. Where a particular business operation within a partner organisation could be extended through that provided by another business partner with similar (but typically more advanced) or different capabilities.

Dependent Sourcing. Where a particular business operation within a partner organisation requires a business operation of another business partner with different capabilities.

Incompatible Sourcing. Where a particular business operation within a partner organisation cannot be used with that of another business partner that has similar or different capabilities.

Anchored Sourcing. Where a particular business operation within a partner organisation by default includes that of another business partner with similar or different capabilities.

The following section expands on the manner in which novation can be specified and utilised. Particular attention is given to its use in the OSS operational environment. However due to space limitations we only elaborate on one scenario.

Scenario: A service specialist can substitute for a customer service agent in a channel and agency for tier 4 services

This scenario corresponds to a *change to the deployment model of an artefact*. The novation requirement is indexed via the Tier 4 service delivery constraint that has corresponding local capabilities at OSS and Agency level. It provides an alternative execution mechanism for Agency service delivery services at agency level, allowing them to also be undertaken by suitably qualified Agency service delivery agents embedded in the OSS channel Fig. 5.

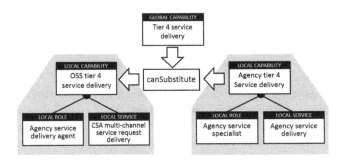

Fig. 5. One stop shop novation example: artefact augmentation

3.2   Case 2: Upstream Oil and Gas

In order to give these novation requirements some broader context, we consider their use in the upstream oil and gas industry, however due to space limitation the case study focuses on only one scenario. Energy has become an influential factor in the global economy. Petroleum oil and natural gas continue to be major energy sources, accelerating development of modern civilization. They are also increasingly dominant resources in the production of man-made materials. This high level of demand necessitates the ongoing search for new oil and gas fields and the development of facilities for the extraction of petroleum and natural gas from the earth. Extraction of petroleum is an expensive operation involving a range of different organizations including government agencies, operating organizations (operation orchestrator), drilling contractors, and service companies. Many major activities are required to support the operating activities of the oil and gas industry ranging from *legal and economic analysis, exploration and development* through to *business administration support*. This case study only focuses on exploration and development, generally referred to as *Upstream Oil and Gas*. Figure 6 provides an overview of the different roles within the range of organizations collaborating in an upstream oil and gas operation. Novations can capture the operational characteristics of this collaborative network to ensure the efficiency of key operational roles as depicted in Fig. 6.

Scenario: A driller from a drilling service provider organization requires a company man from an operating organization (operation orchestrator)

This corresponds to the augmenting an artefact scenario where the skill set of the driller is required in order to broaden the range of capabilities provided by the company man from the operation orchestrator. Figure 7 illustrates the associated novation requirement. In this case, it is indexed via the exploration management capability which has direct local capability analogues at both the drilling service provider organization and the operations orchestrator levels.

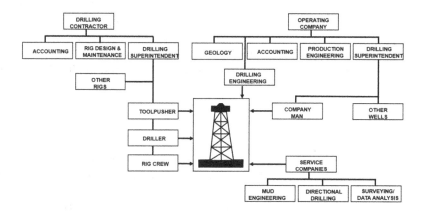

Fig. 6. Key roles in drilling a well

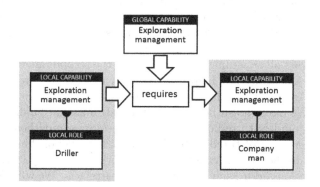

Fig. 7. Oil & gas industry novation requirement

4   Related Work

The following section provides an insight into state-of-the-art EA techniques, methodologies, frameworks and their applications. A spectrum of EA techniques or frameworks are applicable for different situations. Some such as TOGAF, are focused purely on documentation, and the stakeholders [6]. Others such as ArchiMate and RM-ODP are focused on visualization and modeling of key concepts [7]. None of the EA concepts explicitly support external views of organizations [8]. Some of them such as ArchiMate supports services and views that are relevant for business networks. However, it is not clear how internal aspects of EA relate to an external EA supportive of a business network and interactions with business partners. Although EA models provide a means to capture current and to-be states through different modelling techniques, the adequacy of these modelling and analysis concerning the cross-border interactions of an organizations is an open to question. The alignment is not explicit. Furthermore, rules for extending services at business network level as supported by service languages like USDL are not supported by EA models. Taken together, it is remains uncertain both how current EA are applicable to the external view of organizations and also how they can be comprehensively supported and aligned with the internal views in an organization.

5 Conclusions

In this paper, we have argued that EA can be used for business network planning and that current EA methods, while supporting cross-organisational interactions, leave open the modelling of how key organisational artefacts such as resources, services, processes and business objects are reused and extended through external partners (network partners). We have demonstrated a five stage approach to use EA for business network planning. Specifically, we have detailed six novation constraints defining how services and resources, as important artefacts, can be extended or referenced, as warranted by different network domains. At the heart of the paper, we described two case studies, one undertaken for a large, eGovernment network endeavour (a federated One-Stop Shop supporting service delivery across all government agencies) and the second one in upstream oil and gas industry. These cases help illustrate EA extensions through the standard TOGAF/ArchiMate method supporting resource and service reuse at the network level. We have shown how novation constraints can be defined in integrated scenario models to indicate how local resources and their set of skills (capabilities) can be substituted, extended etc. at the level of the network, such that models retain their compact form. Future work will develop further requirements and extensions addressing the full range of artefacts. We will also consider other network situations including contemporary resource models such as liquid workforce and crowdsourcing.

References

1. Ko, R., Lee, S., Lee, E.: Business process management (BPM) standards: a survey. Bus. Process Manag. J. **15**(5), 744–791 (2009)

2. Cardoso, J., Pedrinaci, C., De Leenheer, P.: Open semantic service networks: modeling and analysis. In: Falcão e Cunha, J., Snene, M., Nóvoa, H. (eds.) IESS 2013. LNBIP, vol. 143, pp. 141–154. Springer, Heidelberg (2013)
3. Ahuja, M., Kathleen, M.: Network structure in virtual organizations. J. Comput.-Mediated Commun. **3**(4), 741–757 (1998)
4. Bernus, P., Nemes, L., Schmidt, G.: Handbook on Enterprise Architecture. Springer, Heidelberg (2003)
5. Barros, A., Hettel, T., Flender, C.: Process choreography modeling. In: vom Brocke, J., Rosemann, M. (eds.) Handbook on Business Process Management 1, pp. 257–277. Springer, Heidelberg (2010)
6. Chen, D., Lillehagen, F.: Enterprise architectures - review on concepts, principles and approaches. In: Proceedings of the 10th international conference on concurrent engineering (ISPE CE 2004), pp. 1211–1216. Tsinghua University Press, Beijing (2004)
7. Lankhorst, M.: Enterprise Architecture at Work. Springer, Heidelberg (2005)
8. Kutvonen, L., Metso, J., Ruokolainen, T.: Inter-enterprise collaboration management in dynamic business networks. In: Meersman, R., Tari, Z. (eds.) OTM 2005. LNCS, vol. 3760, pp. 593–611. Springer, Heidelberg (2005)

Towards Flexible and Efficient Process and Workflow Support in Enterprise Modeling

Andreas Demuth[✉], Markus Riedl-Ehrenleitner, Roland Kretschmer,
Peter Hehenberger, Klaus Zeman, and Alexander Egyed

Johannes Kepler University (JKU), Linz, Austria
{andreas.demuth,markus.riedl-ehrenleitner,roland.kretschmer,
peter.hehenberger,klaus.zeman,alexander.egyed}@jku.at

Abstract. In enterprise modeling, organizational structures as well as
an enterprise's processes and important artifacts (e.g., business knowledge stored in documents) are captured formally using different kinds of
models. These models are not only used for documentation purposes, but
they are also used to provide guidance for employees. For example, the
models may impose rules on artifact access (i.e., who is allowed to view or
manipulate certain artifacts) or they may define workflows for individual
processes (e.g., which employees should perform which adaptation steps,
and in which order). However, existing enterprise modeling approaches
typically support only coarse-grained artifacts. For instance, only individual files can be associated with workflow tasks. Unfortunately, enterprise artifacts are typically of high complexity (e.g., spreadsheets contain
millions of data cells). Therefore, it is not sufficient to provide employees only with information about the artifacts involved in a task, but it
is necessary to provide more detailed information (e.g., which cells in a
spreadsheet are relevant).

In this paper, we introduce a novel approach to enterprise modeling that addresses the issue of too coarse-grained support for enterprise
artifacts. Our approach relies on a generic knowledge-sharing platform,
called DesignSpace, in which all aspects of an enterprise are integrated
and stored at a fine level of granularity. The DesignSpace supports fine-
grained representation of enterprise artifacts and their linking to tasks in
defined workflows. Moreover, it enables automatic, efficient, and generic
workflow support. First case studies suggest that the approach is feasible
and provides significant improvements in terms of efficiency compared to
state-of-the-practice enterprise modeling solutions.

Keywords: Enterprise modeling · Workflow support · Consistency

1 Introduction

Generally, enterprise modeling captures the organizational structure as well as
important processes of an enterprise [1–5]. The organizational structure depicts
an enterprise's organizational hierarchies and includes detailed information about
how individual areas of the enterprise are interrelated (e.g., chain of command,
reporting hierarchy) [1,6]. The modeled processes define at a quite abstract level

© Springer International Publishing Switzerland 2015
A. Persson and J. Stirna (Eds.): CAiSE 2015 Workshops, LNBIP 215, pp. 270–281, 2015.
DOI: 10.1007/978-3-319-19243-7_26

which information is available in the enterprise and how information should be shared and propagated [6]. Typically, for each process there is a detailed workflow that defines guidelines for employees about how to execute the process step-by-step; it consists of a series of ordered tasks that have to be perfomed, where each tasks is assigned to either an individual or a group of employees [4,6,7]. For the sake of simplicity, we will refer to those responsible for performing tasks (i.e., individual members of the organization or groups thereof) as *agents* in this paper.

Indeed, capturing these aspects in enterprise models with graphically appealing visual notations is beneficial for building awareness and making communication about the organization more efficient [1,8]. However, capturing these aspects is not enough. Especially for processes, it is crucial that they are not only well defined, but that they are also executed properly. Thus traceability and process enforcement are essential for applying enterprise models successfully and with maximum effectiveness [7,9]. Unfortunately, most existing approaches to enterprise modeling do not support these aspects in enough detail. Specifically, process enforcement is typically limited to the definition of workflows and the assignment of defined tasks to agents (e.g., [5,7,10]). Tasks often including coarse-grained information about the involved enterprise artifacts. After performing an assigned task, it is typically marked as completed by the corresponding agent (e.g., through an enterprise management system) and the next task is started. For example by notifying another agent about the new, pending task. While this is indeed a first step in the right direction, it is by far not sufficient as typically traceability is limited to who performs which task, and which enterprise artifacts are involved (e.g., a spreadsheet for calculating the total personnel costs) [8]. With artifacts of increasing complexity, such as spreadsheets with millions of cells and highly complex calculations, the coarse-grained level of traceability that is available in existing approaches does not suffice to provide meaningful guidance for agents. However, traditional approaches cannot tackle this issue as they generally do not consider enterprise artifacts at a level finer than individual files (at least in a generic fashion) [8].

Furthermore, adaptations to files performed by agents during workflows may introduce contradictions (also called inconsistencies) between knowledge captured in the adapted file and knowledge existing in other files—or even within the same file. For instance, after adding information about a new employee in a spreadsheet, it may be necessary to perform another adaptation that updates the total number of employees for the specific organizational unit in the organization model. Unfortunately, such inconsistencies that may be introduced to enterprise knowledge typically cannot be detected with existing approaches.

In this paper, we present a novel approach to enterprise modeling that addresses the issue of coarse-grained traceability and enterprise artifact integration, and missing guidance and detection of errors made during workflows. We introduce a platform, called DesignSpace, that allows for the integration of enterprise knowledge at arbitrary levels of granularity. The DesignSpace supports enterprise models and artifacts of arbitrary formats and notations, as well as traceability between these models and enterprise artifacts. For efficient process and workflow support, it provides various mechanisms such as incremental consistency checking, automatic change impact analysis, knowledge propagation, or change notifications. First case studies with a prototype implementation of the DesignSpace indicate that the proposed approach is technically feasible, scalable, and usable in practice. Please note that the DesignSpace as a platform for knowledge sharing has been published previously [11]. The novel contribution of this paper is the application of the DesignSpace approach to the domain of enterprise modeling to address the issues discussed above.

2   Illustrative Example

As a simple, yet illustrate example, consider the following scenario that involves the organization model of an enterprise and a spreadsheet that is used for calculating the enterprise's personnel costs, grouped by individual departments. Assume that a large enterprise's European accounting department has just hired an intern for several months. For this hiring process, a workflow is defined that contains two tasks: (i) add the intern's information to the organization model, and (ii) add the intern's information to the enterprise's cost-calculation spreadsheet. For the first task, an agent uses an organization modeling tool and adapts the organization model. To execute the second task, another agent has to add the intern to the list of employees and he must insert the intern's personal information and salary in the corresponding spreadsheet, which is linked with the task. As the agent performs this task, he encounters two challenges. First, he must find the exact location within the document where information about the accounting department is kept. Second, to obtain the correct salary for the cost calculation, the agent must look up the salary for interns in the accounting department, which is already defined in the spreadsheet. Note that for a complex spreadsheet with millions of cells, dozens of pages, and numerous complex calculations, this task becomes quite error prone and the agent may, by accident, add the intern to the wrong department (e.g., the logistics department), or he may use the wrong salary (e.g., the salary for junior accountants, or interns in the logistics department). Moreover, the intern's personal information (e.g., name, social security number) is entered twice by different agents. If either of them enters information incorrectly, an inconsistency is introduced. Unfortunately, this inconsistency likely remains undetected as there is no connection between the organization model and the cost-calculation spreadsheet.

Overall, this simple example highlights how the lack of fine-grained integration of enterprise artifacts and models and the resulting lack of traceability and consistency checking may lead to contradictions in enterprise knowledge.

3   DesignSpace

Next, we discuss in detail the capabilities of the *DesignSpace* with respect to enterprise modeling, workflow support, and knowledge management. The DesignSpace is a cloud-based knowledge integration and service platform that

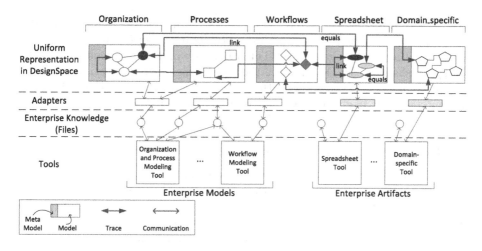

Fig. 1. Approach Overview.

enables effective and efficient knowledge sharing and management by providing an integrated view on knowledge of various sources and in various formats. The DesignSpace also allows arbitrary inter-dependencies to be established within this representation of enterprise knowledge, therefore augmenting the knowledge already available in the individual models and artifacts. Moreover, it provides services that enable agents to work with diverse enterprise artifacts, to handle inconsistencies between individual pieces of enterprise knowledge, and to perform transformations of knowledge during the execution of tasks. An overview of the DesignSpace approach is depicted in Fig. 1.

3.1 Integration Services

The DesignSpace is a mirror of existing enterprise knowledge, reflecting the contents of existing files using a uniform representation. The existence of the DesignSpace is generally transparent to agents as they can continue to work with common modeling or artifact editing tools to edit enterprise knowledge. However, the DesignSpace's integration of knowledge enables a range of knowledge sharing and information services that, for example, allow agents to define inter-dependencies among enterprise models and artifacts—even if these are produced and edited in different tools and stored in different files with different formats. These services will be discussed in detail in Sect. 3.2.

There are two ways of integrating existing enterprise knowledge in the Design Space, which we discuss next: file-based integration and tool-based integration.

File-based Integration. File-based knowledge integration takes as input the existing files that contain enterprise knowledge (e.g., enterprise model files or spreadsheets). The contents of these files and are parsed and mapped to the unified representation used in the DesignSpace by *file-adapters*. For each type of file to be integrated with the DesignSpace, a corresponding, file-type-specific adapter is used. Note that the tool adapter also defines at which level of granularity files are mapped to the DesignSpace's unified representation. For instance, an adapter may work at a very fine-grained level of granularity and map the individual cells of a spreadsheet to the DesignSpace (i.e., for a single spreadsheet, information about each of its cells is available in the DesignSpace). However, for certain primitive enterprise artifacts this may not be required (e.g., for image files). When knowledge—and thus the file in which the knowledge is stored—evolves, this is reflected in the DesignSpace by incrementally updating the uniform representation. This synchronization is fully automated by the file-adapters.

Tool-based Integration. Even though the default way of integrating enterprise knowledge is via file-adapters, the DesignSpace also supports and encourages the use of *tool-adapters* that map tools' internal data structures (and thus the knowledge that is edited with the tool) to the DesignSpace's uniform representation on-the-fly. Tool-adapters have a grey background in Fig. 1. In the figure, tool-adapters are used for enterprise artifacts and file-adapters are used for enterprise models. This is by coincidence and not a prescription of our approach. The major benefit of tool-adapters is that they allow for the augmentation of tools with additional information. For example, inconsistencies may be highlighted directly within a tool.

Overall, the DesignSpace is agnostic to the enterprise knowledge it manages and thus supports arbitrary knowledge. Only adapters are aware of which knowledge is integrated with the DesignSpace and how the mapping to the uniform representation of the DesignSpace is done.

3.2 Knowledge Sharing and Management Services

The DesignSpace provides extensive support for sharing and managing enterprise knowledge efficiently.

Traceability Support. Once an enterprise's knowledge is integrated with the DesignSpace through adapters, as discussed above, traceability information may be added. The DesignSpace allows for the definition of traceability between arbitrary pieces of knowledge. Traces may be used within or between individual enterprise models or artifacts, as shown in Fig. 1. For example, it is possible to link a specific cell in a spreadsheet to another cell within the same file, to link individual cells of a spreadsheet with certain workflow tasks, or to link specific files to certain agents (e.g., to define access rights or responsibilities; not depicted in the figure). Different kinds of traces are available in the DesignSpace: untyped and typed traces.

Untyped traces. Arbitrary pieces of knowledge (i.e., parts of enterprise models or artifacts) can be connected via *untyped traces*. Such traces do simply consist of two connection ends where each end points to at least one piece of knowledge.

Typed traces. Typed traces are defined using meta-information. For typed traces, it is defined explicitly which kinds of knowledge they may link. Moreover, typed traces may have explicit semantics assigned. For instance, to define responsibilities within an enterprise, a typed trace named `responsibility trace` may be defined that allows only the linking of (parts of) enterprise artifacts to agents. Each such trace then defines a specific responsibility. As another example, a simple *equality trace* may be defined for a certain type of enterprise artifact knowledge (e.g., spreadsheet cells) and it may require the linked pieces of knowledge to be actually equal (depicted as traces named *equals* in Fig. 1). The semantics of such a trace are straightforward: it requires the linked spreadsheet cells to have equal values. Similarly, a complex equality traces could be defined between knowledge pieces of different types, along with explicit information about how equality is defined. Such a trace could be established, for example, between spreadsheet cells and enterprise model elements. Equality could be defined as both the spreadsheet cell and the enterprise model element must contain the same value. For every typed trace it can be checked if the trace is correct or if there is a mismatch between the linked knowledge and the desired relation (i.e., the semantics) are violated.

Consistency Checking. A key feature of the DesignSpace is consistency checking. Generally, consistency is given if enterprise knowledge is free of inconsistencies (i.e., contradictions). Such contradiction may occur not only between knowledge stemming from different sources (e.g., a spreadsheet cell and an enterprise model element represent the same knowledge, but both have different values), but also between pieces of knowledge that stem from a single source (e.g., two cells in a spreadsheet that should have the same value actually have different values). Indeed, a contradiction indicates that either an agent made a mistake during knowledge adaptation, or that different agents have a different understanding. In the DesignSpace, consistency checking is done automatically based on defined traces (see above) and also on explicitly stated, domain-specific, and adaptable consistency rules. These rules are defined for certain types of knowledge and specify desired conditions that must hold between individual pieces of knowledge. For instance, a consistency rule may state that each pending task during a workflow must be assigned to an agent, and that the assigned agent must belong to the organizational unit that is responsible for performing that workflow.

Change Impact Analysis and Change Notification. Whenever agents perform tasks during a workflow, they may adapt and change enterprise knowledge. In particular, they may adapt pieces of knowledge that were previously adapted by other agents. Or they may change knowledge which other agents depend on. In the DesignSpace, every single adaptation of enterprise knowledge is analyzed automatically by the change impact service for its potential effects on other agents (based on defined traces). If a piece of knowledge is changed, the agents that are linked to the changed part either directly through a trace or transitively through a chain of traces can be notified about the change. This allows these potentially affected agents to review the change and to react to it accordingly.

Knowledge Transformation and Propagation. As discussed above, adaptations of enterprise knowledge may lead to inconsistencies. In addition to the detection of inconsistencies, the DesignSpace also supports mechanism for repairing inconsistencies and propagating adaptations in a way that re-establishes consistency among pieces of knowledge.

4   Fine-Grained Enterprise Artifact Integration

Let us now discuss specifically how enterprise knowledge can be integrated with the DesignSpace. In particular, we present how traditional enterprise models and arbitrary enterprise artifacts can be integrated.

4.1   Organization, Process, and Workflow Models

In enterprise modeling, models that describe the organizational structure, the processes, and their associated workflows are commonly used. Typically, these models provide fine-grained information and they are stored by modeling tools in common file formats that are well-structured and well-documented (e.g., XML files with defined schemas); the structure of the models typically resembles a graph-structure. Therefore, integration of these models typically requires a straight-forward mapping of the well-structured model file contents to the DesignSpace's uniform representation. For XML files, for example, it is sufficient to use a single, generic adapter that takes as input an XML schema and a model file to perform the integration of the corresponding model with the DesignSpace.

However, even if custom enterprise modeling tools are used that do not allow for the export of models to common file formats, at most one adapter is required per model type; and, indeed, the number of different models is usually quite limited.

4.2   Enterprise Artifact Models

Besides the integration of the typical enterprise models discussed above, other enterprise artifacts must also be integrated with the DesignSpace. Compared to the integration of the typical enterprise models, as discussed above, the integration of arbitrary enterprise artifacts is more challenging. Specifically, this is because of diversity of enterprise artifacts, which range from spreadsheets, over semi-structured documents containing natural language, to domain-specific files. Especially the latter imposes challenges as for different business domains, different domain-specific knowledge is required. For example, technology companies require hardware models and source code of software to be integrated, whereas for commercial banks the domain-specific enterprise artifacts may contain risk-analysis and stock exchange information. Indeed, for each kind of these enterprise artifacts, a corresponding adapter is required that maps the artifact to the DesignSpace. In contrast to Sect. 4.1, this mapping is less straight-forward because the files that contain the domain-specific knowledge are often created by custom-built tools. Moreover, before building an adapter, it must be determined at which level of granularity the knowledge should be reflected in the DesignSpace. The level of granularity necessary does not only depend on the knowledge contained in an enterprise artifact and its structure, but also on how and where the artifact is used in workflows. If an artifact is only used as-is during workflows (e.g., an image for the enterprise's official letter head, which is only embedded in documents for customer correspondence but never changed), it is sufficient to represent the artifact at file-level-granularity. If, however, different parts of an artifact are adapted during workflows (e.g., a spreadsheet containing entry-level salaries for different positions), it may be required to represent the artifact in the DesignSpace at a quite fine-grained level so that for different workflows and different tasks it can be defined exactly which parts of the artifact are to be adapted.

5 Efficient Process and Workflow Support

Next, based on our illustrative example, we discuss how the integration of enterprise knowledge with the DesignSpace makes task execution more efficient for agents and how it prevents inconsistencies from being introduced unnoticed.

First, both required tasks in the workflow, which is highlighted with a green background in Fig. 1, can be linked to specific pieces of knowledge (e.g., to the department that hired the intern in the organization model, or the salary for interns in that department in the spreadsheet). This not only increases efficiency, but it also reduces the chance of errors being made.

Moreover, since the organization model and the enterprise's cost-calculation spreadsheet are integrated with the DesignSpace, consistency can be checked between the knowledge stored in the corresponding files. A consistency rule can be used that expresses, for instance, that for each employee that appears in the spreadsheet there must be a corresponding entry in the organization model that has exactly the same information (e.g., the employee must not belong to different departments). The traces between employee entries in the organization model and the spreadsheet can be generated automatically in the DesignSpace's knowledge transformation service based on unique indentifiers (e.g., the employees name, date of birth, and social security number). Indeed, if such a trace cannot be established, for example because one of the two responsible agents entered an incorrect date of birth, this is identified as an inconsistency by the DesignSpace. If the trace can be created, the consistency checking service can navigate the trace and check whether both pieces of information meet the desired condition (i.e., equality), and detects an inconsistency if there is a contradiction (e.g., the department differs). If an inconsistency is detected either during trace generation or during consistency checking, both agents are informed through the notification service that there is an inconsistency that needs to be fixed. The knowledge involved in this inconsistency is highlighted with red background in Fig. 1. Since the consistency rule requires the specified information to be equal, either of the responsible agents may review in the file linked to his workflow task whether he entered the employee information correctly. If, for example, the agent that adapted the organization model finds that he entered the information correctly, it follows automatically that the information is incorrect in the involved spreadsheet. In this case, the DesignSpace's knowledge transformation and propagation services may be used to automatically propagate the correct information and update the spreadsheet accordingly.

To check whether the correct salary was entered in the spreadsheet during the second task of the workflow, another trace can be generated that, based on the employee's specific job, department, and geographic location automatically traces to the correct salary. This equality trace can then be checked by the consistency checker. If an inconsistency is detected (as illustrated by the elements highlighted with yellow background in Fig. 1), in this case only the agent who performed the second task is informed because the contradiction is within the spreadsheet, which was not edited by the agent that handled the first task. As with the first inconsistency, the change propagation service of the DesignSpace may be used by the agent to establish equality and thus eliminate the inconsistency. Note that in this scenario, the knowledge transformation service of the DesignSpace could have been used to insert the correct salary automatically. However, by detecting an inconsistency and informing the agent, it remains possible to purposely ignore an inconsistency, for example because the intern has negotiated a higher salary. In this section, we have shown by example how the fine-grained integration of enterprise knowledge and the DesignSpace's various services enable efficient detection and handling of inconsistencies during workflows.

6   Validation

To demonstrate the general feasibility of our approach, we used a prototype implementation of the DesignSpace as well as adapters for commonly used modeling and enterprise artifact editing tools. In three case studies the practical applicability and scalability was assessed.

6.1   Prototype Implementation and Tool Integration

To date, the core knowledge integration and knowledge sharing and management services of the DesignSpace, as discussed in Sects. 3.1 and 3.2, have been implemented.[1] These services include: (i) data storage mechanisms that allows for cloud-based mirroring of arbitrary enterprise models and artifacts, (ii) traceability, (iii) consistency checking, (iv) trace-based change notification for knowledge changes, and (v) an editor with basic visualization capabilities.

Currently, tool-adapters are available for various tools to synchronize existing enterprise knowledge automatically with the DesignSpace.

Modeling Tool. For modeling tools, we have developed a tool adapter for the IBM Rational Software Architect (IBM RSA). The RSA does not only support

---

[1] Prototype available at isse.jku.at/tools/dsspc/xadr.zip (pw: dsisse).

software architecture modeling, but it provides general support for building models for diverse domains, including business process models and workflows.

Spreadsheet Tools. For spreadsheet software, we implemented a tool adapter for Microsoft Excel. The adapter performs synchronization with the DesignSpace at cell level—each cell that contains information is mapped to the DesignSpace.

Domain-specific Tools. We have implemented adapters for three tools commonly used by technology companies: (i) Eclipse IDE, a source code development tool commonly used in software engineering, (ii) ProEngineer, an integrated 3D CAD/CAM/CAE solution commonly used in various engineering domains (e.g., mechatronical systems), and (iii) IBM RSA.

6.2   Case Studies

The DesignSpace has been applied in three different case studies.

EPlan. In this case study, engineers used the DesignSpace's services to establish traceability between enterprise artifacts, specifically between EPlan electrical models and Java source code. Consistency between the electrical model and source code was checked based on a set of user-defined, domain-specific rules. Even with large models and source code bases, engineers did not encounter any issues regarding the responsiveness of the DesignSpace. Knowledge adaptations were handled live during workflows by tool-adapters and consistency information as well as change notifications were provided in tools without noticable delays.

ACCM Robot Arm. The DesignSpace has also been used in the mechatronics domain as a platform for designing a robot arm. The project involved various kinds of enterprise artifacts. For example, mechanical calculations were provided in the form of multiple Excel spreadsheets. IBM RSA was used to build models of the robot's controller software. 3D CAD models and Matlab simulation models were also built and integrated with the DesignSpace. All artifacts were represented in the DesignSpace and traceability between the artifacts was established. The DesignSpace's data services were used to check consistency among artifacts and to notify engineers about relevant artifact changes.

ACCM Visualization Experiment. In this application, different enterprise artifacts for mechatronical development projects (e.g., requirements, mechatronic design models) were integrated in the DesignSpace and traces between those artifacts were established by domain experts. Students were then asked to perform defined refactorings (i.e., adaptations of existing knowledge) using the services provided by the DesignSpace, which they did with overall great success.

Summary. Overall, the DesignSpace has been used successfully in different domains to integrate enterprise artifacts, to establish traceability among them, to check consistency, and to notify agents about knowledge changes.

6.3   Threats to Validity

Next, we discuss some possible threats to the validity of our approach.

Integration Effort. While for typical formats of enterprise models it is possible to use standardized adapter, this is often not possible for domain-specific enterprise artifacts that may require specialized adapters. In practice, this means that enterprises adopting our approach will need to consult with information engineering experts to decide on these questions. However, the DesignSpace provides a sophisticated programming interface as well as an extensive documentation. Therefore, building file- or tool-adapters is quite straight-forward.

Trace Creation and Management. Traces are one of the cornerstones of our approach, thus it is crucial that they are established and also managed, which seems to be error-prone when considering the vast amount of knowledge and the diversity of artifacts that exist in today's enterprises. However, the DesignSpace supports different ways of establishing and managing traces. First, heuristic algorithms may be used to generate and maintain traces automatically. Second, the DesignSpace provides tools that support agents in creating and managing traces. In first industrial applications (see above), agents have not encountered any issues with creating or managing traces. Thus, using the DesignSpace to integrate and trace diverse enterprise artifacts has been shown to be feasible.

Kinds of Integrated Models and Artifacts. In the case studies presented above, only enterprise artifacts but no enterprise models have been used. However, in principle there is no difference between tracing enterprise artifacts and enterprise models, as both are represented uniformly within the DesignSpace. Moreover, the software models that have been used in the case studies are structurally quite similar to typical enterprise model (i.e., graph-like data structures). Therefore, we believe that our approach is applicable also to enterprise models.

7   Related Work

Antunes et al. [12] proposed the use of ontologies to enable sophisticed EA analysis through the use of description logics. While the DesignSpace is generally agnostic to ontologies, the ontologies of enterprise models and artifacts can also be managed by the DesignSpace. The additional information can be used by services to perform, for example, more sophisticated consistency checking. A benefit of using the DesignSpace is that it does not require the explicit definition of ontologies. Moreover, the DesignSpace has been built with incrementality as key feature—any change to enterprise knowledge is analyzed immediately and automatically, and feedback to potentially affected agents is available instantly. Florez et al. [1] proposed an approach that allows for the explicit modeling of imperfections in enterprise models that occur because of, for instance, incorrect information or missing information sources. Note that when using the DesignSpace services for modeling an enterprise, such imperfections are detected automatically. Information about these imperfections is available to modelers instantly. However, are free to ignore inconsistencies for the time being, thus accepting the detected imperfections temporarily. Moreover, the DesignSpace is in principle capable of detecting imperfections in enterprise models represented in any language.

8   Conclusion and Future Work

In this paper, we presented how the cloud-based knowledge-sharing platform *DesignSpace* can be applied in enterprise modeling to address common issues of too coarse-grained support for enterprise artifacts in workflows. First case studies with a prototype implementation suggest that the approach is feasible and scalable. For future work, we plan to provide more adapters for different kinds of existing enterprise knowledge and to apply our prototoype in industrial companies.

Acknowledgments. The research was funded by the Austrian Science Fund (FWF): P25289-N15 and P25513-N15, FWF Lise-Meitner Fellowship M1421-N15, and the Austrian Center of Competence in Mechatronics (ACCM).

References

1. Florez, H., Sánchez, M.E., Villalobos, J.: iarchimate: A tool for managing imperfection in enterprise models. In: EDOC Workshops, pp. 201–210 (2014)
2. Pinto, V.A., de Rezende Rohlfs, C.L., Parreiras, F.S.: Applications of ontologies in enterprise modelling: A systematic mapping study. In: ER Workshops, pp. 23–32 (2014)
3. Berio, G., Vernadat, F.B.: New developments in enterprise modelling using cimosa. Comput. Ind. **40**(2), 99–114 (1999)
4. Gudas, S., Lopata, A., Skersys, T.: Approach to enterprise modelling for information systems engineering. Informatica **16**(2), 175–192 (2005)
5. Vernadat, F.: Ueml: towards a unified enterprise modelling language. Int. J. Prod. Res. **40**(17), 4309–4321 (2002)
6. Petrikina, J., Drews, P., Schirmer, I., Zimmermann, K.: Integrating business models and enterprise architecture. In: EDOC Workshops, pp. 47–56 (2014)
7. Sunkle, S., Rathod, H.: Visual modeling editor and ontology api-based analysis for decision making in enterprises - experience and way ahead. In: EDOC Workshops, pp. 182–190 (2014)
8. Frank, U.: Enterprise modelling: The next steps. Enterp. Model. Inf. Syst. Architect. **9**(1), 22–37 (2014)
9. Vernadat, F.B.: Enterprise modeling and integration (emi): Current status and research perspectives. Annu. Rev. Control **26**(1), 15–25 (2002)
10. Barone, D., Yu, E., Won, J., Jiang, L., Mylopoulos, J.: Enterprise modeling for business intelligence. In: van Bommel, P., Hoppenbrouwers, S., Overbeek, S., Proper, E., Barjis, J. (eds.) PoEM 2010. LNBIP, vol. 68, pp. 31–45. Springer, Heidelberg (2010)
11. Demuth, A., Riedl-Ehrenleitner, M., Nöhrer, A., Hehenberger, P., Zeman, K., Egyed, A.: DesignSpace - an Infrastructure for multi-user/multi-tool engineering. In: SAC (2015)
12. Antunes, C., Caetano, A., Borbinha, J.L.: Enterprise architecture model analysis using description logics. In: EDOC Workshops, pp. 237–244 (2014)

RW-BPMS 2015

The Things of the Internet of Things in BPMN

Sonja Meyer[1(✉)], Andreas Ruppen[2], and Lorenz Hilty[3]

[1] Informatics and Sustainability Research Group,
Swiss Federal Laboratories for Materials Science and Technology,
9014 St. Gallen, Switzerland
sonja.meyer@empa.ch
[2] Software Engineering Group, University of Fribourg,
1700 Fribourg, Switzerland
andreas.ruppen@unifr.ch
[3] Department of Informatics, University of Zurich, 8050 Zurich, Switzerland
hilty@ifi.uzh.ch

Abstract. The component "thing" of the Internet of Things does not yet exist in current business process modeling standards. The "thing" is the essential and central concept of the Internet of Things, and without its consideration we will not be able to model the business processes of the future, which will be able to measure or change states of objects in our real-world environment. The presented approach focuses on integrating the concept of the Internet of Things into the meta-model of the process modeling standard BPMN 2.0 as standard-conform as possible. By a terminological and conceptual delimitation, three components of the standard are examined and compared towards a possible expansion. By implementing the most appropriate solution, the new thing concept becomes usable for modelers, both as a graphical and machine-readable element.

Keywords: Internet of things · BPMN · Physical entity · Entity of interest

1 Introduction

Due to the ongoing development of Web technologies the branch of research called *Internet of Things (IoT)* has grown up and meanwhile stucks into its teen shoes. According to the IoT vision, millions of devices such as sensors and actuators can communicate via Web-like structures through standardized software services. From a user and process perspective, these devices are resources that allow to measure or even change properties of entities of interest (i.e. a living room) in the real world. While the individual device used to communicate between the digital and the real world is interchangeable, rather the sensed (i.e. measure temperature) or even modified (i.e. activate cooling) *thing*[1] stands at the center of the application. Hitherto parallel, companies have been modeling their business processes from a process-oriented perspective for many years. Modern BPM systems automate these processes. They distinguish different phases in a life cycle. A fundamental phase before any process

---

[1] The terms physical entity, entity of interest, object and thing are used replaceable.

© Springer International Publishing Switzerland 2015
A. Persson and J. Stirna (Eds.): CAiSE 2015 Workshops, LNBIP 215, pp. 285–297, 2015.
DOI: 10.1007/978-3-319-19243-7_27

automation deals with process modeling. Its main goal is to create a model of the business process by applying a suitable language.

Business processes that integrate the technologies of the IoT differ from conventional processes [2]. So far, modeling languages such as the industry standard BPMN 2.0 and its compliant tools have offered only rudimentary support for expressing the component *thing*. With other words, the things of the Internet do not exist from the perspective of a BPM system. This is surprising, as the IoT promises to change not only our daily lives but also the business world significantly.

We suppose that conventional meta-models can be expanded by the missing concept *thing*. Its implementation shall empower end-users to model the things in business processes alongside to traditional concepts. This paper examines how the IoT domain component *thing* can be represented in the process model. For this purpose, we make the following contributions:

- Based on related contributions, we *identify three concepts* of the BPMN meta-model that are suitable for the representation of a thing.
- Based on the IoT terminology and its domain model [1] we *define detailed requirements* for the new component.
- We investigate to what extent the identified BPMN concepts meet the defined requirements. *For each concept* we introduce a potential *BPMN extension* "Physical Entity" in order to meet all requirements that could not yet be covered by standard elements.
- By *evaluating the extension* we identify the extension "Custom Participant" as the most appropriate thing-representation.
- By further assessing the Custom Participant, we come up with a *solution beyond the BPMN standard*.

2 The Problem

The main components of the IoT are defined in a reference model [1] that potentially may perform tasks in business processes. The central component of these concepts is the *thing*, also named *physical entity*. To integrate the areas IoT and BPM seamlessly with one another, it should be possible to transmit all major components of the IoT meta-model to a corresponding meta-model of the BPM domain, including the concept *thing*. When examining different process modeling standards, it becomes clear that such a BPM counterpart does not exist. Likewise, it is not surprising that the *things* of the IoT are not part of the meta-model of the extensive industry standard BPMN either. This becomes a problem when it comes to the modelling and subsequent dynamic execution of elementary IoT-aware processes following the traditional BPM life cycle.

We consider the following process example: A Web service shall measure the temperature of the physical entity chocolate *by means of one currently available device that is accessible* via *the Internet.*

The product *chocolate* is available as a digital representation, but it remains unclear how it can be taken into account in a BPMN model. According to the IoT domain model [1], the problem area can be structured into four architectural components: the device, the thing, the native service and the IoT service. A *device* in the IoT is a technical artifact that can bridge the physical with the digital world. This connection is enabled via special on-device services (*native services*) such as sensing or actuating abilities. The device can communicate with other devices and is part of a physical construction unit. A *thing* is an identifiable, separable part of the physical environment which is of particular interest for a business process. Thus, a thing can become part of the digital world, if the artificial relation "attached to" is created between a device and the concerned thing (e.g. between the temperature sensor and the chocolate). *IoT services* are software components with standardized interfaces that expose the native interfaces of heterogeneous devices. They augment the functionality of one or more native services. By their well-defined interfaces, they denote an integratable part of a business process and can be bound to a process activity.

BPMN comes with a multitude of components of which some are potentially suitable for the constitutive thing integration. Anyhow, a detailed analysis and a comprehensive solution to the problem, both conceptually and as an implemented standard extension are still missing for the research community as well as for modelling users.

3   The Things in BPMN

The IoT comes with numerous of things being measured and influenced by devices that are able to flexibly perform as resources in business processes in a constantly changing environment. We aim at integrating this potential with traditional BPM systems which focus on executing planned processes with a constant set of resources. Existing BPM environments support a comprehensive lifecycle. One central and initial part of each lifecycle is the creation of a business process model. In order to bring the new IoT element *thing* to the envisioned BPM environment, we aim to provide a process model that includes the *thing* element, as a basis to express this new information. There are various Business Process Notations available, but [2] evaluated the industry standard BPMN 2.0 as the most IoT-aware state-of-the-art process modeling approach. The process model of BPMN comes already with a graphical and a machine-readable notation. The latter can comprise technical details [3] and is executable by a compliant engine. The process model is the outcome of the process design phase and serves as clearly defined interface between the design, resolution and execution phase. It shall cover typical and all needed constructs with the thing element.

4   Details of the Integration

The work of [4] provides a starting point for our work. It identifies three suitable concepts in the BPMN meta-model that can be used for such integration. These concepts are Text Annotation, Data Object and Participant. We compare these three potential elements and evaluate them. To do so, we adopt the IoT terminology and its domain model [1] as a definition and define detailed requirements for the new component *thing* in a first step. Next, we realize a potential extension of the meta-model for each of the three standards concepts. This allows us to examine in detail if the requirements are met. Subsequently, we evaluate how many of the requirements could be met and how many extensions were needed for this purpose. We receive a best standard solution. Finally, we improve this solution by hypothetical extensions that would require a slight change of the BPMN standard.

4.1 Requirements

Table 1 lists the identified requirements for the modeling element Physical Entity and its relations. We focus on two aspects: On the one hand the process modeler should be given the ability to express all important entity components graphically and on the other hand the output model should be machine-readable for the resolution and execution environment.

Table 1. Functional formalization requirements of physical entity element

No.	Requirement	Rationale
1	There must be a way of representing the Physical Entity in the graphical process model as a separate element	The Process Modeler needs standardized rules to express the participation of a Physical Entity in an own element
2	There must be a way of representing the Physical Entity in the machine-readable model as separate element	The process resolution environment [5] needs a schema to identify participating Physical Entities
3	The selected or extended element for representing the Physical Entity must support contentwise its intention	Realized extensions shall not contradict the semantics of any BPMN element [11]
4	The Physical Entity element must not be target or source of a sequence flow	The Physical Entity is a passive element and can neither directly execute tasks nor be instantiated by arriving tokens
5	The Physical Entity element must not be target or source of a message flow	The Physical Entity does neither directly receive nor send messages
6	The Physical Entity element must not be target/source of a data association	The Physical Entity does not contain data objects or data stores
7	The Physical Entity element must support associations as connection type both as target and as source	The Physical Entity can be bi-directionally associated with an IoT service [1]
8	The Physical Entity element must not contain any responsibility assignments	The Physical Entity is a passive object. It can't overtake any execution responsibility.
9	The Physical Entity element must not be assignable to a pool or lane	The Physical Entity is able to have multiple relationships to further process participants. It does not exclusively belong to one single participant that is responsible for the entity

(Continued)

Table 1. (*Continued*)

No.	Requirement	Rationale
10	The Physical Entity must take part in the process collaboration of the XML between further participants	The Physical Entity collaborates with activities of further process participants
11	The Physical Entity element must allow being a multi-instance element. [4]	One entity can be an augmentation of several entities [1]
12	The description model of the Physical Entity must be expressible in the form of entity properties	The work of [6, 7] foresees an entity description model
13	The association between a Physical Entity and an IoT service must be expressible in the graphical and machine-readable process model	Following [1], the Physical Entity can be associated with an IoT service. The resolution environment [5] needs the association in a machine-readable form
14	The direction of association between a Physical Entity and an IoT service must be expressible	[1] distinguishes between the associations "monitors" (gaining entity states) and "acts on" (changing entity states)
15	One Physical Entity element must support multiple associations to different process activities in the same process model [4]	During a process flow even at the same time different IoT services can gain and change states of the same Physical Entity
16	The indirect association between a Physical Entity and an IoT Device must be expressible in the graphical and machine-readable model	In order to enable the resolution of [5] based on [1], the association between Device and Physical Entity has to be mapped to the process model
17	The indirect association between a Physical Entity and a Native Service must be expressible	To provide domain support to the modeler, the association between Native Service and Physical Entity has to be mapped to the process model

4.2   Three Potential Extensions

Since the structure of the three potential extensions is complex, we will summarize the analysis of suitable representations in BPMN for the Physical Entity, considering the defined requirements and rationales. Firstly, the three most similar elements of the BPMN standard are identified and whether the Physical Entity requirements will cope with them is reviewed. Secondly, a potential Physical Entity class extension under or above the individual element class is discussed. In order to keep the BPMN extension conformance, standard classes are not changed.

Text Annotation and Establishment of Custom Artifact. `TextAnnotation` is a subclass of `Artifact`. `Artifacts` are used to specify process-related information, which does not affect the sequence or message flow. `TextAnnotations` define a mechanism to add additional descriptive information, but they are also represented in the machine-readable model. By a non-directional connection `TextAnnotations` can be connected to each object. Graphically they comply with data connections, but the machine-readable model differs in its output. One disadvantage of applying `TextAnnotations` is that the direction of the association is not modifiable and equates to type "none". In addition, it is impossible to forbid that a `TextAnnotation` is assignable to process flow elements contained by a Pool, since this is principally admitted for `Artifact` classes. A multi-instance property is not expected for Artifacts. As all elements, neither a `TextAnnotation` nor an `Artifact` depicts a separate `Physical Entity` element and they are not designed to tie-in to a description model. In parallel to the `TextAnnotation` class, BPMN provides an extension mechanism to create own `Artifacts`, which resolves some of the shortcomings. This approach has the disadvantage that a `Physical Entity` element shall not be assignable to further Pool and Lane containments that cannot be resolved by this class introduction. Figure 1 shows the class diagram.

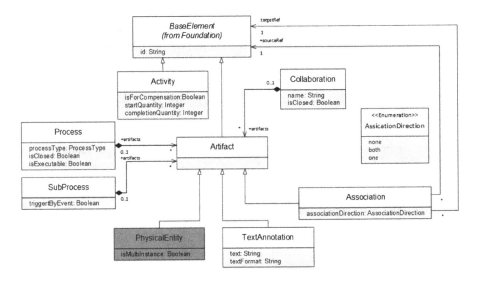

Fig. 1. Artifact subclass extension of BPMN standard

Data Object and Establishment of Custom Item Aware Element. In the BPMN standard, `DataObject` is a subclass of `ItemAwareElement` that is applied to support the process execution. It is used to represent information flowing through the process. As a `FlowElement` the `DataObject` belongs to a process or sub-process and, being an `ItemAwareElement` at the same time, it can reference a data item and a state definition. In a conventional manner, the class `ItemAwareElement` is devoted to detect data structures that are queried, transferred or changed during execution time. This contrasts with the task of a Physical Entity: in its passive role, it is not directly relevant to the final execution, but rather, it is solely used for the resolution in the actual initialization of a model. If the process is resolved as envisioned by [5], the Physical Entity is no longer needed. Nevertheless, the introduction of a new subclass of `ItemAwareElement` such as suggested by [4] is examined (c.f. Fig. 2). Though `ItemAwareElement` initially does not support any sequence or message flows, it may support data connections if it is of the sub-class `DataObject`. In the XML output this inevitably leads to the fact that, once an `ItemAwareElement` contains an association it belongs to the class `DataAssociation`, and not to the class `Association`, because the specification of the graphical model contains the same symbols for both classes. To face this problem [4]. suggests implementing the class `PhysicalAssociation`. This approach in turn leads to redundancies in the meta-model, as `PhysicalAssociation` and the standard class Association do not differ in their meaning. Additionally, a new composition-relation between `Collabora-tion` and `PhysicalEntity` needs to be established to enable the allocation on the process participant level in the XML mode.

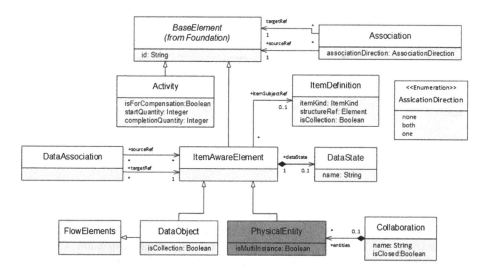

Fig. 2. Item aware element extension of BPMN standard

Participant and Establishment a Custom Participant. `Participant` is a subclass of `BaseElement` and serves as a partner element in `Collaboration` - the representation of a process interaction with one or more `Participants`. Graphically, a `Participant` is represented as a Pool and takes over the task of a container for `FlowElements`. A special kind of a Pool is the Collapsed Pool containing no elements. Following [9] a Collapsed Pool is used to represent a black box pool: i.e. a Pool without any process reference. Consequently, a Collapsed Pool is either a pool in which `FlowElements` are unknown, or that simply does not have any `FlowElements`. The second option would be tantamount to a process participant who has no active execution responsibility, which is consistent with the properties of the `Physical-Entity`. For the supplementary definition, the BPMN standard includes the `Part-nerRole` (e.g. product) and the `PartnerEntity` (e.g. chocolate). With one of these two partner elements the Pool can be designated. A `Participant` can be already defined as a multi-instance element, to have associations, and to be neither a source nor target of a sequence flow or data association. However, the `PhysicalEntity` differs from other black-box process participants in the sense that it can never become part of a message flow. A `PhysicalEntity` is a passive participant whose state can be measured or changed by active resources. Besides the process subscription, the entity does not take over any task or responsibility. By introducing `PhysicalEntity` as a subclass of `Participant` (cf. Fig. 3) a separate element is created, which meets all criteria except that it is still possible to specify message flow connections for the `PhysicalEntity`.

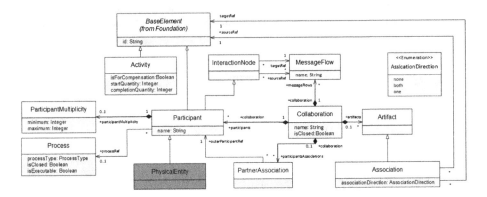

Fig. 3. Participant sub class extension of BPMN standard

4.3   Assessment

Table 2 summarizes whether the defined requirements for a separate `PhysicalEntity` element are satisfied for the three BPMN elements `TextAnnotation`, `DataObject` and `Participant`, as well as for their related extensions `CustomArtifact`, `CustomItemAwareElement` and `CustomParticipant`. The last two lines of the table provide the number of requirements that were met from all requirements and how many extensions were needed to obtain the best possible result. Not fulfilled requirements are marked with "−", fulfilled requirements with "+", and fulfilled requirements by introducing extensions are marked with "O". The outcome is that the `Collapsed Pool` is the most appropriate standard element, fulfilling 13 out of the 16 points. In the case that no IoT-specific extensions are available, the `Collapsed Pool` should be picked for representing a Physical Entity. The following section presents a BPMN standard-compliant extension that introduces a meta-model sub-class below the class `Participant`. This extension even allows for meeting all requirements except the one excluding the definition of message flows.

4.4   Solution Proposal

A solution for meeting all requirements can be achieved through a more fundamental change in the BPMN meta-model. Based on the results of the previous assessment, we suggest a new element, `PhysicalEntity`, meeting all requirements. Therefore we present both a graphical element that is anchored on the `Collapsed Pool` concept,

Table 2. Entity requirement fulfillments of BPMN elements

No.	Text annotation/ custom artifact		Data object/ custom item aware element		participant/ custom psarticipant	
1	−	+	−	+	−	+
2	−	+	−	+	−	+
3	+	+	−	−	+	+
4	+	+	+	+	+	+
5	+	+	+	+	−	−
6	+	+	−	−	+	+
7	+	+	+	−	+	+
8	+	+	+	−	+	+
9	−	−	−	+	+	+
10	+	+	−	O	+	+
11	−	O	+	O	+	+
12	−	O	−	O	−	O
13	+	+	+	+	+	+
14	−	+	+	+	+	+
15	+	+	+	+	+	+
16	+	+	+	+	+	+
17	+	+	+	+	+	+
Fulfilment degree	11/17	16/17	10/17	13/17	14/17	16/17
Extensions		2		3		1

and a machine-readable element that enhances the introduced `Participant` subclass without being restricted by the BPMN extension conformance.

Graphical Model. To integrate a separate `PhysicalEntity` element to the model, the closest related element, `Collapsed Pool`, is extended graphically, representing a `Participant` without having any process reference in the semantic model. We suggest using the significant pool shape that should be labeled with the name of the `PhysicalEntity`. An icon within the `PhysicalEntity`'s pool can be displayed before the lettering to identify its special role. This approach is similar to the one used in the specification to describe the activity character with the aid of a meaningful marker. Based on [10] we propose using a cow when selecting a self-explanatory marker, expressing that the `PhysicalEntity` represents a real-world entity that can even be alive. In comparison to the Collapsed Pool, the `PhysicalEntity` is not expandable, despite the way how it is realized by some tool implementations.

Figure 4 shows a graphical model containing two process participants in collaboration. As advocated by [9], we label the process pool with the name "IoT Process", and it contains flow elements. The `Collapsed Pool` "chocolate" is of type `PhysicalEntity` and cannot be further extended since it is empty. The associations of the IoT-specific activities contain a direction that show the orientation of the association of the `PhysicalEntity`'s state:

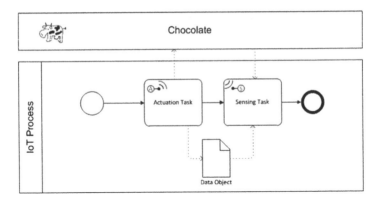

Fig. 4. Graphical process representation of Physical Entity

- From Physical Entity to Sensing Task: measuring of the entity state ("monitor").
- From Actuation Task to Physical Entity: setting the entity state ("act on").

While an Actuation Task with an associated Physical Entity acts as information sink, a Sensing Task acts as information source. Nevertheless, the actual flow of information originates/terminates not at the entity itself, but at the IoT Device, which justifies the type of connection between entity and activity as an association, rather than a flow of information.

Machine-readable Model. Based on the Participant extension discussion, in this subsection we come up with a solution beyond the BPMN standard to represent the Physical Entity as Participant in the meta-model. In contrast to the standard-conforming extension of the former subsection, this solution enables to meet the remaining requirement of the message flow, so that a Participant of type Physical Entity cannot directly send or receive messages.

Figure 5 shows the integration of the proposed extension. The shaded diagram areas represent those concepts that are newly added or changed, while the light areas belong to the unchanged meta-model. The new abstract class `ParticipantContainer` is added and derived from `BaseElement`. This class is used as a superclass for specific types of participants. `ParticipantContainer` contains the two subclasses `Participant` and `PhysicalEntity`. All attributes and associations of the old class `Participant` (c.f. Fig. 3) are attached to `ParticipantContainer`, except for the associations `processRef`, `interfaceRef` and `endPointRef`. These associations are not needed, since the subclass `PhysicalEntity` never contains elements and, none of the references. Given that the new class `Participant` (c.f. Fig. 5) inherits all properties of its superclass, it is also a sub-class of `InteractionNode`, whereby all old properties remain unchanged. In the graphical model, a Participant can still be represented by both a Collapsed Pool and an Extended Pool, depending on whether it references a process. A Participant still supports one or more message flows. In contrast to that, the class `PhysicalEntity` cannot contain any message flows. This is ensured by not deriving `PhysicalEntity` from `InteractionNode`. The added and changed standard attributes and associations refer to the definition for `PhysicalEntity`, `Participant`, `Collaboration` and `ParticipantAssociation` defined by [11].

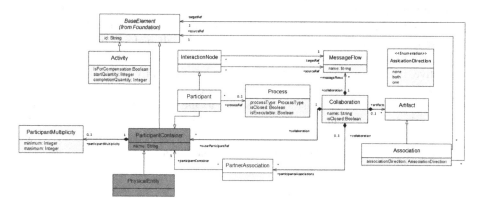

Fig. 5. Non-standard-conform BPMN extension of Physical Entity

Benefits. The extension provides the possibility to uniquely represent the Physical Entity element in the graphical and machine-readable model. The implementation was realized as close as possible to the standard without contradicting restrictions. The relations between the elements `IoT Device`, `IoT Service` and `Native Service` from [1] can still persist in the implementation. The character and intention of the Physical Entity element is kept by respecting the individual properties of the process, data and message flow. This extension proposal leaves open how the resolution of the process model is realized, but assumes that an automatic resolution approach such as envisioned by [5] is applied. This approach allows for the dynamic adaption to the changing availability of Physical Entities and attached devices. As some research efforts [6, 7], suggest semantic models for the description of some of the IoT-specific elements like the Physical Entity, we see the creation and integration of a IoT-specific model to the process modelling notation as a separate problem. Anyhow the problem is related to the refinement of the Physical Entities' representation.

5 Related Work

In this section we summarize ideas of related research initiatives to express the IoT concept Physical Entity in the BPMN process model. Building on this groundwork, we identify problems: [4] states that the Text Annotation to an activity is the state of the art approach for expressing a Physical Entity in the process model. To cover the Physical Entity it is proposed to derive a new sub-class from the `ItemAwareElement` class, called `PhysicalObject`. In order to connect a `PhysicalObject` to an activity, it is proposed to introduce a separate association type called `PhysicalAssociation` derived from the `BaseElement` class. This work was examined (above) to see whether a subclass of `ItemAwareElement` can meet the postulated requirements for a Physical Entity element. In comparison with [4, 5] separates the concepts IoT Device and Physical Entity more clearly. [5] uses the expression "entity" differently and does not clearly distinguish between the terms IoT Device and Physical Entity as it is envisioned by [1]. Nevertheless, a process example includes the Physical Entity "parcel" modeled as a Collapsed Pool, and representing a multi-instance participant. In this case [5] doesn't distinguish between the device itself in form of a tag and the Physical Entity parcel, but abstracts both concepts to the entity parcel. From this perspective, it seems reasonable that a parcel acquires the ability to communicate. This approach is, however, less reasonable for models representing IoT Devices [12] as a maximum of one resource existing in parallel to the Physical Entity element. The device and the entity are clearly separated concepts with their own semantic representation. The used devices, as well as the entities, are of central importance to the business process and cannot be considered in an augmented way.

6 Conclusion and Further Work

The absence of modeling concepts to directly express the *things* of the Internet as elements in a business process model is a significant obstacle to successfully resolve and automatically execute business processes of traditional BPM systems across distributed and Web-integrated devices. With this paper we have identified and investigated to what extent three different modeling elements of the industry standard BPMN are suitable to cover the specificities of the concept *thing*. In order to express the *thing* as an own element fulfilling all defined requirements; we introduced and evaluated for each of the concepts a standard-compliant BPMN extension. For each extension we presented the CMOF meta-model. As a result of the evaluation we conclude that a custom Participant of the semantic model visualized as a Collapsed Pool in the diagram is the closest standard-conform extension to express a thing in a business process.

Our future work will include investigating the significance of using IoT technology in business processes from a sustainability perspective. For this purpose, we will access the life cycle of an IoT-aware business process model towards the application of different wireless communication technologies (e.g. Wifi, Zigbee, Z-Wave, Bluetooth) building on the IoT Reference Architecture [1].

Acknowledgments. The authors would like to thank Alexandre de Spindler, Carsten Magerkurth and Jacques Pasquier for the valuable support.

References

1. Carrez, F. et al.: Final architectural reference model for the IoT v3.0. EC FP7 IoT-A Deliverable 1.5 (2013)

2. Meyer, S., Sperner, K., Magerkurth, C., Pasquier, J.: Towards modeling real-world aware business processes. In: Proceedings of the Second International Workshop on Web of Things, p. 8. ACM (2011)
3. Freund, J., Rücker, B., Henninger, T.: Praxishandbuch BPMN. Hanser (2010)
4. Sperner, K., Meyer, S., Magerkurth, C.: Introducing entity-based concepts to business process modeling. In: Dijkman, R., Hofstetter, J., Koehler, J. (eds.) BPMN 2011. LNBIP, vol. 95, pp. 166–171. Springer, Heidelberg (2011)
5. Concepts and Solutions for Entity-based Discovery of IoT Resources and Managing their Dynamic Associations. EC FP7 IoT-A Deliverable 4.3 (2012)
6. De, S., Barnaghi, P., Bauer, M., Meissner, S.: Service modelling for the internet of things. In: Proceedings of the Federated Conference on IEEE in Computer Science and Information Systems (FedCSIS) (2011)
7. De, S., Elsaleh, T., Barnaghi, P., Meissner, S.: An internet of things platform for real-world and digital objects. Scalable Comput. Pract. Experience **13**(1), 45–57 (2012)
8. Concepts and Solutions for Entity-based Discovery of IoT Resources and Managing their Dynamic Associations. EC FP7 IoT-A Deliverable 4.3 (2012)
9. Silver, B.: BPMN Method and Style. Cody-Cassidy Press, Aptos (2009)
10. The things in the internet of things. Poster at the (IoT 2010). Tokyo, Japan, November 2010
11. Business Process Model And Notation (BPMN). OMG Specification. Object Management Group (2011)
12. Meyer, S., Ruppen, A., Magerkurth, C.: Internet of things-aware process modeling: integrating IoT devices as business process resources. In: Proceedings of the 25th International Conference on Advanced Information Systems Engineering, Valencia, Spain (2013)

Applying Process Mining to Smart Spaces: Perspectives and Research Challenges

Francesco Leotta[1]([⊠]), Massimo Mecella[1], and Jan Mendling[2]

[1] Sapienza Università di Roma, Rome, Italy
{leotta,mecella}@diag.uniroma1.it
[2] Wirtschaftsuniversität Wien, Vienna, Austria
jan.mendling@wu.ac.at

Abstract. A software system managing a smart space takes, among its inputs, models of human behavior; such models are usually difficult to obtain and to validate. The employment of techniques from business process modeling and mining may represent a solution to both the problems, but a set of challenges need to be faced in order to cope with major differences between human activities and business processes. In this work we provide insights about these challenges, and propose further research activities to tackle them.

Keywords: Smart spaces · Process mining · Human habits

1 Introduction

The main goal of a smart space is to employ raw data coming from *sensors* deployed into the environment to make decisions about the environment itself [2]; these decisions are then applied through *actuators*, either virtual or physical, or proposed to the final user in the form of suggestions or alerts.

The reasoning task is performed according to a set of models representing environmental dynamics and, noteworthy, user habits and desires [10]. These models can be either hand-made by experts or automatically extracted (through learning and mining techniques) from previously acquired *sensor logs*. In the latter case, the amount of labeling work in charge of the final user strongly influences how much applicable a specific technique is in a real setting. From this point of view, automatic learning techniques can be classified as "supervised", "semi-supervised" and "unsupervised". The latter ones are particularly interesting in a smart space scenario as they (potentially strongly) reduce the burden on the final users to manually label the dataset fed as input. Semi-supervised learning is often associated with "active learning" approaches, whereas unsupervised techniques are the main tools employed for data mining.

If we focus our attention on models of human habits, many attempts have been made to represent human behavior by means of different kinds of state-based modeling techniques. Supervised solutions (probabilistic models such as Hidden Markov Models or deterministic models such as decision trees) are either

© Springer International Publishing Switzerland 2015
A. Persson and J. Stirna (Eds.): CAiSE 2015 Workshops, LNBIP 215, pp. 298–304, 2015.
DOI: 10.1007/978-3-319-19243-7_28

difficult to read or they require a prohibitively large amount of data to be labeled. Recently, approaches that model human habits as workflows have been proposed, thus opening to the possibility of applying process mining [15] techniques to obtain, in a semi or unsupervised manner, human-readable models that can be easily validated by end-users. Still, many new challenges have to be addressed.

As noted in [4], despite the growing availability and maturity of process mining techniques, their applicability in some contexts still faces the problem of bridging the gap between events given as input and actions composing the models obtained as output. This problem particularly applies to the challenge of mining human habits, as here sensor logs contain very fine grained events whereas mined model should contain actions at a higher level of abstraction.

Moreover, human habits are flexible in their nature. In the vast majority of cases, humans do not follow a precise workflow while performing their daily activities; they instead follow a series of best practices that are difficult to be described using a precise sequence of tasks.

Finally, process mining techniques need a log segmented in traces, which is not a safe assumption in many application scenarios, including smart spaces.

In this paper we identify a set of research challenges behind the above mentioned problems through the analysis of a case study tailored on an established dataset employed in the smart space community [5].

2   Case Study and Research Challenges

We can abstract a smart space as producing, at runtime, a sensor log containing raw measurements from available sensors. Given a set S of sensors, a sensor log is a sequence of measurements of the kind $\langle ts, s, v \rangle$ where ts is the timestamp of the measurement, $s \in S$ is the source sensor and v the measured value, which can be either nominal (categorical) or numeric (quantitative). Measurements can be produced by a sensor on a periodic base (e.g., temperature) or whenever a particular event is detected (e.g., a door opening).

Many solutions, especially those based on pattern analysis, expect as input an *event log* instead. Given a set $E = \{e_1, \ldots, e_n\}$ of event types, an event log is a sequence of pairs $\langle e, t \rangle$ where $e \in E$ and t is an integer, the occurrence time of the event e. Translating a sensor log into an event log may cause a loss of information, especially if discretization of sensor measurements is required.

A typical example of employed sensor is represented by PIR – Presence Infrared – sensors. Usually these sensors are installed on the ceiling following a grid layout; they trigger upon the detection of an object entering their field of view and automatically reset after a fixed amount of time. The CASAS project [5] provides, for example, datasets from different installations and different housing patterns (e.g., number of persons, presence of pets). All these installations contain such a grid of sensors, thus, in the following, we will refer to this particular kind of sensors to provide an insight of the research challenges raised by the application of process mining to the smart space scenario.

2.1   Bridging the Gap Between Sensor Events and Actions

As stated in [4], there exists a clear gap between the granularity of sensor logs and that of traces traditionally employed for process mining. In other words, there is no one-to-one correspondence between sensor measurements and actions performed by a person. Techniques from the machine learning field can be used to aggregate sensor measurements in order to recognize actions. These techniques, originally developed for computer vision applications [13], have been recently moved to a more generic smart space setting [1]. Noteworthy, in smart space literature, the terms "action" and "activity" have a completely different meaning [16]: an activity is a coordinated sequence of actions whose goal is performing a specific daily routine. This distinction influences our approach as well, as we suggest to split the log transformation step from the process mining one.

Sensor measurements and human actions can be directly related, indirectly related or completely unrelated to human actions. In the simplest case, especially when they come from device-attached sensors (e.g., a switch sensor connected to the oven), it is easy to associate sensor measurements to human actions. In other cases, sensors that are, in principle, unrelated to human actions, are instead indirectly influenced by human behavior; as an example, a temperature sensor is usually only influenced by environmental dynamics, but sometimes it may report variations due to the human behavior (e.g., a user is having a shower). In other cases, sensor measurements are completely unrelated to human actions and should be filtered out. Additionally, in some cases sensor measurements are not an effect of human behavior, but act instead as control variables (reflecting some kind of environmental phenomenon) influencing the behavior of the user.

In real usage scenarios, sensor and event logs are affected by a certain degree of uncertainty. Sensors have indeed their own technical limitations as they are prone to breakdowns, disconnections from the system and environmental noise (e.g., electromagnetic noise). As a consequence, measured values can be out of date, incomplete, imprecise, and contradictory to each other. Techniques for cleaning sensor data do exist, but uncertainty of sensor data may still lead to wrong conclusions about the current context.

Referring to our case study, PIR sensors are indirectly influenced by human behavior. In order to (probabilistically) infer human actions from them, it is necessary to first define which devices are installed in correspondence of each one. This association is of the type n-to-n; on the one extreme, a PIR sensor may cover multiple actions (e.g., interacting with both the fridge and the oven), thus limiting the expressiveness of models if only PIR sensors are available; on the other extreme, a single action (e.g., cooking) may cover several PIR sensors.

Another way of looking at this scenario is to think in terms of human action patterns with respect to PIR sensor triggering, e.g., the following ones:

– Static: only one PIR sensor triggers while a human is performing an action. As an example, when the user is chopping vegetables, the only interested sensor will be the one in correspondence of the kitchen table.
– Interleaved: multiple sensors trigger while the user is performing an action. In the CASAS dataset for example, while the user is sleeping, two PIR sensors

interleave, namely the ones over the two sides of the bed. The same pattern applies to higher level actions (e.g., cooking, cleaning the house).
– Movement: a set of PIR sensors quickly trigger in sequence because the user is moving from one place of the house to another to perform different actions.

These considerations make it necessary to preprocess a sensor log containing PIR sensor measurements by filtering certain sensor measurements and aggregating other ones. Methods to do that should take into account *(i)* the position of the sensor, *(ii)* the set of devices which potentially relates to the sensor, and *(iii)* the amount of time that elapses from a sensor measurement to another one. As an example, while a user is moving we will see a quick sequence of sensor triggering one close to the other, all these sensors will probably belong to movement areas of the house (e.g., a corridor); such a sequence should be filtered out. As another example, the interleaving between the two sensors over the bed should be easily aggregated as they have a single device in common (i.e., the bed).

2.2   Improving on Process Mining and Modeling Techniques

A basic question for the application of process mining techniques to human habits is whether human behavior is structured enough to be described using a process model. If the answer to this question is affirmative, the obtained model will probably resemble a "spaghetti" process [15]. Approaches to deal with unstructured processes do exist for both imperative and declarative modeling formalisms.

Declarative modeling formalisms, e.g., DECLARE [12], are usually based on temporal logics; even though different graphical representations are available to describe them, reading a declarative model is not a trivial task, requiring the knowledge of the logic language behind symbols. Additionally, as should be clear from the definitions of sensor and event logs, time is a first-class property of a measurement, but the notion of time in declarative formalisms is qualitative and not quantitative. Nevertheless, attempts to support a quantitative notion of time are available [17], and temporal logics have been applied to smart spaces [11].

Another typical approach to deal with unstructured processes is fuzzy mining [9]; it borrows concepts from the world of maps and cartography and apply them to zoom in and out on a process model highlighting the importance of certain tasks and connection between tasks just like they were points and paths on a map. It is worth to note how the implicit uncertainty coming from the transformation that turns sensor measurements into tasks should be taken into account. As an example, let us consider the derived actions resulting from the filtering and aggregation as described in Sect. 2.1, as task instances and apply a declarative miner [7,8] to the resulting dataset. Assume now that a constraint between two PIR sensors M001 and M002 has been discovered imposing that the former only triggers if the latter has previously triggered. If we say that M001 triggers because of the user interacting with either the device D001 or the device D002, this results in a branching condition. In that case we should take into account the fact that this is the result of a probabilistic decision. From this point of view, techniques like fuzzy mining appear to be particularly suitable in the smart space scenario as, by definition, they support uncertainty.

2.3   Automatic Log Segmentation

A common prerequisite of process mining techniques is to have a trace log explicitly segmented in traces (process instances). This assumption is usually not met by sensor logs as labeling is generally an expensive task to be performed by humans. This problem can be translated into a precise question: what is a habit? Is that a specific routine (e.g., cleaning the kitchen) or is it more generally what happens in a specific time frame of the day (e.g., between 8:00 am and 9:00 am).

On the one hand, choosing the second solution makes it easier to segment the log as we cannot assume that a user will not perform different routines at the same time and there is no way, from the log solely, to identify such a situation. On the other hand, according to what criteria should we choose the time ranges? The trivial solution of segmenting the day in fixed length stints of time fails if something anomalous happens (e.g., holidays). Possible solutions are:

– Associating specific combinations of sensor measurements to the beginning and to the end of a time range. E.g., the morning habit starts whenever a movement sensor different than the ones mounted over the bed triggers and ends whenever the movement sensor in correspondence of the exit door triggers and no other movement sensor triggers for a certain amount of time.
– Active learning. In order to let the system learn his habits, the user explicitly signals to the system the beginning and the end of a specific habit.

However, time is not the only dimension to take into account for segmentation. Differently from the common process mining scenario, usually sensor logs do not contain any information about which user/s caused a certain sensor to trigger or to provide a specific measurement. Thus, mining habits in a multi-user scenario is significantly harder especially with respect to the transformation task introduced in Sect. 2.1. Our use case, based on PIRs, is particularly challenging from this point of view as, even though multiple users can be identified by the spatial distance between PIRs triggering close in time, when trajectories intersect, tracking techniques [14] must be employed to keep following users.

3   Concluding Remarks

Learning human habits is a hot topic in the pervasive computing community. Such models can be employed to assist humans during activities of daily living or for energy saving strategies. Many works faced this challenge proposing techniques from machine learning and data mining. Nonetheless, the proposed approaches produces unreadable models or require an excessive labeling effort.

As shown in [3], using process modeling techniques (workflows in particular) for human habits represents a promising approach to solve the readability. Other approaches instead use techniques from the data mining area to extract subsequences of symbols that represents different activity templates [6].

Process mining could offer the best of two worlds but three research challenges need to be faced, namely *(i)* the gap between sensor logs and tasks employed in process mining, *(ii)* designing process modeling and mining techniques fitting the variability of human habits, and *(iii)* the problem of segmentation of logs. In this paper we briefly discussed them, by providing examples based on the PIR-based CASAS dataset, in order to stimulate further research in the field.

Acknowledgments. The work of F. Leotta and M. Mecella has been partly supported by the EU project VOICE, the Italian clusters SM&ST (Social Museum & Smart Tourism) and Smart Living Technologies, the project RoMA, and the Intel Galileo University Donations.

References

1. Aggarwal, J.K., Ryoo, M.S.: Human activity analysis: a review. ACM Comput. Surv. **43**(3), 16 (2011)
2. Aztiria, A., Izaguirre, A., Augusto, J.C.: Learning patterns in ambient intelligence environments: a survey. Artif. Intell. Rev. **34**(1), 35–51 (2010)
3. Aztiria, A., Izaguirre, A., Basagoiti, R., Augusto, J.C., Cook, D.J.: Automatic Modeling of Frequent User Behaviours in Intelligent Environments. In: Intelligent Environments, pp. 7–12 (2010)
4. Baier, T., Mendling, J.: Bridging abstraction layers in process mining by automated matching of events and activities. In: Daniel, F., Wang, J., Weber, B. (eds.) BPM 2013. LNCS, vol. 8094, pp. 17–32. Springer, Heidelberg (2013)
5. CASAS Project Website. http://wsucasas.wordpress.com
6. Cook, D., Krishnan, N., Rashidi, P.: Activity discovery and activity recognition: a new partnership. IEEE Trans. Cybern. **43**(3), 820–828 (2013)
7. Di Ciccio, C., Maggi, F.M., Mendling, J.: Discovering target-branched declare constraints. In: Sadiq, S., Soffer, P., Völzer, H. (eds.) BPM 2014. LNCS, vol. 8659, pp. 34–50. Springer, Heidelberg (2014)
8. Di Ciccio, C., Mecella, M.: A two-step fast algorithm for the automated discovery of declarative workflows. Symposium on Compututational Intelligence and Data Mining, pp. 135–142 (2013)
9. Günther, C.W., van der Aalst, W.M.P.: Fuzzy mining – adaptive process simplification based on multi-perspective metrics. In: Alonso, G., Dadam, P., Rosemann, M. (eds.) BPM 2007. LNCS, vol. 4714, pp. 328–343. Springer, Heidelberg (2007)
10. Leotta, F.: Instrumenting and Mining Smart Spaces. Ph.D. thesis (2014)
11. Magherini, T., Fantechi, A., Nugent, C.D., Vicario, E.: Using temporal logic and model checking in automated recognition of human activities for ambient-assisted living. IEEE Trans. Hum. Mach. Syst. **43**(6), 509–521 (2013)
12. Pesic, M., Schonenberg, H., van der Aalst, W.M.P.: Declare: full support for loosely-structured processes. In: IEEE Conference on Enterprise Distributed Object Computing (EDOC), pp. 287–300 (2007)
13. Poppe, R.: A survey on vision-based human action recognition. Image Vis. Comput. **28**(6), 976–990 (2010)
14. Smeulders, A., Chu, D., Cucchiara, R., Calderara, S., Dehghan, A., Shah, M.: Visual tracking: an experimental survey. IEEE Trans. Pattern Anal. Mach. Intell. **36**(7), 1442–1468 (2014)

15. Van Der Aalst, W.: Process mining: discovery, conformance and enhancement of business processes, Springer Science & Business Media (2011)
16. Ye, J., Dobson, S., McKeever, S.: Situation identification techniques in pervasive computing: a review. Pervasive Mob. Comput. **8**(1), 36–66 (2012)
17. Westergaard, M., Maggi, F.M.: Looking into the future. In: Meersman, R., Panetto, H., Dillon, T., Rinderle-Ma, S., Dadam, P., Zhou, X., Pearson, S., Ferscha, A., Bergamaschi, S., Cruz, I.F. (eds.) OTM 2012, Part I. LNCS, vol. 7565, pp. 250–267. Springer, Heidelberg (2012)

Factors Affecting Ocean-Going Cargo Ship Speed and Arrival Time

Erwin Filtz$^{(\boxtimes)}$, Emanuel Sanchez de la Cerda,
Mathias Weber, and David Zirkovits

Vienna University of Economics and Business, Vienna, Austria
erwin.filtz@gmail.com, mathias_weber@gmx.at,
{h0850863, david.zirkovits}@wu.ac.at

Abstract. Due to the high density of ocean traffic and the influence of marine weather on the route planning of vessels, as well as berth allocation in harbors, it is important to be able to predict arrival times as precise as possible. This paper shows the influence of marine weather on ship speed by analyzing publicly available ship traffic and weather data from different sources. A linear regression model is created to explain recorded ship speed in terms of certain ship properties and marine weather. The model has an adjusted R^2 value of 83.98% with a significant correlation of many weather related data such as wind direction (0.211), significant wave height (0.195), peak wave period (0.133), as well as ship-related data including ship type, dead weight tonnage, and gross register tonnage. Given the variables in the model the speed of the ship could be estimated fairly well. These variables along with other factors are tested regarding their usefulness for the prediction of arrival times.

Keywords: Cargo ship speed · Marine vessel speed prediction · Marine weather effects · Predicting arrival times

1 Introduction

In 2012 about 9,2 billion tons of goods destined for seaborne trade were loaded in ports worldwide. With a steady growth rate, maritime transport has more than doubled since 1980 and can be considered as one of the most important transport modes in today's global economy. Between 2012 and 2013 the number of seagoing merchant vessels of 100 GT (gross tonnage) and above grew by 6% to a total of 1,628,783 [1]. With this ever increasing number of ships and freight capacity the market is highly competitive and declining freight rates reduce earnings, requiring operators to increase efficiency and to cut costs.

One significant factor for shipping operators is costs caused by vessel delays. This paper aims to determine factors that allow for a better prediction of ship arrival times and therefore enable involved parties in the shipping process to better deal with

The research leading to these results has received funding from the European Union's Seventh Framework Programme (FP7/2007-2013) under grant agreement 318275 (GET Service).

A. Persson and J. Stirna (Eds.): CAiSE 2015 Workshops, LNBIP 215, pp. 305–316, 2015.
DOI: 10.1007/978-3-319-19243-7_29

possible delays. However, it is not only shipping operators but also other businesses holding a stake in ships being on time. In today's logistics where companies usually source from multiple suppliers and production gets ever more time critical it is advantageous to have accurate estimates on the arrival of goods allowing adjusting production and procurement accordingly. By enhancing process management with further information, businesses will be able to increase performance and optimize their processes.

Reasons for cargo vessels not arriving on time are numerous. A classification found in marine delay insurances divide them into shore side incidents and ship related incidents [2, 3]. The former include dock worker strikes, fire, lawful closures, and physical obstructions while the latter comprise crew strikes, collisions, strandings, crew illness, quarantine, and piracy. Another factor affecting vessel speed and therefore arrival time often mentioned is the weather along the shipping route [4], which includes precipitation, water levels, wave height, swell, wind speed and direction and a number of other factors.

Even though all of these can be causes for serious delays, most of them are either hard to predict or not publicly available and therefore not suitable factors for arrival prediction models. For the scope of this research external factors were limited to the effect of marine weather conditions on cargo ship speed.

The main purpose of this research is to identify internal (ship related, e.g. ship type and size, year of build) and external (non-ship related, e.g. weather, waves) variables that affect ship speed. The aim is to create a model with these variables explaining the actual recorded speed of a given ship. It shall be shown which variables and to which extent are useful to this model. To identify the importance of influencing variables a multiple linear regression model is used.

Fig. 1. Conceptual framework

Figure 1 shows the conceptual framework of this research work. Ship data is acquired from two different sources and saved in log files. Parallel to the ship data, weather data is also acquired from the weather source and saved in log files. Afterwards, the log files are combined to get a full log of ship data enhanced with weather data. This data is the basis for analysis via a multiple linear regression and on the predictability of arrival times.

This framework does not represent a monitoring or management system on its own. This work aims to investigate the effects of specific factors on the speed and arrival times of vessels. The findings are ought to be incorporated into models that deal with the prediction of delays of vessels that support business process management systems in the fields of berth allocation and ship operating.

The remainder of this paper is structured as follows: Section 2 describes the data acquisition and preparation process for both the ship and weather data. Section 3 outlines the correlations between variables and the multiple linear regression is explained in Sect. 4. Section 5 provides a closer look into the arrival deviation at the port of Rotterdam. It is followed by Sect. 6 where related work is mentioned. Finally, Sect. 7 concludes the paper.

2 Data

The data used within this research originates from two different sources. Ship movement data is broadcasted by marine vessels worldwide via the Automatic Identification System (AIS) and made available by AIS service providers on the Internet. Weather data required for the model is made available by the Environmental Research Division's Data Access Program (ERDDAP). Both datasets are then combined and used to create the prediction model.

2.1 Vessel Data

As there is no ready-to-use ship movement dataset available free of charge, it is necessary to aggregate this data with specialized scripts.

For the vessel data it was decided to follow two different approaches with two different data sources, namely marinetraffic.com and vesselfinder.com. This approach enables us to try out different ways of data collection and provides us, in case one approach turns out to be a dead end, with data to work with from the other data source.

Based on the data provided by vesselfinder.com an area around the harbor of Rotterdam with a $\sim$ 200 mile radius is selected where all vessels sailing through are recorded at a 15 min interval. While there were millions of data points recorded over the course of four weeks, they are not used for further analysis as it proved too difficult to filter and link them with accurate weather data.

Parallel to the vesselfinder data acquisition, data is also collected from marinetraffic, in which all vessels sailing to Rotterdam are recorded worldwide. This method provides several advantages over the other approach including longer observation periods for each ship, obstacle free tracking and more information provided by the website (e.g. estimated arrival time, vessel status).

The following list describes the data we retrieved from both approaches whereas the source is indicated in brackets after the variables. "m" indicates data retrieved from marinetraffic, "v" data from vesselfinder: timestamps (m, v) of the query and currentness of data, International Marine Organization Number IMO (m), Maritime Mobile Service Identity MMSI (m,v), name (m), call-sign (m), flag (m), ship type (m,v), gross weight and deadweight tonnage (m), length and width (m), built (m), status (m), area (m), latitude and longitude (m,v), activity (m), speed (m,v), course (m,v), draught (m), estimated time of arrival (m), wind speed (m), wind direction as classification (m), wind direction in degrees (m), air temperature in °C (m), departure time at previous port (m), name of previous port (m) and the destination (m).

Not all variables are used in the final prediction model as they are not all contributing to the intended purpose. The finally used variables for the prediction model are described below.

2.2   Weather Data

As our data sources for AIS data do not provide any marine weather information, but wind information only, it is required to get marine weather information.

The marine weather information is provided by ERDDAP which allows downloading marine weather information based on time, latitude, longitude and selected variables as gridded data, which means that it contains the selected variables for a chosen area in a 0.5 degree grid.

The weather information is based on the third-generation wind-wave model WAVEWATCH III developed by the Marine Modeling and Analysis Branch (MMAB) of the Environmental Modeling Center (EMC) of the National Centers for Environmental Protection (NCEP). The third-generation model differs from its predecessors in major points, for instance physical approaches [5].

We do not investigate different possible routes from a vessels origin to a specific destination based on historic ship and current marine weather data as the acquired dataset only includes the current positions of the vessels.

Marine weather information that is available and part of our model includes the peak wave direction in degrees, peak wave period in seconds, significant wave height in meters, swell peak wave direction in degrees, swell peak wave period in seconds, swell significant wave height in meters, wind peak wave direction in degrees, wind peak wave period in seconds and wind significant wave height in meters.

The significant wave height is defined as the average height (trough to crest) of the highest one-third of the waves [6]. The wave period in seconds describes the time between two peaks of a wave at the same point in space. The direction indicates where a wave is coming from.

The different weather information is related to the types of existing waves. Wind waves are generated through wind blowing over large area (called fetch). By contrast, swells are also called surface gravity waves and are caused not by local but distant weather systems.

2.3   Data Preparation

Data preparation is necessary to join ship and weather data. The latitude and longitude of the ships and the weather data is indicated in degrees, but the weather data is provided in a 0.5 degree grid. In order to being able to match both datasets, the ship positions must be adjusted and rounded to next integer or half of an integer. Furthermore, the longitude of the weather data is not indicated in the range ± 180, but 0 to 359 degrees. Hence, the longitude of the ship position must be added to 180. The adjusted position data is then used to join both datasets.

2.4   Data Recorded in Numbers

The data collection phase is divided into two periods. From 14th December 2014 until 23rd December 2014 we collected 55,776 ship positions. The second collection period lasted from 2nd January 2015 till 12th January 2015 and involved 68.395 observations. Hence, in total 124,170 observations. It must be noted that this number refers to the already cleaned dataset as the AIS data might not be updated with every data query, e.g. the ship is not within the range of an AIS receiver. Therefore, duplicate entries have been removed from the dataset.

As the work focuses on vessel highways located in Europe, weather data was only downloaded for that area (02N25W to 72N35E) for both vessel data acquisition periods which resulted in total 3,170,387 observations. The ship observations are then enhanced with marine weather data and result in a new dataset with 54,554 entries. The deviation of the two datasets is caused by the area where weather information is downloaded.

The focus is on the analysis of cargo ships and tankers sailing long distances over the ocean, other special ship types, e.g. "Tug" or "Dredger" not showing the typical behavior of ocean ships are removed from the dataset.

Sailing vessels show the activity "Underway using Engine". For the analysis of the ship speed all other observations with not-sailing activities of the ships, e.g. "Stopped" or "At Anchor" were removed from the dataset to avoid distorting the evaluations. The recorded data also includes inland water, e.g. "Kiel Canal", "Elbe River" or "Europe, Inland", and inter-port traffic through canals, e.g. Rotterdam to Antwerp. These ships are not exposed to equal environmental conditions as ocean ships, e.g. wave height and currents, and therefore as well removed from the dataset.

3   Correlations

As discussed in the previous section, the dataset was cleaned and irrelevant observations removed from the data. Thereafter, a meaningful analysis can be applied on the dataset. The aim is to identify properties that affect the speed of the vessel. Generally, properties are divided into vessel-related and weather-related properties. Correlation tests are used to find out which weather conditions and vessel properties impact the speed of the ocean ships. For the weather related analysis 11 variables as shown in Table 3 were collected.

The absolute wind direction given in degrees (0-360°) was adjusted by each ship's sailing course resulting in a new variable that shows the relative wind direction *appwinddir* ranging from full head winds to full tail winds, but does not indicate port or starboard side. The following method is used to calculate the new variable:

$$AppWindDir = \begin{cases} 360 - |ShipCrs - WindDir|, & if\ |ShipCrs - WindDir| > 180 \\ |ShipCrs - WindDir|, & otherwise \end{cases}$$

The results of our correlation tests are shown in Table 1. The highest correlation is identified between wind direction (degrees) and speed of the vessel. Also the significant wave height and the swell significant wave height show quite a moderate correlation to the speed of the vessel (18%-19%). Wind speed has just a low negative correlation with about -8%. The higher the wind speed, the slower the vessel. Peak wave direction and swell peak wave direction do not correlate with the speed of the vessel. The low P-value in most of the results can be explained by the high number of observations (23,810).

Table 1. Correlation results

Variable	Correlation	P-Value
winddirdeg (wind direction, degrees)	0.2113996	$<2.2*10^{-16}$
windspd (wind speed)	-0.08453314	$<2.2*10^{-16}$
wdir (peak wave direction, degrees)	0.0513367	$2.22*10^{-15}$
tper (peak wave period, seconds)	0.1325658	$<2.2*10^{-16}$
thgt (significant wave height, meters)	0.1947815	$<2.2*10^{-16}$
sdir (swell peak wave direction, degrees)	-0.00387547	0.5629
sper (swell peak wave period, seconds)	0.1088287	$<2.2*10^{-16}$

4   Multiple Linear Regression

The previous section deals with the correlation of weather data on the ship data. This section focuses on applying multiple linear regressions [7] on the data in order to find out if speed of the vessel can be described by corresponding variables. The multiple linear regression consists of two parts, the dependent variable (regressand) and the independent variable (regressor). While the regressand represents the effect of the formula, regressors are input variables that constitute the causes that lead to the effect. In our context, the speed of the ship (effect) has to be predicted by corresponding variables (causes). A variable selection technique lets the algorithm decide which attribute is considered as relevant and which is omitted. Observations with missing values have to be removed, because this technique cannot deal with them.

In our context, not only the weather data is taken into account but also some other attributes that are related to the ships and to the current location of the vessels: deadweight tonnage, gross, built and area. For multiple linear regression analysis, this paper focuses on specific areas on the oceans. These areas have several characteristics in common: Vessels are travelling in a straight line, are not encumbered by other vessels and can get top-speed in these areas. Hence, these areas are named as "vessel highways" and separated based on longitude/latitude specifications. The three vessel highways are: The English Channel, the west coast of Portugal in the Atlantic Ocean and the area between Sicily and Africa in the Mediterranean Sea. After the data filtering, 1,305 observations remained which we used for our analysis (Table 2).

Seven variables were removed from the model after applying the variable selection (see Table 3) via a stepwise regression. All other variables shown in Table 3 were considered as important from the selection algorithm.

Table 2. Linear regression models

Initial model	Results
shiptype, crs, windspd, thgt, whgt, tdir, wdir, sdir, shgt, area, activity, tper, sper, wper, dwt, built, gross, relwinddir	R^2: 87.76% Adjusted R^2: 84.94% P-Value: $<2.2 * 10^{-16}$
Final model	Results
shiptype, windspd, whgt, area, activity, tper, wper, dwt, built, gross, relwinddir	R^2: 86.71% Adjusted R^2: 83.98% P-Value: $<2.2 * 10^{-16}$

Table 3. Eliminated/Important variables

Variable	Description	Eliminated variable	Important variable
wdir	wind peak wave direction, degrees	X	
crs	course of the ship, degrees	X	
shgt	swell significant wave height, meters	X	
tdir	peak wave direction, degrees	X	
thgt	significant wave height, meters	X	
sdir	swell peak wave direction, degrees	X	
sper	swell peak wave period, seconds	X	
shiptype	type of the vessel (cargo, tanker)		X
windspd	windspeed		X
whgt	wind significant wave height, meters		X
activity	activity of the vessel		X
tper	peak wave period, seconds		X
wper	wind peak wave period, seconds		X
dwt	deadweight Tonnage		X
built	year the ship was built		X
gross	gross register tonnage		X
area	area in which the ship is located		X

As a result 86.71 % of the speed values can be explained via corresponding variables. However, these results have to be considered with some caution since variable selection is a dubious method against overfitting. Variable selection is highly discussed in the literature. On the one hand, theory tends to decline this approach while on the other hand it is frequently used in practice. The fact is, that it does not cover all issues with overfitting and even can come with several new problems [8]. An evidence for legitimating the dubiety of this method could be the fact that although variables *shgt* (swell significant wave height) and *thgt* (significant wave height) correlate more with the speed of the vessel than variables *wper* (wind peak wave period) and *tper* (peak wave period) they were removed from the model. What is more, for some variables it is easier to explain effects and correlations with the speed of the vessel than for others. Variable *built* for example, doesn't say anything about maintenance and modifications of a ship. A 10 year old ship could basically be as fast as a 2 year old ship. However, the algorithm decided to consider this variable as important.

5   Arrival Deviation - Harbor of Rotterdam

In order to give the findings of the prior sections a practical value, they are tested for their applicability for predicting the arrival of vessels at their destination. The harbor of Rotterdam is chosen as destination of interest, as the collected data contains information about vessels heading to this harbor.

At first the dataset for arrival deviation analysis is prepared. Then the influence of the destination within the harbor is investigated. After that the findings are adapted to be applicable for testing their correlations with the arrival deviation.

5.1   Dataset for Analyses

For the purpose of investigating the arrival deviations, data about each shipping is needed. Additionally to the variables of the prior sections, the variables *ATA*, *ATA_moored*, *ETA_12hours* and *delay* have to be derived.

The actual time of arrival (*ATA*) is not directly available in the dataset. At the harbor of Rotterdam the *ETA* has to refer to the Maas Center buoy (5200.9'N, 00348.8'E) which is positioned in front of the harbors' main entrance from the ocean [9]. The point in time the vessel passes that point is considered as *ATA*.

The second actual time of arrival refers to the point in time when the vessel finished the mooring operation at the berth (*ATA_moored*).

The derived variable *ETA_12hours* contains the ETA that the vessel was communicating approximately 12 h before *ATA*. The decision of using this 12 hour difference was made, because the maritime weather data near the harbor will be used to investigate its effects on the arrival deviation. The time period 12 to 24 h prior to arrival also has a high impact on the vessel management at the harbor [10].

The *delay* is the difference between *ATA* and *ETA_12hours* in hours. Negative values indicate that the vessel was arriving earlier than expected.

The dataset made for analysis of the arrival deviation consists of one record for each observed shipping. These records contain the derived variables mentioned above and ship related variables necessary for analyses. Additionally each record contains weather related information which is averaged throughout the time period between *ATA* and *ETA_12hours*, in order to observe the influence on the arrival deviation near the harbor.

This dataset is cleaned by the following criteria. Only records with a *delay* ranging from -12 h to +12 h are kept in the dataset. Other delays are not considered as being realistic or considered as errors in the collected data. Furthermore if one of the derived variables is not computable for a record, the whole record is left out. The reasons for that could be incomplete or erroneous information in the collected data or shipping that do not follow the required behavior for this analysis.

5.2 Destination Within the Harbor

As the harbor of Rotterdam consists of many terminals and extends over a wide area it is assumable that the destination of a vessel within the harbor is influencing the vessels behavior. For investigation the area of the harbor is geographically divided into three sectors. Sector 1 is nearest to and sector 3 is farthest away from the ocean entrance to the harbor.

The first assumption is that the further the destination terminal is away from the ocean, the more time it takes from the arrival at the harbor entrance to being moored at the final position. This assumption is approved as the first column of Table 4 shows. The time consumed is continuously increasing along with the distance from the ocean entrance.

The second assumption is that the distance of the destination terminal from the ocean is influencing the delay of the vessel at the harbor entrance. This assumption is partly approved. On the one hand the second column in Table 4 shows that there is no significant difference between sector 1 and sector 2. On the other hand sector 3 shows a significantly lower average delay than the other sections. It can be said that vessels that are heading to terminals in sector 3 tend to be on time as their average delay is close to zero.

Table 4. Delay by sector

	from *ATA* to *ATA_moored*	average *delay*
Sector 1	137 min	141 min
Sector 2	154 min	154 min
Sector 3	196 min	20 min

5.3 Applicability of Findings

In this section the findings of the previous sections are proved regarding their applicability on a prediction of delay. In order to do that the related variables are prepared in a suitable form and then their correlation with the delay is tested.

At first the variables that are found to be useful for predicting the vessels speed are tested. The variables *windspd*, *relwinddir*, *whgt*, *tper* and *wper* are averaged over the 12 h timeframe prior to arrival at the harbor and added to the data records. The variables *shiptype*, *dwt*, *built* and *gross* are not changing over time during one shipping, so they can be added as static values to the data records. The *activity* and the *area* are not considered in this test, as they are used to separate the individual shipping from each other and therefore not giving differences between them. The results of the tests can be seen in Table 5. As a result of these tests, the variables that could be useful for such prediction are only the ones that relate to weather, namely the peak wave period,

Table 5 Correlations between variables and delay

Variable	Correlation	P-Value
tper	-0.271860309754	0.0218218460564
wper	-0.27024008102	0.0226520841171
whgt	-0.229939767856	0.0537246472085

the wind peak wave period and the wind significant wave height. These results emphasize the assumption that the weather conditions mainly influence the delay.

Secondly the findings about the destination terminal within the harbor are tested. To this extent, the ship movements are classified according to the section they are heading to. The result is a correlation coefficient of -0.221585715593 with a p-value of 0.00368431138331. It can be assumed that the destination terminal within the harbor is of importance to the prediction of delay. Future research will investigate how to better define the individual sectors and what could be the reason for the differences.

5.4 Limitations

There are some limitations regarding the results of the arrival deviation analysis. Due to a very short time frame for data collection, the number of usable movements is quite small. Combining these movements with available weather data, the number of useful and complete records decreases even further. It would be of interest to have more data available for analysis and also to be able to investigate seasonal effects on the delay. Another limitation of the analysis is that they rely on the assumption that the delay is caused in the 12 h timeframe prior to the arrival. For a more precise analysis it would be necessary to know how much of the delay has already occurred prior to the investigated time frame. The decision of only collecting data of vessels heading to Rotterdam turned out to have the downside of not knowing about the complete traffic at the harbor. This made the analysis regarding the traffic not feasible with this dataset, although this could be of interest regarding a prediction of delay. It is in the plans to circumvent such limitation in future research.

6 Related Work

There are researches that mainly focus on the methods of berth allocation planning. [11] is dealing with robust berth scheduling and [12] is dealing with dynamic approaches for container handling at the berth. Our work is focusing on making the arrival times of vessels predictable which would be contributing to a more dynamic berth allocation planning. [13] provides approaches for the extraction of vessel routes and anomaly detection in movement patterns for decision support systems. On the other hand [14] is investigating the impacts of tides on seaside operations in container ports. Both are focusing on specific factors that influence the arrival times. Our work is investigating in particular the impacts of weather conditions on the arrival times. [10]

follows a similar approach to our work. A machine learning approach is applied using ship and weather related data for the prediction of arrival times. A main difference is that our work is using publicly available data whereas [10] is using data reported directly by the harbors of Antwerp and Cagliari.

7 Conclusions

There is data publicly available that can be used for estimating ship speed and arrival time. This data includes ship related and non-ship related information. A first challenge was to collect the data from different sources. Then they had to be combined and cleaned resulting in one common data store. After that the data store was used for making predictions on the ship speed at a certain point in time using multiple linear regression. It turned out that weather related data has a strong influence on the ship speed, but also some ship related variables are of importance. Regarding the prediction of arrival times this work can only give suggestions on input variables that could be used for a prediction model, because of the mentioned limitations. What is found to have a significant influence on the arrival time are weather related variables and the geographically location of the destination terminal.

This work serves as a basis for further researches on the prediction of arrival times of ships. We only had the possibility to investigate the effects of certain factors. The influence of the ongoing traffic in the harbor or in front of it is still an open question. The data could also be collected over a longer period of time to investigate seasonal effects. In the end the findings of this work along with other factors could be applied in a prediction model for estimating delays.

References

1. United Nations Conference on Trade and Development, Review of Marine Transport 2013. http://unctad.org/en/PublicationsLibrary/rmt2013_en.pdf
2. RaetsMarine Insurance B.V. http://www.raetsmarine.com/news/marine-delay-insurance
3. Nordic Marine Insurance, General information on fixed premium delay insurance. http://www.nmip.se/dwnds/General_Information_on_Delay_Insurance_Sept_2013.pdf
4. National Imagery and Mapping Agency, Principles of weather routing, http://msi.nga.mil/MSISiteContent/StaticFiles/NAV_PUBS/APN/Chapt-38.pdf
5. Tolman, H.L.: User manual and system documentation of WAVEWATCH III. Environ. Model. Center MMAB 276, 194 (2009)
6. National Oceanic and Atmospheric Administration. http://www.srh.noaa.gov/key/?n=marine_sigwave
7. Brant, R.: Multiple Linear Regression (2007)
8. Babyak, M.A.: What You See May Not Be What You Get: A Brief, Nontechnical Introduction to Overfitting in Regression-Type Models. Psychosom Med. 66(3), 411–421 (2004)
9. Port of Rotterdam, Port Information Guide November 2014. http://www.portofrotterdam.com/en/Shipping/sea-shipping/port-information/Documents/port_information_guide.pdf

10. Pani, C.: Managing vessel arrival uncertainty in container terminals: a machine learning approach, Ph.D.-Thesis (2013)
11. Xu, Y., Chen, Q., Quan, X.: Robust berth scheduling with uncertain vessel delay and handling time. Ann. Oper. Res. **192**(1), 123–140 (2012)
12. Ku, L.P., Chew, E.P., Lee, L.H., Tan, K.C.: A novel approach to yard planning under vessel arrival uncertainty. Flex. Serv. and Manuf. Journal **24**(3), 274–293 (2012)
13. Pallotta, G., Vespe, M., Bryan, K.: Vessel pattern knowledge discovery from ais data: a framework for anomaly detection and route prediction. Entropy **15**(6), 2218–2245 (2013)
14. Du, Y., Chen, Q., Lam, J.S.L., Xu, Y., Cao, J.X.: Modeling the Impacts of Tides and the Virtual Arrival Policy in Berth Allocation. Transportation Science (2015)

Monitoring Batch Regions in Business Processes

Tsun Yin Wong, Susanne Bülow(✉), and Mathias Weske(✉)

Hasso Plattner Institute at the University of Potsdam, Potsdam, Germany
susanne.buelow@student.hpi.uni-potsdam.de, mathias.weske@hpi.de

Abstract. Recently, batch activities have been introduced to improve the execution of business processes by collectively performing batch activities that belong to different process instances. Using traditional techniques to monitor processes with batch activities leads to inadequate representation of process instances, since monitoring is unaware of batch activities. This paper introduces an approach to monitor batch activities, which also takes into account exceptions in batch clusters at different levels of abstraction. The concepts and techniques introduced are evaluated by a prototypical implementation using real-world event data from the logistics domain.

1 Introduction

Many organizations in business and administration represent their working procedures as business processes to improve them and to monitor their execution [1]. Recently, batch activities [2] and batch regions [3] have been proposed to collectively execute activities of different process instances. While methods and techniques for monitoring individual business processes have been proposed, these are inadequate to monitor batch activities. This paper introduces novel concepts and techniques for monitoring batch activities, which also take into account exceptions. The approach is evaluated by a prototypical implementation using real-world event data from the logistics domain.

A batch region [3] of a process model consists of activities that are executed collectively as a batch. We find batch activities in many domains, including health care (many blood samples are analyzed in a batch) and logistics (containers in a vessel are transported together). Since processes are performed non-automatically in these environments, process monitoring uses events that occur while the process is being executed. Events include the arrival of a vessel in a harbor with certain containers or the completion of a blood sample analysis in a hospital.

If traditional techniques for process monitoring were used in these settings, the number of monitoring events would be overwhelming. Using information about batch regions, the number of events to monitor can significantly be reduced. Furthermore, monitoring approaches need to expose the occurrence of irregular

The research leading to these results has received funding from the European Union's Seventh Framework Program (FP7/2007–2013) under grant agreement 318275 (GET Service).

© Springer International Publishing Switzerland 2015
A. Persson and J. Stirna (Eds.): CAiSE 2015 Workshops, LNBIP 215, pp. 317–323, 2015.
DOI: 10.1007/978-3-319-19243-7_30

behaviour, such as exceptions. Therefore, we also provide a classification of different types of exceptions of business processes, involving individual process instances and all process instances in a batch, respectively.

The remainder of this paper is organized as follows: First, the need for batch monitoring is illustrated by a motivating example in Sect. 2. Then, a conceptual approach of batch monitoring is introduced in Sect. 3. In Sect. 4, the prototypical implementation is explained. In Sect. 5, we use the batch monitoring approach for the motivating example. Finally, Sect. 6 concludes this paper.

2   Motivating Example and Requirements

To exemplify the approach, we introduce a real world use case inspired by the GET Service project[1], which is funded by the Seventh Framework Program of the European Union. GET Service aims at supporting efficient transportation planning to reduce both transportation times and empty miles, leading to a reduction of CO_2 emission.

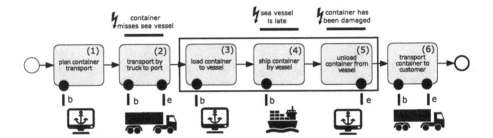

Fig. 1. Process from logistics domain. Events from various sources are related to monitoring points (begin event of activity denoted as 'b', end event denoted as 'e').

The respective process model is shown in Fig. 1; it consists of six sequential activities: At first, the transport planner schedules a container for transport (activity 1). The container is later picked up at the warehouse and transported to the port by truck (2), where the container is loaded on a sea vessel (3). The container is then shipped to another port (4), where it is unloaded (5). Finally, the container is transported to the customer by another truck (6).

As a sea vessel transports multiple containers at a time, activities (3), (4) and (5) form a batch region. Each container is represented by a process instance, whereas a sea vessel is represented by a batch cluster containing all process instances of the containers on the sea vessel. To facilitate process monitoring, we assign monitoring points to each activity, defining its begin and its end event. The set of monitoring points for the given use case is limited to the corresponding real-world events provided by port community systems (1) (3) (5), transport companies (2), (6) and shipping companies (4), resp.

---

[1] http://getservice-project.eu.

In the use case, three exceptions may occur:

- *Container misses sea vessel*: A container arrives with excessive delay at the port of origin and cannot be transported on the sea vessel for which it was scheduled.
- *Sea vessel is late*: The calculated arrival of the ship is after the planned arrival.
- *Container has been damaged*: During the unloading of the containers, customs notice that the container is unsealed and therefore needs further inspection.

From our scenario, we can identify two main requirements for batch monitoring:

R1. In the traditional process monitoring approach, events indicate information about single process instances. In our use case, each container transport would represent one process instance and events about each container would be monitored individually. However, as soon as the container is loaded onto the sea vessel, it would be sufficient to be updated about the progress of the vessel, instead of the progress of the hundreds of containers on the vessel. To enable monitoring of the vessel as a batch cluster containing several process instances, the events arriving for each container must be aggregated. To enable monitoring of a batch cluster, we therefore need a *batch aggregation strategy* for the events on the process instance level.

R2. Exceptions occurring in batch regions need to be handled differently than exceptions during normal process executions. For example, the exception "Ship is late" would normally result in one exception for each container on the ship. In batch monitoring, it would be sufficient, to mark the sea vessel as having an exception. On the other hand, the exception "Container has been damaged" detected for a container should not result in an exception of the whole vessel, but only in an exception for the affected container. Thus, a handling for different *batch exceptions* has to be examined.

3   Batch Monitoring Approach

In this section, an approach for batch monitoring is introduced. Processes are monitored using technical representations of real world happenings, so called *events*. Each event has an event type that defines its structure [4]. A *monitoring point* is a binding of an event type to an activity of a process model. Monitoring points are used to measure the progress of process instances based on events [5].

A *batch region* is a coherent part of a process model with a single entry, in which several process instances with similar characteristics are executed together as *batch clusters*. The assignment of an instance to a cluster is defined by the grouping characteristic of the batch region [3]. *Exceptions* indicate an erroneous execution of a process instance. Several exception types on different levels of a process can be distinguished [6].

Based on this preliminary work, the novel approach for batch monitoring is described, covering requirements R1 and R2 from Sect. 2. To allow monitoring of batch clusters (R1), we introduce two *batch aggregation strategies* for process instance events:

- *Complete Event Set Strategy*: Only if events for all process instances of a batch cluster have been observed, the cluster progress will be recognized. This is a cautious approach that needs additional exception handling in case of missing events.
- *Single Event Strategy*: The first event connected to one process instance within a batch cluster determines the cluster progress. We here assume that the correct execution of one instance directly implies the correct execution of the whole cluster. For our implementation, we chose this approach.

As far as *batch exceptions* (R2) are concerned, those have to be differentiated in exceptions outside of a batch region, which would be normal *process exceptions* and exceptions within a batch region. Moreover, we consider the following two levels for exceptions in a batch region:

- *Batch-level Exceptions*: If the exception affects the whole batch cluster, namely all contained process instances, it is an exception on batch level.
- *Instance-level Exceptions*: If the exception affects only one process instance, this instance is then in exception and cannot be further executed together with the remaining, correct process instances in the batch cluster. It is therefore removed from the cluster and has to be handled separately. This is an exception on instance level.

4   Batch Monitoring Tool

In this section, we present the prototypical implementation of the batch monitoring approach. An overview of the system architecture is presented in Fig. 2. It contains three main components. The *Process Configuration* is accessed by the *Frontend* to create the monitoring points and batch regions as part of a process model. *Monitoring* includes the monitoring of process instances, batch clusters (as described in R1 of Sect. 2) and exceptions (as described in R2) using monitoring points and batch regions specified in the *Frontend*. It communicates with the Event Processing Platform (UNICORN[2]) introduced in [7] that consumes events provided by process engines executing the process model. Information about process instances and batch clusters are propagated to the *Frontend*. The *Frontend* offers an intuitive visualization of the progress of process instances as well as batch clusters and visualizes occurring exceptions using the information propagated from the *Monitoring*. The visualization is limited to sequential processes as the one introduced in Sect. 2. However, the monitoring concept is applicable to all well-formed process models.

The tool is implemented in Java 7, using the Apache Wicket Framework for the frontend. For process import of BPMN-alike signavio.xml-files, we use the libraries jBPT[3] and promniCAT[4]. The ability of this tool for batch and exception

---

[2] http://bpt.hpi.uni-potsdam.de/UNICORN.

[3] https://code.google.com/p/jbpt/.

[4] https://code.google.com/p/promnicat/.

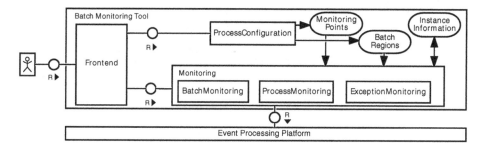

Fig. 2. System architecture of batch monitoring tool

monitoring is demonstrated with an example in Sect. 5 as well as in a screencast of the tool[5], where historic real world data is used to simulate occuring events.

5 Example Use Case

Figure 3 provides a screenshot of the batch monitoring tool, showing an example execution of the scenario described in Sect. 2. Each table row refers to a batch cluster or a process instance. The current activity is indicated by the column in which it is located, i.e. it moves to the right during execution. A circle denotes that the activity is in execution, a green tick marks the completion of the activity. Instances of a cluster are visible only when the cluster is selected (see Fig. 4).

When a freight transport company schedules a container for transport, it also arranges the sea vessel to export its container. On this basis, we identify process instances of the same batch cluster by taking the scheduled sea vessel as the grouping characteristic of the batch region. In Fig. 3, the transport planning for *Container 12* is ongoing. *Container 10* and *Container 11* that have arrived at the port are expected to be grouped in the same batch cluster. The status of a sea vessel progresses as soon as one container of the cluster is updated (follows R1 from Sect. 2).

The three exception types described in Sect. 3 cover the exceptions in our use case (follows R2).

– *Container misses sea vessel*: The corresponding process instance must be removed from the batch cluster for which it was planned. In our example, this applies to the process instance regarding *Container 3*.
– *Sea vessel is not moving*: The whole batch cluster *Sea vessel 4* containing five process instances is affected as shown in Fig. 4. The exception is triggered by an event of the type *ShipNotMoving* bound to the activity *ship container by vessel*.
– *Container has been damaged*: The process instance regarding *Container 2* is removed from its batch cluster and remains at the port.

---

[5] https://owncloud.hpi.de/public.php?service=files&t=f02387692aaa880428905d
30e3f9ab89.

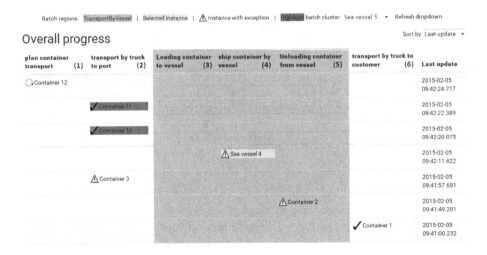

Fig. 3. Visualization of process instances and batch clusters. Containers are represented by process instances, whereas a sea vessel is represented by a batch of all containers on that sea vessel.

The example shows how the batch monitoring concept allows monitoring of single containers, but also of sea vessels containing several containers and their exceptions.

Batch instance Sea vessel 4

Attribute	Value	View process:
Grouping characteristic	2013-05-16T11:00:00.000+0200	Container 6 ▾
Batch region	TransportByVessel	Choose One
		Container 5
Current state	RUNNING	Container 6
		Container 7
Creation time	2015-02-05 09:41:18.242	Container 8
		Container 9
Exceptions		
Event 'ShipDelay' occured in 'ship container by vessel'	2015-02-05 09:42:17.717	

Fig. 4. Details of batch cluster *Sea vessel 4* with five process instances. Its exception has been triggered by an event of type *ShipDelay*.

6   Conclusion and Future Work

In this paper, we have presented an approach with the corresponding implementation which enables the monitoring of batch executions, including their exceptional behaviour. The progress monitoring is driven by monitoring points triggered by events; a direct interaction with our tool to handle exceptions is not in its scope.

As of now, a BPMN process model is loaded into the monitoring tool and then complemented with monitoring points and batch regions afterwards. Future work includes the support of annotations in XML files for BPMN process models as mentioned in [8].

The batch concept presented in [9] includes the application of threshold rules and Event-Condition-Action (ECA) rules. They are currently not considered in our concept and we intend to integrate them to enable the detection of exceptions such as the exceeding of batch clusters.

Since the concept of the monitoring tool is loosely based on workflow exception patterns [6], research in how these patterns are supported in batches is required.

References

1. Weske, M.: Business Process Management: Concepts, Languages, Architectures., 2nd edn. Springer, Heidelberg (2012)
2. Pufahl, L., Weske, M.: Batch activities in process modeling and execution. In: Basu, S., Pautasso, C., Zhang, L., Fu, X. (eds.) ICSOC 2013. LNCS, vol. 8274, pp. 283–297. Springer, Heidelberg (2013)
3. Pufahl, L., Meyer, A., Weske, M.: Batch Regions: Process Instance Synchronization based on Data. Universitätsverlag Potsdam (2014)
4. Etzion, O., Niblett, P.: Event Processing in Action. Manning Publications Company, Greenwich (2010)
5. Herzberg, N., Weske, M.: Enriching raw events to enable process intelligence - research challenges. Technical report 73, Hasso Plattner Institute at the University of Potsdam (2013)
6. Russell, N., van der Aalst, W.M.P., ter Hofstede, A.H.M.: Workflow exception patterns. In: Martinez, F.H., Pohl, K. (eds.) CAiSE 2006. LNCS, vol. 4001, pp. 288–302. Springer, Heidelberg (2006)
7. Bülow, S., Backmann, M., Herzberg, N., Hille, T., Meyer, A., Ulm, B., Wong, T.Y., Weske, M.: Monitoring of business processes with complex event processing. In: Lohmann, N., Song, M., Wohed, P. (eds.) BPM 2013 Workshops. LNBIP, vol. 171, pp. 277–290. Springer, Heidelberg (2014)
8. Baumgrass, A., Herzberg, N., Meyer, A., Weske, M.: BPMN Extension for Business Process Monitoring. In: Enterprise Modelling and Information Systems Architectures, GI (2014)
9. Pufahl, L., Herzberg, N., Meyer, A., Weske, M.: Flexible batch configuration in business processes based on events. In: Franch, X., Ghose, A.K., Lewis, G.A., Bhiri, S. (eds.) ICSOC 2014. LNCS, vol. 8831, pp. 63–78. Springer, Heidelberg (2014)

TEAR 2015

Revealing Hidden Structures in Organizational Transformation – A Case Study

Franz Heiser[1], Robert Lagerström[2(✉)], and Mattin Addibpour[1]

[1] Ericsson AB, Isafjordsgatan 10, 164 80 Stockholm, Sweden
{franz.heiser,mattin.addibpour}@ericsson.com
[2] KTH Royal Institute of Technology,
Osquldas väg 12, 100 44 Stockholm, Sweden
robertl@kth.se

Abstract. EA initiatives are usually spanning the entire enterprise on high level. While, a typical development organization (could be a business unit within a larger enterprise) often has detailed models describing their product, the enterprise architecture on the business unit level is handled in an ad hoc or detached way. However, research shows that there is a tight link between the product architecture and its developing organization. In this paper we have studied an organization within Ericsson, which focuses on the development of large software and hardware products. We have applied the hidden structure method, which is based on the Design Structure Matrix approach, to analyze of organizational transformations. The to-be scenarios are possible alternatives in trying to become more agile and lean. Our analysis shows that one scenario likely increases the complexity of developing the product, while the other two suggestions are both promising to-be scenarios.

Keywords: Enterprise architecture · Organizational transformation · Design structure matrix · Hidden structure

1 Introduction

In Enterprise Architecture (EA) business aspects, software applications, data, and infrastructure are modeled together in a structured way in order to manage the enterprise and make well-informed decisions. In a company where the main business is to develop complex hardware (HW) and software (SW) products the discipline of EA is mainly used to handle the overall commonly used office IT and the processes it supports, more rarely does EA include the development of the customer products. Furthermore, the business units in charge of the development are usually good at modeling the system under development, their product, in a formal way. However, these two approaches rarely meet formally.

Generally speaking, while the product architecture is handled in a formal way and relations between its elements are specified and controlled in a systematic way, the organizational part is not considered to be a part of the architecture and the system as whole. This makes the analysis of the impact between product and organization a very tedious task. In the context of a business unit with strong HW and SW product focus, we propose to consider the organizational part as a legitimated system that has to be

© Springer International Publishing Switzerland 2015
A. Persson and J. Stirna (Eds.): CAiSE 2015 Workshops, LNBIP 215, pp. 327–338, 2015.
DOI: 10.1007/978-3-319-19243-7_31

described, specified, and analyzed in a systematic way in the same manner as the product.

The focus of this paper is to analyze the hidden dependencies in the organization under transformation. We have not explicitly modeled the product and its relation to the organization structure in this paper, but the blueprint of the product architecture is implicitly presented and inherited in the structure of the original organization. For analyzing the hidden relations between organizational elements we have applied an evolution of Design Structure Matrices (DSMs) called "Hidden Structure" [1, 2], a methodology mainly used for analysis of product-related artifacts. We have created a number of to-be scenarios, which are containing mappings of new process proposals on our organizational units. The aim with this transformation is to become more agile and lean, but it is also necessary that this potential organizational architecture is implemented without increasing communication dependencies between different teams. The visualization of the architecture that the hidden structure method provides, including dependency maps, makes it a valuable tool used for identifying impacts on the architecture. Our results show that one of the to-be scenarios dramatically increase the complexity, while the two other are neither increasing nor (remarkably) decreasing the complexity when transforming into a more agile and lean organization.

The paper unfolds as follows: Sect. 2 presents related work and Sect. 3 the hidden structure method. In Sect. 4 our case is described together with its results and a discussion. Future work is outlined in chapter Sect. 5. And finally, Sect. 6 concludes the paper.

2   Related Work

Product architectures have been given a lot of attention throughout the years, both in academia and in practice. Today there are numerous initiatives aiming to guide and aid the design and evolution of product architectures. For instance, in software architecture [3] state "... software architecture has matured to encompass a broad set of notations, tools, and analysis techniques. Whereas initially the research area interpreted software practice, it now offers concrete guidance for complex software design and development." However, there is less focus on the organizational aspects of SW development when it comes to treating the organization as a complex system that needs to be modeled and analyzed to the same extent.

The focus on products is also the case in the community of Design Structure Matrices (DSMs), e.g. [4, 5]. Baldwin et al. [1] developed a method to visualize the hidden structure of software architectures (one example of a product architecture) based on DSMs and classic coupling measures. This method has been tested on numerous software products, such as Linux, Mozilla, Apache, and GnuCash. In one study by MacCormack et al. [6] an early version of this hidden structure method was employed to show the relation between the product architecture and its development organization.

For some time now enterprise architecture models have been used in order to model complex systems including organizations, processes and supporting IT [7–9]. Although modeling has been the main focus of EA initiatives, running analyses on these models is getting more and more attention. Different approaches have been suggested [e.g. 10] and numerous of analyses have been proposed (for instance [11–14]).

Recently the field of enterprise architecture started to test the hidden structure method with the aim to visualize and measure complex systems. In [15] the hidden structure method was used on a Biopharmaceutical case to reveal the hidden dependencies in its enterprise architecture incl. business groups, software applications, databases, schemas etc. Data from this case was then used to show that the cost of changing applications with many indirect dependencies (metrics derived using the DSM based hidden structure method) was more expensive than applications with few [16]. In [17] the authors employed the hidden structure method on application portfolio data from a Telecommunication case.

In this paper we aim to make use of the success of combining DSMs, hidden structure, and EA.

3   The Hidden Structure Method

The method we use for representing architectures is based on and extends the classic notion of coupling. Specifically, after identifying the coupling (dependencies) between the architecture elements, we analyze the architecture in terms of hierarchical ordering and cyclic groups and classify elements in terms of their position in the resulting network (this method is described in [1]).

In a Design Structure Matrix (DSM), each diagonal cell represents an element (node), and the off-diagonal cells record the dependencies between the elements (links): If element i depends on element j, a mark is placed in the row of i and the column of j. The content of the matrix does not depend on the ordering of the rows and columns, but different orderings can reveal (or obscure) the underlying structure. Specifically, the elements in the DSM can be arranged in a way that reflects hierarchy, and, if this is done, dependencies that remain above the main diagonal will indicate the presence of cyclic interdependencies (A depends on B, and B depends on A). The rearranged DSM can thus reveal significant facts about the underlying structure of the architecture that cannot be inferred from standard measures of coupling. In the following subsections, a method that makes this "hidden structure" visible is presented.

3.1   Identify the Direct Dependencies and Compute the Visibility Matrix

The architecture of any complex system can be represented as a directed graph composed of N elements (nodes) and directed dependencies (links) between them. This directed graph can be represented as a DSM. If the DSM is raised to successive powers, the result will show the direct and indirect dependencies that exist for successive path lengths. Summing these matrices yields the visibility matrix V (or VSM), the far right matrix in Fig. 1, which denotes the dependencies that exist for all possible path lengths. The values in the visibility matrix are constrained to be binary, capturing only whether a dependency exists and not the number of possible paths that the dependency can take [1]. The matrix for n = 0 (i.e., a path length of zero) is included when calculating the visibility matrix, implying that a change to an element will always affect itself.

A Directed Graph	Design Structure Matrix	Visibility Matrix $V=\sum M^n$; n=[0,4]
	A B C D E F A 0 1 1 0 0 0 B 0 0 0 1 0 0 C 0 0 0 0 1 0 D 0 0 0 0 0 0 E 0 0 0 0 0 1 F 0 0 0 0 0 0	A B C D E F A 1 1 1 1 1 1 B 0 1 0 1 0 0 C 0 0 1 0 1 1 D 0 0 0 1 0 0 E 0 0 0 0 1 1 F 0 0 0 0 0 1

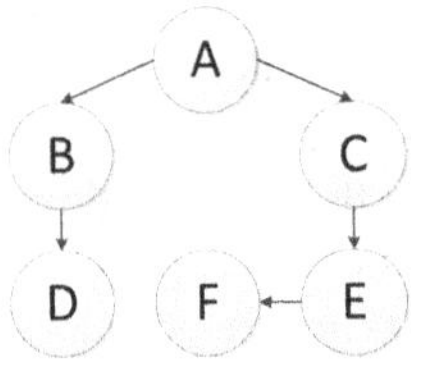

Fig. 1. A directed graph with the corresponding DSM and VSM.

Several measures are constructed based on the VSM. First, for each element i in the architecture, the following are defined:

- VFIi (Visibility Fan-In) is the number of elements that directly or indirectly depend on i. This is found by summing entries in the ith column of V.
- VFOi (Visibility Fan-Out) is the number of elements that i directly or indirectly depends on. This is found by summing entries in the ith row of V.

In Fig. 1, element A has VFI equal to 1, meaning that no other elements depend on it, and VFO equal to 6, meaning that it depends on all other elements in the architecture. To measure visibility at the system level, Propagation Cost (PC) is defined as the density of the VSM. Intuitively, propagation cost equals the fraction of the architecture that may be affected when a change is made to a randomly selected element.

3.2 Identify and Rank Cyclic Groups

The next step is to find the cyclic groups in the architecture. By definition, each element within a cyclic group depends directly or indirectly on every other member of the group. First, the elements are sorted, first by VFI descending then by VFO ascending. Next one proceeds through the sorted list to find different cyclic groups. These groups are referred to as the "cores" of the system. The largest cyclic group is defined as the "Core". Once the Core is identified, the other components in the architecture can be classified into groups, as follows:

- "Core" elements are members of the largest cyclic group and have the same VFI and VFO, denoted by VFIC and VFOC, respectively.
- "Control" elements have VFI < VFIC and VFO ≥ VFOC.
- "Shared" elements have VFI ≥ VFIC and VFO < VFOC.
- "Periphery" elements have VFI < VFIC and VFO < VFOC.

Using the above classification scheme, a reorganized DSM can be constructed that reveals the "hidden structure" of the architecture by placing elements in the order Shared, Core, Periphery, and Control down the main diagonal of the DSM, and then sorting within each group by VFI descending then VFO ascending (cf. Figure 3 for an example of a hidden structure sorted DSM).

The method for classifying architectures into different types is discussed in empirical work by Baldwin et al. [1]. Specifically, the authors find a large percentage of the architectures they analyzed contained a large cyclic group of components that was dominant in two senses: (i) it was large relative to the number of elements in the system, and (ii) it was substantially larger than any other cyclic group. This architectural type is classified as "core-periphery." Where architectures have multiple cyclic groups of similar size, the architecture is referred to as "Multi-Core". Finally, if the Core is small, relative to the system as a whole, the architecture is referred to as "Hierarchical".

4   Case

In this paper we describe; (1) the application of the DSM method in order to reveal the hidden organizational structure of an enterprise architecture, and (2) how the method was used as pilot for a what-if analysis transforming the organization in a large project, developing both HW and SW.

4.1   Motivation

SW and HW design has in the past years seen a transition from waterfall based design approaches towards agile and lean. The main driving force for this transformation is to increase time-to-market of SW and HW features by breakdowns of smaller tasks and by utilization of small cross-functional teams. This transition is quite successful for organizations involving a limited number of designers in total, i.e. with less than 100 people, split up into cross-functional teams with less than 10 team members. However, scaling up these design approaches towards several thousand of designers working for developing large SW/HW products is still a challenge and not fully understood and solved, neither in academia nor in industry (what we are aware of).

Performing such a transition in one big organizational change is therefore a considerable business risk due to the lack of understanding. A step-by-step approach is therefore less risky. However, even with a step-by-step approach there are major risks that need to be considered. It would be of great help if it would be possible to analyze the impact different changes have in each step, in order to understand the consequences.

Given the assumption that an agile and lean project organization will decrease lead-time and increase efficiency at the end of the transition, intermediate steps must not add unnecessary complexity. This is important since the organization must be able to maintain and deliver its SW features and HW deliveries to the customers during the transition period. It is therefore not always about an explicit boost of productivity during a transition step, but also about not destroying the already achieved improvements.

Our case takes place at Ericsson, a large telecom infrastructure provider. We focus on one part of Ericsson, which is basically an enterprise in itself divided into seven organizations (here called A–G). These organizations contain up to eight sub-units each, numbered in sequential order. Customers were also included as the last part of the development chain, the last step out of the development units, i.e. as one sub-unit for each organization The organizations and sub-units are the artifacts/components used in our DSM analysis.

The content of the DSM is realized from use-cases starting with a customer offer and ending with the SW and/or HW being delivered to the customers. Every use-case is modelled as a flow of events through the organizations. Typical examples of elements within our organizations are units or sub-units for product management, early phases investigations (EP), product development (PD), product integration (CI), product and system verification (SV), release management (RM), product packaging (PP), etc.

The DSM was created by analyzing the dependencies and deliveries between the above-mentioned organizations developing the HW and SW. The details of the DSM are not revealed in this paper. Figure 2 shows the DSM together with some high level, schematic outline of the flows used. The example flows are shown to outline the input data for the DSM. The flows are the result of a separate activity within Ericsson to visualize what is called the football field of the organization, i.e. a few pages of explanation of how the organization is working with product development. Thus, the flows are not only revealing the organizational architecture, but also the way of handling the product artefacts in this architecture, i.e. the (SW & HW) elements of the products and their development. For simplicity only the major flows are used, e.g. infrequent feedback loops are not considered. For a better understanding we here provide an example for such a flow. The DSM is created from a number of "send operations" between two organizations or sub-units. Let's assume two sub-units "A" and "B". "A" sends (e.g. an order, SW, HW) to "B", in a flow picture indicated by an arrow from "A" to "B". In the DSM this is modeled as "B" is dependent (on order, on delivery, etc.) on "A". Ericsson realizes SW and HW for multi-standard (e.g. GSM, LTE, WCDMA) networks. An example flow could be that sub-unit Product Line for multi-standard (PL-MS) offers a feature to a customer running a multi-standard network and checks for commercial interest: (DSM operation: Customer dependent on feature offer from PL, Customer => PL-MS). PL-MS orders a consequence impact study from e.g. GSM RAN Product Development Organizations Early Phases (EP) sub-unit, doing such studies (DSM: GSM RAN EP => PL-MS); Next steps are: PL-MS orders feature from e.g. GSM RAN Product Development Program (GSM RAN PD => PL-MS); GSM RAN PD sub-unit sends HW and/or SW with updates to Continuous Integration (CI) sub-unit within GSM RAN (GSM RAN CI => GSM RAN PD). GSM RAN CI sends HW and/or SW with updates to Continuous Integration sub-units in PDU WCDMA RAN (WCDMA RAN CI => GSM RAN CI) and PDU LTE RAN (LTE RAN CI => GSM RAN CI). Then the SW/HW with the feature is sent to the Product packaging (PP) sub-units within all three RAN PDU's and from there to each PDUs Release Management (RM) sub-unit, which next provides the SW/HW in a release together with other features to the multi-standard customer(s). In the DSM, each of those "send operations" is modeled as explained further above and indicated as an arrow in Fig. 2 below.

4.2   Results

Based on the original DSM (see Fig. 2) we derived our VSM, which we used in order to sort the DSM revealing its hidden structure, see Fig. 3.

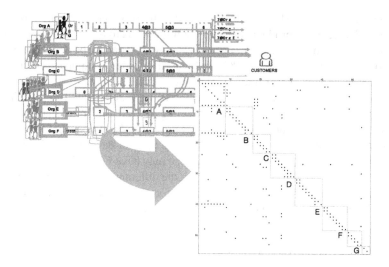

Fig. 2. From high-level process models to DSM.

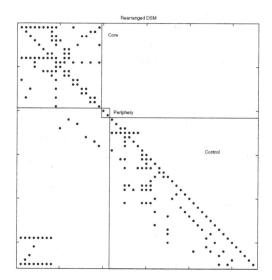

Fig. 3. The organizational architecture DSM, sorted according to the hidden structure method explained in Sect. 3.

From the hidden structure method sorting we can see that the architecture is a core-periphery architecture (or more precise a core-control architecture). We have no elements in the DSM being labeled Shared, and only two units in the Periphery. We have one large Core containing 19 of the total 55 elements. These core units have outgoing dependencies to all other core elements (VFO = 19) and have in-flowing dependencies from 53 units (i.e. the Core and the Control elements, VFI = 53).

The Propagation Cost (PC) of the VSM is calculated to 47 %, meaning that a new request or a change in the product development might need to be communicated through 47 % of the units in the organization. From this analysis, it cannot be derived if 47 % is a good or bad number. However the PC can be used in order to compare different alternatives for changing the organizational architecture. This is further explored in our to-be analysis, e.g. an increase of the PC after a change will reveal increased complexity in the product development. If the PC is neither increasing or decreasing after an organizational change, then it can be concluded that the change did not add additional complexity, e.g. if the organizational change was done to have more parallel development between agile teams and the PC is not increased, then the change may have fulfilled its purpose without increasing the number of dependencies between the different organizational units, i.e. the "complexity" in the interworking is constant before and after the change, which is a positive outcome of the change despite that the PC stayed constant.

4.3   To-Be Analysis

The next step in our organizational architecture analysis was to test the consequence of different changes to the architecture and its elements. All changes shall result in a possibility to implement a transformation from product specific architecture elements to cross-functional elements. The main driving force behind this is the move towards becoming more agile and lean, from now on called "Agilean". Teams (our DSM elements) should be able to pull orders/features from a prioritized list and to take full end-to-end responsibility for such a feature without negotiation between product domains about the allocation of skilled people in a specific domain (which is the case today). The domain specific fan-in and fan-out dependencies are in such a transformation equal for all resulting units, i.e. all such architecture elements would form a cyclic group in the DSM.

We analyzed three possible to-be scenario alternatives: (1) Agilean transformation within existing organizations, with the target to remove dependencies within an organization and maximize parallel work. (2) Agilean transformation on the front-end side of our organizational architecture, with the target to maximize parallel work inside the core. (3) Agilean transformation on the back-end side of our organizational architecture with the target to utilize the fact that some units have the same outgoing dependencies and maximize parallel work.

The organizational transformation in Scenario 1 resulted in one gigantic core (see top-left DSM of Fig. 4), where the propagation cost increased from 47 % to 76 %, thus a scenario in which nearly everything is dependent on everything.

Scenario 2 resulted in a core-control architecture (cf. top-right DSM of Fig. 4) similar to the original DSM in terms of PC, core size, and categorization. Finally, Scenario 3 (see bottom DSM in Fig. 4) that also is a core-control architecture similar to the original. Here propagation cost decreased slightly to 43 %.

4.4   Discussion of the To-Be Analysis Results

An agile and lean transformation that is focusing only on the internal "root" organizational level (Scenario 1), disregarding fan-in and fan-out dependencies has resulted in

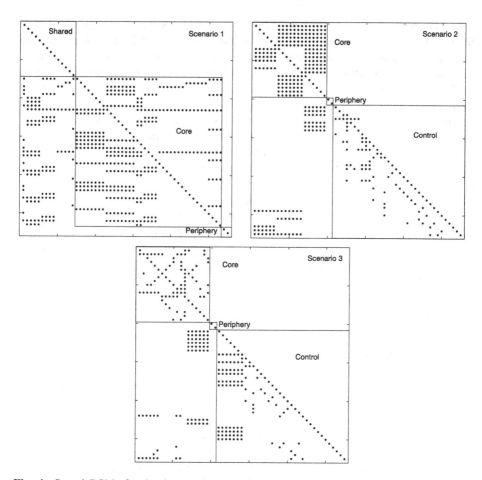

Fig. 4. Sorted DSMs for the three to-be scenarios; top-left Scenario 1, top-right Scenario 2, bottom Scenario 3.

a big increase of propagation cost and a "gigantic" core, covering 76 % of all architecture elements. An explanation for this is that the transformation was driven to maximize the possibility to use any sub-unit for any type of product changes. This is very helpful for the "pull-principle" in agilean development, i.e. that each sub-unit can pull and execute "orders/deliveries" from arrival to delivery, thus there is no longer an internal dependency between sub-units on the cost of an increase in the number of dependencies to/from external sub-units. This low focus on external dependencies caused the PC to double. Two other approaches were then tested; (i) the transformation of the front-end side (optimizing within the core, Scenario (2), and (ii) the transformation of the back-end side (optimizing specifically selected sub-units, Scenario (3). The transformation of Scenario 2 resulted in the same PC as the as-is scenario, while Scenario 3 resulted in a slightly decreased PC. Indicating that the two groups (front-end and back-end) are rather separated in their fan-in and fan-out structure, only a few new dependencies are created during the agilean transformations. In Scenario 2, the PC stayed constant. This can be explained by the fact that the selection of sub-units where the transformation was applied was done in a way that those sub-units already before the transformation had large dependencies between each other and very similar dependencies towards/from external sub-units. The decreased PC in Scenario 3 can be explained by the fact that the agilean transformation within the selected-sub-units decreased the number of dependencies between the sub-units. This decrease (over-) compensate the increased number of external dependencies. The remaining question is, whether there is a fundamental other difference between Scenario 2 and Scenario 3 that would lead to a decision in choosing between them.

When looking on the number of people working the two big groups, we see that the back-end group is a factor of 20–30 larger than the total number of people working in the core. Therefore an agilean transformation of the back-end side has potentially bigger positive scaling impact than the front-end side transformation. As the number of people in the front-end is so much smaller, the examined re-structuring of the core into a structure with very few dependencies inside the core is really feasible and the PC for Scenario 2 is not higher than the PC before the transformation. This means that we can create a large number of cross-functional teams (back-end) that can work almost end-to-end (excluding competence in core) in an agile and lean company environment.

5 Future Work

In this paper we used a rather high-level process model to gather the organizational dependencies. In our model all dependencies are only binary; this will result in a worst-case analysis and not a weighted or probable one. To make the DSM analysis more precise the dependencies between the elements could be weighted.

Our current focus will be extended beyond organizational aspects and include other artifacts in the development system. The intention is to extend the analysis to the whole production architecture, where the organization is only one part. The major components of the production architecture are; Organization, Processes, Development artifacts (tools, production related code, information, and machines). In this work Enterprise Architecture methods for modeling and analysis will play an important role.

Our long-term approach is to map the dependencies between product and production architecture; and to find a set of methodologies that can model these as one interrelated system. The product and the organization should not be considered as independent entities, but as a complex system with many levels of components and relations that are affecting and forming each other. The hidden relations and dependencies between product and organizational parts are vital to understand and analyze in order to foresee the true impact of a change on both, i.e. the two faces of the system are not independent of each other.

Other complementary analytical methods in addition to the hidden structure analysis using DSMs are needed to cover the multifaceted nature of the system. These connected models are intended to be used in the same systematic manner as product architecture models are used today, e.g. to drive the improvements and needed evolution of the production architecture.

6 Conclusions

In this paper we have used the Design Structure Matrix (DSM) based hidden structure method in order to investigation organizational transformation scenarios at Ericsson. In our case this turned out to be an appropriate approach for revealing the unknown dependencies in a complex system of organizational units communicating with each other to develop hardware and software products. We were able to identify impacts on the current as-is architecture and to (re)organize this architecture for three different to-be cases. The results of our to-be analyses show that the organizational transformation must take into account the hidden dependencies that are in part a reflection of the product architecture structures. However, for a more detailed and possibly more accurate analysis, we need to evolve the methodology further by using a less binary approach to dependency schemes. Completing the model with other artifacts such as development tools and related processes will require additional modeling and analysis techniques.

References

1. Baldwin, C., MacCormack, A., Rusnak, J.: Hidden structure: using network methods to map system architecture. Res. Policy, accepted manuscript **43**(8), 1381–1397 (2014)
2. MacCormack, A., Lagerström, R., Baldwin, C.: A Methodology for Operationalizing Enterprise Architecture and Evaluating Enterprise IT Flexibility. Harvard Business School Working Paper, No. 15-060, January 2015
3. Shaw, M., Clements, P.: The golden age of software architecture. IEEE Softw. **23**(2), 31–39 (2006)
4. Steward, D.: The design structure system: a method for managing the design of complex systems. IEEE Trans. Eng. Manage. **3**, 71–74 (1981)
5. Eppinger, S.D., Whitney, D.E., Smith, R.P., Gebala, D.A.: A model-based method for organizing tasks in product development. Res. Eng. Des. **6**(1), 1–13 (1994)
6. MacCormack, A., Baldwin, C., Rusnak, J.: Exploring the duality between product and organizational architectures: a test of the "mirroring" hypothesis. Res. Policy **41**(8), 1309–1324 (2006)
7. Ross, J.W., Weill, P., Robertson, D.: Enterprise Architecture As Strategy: Creating a Foundation for Business Execution. Harvard Business School Press, Boston (2006)
8. Zachman, J.A.: A framework for information systems architecture. IBM Syst. J. **26**(3), 276–292 (1987)
9. The Open Group: The Open Group Architecture Framework (TOGAF). Version 9, The Open Group (2009)
10. Johnson, P., Lagerström, R., Närman, P., Simonsson, M.: Enterprise architecture analysis with extended influence diagrams. Inf. Syst. Front. **9**(2–3), 163–180 (2007)
11. Lagerström, R., Johnson, P., Höök, D.: Architecture analysis of enterprise systems modifiability: models, analysis, and validation. J. Syst. Softw. **83**(8), 1387–1403 (2010)
12. Ullberg, J., Lagerström, R., Johnson, P.: A framework for service interoperability analysis using enterprise architecture models. In: IEEE International Conference on Services Computing (SCC 2008), vol. 2, pp. 99–107 (2008)

13. Saat, J., Franke, U., Lagerström, R., Ekstedt, M.: Enterprise architecture meta models for IT/ business alignment situations. In: EDOC, pp. 14–23 (2010)

14. Simonsson, M., Lagerström, R., Johnson, P.: A Bayesian network for IT governance performance prediction. In: Proceedings of the 10th International Conference on Electronic Commerce (2008)

15. Lagerström, R., Baldwin, C., MacCormack, A., Dreyfus, D.: Visualizing and measuring enterprise architecture: an exploratory biopharma case. In: Grabis, J., Kirikova, M., Zdravkovic, J., Stirna, J. (eds.) PoEM 2013. LNBIP, vol. 165, pp. 9–23. Springer, Heidelberg (2013)

16. Lagerström, R., Baldwin, C., MacCormack, A., Dreyfus, D.: Visualizing and measuring software portfolio architecture: a flexibility analysis. In: Proceedings of the 16th International Dependency and Structure Modelling (DSM) Conference (2014)

17. Lagerström, R., Baldwin, C., MacCormack, A., Aier, S.: Visualizing and measuring enterprise application architecture: an exploratory telecom case. In: Proceedings of the 47th Hawaii International Conference on System Sciences (HICSS), pp. 3847–3856 (2014)

Enterprise Architecture with Executable Modelling Rules: A Case Study at the Swedish Defence Materiel Administration

Mika Cohen[1], Michael Minock[2], Daniel Oskarsson[1(✉)], and Björn Pelzer[1]

[1] FOI, Stockholm, Sweden
{mika.cohen,daniel.oskarsson,bjorn.pelzer}@foi.se
[2] KTH Royal Institute of Technology, Stockholm, Sweden
minock@kth.se

Abstract. Formal modeling rules can be used to ensure that an enterprise architecture is correct. Despite their apparent utility and despite mature tool support, formal modelling rules are rarely, if ever, used in practice in enterprise architecture in industry. In this paper we propose a rule authoring method that we believe aligns with actual modelling practice, at least as witnessed in enterprise architecture projects at the Swedish Defence Materiel Administration. The proposed method follows the business rules approach: the rules are specified in a (controlled) natural language which makes them accessible to all stakeholders and easy to modify as the meta-model matures and evolves over time. The method was put to test during 2014 in two large scale enterprise architecture projects, and we report on the experiences from that. To the best of our knowledge, this is the first time extensive formal modelling rules for enterprise architecture has been tested in industry and reported in the literature.

Keywords: Enterprise architecture · Data quality · Meta-model · Semantics · Business rules · Case study

1 Introduction

An enterprise architecture (EA) model is composed of symbols (boxes, arrows, words, etc.) that combine to make claims about the business being modelled. How the symbols combine to express meaningful statements is given by the model's *semantics*. Part of the semantics is typically governed by an explicit *meta-model*; ideally, the rest is governed by informal or tacit agreement across modellers and model users.

As long as the model semantics is thus fully determined, explicitly or informally, it can, at least in part, be captured by formal (and thus executable) modelling rules[1], e.g. in OCL[2] [8,13,14], forming an *extended meta-model* which can in turn be used to automatically verify that the model complies with the semantics.

---

[1] Sometimes referred to as "compliance rules".
[2] Object Constraint Language.

© Springer International Publishing Switzerland 2015
A. Persson and J. Stirna (Eds.): CAiSE 2015 Workshops, LNBIP 215, pp. 339–350, 2015.
DOI: 10.1007/978-3-319-19243-7_32

But what if part of the semantics are not even implicit but thoroughly undetermined? In a typical modelling scenario, with multiple modellers and stakeholders modifying and interacting with the model over a span of time, the risk is then that semantic underdetermination leads to model inconsistencies that go undiscovered by automatic compliance checking, since that which is undetermined cannot be formalized into compliance rules.

Fortunately, the very process of formulating executable rules lends itself to weeding out vagueness: Since a rule, to be executable, must be expressed in precise concepts, formulating the rule entails specifying those concepts that are yet not precise.

To secure the participation and involvement of a broad range of stakeholders in the rule formulation process, and thus ultimately to ensure the quality of the extended meta-model thus produced, it helps if the rules, in addition to being formal, are expressed in a language that resembles natural language.

So, resting upon the assumptions that (1) it is useful to continually submit an EA model to validation against semantic rules, (2) the process of expressing formal rules has the effect of forcing semantic specification, bringing value by precluding model vagueness, and (3) natural language rules improve quality by involving a wider range of stakeholders in the formulation of the semantics, we propose a method for automatic model validation and continual semantic specification based on semantic rules expressed in a controlled natural language.

We report the results from applying this method within two EA projects at the Swedish Defence Materiel Administration (FMV) in the main section of this paper (Sect. 5). But first, in Sect. 2, we describe the background that lead us to formulate a set of hypotheses about the role of modelling rules in EA projects—listed in Sect. 3—which in turn lead to the formulation of the method—described in Sect. 4. The case study Sect. 5 evaluates the method in terms of the hypotheses, and the verdict is summarized in Conclusions (Sect. 6).

Related Work. The need for enterprise architecture to be correct has been pointed out repeatedly and formal modelling rules have been proposed as a suitable means to enforce correctness [1,4,6,8,10,13,14]. Indeed, several commercial EA-modelling tools allow the user to specify formal modelling rules in OCL; the modelling environment will then warn the user whenever data is entered that violates a rule. To the best of our knowledge, however, no extensive use of formal modelling rules in a large scale industrial EA project has been reported previously in the literature.

The meta-modelling method described in the present paper can be seen as *domain specific modelling* [9], a modelling methodology used in software engineering. In domain specific modelling, the meta-model is tailored to suit a narrow problem domain, e.g. a particular product line or a particular software project. The narrow problem domain allows stronger, more effective modelling rules compared to the rather weak modelling rules that come with general purpose software modelling languages such as UML. Typically, the modelling rules are expressed in OCL or other similarly low-level constraint language inaccessible to stakeholders outside IT.

The rule authoring method described in the present paper, by contrast, follows the *business rules approach* [5]. In particular, the rules are captured in a (controlled) natural language which is subsequently transformed into executable code. In typical business rules applications, the rules capture operational guidelines such as regulatory compliance rules rather than, as in our case, modelling rules for a domain specific modeling language. Moreover, the executable code (that the rules compile to) is typically decision logic (e.g. in a workflow system) rather than database integrity constraints.

Richer, extended EA meta-models are considered in [7], which extends ArchiMate, an enterprise architecture modelling language, with inference rules that derive numerical data attributes in an element from other attributes in the same or related elements. The inference rules reflect empirically established correlations ("laws of causation") rather than an informal intuitive semantics.

The natural language compiler used in the case study is described in [3].

2 Background

During 2013, FOI[3] was called in to lend support to the EA modelling project *SK TS*[4] at the Swedish Defence Materiel Administration (FMV). The SK TS architecture describes, at a high level of abstraction, the dependency relationships between technical systems[5], and how the development, production, use and retirement of the systems is planned over time.

Our task was to design a set of consistency rules and implement them as queries into the EA tool[6] used to host the model. The queries were to be run on a regular basis to uncover inconsistencies in the models, and thus to eschew manual "proof reading" that was becoming intractable as the model was growing in size and complexity.

We discovered at an early stage that having access to the model, attendant meta-model and other documentation was insufficient as specification for the rules to be designed; trying to design rules raised a multitude of questions of interpretation, which we directed at the architecture modelling team. Our second discovery was that these questions often did not have ready answers, but gave rise to discussions that fed into the modelling process itself. We also found that it took a few rounds of execution and redesign of the rule queries for them to mature. Finally, we found that implementing the rules directly as queries into the EA modelling tool offered poor overview over the rule set, and that keeping an informal catalogue of rules as a companion to the queries posed its own problems of synchronization.

---

[3] Swedish Defence Research Agency.

[4] *Systemkarta tekniska system*, Swedish for "system map (over) technical systems".

[5] The term "technical system" can be loosely defined as a category of equipment of non-trivial complexity, encompassing aircraft as well as munitions, but not e.g. clothing.

[6] MooD Business Architect 2010.

These realizations lead to a redefinition of our task, from delivering a bundle of rules, implemented as queries, to handing over a framework for continuous rule development, management and execution. Having expressed the rules in the technical syntax most expedient to the task of implementation, we now turned to a controlled natural language to make the rule design process accessible to all stakeholders. The new approach—detailed in the next section—was applied to the continuation of the SK TS project, as well as to a different EA modelling project, called FM UFS, at FMV.

3   Hypotheses

Based on the SK TS experience during 2013, we formulated a number of hypotheses about the possible role of executable semantic rules in EA modelling:

H1 EA models contain many errors that are missed despite extensive manual auditing, but which can be captured automatically through the execution of formal rules.

H2 EA meta-models contain many poorly defined concepts; the activity of designing and executing formal semantic rules uncovers vagueness, imprecision and ambiguity.

H3 EA modelling tends to require project-specific semantics, even when based on well-established architecture frameworks.

H4 EA model semantics need to evolve with the modelling process.

H5 A natural language format for the rules boosts the semantic specification process by stimulating broader participation in rule development.

The rationale behind that last hypothesis (H5) is that if the model semantics need to be developed continually and specifically for the project, and if—as H2 suggests—this semantic development is to be catalysed by the development and execution of semantic rules, then the design and execution of rules is of concern to a broad range of stakeholders, including non-technical ones. Such broad participation should be facilitated by being able to directly execute natural language formulations of rules.

4   Proposed Method: Rule Authoring as Continual Modelling Support

The method we propose can be described as a business rules approach to EA modelling, where one works simultaneously and iteratively with the architecture modelling process to produce a *rule book* that encodes project specific semantics in SBVR[7] [12], a controlled natural language. The rule book is continually put to use in validating the architecture model as new rules are formulated, catching semantic errors early in the modelling process. Meanwhile, the very process of creating the rule book extends the range of testable semantics, further shoring up the modelling process.

---

[7] Semantics of Business Vocabulary and Rules.

4.1   Executable Natural Language Rules in SBVR

An SBVR model consists of a vocabulary and a set of rules expressed in terms of the vocabulary. The vocabulary is made up of *nouns* (see Fig. 1), naming entities in the architecture model, and *verbs* (see Fig. 2), naming relationships between the entities.

Id	Noun concepts	Attribute	Attribute value	New noun concep
n100	system			
		Definition (informal):	a category of equipment of non-trivial technical comple>	
		Definition (primitive):	(X TS (= X NAME $C1))	
n101	combat unit			
		Definition (informal):	a formal organizational unit able able to perform comba<	
		Definition (primitive):	(X FOERBAND (= X NAME $C1))	
n102	taxonomic rank			
n103	version level system			
n104	life-cycle data			
n105	life-cycle phase			
n106	date			
n107	concept phase			
n108	development phase			
n109	production phase			
n110	use phase			
		Definition (informal):	a life-cycle phase during which a system is used	
		Category of:	life-cycle phase	
		Definition (primitive):	(X LCS (= X LCS "Användning"))	

Fig. 1. Some noun concepts in the SK TS SBVR model, including (optional) informal definitions as well as formal definitions ("Definition (primitive)") in tuple calculus, mapping the nouns to corresponding elements in the database.

The naming of entities and relationships serves the semantic function of appealing to human intuition about what states of affairs in the real world the terms refer to. To provide semantic information to a *machine*, however, we need to specify in what patterns the entities and relationships can appear in the architecture model. This is done by the rule part of the SBVR model.

The rules are statements in the controlled natural language of SBVR, composed of the nouns and verbs of the vocabulary, bound together by generic operators, such as *and, or, not, it is necessary that*, to specify allowable patterns in the EA model. As an example, take the last rule in Fig. 3 (r115), *"It is necessary that a system1 that is part of a system2 that has a use phase2, have a use phase1"*. It uses the nouns *system* and *use phase* (with indices to identify distinct variables of the same class) and the verbs *system1 is part of system2* and *system has life-cycle phase*, connected into a meaningful statement by the modal operator *It is necessary that*, the existential quantifier *a* and the specifying operator *that*. The rule disallows the pattern where a sub-system lacks a use phase while its super-system has one.

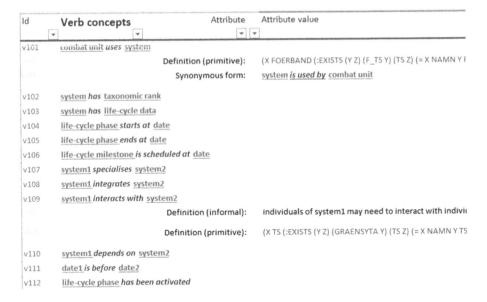

Id	Verb concepts	Attribute	Attribute value
v101	combat unit *uses* system		
		Definition (primitive):	(X FOERBAND (:EXISTS (Y Z) (F_TS Y) (TS Z) (= X NAMN Y F
		Synonymous form:	system *is used by* combat unit
v102	system *has* taxonomic rank		
v103	system *has* life-cycle data		
v104	life-cycle phase *starts at* date		
v105	life-cycle phase *ends at* date		
v106	life-cycle milestone *is scheduled at* date		
v107	system1 *specialises* system2		
v108	system1 *integrates* system2		
v109	system1 *interacts with* system2		
		Definition (informal):	individuals of system1 may need to interact with indivi(
		Definition (primitive):	(X TS (:EXISTS (Y Z) (GRAENSYTA Y) (TS Z) (= X NAMN Y TS
v110	system1 *depends on* system2		
v111	date1 *is before* date2		
v112	life-cycle phase *has been activated*		

Fig. 2. Some verb concepts in the SK TS SBVR model, including (optional) informal definitions as well as formal definitions ("Definition (primitive)") in tuple calculus, mapping the verbs to corresponding elements in the database. Attributes shown here only for a subset of the verbs.

Since the rules follow the controlled grammar of SBVR, they are machine-readable and can be "executed", in the sense of generating reports of rule violations committed by the architecture model. Figure 4 shows an example of a violations report produced by executing a rule.

The execution of rules over the architecture model is made possible by compiling them into SQL code that queries the architecture model—that is, the database representation of it in the particular EA modelling tool used—for violations against the rules. To enable such compilation, the nouns and verbs in the SBVR vocabulary must be formally mapped onto entities and relationships of the model, as represented in the database. In our current implementation, the mappings are encoded in Codd's tuple calculus [2] (as can be seen in Figs. 1 and 2), and the compilation is performed by a modified version [3] of the natural language question-answering engine C-Phrase [11].

4.2   Process

The semantic rules should be developed in parallel with the meta-model, as an integral part of the meta-model development itself, with the participation of as broad a range of stakeholders as possible: enterprise architects, problem owners, domain experts, database technicians, etc. As long as the meta-model has not been set in stone, the rule book should equally be considered a living document.

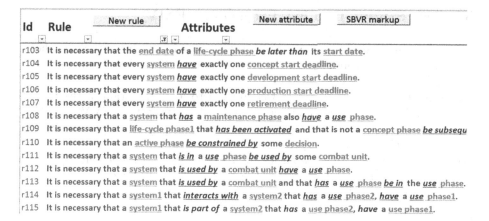

Id	Rule	New rule	Attributes	New attribute	SBVR markup
r103	It is necessary that the end date of a life-cycle phase *be later than* its start date.				
r104	It is necessary that every system *have* exactly one concept start deadline.				
r105	It is necessary that every system *have* exactly one development start deadline.				
r106	It is necessary that every system *have* exactly one production start deadline.				
r107	It is necessary that every system *have* exactly one retirement deadline.				
r108	It is necessary that a system that *has* a maintenance phase also *have* a *use* phase.				
r109	It is necessary that a life-cycle phase1 that *has been activated* and that is not a concept phase *be subsequ*				
r110	It is necessary that an active phase *be constrained by* some decision.				
r111	It is necessary that a system that *is in* a *use* phase *be used by* some combat unit.				
r112	It is necessary that a system that *is used by* a combat unit *have* a *use* phase.				
r113	It is necessary that a system that *is used by* a combat unit and that *has* a *use* phase *be in* the *use* phase.				
r114	It is necessary that a system1 that *interacts with* a system2 that *has* a *use* phase2, *have* a *use* phase1.				
r115	It is necessary that a system1 that *is part of* a system2 that *has* a use phase2, *have* a use phase1.				

Fig. 3. Some rules in the SK TS SBVR model.

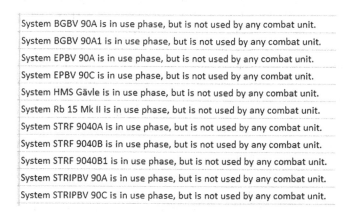

System BGBV 90A is in use phase, but is not used by any combat unit.

System BGBV 90A1 is in use phase, but is not used by any combat unit.

System EPBV 90A is in use phase, but is not used by any combat unit.

System EPBV 90C is in use phase, but is not used by any combat unit.

System HMS Gävle is in use phase, but is not used by any combat unit.

System Rb 15 Mk II is in use phase, but is not used by any combat unit.

System STRF 9040A is in use phase, but is not used by any combat unit.

System STRF 9040B is in use phase, but is not used by any combat unit.

System STRF 9040B1 is in use phase, but is not used by any combat unit.

System STRIPBV 90A is in use phase, but is not used by any combat unit.

System STRIPBV 90C is in use phase, but is not used by any combat unit.

Fig. 4. Violations report produced when executing the rule *"It is necessary that a system that is in a use phase be used by some combat unit."*. Results shown here are from a public demo release of SK TS, not the actual SK TS model, which is confidential.

The process we propose can be roughly summarized in the following steps, to be repeated indefinitely:

1. Express intended model semantics as rules (either by adding new rules or modifying existing ones). If questions are raised as to what is meant by some of the terms, engage in a discussion, agree upon a meaning, and let the rules reflect the agreement.
2. Execute rules to generate violation reports.
3. Examine the violation reports and figure out to what extent they indicate errors in the model, errors in the meta-model (the rules), or temporary and tolerable incongruence between them.
4. Act accordingly, that is, correct the model, modify the rules, or tolerate.

5   Case Study: Two EA Projects at FMV

In this section, we evaluate the method just proposed, in terms of the hypotheses that underpin it (as listed in Sect. 3), in the context of two EA modelling projects at FMV.

Throughout 2014 the method was applied to a continuation of the SK TS project and to FM UFS[8], another EA modelling project at FMV. FM UFS describes the capabilities, current and targeted, of military units at different levels of aggregation, what types of tasks the units are expected to perform, and the relationships between capabilities and tasks. Both cases differ somewhat from the ideal application scenario in that the rule development process was initiated well into the EA modelling process.

5.1   Executing Rules to Find Errors (H1)

Executing the rule book for SK TS produced a list of several thousand violations—despite the extensive manual validation and verification that had already been performed on the model. Most of the rule violations trace back to errors in the various data sources that feed the SK TS model, and to inconsistencies between the data sources. As an example, the rule *"It is forbidden that a system that specialises an abstract system has an object-group1 that generalises the object-group2 of the abstract system"* identifies cases where the *object group* hierarchy (imported from one particular data source) and the system hierarchy (imported from another data source) run in different directions of abstraction. More than 10 % of all systems in SK TS violate this particular rule; one instance is the system *Grävmaskin hjul* ("Wheeled excavator"), of object group *L151* and with the specialisation *GM HB 19T* ("Wheeled excavator 19T"), of object group *L15*, which is a more general group than *L151*.

Executing rules also uncovered more trivial inconsistencies in SK TS. For instance, the rule *"The start date of a life cycle phase must precede its end date"* identifies several life cycle phases with inconsistent start- and end dates.

In addition to uncovering inconsistencies, executing the SK TS rule book also uncovered incompleteness in the model. The rule *"Every system in use phase must have a decision of use"*, for instance, identified more than a hundred incompletely specified systems, that is, systems that were required to have been cleared for use according to FMV policy, but where this use decision had not been entered into the model.

We do not report error rates in the FM UFS model, since at the time of writing, the version of model for which we designed rules has not yet been released, except for a small preview sample. However, FMV plans to use the rule book as part of the validation step prior to the release of the model. Presently, the UFS rule book contains approximately 100 rules.

---

[8] *Försvarsmaktens uppgifts-, förmåge- och systemkartor*, Swedish for "the Armed Forces' maps over tasks, capabilities and systems", with "systems" in this case referring roughly to military units.

5.2   Specifying the Semantics Through Rules (H2)

The rule authoring process quickly uncovered ambiguities in both SK TS and FM UFS meta-models—some local, others affecting the entire architectures. Throughout the efforts of formulating rules for both SK TS and FM UFS, questions of interpretation kept coming up for the modelling teams to address. Some were answered promptly because the interpretation, while not being explicitly encoded in any meta-model, was a matter of implicit consensus among the modellers. Some questions triggered discussions about the meaning of terms and how they should relate to each other. Both modelling teams stated that these discussions brought clear value to their respective modelling efforts.

The rule authoring process for FM UFS uncovered ambiguity in each and every relation (both properties and associations) in the FM UFS meta-model. For instance, when discussing the rule *"A combat unit that performs a task that supports a capability, must have the capability."* we found that the relation *task supports capability* was interpreted differently by different members of the modelling team. Some understood it to mean that the task single-handedly realises the capability; others, that the task is one of a possible multitude of tasks that together realise the capability. The ambiguity had not been spotted before, and there was nothing in the meta-model to resolve it.

The process of authoring rules for the SK TS model also uncovered many ambiguities. As an example, when evaluating the rule *"Every system used by a combat unit must be in its use phase."* it was discovered that the relation *system is used by combat unit* is used in two different senses, namely: (1) "the system has been allocated to the combat unit in the defence planning" and (2) "the combat unit has requested the system". The rule in question is valid only under the first interpretation.

We also found that being able to execute the rules under design provided input to that design, and hence helped specify the semantics thus expressed. As an example, executing the rule *"Each system that is used by a combat unit must be in use phase."*, intended to capture cases of erroneously planned use phases, returned instances of systems that, for acceptable reasons (according to the modellers), did not have a use phase registered. The rule was then changed to *"Each system that is used by a combat unit that has a use phase must be in the use phase."*. In this and many more cases then, an iterative rule design-execution process was key to uncovering semantic subtleties that needed to be sorted out.

The previous example highlights an all-encompassing case of semantic underdetermination in the SK TS meta-model that kept coming up during rule authoring, namely: What is the meaning of absent data? For example, what is the meaning of an absent system life-cycle phase? That no such phase has in fact (yet) been planned? That data about a possible plan has not been entered into the model? Or, that life-cycle phases of systems at this level of abstraction are to be inferred from those of higher or lower level systems?

5.3   Project-Specific Semantics (H3)

Both SK TS and FM UFS modelling efforts were based on the MODAF[9] architecture framework and its attendant meta-model M3[10], and the modellers were
experienced MODAF practitioners. Yet the two projects took quite different
approaches to the application of M3.

For reasons of practical expediency, SK TS redefined how concepts such as
the life-cycle phases of systems and resource interactions between systems where
to be represented in M3 terms. While these redefinitions did not introduce any
concepts that couldn't have been represented in an orthodox application of M3,
they did shuffle the relationships between terms and referents, invalidating any
inheritance of meaning from M3.

FM UFS also departed quite radically from orthodox M3 usage, but in a
different way. MODAF is designed to support *capability based planning*, whereby
plans are initially expressed at a high level of abstraction ("what"-questions),
deferring specifics ("how"-questions) to a later time and lower-level decision-
making. M3 thus has *capabilities* at a "strategic" level, that are realised by
nodes that perform *operational activities* at an "operational" level; *nodes* are
then further realised by *resource configurations* at the lowest, "systems" level.
In FM UFS, though, *capabilites* and *operational activities*—rebranded as *tasks*—
do not express different levels in a realisation hierarchy; instead, the *task* concept
is fused into the *capability* concept by being seen as its qualitative component.

5.4   Semantic Evolution (H4)

Both SK TS and FM UFS projects kept developing their meta-models—and more
generally their semantics—in parallel with architecture modelling. While the SK
TS meta-model only underwent minor modifications to its original version, the
FM UFS meta-model changed frequently, and at one point, radically.

A notable change to the SK TS meta-model was in the handling of system lifecycle phases. Originally, a system use phase could include, within its time span,
a number of maintenance phases. This was changed such that a maintenance
phase would end its preceding use phase and then engender a new use phase after
its completion. In addition to this modification, and as noted in Sect. 5.2, several
semantic decisions where made along the way, triggered by rule development.

The redefinition of the relationship between *capabilities* and *tasks* in FM
UFS (described in the previuos section), which was done way into the architecture modelling process, was the most radical semantic shift of the the FM UFS
project. In addition, a number of more specific semantic modifications where
made along the way. An example is the relation *combat unit has capability*, whose
interpretation was changed from "the combat unit is required by its specification
to have the capability" to "the combat unit will realise the capabaility according to the plan". Another example is the rule-of-thumb *"Each combat unit type*

---

[9] Ministry of Defence Architecture Framework.
[10] MODAF Meta-Model.

is realised by at most one combat unit", which was enacted a few months into modelling, when it was discovered that this was the pattern of the data being used to populate the model (thus deviations from the pattern could be flagged as possible errors).

5.5   Natural Language Rules (H5)

Because of the evolving and project-specific nature of the semantics of the architecture modelling projects we observed (as described in Sects. 5.3 and 5.4), and because, as described in Sect. 5.2, the activity itself of developing and executing rules contributed in a significant and positive way to the semantic evolution, we found it fruitful to have regular discussions, centered around rules, with the modelling teams at FMV. During the 2013 SK TS project, before natural language rules were introduced, resolving ambiguities uncovered through rule authoring was an active initiative on our part—alternating between designing rules, executing them and directing questions at the SK TS modellers. With rules in natural language, however, we found that simply handing over the rule book to the modellers triggered discussions that propelled semantic specification forward with much less active effort required from our part—the modellers became a part of the rule formulation process, rather than just being passive receivers of its output.

Natural language rules also facilitated the participation of business stakeholders outside the modelling teams in the rule authoring process.

6   Conclusions

Formal modelling rules are rarely used in industrial EA-projects, despite their apparent utility and despite mature tool support. In this paper we have reported on their use in two large scale EA-projects at the Swedish Defence Materiel Administration. Both case studies confirmed the utility, by showing that formal modelling rules effectively capture errors missed by manual auditing, and that the rule authoring process uncovers vagueness, imprecision and ambiguity in the meta-model. Moreover, the case studies confirmed a claim often made in the business rules community: that it is easy to engage business architects and other stakeholders in the rule authoring process if rules are formulated in a (controlled) natural language.

It might be argued that engaging business architects and other stakeholders in the rule authoring is unnecessary—why not simply let the formal modelling rules be built in as part of a generic architecture framework or EA-tool that the business architects can use out of the box? However, and perhaps somewhat surprisingly, the case studies showed that meta-models are project specific—even when the organisation has agreed upon a common architecture framework—and the project specific meta-model evolves along with the architecture model itself. Consequently, modelling rules need to be formulated by the EA-project itself and the rules need to be continually updated during the project, which suggests a need for a natural and accessible rule format.

References

1. Aier, S., Buckl, S., Franke, U., Gleichauf, B., Johnson, P., Närman, P., Schweda, C.M., Ullberg, J.: A survival analysis of application life spans based on enterprise architecture models. In: EMISA, pp. 141–154 (2009)
2. Codd, E.F.: A relational model of data for large shared data banks. Commun. ACM **13**(6), 377–387 (1970)
3. Cohen, M., Minock, M.J., Oskarsson, D., Pelzer, B.: Natural language specification and violation reporting of business rules over er-modeled databases. Accepted and to appear in Proceedings of the 18th International Conference on Extending Database Technology (2015)
4. Dam, H.K., Lê, L.S., Ghose, A.: Managing changes in the enterprise architecture modelling context. Enterp. Inf. Sys. (ahead-of-print), 1–31 (2015)
5. Date, C.J.: What Not How: The Business Rules Approach to Application Development. Addison-Wesley Professional, Reading (2000)
6. Fischer, R., Aier, S., Winter, R.: A federated approach to enterprise architecture model maintenance. Enterp. Model. Inf. Syst. Architect. **2**(2), 14–22 (2007)
7. Johnson, P., Ekstedt, M.: Enterprise Architecture: Models and Analyses for Information Systems Decision Making. Studentlitteratur, Pozkal (2007)
8. Johnson, P., Ullberg, J., Buschle, M., Franke, U., Shahzad, K.: P^{2}AMF: predictive, probabilistic architecture modeling framework. In: van Sinderen, M., Oude Luttighuis, P., Folmer, E., Bosems, S. (eds.) IWEI 2013. LNBIP, vol. 144, pp. 104–117. Springer, Heidelberg (2013). doi:10.1007/978-3-642-36796-0_10
9. Kelly, S., Tolvanen, J.P.: Domain-Specific Modeling: Enabling Full Code Generation. Wiley, Hoboken (2008)
10. Lankhorst, M.M.: Enterprise architecture modelling–the issue of integration. Adv. Eng. Inform. **18**(4), 205–216 (2004)
11. Minock, M.J.: A step towards realizing codd's vision of rendezvous with the casual user. In: Proceedings of the 33rd International Conference on Very Large Data Bases, pp. 1358–1361. VLDB Endowment (2007)
12. Semantics of business vocabulary and rules (sbvr), version 1.2. OMG (2013)
13. Sousa, P., Caetano, A., Vasconcelos, A., Pereira, C., Tribolet, J.: Enterprise architecture modeling with the unified modeling language. In: Enterprise Modeling and Computing with UML, pp. 69–97. IGI Global (2006)
14. Steen, M.W., Akehurst, D.H., ter Doest, H.W., Lankhorst, M.M.: Supporting viewpoint-oriented enterprise architecture. In: Proceedings of the Eighth IEEE International Enterprise Distributed Object Computing Conference, EDOC 2004, pp. 201–211. IEEE (2004)

Modeling Decisions for Collaborative Enterprise Architecture Engineering

Dierk Jugel[1,2]([envelope]), Christian M. Schweda[1], and Alfred Zimmermann[1]

[1] Reutlingen University, Reutlingen, Germany
{dierk.jugel,christian.schweda,
alfred.zimmermann}@reutlingen-university.de
[2] Rostock University, Rostock, Germany
dierk.jugel@uni-rostock.de

Abstract. New or adapted digital business models have huge impacts on Enterprise Architectures (EA) and require them to become more agile, flexible, and adaptable. All this changes are happening frequently and are currently not well documented. An EA consists of a lot of elements with manifold relationships between them. Thus changing the business model may have multiple impacts on other architectural elements. The EA engineering process deals with the development, change and optimization of architectural elements and their dependencies. Thus an EA provides a holistic view for both business and IT from the perspective of many stakeholders, which are involved in EA decision-making processes. Different stakeholders have specific concerns and are collaborating today in often-unclear decision-making processes. In our research we are investigating information from collaborative decision-making processes to support stakeholders in taking current decisions. In addition we provide all information necessary to understand how and why decisions were taken. We are collecting the decision-related information automatically to minimize manual time intensive work as much as possible. The core contribution of our research extends a decisional metamodel, which links basic decisions with architectural elements and extends them with an associated decisional case context. Our aim is to support a new integral method for multi-perspective and collaborative decision-making processes. We illustrate this by a practice-relevant decision-making scenario for Enterprise Architecture Engineering.

Keywords: Enterprise architecture · Decision modeling · Collaborative decision-making process

1 Introduction

The constant change in modern business models requires an enterprise to continuously adapt its business processes, its information systems, and the underlying IT infra-structure, which together form the enterprise architecture (EA). Different stakeholders, e.g. from senior management, but also from IT-operations take different perspectives on the EA and have different concerns in the evolution of the EA. Collaborative support by current developments in social and collaborative media and in adaptive case manage-ment has inspired the upcoming wave of collaborative enterprise architecture. The main

© Springer International Publishing Switzerland 2015
A. Persson and J. Stirna (Eds.): CAiSE 2015 Workshops, LNBIP 215, pp. 351–362, 2015.
DOI: 10.1007/978-3-319-19243-7_33

challenging recommendations from [1] for a successful collaborative EA are: establish a lean set of processes and rules instead of overloading stakeholders with bureaucratic processes and unsolicited artifacts, adopt evolutionary problem solving instead of extensively blueprinting the future rigidly, and foster and moderate open participation in decisions on the ground instead of relying on experts and top-down wisdom.

Decision processes in such complex environments have to balance these various concerns and stakeholder collaboration is a prerequisite therefore. It is nevertheless very difficult to reflect on the decision processes after the fact, especially to revisit on the perspectives that had been considered and the analysis techniques that had been applied.

These deficiencies are imminent also in the closely related field of software architecture. Tang et al. [2] elicited in a survey, that capturing decisions and rationale is very important. Without information on decisions and rationale, stakeholders find it difficult to understand the architecture. This is also already reflected in the definition of the term architecture provided in the broader context of the ISO Standard 42010 [3]: the architecture is the fundamental organization of a system, embodied in its components, their relationships to each other and to the environment, and the **principles** guiding the decision and evolution. In particular these principles are often not documented explicitly, but implicit in the reasoning and rationale behind architecture decisions. In this light, another observation of Tang et al. [2] can be considered critically as well: stakeholders tend to forget their decisions over time. Combined with the fact that architecture decisions have a long-term impact, but often short-term contracted consultants are involved in decision-making, a significant part of the knowledge about an architecture gets lost over time.

EA Management is in its very nature a knowledge-intense activity and as such the decision-making processes are not formal, but driven by ad hoc information that is collected during the decision-making process and by assumptions made in the stakeholders' discussions. The stakeholder-specific views showing different perspectives on the EA are in this vain a starting point for decision making, but are enriched with additional information during the process. This yields a threefold challenge for EAM decision-making:

- Support different stakeholders in collaborative decision-making needed to balance different concerns.
- Capture the discussions and argumentation that lead to a distinct decision needed to facilitate organizational learning.
- Document the decision taken and its impact in various perspectives.

At the same time, in particular the capturing of discussions and argumentations should be automated as far as possible, as manual documentation after the fact is costly and time consuming.

In this paper, we present a method for documenting the decision-making processes in EAM. The method builds on the well-established work in the field of EAM, revisited in Sect. 2. In particular, we build on the EA Anamnesis method of Plataniotis et al. [4], which we extend in Sect. 3 to a method for multi-perspective and collaborative decision-making. A collaborative decision-making scenario in Sect. 4 exemplifies the method and its modeling concepts. Final Sect. 5 concludes our findings, reflects on limitations of the approach and outlines future streams of research.

2   Related Work

ArchiMate [5] is a modeling language that also defines a notation for visualizing Enterprise Architectures. The underlying metamodel comprises several concepts on different layers and relationships between them. In its core ArchiMate focuses on modeling a static state of the EA, being the current or an intended future state. Two extensions to ArchiMate address more transformation-oriented aspects of EAM.

The motivational extension [5] allows to model incentives and reasons for EA design. A *Stakeholder* is associated with a so-called *Motivational Element*. There are several characteristics of such an element. A *Motivational Element* e.g. can be a *Driver, Goal, Principle, Requirement* or *Constraint*. These concepts are related with each other and are useful to capture the reasons of designing EAs.

The implementation and migration extension to ArchiMate [5] describes EA transformations in more detail. Thereby a *Gap* describes the differences of two states. The states are defined as *Plateau*. A *Plateau* is realized by *Deliverables*. The detailed work that has to be done is modeled with *Work Packages*. *Work Packages* are similar to a project that has *Deliverables* as outcome.

While both extensions deal with decisions, either from the side of their motivations or the side of their impact on the architecture, an explicit decision concept focusing on the decision-making process, is missing.

In a similar manner, Buckl et al. discuss motivation and impact of EA transformations [6]. They combine the approach of Aier et al. described in [7] for modeling Work Packages and their impact on the EA with the i* modeling method [8] for describing motivations. While the employed modeling of transformations can be regarded as a refinement of implementation and migration extension, and i* modeling of motivation provides a refined perspective on e.g. soft goals, the approach does not provide an explicit concept for reflecting decisions.

Plataniotis et al. recognize the insufficiencies of above approaches and describe in [4] an approach called EA Anamnesis focusing on ex-post modeling Enterprise Architecture decisions and the decision-making process. They develop a metamodel for this purpose. An *EA Issue* represents the starting point of a decision-making process. It describes the design problem that has to be addressed. The *EA Decision* is described as a representation of a design decision that is taken. *EA Decisions* result in an *EA Artifact*. The *EA Artifact* is defined as result produced by an *EA Decision*. Furthermore it is described as representation of the result. The intention is to use this concept to relate an *EA Decision* with a visual representation of ArchiMate. In addition an *EA Decision* is associated with a *Layer* of ArchiMate.

Furthermore the approach provides four different relationships to relate *EA Decisions* with each other. *EA Decisions* can be translated into others using the *Translation Relationship*. This relationship enables deriving *EA Decisions*. For instance, a stakeholder takes a decision on Business Layer. This decision has impacts on the underlying Application Layer. Therefore the *EA Decision* on Business Layer has to be translated into an *EA Decision* on Application Layer and so on. Using *Decomposition Relationships* enables decomposing into more detailed ones. Before a decision is taken, the responsible usually has to choose between several alternatives. Such alternatives between *EA Decisions* can be modeled using the *Alternative Relationship*. Thus *EA Decisions* may have negative impacts on the Enterprise Architecture, the *Substitution Relationship* enables modeling how these negative impacts can be repaired. Furthermore the approach comprises concepts to model strategies for decision-making. These strategies e.g. include requirements that form a framework for decision-making. For instance, there are standards determined by governance processes that have to be involved in decision-making.

While the approach of Plataniotis et al. provides a significant contribution in the field, it is limited with respect to the challenges outlined in Sect. 1. Firstly, the authors assume that a single stakeholder takes the decisions and the proceeding is straightforward. In practice many stakeholders are involved in decision-making. Secondly, the approach's intention is an ex-post documentation of decisions. While this is possible, we regard it to be time-consuming and not adequate in particular in a collaborative setting. Thirdly, an *EA Decision* is associated with exactly one layer of ArchiMate. The layers describe non-overlapping subsets of the EA. We assume that complex interdependencies within the EA make it impossible to confine a decision to a single layer.

3 Collaborative Decision Modeling

In this section we present an adapted metamodel based on Plataniotis et al. [4] targeting collaborative decision modeling. We further adopt relevant concepts from the ArchiMate implementation and migration extension [5] to more clearly elaborate on the impact of a decision. Especially in the field of EAM, where typically several stakeholders are involved, (1) collaboration support, (2) multiple viewpoints and (3) early documentation are necessary during the decision-making process. The adapted metamodel is shown by Fig. 1. Therein, we highlight added concepts, whereas the other concepts are adopted from [4].

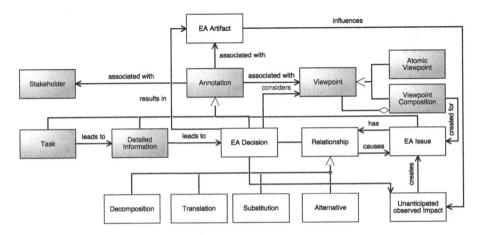

Fig. 1. Collaborative decision metamodel

A key differentiation to Plataniotis et al. [4] is the relationship from *EA Decision* to a *Viewpoint*. In their work, the authors relate an *EA Decision* to a particular *Layer* of ArchiMate [5]. Layers can be regarded as specific viewpoints in line with the ISO Std. 42010 [3], i.e. as "work product establishing the conventions for the construction, interpretation and use of architecture views". The layers are nevertheless specific as they target non-overlapping subsets of the EA. Like described in Sect. 2 complex interdependencies within the EA make it impossible to confine a decision to a single layer. Thus, we understand a decision to consider different, potentially overlapping viewpoints, instead of layers. In [9] we presented an interactive cockpit approach using a viewpoint composition consisting of several coherent viewpoints. Analyzing EAs using a viewpoint composition that can be considered in parallel supports stakeholders in the decision-making process and prohibits loosing the overall context. Thus we distinguish two types of viewpoints: Atomic Viewpoint and Viewpoint Composition.

Atomic Viewpoint: An *Atomic Viewpoint* is a single Viewpoint.
Example: "Application Usage Viewpoint" (see [5]).

Viewpoint Composition: A *Viewpoint Composition* forms a composite structure and consists of coherent Atomic Viewpoints or other *Viewpoint Compositions* needed by stakeholders to satisfy their information demands. Furthermore a *Viewpoint Composition* is assembled to consider an *EA Issue*.
Example: A *Viewpoint Composition* considering the *EA Issue* "Outdated Technologies" consisting of several *Atomic Viewpoints*, like "Application Usage Viewpoint" or "Infrastructure Usage Viewpoint" (see [5]).

We extend the metamodel of Plataniotis et al. [4] with the concept of the stakeholder – in line with the ISO Std. 42010 [3] – reflecting a person, role, or group having a concern in the EA and hence being involved in the decision-making process.
Example: Software Engineer, Business Process Owner, or Technology Expert.

Stakeholders provide different contributions during a decision-making process: they raise *EA Issues* to be addressed, provide relevant *Detailed Information* on the EA not covered by the model, assume responsibility for *Tasks*, or take *EA Decisions*. EA Issues and *EA Decisions*, as already present in the model of Plataniotis et al. [4], very much reflect the ex-post perspective of decision-making, whereas Detailed *Information* and *Tasks* are intermediary in the process. By making them explicit, we provide a means to document the rationale of a decision.

Detailed Information: Detailed Information enables modeling considerations, discussions and findings during the decision-making process that are necessary for taking a decision.
Example: Stakeholder A wants to highlight three architectural elements and assign them with a comment, because the stakeholders discuss about these elements.

Task: By using the *Task* concept open questions can be documented that have to be clarified by a stakeholder until the next meeting. A *Task* leads to *Detailed Information*.
Example: Stakeholder B has to identify the responsible for a particular part of the EA that they want to retire.

The different stakeholders' contributions in the decision-making process, ranging from *EA Issues*, over *Detailed Information* and *Tasks*, to *EA Decisions*, impact specific parts of the overall EA. In [4] these "parts" are alluded to as *EA Artifacts*. The contributions on the other hand are contextual, i.e. depend on the decision-making process in which they are created. Hence, we identify the contributions with the concept of the *Annotation* as introduced in [9]. This approach uses annotations to enrich the EA description with additional knowledge. We defined several interactive functions that support stakeholders in analyzing and planning an EA. An impact analysis is an example for such an interactive function. Each function enriches the description of the EA with an *Annotation* that explicitly represents analyzing and decision-making information. Accordingly, *Annotations* are associated with stakeholders, who performed the function and elements of the EA, i.e. the *EA Artifacts* of [4].

In the following we want to detail the concept of *EA Decisions*. Plataniotis et al. define an *EA Artifact* as a result of an *EA Decision*. We want to detail this definition. Aier et al. [7] describe three types of changing elements of an EA. Thereby elements can be introduced, retired or optimized. In other words an *EA Decision* is based on current valid *EA Artifacts* (as-is landscape) and transfers them into *EA Artifacts* in the future (to-be landscape). According to this approach we refine the "results in" relationship to be these three types. Moreover *EA Artifacts* need to have a period they are valid. Moreover *EA Artifacts* are affected by an *EA Change* and need to have a period they are valid. Thus this period is independent of an introduction or retirement, we added a particular date for both concepts. Through the relative independency of life-cycle planning information, which is manifested by the validity attributes, and the decision related controlling information of changes there could be three scenarios and their possible combinations: (1) consistent decisions of change in accordance with the specified lifecycle, (2) premature introduction of *EA Artifacts* before starting the life-cycle and (3) deferred retirement of *EA Artifacts* after the specified artifact" lifecycle. Figure 2 shows these metamodel changes in detail.

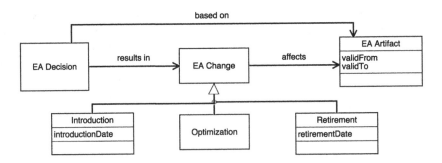

Fig. 2. EA Decision Consequences on EA Artifacts

The metamodel of [4] also includes a concept named *Unanticipated observed impact*. However such impacts can only be documented after taking a decision, because such impacts can only be found after implementation. Furthermore the authors describe decision strategies to document which criteria are used to take the decision.

To support stakeholders in decision-making, in line with Plataniotis et al. [10], we suggest a Decision Viewpoint that provides all collected information during the decision-making process and the current state. At the end the Decision Viewpoint can be used as documentation and stored in a central knowledge base. The knowledge base affords stakeholders to learn about decisions from the past to take better decisions in the future. Another advantage of such a knowledge base is that new employees get a fast insight about the architecture and what the reasons are how the architecture looks like. An example of such Decision Viewpoint is exemplarily described in Sect. 4.

4   Collaborative Decision-Making Scenario

In this section we adapt the example case of Plataniotis et al. [4] to illustrate our collaborative decision modeling approach. The example case is based on ArchiSurance that is a virtual insurance company introduced to demonstrate the capabilities of ArchiMate [5].

ArchiSurance hired an external consultant named John. He is a business consultant with experience in changing business models. His mandate is to change ArchiSurance's sales model towards an intermediate one. As changing business models has impact on the underlying applications and the IT infrastructure, he involve Mike – an application responsible – and Jack – an infrastructure and security expert. They both have particular concerns and need specific viewpoints to satisfy their information demands, i.e., to assess the impact of the business model change.

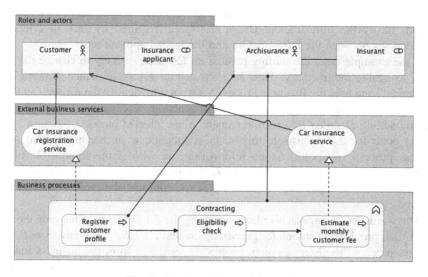

Fig. 3. Business Process Viewpoint

To analyze the current state of the EA and to generate implementation alternatives, they meet at an Architecture Cockpit like described by Jugel et al. [9]. The cockpit provides a *Viewpoint Composition* consisting of three different ArchiMate viewpoints

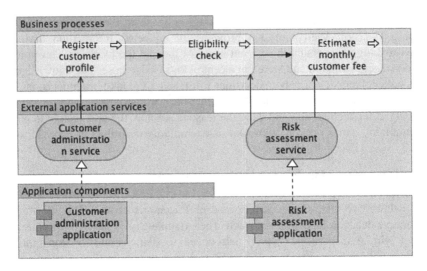

Fig. 4. Application Usage Viewpoint

side-by-side, namely the Business Process Viewpoint, the Application Usage Viewpoint and the Infrastructure Usage Viewpoint. Exemplarily Fig. 3 shows the Business Process Viewpoint and Fig. 4 the Application Usage Viewpoint. The Business Process Viewpoint shows the overall context about ArchiSurance's sales model. By using this information, John wants to adapt the sales model. The Application Usage Viewpoint describes the applications, their application services and the business processes they support. Lastly the Infrastructure Usage Viewpoint required by Jack describes the dependencies between the infrastructure and the hosted applications.

In the example case, the starting point is an *EA Issue*, namely to change the sales model to enable intermediary. Thus John creates an *EA Issue* named "Intermediary sales model" and uses the Business Process Viewpoint to identify the *EA Artifact* that is affected by the *EA Issue*. This is the business function "Contracting", which he indicates by adding *Detailed Information* named "Main affected business function". As a starting point for the discussion, this business function is further highlighted in the business process viewpoint. As no information, on who is the responsible of this business function, is given, John creates a *Task* named "Clarify responsibilities" setting a schedule to the next meeting, because this is an additional stakeholder that has to be involved.

Afterwards John suggests his idea by creating the *EA Decision* "Changing the sales model" that provides a solution for previously created *EA Issue*. John envisions that the business process "Register customer profile" is separated from the business function "Contracting". Instead he recommends creating a new business function named "Create customized insurance package". The results of his suggestion can be modeled according to [7] by relating the impacted *EA Artifacts* by one of the defined relationship types. For example, a new *EA Artifact* named "Create customized insurance package" of the type business function is needed that has to be related to the *EA Decision* by an

Introduction concept. Furthermore, the business process "Register customer profile" has to be retired to realize the new demand by superseding it with a new business interaction named "Customer profile registration". Mike recognizes that changing the business process "Register customer profile" is the only change in the business model that may have impacts on underlying applications and infrastructure. He documents this finding by adding *Detailed Information* named "May have impacts on applications and infrastructure" and relating it with the business process "Register customer profile".

The state of the discussion after these initial considerations is represented in Fig. 5. The figure uses color-coding and comment-like symbols to indicate the different decisions. Thereby elements with a green fill color represent *EA Artifacts* that have to be introduced whereas elements that have to be retired are represented with a red fill color. Furthermore, the *EA Artifact* with the blue fill color represents the starting point and bears the *Detailed Information* "Main affected business function" described above.

Next they analyze the impacts of the business process change on application services and applications by using the impact analysis function. Thereby affected elements are assigned to new *Detailed Information* named "Impact Analysis of Register Customer profile" representing the analysis result and are highlighted on the views with a brown fill color. The result is, that the application service "customer administration service" has to be adapted to the new situation.

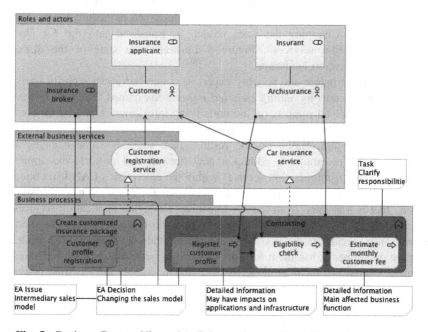

Fig. 5. Business Process Viewpoint (Sales model adaptions) (Color figure online)

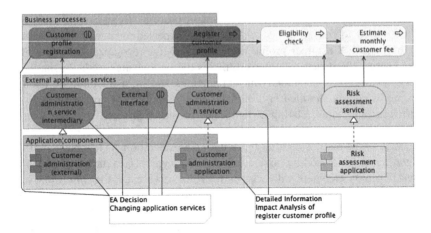

Fig. 6. Application Usage Viewpoint (with adaptations)

Mike recommends retaining the application service, but to use an external application service named "Customer administration service intermediary" that provides customer information from intermediary. An interface is created to link the two application services, enabling the external service to provide customer information to the internal one. Mike documents his idea by creating a correspondent *EA Decision* "Changing application services" according to the described procedure above. Thereby the *EA Decision* "Changing the sales model" is translated into the *EA Decision* "Changing application services". Figure 6 illustrates the state of the discussion regarding the application landscape.

Jack, the infrastructure and security expert, is concerned about security issues. He documents his concerns by adding *Detailed Information* named "Security Issues". He demands to consider all impacts on the underlying infrastructure and hence they perform an impact analysis choosing the application "Customer administration application" as starting point. Based on the results, Jack suggests some changes at the infrastructure. He recommends adding a new firewall that protects the application service "Customer administration service" within the enterprise's LAN from undesired external access. The group agrees and they take an *EA Decision* named "Adding a Firewall" that is translated from the *EA Decision* "Changing application services".

Concluding they discuss whether the proposed and taken *EA Decisions* should be realized. They decide to discuss the implications with other employees from their respective departments, ask them for opinions and possible alternatives that should be taken into account. To facilitate these discussions, they apply the Decision Viewpoint that shows all relevant information during the process. In this example case the Decision Viewpoint (see Table 1) is illustrated using a table. Alternatively decision graphs like described in [10] can be used.

Table 1. Decision Viewpoint

Decision Viewpoint		
Stakeholder	Annotation	EA Artifacts & Viewpoints
John	EA Issue "Intermediary sales model"	Business Process Viewpoint
John	Information "Main affected business function"	Contracting
John	Task "Clarify responsibilities"	Contracting
John	EA Decision "Changing the sales model"	**Introduce:** Create customized insurance package, Customer profile registration, Insurance broker **Retire:** Register customer profile
...	...	...

5 Conclusion and Outlook

Our research raised the question how a framework for supporting collaborative decision-making in the EA context looks like. We have analyzed and extended related work about fundamental decisional support for enterprise architectures by introducing our generic decisional metamodel for collaborative enterprise architecture engineering. To close the connection between the *EA Decision* and the *EA Artifact* we have extended related work results and mapped our decisional metamodel to the viewpoint-supported Enterprise Architecture approach form ArchiMate and other standards. The illustration of a working decision-making scenario aims to show the usage of our decisional metamodel into a real-life EA scenario. We are planning to validate our decisional framework in our current and future research with selected industrial partners. Currently we are performing case studies with enterprise architects and students in the architecture cockpit at Reutlingen University. We have to investigate in our future research and work out the limitations of the approach. Future work should also respect extended decisional contexts, like the decisional case and inputs from adaptive case management and new elements from knowledge management. Another important idea we are currently researching is about connecting architectural decisions with rationales and in a planned extension with explanations and semantic-supported inferences for architectural impacts.

References

1. Bente, S., Bombosch, U., Langade, S.: Collaborative Enterprise Architecture. Morgan Kaufmann Elsevier, Waltham (2012)
2. Tang, A., Babar, M.A., Gorton, I., Han, J.: A survey of architecture design rationale. J. Syst. Softw. **79**(12), 1792–1804 (2006)

3. International Organization Of Standardization: ISO/IEC/IEEE 42010:2011 - Systems and software engineering - Architecture description (2011)

4. Plataniotis, G., De Kinderen, S., Proper, H.A.: EA anamnesis: an approach for decision making analysis in enterprise architecture. Int. J. Inf. Syst. Model. Des. **4**(1), 75–95 (2014)

5. The Open Group: ArchiMate 2.0 Specification (2012)

6. Buckl, S., Matthes, F., Schweda, C.M.: Socio-technic dependency and rationale models for the enterprise architecture management function. In: 5th International Workshop on Ontology, Models, Conceptualization and Epistemology in Social, Artificial and Natural Systems (ONTOSE 2011), London (2011)

7. Aier, S., Buckl, S., Gleichauf, B., Matthes, F., Schweda, C.M., Winter, R.: Towards a more integrated EA planning: linking transformation planning with evolutionary change. In: 5th International Workshop on Enterprise Modelling and Information Systems Architectures, Hamburg (2011)

8. Yu, E.S.K.: Towards modelling and reasoning support for early-phase requirements engineering. In: Proceedings of the 3rd IEEE International Symposium on Requirements Engineering, Annapolis, pp. 226–235 (1997)

9. Jugel, D., Schweda, C.M.: Interactive functions of a cockpit for enterprise architecture planning. In: 18th International Enterprise Distributed Object Computing Conference Workshops and Demonstrations (EDOCW), Ulm, pp. 33–40 (2014)

10. Plataniotis, G., De Kinderen, S, Proper, H.A.: Relating decisions in enterprise architecture using decision design graphs. In: 17th IEEE International Enterprise Distributed Object Computing (EDOC), Vancouver, pp. 139–146 (2013)

Towards an Enterprise Architecture Benefits Measurement Instrument

Henk Plessius[(⊠)], Marlies van Steenbergen, and Raymond Slot

University of Applied Sciences Utrecht, Utrecht, The Netherlands
{henk.plessius,marlies.vansteenbergen,
raymond.slot}@hu.nl

Abstract. Based on the Enterprise Architecture Value Framework (EAVF) - a generic framework to classify benefits of Enterprise Architecture (EA) - a measurement instrument for EA benefits has been developed and tested in a survey with 287 respondents. In this paper we present the results of this survey in which stakeholders of EA were questioned about the kind of benefits they experience from EA in their organization. We use the results of the survey to evaluate the framework and develop a foundation for the measurement instrument. The results of the survey show a moderate support for the assumptions underlying the framework. Applying ordinal regression, we derived sets of questions for ten out of the twelve classes in the framework. These sets constitute the first step in defining a final EA measurement instrument for establishing actual benefits in the classes of the framework.

Keywords: Enterprise architecture · Benefits · Value framework · Benefits measurement instrument

1 Introduction

Enterprise Architecture (EA) is an instrument for decision makers to structure and manage organizations from an integral perspective. EA provides a holistic view of the organization, including customer offerings, business processes, information systems, technical infrastructure and the relations between these aspects. The purpose of EA is twofold: on the one hand it provides insight into the actual state of the organization, enabling the organization to determine the impact of changes. On the other hand it gives direction to such changes by sketching the design principles and designs that best fit the organization's ambitions and goals. EA is the bridge between strategy and execution [1].

EA is seen as an instrument for organizations to achieve their business goals. The argument behind this view is that a well-structured, well-aligned organization is more cost-effective, agile and effective. The actual benefits of EA have been subject to academic research by different authors. The number of benefits claimed by authors is large, though proof of actual benefits is less abundant [2, 3]. For example, Boucharas et al. [2] found in a structured literature review 107 academic publications mentioning benefits, of which 33 were found relevant to the question of relating EA to benefits but only 14 fulfilled the qualitative requirements of the literature review. In these 14

© Springer International Publishing Switzerland 2015
A. Persson and J. Stirna (Eds.): CAiSE 2015 Workshops, LNBIP 215, pp. 363–374, 2015.
DOI: 10.1007/978-3-319-19243-7_34

publications, 100 different benefits are mentioned. In recent years various literature studies [2–7] as well as empirical studies on actually achieved benefits have appeared [8–10]. In these publications all authors define EA benefits in their own way. Where most authors introduce some kind of categorizing of benefits, these categorizations differ between authors as well. This lack of a common framework of EA benefits makes it difficult to compare different studies and is an obstacle in augmenting other research results.

In an earlier paper [11] we introduced a generic framework for classifying EA benefits, the Enterprise Architecture Value Framework (EAVF). We have used this framework as a starting point for a survey concerning perceived benefits in organizations. The first results of this survey [10] not only provide an interesting insight into the kind of benefits that are actually perceived within organizations, but they can be used to develop the EAVF into a EA benefits measurement instrument as well.

The research question we aim to answer in this paper is: *Is it possible to develop an EA benefits measurement instrument based on the EA Value Framework?*

In the next section of this paper we sketch the theoretical background to our research question, followed in Sect. 3 by an overview of the research method used in further developing the EAVF and the derived benefits measurement instrument. The results are presented and discussed in Sects. 4 and 5 and followed by conclusions, limitations and further research in Sect. 6.

2   Theoretical Background

In the literature, no common framework for classifying EA benefits can be found. The framework we developed in our research [11] is based on two theses:

1. Organizations benefit from EA when EA contributes towards their business goals.
2. Benefits may evolve from the inception of the architecture towards the implementation of architectural designs.

For the contribution towards business goals, we decided to use the four well-known categories of the Balanced Scorecard [12, 13]: the Financial, Customer, Internal and Learning and Growth perspectives as many organizations use these to classify their goals and it has been used by other authors to classify benefits as well [2, 5].

In order to follow the evolution of benefits in time, we introduce the lifecycle of EA in which we distinguish three main phases:

- the *Development* of the architecture where principles and models are developed and registered. In this phase, usually the architects are leading;
- the *Realization* phase where architectural designs are implemented and projects have to comply with the architecture. In most enterprises, project managers are in the lead in this phase;
- the *Use* phase, where (parts of) the new architecture have been implemented and used in operations. In this phase, the actual operational benefits are obtained and the lead is with business line managers.

The idea of benefits developing in time can be found with other authors as well. For example, Foorthuis et al. [8] explicitly distinguish benefits in the project execution phase from other benefits where Tamm et al. [3] distinguish between benefits flowing directly from EA and benefits resulting from the implementation of EA plans.

Combining the two mutually independent axes results in the EA Value Framework (EAVF) as depicted in Fig. 1. The EAVF essentially divides the field of EA benefits in twelve classes of EA benefits: four perspectives times three phases.

BSC Perspective / Phase	Financial	Customer	Internal	Learning & Growth
Development				
Realization				
Use				

Fig. 1. The Enterprise Architecture Value Framework

The EA benefits measurement instrument we are developing is based on this framework and essentially consists of a series of questions that may be used to determine the perceived and realized benefits in every cell of the framework. These questions are derived from benefits as reported in the literature, especially from the work of Boucharas et al. [2]. Examples of these questions are given in Plessius et al. [11].

3   Research Method

In order to validate the EAVF and the EA benefits measurement instrument we conducted a survey. In this survey we defined for each cell in the EAVF one overall statement representing the class of benefits corresponding with that cell, as well as a number of questions representing the specific benefits belonging to that class. For instance, for the Learning and Growth perspective in the Realization phase we defined the main (class-representing) statement as:

- By applying Enterprise Architecture in projects the learning and innovative capacity of the organization is better.

with the following questions on specific benefits in the class:

- Projects carried out under architecture provide a better understanding of the limitations of the solution.
- Projects carried out under architecture feature a more substantive decision-making process.

- Projects carried out under architecture feature better sharing of knowledge.
- Projects carried out under architecture more often produce results that fit the operational management.
- Projects carried out under architecture produce more agility (flexibility).

The questions that ask about specific benefits, can be regarded as reflective measures of each main statement, giving a generic view on that class of benefits. In Sect. 5.2 we will examine which questions are most representative for each class.

All statements and questions were scored on a 5-point Likert scale. The survey was targeted at stakeholders of architecture in organizations. We included a question to be able to discern between the three roles that correspond with the rows of the EAVF:

- *Developers* of architecture such as enterprise and domain architects.
- *Implementers* of architecture, such as solution architects, designers, developers and project managers.
- *Users* of architecture such as business line managers, IT managers and staff.

Based on their answer to this question, the respondents were presented with the questions on benefits related to the corresponding row. We included some questions on the background of the respondents as well. The survey consisted of 97 questions and in this way less than 50 questions were presented to all respondents.

From over 3000 mailings we received 287 fully completed responses where 110 respondents have answered the questions on the Development of architecture, 68 on the Realization of architecture and 109 on the architecture in Use. Based on the general questions on their background, we found the characteristics of the respondents congruent with the results found in other surveys (see for example [8, 14]) and as they are encountered in practice.

For the statistics in the next sections we have used SPSS edition 22 (Statistical Package for the Social Sciences, nowadays an IBM product). In most questions, the extremes of the Likert scale were hardly used and in order to reduce the number of possibilities - especially for the regression analysis (as described in Sect. 5.2) - we decided to bundle the answers in three categories:

- (very) negative benefits reported (Likert categories 1 and 2);
- neutral, neither positive nor negative benefits reported (Likert category 3);
- (very) positive benefits reported (Likert categories 4 and 5).

By combining the original answers in these three categories we reduced the original questions to questions if benefits could be reported and if these benefits were deemed positive, negative or neutral. Given the small number of extremes in the original answers, we consider this reduction justified.

The survey has been carried out in the Netherlands with statements and questions in Dutch. For this paper all statements and questions have been translated into English, but there may be slight differences in meaning between the translated statement or question and the original one.

4   Benefits Perceived

In this section we present the results of the survey providing an overall picture of the kinds of EA benefits (positive and negative) that are actually perceived by organizations. Next, in Sect. 5, we will use the survey results to validate the EAVF and the survey questions as a measurement instrument for the twelve EA benefit classes.

4.1   Statements on the Benefits Classes

All respondents – regardless of their role - answered the twelve generic statements for the twelve classes of the EAVF. The results are presented in Fig. 2 where the numbers in each cell are the percentage of respondents who found that EA had a positive effect in that particular area, respectively found no effect of EA or found a negative effect of EA. The numbers are statistically significant as shown in Plessius et al. [10].

BSC Perspective / Phase		Financial	Customer	Internal	Learning & Growth
Development	+	78.1	48.4	78.2	82.1
	0	21.5	51.2	19.6	15.7
	-	0.4	0.4	2.2	2.2
Realization	+	75.9	47.5	50.0	53.0
	0	21.7	50.2	42.9	43.0
	-	2.4	2.3	7.1	4.0
Use	+	47.8	29.8	57.9	77.6
	0	50.0	67.6	38.8	21.2
	-	2.2	2.6	3.3	1.2

+ : percentage (very) positive; 0 : percentage neutral; - : percentage (very) negative

Fig. 2.   Perceived benefits of Enterprise Architecture in the EAVF

From Fig. 2 it is clear that – except in the Customer perspective – respondents perceive an overall positive effect of EA. Even where the percentage of positive responses is less than fifty percent, the overall effect is neutral rather than negative. These effects are consistent over the three roles: it seems there is consensus between stakeholders on the benefits of EA in each cell of the framework.

4.2   Questions on Specific Benefits

In all, we asked 70 questions about the occurrence of specific benefits distributed over the twelve cells. Of these questions, 17 questions did not show a significant result in the one-sided binominal test we performed ($p < 0.05$). These questions are not included in this section. In the following tables we present for each row in the EAVF the 3 questions that received the highest percentage of (very) positive answers and the 3 questions that received the lowest percentage of (very) positive answers.

In the development phase (Table 1) we find that the benefits perceived by most respondents are concerned with providing insight. The benefits perceived the least are related to the effect of EA on governance. One might conclude that the development phase provides insight, but that to turn these insights into decision-making lags behind. This is in line with previous research [8]. Still, more than fifty percent of the respondents indicate perceived benefits for each of the bottom 3 benefits.

Table 1. Top and bottom benefits perceived in the development phase

Perspective	Question	+ (%)	0 (%)	− (%)
Top 3				
Internal	By developing Enterprise Architecture more insight into the target architecture has been gained	88.7	11.3	0.0
Internal	By developing Enterprise Architecture the organization has more grip through a coherent set of principles	85.3	12.7	2.0
Financial	By developing Enterprise Architecture the risks involved in business processes and IT are more evident	81.6	17.4	1.0
Bottom 3				
Learning and growth	By developing Enterprise Architecture the governance structure of the organization has become better	51.5	48.5	0.0
Internal	The final products of the Enterprise Architecture (baseline, target architecture, goals, principles) have received much support from the accountable management	54.1	36.7	9.2
Financial	By developing Enterprise Architecture compliance with laws and regulations is better	59.8	38.2	2.0

In the realization phase (Table 2) we find a similar distinction. The top 3 contains benefits concerned with insight, while the bottom 3 consists of benefits related to actual project performance. Architecture does seem to contribute to better decision-making at the project portfolio level, but at the level of cost and time of individual projects EA does not seem to generate improvements.

In the use phase (Table 3) we find a less clear-cut situation. The alignment between business processes and IT is in the top 3, but better cooperation within the organization is in the bottom 3. It seems as though business and IT have started to communicate with each other, but there is still space for improvement. Clearly the respondents see no effect from EA on market shares for most organizations.

The results shown in Tables 1, 2 and 3 are in line with previous research [8]. As the responses seem representative for the field, they present a good starting point for

Table 2. Top and bottom benefits perceived in the realization phase

Perspective	Question	+ (%)	0 (%)	− (%)
Top 3				
Internal	In projects carried out under architecture the architecture has contributed to making the project's impact on the organization more clear	89.2	10.8	0.0
Learning and growth	Projects carried out under architecture provide a better understanding of the limitations of the solution	84.4	14.0	1.6
Internal	In portfolio decisions architecture contributes to good decision-making	83.6	16.4	0.0
Bottom 3				
Financial	Projects carried out under architecture have lower cost than other projects	19.5	43.9	36.6
Internal	Projects carried out under architecture have a better record of on-time completion	23.5	56.9	19.6
Internal	Projects carried out under architecture have a better record of staying within budget	24.1	59.2	16.7

Table 3. Top and bottom benefits perceived in the use phase

Perspective	Question	+ (%)	0 (%)	− (%)
Top 3				
Customer	Since the organization has been using Enterprise Architecture supply chain integration has been better	71.4	23.5	5.1
Internal	Since the organization has been using Enterprise Architecture the alignment between the business processes and IT has been better	70.5	25.3	4.2
Internal	Since the organization has been using Enterprise Architecture the IT infrastructure has been utilized better	68.4	26.5	5.1
Bottom 3				
Customer	Since the organization has been using Enterprise Architecture market share has grown	8.6	84.3	7.1
Internal	Since the organization has been using Enterprise Architecture cooperation within the organization has grown	48.9	44.7	6.4
Financial	Since the organization has been using Enterprise Architecture compliance with laws and regulations has been better	49.5	49.4	1.1

validating the EAVF and the measurement instrument based on the EAVF. We will discuss this in the next section.

5   Evaluation

5.1   Propagation of Benefits

From the meaning of the EAVF dimensions it may be expected that there exist positive relationships:

- *Horizontally* from right to left as the Balanced Score Card argues that results in the learning and growth perspective should impact the customer and internal process perspectives, whereas the latter two should impact the financial perspective.
- *Vertically* from top to bottom as the Architecture life cycle implies that results from the development phase should impact the realization phase and the results from the realization phase should impact results in the use phase.

We tested if these relationships hold in the EAVF as well by calculating the correlations between cells horizontally and vertically. Figures 3 and 4 show the Spearman's rho values found with p < 0.05.

	Spearman's Rho
Customer -> Financial	0.486
Internal -> Financial	0.349
Learning & Growth -> Customer	0.332
Learning & Growth -> Internal	0.261

Fig. 3.   Horizontal correlations between cells in the use phase

	Financial	Customer	Internal	Learning & Growth
Development -> Realization	0.484	0.586	0.140	0.359
Realization -> Use	0.224	0.292	0.362	0.362

Fig. 4.   Vertical correlations between phases

The horizontal relationships (between the perspectives of the Balanced Scorecard) were only tested for the use phase, as this is the phase in which the end results of EA are realized. The results in Fig. 3 show a moderate correlation from the customer and internal perspectives with the financial perspective. The relation between customer and financial is largest. This stresses the importance of the customer perspective, which in practice often gets little exposure (see Fig. 2).

Looking at correlations between the phases we find correlations with a Pearson's rho > 0.300 between most phases. The correlation between development and realization in the internal perspective is lowest.

The correlation results seem to support the underlying assumptions of the EAVF (EA benefits can be related to organizational goals and the benefits may evolve in time).

5.2   The EA Benefits Measurement Instrument

In order to develop the benefits measurement instrument we researched if the questions defined for each class cover the main statement of that class, or, stated differently, can we predict the outcome of the main statement (the view on the EAVF-class as a whole) from the corresponding questions (the actual benefits in that class)? If this is possible, the questions form a sound basis for a questionnaire.

To research this question we used the method of ordinal regression for each cell with the main statement as dependent variable and the questions as independent variables. The link variable used is the logit as the distributions were varying across different cells and we wanted to use the same link function for every cell.

For each cell we built several models; starting with individual questions we took the best fitting question and added questions while the prerequisites were satisfied. The prerequisites we used to accept a question in the model are: significance of model fit < 0.05, Pearson's goodness of fit > 0.05 and significance of parallel lines > 0.05.

In ten out of the twelve cells of the EAVF we found a relation between the dependent variable (the overall statement) and some of the independent variables (the questions). As a threshold for acceptance we used a Nagelkerke pseudo $R^2 > 0.250$, which in itself is low but can be defended as this is a first try at validating the instrument and we did not want to reject possible relations prematurely. For discussion purposes we present here one of the results (Table 4), corresponding with the Learning and Growth perspective in the Realization phase. All results can be requested from the authors.

Table 4. Model example

Phase	Realization
View	Learning and growth
Statement (dependent variable)	By applying Enterprise Architecture in projects the learning and innovative capacity of the organization is better
Questions included in model	- Projects carried out under architecture provide a better understanding of the limitations of the solution
	- Projects carried out under architecture feature better sharing of knowledge
	- Projects carried out under architecture more often produce results that fit the operational management
	- Projects carried out under architecture produce more agility (flexibility)
Questions not included in model	- Projects carried out under architecture feature a more substantive decision-making process
Statistics	Nagelkerke: 0.499
	Significance of model fit: 0.000
	Pearson's goodness of fit: 0.256
	Significance parallel lines: 0.812

As can be seen from Table 4, from four out of the five questions around 50 % of the overall statement can be explained, whereas for the fifth question no statistical evidence was found, as adding this question gave rise to a quasi-complete separation of data.

In most cells, adding the excluded questions to the model made the model fit statistically not significant ($p >= 0.05$) or the test of parallel lines failed. Adding more responses could help to overcome this. In Fig. 5 we have summarized the results in the framework, where the number gives the Nagelkerke pseudo R^2 of the best-fitting model found.

	Financial	Customer	Internal	Learning &Growth
Development		0.299	0.371	
Realization	0.363	0.444	0.620	0.499
Use	0.399	0.301	0.549	0.303

Fig. 5. Model fit in the cells of the EAVF

In the empty cells there seemed to be a quasi-complete data separation for all individual questions, so we could not use ordinal regression for model building.

6   Conclusions and Further Research

The contribution of this paper is twofold: we introduce a framework, the EA Value Framework, for classifying EA benefits that combines the aspects of goal and time. To be able to compare results from different EA benefit research initiatives and to enlarge our knowledge base on EA benefits by building on each other's research, it is important to share a common framework. Supplementing this framework we show the current state regarding EA benefits in the Netherlands, based on a survey held in the first months of 2014.

The results of this survey show the kind of benefits organizations experience at the moment. The main conclusions we can draw from the results are first of all that regarding the customer perspective, benefits reported are low. This is consistent with findings in the literature (for example, Boucharas et al. [2] found only two benefits in the Customer perspective out of 100 benefits) and our observation that many architects are focused on the internals of the organization (processes and information) and not on the relation with the outside world. Secondly, we found that most benefits seem to occur in the Development phase, which may be caused by the fact that in the Realization phase project managers may perceive EA primarily as a constraint instead of a support and in the Use phase results can not be attributed to EA only. In future research we want to explore these hypotheses in case studies.

The results of the survey appear to be representative of the EA field (as discussed in Sect. 3), so we used them to evaluate the EAVF as well. We found moderate support for the assumed underlying relations between the cells of the framework which in turn give support to the validity of our framework.

Finally, we used the results to continue the development of an EA benefits measurement instrument based on the EAVF. This instrument consists of a series of questions for every cell in the EAVF, which are derived from benefits as reported in the literature. These questions have been used to predict the overall outcome in the cell, as measured in an overall statement for that cell. Using ordinal regression, we found valid models for ten of the twelve cells. These models constitute the first step in defining a final questionnaire to measure actual benefits for a specific cell.

Our research has its limitations. As our survey asks for the perception of the respondents concerning EA benefits, the outcome is subjective. This is a frequently occurring phenomenon with evaluative surveys but there are indications that this kind of survey leads to reliable results. For example Wall et al. [15] show that perceptions are a reliable indicator of actual organizational performance. Secondly, the respondents to our survey are self-selected and therefor are not a random sample of the EA community. As a consequence some bias in the answers may be present. Moreover, as the survey is conducted in the Netherlands, care must be taken in generalizing the results. Finally, as the twelve main statements are generic by nature, they leave room for different interpretations.

In order to examine if the overall statements cover the cells fully and to further refine the results from our survey, we plan to perform case studies in organizations with the EA benefits measurement instrument. In that way, we expect to get a better understanding which benefits are most important for organizations and gather 'best practi-ces' on how to maximize the benefits of EA.

Acknowledgment. The authors wish to thank all respondents to the survey. Without their diligent answering our questions, this research would not have been possible.

References

1. Federation of EA Professionals Organizations.: A common perspective on enterprise architecture. Archit. Governance Mag. **9**(9–4), 11–17 (2013)
2. Boucharas, V., Steenbergen, M., van Jansen, S., Brinkkemper, S.: The contribution of enterprise architecture to the achievement of organizational goals: establishing the enterprise architecture benefits framework. Technical report UU-CS-2010–2014, Utrecht (2010)
3. Tamm, T., Seddon, P.B., Shanks, G., Reynolds, P.: How does enterprise architecture add value to organizations? Commun. Assoc. Inf. Syst. **28**, 141–168 (2011). Article 10
4. Niemi, E.: Enterprise architecture benefits: perceptions from literature and practice. In: Niemi, E., Ylimäki, T., Hämäläinen, N. (eds.) Evaluation of Enterprise and Software Architectures: Critical Issues, Metrics and Practices: [AISA Project 2005–2008], University of Jyväskylä, Information Technology Research Institute, Jyväskylä (Tietotekniikan tutkimusinstituutin julkaisuja, ISSN 1236-1615; 18), (CD-ROM) (2008). ISBN 978-951-39-3108-7
5. Schelp, J., Stutz, M.: A balanced scorecard approach to measure the value of enterprise architecture. J. Enterp. Architect. **3**(1), 5–12 (2007)
6. Lange, M., Mendling J., Recker, J.: A comprehensive EA benefit realization model – an exploratory study. In: 45th Hawaii International Conference on System Science (HICSS), pp. 4230–4239. IEEE (2012)

7. Wan, H., Luo, X., Johansson, B., Chen, H.: Enterprise architecture benefits. In: ICISO 2013, p. 62 (2013)
8. Foorthuis, R., Steenbergen, M., van Mushkudiani, M., Bruls, W., Brinkkemper, S.: On course but not there yet: enterprise architecture conformance and benefits in systems development. In: ICIS 2010 Proceedings, Paper 110 (2010)
9. Steenbergen, M. van Foorthuis, R., Mushkudiani, N., Bruls, W., Brinkkemper, S., Bos, R.: Achieving enterprise architecture benefits – what makes the difference? In: Proceedings of the 15th IEEE International Enterprise Distributed Object Computing Conference Workshop Trends in Enterprise Architecture Research, pp. 350–359 (2011)
10. Plessius, H., Steenbergen, M., van Slot, R.: Perceived benefits from enterprise architecture. In: Eighth Mediterranean Conference on Information Systems, Verona, pp. 1–14 (2014)
11. Plessius, H., Slot, R., Pruijt, L.: On the categorization and measurability of enterprise architecture benefits with the enterprise architecture value framework. In: Aier, S., Ekstedt, M., Matthes, F., Proper, E., Sanz, J.L. (eds.) TEAR 2012. LNBIP, vol. 131, pp. 79–92. Springer, Heidelberg (2012)
12. Kaplan, R.S., Norton, D.P.: The balanced scorecard—measures that drive performance. Harv. Bus. Rev. **70**(1), 71–79 (1992)
13. Kaplan, R.S., Norton, D.P.: Strategy Maps: Converting Intangible Assets into Tangible Outcomes. Harvard Business Press, Boston (2004)
14. Obitz, T., Babu K.M.: Enterprise Architecture Expands its Role in Strategic Business Transformation. Infosys Enterprise Architecture Survey 2008/2009 (2009)
15. Wall, T.D., Michie, J., Patterson, M., Wood, S.J., Sheehan, M., Glegg, C.W., West, M.: On the validity of subjective measures of company performance. Pers. Psychol. **57**(1), 95–118 (2004)

Modelling Value with ArchiMate

Adina Aldea[1,2(✉)], Maria Eugenia Iacob[1], Jos van Hillegersberg[1],
Dick Quartel[2], and Henry Franken[2]

[1] Centre for Telematics and Information Technology, Twente University,
Enschede, Netherlands
{a.i.aldea,m.e.iacob,j.vanhillegersberg}@utwente.nl
[2] BiZZdesign, Enschede, Netherlands
{d.quartel,h.franken}@bizzdesign.nl

Abstract. This paper investigates the suitability of the ArchiMate modelling language for the purposes of modelling value and related concepts and approaches. Based on this we propose several improvement which can help enterprise architects come one step closer to being able to model all aspects of an organisation, from its strategy, to the value it should create and deliver, to the abilities which are needed to realise this value, and to the architecture which supports this value creation and delivery. This can aid with motivating the value of a project, making changes directly aimed at improving customer value, and visualising the value exchanges within the value network of the organisation.

Keywords: Value · Value network · e3value · Value exchange · Value stream · Enterprise architecture · ArchiMate

1 Introduction

The concept of value has been discussed since the days of Aristotle [1], and to this day it is still a point of debate for many scholars [2]. It is used in many different domains such as strategy, marketing, purchasing, supply chain management, etc. [3]. Therefore it is no surprise that value has a central role in debates about why an organisation exists. The creation and delivery of value is considered to be the core purpose of organisations [1]. The survivability and continued profitability of organisations are linked to their ability to fulfil their economic purpose, which is to create and distribute sufficient value to each primary stakeholder from their value network [4, 5].

In practice, the term of value is a common occurrence in discussions of business strategy [6]. A business strategy typically describes, at a high level, how an organisation intends to create and deliver value to its stakeholders. The execution of the strategy addresses the mobilisation and alignment of specific resources and capabilities [7]. Therefore, the change associated to strategy needs to realise a specific value.

Enterprise Architecture (EA) is a discipline which is focused on designing, planning and implementing of organisational change. A commonly used approach to illustrate the architecture of an organisation, in the context of EA, is the ArchiMate modelling language. This language supports the modelling of motivational elements (stakeholder, goal, assessment, driver, etc.), business elements (actor, value, business

© Springer International Publishing Switzerland 2015
A. Persson and J. Stirna (Eds.): CAiSE 2015 Workshops, LNBIP 215, pp. 375–388, 2015.
DOI: 10.1007/978-3-319-19243-7_35

process, business service, etc.), application elements (application service, application component, etc.), technology elements (network, device, node, etc.), and implementation and migration elements (plateau, work package, gap, etc.). Therefore it should be possible to use the ArchiMate language to model the strategy of the organisation, the value it should create and deliver, the abilities which are needed to realise this value, and the architecture which supports this value creation and delivery.

The main goal and contribution of this paper is an investigation into the suitability of the ArchiMate language for modelling value and value-related concepts and approaches. Based on a review of current literature we can provide a definition of value, identify the value-relating concepts, and determine relevant value-related approaches. We apply this knowledge to ArchiMate and assess if the current specification of the language is sufficiently developed for the purpose of value modelling. Based on this we suggest the adjustment of several definitions of ArchiMate concepts. Furthermore, we propose an extension to the current metamodel to support the modelling of these concepts and relationships. With the help of a case we demonstrate how value modelling can be done with ArchiMate.

Being able to model the relation between the architecture of an organisation and the value it intends to generate can have several benefits. First of all, it can become easier to motivate the value of specific projects that implement organisational change. By modelling the value that a goal is supposed to realise, we can reason that a project which realises that goal also contributes to realising the value. Second, by relating the value creation to elements of the architecture, an organisation can make changes to the value they create by making more precise adjustments to the specific elements of the architecture that help create the value. Last but not least, the exchanges that occur within the network of an organisation can be modelled by abstracting from how they are actually realised and focusing on the value that is being exchanged.

The research methodology we follow in this study is design science as proposed by [8]. The remainder of this paper has been structured according to the activities described in [8]. Hence, Sect. 2 includes a presentation of the current literature on value. Section 3 introduces the ArchiMate modelling language in its current specification. In Sect. 4 we assess the suitability of the ArchiMate modelling language and propose several adjustments together with a value centred metamodel. Section 5 contains a demonstration of our proposed metamodel with the help of a case study. The paper ends with some conclusions and pointers to future work (Sect. 6).

2   Value and Value-Related Concepts and Approaches

The purpose of this section is to present the current state of research relate the topic of value, the different types of approaches to value, and identify which concepts are used in relation to value. Based on this we propose a definition to value, identify relevant approaches and related concepts to be modelled with ArchiMate.

Many different definitions and meanings have been attributed to the concepts of value. The two most predominant views on value, which have been originally identified by Aristotle, are value-in-use and value-in-exchange.

Value-in-use represents the quality of something as perceived by users in relation to their needs [9]. This quality refers to how much that something is worth to someone. Value-in-use is created by integrating resources and applying competencies [1].

Value-in-exchange refers to the amount paid by the user to the seller for the value-in-use of something [9] which was created by the seller and distributed in the market [1]. This second view on value is related to the idea of bartering in which one party offers something to another party, which in return will offer something of equal value. The value (i.e., price of the exchange) is determined based on the supply and demand. By looking at value-in-exchange in this way it can be said that it represents the price the buyer is willing to pay in order to benefit from something produced by the seller.

The concept of value is used in many different domains such as strategy, marketing, purchasing, supply chain management, etc. [3]. Therefore it is no surprise that is has a central role in debates about why an organisation exists. Peter Drucker has defined the role of an organisation as a creator of value for the customer and society and not for the organisation and its shareholders [10, 11]. As a response to this view on value, a trend has emerged which states that organisations should create and maximize **value for all stakeholders** alike [12], whether they are shareholders, employees, customers, suppliers, community residents, natural environment [5]. By pursuing this approach to value generation, an organisation integrates short and long-term results and ties its operations to its financial needs and results [12].

2.1   Value Definition

Based on the different views presented on value, we formulate a basic and general definition of value. Simply said, *a value is the quality (worth) of something (tangible or intangible) as perceived by a stakeholder (in relation to their goals/needs).* This value can be realised by an actor and exchanged with other actors. This definition will be used as a basis for investigating the suitability of the current concept of value in ArchiMate.

2.2   Value-Related Concepts

Value within an organisation is not an isolated concept. By looking at the definition of value proposed in Sect. 2.1 of this paper, we can deduce that value is relative to a **stakeholder** and thus it does not exist independently of a stakeholder. Other interesting relationships to investigate are between value and strategic intent (strategy, goal, objective, etc.) and between value and capability (what an organisation can do to achieve a certain strategic intent).

As mentioned before, the generation of value for stakeholders is often used as an explanation for why an organisation should exist. By itself the pursuit of value generation does not give guidelines on how this value can be created or delivered, or which activities of an organisation generate the specific value [13]. The **strategy** of an organisation is typically used to describe how an organisation creates this value for its stakeholders [7]. The strategy can be further decomposed in long and short term goals/objectives which are aimed at achieving stakeholder value. Therefore we can say that each strategy, goal, objective has a specific value for a stakeholder.

Current literature has proposed **capabilities** as the way to link business and IT [14, 15] because they are focused on business outcomes [16]. Typically business outcomes are quantitative in nature. Another approach to capabilities presents them as what is required to produce any type of value within an organisation. This implies that an organisation's value creation is highly related to its various capabilities [17].

2.3   Value-Related Approaches

Over the years several approaches have been developed to support value, within different disciplines. In business management, Porter has introduced the **value chain** as an approach for analysing the sources of competitive advantage by examining the activities of an organisation and their interactions [18]. In essence, a value chain describes the sequence of value adding activities to bring products and services to the market [19]. Although the value chain has proven very useful in the past decades, it has become an inappropriate tool to analyse many industries today and uncover sources of value, particularly in sectors such as banking, insurance, telecommunication, news, entertainment, some areas of the public sector, etc. [20]. There are several reasons for this: products and services have become more dematerialised, the value chain no longer has a physical dimension, industries are constantly changing and evolving which makes the traditional view on value chains incompatible, and there is a strong co-operative behaviour [20].

The modern version of the value chain is the **value network**. The main difference between the two approaches is that the focus is not on the organisation or the industry (value chain), but on the value-creating system itself, in which different actors co-produce value (value network) [20]. The value network creates value through complex dynamic exchanges between one or more actors [21]. The **value exchange** represents the total pattern of values received, created, generated, and distributed by an organisation in all of its ongoing relationships with other actors [22]. These value exchanges can take the form of (1) goods, services and revenue (including contracts, invoices, confirmations, payment, etc.), (2) knowledge (strategic information, planning knowledge, technical know-how, etc.), (3) intangible benefits (customer loyalty, image enhancement, etc.) [21]. The e3value ontology [23] is an economic value-based modelling approach which incorporates ideas of the value chain, value network with value exchanges. Besides describing value exchanges of the value network, this ontology also captures behavioural aspects of such networks by using value activities, start and end stimuli and dependency paths. Another modelling approach, coming from lean management, is **value stream** mapping. Traditionally, it is used as a visual representation of all the activities needed to bring a product from raw material, through manufacturing, to the customer [24]. An organisation can have multiple of these value streams, each corresponding to one product/service. This type of approach to value is used to link the value creating activities of an organisation to the customer. Even though this approach was developed with the manufacturing sector in mind, it is now also used in service driven other sectors which are focused on delivering services, such as health care [25]. The activities of a value stream might differ, but the main principle of value stream mapping remains true: mapping of the activities that generate value for the customer. In the context of value networks and e3value, it can help with detailing, if so desired, of the activities/processes that create value for the customer. An organisation can use this information for improvements that are directly targeted at changing the value that is delivered to their customers.

3 ArchiMate

The core language distinguishes between three layers: business, application, and technology layer. Each of these layers contains structural, behavioural and informational aspects, and also defines relationships between and within the layers Fig. 1. A complete description of the ArchiMate language (core, motivation extension, implementation and migration extension) is offered by [26].

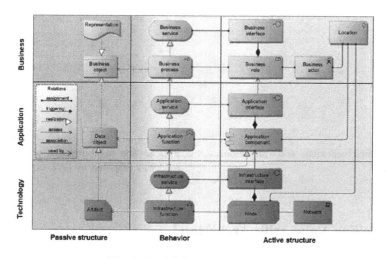

Fig. 1. ArchiMate core metamodel

The role of the motivation extension is to allow for the modelling of motivations or reasons that underlie the design or change of some enterprise architecture (Fig. 2).

The implementation and migration extension describes concepts that support the modelling of the architectural change process and provides insight into these changes and into portfolio and project management decisions (Fig. 3).

Iacob et al. [27] investigate if ArchiMate is suitable for modelling business strategy and value-related concepts. The conclusion of this research is that ArchiMate 2.1 Specification does not include all the necessary concepts, including the Capability concept. The authors also propose a metamodel for these new concepts, together with their relation to existing ArchiMate concepts (Fig. 4). In this metamodel we can see that the association relationship is used to model the relation between Value and other concepts.

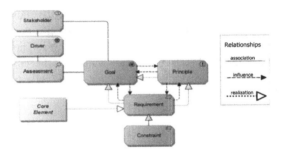

Fig. 2. Motivation extension metamodel

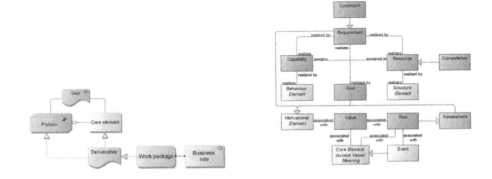

Fig. 3. Implementation and migration metamodel

Fig. 4. The capability and resource metamodel as proposed by [27]

4   Modelling Value with ArchiMate

Several relevant concepts can be identified based on the literature review presented in Sect. 2. By using these concepts as a base, we can determine if the current specification of the ArchiMate modelling language [26] is sufficiently developed to model value, and the related approaches and concepts. Table 1 contains the assessment of current ArchiMate concepts and proposes several improvements to each of them, including the addition of the concept of Capability to the language.

From this we can conclude that the current specification of the ArchiMate language is not sufficient for modelling value, and value-related approaches and concepts. Therefore we propose the modification of the definition for Value and Stakeholder, the addition of the Capability concept as proposed by [27, 29] and the use of the realisation relationship to link Value to other ArchiMate concepts (goal, capability, core elements, work packages, plateaus).

Table 1. Assessment of ArchiMate 2.1 specification and suggested improvements

Concept/ Relationship	ArchiMate definition	Assessment	Improvement
Value	The relative worth, utility, or importance of a business service or product.	Definition is limited as it does not define value as being relative to a stakeholder. It does not reflect the relationship between the relative worth (value) and the needs and goals of stakeholders. It limits the value to being associated only with a business service or product.	**New definition**: the quality (worth) of something (tangible or intangible) as perceived by a stakeholder (in relation to their goals/needs).
Stakeholder	A person or a team that has interests or concerns regarding the outcome of the architecture.	Definition is limited by describing only the stakeholders that have an interested regarding the outcome of the architecture of an organisation. It considers only individuals and teams of individuals as possible stakeholders, and not organisations.	**New definition**: a person, a group of persons, or an organisation that has interests or concerns regarding the organisation, which is described by its architecture.
Business actor	An organisational entity that is capable of performing behaviour.	The business actor represents the actual entity that can have the role of Stakeholder.	No change
Goal	An end state that a stakeholder intends to achieve.	There is no distinction between the different strategic concepts such as Vision, Mission, Strategy, Objective.	Aldea et al. [28] have proposed using different profiled for Goal to model the different strategic concepts.
Capability	Does not exist in the current ArchiMate specification	It has already been proposed as an addition to the language by [27, 29]	**New concept definition**: the ability of an organization to employ resources to achieve some goal.

(Continued)

Table 1. (*Continued*)

Concept/ Relationship	ArchiMate definition	Assessment	Improvement
Association relationship	Models a relationship between objects that is not covered by another, more specific relationship.	This relationship is currently being used to link Value to other concepts of ArchiMate. We consider this relationship too weak for the purposes of modelling what creates value in an organisation.	We propose the use of a realisation relationship, in addition to the association relationship.
Realisation relationship	Links a logical entity with a more concrete entity that realises it.	The Value concept should be used to model what value is being created by an organisation. Thus not what value is being associated to a specific element, but what value is being realised by a specific element. By having this relationship to value it can become easier to determine where changes need to occur in order to influence that value that is being created.	**New relationship**: We consider this relationship to be more appropriate for modelling the relation between Value and other ArchiMate concepts. Use of this relationship does not exclude the use of the association relationship.
Flow relationship	Describes the exchange or transfer of information or value between processes, functions, interactions, and events.	The definition is limited because it does not include the possibility to model the value transfer between actors. Flow can be used to model value exchanges between the actors in a value network.	**New definition**: The exchange or transfer of information or value between actors, processes, functions, interactions, events.

Figure 5 shows how the concept of Value can be related to the proposed and current ArchiMate concepts. This metamodel includes all the required relationships for modelling all the value-related approaches presented in Sect. 2.

Even with the proposed extension there are still certain limitations to what can be modelled with ArchiMate, especially concerning value networks and e3value. The value exchanges between the actors of a network can be modelled in ArchiMate by using the flow relationship. Although this relationship expresses that there is a transfer of information, knowledge or value between two actors, it does not specify exactly what is being transferred.

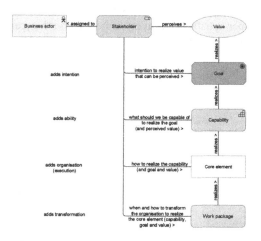

Fig. 5. Value and related concepts metamodel

We propose that in the case of flow relationships, the actual value that is being transferred should be associated to the flow relationship. Figure 6 illustrates our proposed idea of associating the value to the flow relationship.

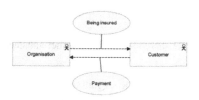

Fig. 6. Value associated to the flow relationship

Another limitation regarding value networks comes from the fact that the ArchiMate modelling language does not support at the moment a distinction between AND/OR junctions. Thus we cannot make the distinction between value exchanges that take place together in the same scenario (AND) or value exchanges that happen in alternative situations (OR).

5 Demonstration

Throughout this section we demonstrate how the value concept and its related concepts and approaches can be modelled. We take the example case study of the fictitious but realistic ArchiSurance organisation as described by [30]. This case study is published by the Open Group and is used to portray the use of the ArchiMate in the context of TOGAF. The following is a short summary of the case study.

The ArchiSurance organisation is the result of a merger between three independent insurance organisations. The main reason that leads to this merger is that the three independent organisations could not remain competitive without significant investments in IT. By combining into one organisation they would be able to control their costs, maintain customer satisfaction, invest in new technology and take advantage of the emerging high growth potential markets.

Fig. 7. Example shareholder and customer satisfaction strategy

The management team (MT) of the organisation has two main concerns: the satisfaction of the organisation's shareholders and customers. In terms of shareholders, the main concerns are the stock value and the profit. In terms of customers the main concerns are the customer complaints and leaving customers. An analysis of the profit concern reveals that application and employee costs are too high. An analysis of the customer complaints concern reveals that there is a lack of insight in claim status and insurance portfolio, and an inconvenient claim submission process. As a result of this assessment, the MT formulates several goals. For example, in order to deal with the high application costs the maintenance costs and the direct application costs need to be reduced. Similarly, for the lack of insight into the insurance portfolio the goal formulated is to improve the portfolio management. For each of these goals there are several requirements formulated. These requirements are realised by several capabilities of the organisation. Figure 7 illustrates the example of the stakeholders, concerns, goals, requirements and corresponding capabilities of the ArchiSurance organisation.

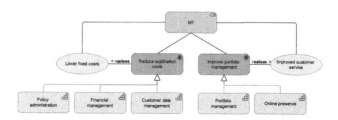

Fig. 8. Example goals that realise values, as perceived by the stakeholder

The MT expects a certain value to be realised by each goal. For example, the reduced application costs are supposed to realise the value of lower fixed costs. Similarly, the goal to improve portfolio management is supposed to realise the value of improved customer service. Figure 8 illustrates the relation between these goals and values as perceived by the MT. All the sub-goals, capabilities and projects that help realise these main goals are also realising the values or parts of the values.

The previous example shows how value can be perceived by an internal stakeholder of the organisation. It also shows how the organisation, at strategic level, intends to create value for their shareholders and customers. However the organisation does not realise this value alone, but it is part of a value network. The organisation has value exchanges with intermediaries and the customer. Figure 9 illustrates these value exchanges related to the main value creating processes, within the value network of the ArchiSurance organisation. In this the values exchanged between the actors of the value network are named on top of the flow relations.

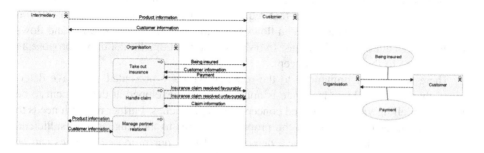

Fig. 9. Example value network with value exchanges and value creating activities

The ArchiSurance organisation wishes to improve the value it delivers to its customers. They can do this by having a closer look at its value streams. From the value network example presented above we can see that there are two main processes that deliver value to the customer. Figure 10 illustrates the value streams for the two processes. In this figure we can see in detail the processes that realise the services that have a particular value for the customers. Any change that is aimed at improving the values delivered to the customer should be made within these processes.

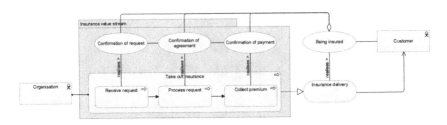

Fig. 10. Example value stream(s)

6   Conclusions, Limitations and Further Research

In this paper we have proposed an approach which will allow for Value and related concepts to be modelled with ArchiMate. Based on a literature review, we are able to put forward an improved definition of the Value and Stakeholder concepts of Archi-Mate. Furthermore, we determine which concepts can have a relationship with Value (Stakeholder, Actor, Goal, Capability, core elements, and implementation and migration elements), and also specify what kind of relationships are possible (realization and flow). The current AchiMate specification allows for the concept of Value to be related to all other concepts by using the association relationship. We consider this relationship to be too weak for expressing what actually creates value in an organisation. For the purpose of modelling a value network we propose the use of the flow relationship. This allows for modelling that there is a transfer between actors but does not specify what is actually being transferred. In order to be able to model the actual value that is being exchanged, we propose to use an association relationship to connect the value to the flow relationship. Another aspect that requires attention is the fact that no distinction can be made at the moment between flows that happen in the same situation and flows that happen in alternative situations. In order to deal with this limitation we propose an improvement to the junction concept.

There are several limitations to the research we have presented. We have determined that the ArchiMate language is not sufficiently developed at the moment to be use for modelling value and related concepts and approaches. Further research needs to be done in order to determine if the proposed changes to the language are sufficient. Furthermore, in this paper we have demonstrated how our proposed changes can be used with the help of a fictitious case study. Even though this is sufficient for illustration purposes, further research needs to be done in order to investigate the applicability and generalizability of our proposed extension in practice. Another point of interest for further research would be to determine if automated model transformations between e3value and ArchiMate are possible with the help of our proposed changes.

References

1. Vargo, S.L., Maglio, P.P., Akaka, M.A.: On value and value co-creation: a service systems and service logic perspective. Eur. Manage. J. **26**(3), 145–152 (2008)
2. O'Cass, A., Ngo, L.V.: Examining the firm's value creation process: a managerial perspective of the firm's value offering strategy and performance. Br. J. Manag. **22**(4), 646–671 (2001)
3. Lindgreen, A., Wynstra, F.: Value in business markets: what do we know? Where are we going? Ind. Mark. Manage. **34**(7), 732–748 (2005)
4. Clarkson, M.E.: A stakeholder framework for analyzing and evaluating corporate social performance. Acad. Manag. Rev. **20**(1), 92–117 (1995)
5. Hillman, A.J., Keim, G.D.: Shareholder value, stakeholder management, and social issues: what's the bottom line? Strateg. Manag. J. **22**(2), 125–139 (2001)
6. Brandenburger, A.M., Stuart, H.W.: Value-based business strategy. J. Econ. Manag. Strateg. **5**(1), 5–24 (1996)
7. Kaplan, R.S., Norton, D.P.: The strategy map: guide to aligning intangible assets. Strateg. Leadersh. **32**(5), 10–17 (2004)
8. Peffers, K., Tuunanen, T., Rothenberger, M.A., Chatterjee, S.: A design science research methodology for information systems research. JMIS **24**(3), 45–77 (2007)
9. Lepak, D.P., Smith, K.G., Taylor, M.S.: Value creation and value capture: a multilevel perspective. Acad. Manag. Rev. **32**(1), 180–194 (2007)
10. Drucker, P.F.: The Practice of Management. Harper and Row Publishers, New York (1954)
11. Martin, J.D., Petty, J.W., Wallace, J.S.: Value-based Management with Corporate Social Responsibility. Oxford University Press, New York (2009)
12. Drucker, P.F.: A Functioning Society: Selections from Sixty-five Years of Writing on Community, Society, and Polity. Transaction Publishers, New Brunswick (2003)
13. Jensen, M.C.: Value maximization, stakeholder theory, and the corporate objective function. J. Appl. Corp. Finance **14**(3), 8–21 (2001)
14. Danesh, M.H., Yu, E.: Modeling Enterprise capabilities with i*: reasoning on alternatives. In: Iliadis, L., Papazoglou, M., Pohl, K. (eds.) CAiSE Workshops 2014. LNBIP, vol. 178, pp. 112–123. Springer, Heidelberg (2014)
15. Stirna, J., Grabis, J., Henkel, M., Zdravkovic, J.: Capability driven development – an approach to support evolving organizations. In: Sandkuhl, K., Seigerroth, U., Stirna, J. (eds.) PoEM 2012. LNBIP, vol. 134, pp. 117–131. Springer, Heidelberg (2012)
16. Miklos, J.: A meta-model for the spatial capability architecture. J. Theor. Appl. Inf. Technol. **43**(2), 301–305 (2012)
17. Möller, K.K., Törrönen, P.: Business suppliers' value creation potential: a capability-based analysis. Ind. Mark. Manage. **32**(2), 109–118 (2003)
18. Porter, M.E.: Competitive Advantage: Creating and Sustaining Superior Performance. Free Press, New York (2008)
19. Sato, Y., Fujita, M.: Capability matrix: a framework for analyzing capabilities in value chains, IDE Discussion Paper 219, Institute of Developing Economies (2009)
20. Peppard, J., Rylander, A.: From value chain to value network: insights for mobile operators. Eur. Manag. J. **24**(2), 128–141 (2006)
21. Allee, V.: Reconfiguring the value network. J. Bus. Strateg. **21**(4), 36–39 (2000)
22. Miller, R.L., Lewis, W.F.: A stakeholder approach to marketing management using the value exchange models. Eur. J. Mark. **25**(8), 55–68 (1991)
23. Gordijn, J., Akkermans, J.: Value-based requirements engineering: exploring innovative e-commerce ideas. Requirements Eng. **8**(2), 114–134 (2003)

24. Gracanin, D., Buchmeister, B., Lalic, B.: Using cost-time profile for value stream optimization. Procedia Eng. **69**, 1225–1231 (2014)
25. Lummus, R.R., Vokurka, R.J., Rodeghiero, B.: Improving quality through value stream mapping: a case study of a physician's clinic. Total Qual. Manag. **17**(8), 1063–1075 (2006)
26. The Open Group: ArchiMate® 2.1 Specification. Van Haren Publishing, Zaltbommel (2013)
27. Iacob, M.E., Quartel, D., Jonkers, H.: Capturing business strategy and value in enterprise architecture to support portfolio valuation. In: 16th International Enterprise Distributed Object Computing Conference (EDOC 2012), pp. 11–20. IEEE, Bejing (2012)
28. Aldea, A., Iacob, M.E., van Hillegersberg, J., Quartel, D., Franken, H., Bodenstaff, L.: Modelling strategy with ArchiMate. In: Proceedings of the 30th ACM/SIGAPP Symposium on Applied Computing (SAC 2015), 13–17 April, Salamanca, Spain (2015, accepted)
29. Azevedo, C.L.B., Iacob, M.E., Almeida, J.P.A., van Sinderen, M., Pires, L.F., Guizzardi, G.: An ontology-based well-founded proposal for modeling resources and capabilities in ArchiMate. In: 17th International Enterprise Distributed Object Computing Conference (EDOC 2013), pp. 39–48 (2013)
30. Jonkers, H., Band, I., Quartel, D.: The ArchiSurance Case Study, White paper, The Open Group, Spring (2012)

Implementing Architectural Thinking

A Case Study at Commerzbank AG

Stephan Aier[1(✉)], Nils Labusch[1], and Patrick Pähler[2]

[1] Institute for Information Management, University of St. Gallen,
St. Gallen, Switzerland
{stephan.aier,nils.labusch}@unisg.ch
[2] Commerzbank AG, Frankfurt/Main, Germany
patrick.paehler@commerzbank.com

Abstract. The discipline of enterprise architecture (EA) has become well-established in many organizations and is continuously discussed in academic literature. However, EA's effectiveness beyond IT is limited. The paradigm of architectural thinking aims at reaching the 90 % of an organization that is not related to IT. The paper contrasts the abstract definitions of architectural thinking with empirical case study data. We find that practice has developed implementations of these abstract definitions. However, we also find new characteristics of architectural thinking that have not yet been discussed in literature. Specifically, these are the role of decisions and the role of formal governance mechanisms.

Keywords: Enterprise architecture · Enterprise architecture management · Architectural thinking · Case study

1 Introduction

The discipline of enterprise architecture (EA)has become well-established in many organizations and is continuously discussed in academic publications [1]. The achievements of the discipline in the practitioner's domain are documented for example in EA frameworks out of which The Open Group Architecture Framework (TOGAF) [2] has received most attention in recent years [3, 4]. Achievements of academic research are published in numerous method fragments [for overviews see 1, 3, 5–7] covering EA modeling, EA planning, EA principles, etc.

Enterprise architecture describes the fundamental structures of an organization. Enterprise architecture management (EAM) is concerned with guiding changes and developments of EA. As such, the notion of EAM goes beyond EA modeling and includes the management tasks of planning and controlling business changes from an architectural perspective [8].

What defines the architectural perspective and differentiates EAM from other management disciplines, such as business process management or project management, is its holistic scope which spans three dimensions [9, 10]: (1) on a horizontal dimension, EAM often covers the entirety of artifacts of a specific artifact type (e.g., all applications or all processes) of an organization. (2) On a vertical dimension,

A. Persson and J. Stirna (Eds.): CAiSE 2015 Workshops, LNBIP 215, pp. 389–400, 2015.
DOI: 10.1007/978-3-319-19243-7_36

EAM often covers all layers of an organization's business-to-IT stack. (3) In a dimension of time, EAM is not limited (e.g., to a project or program), but covers changes of several projects or programs linking an EA's as-is state to one or several to-be states.

Due to this holistic perspective, EAM is expected to identify and leverage those potential synergies in an organization that cannot be identified, having a partial perspective, e.g., of a single project, in a single process, or a single organizational unit. This is because all these entities often have their particular but locally restricted perspectives and strive for achieving their respective local goals. From a holistic perspective, the set of local, and in this matter uncoordinated, decisions often results in inconsistent, redundant, and/or conflicting solutions.

In practice, however, EAM's impact often falls short of its potential benefits. One of the reasons is that EAM's range of influence is often restricted to IT departments only [11]. In fact, EAM often has an "image problem", and once people use the word enterprise architecture, "eyes start to roll" [12]. Involving business departments seems to be a difficult task on which EAM regularly fails to deliver. Thus, a relevant question for EAM is how to reach "that other 90 %" of an organization that are not related to IT [13]. This question is crucial since Ross and Quaadgras [14] found that more mature EAM functions "do not necessarily lead to business value" but that "business value accrues through management practices that propagate architectural thinking throughout the enterprise." [14] Given a certain maturity level, EAM should not aim at further improving EAM methods, tools, and processes. Instead, the underlying philosophy of EAM, taking decisions informed by a holistic perspective, should be internalized by a broad range of decision makers across hierarchical levels.

Ross and Quaadgras [14] define *architectural thinking* as the way of thinking and acting throughout an organization that considers holistic, long-term system aspects as well as fundamental system design and evolution principles in everyday decision making, which is not restricted to architects or system developers. According to Winter [15], architectural thinking is supposed to be a lightweight, less formalized, and utility-centered approach that aims to support non-architects and people outside the IT function to understand, analyze, plan, transform, and communicate fundamental structures as well as design/evolution principles of what they perceive as their work system. Architectural thinking aims at educating these people in adopting holistic, long-term considerations in their daily decisions.

The concept of architectural thinking occurred fairly recently in academic literature and remains abstract. Therefore, our research aims to contrast the concept of architectural thinking found literature with empirical case study data. We further aim to understand whether corresponding concepts can be identified from empirical data and where existing conceptualizations can be extended. Therefore, this research provides an overview of the existing literature on architectural thinking and derives a corresponding research lens. We follow an interpretive (antipositivist) approach. Our aim is to add to the understanding of the phenomenon of architectural thinking since there is no other empirical foundation to discuss the phenomenon, yet. We contribute new aspects of architectural thinking and we add empirical instances to so far only theoretically described constructs.

We proceed as follows: in Sect. 2 we present the conceptual lens of architectural thinking and introduce related literature. We provide empirical data from a case study at Commerzbank AG in Sect. 3, followed by a discussion of the data through our conceptual lens in Sect. 4. We conclude by a summary in Sect. 5.

2 Conceptual Foundations

2.1 Differentiating Architectural Thinking from EAM

Architectural thinking has only recently been discussed as an addition to traditional EAM [14]. This shift in perception is rooted in the finding that EAM practices differ from the descriptions that are often subjected in EAM discussions. While traditional EAM oftentimes focusses on the results of architectural work, it may become much more valuable to focus on the process of gathering information relevant for architectural decisions [16] and thus involving the relevant stakeholders. Winter [15] details this perception by identifying commonalities and differences between the two concepts of EAM and architectural thinking. Both approaches share the scope concerning the fundamental structures of the organization and the principles guiding its design and evolution. The goals of both approaches are the reduction of redundancies, increasing consistency, increasing manageability, leveraging synergies, and increasing flexibility, respectively. Their scope regarding time is long-term rather than short-term.

However, Winter [15] mentions important differences (see Table 1). While EAM describes architects as the driving actors, architectural thinking promotes the individual decision-maker within the organization to taking responsibility. Local, often non-IT decision-makers are responsible, not only for achieving their respective goals, but also for contributing to the enterprise-wide goal achievement. In order to facilitate architectural thinking, the focus needs to be both extended to long-term goals of the

Table 1. Differences between EAM and architectural thinking [15]

Differentiating Characteristics	Traditional EAM	Architectural Thinking
Driver/owner	Architects	Individual decision-makers
Hosting organizational unit	Primarily IT; sometimes corporate center	Business lines
Addressed stakeholders	Various (IT, corporate management, business lines)	Individual decision-maker (= owner)
Benefit type	Enterprise-wide, long-term: "what's in it for the enterprise"	Local utility, medium-term: "what's in it for me and why is it beneficial for all of us"
Threats for benefit realization (and solution strategy)	"ivory tower" → engage architects in changing projects	"local" architectures → bottom-up consolidation
Method support	Dedicated, sophisticated methods and tools: expert users!	Lightweight, pragmatic (e.g., principle catalogues, calculation templates, charts): users are no architecture experts!

organization and aligned with the short-term goals of decision makers. In order to mitigate the risk that architectural thinking is misunderstood as set of local optimizations, the trade-off between local and enterprise-wide goals need to be addressed and reduced. Opposed to existing, often sophisticated EAM approaches, the architectural thinking approach is supposed to be lightweight and targeted at supporting non-architects.

Some confusion may arise on how architectural thinking differs from strategy making and concrete design of the organization. Proper [17] deals with this confusion and positions architectural thinking between the strategic and the design level. The strategic level deals with definitions and evolutions of the corporate strategy. The design level copes with decisions that are related to each team's work processes and project organization. The intermediary architecture level, which involves architectural thinking, is positioned to focus on the requirements that can be gathered from the strategic level as well as from goals and concerns of the stakeholders in the organization.

2.2   Adoption of Architectural Thinking in an Organization

The core of architectural thinking is the establishment of the architectural perspective in the organization. Lattanze [18] particularly articulates the need of EAM training programs to have the long-term goal of establishing the architectural perspective throughout the organization. He aims not only at training employees in architecture theory and principles, but also at achieving a state, where designing organizational elements, such as products etc., is a deeply rooted paradigm within the organization. This could be achieved by providing formal roles and career paths for people involved in architecture. Furthermore, architects need to be trained in marketing and communication concepts; processes need to be constructed/changed by involving architects in an early stage. This is in line with Ross [14], who states that, in order to drive the value from enterprise-wide activities, management mechanisms need to be implemented, allowing people to continuously learn how to improve their platforms.

Van der Raadt et al. [19] emphasize the origin of the "architecture lobby" when aiming at the establishment of architectural thinking. According to the authors, "an organization where architecture awareness originates with business management has different ideas about architecture and has a different momentum than an organization in which architecture awareness starts in the IT-department."

Weiss et al. [20] describe antecedents that need to be considered for establishing an architectural perspective. They ground their research in institutional theory [21–23]. According to the authors, benefits through EAM are achieved when EAM has a "rule-like status in social thought and action", provides social legitimacy and efficiency, and when it is grounded in the organization [24].

Winter [15] finds that the antecedents for establishing EAM are also relevant for the adoption of architectural thinking throughout the organization. Based on the work by Weiss et al. [20], Winter [15] derives challenges for the adoption of architectural thinking in organizations (Table 2):

Table 2. Challenges for the adoption of architectural thinking [based on 15; 20]

Adoption Challenge	Role of the Challenge for Establishing Architectural Thinking
Creating social fitness and architectural compliance	When decisions of decision-makers do not only contribute to his or her local goals but are architecturally compliant and thus contribute to enterprise-wide goals, such decisions should be socially recognized and should foster the decision-maker's legitimacy within the organization.
Understanding use situations and efficiency	In order to make architectural thinking effective and to contribute to decision-makers efficiency different situations and their specific decision types need to be addressed.
Development of architects as business supporters	Architects are required being the facilitators of architectural thinking and the ones providing the holistic perspective to decisions-makers. Architecture roles need to be developedto provide this business support.
Communication of architects' value contribution	In order to grow the trust in architects as well as in architectural thinking,architects' value contribution needs to be communicated.

In the following we use the dimensions from Tables 1 and 2 as the conceptual lens to analyze the empirical data presented in the next section.

3 Case Study Commerzbank AG

In this section we present case study data on architectural thinking, collected from Commerzbank AG. Two of the three authors are university-scientists and part of an applied research project at the case company. The third author is employed with the case company as an enterprise architect and involved in the initiative reported here. The goal of the case study is to contrast the perceptions from practice with the early conceptualizations of architectural thinking from academia.

3.1 About the Case Company

Commerzbank is the second-largest German bank, located in Frankfurt/Main. The company is providing services for the global banking business, having more than 52,000 employees. Similar to other companies in the banking sector, Commerzbank has to deal with challenges imposed by the recent financial crisis and the subsequent regulatory requirements, significantly impacted by low interest rates in their daily business operations. In order to cope with these challenges, Commerzbank aims at further reducing risks, optimizing the capital base, pursuing cost management, and simultaneously making long-term investments in the core bank's earnings power, while rigorously orienting the business model toward the needs of customers and the real economy [25].

Within Commerzbank, the EAM function is part of the IT-organization and directly reports to the group chief information officer (CIO). One of the main goals of the EAM function is to support the joint definition of target processes and to align system architectures with business and IT units. Architects thereby serve as drivers of the target architecture definition process and as method providers. Target architectures are always developed within a business-driven change project or program.

3.2 About the Project

Commerzbank has recently launched a strategic investment program called *Group Finance Architecture* (GFA), aimed at redesigning the process and system architecture of the Commerzbank group finance function. The sponsor of the strategic initiative is the chief financial officer (CFO). The main goals of the program comprise delivering on the latest regulatory requirements, integrating financial accounting and management accounting in order to significantly faster processes, and improving the financial analysis options.

To achieve these goals, a new finance architecture needs to be designed and implemented in an almost greenfield approach. The new finance architecture serves as the nucleus for a more integrated bank steering platform. The project is supported by the EAM function for supporting and guiding the design of the new target architectures. EAM always needs to be involved in large projects and programs that are conducted at Commerzbank. The new layered architecture is based on a state of the art standard accounting software and a data warehouse, resembling the new single source of facts.

The architecture work focuses on ensuring that the new solution fulfills the defined functional and non-functional requirements. The top priority is to ensure that the results of this investment will actually serve as the core for the new finance architecture and thus as a substantial nucleus for future projects. Although a single project is usually not a suitable case for demonstrating architectural work, this particular project is a nice exemplar for demonstrating architectural work in general and architectural thinking in particular. This is due to the size of the project, where up to 150 project members need to take decisions during the five years of the project, and it is due to the fact that this project is sponsored by the CFO, i.e., from outside the IT organization. This project has to address both the long-term holistic perspective as the future nucleus for further projects as well as the local project perspective to deliver in time, in budget, and in quality.

3.3 Architectural Thinking in the Project

To align decisions of the project members, Commerzbank uses the capabilities of the EAM function. The EAM approach focusses on demonstrating its value contribution to the project members. For this purpose, EAM starts with project scoping and is primarily involved during the functional design phase; EAM is less involved when it comes to the subsequent IT development.

An important step to ensure the acceptance of architectural work is to formulate business-driven goals that need to be met by the final solution. Thus, the focus is on the solution (what does the business want to achieve?) and not, like oftentimes before in similar projects, on the way to achieve the goal (how do we want to achieve the goal?). Exemplary business goals are the convergence of finance and risk data, the support of very short time-to-market-cycles for new products, fast consideration of new (regulatory) requirements, and an overall cost efficiency. Based on these high-level business goals, more specific goals for the overall solution are formulated. Examples for such goals are:

- The solution provides a convergent storage.
- The solution is designed to enable short change cycles.
- The solution design is cost efficient.

These goals are focusing on the solution and do not mention any architectural rule or paradigm. The designs are evaluated concerning their contribution to the solution's goals. These solution goals are transparently linked to business goals. They are not the result of an architect's or engineer's opinion on what a favorable solution would look like.

To support the practical implementation of the solution's goals, rules are defined for each solution layer (e.g., data warehouse, accounting solution, and reporting). Yet, those rules are formulated in a way that any design can be evaluated regarding its contribution to the solution's goals. Exemplary rules are:

- The implementation is achieved by customizing.
- Each rule references a business goal that the rule should contribute to.

If a situation occurs, where the use of a rule would not contribute to the business goal, the rule is not supposed to be applied. For reasons of governance, it was necessary to communicate this set of business and solution goals as an official and binding document within the project. However, this formal binding stays effective only as long as there is good reason. The Commerzbank approach is not to rely on any formal status of architecture documents, but to rely on the good and comprehensible reasons for the business and solution targets.

3.4   Project Learnings

In this project, the most important philosophy to foster business stakeholders' architectural thinking is to handle design and implementation decisions in a consensual way. The consensus, however, always has two components: the business driven goal definitions and the holistic architectural perspective. Sound design, from an architectural point of view, became a self-runner after the first phase of intensive collaboration between the architecture and the design team. In conflicting situations, where someone argues for a design that does not comply with the current architectural rules, and still was able to explain why the proposed design contributes to the overall goals, this new design was handled as the new architectural standard. If the respondents were not able to provide a reasonable explanation, they were in charge to argue, why in this case it might be more appropriate not to contribute to the overall solution's goals. Thus, in this project architectural thought and action were focused on the individual decision and the respective justification in a given situation rather than on the codified architectural rules. However, discussing the individual decisions fosters the understanding of the various and possibly conflicting perspectives of the involved parties. It also fosters the conscious and deliberate decision-taking, since every decision potentially serves as the architectural standard in subsequent comparable situations. This decision focus is similar to the "case-law" in the US legal system, contrary to codified law, which is prevalent in European countries. Finally, the developed solution at Commerzbank, designed by the project team, serves as one of the best solutions in the market, but even more important as the gold standard within the organization itself.

Discussing success factors of architectural thinking at Commerzbank, stakeholders mentioned the definition of architectural thinking as an important goal. Thus, the restriction of conflicting goals, appropriate performance management and incentive systems, the involvement of long-term beneficiaries in the project as well as a shared mental model among stakeholders have become critical success factors; silo-mentality, unknown or ignored interrelations, locally focused performance indicators, missing boundary spanners such as architects, and "content-free" project manages whose involvement ends with the project, were characterized as major challenges in this context.

4 Discussion

In Sect. 2 we introduced the currently scarce and abstract concepts of architectural thinking. In Sect. 3 we presented case data concerning the topic of architectural thinking aimed at contrasting the abstract concepts. Here we discuss how architectural thinking was applied in the described project, aimed at answering the research question, what the constituents of architectural thinking in practice are. Therefore we employ the conceptual lens codified in Tables 1 and 2 in order to analyze the empirical data. The results of this analysis and the answer to our research question are summarized in Table 3.

One of the most important determinants of architectural thinking is the ownership of architectural considerations by all stakeholders in the project. This is given in the case described above—the sponsor is as much involved in architectural considerations as the individual project members, and can therefore improve the architectural rules by providing better ones.

Concerning the hosting organizational unit, architectural thinking was rather hosted in the program management than in the involved business lines. This might be an intermediary step of introducing architectural thinking. Program management is more often regarded closer to the business units than the EAM function. However, a high degree of architectural thinking would even further include business units.

Individual decision-makers have been identified as the addressed stakeholders. As described earlier, they had the opportunity and responsibility to participate in the architecture process and were encouraged to contribute their ideas.

The provided benefits were discovered to exist both locally and globally, i.e., enterprise-wide. Concerning the first dimension, the architecture guidance has

Table 3. Architectural thinking and the case study findings

Characteristics of Architectural Thinking	Abstract Definition of Architectural Thinking	Constituents of Architectural Thinking at Commerzbank
Driver/owner	Individual decision-makers	Main driver of the project is the CFO, but relevant for a sustainable solution are the project management team and every individual project member providing solution designs. Therefore, the main stakeholders are the project management team and the design team
Hosting organizational unit	Business lines	Program management
Addressed stakeholders	Individual decision-maker (= owner)	See driver/owner
Benefit type	Local utility, medium-term: "what's in it for me and why is it beneficial for all of us"	Locally helpful by delivering a successful project and reaching the efficiency goals for the specific long-term solution
Threats for benefit realization (and solution strategy)	"local" architectures → bottom-up consolidation	Local project architecture not delivering the nucleus for further projects.
Method support	Lightweight, pragmatic (e.g., principle catalogues, calculation templates, charts): users are no architecture experts!	Business driven design guidelines and rationales for design decisions (e.g., business driven goals, solution goals, rationales per goal/rule)
Role of decisions	--	Focus is on the decision process since it not only delivers a decision but also a standard for subsequent comparable situations
Adoption Challenge	**Abstract Definition of Adoption Challenge**	**Adoption Mechanisms at Commerzbank**
Creating social fitness and architectural compliance	When decisions of decision-makers do not only contribute to his or her local goals but are architecturally compliant and thus, contribute to enterprise-wide goals, such decisions, should be socially recognized and should foster the decision-maker's legitimacy within the organization.	It is defined in the core of the project that both, local and enterprise-wide perspectives are addressed and recognized as a team effort and team success/failure.
Understanding use situations and efficiency	In order to make architectural thinking effective and to contribute to decision-makers efficiency different situations and their specific decision types need to be addressed.	Specific situation was the design of a target architecture that is the reference for future projects. In the same way decision taking was designed. Every decision could be the standard for future decisions.

(Continued)

Table 3. (*Continued*)

Development of architects as business supporters	Architects are required being the facilitators of architectural thinking and the ones providing the holistic perspective to decisions-makers. Architecture roles need to be developed to provide this business support.	Architects facilitated the definition of goals, rules, and rationales but they did not define these goals, rules, and rationales. Instead architects supported the decision-making by consensus processes.
Communication of architects' value contribution	In order to grow the trust in architects as well as in architectural thinking, architects' value contribution needs to be communicated.	Communication of architects' value contribution is a core activity of the architecture unit in the project.
Governance, goal alignment, and enforcement	--	Architectural thinking is guided and controlled by "defined" consensus processes. Project goals and therefore the goals of the individuals are defined in a way to contribute to enterprise-wide goals.

proven to be a useful instrument to achieve local projects goals. Globally, the overall solution was successfully delivered, too.

The threat for a beneficial realization is a local project architecture that does not deliver the nucleus for further projects and thus, limits the overall impact to a local solution.

The method was strongly influenced by the EAM experts. Guidelines were collected and managed in order to achieve a business-driven design. However, all the goals, rules, and rationales are formulated in a non-architect-language, i.e., using the vocabulary of the project's sponsors.

Another newly discovered aspect complements the findings by Winter [15] and others. While traditional EAM oftentimes performs governance by stating rules or principles as well as by enforcing a project's compliance, architectural thinking in the presented case focuses on the consensus for each decision and thus establishes case-law thinking. Such a philosophy is much more flexible in adapting to new situations, stakeholder requirements and benefits, since the actual context of the decision is well documented.

Similar results are found regarding the adoption challenges for architectural thinking. Table 3 lists the specific implementations of adoption mechanisms discussed in [15, 20] for the presented project. However, beyond the "softer" factors described by Winter [15] the case data also delivers examples for the more formal mechanisms of governance and rule enforcement as such described by Weiss et al. [20]. These governance mechanisms, however, are no classical EAM governance mechanisms like project proposal or milestone reviews for architectural compliance. Instead, the processes of decision-making and the role of decisions are established and fostered in governance mechanisms.

Summarizing our analysis leaves the specific project reported herewith most characteristics of architectural thinking and challenges for adopting architectural thinking being addressed. In addition, we find a new characteristic that has not yet been described in architectural thinking literature. Although the project has been set up with the general idea of architectural thinking in mind, it did not follow any blueprint of architectural thinking. Therefore, the project can only partially serve as a demonstration or even an evaluation of the architectural thinking paradigm. It is rather a case that reflects the abstract concepts of architectural thinking. Also, the intended dimensions of architectural thinking, i.e., to reach "that other 90 %" of an organization that are not related to IT [13] are not met by the case. Rather the project represents a sandbox for architectural thinking. In fact, it is much easier to establish architectural thinking in a team of 150 project members, sharing an overall project goal, than in an entire organization where the overall goals and the individuals' goal contributions might be much less recognizable. Given the limits of effectiveness of traditional EAM and the proposed approaches of architectural thinking, the case data nevertheless deliver an encouraging statement for following this research avenue.

5 Conclusion

In this paper we illustrate the concept of architectural thinking, which aims at reaching "that other 90 %" of an organization that classical EAM does not reach, with empirical cases study data. Therefore we contribute practical implementation exemplars of architectural thinking beyond the abstract definitions of architectural thinking proposed in academic literature so far. We find all of the dimensions and challenges mentioned in literature to be applicable in practice.

References

1. Simon, D., Fischbach, K., Schoder, D.: An exploration of enterprise architecture research. Commun. Assoc. Inf. Syst. **32**, 1–72 (2013)
2. The Open Group: TOGAF Version 9.1 – The Open Group Architecture Framework. The Open Group (2011)
3. Buckl, S., Ernst, A.M., Lankes, J., Matthes, F., Schweda, C.M.: State of the Art in Enterprise Architecture Management 2009. Technische Universität München, Chair for Informatics 19 (sebis), Munich (2009)
4. Buckl, S., Schweda, C.M.: On the State-of-the-Art in Enterprise Architecture Management Literature. Technische Universität München, Chair for Informatics 19 (sebis), Munich (2011)
5. Aier, S., Riege, C., Winter, R.: Unternehmensarchitektur – literaturüberblick und stand der praxis. Wirtschaftsinformatik **50**, 292–304 (2008)
6. Schelp, J., Winter, R.: Language communities in enterprise architecture research. In: Vaishanvi, V., Baskerville, R. (eds.) Proceedingss of the 4th International Conference on Design Science Research in Information Systems and Technology (DESRIST 2009). ACM, Philadelphia (2009)

7. Mykhashchuk, M., Buckl, S., Dierl, T., Schweda, C.M.: Charting the landscape of enterprise architecture management. In: Bernstein, A., Schwabe, G. (eds.) International Conference on Wirtschaftsinformatik, Zurich, vol. 1, pp. 570–577 (2011)

8. Aier, S., Gleichauf, B., Winter, R.: Understanding enterprise architecture management design – an empirical analysis. In: Bernstein, A., Schwabe, G. (eds.) International Conference on Wirtschaftsinformatik, Zurich, vol. 2, pp. 645–654 (2011)

9. Winter, R., Fischer, R.: Essential layers, artifacts, and dependencies of enterprise architecture. J. Enterp. Archit. **3**, 7–18 (2007)

10. Lankhorst, M.: Enterprise Architecture at Work: Modelling, Communication and Analysis. Springer, Berlin (2005)

11. Winter, R., Townson, S., Uhl, A., Labusch, N., Noack, J.: Enterprise Architecture and Transformation: The Differences and the Synergy Potential of Enterprise Architecture and Business Transformation Management. 360° Bus. Transform. J. (5), 22–31 (2012)

12. Asfaw, T., Bada, A., Allario, F.: Enablers and challenges in using enterprise architecture concepts to drive transformation: perspectives from private organizations and federal government agencies. J. Enterp. Architect. **5**, 18–28 (2009)

13. Gardner, D., Fehskens, L., Naidu, M., Rouse, W.B., Ross, J.W.: Point-counterpoint: enterprise architecture and enterprise transformation as related but distinct concepts. J. Enterp. Transform. **2**, 283–294 (2012)

14. Ross, J.W., Quaadgras, A.: Enterprise Architecture Is Not Just for Architects. Center for Information Systems Research Sloan School of Management, vol. 7. Massachusetts Institute of Technology, Cambridge (2012)

15. Winter, R.: Architectural thinking. Bus. Inf. Syst. Eng. **6**, 361–364 (2014)

16. Abrams, S., Bloom, B., Keyser, P., Kimelman, D., Nelson, E., Neuberger, W., Roth, T., Simmonds, I., Tang, S., Vlissides, J.: Architectural thinking and modeling with the architects' workbench. IBM Syst. J. **45**, 481–500 (2006)

17. Proper, H.A.: Enterprise architecture: informed steering of enterprises in motion. In: Hammoudi, S., Cordeiro, J., Maciaszek, L.A., Filipe, J. (eds.) Data Mining and Knowledge Discovery for Big Data. LNCS, vol. 1, pp. 16–34. Springer, Heidelberg (2014)

18. Lattanze, A.J.: Infusing architectural thinking into organizations. IEEE Softw. **29**, 19–22 (2012)

19. Raadt, B.V.D., Soetendal, J., Perdeck, M., Vliet, H.V.: Polyphony in architecture. In: Proceedings of the 26th International Conference on Software Engineering (Isce 2004), pp. 533–542. IEEE Computer Society, Washington, DC (2004)

20. Weiss, S., Aier, S., Winter, R.: Institutionalization and the effectiveness of enterprise architecture management. In: International Conference on Information Systems (ICIS 2013). Association for Information Systems, Milano (2013)

21. Scott, W.R.: Institutions and organizations: ideas and interests. Sage Publications, London (2008)

22. DiMaggio, P.J., Powell, W.W.: The iron cage revisited: institutional isomorphism and collective rationality in organizational fields. Am. Sociol. Rev. **48**, 147–160 (1983)

23. Oliver, C.: Strategic responses to institutional processes. Acad. Manag. Rev. **16**, 145–179 (1991)

24. Meyer, J.W., Rowan, B.: Institutionalized organizations: formal structure as myth and ceremony. Am. J. Sociol. **83**, 340–363 (1977)

25. Commerzbank, A.G.: Annual Report 2013. Commerzbank AG, Frankfurt, Germany (2013)

Data Governance on EA Information Assets: Logical Reasoning for Derived Data

Bernhard Waltl, Thomas Reschenhofer, and Florian Matthes$^{(\boxtimes)}$

Software Engineering for Business Information Systems,
Department of Informatics,
Technische Universität München,
Boltzmannstr. 3, 85748 Garching Bei München, Germany
b.waltl@tum.de, {reschenh,matthes}@in.tum.de

Abstract. Today's companies face increased pressure regarding compliance to legal obligations. Regulations for the financial sector such as Basel II and III, Solvency II, or the Sarbanes-Oxley-Act explicitly demand various requirements. Many of those requirements address the governance and management of information assets, such as data. Companies need to report and track their information architecture, and furthermore have to provide accountability and responsibility information on their data to, e.g., supervisory authorities.

Additionally, the tracking of processed data becomes increasingly difficult since the software systems and their interactions throughout the enterprise are highly complex. This paper argues for a consistent and comprehensive assignment mechanism on data governance roles. Based on logical inferences, we are able to show how accountability and responsibility can be assigned throughout processed data. Thereby, we analyze the limitations of traditional logic, such as propositional logic, and exemplarily show how non-monotonic defeasible logic can be used to keep the assignment of roles on information assets consistent.

Keywords: Data governance · Enterprise architecture · EA metrics · Logical Reasoning · Defeasible logic

1 Introduction

The increasing organizational complexity of today's enterprises requires a strategic approach to align the enterprise's IT to its business [1]. In this sense, an Enterprise Architecture (EA) represents the holistic organization of an enterprise consisting of its components, relations, and environment [2]. Thereby, EA is understood as a descriptive and holistic model of the enterprise [3]. The corresponding management discipline—Enterprise Architecture Management (EAM)—is a function for planning, developing, and controlling an EA and its evolution, and thus to ensure its flexibility, efficiency, and transparency. Consequently, EAM fosters business IT alignment [4] and potentially improves the enterprise's business performance [1]. To cope with the increasing size and

© Springer International Publishing Switzerland 2015
A. Persson and J. Stirna (Eds.): CAiSE 2015 Workshops, LNBIP 215, pp. 401–412, 2015.
DOI: 10.1007/978-3-319-19243-7_37

complexity of an EA, there are various tools supporting enterprise architects by providing methods for gathering, modeling, and analyzing EA data [5]. Analyzing an EA also includes the computation of EA metrics allowing a reliable assessment of the current state as well as the evolution of the EA [6]. Thereby, EA metrics generate derived EA data [7].

Due to EAM's goal to establish a shared understanding of the enterprise's current state among the whole organization, it involves a variety of stakeholders, e.g., enterprise architects, EA repository managers, and data owners [8]. However, there is an increasing pressure to legal compliance forcing companies to ensure transparency and provenance of their data. In the financial industry regulatory frameworks like Basel II [9], respectively Basel III, Solvency II and the Sarbanes-Oxley Act [10] were promulgated to ensure proper risk management and to reduce the vulnerability to systemic risks. Although the concrete measures vary throughout the different regulations, they share common principles regarding transparency and provenance of data. Additionally, the German implementation of Basel II in the banking act [11] has a strong focus on auditing of processes, data, business entities, etc. [12,13]. In this sense, specifying and documenting roles, rights and responsibilities of all stakeholders is indispensable for today's companies.

There are various frameworks to document the roles of stakeholders with regard to specific entities of an EA. For example, the RACI matrix [14] links a stakeholder to certain activities or processes by specifying this person to be responsible (R), accountable (A), consulted (C), or informed (I) regarding the respective process. On another note, the Data Governance Framework (DGF) addresses responsibilities and accountability of stakeholders on data itself. Therefore, there are frameworks providing a way of explicitly specifying which persons are responsible and accountable for processes and data in EA. However, it is still an open question whether these frameworks also fit to derived EA data generated by EA metrics. Furthermore, since the data itself is derived through EA metrics, the question arises if roles for derived EA data are also derivable from the metric and its input. Trends in data science, such as big data, really push the necessity to provide consistent frameworks of semi-automatic determination of responsibility and provenance of data. Who is responsible, respectively accountable, for data that was automatically created by algorithms? Based on existing information about the assignment of roles of either processes and data, algorithms based on logical frameworks can deduce the roles for the derived properties. A consistent logical framework helps to generate reproducible and reliable results [15].

Consequently, answering the following research questions constitutes this work's contribution: What is a framework for the specification of roles on EA data governance? And what is a logical framework to infer roles on derived EA data based on the corresponding EA metric and its input?

This paper describes an approach to cope with the assignment and derivation of roles on data, representing information about an enterprise architecture. Thereby, we briefly sketch prior and related work in Sect. 2. Section 3 will give an overview about models and roles for relevant information assets (e.g., data, metrics, and derived data) in the EA domain. The paper continues with the adaption of an existing and well studied logical framework, namely the defeasible logic, in Sect. 4. Finally, Sect. 5 summarizes its contribution and sketches further research directions.

2   Related Work

One of the most common tools for documenting the roles of persons on activities is the RACI (Responsible, Accountable, Consulted, Informed) matrix [16]. The RACI matrix was already applied in software development governance [16], but also in the domain of EAM. Thereby, Fischer et al. [8] used the RACI matrix for the EA maintenance process, i.e., they specify roles for EA stakeholders on activities related to the maintenance of the EA model. However, they did not discuss roles for derived EA information.

How to govern enterprise data was discussed by the Data Governance Institute (DGI). The DGI proposed the Data Governance Framework (DGF), which is a "logical structure for classifying, organizing, and communicating complex activities involved in making decisions about and taking action on enterprise data" [17]. The framework argues for an extensive system analysis to trace unclear accountabilities along the data flow. This manual tracing might work out for small programs with well defined data flows, but exceeds its applicability in complex enterprise structures.

As an extension to the DGF, Khatri and Brown [18] analyzed different facets of "data as an asset" with a strong focus on the provision of a framework for data governance. They also admit that data assets are moving more and more in the focus of legislative compliance and related reporting. The outcome of a case study they conducted in the insurance industry is a differentiation between five interrelated decision domains for data governance, namely data principles, data quality, meta-data, data access, and data life-cycle. For each of the provided domains the driving decisions are stated out and potential roles are given.

Yogesh et al. [19] argue that data provenance is crucial for the reuse of data. Thereby, data tracking can be ensured using meta-data, pertaining the complete derivation history starting from its original source. Analyzing the scientific workflows, they created a taxonomy of data provenance characteristics. The taxonomy differentiates between five main headings, namely application of provenance, subject of provenance, representation of provenance, provenance storage, and provenance dissemination. The differentiations are discussed regarding their characteristics, but miss a normative guideline how to derive the provenance information for data from its sources.

The usage of logical frameworks to enrich existing frameworks with consistent logical conclusions was also subject of prior research. Ninghui et al. [15] developed a logic-based language, namely delegation language, with the objective to represent policies, credentials, and requests allowing inferences based on logical conclusions. Their research focused on the support of decentralized aggregation of data, in which the derivation and inference on data plays a significant role.

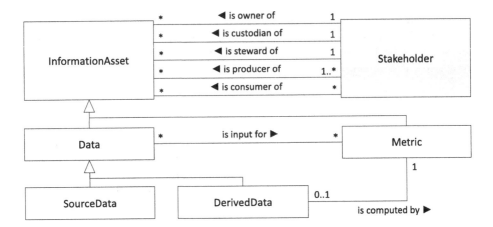

Fig. 1. A conceptual model of EA information assets including EA data, metrics, and derived data. Each information asset is associated with stakeholders through specific roles (see Table 1).

The possibility to express complex policies allows a fine granular declaration and delegation of data authority. The delegation language only supports monotonic reasoning, which was also identified as drawback by the authors. They later on worked on a non-monotonic delegation logic to handle with conflicting policies, but the manuscript was never officially published [20].

Gaaloul et al. [21] used a logical framework to reason about delegation events to model task delegation. The usage of formal logical engines, such as event calculus, allows the definition of delegation policies. Their overall objective is the automated assignment of delegation policies. Once the delegation policies are specified, a discrete event calculus reasoner can efficiently solve the problem by transforming it into a satisfiability (SAT) problem. They showed that formal reasoning increases the compliance regarding delegation changes in existing policies.

3   A Model of Roles for EA Data and Metrics

In the context of this work, we define derived EA data as the output of EA metrics, which performs a computation based on input data. Thereby, we differentiate between source data which has to be provided by one or more EA stakeholders, and derived data which is computed by an EA metric based on respective input data. In this sense, not only data itself is considered to be an information asset, but also the metric capturing the actual computation prescription. Figure 1 gives an overview of the information assets, and their relationships. In this context, a metric has an arbitrary amount of input data, and produces a derived datum. The corresponding roles are described bellow in Table 1.

For example, Schneider et al. [22] describe the metric *Average Functional Scope* computing the average number of function points of business applications

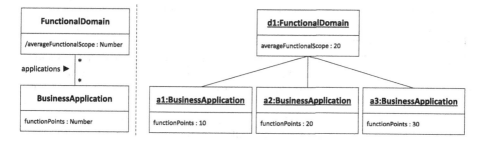

Fig. 2. An excerpt of the information model for the metric *Average Functional Scope* as described by Schneider et al. [22], as well as a corresponding and exemplary UML object diagram.

within a certain business domain. In this sense, function points are a quantification of how much business functionality a business application provides. An excerpt of the corresponding information model as well as a proper exemplary object diagram is depicted in Fig. 2. A formal computation prescription for this metric can be expressed with the Object Constraint Language (OCL) as follows:

context FunctionalDomain :: averageFunctionalScope : Number
derive :
　　self . applications -> collect (functionPoints) -> sum ()
　/ self . applications -> size ()

Based on the exemplary object diagram in Fig. 2, the evaluation of the metric *Average Functional Scope* for the functional domain *d1* generates a derived datum, namely the value 20 for the attribute *Average Functional Scope*.

To relate the exemplary information model in Fig. 2 to the conceptual model of information assets as depicted in Fig. 1, we consider the attribute values in Fig. 2 to be objects of class *Data* as defined in the conceptual model. Furthermore, also whole entities are information assets. More specifically, the function points of business applications *a1*, *a2*, and *a3* are *Source Data*, and the derived attribute's value is *Derived Data*. The entities themselves (business applications *a1*, *a2*, and *a3* as well as functional domain *d1*) are *Information Assets*. Moreover, the metric *Average Functional Scope* with its computation prescription is an object of class *Metric*. While this is a very concrete example of a model-based metric, we could use any other metric which is defined based on an information model.

Depending on the level of granularity of data management and governance, various roles have to be specified to govern *Information Assets* (see Fig. 1). According to Kathri and Brown [18], five interrelated decision domains are common (see Sect. 2), whereas the "data principles" domain is responsible for the linkage with the business. Consequently, the data principles domain clarifies the extent to "which data is an enterprise-wide asset, and thus what specific policies, standards and guidelines are appropriate." [18]. In order to achieve clarification, a differentiation according to roles for accountability for data is necessary. The differentiation as used in our research was derived from Khatri and Brown is provided in Table 1.

Table 1. Roles for accountability and responsibility of information assets [18].

Role	Description
Data owner	The data owner has to ensure the data quality and develop and implement the data definition. Furthermore, he is responsible for interpreting and ensuring compliance to Federal, State and other policies.
Data custodian	The data custodian ensures that the access to the data is authorized and controlled. He is responsible for safe custody, transport, storage and implementation of business rules.
Data steward	The data steward ensures that each data element has a clear and unambiguous definition. He also has a respective documentation on usage.
Data producer	Everyone that creates data elements and persists them is a data producer. This is not necessarily a person but can also be an application.
Data consumer	The data consumer is the opposite role to the data producer. Data consumers read, transform, or process existing data elements.

In the domain of EAM, Matthes et al. [23] proposed two different roles on metrics, namely the owner and consumer. As proposed by Kathri and Brown [18] and by considering metrics as information assets, we extend this existing set of two roles on metrics to enable comprehensive data governance regarding information assets. Thereby, we are adding the roles of the data custodian, data steward and data consumer to metrics. As shown in Fig. 1, data as well as metrics can now be subsumed as information assets, which also holds the required relationships (data governance roles expressed by associations) between stakeholders and the information asset.

4   Defeasible Derivation of Roles for Derived EA Data

Just as Ninghui et al. [20] used a "delegation logic" to derive policies (see Sect. 2), we argue now for an existing logic system, namely "defeasible logic".

4.1   An Introduction to Defeasible Logic

Defeasible logic has been investigated extensively and is well known in the domain of artificial intelligence, especially its usage as argumentation logic [24]. Nute has shown the advantage of the defeasible logic over other logic systems [25]. The main advantage is the capability of non-monotonic reasoning. Monotonic logic systems fail if new information and conclusions contradicting prior reasoning results are added. Due to contradictions the logic framework gets inconsistent. This inconsistency does no longer allow the derivation of true and reliable results and can lead to undecidable problems for first order logic [25]. Therefore, the defeasible logic differentiates between different types of rules. Since it is not necessary to introduce and discuss all the possible rules and their relationships, we just restrict ourselves to the two most important:

$A \rightarrow \phi$ **(strict rule)** ... Strict rules can never be defeated. They do not have exceptions and consequently it is a *necessary* connection between antecedent (A) and consequence (ϕ), e.g., "Penguins are birds".

$A \Rightarrow \phi$ **(defeasible rule)** ... Defeasible rules represent weaker connections that can be defeated by a strict rule or a defeasible rule, e.g., "Birds can fly".

Without introducing all formalism required to fully understand the defeasible logic system, we will just briefly sketch out the symbols and predicates that we are using:

Predicate: P(X,Y) ... The predicate specifies the properties of some entity. For instance if someone wants to set the data owner of data entity d to the person p this can be denoted as dataOwner(d, p).

Logical Conjunction: , ... The comma is an abbreviation for the logical conjunction (AND, &, $\wedge$). E.g., "isData(d), isData(d')" represents the fact that both d *and* d' are data entities.

Logical Consequence: $\Sigma \vdash \phi$ ... The symbol represents the consequence relation. Informally spoken does this mean, that based on the given set of facts and rules Σ the logical system allows to derive the information ϕ. To express which information should be derived, it is possible to write a predicate, specifying the queried information.

Contradiction: $\bot$ ... To represent a contradiction in a logical system, for example inferred by conflicting rules or facts, the $\bot$ symbol (bottom) can represent this. This is usually a most unwanted state, since the logic system does not longer allow true and proofed inferences.

Inference: $\rightarrow$, $\Rightarrow$ ... To enable the derivation of new information, existing information has to be combined in rules. The two rule types are described above.

The applicability of the logic system is now discussed by a small example. Firstly, several facts are defined. In this case, there are two persons, namely p and q, and there are two data elements, namely d and d', whereas d' is derived data from d. Furthermore, the role of the data owner of d is kept by person p. We can now define the defeasible rule, that if a person is the data owner of some data element, and there is some other data element, that was derived from this data, then this person automatically becomes the data owner of the derived data element, i.e., dataOwner(d', X) $\vdash$ X = p. If someone now adds an additional fact, e.g., the data owner of d' is explicitly set to person q, then traditional logic systems, such as propositional logic systems, would determine a contradiction, which consequently would cause inconsistency and therefore the end of the logic engine as is. This inconsistency does not arise in defeasible logic, since theimplications that can be drawn using defeasible rules, are "soft" and can be overwritten by other rules and facts. Consequently, person q is the data owner of d', i.e. dataOwner(d', X) ⊢ X = q. This example can be formally expressed as follows:

> **Facts:**   isPerson(p), isPerson(q), isData(d), isData(d'),
>   isDerivedData(d', d), dataOwner(d, p)
> **Def. rule:** isDerivedData(D, S), dataOwner(D,X) ⇒ dataOwner(D, X)
> **Query 1:**   dataOwner(d', X) ⊢ X = p
> **Fact:**   dataOwner(d', q) (⊢ ⊥, in traditional logic systems)
> **Query 2:**   dataOwner(d', X) ⊢ X = q

To avoid problems of decidability, defeasible rules can and should be enriched with priorities clarifying the precedence between defeasible rules (see [25]). According to Nute, it is reasonable to prioritize regarding the specificity of rules. Thereby, one possible assignment could be *lex specialis derogat legi generali*. This means, that the more specific rule (*lex specialis*) takes precedence over the more general rule (*lex generali*). But there are also other ways to assign priorities to rules. Nute argues, just as legal sciences does in some cases, for the *lex superior derogat legi inferiori*, that higher-ranked rules (*lex superior*), such as the federal law, should have a higher priority than lower-ranked rules (*lex posterior*), such as state law. Different other priority assignments would be possible, depending on the concrete use case and implementation. Recent implementations of defeasible logic, e.g. Spindle [26], allow to explicitly assign priorities to express the conflict solution between rules.

4.2 Defeasible Derivation of Accountability and Responsibility Roles on Information Assets

As described in Sect. 3, every information asset needs to have roles governing the accountability on various levels. Although the number of roles, their name and their description may vary between enterprises, the need for assignment throughout dependent information assets remains. In the following we exemplarily show the applicability of defeasible logic as consistent and comprehensive method to assign roles with dependencies and resolve contradicting assignments.

Combining the roles as defined by Khatri and Brown (see Table 1), and nonmonotonic reasoning of defeasible logic as described by Nute (see Sect. 4.1), it is possible to extend this reasoning to a comprehensive and consistent role derivation framework. Based on the assumption, that information assets of an enterprise, namely data, which can be differentiated into source data and derived data, and EA metrics, need to have a complete and unambiguous assignment of accountability and responsibility roles, we can model a situation as shown in Fig. 3.

The model visualizes the situation as already described in Fig. 2. We have three different business application entities, *a1*, *a2*, and *a3*, which have respective function points as attribute values. The function points of those business

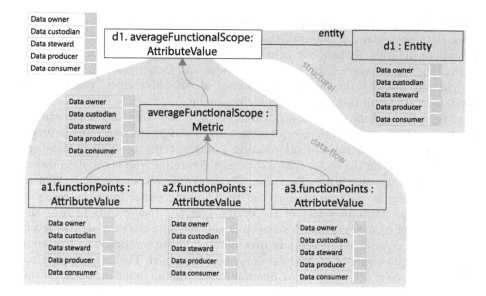

Fig. 3. Structural and data-flow influence factors of an attribute value.

applications are aggregated by an EA metric, which solely measures the mean value. The result of the metric is the value of the attribute *averageFunctionalScope* of the entity *d1* and consequently an information asset. Therefore, the holistic perspective on this particular attribute shows that it has two influence factors, i.e. data-flow and structure (see Fig. 3). The data-flow arises through metric and their calculation, whereas the structural influence factor is given through the data model, since every attribute value belongs to an entity. Both, the entity and the attribute definition are considered to be information assets and therefore have well-defined roles.

The situation as described has some obvious challenges. The derived attribute, namely averageFunctionalScope, is an information asset itself and is also part of other information assets. As an information asset it is necessary to have well-defined roles regarding accountability and responsibility. Hereby three determination scenarios are possible:

1. The roles are derived from the entity to which the derived attribute belongs.
2. The roles are derived from the data-flow influence factors, namely the data sources and metric from which it was calculated.
3. The roles are manually assigned for each information asset.

Which of the three scenarios is going to be applied depends on various factors and the enterprise's data governance strategy. It could also be a combination of all of the mentioned strategies, depending on the situation and data. However, using defeasible logic it is possible to specify the derivation rules accordingly. The possibility to set priorities between roles, as explained in Sect. 4.1, can be used to create a logically consistent and comprehensive data governance derivation framework. The combination of strict and defeasible rules is then the key to set up a data governance framework that allows logical inference regarding roles, i.e. responsibilities. Although it is in principle possible to create contradictions within the logical system, by using strict rules and facts, this can and should be circumvented by the priority mechanism of defeasible rules, which is the fundamental idea of this non-monotonic reasoning.

The example bellow shows a possible scenario how defeasible logic can be used to update data governance principles, facts and interconnections between the data governance roles of information assets. At the beginning, facts are provided. Based on the facts, *Query 0* cannot determine who is the data owner of the attribute value *d1.avgFctScope*. The first rule allows the derivation of data ownership from the containing entity. The data owner from the entity is passed to the attribute values of the entity. *Query 1* now results in p as the data owner of *d1.avgFctScope*, because p is also the data owner of *d1*. However, a succeeding defeasible rule can now overrule this derivation. Based on the input values, the data owner of derived data may be determined. The facts define, that *d1.avgFctScope* is derived from *a1.functionPoints* and *a2.functionPoints*. So the data owner of the input variables is passed towards the derived data, which is then q (see *Query 2*). The metric, i.e. the combination of the input variables, might be more important than the source data, the defeasible rule 3 now allows the derivation of the data owner. The data owner of *d1.avgFctScope* will then be the same as the data owner of the metric *avgFctScope*, which is r (see Query 3).

Facts:	isEntity(d1), isEntity(a1), isEntity(a2), isMetric(avgFctScope), isData(d1.avgFctScope), isData(a1.functionPoints), isData(a2.functionPoints), isDerivedData(d1.avgFctScope, a1.functionPoints), isDerivedData(d1.avgFctScope, a2.functionPoints), isPerson(p), isPerson(q), isPerson(r), dataOwner(d1, p), dataOwner(a1, q), dataOwner(a2, q), dataOwner(avgFctScope, r)
Query 0:	dataOwner(d1.avgFctScope, X) ⊢ X = *undecided*
Def. rule 1:	isEntity(E), dataOwner(E,X), isDataOfEntity(D,E) ⇒ dataOwner(D, X)
Query 1:	dataOwner(d1.avgFctScope, X) ⊢ X = p
Def. rule 2:	isDerivedData(D', D), dataOwner(D,X) ⇒ dataOwner(D', X)
Query 2:	dataOwner(d1.avgFctScope, X) ⊢ X = q
Def. rule 3:	isMetric(M), dataOwner(M, X), calculates(M, D) ⇒ dataOwner(D, X)
Query 3:	dataOwner(d1.avgFctScope, X) ⊢ X = r

This example shows the applicability of non-monotonic reasoning in the data governance process of EA information assets. The focus was rather the provision of a methodology than focusing on concrete rules, since those may vary throughout enterprises. However, the defeasible logic allows continuous adaption of rules, without being inconsistent, i.e. contradicting, at any time.

5   Conclusion

This paper is an attempt to support data governance in enterprises by using non-monotonic logic, i.e. defeasible logic. We developed a model for information assets in enterprise architectures and identified existing roles for accountability and responsibility. The synthesis with a respective meta-model that was used in prior research leads to a model on information and governance structure. The assignments of five different governance roles to each information asset assures tracking and well-defined accountability but can lead to a managerial overhead due to the amount of assignment.

The interconnectedness of data in enterprises and the derivation of data by metrics calls for a consistent framework that ensures the derivation of data governance roles. In this paper we argue for an existing logic, namely defeasible logic. Thereby it is not only possible to provide rules for derivation but also to continuously adapt the existing set of rules. In contrary to other logic frameworks, existing rules can be overwritten and priorities between rules can be specified. This allows seamless adaptation to changed data governance policies.

This paper proposes a framework for roles on EA data governance and shows how a defeasible logic can be used to support data governance, and thus answers the research questions as raised in Sect. 1. Open research questions could address the role of time in data governance principles, but could also focus on a more practical research such as using a defeasible logic engine to simulate and analyze the impact of changes in data governance policies.

References

1. Ahlemann, F., Stettiner, E., Messerschmidt, M., Legner, C.: Strategic Enterprise Architecture Management. Springer, Heidelberg (2012)
2. International Organization for Standardization: ISO/IEC 42010:2007 Systems and Software Engineering – Recommended Practice for Architectural Description of Software-Intensive Systems. Switzerland, Geneva (2007)
3. Zachman, J.A.: A framework for information systems architecture. IBM Syst. J. **26**, 276–292 (1987)
4. Buckl, S., Matthes, F., Monahov, I., Roth, S., Schulz, C., Schweda, C.M.: Towards an agile design of the enterprise architecture management function. In: Proceedings of the Enterprise Distributed Object Computing Conference Workshops (2011)
5. Matthes, F., Buckl, S., Leitel, J., Schweda, C.M.: Enterprise Architecture Management Tool Survey 2008. Technical report (2008)
6. Monahov, I., Reschenhofer, T., Matthes, F.: Design and prototypical implementation of a language empowering business users to define key performance indicators for enterprise architecture management. In: Proceedings of the Trends in Enterprise Architecture Research Workshop (2013)
7. Reschenhofer, T., Monahov, I., Matthes, F.: Type-safety in EA model analysis. In: Proceedings of the Trends in Enterprise Architecture Research Workshop (2014)
8. Fischer, R., Aier, S., Winter, R.: A federated approach to enterprise architecture model maintenance. Enterp. Model. Inf. Syst. Archit. **2**(2), 14–22 (2007)

9. Basel Committee on Banking Supervision, International Convergence of Capital Measurement and Capital Standards: A Revised Framework Comprehensive Version, June 2006

10. Aleatrati, P., Hauder, M., Roth, S.: Impact of solvency II on the Enterprise architecture of insurances - a qualitative study in Germany. In: Multikonferenz Wirtschaftsinformatik (MKWI 2014) (2014)

11. Bundesbank, D.: Banking Act: 2009 (2009)

12. Bretz, J.: Prüfung IT im Fokus von MaRisk und Bundesbank: Verstärkter IT-Fokus in Sonderprüfungen. Finanz Colloquium Heidelberg (2012)

13. Waltl, B., Schneider, A.W., Matthes, F.: Deriving and modelling compliance requirements from legal audits, In: 23rd Annual EICAR Conference: Trust and Transparency in IT Security (2014)

14. Hallows, J.E.: The Project Management Office Toolkit. American Management, New York (2002)

15. Ninghui, L., Benjamin, N.G., Joan, F.: Delegation logic: a logic-based approach to distributed authorization. ACM Trans. Inf. Syst. Secur. 6(1), 128–171 (2003)

16. Kofman A., Klinger, T.: Roles, rights, and responsibilities: better governance through decision rights automation, In: Proceedings of the Workshop on Software Development Governance (2009)

17. Data Governance Institute, The DGI Data Governance Framework (2009)

18. Khatri, V., Brown, C.V.: Designing data governance. Commun. ACM 53(1), 148–152 (2010)

19. Yogesh, L.S., Beth, P., Dennis, G.: A survey of data provenance in e-science. SIGMOD Rec 34(3), 31–36 (2005)

20. Li, N., Grosof, B.N., Feigenbaum, J.: A nonmonotonic delegation logic with prioritized conflict handling. Technical report (2000)

21. Gaaloul, K., Proper, H.A., Zahoor, E., Charoy, F., Godart, C.: A logical framework for reasoning about delegation policies in workflow management systems. Int. J. Inf. Comput. Secur. 4(4), 365–388 (2011)

22. Schneider, A.W., Reschenhofer, T., Schütz, A., Matthes, F.: Empirical results for application landscape complexity. In: Proceedings of the Hawaii International Conference on System Sciences (2015)

23. Matthes, F., Monahov, I., Schneider, A.W., Schulz, C.: Towards a unified and configurable structure for EA management KPIs. In: Proceedings of the Trends in Enterprise Architecture Research Workshop (2012)

24. Ashley, K.D.: Toward a computational theory of arguing with precedents. In: Proceedings of the 2nd international conference on Artificial intelligence and law, pp. 93–102. ACM, Vancouver (1989)

25. Nute, D.: Defeasible logic. In: Bartenstein, O., Geske, U., Hannebauer, M., Yoshie, O. (eds.) INAP 2001. LNCS (LNAI), vol. 2543, pp. 151–169. Springer, Heidelberg (2003). http://dx.doi.org/10.1007/3-540-36524-9_13

26. Lam, H.-P., Governatori, G.: The making of SPINdle. In: Governatori, G., Hall, J., Paschke, A. (eds.) RuleML 2009. LNCS, vol. 5858, pp. 315–322. Springer, Heidelberg (2009). http://dx.doi.org/10.1007/978-3-642-04985-9_29

Success Factors for Federated Enterprise Architecture Model Management

Pouya Aleatrati Khosroshahi[1(✉)], Stephan Aier[2], Matheus Hauder[1],
Sascha Roth[1], Florian Matthes[1], and Robert Winter[2]

[1] Chair for Informatics 19 (Sebis), Technische Universität München,
Boltzmannstrasse 3, 85748 Garching b. Munich, Germany
{p.aleatrati,matheus.hauder,roth,matthes}@tum.de
[2] Institute for Information Management, University of St. Gallen,
Mueller-Friedberg-Strasse 8, 9000 St. Gallen, Switzerland
{stephan.aier,robert.winter}@unisg.ch

Abstract. Recent approaches for managing Enterprise Architecture (EA) models provide technical systems to procure information from existing repositories within the application landscape of an organization. Beyond technical solutions, social factors are of utmost importance to implement a successful EA initiative. Institutional theory has for example been employed to understand crucial factors for realizing EA Management (EAM) benefits through architectural thinking. Yet, it remains unclear how these social factors influence a federated approach for EA model management. Based on a socio-technical systems perspective, we investigate success factors for Federated EA Model Management (FEAMM) by conducting qualitative interviews with industry experts. Our findings suggest that success factors for FEAMM are related to the model sources, modeling instruments, and model integration aspects from a technical perspective as well as to organizational grounding, governance, enforcement, efficiency, goal alignment, and trust from a social perspective.

Keywords: Federated enterprise architecture model management · Institutionalization · Socio-technical system

1 Motivation

Increasing complexity of business transactions as well as an accelerated rate of change due to globalization and fierce competition demand for continuous alignment of organizational structures with strategic goals. Enterprise Architecture and the corresponding management function are discussed as an effective means to improve alignment of business with its supporting information systems (IS) and technology (IT) [5, 37]. Empirical data confirm the potential of this discipline to achieve and maintain IS/IT efficiency and effectiveness while contributing to the business value of an organization [9, 20]. Among others, one of the essential requirements to realize these benefits is the creation of transparency about the current and future state of the organization's architecture among relevant stakeholders.

EA models facilitate this transparency and provide the foundation for measurability, consistency, as well as a shared language and understanding among diverse

© Springer International Publishing Switzerland 2015
A. Persson and J. Stirna (Eds.): CAiSE 2015 Workshops, LNBIP 215, pp. 413–425, 2015.
DOI: 10.1007/978-3-319-19243-7_38

stakeholders [1, 2, 10, 21, 33, 34]. EA modeling is a cross-cutting effort that documents the organization's structure, e.g., IS, business processes, infrastructure components as well as their relationships. Particularly in medium and large organizations, EA models grow huge. Creating and maintaining these models can only be achieved by division of labor and the reuse of available data. Several already existing models might be maintained for specialized purposes in the organization, e.g., configuration management databases, license management and project portfolio management tools [17]. FEAMM is an approach to integrate existing special purpose models by transforming relevant horizontal (enterprise-wide), vertical (business-to-IT), and time dimensions (planning) of the information [18]. In FEAMM formerly independent models providing partial perspectives of an organization are linked to an EA repository through meta-model integration.

Successful management of the EA relies on solid and up to date information provided by these federated models. Ensuring topicality and consistency of the EA model requires maintenance processes that are either run periodically or triggered by specific events, e.g., certain project milestones [4, 18]. These maintenance processes require the active involvement of EA stakeholders and data owners that provide the information from federated models and revise inconsistencies during the integration with the EA meta-model [18]. While research recently promotes technical systems that attempt to support stakeholders of FEAMM with the automated provisioning of aggregated information from existing specialized models [14, 31], the enterprise-wide stakeholder engagement for sharing local data and contributing to an enterprise-wide EA model remains a major challenge. The active engagement of stakeholders during the creation and maintenance processes requires an institutionalization of EA in the organization. Next to strict governance mechanisms that enforce the involvement of stakeholders in maintenance processes, successful FEAMM relies on the organizational grounding, social legitimacy, efficiency, and trust of EA in the organization [38]. Governance aspects that are important for the successful establishment of FEAMM need to consider these social as well as technical aspects. Against this background we formulate the following research question:

What are social and technological success factors for Federated EA Model Management?

Our findings summarize novel and integrated success factors that are crucial for the establishment of a successful FEAMM in order to maintain a solid and up to date model that can serve as a foundation for successful EA management. While existing research mainly investigates technology to automate the provision of EA information from existing specialized models in the organization [14, 29], this paper considers the socio-technical perspective in which FEAMM is embedded.

2   Related Work

In this section we discuss related work regarding the general idea of FEAMM, methods and techniques used, and the social aspects of anchoring the general idea of EA and FEAMM in an organization.

Roth coined the term FEAMM [28] describing a phenomenon often observed in industry during the procurement of information for an EA model. FEAMM is an organizational setting in which a central EA management function integrates models of highly specialized, semi-autonomous IT management functions referred to as communities. Each community performs tasks which follow processes defined either explicitly or implicitly. These processes are supported by technology. In [28] we report that each modeling community can be considered a separate linguistic community. That means each community describes real-world objects with their own terminology. Although the modeling communities may refer to the same real-world objects, they use different names and attributes to describe them. Multiple modeling communities perform their tasks employing highly specialized repositories incorporating best-practice knowledge. In [22], Goodhue and Thompson observe a phenomenon and coined the phrase 'task technology fit'. The authors highlight that individual performance rises if a good fit prevails between employed technologies and the task. Hence we conclude that the repositories employed by the different communities are intended to fit best for the tasks at hand for this particular community.

The concept of FEAMM embraces technical details, relevant information sources, data quality aspects, documentation processes, and respective challenges that arise when procuring information from existing repositories. These aspects have been investigated by different research groups, e.g. Farwick et al. [15], Buschle et al. [11], or Roth et al. [31]. Further, requirements [16], governance and processes [15, 18], case studies [17], and issues [23] are pointed out by these research groups. Roth et al. note that the teams of modeling communities are aware that the information they maintain may contribute to the overall performance of an organization and proposes an approach for FEAMM assuming that the modeling communities are willing to share information, which, however, might not always be the case. Important for a successful FEAMM are governance aspects such as role allocations [28, 31] and a clear definition of responsibilities [28] and escalation paths in case a conflict between two repositories describing the same real-world object occurs [30].

Closely related to our work are the findings reported by Lange et al. [25]. The researchers report on success factors found in literature and explain a theoretical model that aims at the realization of EA benefits. Schmidt and Buxmann perform a field survey on outcomes and critical success factors for EA management [13]. While both, the research group around Lange et al. and Schmidt and Buchmann, investigate EA management function in general, we focus on success factors with respect to FEAMM.

As of today, no research group investigated how to get stakeholders to share EA information. In contrast, Hauder et al. [23] report that sharing information without clear benefits is often an issue of EA management initiatives. We argue that sharing EA information among communities requires prior institutionalization of EA management. Despite the maturity of EA methods and techniques, it remains challenging to effectively anchor, i.e., institutionalize EA in an organization [33, 38]. Ross and Quaadgras [27] found that "business value accrues through management practices that propagate architectural thinking throughout the enterprise". What is needed is an *architectural thinking* as "the way of thinking and acting throughout an organization, i.e. not restricted to architects and system developers" [40].

Weiss et al. [38] therefore propose an institutional theory perspective on EA research. They employ institutional theory in order to understand how organizations and individuals respond to pressures - in our case the need to share and integrate their local EA models. They find that the stakeholders' response towards EA is influenced by the social legitimacy and efficiency stakeholder's gain, by the organizational grounding of EA, and by the trust stakeholders have in the EA unit. They also find that governance mechanisms, stakeholders' goal alignment with general EA goals, and enforcement of EA foster EA consistency and adoption. Wieland et al. first propose to deal with model conflicts and merging with human intervention [39]. However, their approach addresses software models and thus cannot be directly applied to EA models.

While methods and models for an automation of FEAMM are elaborated at a rather technical level by research outlined above, in line with Roth [28], we identify a research concerning governance aspects, role integration in organizational processes, and the complex social interactions across diverse communities in an organization.

3   Research Methodology

3.1   Research Model

In the paper at hand we analyze our empirical data through the lens of socio-technical systems theory and its four perspectives of task, technology, people, and structure (cf. Fig. 1) [7]. Socio-technical systems theory conceptualizes an organization as a system with two interrelated subsystems, the technical system and the social system.

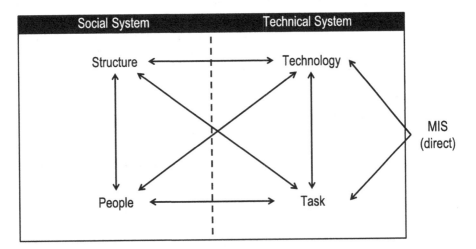

Fig. 1. Interacting classes and their relationships in socio-technical systems theory [7]

The technical system is concerned with the processes, tasks, and technology needed to transform inputs such as materials or information to outputs such as products or services. The social system is concerned with the relationships among people and the attributes of these people such as attitudes, skills, and values. The outputs of the entire system are a result of the joint interaction between these two systems [8]. System designs that ignore one of these dimensions are expected to perform worse or even fail to achieve their goals compared to designs that cater for all four perspectives.

3.2   Research Approach

FEAMM is rarely discussed in academia and practice. *Thus, we conducted 11 interviews with EA experts across various industries and various job positions to get different views on how EA experts deal with FEAMM practices and which governance structures support these.* Table 1 gives an overview of the interview participants.

Table 1. Overview of interview participants

#	Position	Industry	No. of Employees
1	Enterprise Architect	Insurance	~5.000
2	Enterprise Architect	Manufacturer	~50.000
3	IT Architect	Manufacturer	>100.000
4	Enterprise Architect	Insurance	~10.000
5	Senior Manager	Consulting	>100.000
6	Enterprise Architect	Public Sector	Ns.
7	Senior Consultant	Consulting	<1.000
8	Executive Assistant	Insurance	~50.000
9	IT Architect	Insurance	~10.000
10	Enterprise Architect	Insurance	~100.000
11	Professor	Research	<1.000

To ensure anonymity of participants, an aggregated view on the interview data is provided [35]. We employ semi-structured interviews with open questions to create the opportunity for EA experts to discuss a broad range of aspects of FEAMM [24]. We provided the interviewees with an interview guideline illustrating the research topic. *Although, the interviews followed a semi-structured style, we pay attention to include questions referring to preferred role allocations, governance principles and used methods in case of establishing a FEAMM within the corresponding organization.* The interview duration ranges from 23 to 120 min (68 min in average). All interviews were recorded, transcribed, and sent back to the participants to ensure the correctness of the transcripts [19]. The experts interviews were analyzed according to a concept matrix based method by Webster and Watson [36].

4   Empirical Findings

Our empirical data cover organizational aspects and technical aspects of FEAMM. The organizational aspects provide information about preferable governance structures, such as role allocation and non-technical prerequisites. Moreover, we analyzed incentives that might increase the participation in FEAMM activities, for instance use cases that benefit from FEAMM. Technical aspects include information about the direction of data flow between communities, the EA model and the application of ontologies when maintaining FEAMM. Moreover, the empirical data provide information about the current status of EAM within the respective organizations and reflect specific use cases that might benefit from establishing FEAMM.

4.1   Use Cases of Federated EA Model Management

Most of the interviewed EA experts stated that EAM is perceived as a significant asset within their respective organization. EAM supports running business activities by identifying relevant information sources, transforming the EA landscapes to provide appropriate data flows for business requirements and supports mandatory tasks, such as the implementation of regulatory requirements [6]. *Most of the interviewees stated that EAM is driven by IT departments and rather by than business departments. The problem is that business departments neither observe any benefit from EAM nor believe that their running business would change.* Furthermore, the interviewees face the problem of missing management support and a low priority of EAM. Daily business activities and mandatory issues such as regulatory requirements receive higher priorities. Thus, we asked the EA experts for use cases in which a federated EA model would realize a benefit for the majority of the stakeholders within the respective organization. *We received the following use cases from the conducted expert interviews:*

IT Controlling: These days, there are several possibilities to allocate overhead to specific products within a company, such as the marginal planned cost accounting approach. Groups operate across various countries and run thousands of IT applications and databases. Moreover, current IT landscapes of today's organizations face frequent changes with respect to daily migrations and software implementation projects. As a consequence, companies have an issue to both comprehensively and correctly capture the status quo of IT landscapes. 7 out of 11 EA experts stated that a federated EA model can be a useful information source for IT controlling purposes: All EA related information are stored within a federated EA model and provide the required information to identify used IT components within an organization and allocate them to products or specific communities.

Trends and Forecasting: Depending on the defined or available attributes for the considered entities within a federated EA model, the single instances might provide information regarding their storage, the supported business processes or the current status of issues within the specific instance (such as failed interface transfers between two databases). 5 out of 11 EA experts stated that this information would support forecasting activities with regard to the current EA landscape.

Planning and Controlling the EA Landscape: Within large organizations, IT landscapes have developed in a heterogeneous way and contain various IS components.

One EA expert mentioned that his organization runs over 150 information systems. The respective company is facing the challenge of missing transparency and non-existing documentation of the introduced ISs. A federated EA model helps to cope with these barriers by providing a clear overview of the current IT landscape and thus supports the strategic planning of the EA. 4 out of 11 interviewed EA experts confirmed this use case. Single EA experts mentioned further use cases that do not fit to all organizations and depend on characteristics of specific markets.

Regulatory Requirements: Financial service providers in particular face the problem of upcoming Solvency II or IFRS 4 Phase 2. These regulatory requirements ask among other for the used ISs with regard to risk management purposes. A federated EA model can provide required information.

Chief Information Officer (CIO) Reporting: IT departments are encouraged to report the current status—such as used IS components—to the CIO of the organization. A federated EA model provides the information to facilitate this reporting.

Transformation Projects: Companies put much effort in solving the obstacle of heterogeneous IT landscapes by conducting IS harmonization and migration projects, i.e., transformations. A clear overview of the EA landscape and the implemented data flows between the ISs are the foundation of transformation projects. A holistic EA model provides this information.

4.2   Lean Role Allocation Approach

During the expert interviews, it turned out that industry experts prefer a pragmatic approach with fewer roles. The involvement of too many roles lead to bureaucratization of the maintenance process and influence the efficiency of it. Moreover, all interviewed EA experts prefer to involve the Domain Architect within the maintenance activities of the EA model. A Domain Architect acts as a specialist for a specific business or technology domain such as IBM DB2. The Enterprise Architect has an overarching role within the maintenance process and is involved in the majority of the conducted activities. EA experts prefer to limit the involvement of different roles to a minimum.

4.3   Incentives to Participate in FEAMM

The participation of business stakeholder and all communities is mandatory to keep a federated EA model up to date. We asked the EA experts, how to convince business stakeholder to participate in FEAMM activities. Two different strategies to convince the communities to participate in FEAMM have been identified:

Social Methods: One mentioned possibility is to provide incentives that convince organizational members on a social level to participate in FEAMM activities. Incentives might be the agreement on objectives or an extra bonus. 4 out of 11 EA experts tries to convince Data Owners for providing necessary EA information by using social methods.

Governance Pressure: A dedicated supervisory makes use of governance procedures to ensure that single communities provide the information on a granular level. This method requires the support of upper management, strict EA principles and the definition of escalation paths. 5 out of 11 EA experts make use of governance pressure to get EA information by single communities.

4.4   Terminology Alignment Is a Necessity

Conflicts between instances lead to model inconsistency issues and have to be solved within the staging area. Conrad [12] provides a categorization of data conflicts—such as semantic conflicts or structural conflicts—in terms of federated databases that might also occur in a federated EA model. In order to guard against the majority of conflicts, the EA experts mentioned that an aligned EA terminology is a mandatory prerequisite before starting to design, develop, and maintain a federated EA model. The alignment process requires the participation of all modeling communities, Enterprise Architects, and of an EA board or a comparable supervisory. The alignment process can be divided in three phases:

General Setup Activities: In this starting phase, the EA board and the Enterprise Architects set the scope of the alignment—such as the considered entities—and define governance principles for the alignment process. Furthermore the process will be tested with one community in form of a pilot study to identify missing unnoticed circumstances and obstacles. The results of the pilot study will be evaluated and used for re-scoping the planned alignment process. The finalized governance structure and the alignment scope will be communicated to all communities

Iterative Standardization: Enterprise Architects conduct workshops with the single communities to define the necessary terminology adjustment for the respective entity. The standardization process follows an iterative approach: An iteration is always comprised of one entity such as application or platform.

Final Sign-off: The finalized EA terminology needs to be signed-off by the EA board.

The majority of the EA experts prefers a lean, pragmatic, and agile alignment process with less involvement of stakeholders. Moreover, EA experts asked for stronger business involvement and think that escalation paths to the EA board within all activities are mandatory to solve disputes between communities.

4.5   Application of Ontologies

Ontologies relate to semantic web technologies that can be used to integrate heterogeneous data sets into a formalized structure [32]. Referring to the conflict resolution process, ontologies support the identification of conflicts in an automated way.

It turned out that ontologies are not a preferred supporting option for the conflict resolution process of FEAMM. All interviewed EA experts disagreed to use ontologies within a FEAMM. Rather, it has only significance in the academics area of EA.

These EA experts that were familiar with the concept mentioned that ontologies could be interesting in the future: The application of ontologies requires highly homogenous data sets and major efforts (referring to data standardization and customization of running ISs). Moreover, other issues, such as the implementation of regulatory requirements in the insurance sector, have a higher priority.

4.6   Unidirectional vs. Bidirectional Data Flow

Communities have to transfer the EA model information – either automatically or manually—to the centralized EA model. There is the possibility to transfer information from the EA model to the communities as well. We evaluated whether the experts prefer a unidirectional or a bidirectional data flow.

- *Machine-to-machine communication:* The EA repository system can change or transfer data sets within the ISs of the single communities.
- *Machine-to-person communication:* The EA repository responsibility communicates information to the communities, but is not authorized to change or transfer data sets within the ISs of the communities.

The communication of EA model information to the community supports data standardization issues and provides useful means to communicate new governance standards to the communities. However, the communities have to ensure the full control about their productive data. EA experts mentioned that wrong data changes might impact the running business of the communities.

5   Discussion

We analyze the empirical data of the expert interviews using the socio-technical system theory framework to structure our research results (cf. Fig. 2). Key findings of the empirical analysis are placed in four areas of the socio-technical system: *Structure, People, Technology,* and *Task.* We allocate the key findings to institutional factors, partly provided by Weiss et al. [38] that influence FEAMM.

This view places the key findings of the empirical data on the four areas of the socio-technical system: Structure, People, Technology and Task. Moreover, we allocated the key findings to institutional factors, partly provided by Weiss et al. [38] that impact the management of a federated EA model.

Structure: Ross [26] states business stakeholders rarely participate in EAM activities because it lacks direct value for them. Our empirical findings show that the participation of all modeling communities is mandatory to ensure a comprehensive and correct federated EA model. For this purpose, FEAMM demands strict EAM principles, escalation paths, and governance pressure (cf. [28]). The definition and operation of these measures influence the *Governance* of FEAMM. Moreover, the current priority of EAM within an organization influences the *Organizational Grounding* of FEAMM.

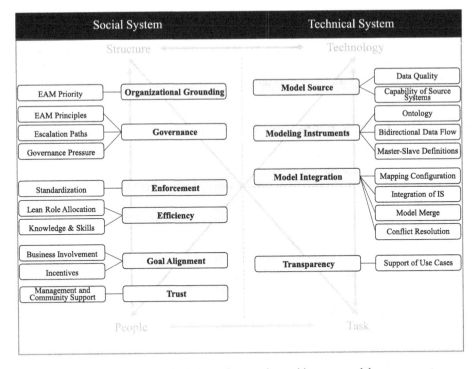

Fig. 2. Success factors of a federated enterprise architecture model management

People: EA experts mentioned they prefer a lean role allocation across all FEAMM activities and face the problem of missing documentations regarding their productive ISs and skills to alter the IS. These two factors influence the *Efficiency* gains through FEAMM. The definition of too many roles within FEAMM leads to bureaucracy and might impact the efficiency of FEAMM negatively. Moreover, missing documentations about the productive ISs lead to major efforts for transformation activities. EA experts also pointed out that the involvement of business stakeholder is mandatory for the efficient FEAMM. Use cases—such as the implementation of regulatory requirements—relate to business issues. Thus, a federated EA model should provide appropriate information. In line with Ahlemann et al. [3], EA experts also confirmed that incentives to participate in FEAMM activities are an essential factor. These factors attract further attention regarding *Goal Alignment* measures between FEAMM and business goals. Moreover, EA experts confirmed that the support of the upper management and the conviction of non-EAM stakeholder in the meaningfulness of FEAMM are mandatory. Organizations stakeholder have to *trust* the EAM function.

Technology: Hauder et al. [23] already highlighted that issues in data quality have a severe impact on EA documentation activities and hence on FEAMM. The interviewees confirmed this issue. As aforementioned, one EA expert pointed out the problem of missing scalability of source systems. These two factors can be aggregated as *Model Source* factors. Furthermore, the empirical data reveals opinions about ontologies, data flow directions, and further technology based factors that can be summarized in *Modeling Instrument* factors.

Task: Considering FEAMM on a higher level, the overarching goal is to improve EAM *Transparency* within an organization. The increased transparency supports the operation of specific use cases, such as IT controlling. *Model Integration* embraces organizational roles and responsibilities for the configuration of a mapping between the information sources and the EA repository, which is part of the initial integration process (cf. [28]). This integration is the foundation for importing information to merge the different (partial) models into the EA model. During such a merge it is of utmost importance to resolve responsible roles for the conflict resolution sub-process.

6   Conclusion

In this paper, we provide empirical insights on important success factors for FEAMM. We took a socio-technical systems perspective to present our results to illustrate factors that influence the implementation and maintenance of FEAMM.

The results show that today's organizations prefer a pragmatic FEAMM approach with strong business involvement and a lean role allocation. However, it turned out that the implementation of FEAMM meet various organizational challenges that need to be resolved previously such as the establishment of a standardized EA terminology. Moreover, technical requirements such as an adequate tool support need to be considered (cf. [28]).

Further research may provide quantitative evidence of these success factors and reveal other important factors for successful FEAMM initiatives. Moreover, the role of business stakeholders within FEAMM in terms of implementation and maintenance activities have to be evaluated.

References

1. Abraham, R.: Enterprise architecture artifacts as boundary objects – a framework of properties. In: European Conference on Information Systems (ECIS 2013) Utrecht, The Netherland, 5–8 June 2013
2. Abraham, R., Niemietz, H., de Kinderen, S., Aier, S.: Can boundary objects mitigate communication defects in enterprise transformation? findings from expert interviews. In: Proceedings of the 5th International Workshop on Enterprise Modelling and Information Systems Architectures (EMISA 2013), St. Gallen, Switzerland (2013)
3. Ahlemann, F., Stettiner, E., Messerschmidt, M., Legner, C.: Strategic Enterprise Architecture Management: Challenges, Best Practices, and Future Developments. Springer, Heidelburg (2012)
4. Aier, S., Buckl, S., Franke, U., Gleichauf, B., Johnson, P., Närman, P., Schweda, C., Ullberg, J.: A survival analysis of application life spans based on enterprise architecture. In: Proceedings of the 3th International Workshops (EMISA 2009) Ulm, Germany, 09–11 September 2009

5. Aier, S., Gleichauf, B., Winter, R.: Understanding enterprise architecture management design - an empirical analysis. In: Proceedings of the 10th International Conference on Wirtschaftsinformatik (WI 2011) Zurich, Switzerland, 16–18 April 2011

6. Aleatrati Khosroshahi, P., Roth, S., Hauder, M.: Impact of solvency II on the enterprise architecture of insurances: A qualitative study in Germany. In: Multikonferenz Wirtschaftsinformatik (MKWI 2014) Paderborn, Germany, 26–28 February 2014

7. Bostrom, R.P., Heinen, S.: MIS, problems and failures – a socio-technical perspective. Part I - the causes. MIS Q. 1(3), 17–32 (1977)

8. Bostrom, R.P., Heinen, S.: MIS problems and failures – a socio-technical perspective. Part II – the application of the socio-technical theory. MIS Q. 1(4), 11–28 (1977)

9. Boucharas, V., van Steenbergen, M., Jansen, S., Brinkkemper, S. The contribution of enterprise architecture to the achievement of organizational goals: establishing the enterprise architecture benefits framework. Technical report UU-CS-2010-014, Utrecht University, Utrecht (2010)

10. Buckl, S., Matthes, F., Roth, S., Schulz, C., Schweda, C.M.: A conceptual framework for enterprise architecture design. In: Proper, E., Lankhorst, M.M., Schönherr, M., Barjis, J., Overbeek, S. (eds.) TEAR 2010. LNBIP, vol. 70, pp. 44–56. Springer, Heidelberg (2010)

11. Buschle, M., Holm, H., Sommestad, T., Ekstedt, M., Shahzad, K.: A tool for automatic enterprise architecture modeling. In: Nurcan, S. (ed.) CAiSE Forum 2011. LNBIP, vol. 107, pp. 1–15. Springer, Heidelberg (2012)

12. Conrad, S.: Föderierte Datenbanksysteme – Konzepte der Datenintegration. Springer, Heidelberg (1997)

13. Schmidt, C., Buxmann, P.: Outcomes and success factors of enterprise IT architecture management: empirical insight from the international financial services industry. Eur. J. Inf. Syst. 20(2), 168–185 (2011)

14. Farwick, M., Schweda, C., Breu, R., Hanschke, I.: A situational method for semi-automated enterprise architecture documentation. Softw. Syst. Model. 1–30 (2014). doi:10.1007/s10270-014-0407-3

15. Farwick, M. Agreiter, B. Breu, R. Ryll, S. Voges, K. Hanschke, I.: Automation processes for enterprise architecture management. In: Enterprise Distributed Object Computing Conference Workshops (EDOCW 2011), Helsinki, Finnland, 29 August–2 September (2011)

16. Farwick, M. Agreiter, B. Breu, R. Ryll, S. Voges, K. Hanschke, I.: Requirements for automated enterprise architecture model maintenance – a requirements analysis based on a literature review and an exploratory survey. In: Proceedings of the 13th International Conference on Enterprise Information Systems (ICEIS 2011) Beijing, China, 8–11 June 2011

17. Farwick, M., Breu, R., Hauder, M., Roth, S., Matthes, F.: Enterprise architecture documentation: empirical analysis of information sources for automation. In: 46th Hawaii International Conference on System Sciences (HICSS 2013) Maui, Hawaii, 7–10 January 2013

18. Fischer, R., Aier, S., Winter, R.: A federated approach to enterprise architecture model maintenance. Enterp. Model. Inf. Syst. Archit. 2(2), 14–22 (2007)

19. Flick, U., von Kardorff, E., Steinke, I.: An Introduction to Qualitative Research, 4th edn. Sage Publications, London (2006)

20. Foorthuis, R., van Steenbergen, M., Mushkudian, N., Brinkkemper, S., Bos, R.: On course, but not there yet: Enterprise architecture conformance and benefits in systems development. In: International Conference on Information Systems (ICIS 2010) Saint Louis, USA, 12–15 December 2010

21. Frank, U., Strecker, S., Fettke, P., Brocke, J., Becker, J., Sinz, E.: The research field "modeling business information". Bus. Inf. Syst. Eng. 6(1), 39–43 (2014)
22. Goodhue, D.L., Thompson, R.L.: Task-technology fit and individual performance. MIS Q. 19(2), 213–236 (1995)
23. Hauder, M., Matthes, F., Roth, S.: Challenges for automated enterprise architecture documentation. In: Aier, S., Ekstedt, M., Matthes, F., Proper, E., Sanz, J.L. (eds.) PRET 2012 and TEAR 2012. LNBIP, vol. 131, pp. 21–39. Springer, Heidelberg (2012)
24. Kvale, S.: Doing interviews. Sage Publications, London (2008)
25. Lange, M., Mendling, J., Recker, J.: A comprehensive EA benefit realization model – An exploratory study. In: 45th Hawaii International Conference on System Sciences (HICCS 2012), Maui, Hawaii, 4–10 January 2012
26. Ross, J. W.: Creating a Strategic IT Architecture Competency: Learning in Stages, April 2003
27. Ross, J., Quaadgras, A.: Enterprise Architecture Is Not Just for Architects. Center for Information Systems Research, Sloan School of Management, Massachusetts Institute of Technology, Cambridge, USA (2012)
28. Roth, S.: federated enterprise architecture model management – conceptual foundations, collaborative integration, and software support. Ph.D. thesis, Technische Universität München (2014)
29. Roth, S., Hauder, M., Farwick, M., Matthes, F., Breu, R.: Enterprise architecture documentation: current practices and future directions. In: 11th International Conference on Wirtschaftsinformatik (WI 2013) Leipzig, Germany, 27 February–01 March 2013
30. Roth, S., Hauder, M., Matthes, F.: Facilitating conflict resolution of models for automated enterprise architecture documentation. In: 19th Americas Conference on Information Systems (AMCIS 2013) Chicago, Illinois, USA, 15–17 August 2013
31. Roth, S., Hauder, M., Münch, D., Michel, F., Matthes, F.: Facilitating conflict resolution of models for automated enterprise architecture documentation. In: 19th Americas Conference on Information Systems (AMCIS 2013), Chicago, Illinois, USA, 15–19 August 2013
32. Shadbolt, N., Hall, W., Berners-Lee, T.: The semantic web revisited. IEEE Intell. Syst. 21(3), 96–101 (2006)
33. Tamm, T., Seddon, P.B., Shanks, G., Reynolds, P.: How does enterprise architecture add value to organisations? Commun. Assoc. Inf. Syst. 28(1), 141–168 (2001)
34. van der Raadt, B., Bonnet, M., Schouten, S., van Vliet, H.: The relation between EA effectiveness and stakeholder satisfaction. J. Syst. Softw. 83(10), 1954–1969 (2010)
35. Walsham, G.: Doing interpretive research. Eur. J. Inf. Syst. 15(3), 320–330 (2006)
36. Webster, J., Watson, R.T.: Analyzing the past to prepare for the future: writing a literature review. MIS Q. 26(2), 13–23 (2002)
37. Weill, P., Ross, J.W.: IT Savvy What Top Executives Must Know to Go from Pain to Gain. Harvard Business Press, Boston (2009)
38. Weiss, S., Aier, S., Winter, R.: Institutionalization and the effectiveness of enterprise architecture management. In: Proceedings of the International Conference on Information Systems (ICIS 2013), Milano, Italy, 15–18 December 2013
39. Wieland, K., Langer, P., Seidl, M., Wimmer, M., Kappel, G.: Turning conflicts into collaboration. Comput. Support. Coop. Work 22(2–3), 181–240 (2012). Springer Verlag GmbH
40. Winter, R.: Architectural Thinking. Bus. Inf. Syst. Eng. 56(6), 395–398 (2014)

Aligning Enterprise Architecture
with Strategic Planning

Carlos L.B. Azevedo[1,2(✉)], Marten van Sinderen[2],
Luís Ferreira Pires[2], and João Paulo A. Almeida[1]

[1] Ontology and Conceptual Modeling Research Group (NEMO),
Federal University of Espírito Santo (UFES), Vitória, ES, Brazil
clbazevedo@inf.ufes.br, jpalmeida@ieee.org
[2] Services, Cybersecurity and Safety Research Group, Centre for Telematics and
Information Technology, University of Twente, Enschede, The Netherlands
{m.j.vansinderen,l.ferreirapires}@utwente.nl

Abstract. Strategic planning improves both the financial and behavioral performance of an enterprise. It helps the enterprise set priorities, focus capabilities and resources, strengthen operations, ensure that stakeholders are working toward common goals and assess and adjust the enterprise's direction. Strategic planning is currently not explicitly represented in EA, although it motivates enterprise architecture choices. This paper studies strategic planning approaches and discusses their potential relation with EA. The paper focuses on how EA can contribute to strategic planning, discussing requirements on EA extensions to support strategic planning and pointing to solutions. A general approach to support strategic planning using EA should mutually benefit the practices of strategic planning and EA.

Keywords: Enterprise architecture · Strategic planning · Strategy · Capability · Goal

1   Introduction

Strategic planning is an organizational management activity that is used to set the priorities of an enterprise. It defines what an enterprise wants to achieve in the future and outlines how it is supposed to achieve it. Accordingly, it establishes where the enterprise should focus its energy and resources, and which operations it needs to strengthen. It also helps stakeholders work toward common goals and assess how to achieve those goals [1]. Empirical studies have shown that strategic planning can improve the financial and behavioral performance of an enterprise, as well as the alignment between its operations towards common goals [2–5].

Strategic planning consists of intentionally setting goals (i.e., choosing a desired future) and developing a plan to achieve those goals. The plan focuses on decisions about what to do, why to do it, and how to do it. These strategic level plans provide an initial direction for the Enterprise Architecture (EA) and motivate choices on the EA.

A change in the enterprise's strategy affects the enterprise as a whole. It affects the products and services the enterprise is delivering and also how they are delivered inside

© Springer International Publishing Switzerland 2015
A. Persson and J. Stirna (Eds.): CAiSE 2015 Workshops, LNBIP 215, pp. 426–437, 2015.
DOI: 10.1007/978-3-319-19243-7_39

the organization. EA aims to have the complete enterprise aligned and integrated [6]. These changes usually imply in reconfiguring the activities that support the delivery of products and services, and thus, in the EA. An explicit relation between strategic planning and EA is therefore desirable. With such a relation, whenever there are changes on the strategic planning, the EA would accordingly change to support the provision of enterprise's products and services. The planning of EA would also benefit from this relation with strategic planning. A strategic plan can be seen as requiring various EAs at different points in time, requiring a sequence of EA transformations, which, by its turn, would benefit from the previous knowledge of the products and services to be supported.

Further, strategic planning can also benefit from EA. Strategists frequently want to analyze possible impacts triggered by changes in strategic planning, and EA, which provides a common view on the whole enterprise, can be used to support this analysis. Additionally, according to the Forbes management magazine [7], one of the main reasons strategic planning implementation fails is the lack of monitoring. EA, as middle ground between enterprise's operations and strategy, could support this monitoring.

There are efforts in EA to address (part of) the motivational aspect of an enterprise as an attempt to address these concerns [8]. Despite that, little effort has been made to explicitly represent strategic planning in EA. Most enterprise architectures do not deal with the strategic planning of organizations [8].

In this paper, we study strategic planning approaches and discuss their potential relation with enterprise architecture, with special interests in how strategic planning impacts in EA transformations over time and how EA can contribute to improve the support for strategic planning and the subsequent monitoring of its execution. We observed gaps in this area of enterprise architecture and we outline a research agenda on the incorporation of strategic planning into EA. EA could support strategic planning description, implementation and monitoring, both in the achievement of enterprise's low-range and mid-term goals, as, most importantly, in the achievement of enterprise's long-term goals. We describe the gaps that EA needs to overcome and point to required extensions to explicitly address strategic planning description, implementation, monitoring and management.

This paper is organized as follows: Sect. 2 describes management theories in strategic planning and strategic planning models in order to recognize what is required to represent strategic planning. Section 3 presents the current support for motivational aspects in EA, including strategic planning. Section 4 discusses requirements to support strategic planning in EA and how EA approaches could contribute to strategic planning, pointing to solutions to fulfill these requirements and Sect. 5 presents our conclusions and future work.

2 Strategic Planning

A variety of perspectives, models and approaches has been used in strategic planning [9–11]. Strategic planning often focuses on an entire enterprise, although a strategic plan can also be made for a specific part or department of an enterprise. The outcomes and the way in which a strategic plan is developed depend on the nature of the enterprise and on the nature of the challenges the enterprise is facing.

2.1 Strategic Planning Theories

Two main categories of theories are used to support strategic planning in the management area: *prescription theories*, also known as deliberate strategies; and *description theories*, also known as emergent strategies [12].

Prescription theories are based on a clear distinction between the design of the strategic plan and its implementation. On the design part, one or more executives and consultants define the strategy to be followed in the enterprise. The strategy can be unique and tailored to a specific enterprise, or it can be defined from a generic one, after some analysis of the enterprise in its particular circumstances and selecting the strategy that should fit the enterprise best [10, 11]. After the strategy is completely designed in terms of the goals the enterprise wants to achieve, when and how, the strategy is then communicated to the enterprise and the defined plan is implemented.

In contrast, *description theories* assume that the realm of strategies is too complex and that the design approach underestimates it, so that it is not possible to define what goals to achieve and how to achieve them a priori. Description theories assume the strategy to be designed during its implementation. According to these theories, strategy does not emerge from planning, it emerges within an enterprise taking a series of actions repeatedly. Once recognized as recurrent, these series of actions might be made formally deliberate and, then, guide the overall behavior, as an enterprise's pattern of behavior. These patterns of behavior are called the enterprise strategy and are not initially anticipated or intended [12]. Additionally, since there is no a priori design, description theories state that changes are easily accommodated.

Few, if any, strategies are purely prescriptive, just as few are purely emergent. Pure prescriptive strategic planning would imply in no adaptation and pure emergent strategic planning would imply in no control. Strategy in the real world invariably involves both planning on the future and adapting the plan during the operation. Most companies pursue a strategy informally termed as 'umbrella strategy', in which there is a mix of deliberate and emergent strategies [12]. In this case, the general guidelines are deliberated and the details are left to be deliberated (or emerge) later in the process [12]. Effective strategists mix prescriptive and emergent strategies to reflect the conditions at hand, notably the expectation to deal with unknown elements, as they need to handle partial knowledge of future matters and to react to unexpected events.

2.2 Strategic Planning Models

Although strategic planning depends on the theory used (prescriptive or descriptive), it is essentially defined in a few types of models [9, 13]. The most common model of strategic planning is the Goal-Based, also called Vision-Based. The models described here are mainly based on descriptions in [9, 12, 13].

2.2.1 Goal-Based Strategic Model

The *Goal-Based* strategic model is related to the prescriptive theories and the 'umbrella strategy'. To describe the *Goal-Based* strategic model, it is necessary to express the enterprise mission, vision and its planned goals.

The planned enterprise goals are among the most important elements of the *Goal-based* strategic model. Goals should be accomplished in timing constraints. Usually, the first goals described are to be achieved on the long-term (e.g. five years from 'now'). They encompass the enterprise's mission and vision. Further, it is common that intermediate goals or milestones are described, as well as short-term goals (e.g., one year or less). Each of these goals can be related to other goals, usually to facilitate their achievement, in a decomposition, refinement or contribution type of relation. In a decomposition relation, goals are decomposed, in the sense that achieving the low level goals defined in the decomposition guarantees the achievement of the higher-level goals. In the refinement, the achievement of each (or all) of the underlying goals contributes to the achievement of the higher-level goal, without guaranteeing its achievement. Each of the goals might have one or more possible decompositions or refinements, and the usage of one decomposition or refinement does not entail that other decompositions or refinements might not be possible as different forms of achieving the same goal; usually to increase the probability of success or decrease risks during strategy implementation.

Further, goals might have a precedence order or might need to be accomplished before or after a certain date. Additionally, goals might require a time window in which they should be addressed and achieved (e.g. because of regulatory compliance; in the case of perishable products).

Goals might also be treated by the enterprise individually or in a bundle and might influence one another. Particularly, it should be assessed whether goals being planned are compatible with previously defined goals. In case a goal contradicts a previously defined goal, one of them should be revised. Goals can be the responsibility of specific departments, of individuals or the whole enterprise.

In addition, organizations need to plan how its goals should be achieved. For short-term goals, it might be relevant to describe which are the operations required to realize them. It also might be relevant to describe their required capabilities and resources. For mid-term and long-term goals, although the same approach can be applied, the enterprise might prefer not to detail the achievement of the goal, or might choose to refer only to the capabilities and resources required for achievement, in a strategy as capability-based planning [14].

In some organizations the strategic planning is separately performed into different departments as well as different management levels, in which each department and management level has different responsibilities on the strategic planning. For example high-level managers may describe the strategic part of the strategic planning and releases it to lower-level managers, which refine the plan and describe how that plan should be implemented.

2.2.2 Other Models

The *Issue-based* strategic planning model [9] defines how to overcome issues the enterprise is facing, instead of defining and planning on a future state in terms of goals. The issue-based model is concerned with a shorter period of time (e.g., a one-year plan) and is usually performed when the enterprise faces difficulties. To express the approach, it is necessary to express the perceived issues as well as their solution requirements. The Issue-based strategic planning is similar in its conceptualization to the goal-based strategic planning model, if we consider "solving an issue" as a goal.

The Alignment model is useful for enterprises that need to find out why their strategies are not working [9]. The overall steps of this model consists of: (i) outlining the enterprise's mission, programs and resources; (ii) identifying what is working well and what needs adjustment; (iii) identifying how these adjustments should be made and; (iv) include these adjustments in the strategic plan.

The Scenario Planning model [13] is usually used in conjunction with other strategic planning models to enhance strategic thinking. It assists in identifying strategic issues and goals using different views. Scenario planning consists of selecting several external forces and devising changes related with each of them, which might influence the organization (e.g., change in regulations, competition, new products or services included in the market). For each force, it discusses different future organizational scenarios (usually best, worst and reasonable cases), which might result from a change. Then, potential strategies to each of these scenarios are identified. With that information, enterprises usually detect common strategies that can be employed to respond to multiple possible scenarios. The review of the worst cases usually identifies enterprise's weaknesses and motivates changes in the enterprise.

In order for the enterprise to achieve its results and improve its business it is necessary to implement and monitor the strategic planning [15]. The reasons why enterprise's strategic planning fails includes the lack of monitoring on the strategic planning achievement and implementation, and the lack of adaptation after the strategic plan is defined [7]. EA could be used to support overcome these problems, as well as to support the description, implementation, monitoring and management of strategic planning.

3   Current Support for Strategic Aspects in EA

The importance of enterprise strategy for Enterprise Architecture was recognized at least two decades ago with the addition of the Motivation column to the Zachman framework [16]. However, most EA approaches are still struggling with the goal domain and its modeling, and are not yet designed to deal with enterprise's high-level concerns, such as enterprise strategy and strategic planning [8]. In this section we analyze the frameworks: Zachman, MoDAF, DoDAF, ISO RM-ODP, TOGAF and its ArchiMate modeling language, ARIS and the OMG BMM according to its strategic aspects concerns.

The concept of mission was not introduced in any EA framework. The concept of vision is present in the MoDAF and DoDAF frameworks, in which the vision concept can be related to, *desired effects* and *goals*, respectively. However, the MoDAF framework adds two more concepts to describe the strategic aspect of enterprises and the possible relations in the framework, namely that *Enterprise Phase has vision Enterprise Vision* and *Enterprise Vision has tasks Enterprise Tasks*. The DoDAF framework, in turn, adds the *desired effect* concept. The existent relations are to represent that *vision is realized by desired effect.* There is also an *activity* concept, used to relate the *desired effect* to activities, in which a *desired effect directs* an *activity*.

The concept of *strategy* is supported by the Zachman framework [16], together with the concept of *objective*. The concepts can be related by means-ends-relations between *objectives* and *strategies.* There is also a *conflict* relation in the framework that can be used between *objectives.*

The concept of *goal*, sometimes called *objective*, which is a crucial concept for strategic planning, also appears in the ARIS, ISO RM-ODP and the TOGAF (Archi-Mate) frameworks. In the ARIS framework, the concept can *belong to* another *objective* and might be supported by a *function.* In the ISO RM-ODP, an *objective* can be *refined* into other *objectives.* This concept can be related to *process, community* or *roles.* Possible relations are that a *community has an objective,* which might represent ownership, and *refined goals* can be *assigned* to both *processes* or *roles.* The *goal* concept appears in TOGAF in its ArchiMate modeling language. In ArchiMate, a *goal* can be *influenced* by another *goal.* ArchiMate also defines concepts such as *Driver, Assessment, Requirement and Principle,* which all can *influence* a *goal* or one another. The relation between these concepts and the EA is indirect through the *requirement* concept, in which its instances need to have *requirements* in order for the *requirements* to be related to an enterprise structure concept.

The OMG BMM framework, in its turn, uses the concepts of *means, ends, assessment and influencer.* These concepts can be related by *means-ends* relations. The OMG BPMN notation, which can be used in conjunction with BMM, introduces concepts, such as *Organizational Unit.* The *Organizational Unit* defines *Ends,* estab-lishes *Means,* makes *Assessments,* recognizes *Influencers, may be defined by a Strategy* and *may be responsible for Business Processes. Business Processes* might be *guided* by a *Business Rule, which is* derived from a *Business Policy.*

None of the frameworks supports the explicit representation of strategic planning concepts and its relations as described in Sect. 2. There are not enough concepts to represent strategic planning in any of the EA approaches. EA frameworks need to be able to express goal relationships and its properties, such as specifying when each goal should be accomplished, as well as to address precedence and priority between goals. Further, the frameworks do not express different opportunities to achieve a goal. Plans (and consequently EA projects) are made under assumptions about circumstances that might not be under enterprise's control, usually referred to as enterprise's context. The enterprise may use scenario planning to overcome those risks and the frameworks should support planning a proper EA based on the prospected scenarios. We sum-marize the limitations we identified for strategic planning in EA frameworks as follows:

– Limited support for expressing goal relationships as stated in Sect. 2;
– Limited support for context modeling and how context can affect strategic planning and long-term EA;
– Limited support for the planning of different scenarios and the description of what strategy to follow in which scenario;
– Limited support for partial planning of the enterprise strategy, leaving details to emerge and have the EA support for that set of strategic goals;
– Limited support for linking strategy with the EA;

- Limited support for relating strategic planning goals to enterprise architecture elements, allowing the specification of required elements for each goal.
- No support for stating when a goal or milestone should be achieved, including precedence between goals.

4   EA Required Extensions for Strategic Planning

This section discusses how EA can contribute to strategic planning, by identifying requirements for EA to support strategic planning and pointing to general solutions to address these requirements. All proposals on this section are subject to further work as a research agenda. A general approach to support strategic planning description, implementation, monitoring and management using EA should mutually benefit the practices of strategic planning and EA.

4.1   Strategic Planning Representation

Limited support is available for describing enterprise's strategic planning in EA. EA frameworks need to be extended to express goal relationships and its properties requirements, such as specifying when each goal should be accomplished, address precedence, priority, express different opportunities to achieve a goal and express context and its possible impacts. We believe that a graph-based notation could address some of the limitations described in Sect. 3 and could provide a useful visualization of strategic plans. Goal-based languages, such as i*/Tropos [17] and Kaos [18], could also be used as a starting point to develop a notation for strategic planning, provided their limitations concerning timing, scenario planning and support to context description are addressed.

4.2   Capabilities, Resources and Their Relation with Strategic Planning

The importance of capabilities and resources for business strategy has been recognized in the management literature [19–22]. Achieving a planned goal on strategic planning requires the availability of capabilities and resources. Organizational capabilities and resources are related to strategic planning in enterprises in order to support and maintain competitive advantage [19, 20], as well as to improve performance, quality and to reduce costs [21, 22].

According to capability-based theories [19], the enterprise needs to know the capabilities it wants to leverage in order to plan to acquire resources and abilities in an intended manner. The emphasis is on adapting, integrating, and re-configuring internal and external organizational skills, resources, and functional competences toward a changing environment. Accordingly, the transition from enterprise's current state towards the goal-state can indicate that superfluous capabilities and resources should be abandoned while new capabilities and resources should be acquired. Further, modeling the transition from enterprise's current EA baseline towards the target EA would benefit from capability-based modeling, in a similar manner as presented in [23]. The paper presents an ArchiMate extension proposal which allows the enterprise to consider the required capabilities and resources to achieve a desired state (e.g., a planned goal), without actually having to pursue a complete and extended view on the business processes and tasks that are necessary to realize that state. The extension proposed in [23] could be extended once more in order to properly address strategic planning concerns.

4.3   Capabilities and Operations

The capability concept denotes the ability to bring about a desired outcome. This ability should be understood in a broad sense. Capabilities are used to state a broad range of behaviors, which can be assumed to inhere in an enterprise or in a specific individual. We argue that modeling resources and capabilities for decision making purposes at strategic level must simplify models and hide the complexity of architecture models which is of no relevance at that abstraction level, where decision makers are mostly interested in means (i.e., resources & capabilities) and goals (i.e., motivation). In contrast, resources and capabilities can be linked to the architecture fragments that implement their behavior, thus enabling an end-to-end traceability from strategic decisions to implementation and architecture change. An initial approach to this has been presented in [23], which captures the notions of capabilities and resources in ArchiMate, focusing on how capabilities are related to enterprise's resources, behavior and structural elements. This could support analysis on what becomes irrelevant or important on the strategic planning follow up. Further, an enterprise could even combine capability with planning analysis models to plan on which area to allocate investments [24].

4.4   EA Transformations Over Time

The strategic plan states on a continuum of the enterprise, describing multiple states that the enterprise is expected to achieve over time. It states the enterprise long-term, through the envisioned period. Thus, strategic planning is not related to an enterprise specific snapshot. A strategic plan thus requires various EAs at different points in time. To obtain these EAs it requires a sequence of EA transformations. The EA transformation over time should be planned to assure that the EA supports the provisioning of enterprise's products and services by the time they are required, in order to support the achievement of enterprise's goals.

Figure 1 illustrates various EAs over time related to the accomplishment of different goals of the strategic planning. Figure 1 also illustrates the EA transformations that are necessary, which are represented by the arrows between EAs. When the EA is implemented, the organization is at some state, represented as S1 in Fig. 1. The EA is then implemented and targeted to support the organization as it is at that specific moment, or to support the enterprise in its transformation to achieve its next goal or set of goals (e.g., improve efficiency, support new service, support new process), illustrated as G1 in Fig. 1. Therefore the EA needs to provide the requirements for achieving G2 in time.

Further, different transformation should be defined to address different scenarios, as the enterprise has unknown future on the strategic planning time and could adopt different goals depending on the context it is required to deal. Figure 1 represents this in the branch leading to G2'.

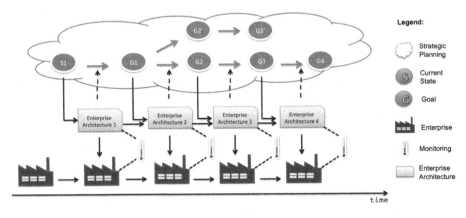

Fig. 1. General Approach

Enterprise architecture frameworks must not be concerned with a single snapshot of the enterprise. They must be concerned with the controlled and continuous change of the EA in order to properly support strategic planning and its implementation.

4.5   Strategic Planning Revisions

Strategic planning is usually reviewed after some period of time (e.g., each year). The revision usually verifies if the strategic planning goals are still relevant to the enterprise. Further, based on monitoring, the enterprise assesses if the strategy to achieve the goal is to be maintained, or should be changed or adapted. The support for strategic planning revision within EA can allow the assessment of change impacts. An approach to strategic planning and enterprise traceability as discussed in Sects. 4.2 and 4.3 using capabilities could be used to support that task.

4.6   Strategic Planning Monitoring

An enterprise should be instrumented to enable the collection of enterprise data. The collected data can be related to Key Performance Indicators (KPI) or milestones, defined in terms of the strategic plan goals. Two outcomes are possible due to the monitoring: (i) indication that goals are to be achieved 'as is' or (ii) indication that the goals will not be achieved under the current circumstances. If the monitoring indicates that goals are to be achieved, the enterprise should keep on performing as planned and continue to monitor and analyze its results. However, if the analysis indicates that goals might not be achieved, the enterprise needs to (i) change its operations in order to achieve the desired effect or, (ii) change its strategic plan properties (e.g., change a goal or its expected time realization), in order to adapt it to the current reality.

In case of (i), EA could support the analysis of which part of the enterprise might be responsible for enterprise's underperformance and, hence, help enterprise reorganization. In both cases, any change might trigger EA changes. The effort to understand which parts are required to change in the EA should be facilitated, since EA elements would be related and traced to both enterprise's operations and strategic planning.

Additionally, on the trajectory between goals, the collected data should be used to analyze if enterprise's subsequent goals are going to be achieved, triggering corrections enterprise's operation, if necessary, or triggering adaptations in enterprise's strategy, if the planned goals are not achievable from current state. Further, the analysis can be also relevant to decisions on which goals to pursue, if a scenario planning approach has been applied. Figure 1 illustrates the monitoring of the enterprise (as a thermometer), which is related to the EA and then, to the strategic planning.

4.7   Coherent Architectural Descriptions

A main challenge related to the alignment of strategic planning and EA is in the identification of a precise conceptualization for these notions. Without a precise conceptualization, rigorous definition of the semantics of the proposed elements is problematic, and modeling and communication problems arise [25]. In particular, we point to the usage of foundational ontologies for semantically anchoring concepts definitions. A foundational ontology defines a system of domain-independent categories and their relations, which can be used to articulate conceptualizations of reality. The use of foundational ontologies aims to ensure ontological correctness of the language and the models described within the language. In particular, we point to the works developed in [23, 26], in which an ontological foundation has been used to define the semantics of concepts of an EA modeling language. The introduction of strategic planning concepts to EA frameworks should have a precise conceptualization in order to avoid ambiguity and communication problems.

5   Conclusions

In this paper, we have presented general requirements towards the extension of enterprise architecture frameworks to express and align it with strategic planning. We argue that there is a limited support for describing enterprise's strategic planning in EA and that the usage of EA for strategic planning should be mutually beneficial to the practices of strategic planning and EA.

We list several limitations of the current frameworks and identify requirements to align strategic planning with EA. In particular, we state that EA frameworks should not be concerned with single snapshots of the enterprise and must be concerned with the controlled transformations of EA over time. We argue that the planning of EA transformations could be enhanced if aligned with strategic planning. We have also outlined an initial approach for extending EA to achieve an end-to-end traceability between strategic planning, EA and enterprise's operations based on the concept of capabilities, as introduced in [23].

Nevertheless, we also focus on how EA can improve enterprise's strategic planning monitoring and management. EA can be used as a middle ground between enterprise's operations and enterprise's strategic planning. EA can also be used for strategic planning on design time for the verification of change impact.

The required extensions are intended to model enterprise's strategic planning and to relate it to the whole enterprise, including its operation. The introduction of the requirements into EA and its usage should improve the traceability between the enterprise's strategic planning and EA choices. The continuous transformations from baseline EA to target EA could benefit from this approach, in which the EA transformations are planned in accordance to the goals each EA version has to support.

Additionally, on the trajectory between goals, EA could help predict if enterprise's subsequent goals are going to be achieved, triggering corrections on the operation or revisions on the strategic planning of the enterprise. Further, the analysis can be relevant on decision-making whenever a scenario-based approach has been performed.

In our future efforts, we intend to further detail on how to overcome the identified limitations and to implement the extensions proposed in this paper. We intend to integrate these results with our results of [23, 26], which addresses capabilities and some motivational concepts for EA. We also intend to interpret new proposed modeling concepts using the Unified Foundational Ontology [27, 28], in an effort to have coherent and aligned enterprise models.

Acknowledgments. This paper is partially funded by FAPES (grant number 59971509/12) and CNPq (grants number 310634/2011-3, 485368/2013-7 and 201495/2014-7).

References

1. Bryson, J.M.: A Strategic Planning Process for Public and Non-profit Organizations. Jossey-Bass Publishers, San Francisco (1988)
2. Miller, C.C., Cardinal, L.B.: Strategic planning and firm performance: a synthesis of more than two decades of research. Acad. Manag. J. **37**, 1649–1665 (1994)
3. Song, M., Im, S., Van Der Bij, H., Song, L.Z.: Does strategic planning enhance or impede innovation and firm performance? J. Prod. Innov. Manag. **28**, 503–520 (2011)
4. Ansoff, H.I.: Critique of Henry Mintzberg's "the design school: reconsidering the basic premises of strategic management". Strateg. Manag. J. **12**, 449–461 (1991)
5. Al-Shammari, H.A., Hussein, R.T.: Strategic planning-firm performance linkage: empirical investigation from an emergent market perspective. Adv. Compet. Res. **15**, 15–26 (2007)
6. Lankhorst, M.: Enterprise Architecture at Work: Modelling, Communication and Analysis. Springer, Heidelberg (2005)
7. Forbes Magazine: 10 Reasons Why Strategic Plans Fail (2011). http://forbes.com/sites/aileron/2011/11/30/10-reasons-why-strategic-plans-fail/
8. Cardoso, E.C.S., Almeida, J.P.A., Guizzardi, R.S.S.: On the support for the goal domain in enterprise modelling approaches. In: 2010 14th IEEE International Enterprise Distributed Object Computing Conference Workshops, pp. 335–344 (2010)

9. McNamara, C.: Strategic planning (in nonprofit or for-profit organizations). Free Manag. Libr. (2001). http://managementhelp.org/plan_dec/str_plan/str_plan.htm. Accessed 19 April 2010

10. Porter, M.E.: Competitive strategy. Tech. Anal. Ind. Compet. **1**, 396 (1980)

11. Porter, M.E.: Towards a dynamic theory of strategy. Strateg. Manag. J. **12**, 95–117 (1991)

12. Mintzberg, H., Ahlstrand, B., Lampel, J.: Strategy Safari: A Guided Tour through the Wilds of Strategic Management. Free Press, New York (1998)

13. Bryson, J.M.: Strategic Planning for Public and Nonprofit Organizations: A Guide to Strengthening and Sustaining Organizational Achievement. Wiley, New York (2011)

14. Stirna, J., Grabis, J., Henkel, M., Zdravkovic, J.: Capability driven development – an approach to support evolving organizations. In: Sandkuhl, K., Seigerroth, U., Stirna, J. (eds.) PoEM 2012. LNBIP, vol. 134, pp. 117–131. Springer, Heidelberg (2012)

15. Ross, J.W., Weill, P., Robertson, D.: Enterprise Architecture as Strategy: Creating a Foundation for Business Execution. Harvard Business Press, Watertown (2006)

16. Kappelman, L.A., Zachman, J.A.: The enterprise and its architecture: ontology & challenges. J. Comput. Inf. Syst. 53 (2013)

17. Mylopoulos, J., Castro, J., Kolp, M.: The evolution of Tropos. In: Seminal Contributions to Information Systems Engineering. pp. 281–287. Springer, Heidelberg (2013)

18. Van Lamsweerde, A.: Others: Requirements engineering: From System Goals to UML Models to Software Specifications. Wiley, New York (2009)

19. Barney, J.: Firm resources and sustained competitive advantage. J. Manage. **17**, 99–120 (1991)

20. Helfat, C.C.E., Winter, S.G.S.: Untangling dynamic and operational capabilities: strategy for the (N) ever-Changing world. Strateg. Manag. J. **1250**, 1243–1250 (2011)

21. Ray, G., Barney, J.B., Muhanna, W.A.: Capabilities, business processes, and competitive advantage: choosing the dependent variable in empirical tests of the resource-based view. Strateg. Manag. J. **25**, 23–37 (2004)

22. Baines, T.S., Lightfoot, H.W., Benedettini, O., Kay, J.M.: The servitization of manufacturing: a review of literature and reflection on future challenges. J. Manuf. Technol. Manag. **20**, 547–567 (2009)

23. Azevedo, C.L.B., Iacob, M.-E., Almeida, J.P.A., van Sinderen, M., Pires, L.F., Guizzardi, G.: An ontology-based well-founded proposal for modeling resources and capabilities in ArchiMate. In: 2013 17th IEEE International Enterprise Distributed Object Computing Conference (EDOC), pp. 39–48 (2013)

24. Quartel, D., Steen, M.W.A., Lankhorst, M.: IT Portfolio valuation - using enterprise architecture and business requirements modeling. In: 2010 14th International Enterprise Distributed Object Computing Conference, pp. 3–13 (2010)

25. Guarino, N.: Formal Ontology and Information Systems, pp. 3–15 (1998)

26. Azevedo, C.L.B., Almeida, J.P.A., van Sinderen, M., Quartel, D.A.C., Guizzardi, G.: An Ontology-Based Semantics for the Motivation Extension to ArchiMate (2011). http://ieeexplore.ieee.org/lpdocs/epic03/wrapper.htm?arnumber=6037557

27. Guizzardi, G.: Ontological Foundations for Structural Conceptual Models (2005). http://doc.utwente.nl/50826

28. Almeida, J.P.A., Guizzardi, G.: An ontological analysis of the notion of community in the RM-ODP enterprise language. Comput. Stand. Interfaces **35**, 257–268 (2013)

Enterprise Architecture in the Age
of Digital Transformation

Zia Babar[1(✉)] and Eric Yu[1,2]

[1] Faculty of Information, University of Toronto, Toronto, Canada
zia.babar@mail.utoronto.ca, eric.yu@utoronto.ca
[2] Department of Computer Science, University of Toronto, Toronto, Canada

Abstract. Recent advances in digital technologies are enabling enterprises to undergo transformations for streamlining business processes, offering new products and services, expanding in new areas, and even changing their business models. Current enterprise architecture frameworks are used for analysis, design, and strategy execution, helping an enterprise transition from an as-is state to a to-be state. However emerging trends suggest the need for richer models to support on-going adaptations and periodic transformations. The scope of enterprise architecture modeling needs to be expanded to include the multiple levels of dynamics that exist within any enterprise, the sense-and-respond pathways that drive change at operational and strategic levels, and the tension between centralized control and local autonomy.

Keywords: Enterprise architecture · Adaptive enterprise · Requirement engineering · Enterprise modeling · Digital transformation · Emerging technologies

1 Introduction

Modern enterprises face immense pressure to continuously grow or reinvent themselves in a fast-moving, ever-changing and integrated world. To successfully survive in such evolving and uncertain conditions, enterprises are expected to continuously adapt to changing environments [1, 2]. The nature of change may be along various perspectives such as strategic vs. operational, transformational vs. transactional, discontinuous vs. continuous, revolutionary vs. evolutionary etc., involving diverse areas such as people, culture, processes, and technology [3].

The widespread adoption of technologies, such as social media, mobile, big data analytics and cloud computing, in enterprises is enabling a change in business model, improved customer experiences, and optimized operational processes [4, 5]. Such a transformation is a significant shift from the previous *modus operandi* and results in broad-ranging and potentially disruptive enterprise-wide transformation enabling enterprises to move from a brick-and-mortar style operation to one that is more encompassing of digital technologies [6]. Digital transformation permeates industry segments, take many forms and exist at many levels within an enterprise. The focus of transformation should not be on individual systems or processes but should rather be viewed holistically and at an enterprise level. All these approaches can be considered

© Springer International Publishing Switzerland 2015
A. Persson and J. Stirna (Eds.): CAiSE 2015 Workshops, LNBIP 215, pp. 438–443, 2015.
DOI: 10.1007/978-3-319-19243-7_40

more conceptually and be thought of as a series of on-going transformative demands on the enterprise at an operational and strategic level.

2   Emerging Requirements for EA Modeling

Enterprise characteristics are traditionally captured through various enterprise architecture frameworks for the purpose of design, analysis, planning and strategy execution. As enterprises are fairly complex entities, a number of enterprise modeling techniques exist with each providing a different view of the enterprise. These modeling techniques are generally used for static as-is and to-be representations of the enterprise and are unable to support the wide range of dynamics that are present in an enterprise. They do not cater to periodic, variable and continuous change including the ability to decide between multiple alternate enterprise configurations at run-time [7]. A review of industry literature highlighting trends in digital transformation suggests the scope for enterprise architecture framework(s) to be broadened so as to consider multi-level dynamics, data-driven sensing and acting, and actor autonomy.

2.1   Multi-level Dynamics

Every organization relies on many processes that together ensure its success and viability. Different types of processes, for example, operational and transactions processes, planning processes, design process, innovation processes, etc., may take place over different timescales and have different frequencies of occurrence. While current enterprise architecture frameworks can model various business process, they are lacking in the ability to express and reason about the nature of the relationships among them; such as the relationship between a planning process and the process that executes the plan, or the relationship between a design process and the process that exploits the new capability, artifact, or tool produced by that design process. The relationships are important in the current context of digital transformation, as these relationships are themselves subject to change. For example, some product design decisions can be deferred closer to the time of usage by allowing customization, user configuration, or even automated personalization. Some activities may be moved from a planning process to the execution process ("run-time") in order to take advantage of the most up-to-date data (e.g., real-time analytics from Internet of Things). We consider examples from various industry sectors.

- Banks are increasingly relying on alternate digital channels (such as mobile and internet) which function at different levels and timescales compared to the more traditional banking channels such as bank branches. Branches are heavy on processes and human interaction thus operating at a slower timescale than the internet and mobile channel. The nature of product and service offerings also varies across these channels. A seamless "omni-channel" experience to customers across all channels is becoming essential, which require careful coordination of the processes across levels of dynamics [8, 9].

- The development of mobile enterprise systems is indicative of two separate and distinct levels with different characteristics and timescales. The front-end mobile app development is characterized by quick development and deployment cycles with customers providing immediate feedback through the app store rating whereas back-end enterprise systems have longer, more cautious development cycles [10]. Thus a new business feature affecting both mobile front-end and enterprise back-end systems would be managed, developed and delivered differently based on the different enterprise levels, methodologies, tools, and timescales.
- The telecommunication industry contains numerous internal operational processes and procedures such as billing operations. Billing operations encompass multiple levels across multiple organizational departments leading to process inefficiencies and possible issues with bill accuracy [11].

These multiple levels of dynamics are not entirely evident to the casual observer nor are the boundary transitions apparent. The enterprise architect would need to understand the differentiating attributes of the levels with the placement of enterprise activities within each. The constituent activities of any process could be moved across level boundaries however there would be resulting implications which need to be understood. For example, in the case of mobile app development above, certain back-end enterprise system development activities can be made part of the mobile app development level (i.e., both front-end and back-end systems follow the same development and deployment methodology) however there might be consequences with regards to the back-end enterprise system testing and platform stability. The identification of such levels, the placement of activities within each level, the possibility of movement of the activities across level boundaries and the possible implications are considerations that have to be understood and captured by the enterprise architect.

2.2   Data-Driven Sensing and Acting

Enterprise change is being influenced by both the internal adoption of technologies and the general pervasiveness of digital technologies in the environment that they operate in. The enterprise needs to "observe" and be aware of such situations based on which it would initiate and undertakes activities of adaptation and change. Such paths of change can be analyzed in terms of sense-and-response loops through which the enterprise continuously adapts and improves [12]. In the sensing part the enterprise would (proactively or reactively) determine the cause and need for change. In the responding part, the enterprise would determine the best possible alternate for change. Sensing and responding take place in processes that exist at different levels of dynamics and timescales. For example the sensing part can happen at machine-scale time (through the use of automated data driven systems) with the acting part existing in human-scale (through managerial decision making). Such data-driven sense-and-respond loops for ongoing enterprise transformation already exist in multiple industries.

- Big data analytics is helping banks make conscious decisions in identifying areas where investment should be made towards the digitization of business operations thus helping banks manage their limited budgets more effectively. Analytics help identify inefficient business processes which are then optimized and improved upon [8, 13].

- The retail industry relies heavily on big data analytics to sense short-term and long-term trends that loom on the horizon. These are then acted upon by the responding side by at an operational and strategic level. Sensing aspects include customers demanding a better shopping experience, increasing competition because of technology improvements, entry of non-traditional competitors, changes in the supply chain etc. [14]; these changes would have to be sensed, understood and appropriate actions taken which would be operational or strategic in nature.

- The healthcare industry is using big data and predictive analytics to produce new innovation in biometrics and bioinformatics. This is in addition to using machines for generating preliminary diagnoses which aid and guide physicians in patient diagnoses and treatment regime [15].

Enterprise architects need to have methods that can help them sketch out such linear paths or cyclic loops as they exist in any enterprise, the various levels and timescales that they transition through, the interactions that the paths may have with other paths or enterprise objects, the sensory inputs to the sensing part and the corresponding balance that the responding part should bring.

2.3   Actor Autonomy Review

Enterprises are complex and collaborative environments with a multitude of human and non-human (system) actors. Each actor possesses their own intentions, goals and objectives which may or may not align with those of other actors or even the enterprise itself. Thus there exists a certain degree of actor autonomy within the overall enterprise. Any enterprise transformation would typically be a disruptive exercise and one that would positively, as well as, negatively affect actors. The expectation is that while the overall enterprise would benefit from such a transformative exercise, it may go against the individual interests of some actors. As before, enterprise actors can exist across the various enterprise levels and even participate in sense-and-respond loops. For an individual actor, their objectives and goals may also span these levels. The actor interests may, at times, align with enterprises hierarchies and divisions whereas on other occasions it may cut across those structures. Actors may support or oppose the goals of any transformative exercise and even change states between the two. Opposition to enterprise objectives may manifest itself as change rigidities in the enterprise.

- Financial institutions have a level of actor autonomy in order to counteract threats from new entrants in the financial services sector. Fintech startups and technology companies (like Google and Apple) are offering competing financial products and services which are eroding into the profitability margins of traditional banks [9]. As a result, banks are digitizing their core products like credit cards, loans and payments to better compete with these entrants. They can better do so if there is some level of distributed autonomy in the enterprise so that digitalization efforts can be executed and delivered independent of other enterprise divisions and inherent enterprise rigidities.

- The ultimate goal (i.e., the implementation of a required business feature) of a mobile enterprise system is the same yet the front-end mobile and the back-end enterprise systems have significant autonomy with defined integration points for the successful completion of this business objective [10]. This allows both areas to maintain distinct culture, processes, methodologies, software tools and environment that are more conducive to their particular needs.
- The retail industry provides an excellent example for *decreasing* actor autonomy in the case of online vs. retail stores. Traditional retailers are attempting to provide a more uniform shopping experience across both segments (i.e., an omni-channel experience) but having two separate segments with significant actor autonomy would not produce the desired end-result [14]. So while the execution specifics between both segments may differ, there is a certain consolidation of actor autonomy with respect to higher level objectives.

Enterprise architects would have to be able to depict actor autonomy, actor objectives and goals, boundaries of actor influence, multiple levels at which these objectives and influences span and interactions between actors. They would also want to show any alignment (or misalignment) of actor objectives with the enterprise-level objectives.

3   Conclusions and Future Work

Transforming enterprises as a response to on-going digital change demands is rather difficult and needs to be considered in a structured manner particularly as enterprises are complicated entities with multifaceted social, process and technological elements; all of which can determine the success or failure of any adaptation exercise. The nature, complexity and texture of any enterprise adaptation may vary significantly and can cut across multiple industry segments. Current enterprise modeling approaches will need to be extended to better acknowledge and support today's highly dynamic environments. Enterprise architects would be expected to be more involved in the strategizing, planning and execution of digital transformation so that they can correctly design and devise the various alternate to-be configurations.

In [7] we attempted a preliminary characterization of an adaptive enterprise. We are exploring methods and techniques from diverse areas, including requirements engineering, system dynamics, and management frameworks, to contribute towards a framework for adaptive enterprise architecture. We envision a framework that would assist enterprises to deal with on-going adaptation demands such as those posed by digital transformation. We wish to understand the nature and texture of such enterprise "adaptiveness" requirements and the ways to capture the as-is and to-be adaptiveness characterization of the enterprise. Additions and enhancements to existing enterprise modeling techniques would be considered for assisting with visualization and analysis of these requirements. On the sensing side, the awareness requirements would be monitored and evaluated on an on-going basis for satisfaction of enterprise adaptive objectives. On the responding side, any dissatisfaction of these requirements results in the selection and implementation of a suitable to-be alternative that enables the enterprise to adapt to changing circumstances. The alternative(s) would be selected while considering the tradeoffs between various factors existing at a social, contextual, process, and technological level.

References

1. Wilkinson, M.: Designing an 'adaptive' enterprise architecture. BT Technol. J. **24**(4), 81–92 (2006)
2. The Economist: Organisational Agility: How Business can Survive and Thrive in Turbulent Times. A report from The Economist Intelligence Unit (2009)
3. Burke, W.: Warner: Organization Change: Theory and Practice. Sage Publications, Los Angeles (2013)
4. Yu, E., Lapouchnian, A.: Architecting the enterprise to leverage a confluence of emerging technologies. In: Proceedings of the 2013 Conference of the Center for Advanced Studies on Collaborative Research. IBM Corp. (2013)
5. Lapouchnian, A., Yu, E.: Exploiting emergent technologies to create systems that meet shifting expectations. In: Proceedings of the 2014 Conference of the Center for Advanced Studies on Collaborative Research. IBM Corp. (2014)
6. Westerman, G., Bonnet, D., McAfee, A.: The Nine Elements of Digital transformation. MIT Sloan Management Review (2014)
7. Yu, E., Deng, S., Sasmal, D.: Enterprise architecture for the adaptive enterprise – A vision paper. In: Aier, S., Ekstedt, M., Matthes, F., Proper, E., Sanz, J. (eds.) PRET 2012 and TEAR 2012. LNBIP, vol. 131, pp. 146–161. Springer, Heidelberg (2012)
8. Olanrewaju, T.: The Rise of the Digital Bank, McKinsey on Business Technology, p. 33. McKinsey & Company, Washington, DC (2014)
9. Denecker, O., Gulati, S., Niederkorn, M.: The Digital Battle That Banks Must Win. McKinsey & Company, New York (2014)
10. Wasserman, A.: Software engineering issues for mobile application development. In: Proceedings of the FSE/SDP workshop on Future of software engineering research, pp. 397–400. ACM (2010)
11. Accenture: How Communications Service Providers Can Transform Telecom Billing Operations to Support a New Convergent, Digital Business (2012)
12. Haeckel, S.H.: Adaptive Enterprise: Creating and Leading Sense-And-Respond Organizations. Harvard Business Press, Boston (1999)
13. Aritomo, K., Desmet, D., Holley, A.: More Bank for your IT buck. McKinsey & Company, Liverpool (2014)
14. Desai, P., Potia, A., Salsberg, B.: Retail 4.0: The Future of Retail Grocery in a Digital World, McKinsey & Company, Tokyo (2012)
15. Vitalari, N.: A Prospective Anaysis of the Future of the U.S. Healthcare Industry, Center of Digital Transformation White Paper Series, UC Irvine

WISSE 2015

Optimizing Information Systems Security Design Based on Existing Security Knowledge

Andreas Schilling[(✉)] and Brigitte Werners

Faculty of Management and Economics, Ruhr University Bochum,
Universitätsstraße 150, 44780 Bochum, Germany
{andreas.schilling,or}@rub.de
http://www.rub.de/or

Abstract. Information systems and the information enclosed are of significant value and it is indispensable for organizations to ensure their protection. To achieve high security, existing knowledge is available and provides recommendations and guidelines to follow. Due to the large amount of data and the complex dependencies within their structure, it is often challenging to make informed design decisions. This paper proposes a quantitative model that is tailored to the optimal selection of security safeguards from an existing security knowledge base. The input data are extracted from the extensive IT baseline protection catalogues of the German Federal Office for Information Security (BSI). The total amount of data include more than 500 threats and 1200 safeguard options. In an application example, we illustrate that an optimal decision can reduce the number of required safeguards substantially while still maintaining a high security level.

Keywords: Information security · System security design · Decision support model · Combinatorial optimization

1 Introduction

Information technology (IT) has become a critical factor for organizations and continuously spreads into more and more areas. The loss, manipulation, disclosure, or simply the unavailability of information may lead to expenses, missed profits, or even legal consequences. If security is weak, attackers will eventually find a weak spot and cause damage. One approach to deal with information security design is to follow common information security practices and guidelines which are available from various sources including, but not limited to, the International Organization for Standardization (ISO), National Institute of Standards and Technology (NIST), and German Federal Office for Information Security (BSI). These practices can help organizations by guiding them on how to establish an effective basis for security. The information is mostly available in form of standards that have to be followed more or less strictly.

For our analysis, we chose on the IT baseline protection catalogues (or IT-Grundschutz catalogues) [4] which are part of a standard provided by the BSI.

© Springer International Publishing Switzerland 2015
A. Persson and J. Stirna (Eds.): CAiSE 2015 Workshops, LNBIP 215, pp. 447–458, 2015.
DOI: 10.1007/978-3-319-19243-7_41

The catalogues are publicly available, free of charge, and offer an extensive repository of technical, organisational, personnel, and infrastructural information security knowledge to protect information systems (IS). The catalogues are also in line with the ISO 27000 series which makes them internationally applicable. Organizations trying to improve security face the challenge of selecting appropriate safeguards from the given catalogues. There is, however, no practical solution available to optimally select safeguards that result in a desired security level. Since most companies have no specialized information security knowledge, this decision process has to be outsourced to a specialized service provider (e.g., a consulting company) which causes additional costs.

This paper presents an approach to optimize information security design by using large amounts of available information. For this purpose, we propose a combinatorial optimization model which makes use of the entire IT baseline protection catalogues. Our model is also applicable to an arbitrary subset of components which makes it usable for any use case covered by the knowledge base of the catalogues. The presented model can help to automate the decision process or at the very least support security design decisions.

The remainder of the paper is organized as follows: Sect. 2 outlines literature related to decision making in IT security. Section 3 discusses the general security investment problem and introduces the source of data which we used as basis for our analysis. Section 4 presents a mathematical model and shows how available data are utilized to support decision making in information security. In Sect. 5, we conceive a realistic case study to demonstrate the application of our model and discuss respective results. Section 6 concludes the paper.

2   Related Work

In recent years, the interest in quantitative models for information security investment decisions has increased significantly. This trend is driven by the fact that system complexity continuously increases and a growing amount of data is available to support decision making. There are several research streams which basically try to solve the security investment problem from different angles. In this analysis, we focus on the selection problem, i.e., what security safeguards should be selected for implementation?

Most approaches addressing this question apply management tools and financial analysis based on measures like annual loss expectancy, return on investment, internal rate of return, net present value, etc. [2,10,11,13]. Other approaches use real options analysis where dynamic aspects of investments are considered and the flexibility of decision making is utilized [6,12,14]. An optimization driven approach to select security safeguards is proposed by Sawik [9] which produces optimal safeguard portfolios. In their study, they used a bi-objective model to minimize expected and worst case losses applying the value-at-risk. Viduto et al. [15] proposed a multi-objective model that also factors in financial costs in addition to losses. Rakes et al. [8] argue that, in addition to expected losses, sparse events that might result in high-impact losses should be considered, too. They propose a model which considers the trade-off between expected and worst-case losses. If it is not sufficient or possible to deploy safeguards to achieve sufficient security, cyber insurance is also an option [1,7].

These approaches either use a small set of very generic data or require the decision maker to collect most of it before the optimization can be conducted. Our model builds on the foundation and ideas established in previous work but requires less information input which makes it more applicable to practical use cases. Using an existing knowledge base significantly reduces workload during a risk assessment and ensures that the data meet a certain quality threshold. To the best of our knowledge, no model exists to support concrete investment decisions of security safeguards which incorporates large amount of data of an existing knowledge base and is still practically applicable in terms of information requirements and computational time.

3   Problem Description

An organization usually runs several business processes and operates a number of information systems. The continuous operation of these systems and the security of processed information is considered to be of high priority for every organization. For this reason, organizations try to achieve high security of such systems by deploying security safeguards. In order to adequately protect IS, organizations can make use of existing information security knowledge. In the following, we use the IT baseline protection catalogues which consist of components (or modules) that comprise all relevant parts of the processes, applications, and systems of an organization. The IT baseline protection catalogues define 80 components which are grouped into 5 categories: general aspects, infrastructure, information systems, networks, and applications. Each component contains a description of the subject, a list of threats, and a set of applicable safeguard options. In total, the IT baseline protection catalogues contain 518 threats and 1244 safeguards.

The catalogues specify that the security of each component is endangered by a number of threats. Depending on the nature of the threat, it is possible that it applies to more than one component. Each threat has a particular criticality, that can be obtained in an automatic manner from the existing knowledge base. To counteract threats, the organization can deploy various safeguards which reduce the criticality of a specific subset of threats according to the safeguards effectiveness. To use this information, we extracted the information from the catalogues and generated an SQLite database serving as a knowledge base for our evaluation.

If an organization intends to obtain a valid ISO or BSI certificate, there are predefined selections available to achieve different security levels. An entry level certificate requires the implementation of 46 % of the safeguards and the ISO 27001 certificate requires 79 % of all safeguards to be implemented. If a certificate is not required, a smaller subset may be sufficient to achieve a desired security level. The model presented in this paper can be used to obtain an initial selection of safeguards that may be further customized according to additional requirements.

4 Model Formulation

In this section, we consider a single-stage combinatorial optimization model which is set up as a mixed integer linear programming (MILP) problem. The goal is to select a feasible subset of safeguards that maximizes security and meets a number of linear constraints. We first establish a nonlinear formulation in Sect. 4.1 and then use the natural logarithm to linearize it in Sect. 4.2. Table 1 lists parameters and decision variables which are used in the following.

Table 1. Parameters and decision variables.

Indices and sets	
$\mathcal{P}$	Index set of components (indexed by p)
$\mathcal{I}$	Index set of threats (indexed by i)
$\mathcal{K}$	Index set of safeguards (indexed by k)
Parameters	
σ_k	Effectiveness coefficient of a safeguard
γ_i	Criticality coefficient of a threat
$C_{i,p}$	Connection between component and threat, $C_{i,p} \in \{0,1\}$
$T_{k,i}$	Connection between threat and safeguard, $T_{k,i} \in \{0,1\}$
$\overline{N}$	Maximum number of safeguards
Decision variables	
s_k	Selection of safeguards, $s_k \in \{0,1\}$
t_i	Threat criticality index (TCI)
c_p	Component criticality index (CCI)

Let $p \in \mathcal{P}$ denote a component of the system in question and let $i \in \mathcal{I}$ denote a threat. Matrix $C_{i,p} \in \{0,1\}$ denotes whether threat i endangers component p ($C_{i,p} = 1$) or not ($C_{i,p} = 0$) and is given in an extension to the IT baseline protection catalogues. Each threat has a preset criticality coefficient $\gamma_i \geq 0$ and a variable criticality index $t_i \geq 0$. The criticality coefficient of a threat is an input to the model and expresses how severe a threat is without investing in security. The criticality index, on the other hand, is variable and determined during optimization. It is reduced if safeguards are deployed which are applicable to the threat in question. The criticality coefficient is not directly provided by the catalogues and we use a generated value based on available data (see Sect. 5.2).

To determine the criticality of a component, we use variable c_p which is called component criticality index (CCI). Due to the fact that the highest threat is the most critical indicator of security, c_p is defined as the maximum of all criticality indexes of threats associated with the component in question, i.e.,

$$c_p = \max_{i \in \mathcal{I}} \{t_i | C_{i,p} = 1\} \quad \forall p \in \mathcal{P}. \tag{1}$$

Whether threat i is associated with component p is defined by the corresponding value of matrix $C_{i,p}$ and can be obtained from the IT baseline protection catalogues. The definition of c_p is based on the assumption that the security of a component depends on the most critical of its threats, i.e., the weakest link in the security chain. Therefore, to reduce the criticality of a component, the criticality index of its most critical threat has to be reduced first.

By deploying safeguards, the criticality index of a threat is reduced. If no safeguards are deployed for a particular threat, we have $t_i = \gamma_i$. A safeguard only reduces the criticality of a threat if it is associated with this threat ($T_{k,i} = 1$) and if it is implemented ($s_k = 1$). In case an applicable safeguard ($T_{k,i} = 1$ and $s_k = 1 \Leftrightarrow T_{k,i} \cdot s_k = 1$) is deployed, the criticality index of an associated threat is reduced from γ_i to $\gamma_i \cdot \sigma_k$, where $\sigma_k \in [0,1]$ is the effectiveness coefficient of the deployed safeguard. To generalize this expression for multiple safeguards, we multiply γ_i by

$$\sigma_k{}^{s_k \cdot T_{k,i}} = \begin{cases} \sigma_k & \text{if } s_k = 1 \text{ and } T_{k,i} = 1 \\ 1 & \text{if } s_k = 0 \text{ or } T_{k,i} = 0 \end{cases} \quad \forall\, k \in \mathcal{K}, \tag{2}$$

which only takes value σ_k if both $s_k = 1$ and $T_{k,i} = 1$ and defaults to 1 otherwise. In case the expression takes value 1, the criticality index of a threat is not reduced. Considering all safeguards at once we get the following equation to calculate the remaining criticality index of threat i:

$$t_i = \gamma_i \cdot \prod_{k \in \mathcal{K}} \sigma_k{}^{s_k \cdot T_{k,i}} \quad \forall\, i \in \mathcal{I}. \tag{3}$$

4.1 Nonlinear Model for Determining an Optimal Selection of Safeguards

Based on these definitions, we establish the optimization model as follows:

$$\min \quad \left[\max_{p \in \mathcal{P}} c_p \right] \tag{4}$$

$$\text{s.t.} \quad c_p = \max_{i \in \mathcal{I}} \{ t_i | C_{i,p} = 1 \} \qquad \forall\, p \in \mathcal{P} \tag{5}$$

$$t_i = \gamma_i \cdot \prod_{k \in \mathcal{K}} \sigma_k{}^{s_k \cdot T_{k,i}} \qquad \forall\, i \in \mathcal{I} \tag{6}$$

$$\sum_{k \in \mathcal{K}} s_k \leq \overline{N} \tag{7}$$

$$s_k \in \{0,1\} \qquad \forall\, k \in \mathcal{K} \tag{8}$$

$$t_i \geq 0 \qquad \forall\, i \in \mathcal{I}. \tag{9}$$

The objective function (4) minimizes the maximum of all CCIs. This formulation assumes that all components are equally important for the overall security of the system. If this is not the case, it would be possible to weight components differently by multiplying their indexes with an additional weighting factor. The objective value characterizes the overall security of the system in question and is called the system security index (SSI). Constraint (5) defines CCI c_p as the maximum of associated threat criticality indexes (TCIs). The total number of safeguards is limited to $\overline{N}$ in constraint (7). Finally, the decision regarding the selection of safeguards is binary (8) and all threat criticality indexes have to be nonnegative (9).

4.2   Linearization Using the Natural Logarithm

The established formulation of the problem has some drawbacks regarding its solvability due to its nonlinearity in constraint (6). Nonlinear problems are substantially more difficult to solve than linear problems. We will show in the following how to obtain a MILP formulation of the problem. Constraint (6) is the only nonlinear equation where the product of multiple decision variables is calculated. To reformulate this constraint, we take the natural logarithm of t_i and thus eliminate the multiplication of decision variables:

$$t_i = \gamma_i \cdot \prod_{k \in \mathcal{K}} \sigma_k^{s_k \cdot T_{k,i}} \tag{10}$$

$$\Leftrightarrow \qquad \ln(t_i) = \ln(\gamma_i) + \sum_{k \in \mathcal{K}} s_k \cdot T_{k,i} \cdot \ln(\sigma_k) \tag{11}$$

To replace constraint (6) with (10), we have to precompute $\ln(\gamma_i)$ and $\ln(\sigma_k)$ which can be done before starting the optimization. Since $\ln(.)$ is a strictly monotonic function, it is order-preserving which means it is still possible to differentiate between t_i values.

The resulting MILP problem is a lot easier to solve with respect to computational complexity. There are several solvers available which can solve large instances within a reasonable solution time. The following version of the problem can be implemented as a linear model and is written as

$$\min \quad \left[\max_{p \in \mathcal{P}} \ln(c_p) \right] \tag{12}$$

$$\text{s.t.} \quad \ln(c_p) = \max_{i \in \mathcal{I}} \{ \ln(t_i) | C_{i,p} = 1 \} \qquad \forall p \in \mathcal{P} \tag{13}$$

$$\ln(t_i) = \ln(\gamma_i) + \sum_{k \in \mathcal{K}} s_k \cdot T_{k,i} \cdot \ln(\sigma_k) \qquad \forall i \in \mathcal{I} \tag{14}$$

$$\text{and} \quad (7,8).$$

Constraint (14) now defines the logarithmic TCI and $\ln(c_p)$ is defined accordingly in constraint (13). The objective function (12) has also been adjusted and now minimizes the maximum logarithmic CCI.

5   Application Scenario

In this section, we give an illustrative example to show some details of the presented model and its application. For this purpose, we use a system which

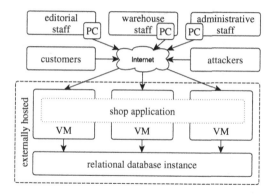

Fig. 1. Externally hosted exemplary e-commerce IS with components and actors.

represents a typical setup for providing a cloud-based e-commerce service. The setup includes a relational database, a shop application running on multiple virtual computing instances (i.e., virtual machines (VMs)), and 5 categories of users. It is visualized in Fig. 1. The computing instances process user requests and access a dedicated database instance to access persistent data. The system is maintained by editorial staff, warehouse staff, and administrative staff. In addition to normal customers which are using the system in the intended way, attackers are threatening the security of the system and data.

The model was implemented in Xpress-Mosel, a modeling and programming language that is part of the FICO® Xpress Optimization Suite [5]. We used the 64 bit version of FICO® Xpress Optimization Suite 7.6 with default settings. Additional data processing, including data extraction and solver input generation was implemented in Python 2.7.

5.1   Data

For our analysis, we extracted 16 components (7 non-technical and 9 technical ones) from the IT baseline protection catalogues which are directly applicable to the system in question. From these components, a list of threats per component and potential safeguards per threat was compiled. All components including the number of threats and safeguards per component are listed in Table 2. For a detailed description of components and a list of corresponding threats, we refer the reader to [4].

To extract information on the connection of threats and safeguards, we used cross-reference tables which are available as an extension to the IT baseline protection catalogues [3]. Since threats may be connected to more than one component and safeguards may be connected to more than one threat, the total number of 190 threats and the total number of 337 safeguards are less than the sum of the columns in Table 2. As a result, the size of matrix $C_{i,p}$ is 16×190 and 190×337 for matrix $T_{k,i}$.

Table 2. System components.

No.	Component	# Threats	# Safeguards
Non-technical			
1	Security management	4	14
2	Organisation	18	17
3	Personnel	21	15
4	Handling security incidents	3	24
5	Outsourcing	26	17
6	Patch and change management	22	18
7	Internet use	23	16
Technical			
8	Data protection	13	16
9	Protection against malware	16	13
10	General server	33	33
11	Servers under Unix	7	26
12	Internet PCs	20	17
13	Client under Windows 7	32	45
14	Web servers	27	27
15	Databases	23	32
16	Web applications	39	38

5.2   Generation of Additional Parameters

The catalogues do not provide an effectiveness coefficient σ_k in the form required for our model. However, each safeguard is assigned a qualification level (A, B, C, Z, W) indicating for which certification it is required (with A being the highest level). For the purpose of our example, we assume that the effectiveness of safeguards is correlated to its qualification level, i.e. a higher qualification level indicates a higher effectiveness. Thus, σ_k is defined as

$$\sigma_k = \begin{cases} 0.5 & \text{if qualification level} = A \\ 0.6 & \text{if qualification level} = B \\ 0.7 & \text{if qualification level} = C \quad \forall k \in \mathcal{K} \\ 0.8 & \text{if qualification level} = Z \\ 0.9 & \text{if qualification level} = W \end{cases} \qquad (15)$$

where, for example, $\sigma_k = 0.7$ indicates that a safeguard reduces a threat's criticality index t_i by $1 - 0.7 = 30\%$ if deployed, hence $t_i = \gamma_i \cdot \sigma_k = \gamma_i \cdot 0.7$.

The second required parameter is the criticality coefficient γ_i of a threat. Since it is also not directly provided by the official standard, we generate it based on the available information. For this purpose, we assume that the criticality of a threat is determined by the number and qualification of safeguards associated with it. This means if a threat has more and higher qualified safeguards associated with it, it is assumed to be more critical. We use the following calculation to generate γ_i:

$$\gamma_i = \sum_{k \in \mathcal{K}} T_{k,i} \cdot g(\sigma_k) \text{ with } g(x) = \sqrt{x} \quad \forall i \in \mathcal{I}. \tag{16}$$

Equation (16) states that the threat criticality coefficient γ_i is the sum of associated $g(\sigma_k)$ values where $g(.)$ returns a numeric value for each value of σ_k. Threat i is associated with safeguard k if $T_{k,i} = 1$. For this example, we chose a concave square root function. As a result, safeguards with higher qualification levels influence the criticality index of associated threats at a diminishing rate.

5.3   Results

To evaluate the model, we compare its results with official BSI and ISO certificates. The BSI entry level certificate requires all A level safeguards to be implemented and for an ISO 27001 certificate, all A, B, and C level safeguards are required. In our example, this would require implementing 177 safeguards for an entry level certificate. To fulfill the conditions of an ISO 27001 certificate, 270 safeguards have to be implemented.

To establish a baseline, Fig. 2 shows the component criticality indexes (CCIs) of an unprotected system compared with the entry level and ISO 27001 certifications. In case of an unprotected system, no safeguards are implemented ($s_k = 0, \forall k \in \mathcal{K}$). To obtain the results for the entry level and ISO 27001 certificates, we fixed the values of s_k to 1 if safeguard k is required by the corresponding certificate (and to 0 otherwise). Note that, although we compute these values using the introduced model, no optimization is carried out at this point, since all decision variables are preset by fixating s_k.

Figure 2 shows that both certifications increase security by reducing the criticality of all system components. The components are displayed on the x-axis

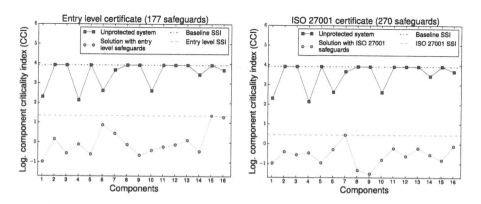

Fig. 2. Logarithmic component criticality indexes (CCIs) of an unprotected system compared with solutions corresponding to entry level and ISO 27001 certifications.

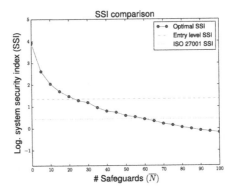

Fig. 3. SSIs of multiple optimal solutions compared with entry level and ISO 27001 certifications.

and the logarithmic CCI is measured on the y-axis. We use logarithmic values to improve readability. In each subplot, the square dots indicate the logarithmic CCIs of an unprotected system and the round dots represent the reduced logarithmic indexes. The dotted line is the objective value of the model, which is the maximum of all component criticality indexes (1). Since the most critical component is the weakest link in the security chain of the system, we call this value the system security index (SSI). We use this value to compare alternative solutions and find that by implementing all entry level safeguards, the logarithmic SSI is reduced by 65.3 % from 3.92 to 1.36 and in case of the ISO 27001 certification by 88.6 % to 0.45. When compared to the actual SSI values, this corresponds to a reduction of 92.3 % and 96.9 % respectively.

Now we are trying to find a smaller selection of safeguards than defined by the standards but one that offers a comparable security level. The questions for an organization trying to do this are: is it possible to achieve a similar security level (i.e., a similar SSI value) by implementing less safeguards? And if so, how many safeguards are necessary for a similar level of security? To answer these questions, we compute several optimal solutions and relax the safeguard limitation (7) in the process. Figure 3 shows the SSIs of 20 optimal solutions where each solution corresponds to an optimal selection of safeguards with a fixed maximum $\overline{N}$ of implemented safeguards. To improve readability, the figure again visualizes the logarithmic SSI values. The dashed and dotted lines mark the SSI of the entry level and ISO 27001 certificates respectively.

As can be seen in Fig. 3, by implementing an optimal solution with a maximum of between 20 and 25 safeguards, it is possible to realize an SSI value similar to the one of the entry level certification. In other words, it is possible to achieve a similar security level with approximately 86 % to 89 % less safeguards. In comparison to the ISO 27001 certificate, the implementation of around 60 safeguards is sufficient for a similar security level which cuts the number of required safeguards by nearly 78 %. These numbers show that an optimal decision with respect to the assumptions outlined can make a significant difference.

However, it should be noted that we do not expect an organization to follow a given solution strictly. Any solution may be used as a starting point for further analyses and design decisions.

6 Conclusion

The security design of information systems is a difficult task due to high system complexity and large amounts of relevant data. To address this problem, a considerable amount of research has been done to determine how to invest based on risk and financial measures. The problem is that existing approaches require the decision maker to provide a lot of exact input data like exact threat and vulnerability probabilities, asset valuations, and other fine-grained parameters. However, these values are very difficult to obtain in practice and, in addition, are critical to the solution. Approaches that require less information often remain vague in their results and require the decision maker to fill in the gaps himself.

The approach presented in this paper is designed to give very concrete decision support and at the same time does not require the decision maker to provide extensive input data. We established a knowledge base with data from the IT baseline protection catalogues of the BSI and developed a combinatorial optimization model to determine an optimal selection of safeguards. The decision maker only has to define the system in question by specifying relevant components. By choosing the maximum number of safeguards, the decision maker can influence the security level of the system according to his risk-preference. We applied our model to an exemplary information system and were able to demonstrate that security levels similar to the ones defined by the BSI and ISO 27001 certificates can be obtained with less safeguards. Using these results as a starting point for further analyses reduces workload and strengthens security.

Future research may include extending the scope of the model by taking additional factors into account. An interesting extension would be a multi-stage model to take into consideration that a system is operated over time. An adaptive multi-stage model could be used during the entire operation of a system to add, exchange, or remove safeguards and thereby adapt to a changing threat environment. To improve the quality of solutions, it is possible to introduce uncertainty of some of the input parameters. In doing so, more robust solutions can be obtained that also yield good security if some input parameters were determined inaccurately.

Acknowledgment. This work was partially supported by the Horst Görtz Foundation.

References

1. Baer, W.S., Parkinson, A.: Cyberinsurance in IT security management. IEEE Secur. Priv. **5**(3), 50–56 (2007)
2. Bojanc, R., Jerman-Blažič, B.: Quantitative model for economic analyses of information security investment in an enterprise information system. Organizacija **45**(6), 276–288 (2012)

3. Federal Office for Information Security: 13. EL: Cross-reference tables of the IT-Grundschutz catalogues: 13th version (2013). https://www.bsi.bund.de/DE/Themen/ITGrundschutz/ITGrundschutzKataloge/Inhalt/_content/hilfmi/checklisten/checklisten.html
4. Federal Office for Information Security: IT-Grundschutz-Catalogues: 13th version (2013)
5. FICO: Xpress-SLP: Program Reference Manual (2008)
6. Gordon, L.A., Loeb, M.P., Lucyshyn, W.: Information security expenditures and real options: a wait-and-see approach. Comput. Secur. J. **19**(2), 1–7 (2003)
7. Mukhopadhyay, A., Chatterjee, S., Saha, D., Mahanti, A., Sadhukhan, S.K.: Cyber-risk decision models: to insure IT or not? Decis. Support Syst. **56**, 11–26 (2013)
8. Rakes, T.R., Deane, J.K.: Paul Rees, L.: IT security planning under uncertainty for high-impact events. Omega **40**(1), 79–88 (2012)
9. Sawik, T.: Selection of optimal countermeasure portfolio in IT security planning. Decis. Support Syst. **55**(1), 156–164 (2013)
10. Schilling, A., Werners, B.: A quantitative threat modeling approach to maximize the return on security investment in cloud computing. In: Endicott-Popovsky, B. (ed.) Proceedings of the International Conference on Cloud Security Management. Academic Conferences and Publishing International, Reading (2013)
11. Sonnenreich, W., Albanese, J., Stout, B.: Return on security investment (ROSI) - a practical quantitative model. J. Res. Pract. Inf. Technol. **38**(1), 45–56 (2006)
12. Tatsumi, K., Goto, M.: Optimal timing of information security investment: a real options approach. In: Moore, T., Pym, D., Ioannidis, C. (eds.) Economics of Information Security and Privacy, pp. 211–228. Springer, US (2010)
13. Tsiakis, T.: Information security expenditures: a techno-economic analysis. Int. J. Comput. Sci. Netw. Secur. **10**(4), 7–11 (2010)
14. Ullrich, C.: Valuation of IT investments using real options theory. Bus. Inf. Syst. Eng. **5**(5), 331–341 (2013)
15. Viduto, V., Maple, C., Huang, W., López-Peréz, D.: A novel risk assessment and optimisation model for a multi-objective network security countermeasure selection problem. Decis. Support Syst. **53**(3), 599–610 (2012)

Towards the ENTRI Framework: Security Risk Management Enhanced by the Use of Enterprise Architectures

Nicolas Mayer[(✉)], Eric Grandry, Christophe Feltus,
and Elio Goettelmann

Luxembourg Institute of Science and Technology,
5 Avenue des Hauts-Fourneaux, L-4362 Esch-sur-Alzette, Luxembourg
{nicolas.mayer,eric.grandry,christophe.feltus,
elio.goettelmann}@list.lu

Abstract. Secure information systems engineering is currently a critical but complex concern. Risk management has become a standard approach to deal with the necessary trade-offs between expected security level and control cost. However, with the current interconnection between information systems combined with the increasing regulation and compliance requirements, it is more and more difficult to achieve real information security governance. Given that risk management is not able to deal with this complexity alone, we claim that a connection with Enterprise Architecture Management (EAM) contributes in addressing the above challenges, thereby sustaining governance and compliance in organisations. In this paper, we motivate the added value of EAM to improve security risk management and propose a research agenda towards a complete framework integrating both domains.

Keywords: Security risk management · Enterprise Architecture · Governance · Compliance

1 Introduction

Today, a strong emphasis is put on the security of Information Systems (IS) and on the management of security risks. For example, a new national regulation in Luxembourg about records management [1] concentrates on security and authenticity of records, and imposes a risk-based approach to service providers. *CSSF,*[1] as the National Regulation Authority (NRA) for the financial sector, has defined rules that emphasize IS security; the recent regulation *"Circulaire CSSF 12/544"* [2] has introduced a "risk-based approach" for financial service providers. Last but not least, in the telecommunication sector, the service providers have to comply with the EU Directive 2009/140/EC [3], which Article 13a on security and integrity of networks and services constraints Member States to ensure that providers of public communication networks manage the security risks of networks and services.

---

[1] *Commission de Surveillance du Secteur Financier.*

© Springer International Publishing Switzerland 2015
A. Persson and J. Stirna (Eds.): CAiSE 2015 Workshops, LNBIP 215, pp. 459–469, 2015.
DOI: 10.1007/978-3-319-19243-7_42

Although managing risks is constrained by regulators, modern day enterprises consider their Risk Management (RM) capabilities as an opportunity to drive competitive advantage. In its 2011 study on Global Risk Management [4], Accenture has identified that "*risk management is now more closely integrated with strategic planning and is conducted proactively, with an eye on how [risk management] capabilities might help a company to move into new markets faster or pursue other evolving growth strategies*". From a security perspective, IS Security RM (ISSRM) supports enterprises to adopt cost-effective security measures: security threats are so numerous that it is impossible to act on all and enterprises are looking for a positive Return On Security Investment (ROSI). In this sense, ISSRM plays an important role in the alignment of a company's business with its IT strategy [5].

Beside the increasing regulatory compliance, enterprises have to deal with disruptions that increase the complexity of their environment: the continuous enterprise evolution (planned evolution and/or unplanned and emergent changes), the disruption in the usage of traditional business solutions (*e.g.*, Dropbox), the heterogeneity of the stakeholder's profile and ability to address security risks, etc. In this enterprise "in motion" [6], new security risks constantly appear and new solutions are required to address them.

Enterprise Architecture Management (EAM) have appeared to be a valuable and engaging instrument to face enterprise complexity and the necessary enterprise transformation [7, 8]. EAM offers means to govern complex enterprises, such as, *e.g.*, an explicit representation of the enterprise facets, a sound and informed decisional framework, a continuous alignment between business and IT, and so forth [9].

Given that the ISSRM discipline is not able to deal with this increasing complexity alone (see Sect. 2), we claim in this paper that a connection with EAM (see Sect. 3.1) contributes in addressing the above challenges (see Sect. 3.2), thereby sustaining governance and compliance in enterprises in motion (see Sect. 3.3).

Section 2 describes the background of our work, and focuses on our preceding works and their drawbacks. Section 3 presents the state of the art in the field of EAM, its links with ISSRM and the evolution of RM towards the GRC concept (Governance, RM, and Compliance). Our research objectives are then defined in Sect. 4. Section 5 presents the research method we currently follow. Finally, Sect. 6 is about current state of the research work, conclusion and future work.

2   Background on Information System Security and Risk Management and Problem to be Tackled

In our preceding works, the concepts of ISSRM have been formalised as a domain model, i.e. a conceptual model depicting the studied domain [10]. The ISSRM domain model was designed from related literature [11]: risk management standards, security-related standards, security risk management standards and methods and security requirements engineering frameworks. The ISSRM domain model is composed of 3 groups of concepts: Asset-related concepts, Risk-related concepts, and Risk treatment-related concepts. Each of the concepts of the model has been defined and linked one to the other [11], as represented in Fig. 1.

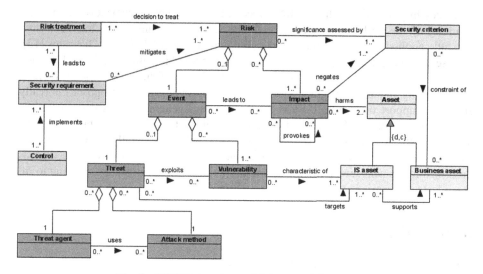

Fig. 1. ISSRM domain model (extracted from [11])

Asset-related concepts describe assets and the criteria which guarantee asset security. An *asset* is anything that has value to the organisation and is necessary for achieving its objectives. A *business asset* describes information, processes, capabilities and skills inherent to the business and core mission of the organisation, having value for it. An *IS asset* is a component of the IS supporting business assets like a database where information is stored. A *security criterion* characterises a property or constraint on business assets describing their security needs, usually for confidentiality, integrity and availability.

Risk-related concepts present how the risk itself is defined. A *risk* is the combination of a threat with one or more vulnerabilities leading to a negative impact harming the assets. An *impact* describes the potential negative consequence of a risk that may harm assets of a system or organisation, when a threat (or the cause of a risk) is accomplished. An *event* is the combination of a threat and one or more vulnerabilities. A *vulnerability* describes a characteristic of an IS asset or group of IS assets that can constitute a weakness or a flaw in terms of IS security. A *threat* characterises a potential attack or incident, which targets one or more IS assets and may lead to the assets being harmed. A *threat agent* is an agent that can potentially cause harm to IS assets. An *attack method* is a standard means by which a threat agent carries out a threat.

Risk treatment-related concepts describe what decisions, requirements and controls should be defined and implemented in order to mitigate possible risks. A *risk treatment* is an intentional decision to treat identified risks. A *security requirement* is the refinement of a treatment decision to mitigate the risk. *Controls* (countermeasures or safeguards) are designed to improve security, specified by a security requirement, and implemented to comply with it.

After having defined the ISSRM domain model, our contributions has been focused on having a model-based approach for ISSRM. It has been motivated both by an efficiency improvement of the ISSRM process, and by the enhancement of the product resulting of the performed process [11]. The ISSRM domain model has been successfully applied to analyse different modelling languages: Mal-activity Diagrams [12], Misuse Case [13], Secure Tropos [14], Business Process Modelling Notations [15], and KAOS extended to security [11]. As a general conclusion of these assessments, none of the preceding modelling languages (even when improvements are proposed) is really suited to support the whole ISSRM steps. They are generally focused on a limited number of activities of ISSRM and do not cover its full scope (*i.e.* the business-to-IT stack). Another (related) drawback we observed is that it is generally difficult to model (business and IS) assets in a meaningful manner for ISSRM. In this frame, and as described in the next section, EAM techniques and related benefits are promising to fill these gaps.

3   State of the Art

3.1   Enterprise Architecture Management

Lapalme has extensively reviewed the Enterprise Architecture (EA) literature and has identified three schools of thought, each with its own scope and purpose [16]: Enterprise IT Architecting (EA is the glue between business and IT), Enterprise Integrating (EA is the link between strategy and execution) and Enterprise Ecological Adaptation (EA is the means for organisational innovation and sustainability). Considering the increased competition and disruptions in the markets, Lapalme's taxonomy demonstrates the evolution of EA from an instrument supporting IT and business strategy execution to a management instrument for sustainable innovation and enterprise transformation [17]. As formulated by Op't Land *et al.* [18], the suggested mission of EAM is to add value by providing to the management means for informed governance of enterprise transformation. Next to top-down changes dictated by the strategy, enterprises are subject to a continuous stream of bottom-up changes, which are neither planned nor controlled: from minute adjustments in business processes, simply to make things "work", to the introduction of "shadow IT" (not formally introduced/supported ICT) in the form of cloud services, social media and BYOD.[2] As a consequence, enterprises are in constant motion [19], increasing the governance complexity. EAM, as a management science, provides the optimal platform for managing complexity [8], and making organisations more resilient in the face of disruption, leading to sustainable benefits: Ross *et al.* [20] show how constructing the right EA enhances profitability and time to market, while it improves strategy execution.

EAM is supported by multiple approaches [9, 21–24]. TOGAF [25] is an open EA framework proposed by The Open Group (TOG) and established as a standard. First published in 1995, TOGAF is based on the US Department of Defense Technical Architecture Framework for Information Management (TAFIM). From this sound foundation, TOG's Architecture Forum developed successive versions of TOGAF at regular intervals and published them on TOG's public web site. The framework is

---

[2] Bring Your Own Device.

mainly composed of a method (the Architecture Development Method, ADM) and a meta-model for architectural artefacts (the Architecture Content Framework, ACF). TOG proposes ArchiMate [26] as a standard EA Modeling Language, providing the capability to represent an enterprise in a uniform way, according to the multiple stakeholders' viewpoints [9]. ArchiMate introduces a layered representation of the EA: business, application and technology. Furthermore, two extensions are introduced since version 2.0 of the language: the Motivation Extension and the Implementation and Migration Extension. The TOGAF framework and the ArchiMate modelling language, as current EA standards, are of particular interest in our context.

3.2   EAM as ISSRM Facilitator

Connecting ISSRM and EAM has been investigated by academic works. Saeki *et al.* [27] underline that EAM is not only for IS/IT planning, but is also an instrument for *corporate planning and business function*, e.g., compliance management or RM. Innerhofer-Oberperfler and Breu [28] propose an approach for a systematic assessment of IT risks using EAM. The goal of the approach is to bridge the different views of the stakeholders involved in security management. They propose an information security meta-model and consider the security management process to be performed by security micro-processes executed by domain owners. In the same way, Ertaul and Sudarsanam [29] propose to exploit the Zachman framework [7] for defining and designing tools for securing an enterprise. This helps, *in fine*, to support security planning especially for IT. Leveraging EAM to defragment the identification of risks and to manage them in an holistic way was also recently proposed in Barateiro *et al.* [30]: EA description is used to model complex business system at the desired level of abstraction, and to cover the views of the enterprise relevant to assess and manage the different kinds of risks. All of the preceding research works are providing some initial and promising inputs towards leveraging EAM to deal with security and/or RM issues. However, to the best of our knowledge, there is no extensive and mature research work trying to benefit from research in EAM to improve RM in the specific field of information security and proposing a completely integrated approach: modelling language, method and tool.

In terms of industry standards, TOGAF [25] states that the enterprise architects are in good place to identify and mitigate risks. TOG's Architecture Forum is currently investigating the integration of security within EA, making it integrally part of the development of EA, and the ArchiMate Forum investigates extending ArchiMate concepts in order to support risk modelling, notably based on our previous works [31]. We have indeed proposed a conceptual mapping of EAM and ISSRM (first step in conceptual integration) [32] and have demonstrated that ArchiMate can be used to model the subject of the security risk assessment (the assets), but also that security risks and controls can be modelled with the existing ArchiMate constructs. This previous work represents a proof-of-concept in the conceptual integration of ISSRM-EAM: we have indeed identified gaps that require further theoretical and conceptual analysis. These different industrial initiatives confirm the interest of practitioners in the integration of EAM and ISSRM, as well as the need to develop the theoretical foundation for this integration.

3.3   From Risk Management to GRC

Today, RM is part of the integrated GRC concept: Governance, RM, and Compliance. According to the literature [25, 33, 34], "governance" evaluates, directs, and monitors the enterprise strategic objectives. To that end, the corporate governance aims at sustaining the relation between the management, the board of direction, and the shareholders [33, 34]. It also expresses the decision making policies related to corporate issues with the intent to ensure the adequacy of the resources usage according to the strategic objectives of the organisation [35]. The international standard ISO/IEC 38500 [36] is a high level framework that confers guidance on the role of governing body. It provides a set of six high level principles for the managers of the company to help them in evaluating, directing and monitoring the use of the information system of the company. COBIT [37] is a framework that enables the development of clear policies and good practice for IT control throughout enterprises. It is a framework and a supporting toolset that allow managers to bridge the gap with respect to control needs, technical issues and business risks, and communicate this level of control to employees.

GRC is also tackled by academics. Racz *et al.* [38] observe the few existing scientific researches in GRC as an integrated concept, despite the amount of research in the three topics separately. They also identify the main drivers for GRC: the regulatory compliance, followed by RM. The authors define GRC as "*an integrated, holistic approach to organisation-wide governance, risk and compliance ensuring that an organisation acts ethically correct and in accordance with its risk appetite, internal policies and external regulations through the alignment of strategy, processes, technology and people, thereby improving efficiency and effectiveness*". Bonazzi *et al.* [39] propose a process that achieves the regulatory compliance by aligning governance activities and RM. Vicente and da Silva also acknowledge the lack of scientific references related to GRC [40] and define an innovative GRC conceptual model, which strengthens the connections between risk and governance in the sense that governance aims at understanding and foreseeing the vulnerabilities of an organisation. The authors also claim that the alignment between business and risks is enforced by structured governance and compliance management. Another approach [41] proposes to use Situational Method Engineering and method fragments [42] to implement GRC. Once again, in this broader domain of GRC, to the best of our knowledge, there is no extensive and mature research work trying to benefit from research in EAM to improve ISSRM for compliance and governance purpose.

4   Research Objectives

Our proposal aims at connecting RM and EAM, in the area of IS security. We claim that such a connection shall help to reduce GRC complexity and associated cost. Our objective is therefore to answer the following research question (Fig. 2): **How to improve ISSRM using results from EAM for Compliance and Governance purpose?**

To answer this research question, the following objectives with the associated contributions have been specifically defined:

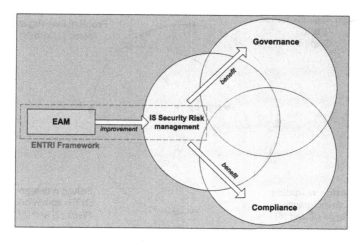

Fig. 2. Research outcome

1. To assess and integrate the conceptual models of EAM and ISSRM domains [contribution 1 = EAM-ISSRM integrated model]
2. To assess and improve the ArchiMate modelling language to support the integrated conceptual model of EAM and ISSRM [contribution 2 = EAM-ISSRM extended language]
3. To analyse the processes supporting both ISSRM and EAM, and to define relevant method fragments/chunks allowing to link both domains at the methodological level [contribution 3 = EAM-ISSRM catalogue of method fragments/chunks]
4. To analyse and position the integrated EAM-ISSRM framework (conceptual model, modelling language and method chunks/fragments), called "ENTRI framework", with regards to GRC models [contribution 4 = GRC-aware ENTRI model, language and method]
5. To implement the designed artefacts on a technological platform called the "ENTRI platform" [contribution 5 = ENTRI platform prototype]

5   Methods and Approach

This research work is especially motivated by the need to fill the gap between GRC and EAM from the IS security perspective. It falls in the frame of Design Science Research (DSR) that tends to design a solution for a specific problem [43]. The research method we want to follow is inspired by the "regulative cycle" approach established by Wieringa [44], that is instantiated to our case in Fig. 3.

Step (1): The motivation of the research work resulted from the observation that ISSRM methods could be improved using EAM, as explained in Sect. 2. This statement is also shared by EBRC (E-Business & Resilience Centre),[3] a leading European datacentre

---

[3] http://www.ebrc.com.

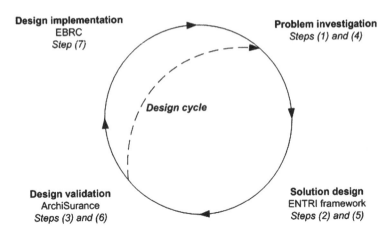

Fig. 3. Research method: A Design Science Research (DSR) approach

operator and our industrial partner, both of us being experienced in running ISSRM methods. EBRC is particularly exposed to governance and compliance problems requiring to perform ISSRM: EBRC holds several certifications (especially the ISO/IEC 27001 certification [45]) and is subject to a set of regulations (financial regulation, tier certification, etc.) many of them involving ISSRM activities having different scopes.

Step (2): In order to achieve our research objectives (Sect. 4), we plan to produce a set of design artefacts called the ENTRI framework and composed of:

- An integrated EAM-ISSRM model
- A integrated modelling language
- A catalogue of method fragments/chunks
- A prototype integrating the preceding results

Step (3): The design validation activity includes the use of the ENTRI framework to run a lab-case study called ArchiSurance [46].

Step (4), (5) and (6): After this first design research iteration, we plan to perform a new design cycle in order to improve our artefacts based on the feedback obtained during the design validation step.

Step (7): Finally, the ENTRI framework will be assessed on a real-world case by EBRC in the frame of improvements of IS security compliance and governance. The ENTRI framework could be compared to their current practices and used in the context of ISO/IEC 27001 certification maintenance [45] and "*Circulaire CSSF 12/544*" [2] compliance for defining an integrated ISSRM system for the company. It is also possible to consider other contractual or regulatory frameworks during this implementation step if additional compliance issues related to our scope apply to EBRC during the design time.

6 Conclusions and Future Work

In this paper, we have described our research background, objectives and agenda in the frame of integrating ISSRM and EAM domains. After having explained the context of our work, we have introduced the current drawbacks of ISSRM approaches: it is generally difficult to model assets, risks and related countermeasures in a meaningful manner, in particular all along the business-to-IT stack. An extensive state-of-the-art has then been established in order to survey the current situation in the field of EAM, its integration with ISSRM and its contextualisation to the emerging GRC field. Our position is that a global framework, encompassing an integrated conceptual model, a modelling language, method(s) and a tool, should be useful to improve the state-of-practice. The expected benefits of such a contribution are numerous: better information security governance, reduction of time and effort dedicated to ISSRM, support in compliance to legal or normative requirements, etc. We plan to demonstrate these benefits through a real-world case-study, with the help of performance indicators.

Regarding current state of the work, the problem investigation step of our research method has been performed and the main observations have been reported in this paper. We are now designing the integrated EAM-ISSRM conceptual model and refining in parallel our coarse-grained research method in a detailed one, taking into account best practices of DSR [44]. Our future works will naturally be focused on following this research method.

Acknowledgments. Thanks to Roel J. Wieringa for his valuable inputs and recommendations about Design Science Methodology. Supported by the National Research Fund, Luxembourg, and financed by the ENTRI project (C14/IS/8329158).

References

1. ILNAS: Technical regulation requirements and measures for certifying Digitisation or Archiving Service Providers (PSDC) (2013). http://www.ilnas.public.lu/fr/confiance-numerique/archivage-electronique/documents-obtention-statut-psdc/index.html
2. CSSF: Circulaire CSSF 12/544 - Optimisation par une approche par les risques de la surveillance exercée sur les "PSF de support" (2012)
3. Official Journal of the European Union: Directive 2009/140/EC of the European Parliament and of the Council of 25 November 2009 (2009)
4. Accenture: Report on the Accenture 2011 Global Risk Management Study (2011). http://www.accenture.com/SiteCollectionDocuments/PDF/Accenture-Global-Risk-Management-Study-2011.pdf
5. Henderson, J.C., Venkatraman, N.: Strategic alignment: leveraging information technology for transforming organizations. IBM Syst. J. **38**, 472–484 (1999)
6. Proper, H.A.: Enterprise architecture: informed steering of enterprises in motion. In: Hammoudi, S., Cordeiro, J., Maciaszek, L.A., Filipe, J. (eds.) ICEIS 2013. LNBIP, vol. 190, pp. 16–34. Springer, Heidelberg (2014)
7. Zachman, J.A.: A framework for information systems architecture. IBM Syst. J. **26**, 276–292 (1987)
8. Saha, P. (ed.): A Systemic Perspective to Managing Complexity with Enterprise Architecture. IGI Global, Hershey (2013)

9. Lankhorst, M.: Enterprise Architecture at Work – Modelling Communication and Analysis. Springer, Heidelberg (2013)
10. Dubois, E., Heymans, P., Mayer, N., Matulevičius, R.: A systematic approach to define the domain of information system security risk management. In: Nurcan, S., Salinesi, C., Souveyet, C., Ralyté, J. (eds.) Intentional Perspectives on Information Systems Engineering, pp. 289–306. Springer, Heidelberg (2010)
11. Mayer, N.: Model-based Management of Information System Security Risk (2009)
12. Chowdhury, M.J.M., Matulevičius, R., Sindre, G., Karpati, P.: Aligning mal-activity diagrams and security risk management for security requirements definitions. In: Regnell, B., Damian, D. (eds.) REFSQ 2011. LNCS, vol. 7195, pp. 132–139. Springer, Heidelberg (2012)
13. Matulevičius, R., Mayer, N., Heymans, P.: Alignment of misuse cases with security risk management. In: Proceedings of the 4th Symposium on Requirements Engineering for Information Security (SREIS 2008), in Conjunction with the 3rd International Conference of Availability, Reliability and Security (ARES 2008), pp. 1397–1404. IEEE Computer Society (2008)
14. Matulevičius, R., Mayer, N., Mouratidis, H., Martinez, F.H., Heymans, P., Genon, N.: Adapting secure tropos for security risk management in the early phases of information systems development. In: Bellahsène, Z., Léonard, M. (eds.) CAiSE 2008. LNCS, vol. 5074, pp. 541–555. Springer, Heidelberg (2008)
15. Altuhhova, O., Matulevičius, R., Ahmed, N.: Towards definition of secure business processes. In: Bajec, M., Eder, J. (eds.) CAiSE Workshops 2012. LNBIP, vol. 112, pp. 1–15. Springer, Heidelberg (2012)
16. Lapalme, J.: Three schools of thought on enterprise architecture. IT Prof. **14**, 37–43 (2012)
17. Vernadat, F.: Enterprise Modelling: Objectives, Constructs and Ontologies. Presented at the CAiSE Workshops, vol. 3 (2004)
18. Op't Land, M., Proper, H.A., Waage, M., Cloo, J., Steghuis, C.: Enterprise Architecture - Creating Value by Informed Governance. Springer, Heidelberg (2008)
19. Lankhorst, M., Proper, H.A.: Enterprise architecture - towards essential sensemaking. Enterp. Model. Inf. Syst. Archit. **9**(1), 5–21 (2014)
20. Ross, J.W., Weill, P., Robertson, D.C.: Enterprise Architecture As Strategy: Creating a Foundation for Business Execution. Harvard Business School Press, Boston (2006)
21. Greefhorst, D., Proper, H.A.: Architecture Principles - The Cornerstones of Enterprise Architecture. Springer, Heidelberg (2011)
22. Giachetti, R.E.: Design of Enterprise Systems: Theory, Architecture, and Methods. CRC Press, Boca Raton (2010)
23. The Architecture Working Group of the Software Engineering Committee: Recommended Practice for Architectural Description of Software Intensive Systems. IEEE, Piscataway, New Jersey (2000)
24. Anaya, V., Berio, G., Harzallah, M., Heymans, P., Matulevičius, R., Opdahl, A.L., Panetto, H., Verdecho, M.J.: The unified enterprise modelling language—overview and further work. Comput. Ind. **61**, 99–111 (2010)
25. The Open Group: TOGAF Version 9.1. Van Haren Publishing, The Netherlands (2011)
26. The Open Group: ArchiMate 2.0 Specification. Van Haren Publishing, The Netherlands (2012)
27. Saeki, M., Iguchi, K., Wen-yin, K., Shinohara, M.: A meta-model for representing software specification & design methods. In: Proceedings of the IFIP WG8.1 Working Conference on Information System Development Process, pp. 149–166. North-Holland Publishing Co., Amsterdam (1993)

28. Innerhofer-Oberperfler, F., Breu, R.: Using an Enterprise Architecture for IT Risk Management. Presented at the Information Security South Africa 6th Annual Conference (2006)
29. Ertaul, L., Sudarsanam, R.: Security planning using Zachman framework for enterprises. In: Proceedings of EURO mGOV 2005 (2005)
30. Barateiro, J., Antunes, G., Borbinha, J.: Manage risks through the enterprise architecture. In: 45th Hawaii International Conference on System Science (HICSS), pp. 3297–3306 (2012)
31. Band, I., Engelsman, W., Feltus, C., Paredes, S.G., Hietala, J., Jonkers, H., Massart, S.: Modeling Enterprise Risk Management and Security with the ArchiMate® Language. The Open Group (2015)
32. Grandry, E., Feltus, C., Dubois, E.: Conceptual integration of enterprise architecture management and security risk management. In: Enterprise Distributed Object Computing Conference Workshops (EDOCW), 17th IEEE International Enterprise Distributed Object Computing Conference, pp. 114–123 (2013)
33. OECD: OECD Principles of Corporate Governance 2004. OECD Publishing (2004)
34. Committee on the Financial Aspects of Corporate Governance: Report of the Committee on the Financial Aspects of Corporate Governance. Gee (1992)
35. Managing development: the governance dimension: a discussion paper. World Bank (1991)
36. ISO/IEC 38500: Corporate governance of information technology. International Organization for Standardization, Geneva (2008)
37. COBIT 5: Implementation. ISACA (2012)
38. Racz, N., Weippl, E., Seufert, A.: A frame of reference for research of integrated governance, risk and compliance (GRC). In: De Decker, B., Schaumüller-Bichl, I. (eds.) CMS 2010. LNCS, vol. 6109, pp. 106–117. Springer, Heidelberg (2010)
39. Bonazzi, R., Hussami, L., Pigneur, Y.: Compliance management is becoming a major issue in IS design. In: D'Atri, A., Saccà, D. (eds.) Information Systems: People, Organizations, Institutions, and Technologies, pp. 391–398. Physica-Verlag, Heidelberg (2010)
40. Vicente, P., Mira da Silva, M.: A conceptual model for integrated governance, risk and compliance. In: Mouratidis, H., Rolland, C. (eds.) CAiSE 2011. LNCS, vol. 6741, pp. 199–213. Springer, Heidelberg (2011)
41. Gericke, A., Fill, H.-G., Karagiannis, D., Winter, R.: Situational method engineering for governance, risk and compliance information systems. In: Proceedings of the 4th International Conference on Design Science Research in Information Systems and Technology, pp. 24:1–24:12. ACM, New York (2009)
42. Mirbel, I., Ralyte, J.: Situational method engineering: combining assembly-based and roadmap-driven approaches. Requir. Eng. 11, 58–78 (2005)
43. Hevner, A.R., March, S.T., Park, J., Ram, S.: Design science in information systems research. MIS Q. 28, 75–105 (2004)
44. Wieringa, R.J.: Design Science Methodology for Information Systems and Software Engineering. Springer-Verlag, Heidelberg (2014)
45. ISO/IEC 27001: Information technology – Security techniques – Information security management systems – Requirements. International Organization for Standardization, Geneva (2013)
46. Jonkers, H., Band, I., Quartel, D.: The ArchiSurance Case Study. The Open Group (2012)

Towards the Development of a Cloud Forensics Methodology: A Conceptual Model

Stavros Simou[1(✉)], Christos Kalloniatis[1], Haralambos Mouratidis[2], and Stefanos Gritzalis[3]

[1] Cultural Informatics Laboratory,
Department of Cultural Technology and Communication,
University of the Aegean, University Hill, 81100 Mytilene, Greece
{SSimou, chkallon}@aegean.gr
[2] School of Computing, Engineering and Mathematics, University of Brighton,
Watts Building, Lewes Road, Brighton BN2 4GJ, UK
H.Mouratidis@brighton.ac.uk
[3] Information and Communication Systems Security Laboratory,
Department of Information and Communications Systems Engineering,
University of the Aegean, 83200 Samos, Greece
sgritz@aegean.gr

Abstract. Cloud Computing technology and services despite the advantages they bring to the market have created number of issues regarding the security and trust of the individuals using them. Incidents occurring in cloud computing environments are hard to be solved since digital forensic methods used to conduct digital investigations are not suitable for cloud computing investigations since they do not consider the specific characteristics of the Cloud. However, designing services over the cloud that will support and assist an investigation process when an incident occurs is also of vital importance. This paper presents a conceptual model for supporting the development of a cloud forensics method and process, thus assisting information systems developers in building better services and investigators to be able to conduct forensics analysis in cloud environments.

Keywords: Cloud forensics · Review · Cloud forensics process · Cloud forensics challenges · Cloud forensics solutions

1 Introduction

The increase of users using applications and infrastructures based on cloud computing technology, lead the investigators and law enforcement agents to introduce a new field in digital forensics called cloud forensics. This new "science" is a subset of digital forensic and it was first introduced by Ruan [1], to designate the need for digital investigation in cloud environments, based on forensic principles and procedures. The rise of criminal behavior on these environments the past years, causes great concern among Cloud Service Providers (CSPs), users and law enforcements due to the lack of techniques and methodologies, policies and standards. During its first steps many issues encountered and the people involved in, adopted the same concept for digital

© Springer International Publishing Switzerland 2015
A. Persson and J. Stirna (Eds.): CAiSE 2015 Workshops, LNBIP 215, pp. 470–481, 2015.
DOI: 10.1007/978-3-319-19243-7_43

forensics. The two forensic techniques (digital and cloud), although they are very close to each other, they do have fundamental differences. The most important difference is the access to devices and evidence. In a traditional investigation to seize the hardware containing the data and have access to hard drives and evidence is a "simple" process. In cloud environments where data is stored in unknown locations around the world due to systems' distribution, seizing (physically) the devices is an issue and also a painful process with unpredictable results. Based on National Institute of Standards and Technology (NIST), *"Challenges, such as those associated with data replication, location transparency, and multi-tenancy are somewhat unique to cloud computing forensics"* [2].

Over the past years, various frameworks and models have been introduced in digital forensics area and few are focusing on cloud forensics (i.e. Integrated Conceptual Digital Forensic Framework [3], Advanced Data Acquisition Model [4]). A detailed review at the respective methods has been conducted in [5, 6]. Through this review we have identified the main challenges related to cloud forensics and we have concluded that the literature fails to provide evidence of a well structured and defined framework to support cloud forensics based on a clear set of cloud investigation concepts and entities and the relations between them.

This paper advances the state of the art by proposing the first effort, to the best of our knowledge, to define a conceptual model for cloud forensics. The paper is organized as follows. Section 2 summarizes related work and lists a number of challenges related to the development of a conceptual model for cloud forensics, while Sect. 3 introduces the main concepts of the conceptual model based on the challenges presented in Sect. 2 along with the proposed conceptual model. In Sect. 4, the applicability of the conceptual model is demonstrated with the aid of a case study related to a forensic investigation scenario. Finally, Sect. 5, concludes the paper by raising future research on this innovative research field.

2   Related Work

Over the last few years a number of researchers have attempted to identify cloud forensics' issues and challenges and find the suitable solutions to mitigate them. Ruan [1], was one of the first researchers who dealt with cloud forensics and revealed the differences between cloud and digital forensics. Unfortunately, and despite the existing effort in the literature, there are still plenty of open issues concerning acquisition, analysis and presentation of digital evidence. Our analysis [5, 6] revealed the challenges and the open issues in cloud forensics, together with the proposed solutions of these challenges. It has also highlighted that there is an urgent need for designing new methodologies and frameworks on cloud forensics. To the best of our knowledge, the literature fails to provide evidence of a methodology, concerning cloud forensics, which covers every aspect and every phase in a cloud forensic investigation. In particular, two issues are important: (i) there are some processes such as preservation and documentation that should be running concurrently with all the other processes. They should be carried out throughout the cloud investigation process and (ii) most authors dealing with cloud forensic solutions have focused on specific challenges such as access to evidence in logs, privacy and SLAs. There is a lack of solutions for the rest of the challenges; there are still open issues to be explored. Unless there is a proper solution on these matters cloud forensics could not cope with cyber-crime.

3 Conceptual Model for Cloud Forensics

In order to develop a new methodology on cloud forensics all possible aspects and elements must be identified. To identify the main concepts for building a conceptual model for cloud forensics, a literature review has been conducted [7–11]. Based on this review analysis the most important components are presented below.

3.1 Concepts

Incident. This concept includes terms such as evidence, initiation, identification, authorization, security and preservation. A cloud forensic investigation is being initiated when an incident occurs (or being discovered). The staff is informed about the activities of the incident and monitors the system. A team is formed in order to deal with the incident and try to eliminate the risks. The main objective is to identify the incident, secure the evidence and find as much information and details about it. Evidence forms the very foundation of any legal system [12]. Digital evidence in cloud computing is the information (data) stored on any digital device in the distributed data centers around the world. The most important element in the digital forensics is to maintain the integrity and the chain of custody of the digital evidence. Identification of evidence in cloud environments is a difficult process due to the different deployment and service models and also the limitation of seizing (physically) the computer device containing the evidence. To win a case in court of law concrete evidence should be produced and presented. In cases where evidence could not be identified as relevant evidence, there is a possibility of never being collected or processed at all, and by the time it will be discovered to have relevance they might not exist in digital form (erased, deleted, reboot machine, etc.) [13]. Besides identifying evidence, the type of environment and configuration of the system should also be examined and identified and the location of data should be determined. A good knowledge on the environment means that the investigator can decide what type of method and tools will be used to secure and acquire data. Securing and preserving data should be one of the first priorities practitioners should accomplish. They should require cooperation of the CSP to place a "litigation hold" on the account and prevent any further changes to the data [3]. Authorization is another element that should be highly considered. To receive authorization to investigate an incident it could be a painful process. Law enforcement agents usually require a search warrant or other legal approval describing in details the terms and limits of the investigation [14, 15]. There are different types of authorization provided by several discrete aspects such as internal, law or external [4].

Organization Stakeholder. There is a number of different people and activities involved in this concept such as training, team members, duties, expert testimonies, external assistance. The objective is to form a team that will have the ability to deal with an incident (criminal behavior) when it occurs and also to be able to manage all human resources to the best of the organization and the investigation. Due to the distributed systems and different environments the technical staff should have great knowledge on networks, security issues and also on new technologies. Legal staff should be part of the team with knowledge on multi-jurisdictional issues and to be able to overcome any legal problems that may arise. Trying to follow the new technologies in a changeable environment is almost impossible. Many organizations do not have the ability to hire all the specialized personnel in order to keep the systems up and running. External assistance could be hired to help organizations' staff in a cloud investigation. Experts' testimony plays an important role to the outcome of the trial where the jury (often) consists of people with only the basic knowledge in computer systems. Depending on the complexity of the evidence a person with knowledge both on legal and technical issues may be needed.

Planning. According to Ciardhuain *"The planning concept is strongly influenced by information from both inside and outside the investigating organizations"* [15]. Under the planning there are concepts such as preparation, implementation, service level agreements (SLAs), team and training. The main objective of this concept is to prepare and ensure that personnel, operations and infrastructures are able to support an investigation in case of an incident [14]. A well-organized preparation can improve the quality and availability of digital evidence collected and preserved, while minimizing cost and workload [16]. When an incident occurs in cloud environments the response time is critical and every second counts. Develop an incident response plan, ensuring that it was taken under consideration all possible calculated risks [16]. Policies and procedures should be clearly defined and as many likely scenarios should be considered and tested. "Forensic polishes deal mainly with the responsibilities of a forensic team, such as what aspects of a forensic investigation should be handled by which personnel" [17]. SLAs are contracts providing information on how a cloud forensic investigation will be handled, usually signed between consumers and CSPs [18]. Well-written and robust SLAs should be considered in order to provide technical and legal details about the roles and responsibilities between the CSP and the cloud customer, security issues in a multi-jurisdictional and multi-tenant environment in terms of legal regulations, confidentiality of customer data, and privacy policies.

Cloud Service Provider (CSP). Based on Liu *"Cloud provider is a person, organization, or entity responsible for making a service available to interested parties"* [19]. Cloud forensics deals with the incidents occur in cloud environments at CSPs premises and infrastructures. Access to evidence, trust, transparency and third parties are concepts closely-related to CSPs. The objective of this concept is to build solid relationships between CSPs and investigators and eliminate the dependencies. CSPs should be responsible to assist and help practitioners and consumers with all the information and evidence found in their infrastructures. They should be willing to provide the right access to potential evidence shortly after a request has been placed, without compromising the privacy and security of their tenants. As CSPs have full control of their infrastructures' data they should ensure that their staff are capable and trained to conduct an investigation and they should not tamper any data. A communication channel with the practitioners should be open during the investigation to exchange knowledge. In order to build a good relationship and trust with the consumers, transparency should be provided by CSPs. Information about the system environment and the location of users' data should be provided otherwise the evidence may be untrustworthy and the investigation may lead to nowhere [20]. Open-source software frameworks should be developed [21] to ensure the transparency for a strong relationship. Consumers should have all the necessary mechanisms to check whether cloud is performing as agreed [22]. Many CSPs have dependencies on third parties (other CSPs). For example a consumer may have an e-mail account on a CSP, who in turn may depend on a third party (partner) to provide infrastructure to store data [1]. All the third parties involved with a CSP should sign contracts clearly stating that their services will be at a consistent level according to the contractual obligations with the consumer [23].

Law Enforcement Agents (LEA). The people responsible for conducting (cloud) forensic investigations are called law enforcement agents. This is an important concept the absence of which will lead to no investigation progress. The objective of this concept according to Association of Chief Police Officers is *"the officers to ensure compliance with legislation and, in particular, to be sure that the procedures adopted in the seizure of any property are performed in accordance with statute and current case law"* [24] and also to track-down the people responsible for a criminal activity. LEA are government agents such as police officers, federal agents, customs, etc. which have the ability to apply their powers to specific jurisdictions. Procedures methods and guidelines that officers should follow are specified in the ACPO Good Practice Guide for Computer-Based Electronic Evidence [24]. The document specifies the rules and principles that all officers should follow when they are dealing with a digital investigation and evidence. According to the complexity of the incident LEAs can ask for the assistance of external consultants to advise them with the process of the investigation.

Documents. Documentation is important for an investigation and runs in parallel throughout the investigation in cloud forensics. Based on Adams *"Documentation is vital to ensure that a record is kept of all activity associated with the acquisition of the electronic data and subsequent transportation and storage as there is the potential for the whole process to come under close scrutiny in court"* [4]. Documentation includes concepts such as chain of custody, people and process. The main objective is to keep the investigation proper documented in order to increase the probabilities of winning a case in a court of law or in an internal investigation. When an incident occurs personnel should be ready to follow specific steps according to the incident. These steps/guidelines should be referred in a manual and should be followed by all people involved in. Documentation at the early stages of the incident also helps to keep track of all the actions have been taken and to proceed with different techniques. Any risk analysis or assessment tests performed during the training and preparation should be documented in order to assist the team. All tools, processes, methods and principles performed should be documented properly in order to maintain the chain of custody. Any changes made to the evidence should be also recorded. According to Grispos et al. *"A properly* *maintained chain of custody provides the documentary history for the entire lifetime of evidence discovered during an investigation*" [25]. To present the evidence in a court as admissible, all the parties (staff, CSPs, third parties) conducted the investigation should record their actions through logs and notes e.g. who handled the evidence, how was it done, did the integrity of the evidence maintained, how was it stored, etc.

Investigation (Process). Starting an investigation, processes and methodologies should be defined in order to achieve a digitally forensic environment [5]. According to Kruse [26] the basic forensic methodology remains consistent and it is based on three activities: (a) acquiring the evidence without altering or damaging the original, (b) authenticating that the recovered evidence is the same as the original seized data, and (c) analyzing the data without modifying it. Terms such as acquisition, analysis, method and integrity are familiar to this concept. The objective is to ensure that the integrity of evidence maintained (not compromised), and the chain of custody remains unbroken. Cloud forensic acquisition typically is a process to collect identified evidence stored in cloud data centers. These data centers store critical information, applications and running services; therefore their operation cannot be stopped. The acquisition must take place while the system is running and the methods will be used should ensure the privacy of the tenants and the efficiency of the operation. At first stage a search warrant need to be executed followed by the mechanisms and tools that will collect the evidence ensuring the integrity is maintained. Integrity can prove if any data being used as evidence from the time of its acquisition has not been modified during the investigation. Transferring evidence through Internet could be with different methods but the outcome of the transmission is to ensure that the evidence remains valid for later use [15]. The same principle applies with the storage of the evidence; the integrity of them cannot be affected. Analysis of digital evidence requires the processing and interpretation of digital data in a humanly meaningful manner [27]. Data should be transformed into a more manageable size and form. A timeline with the evidence information should be built in order to get answers in critical questions. Time is critical for the reconstruction of an incident and it should be handled carefully especial in cloud environments with all the different time zones.

Solution. Solution in general is a concept that deals with the identification of all possible answers to an issue or a challenge. In cloud forensics according to [1] there are three different dimensions (categories): legal, organizational and technical. Therefore the solutions can be categorized into these three dimensions. Legal category mostly involves any aspect that has to do with the law. Due to data distribution evidence can reside in data centers spread across the world. Different legal system means laws and regulations that apply to one country may not apply to the other. Hence, there are multiple jurisdictions that the investigators need to deal with. Special treaties should be followed and international collaborations should be established. On the other hand, SLAs need to be more effective. The organizational category covers the people that work in a company, the provider(s) and all the third parties that provide services to the company through the CSP. The team that will be formed to cope with the incident, should be well-trained to follow the right procedures in order to preserve the integrity of the evidence and maintain the chain of custody. The technical category involves technical issues such as methods, procedures and tools. Methods and procedures should be clearly defined proposing the best available solution according to the incident. The techniques will be used by the investigators should be implemented and documented. In cloud forensics the right tools should be developed to handle incidents and assist on the investigation.

Report. The report concept is different from the documentation. With the term report the study mostly focuses on the case preparation and presentation in a court of law or corporate management. All the information gathered from the analysis of the evidence should be transformed into reports. In most of the times the outcome of a case depends on the presentation of the report. Therefore experts should be chosen with personal knowledge of the procedures that generated the records, having participated in or observed the event [28]. Experts should be prepared to confront the jury who lacks knowledge of cloud computing and try to present the information in a language that anyone can understand. The reports concerning the legal aspect of the presentation should be presented by people with great knowledge of the law issues and not only from people with a good technical background.

3.2   Conceptual Model

Taking into consideration all the respected literature the proposed conceptual model for cloud forensics is presented in this section. Figure 1 summarizes the critical components of the model. After identifying and presenting the concepts and their categories (sub-activities) the bonds and the relationships between the concepts have been imprinted.

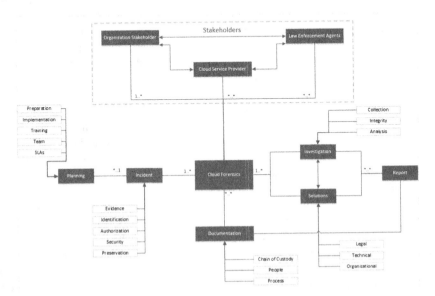

Fig. 1. Conceptual model for cloud forensics

In the planning concept there are a lot of activities that need to be considered in case of an incident. There would be a lot of preparation with all the possible scenarios dealing with the incident; hence, there will be many plans to one incident. In case of an incident the cloud forensic investigation is initiated, which involves organization stakeholders, CSPs and LEAs. Actually the investigation starts the time that an incident has been detected (not occurred). The relationship between incident and cloud.forensics is one to many due to the fact that all the different concepts are been involved to produce the desirable results in order to eliminate the risks.

The three concepts (organization stakeholder, CSP and LEAs) are depended on each other in order to have a smooth and effective investigation. They should co-operate with each other to exchange knowledge and information. Mostly, organization stakeholders and LEAs are waiting from the CSPs to give them access to their data and assist them to proceed with the investigation. The relationship between the organization stakeholders and the CSPs is one to many (it is very common a CSP to sign contracts with third parties) and the same applies between the organization stakeholders and the LEA (they may use external professionals to assist them). On the other hand the relationship between the CSP and the LEA is many to many. Again, all these three are been involved during the whole process of cloud forensics.

As chain of custody and integrity must be maintained at any time, documentation becomes one of the most important elements of the conceptual model. Documentation should run concurrently with all the other concepts from the beginning to the end of the investigation. All the steps should be documented properly according to the procedures, thus, the relationship between this concept and cloud forensics is many to many. Investigation and solution concepts are running in parallel because each one of them gives feedback to other. Depending on the proposed solution the investigation carries on and the opposite, depending on the investigation a solution is proposed. Taking into consideration the findings of these three concepts, the report category generates reports to be presented in a court of law or for an internal investigation, resulting for a relationship many to many between them.

The proposed conceptual model gives the possibility to understand all the different entities involved in a cloud forensic investigation and the role they play. Understanding the exact scope of the concepts, the relations between them and what they represent is easier to develop an accurate and efficient framework for cloud forensic investigation. Adopting a conceptual modelling approach usually allows providing solid foundations to development/analysis methodologies.

4 Case Study

In this section, a case study is presented to demonstrate all the activities that might occur in an investigation in relation to the proposed concepts. The case study deals with a corporate server intrusion and stealing data from cloud scenario. The scenario is similar to [14, 16]. The scenario is based on real incidents. It involves the investigation of cloud computers for stealing corporate material. A Greek company called ABC is using Software as a Service CSP's to run their services and a foreign non-European citizen managed to break into their server and stole confidential information concerning the Greek transportation network. The attacker stores data into cloud in a provider who is running its business in its country. The company was notified about the incident and the investigation was initiated.

Planning includes activities conducted prior to the incident. ABC implemented procedures, hired an external person specialized in forensic procedures and techniques and sent an administrator to be trained in cloud forensic investigation. When the administrator was well-trained a team of three people formed to monitor and test their system with possible scenarios. The administrator was in command of the team and the consultant played the assistant role. A legal officer from inside the company was also trained in cloud forensic matters and in multi-jurisdictional issues. The rest of IT staff trained on the basic concepts of forensics. Evidence preservation procedures were developed, new forensic tools were bought and the company's equipment has been upgraded. Before hiring CSP, ABC made a market research to find the most appropriate provider to suit their needs. They signed a service level agreement stating the rules of using SaaS and their obligations.

In the *incident* phase, when an instance of incidence occurs, the administrator is informed from personnel that some files are missing from the servers. Their allegations are checked to determine if they are valid and confirmed via system analysis. The authentication system between ABC and CSP traces logs of the intrusion and appropriate tools are used in order to identify and preserve potential evidence. A restoration of data from a previous version of backup is activated in order to assess the damage.

From the *organization stakeholder* perspective, the administrator contacts the provider and a communication channel between company and CSP is open to determine the importance of the problem. More information and access to provider's logs about the incident is being asked and the SLA is initiated. The administrator demands from provider's personnel not to proceed on any action unless they are trained to do so. The consultant discusses with the administrator the different procedures they should follow and they are informed by the CSP that the incident involves an IP address from another country. Legal officer is now aware that CSP is relying on a third party for storage of their data and calls the Law Enforcement Agents (LEA) to notify them about the incident and ask for help in jurisdictional issues.

Law Enforcement Agents (LEAs) also are involved prior to the incident. Law enforcement agency conducted training to their staff on handling electronic evidence, techniques and procedures of cloud forensics and legal issues about jurisdictions and regulations. They are equipped with state-of-the-art computer technology and they hired the best investigators with legal and technical background in cloud forensics. LEAs are engaged into investigation after receiving a phone call from ABC's legal officer that a criminal activity is reported. They've been informed that evidence resides in different jurisdiction and try to conduct third party CSP to ask for permission to access log files. Agents are gathering information about the criminal activities and a search warrant is obtained. Due to jurisdiction problem the search warrant does not cover the area where the perpetrator belongs to and agents conduct the law authorities of that country to coordinate their movements and authorize them to proceed. LEAs order to place a litigation hold on the perpetrator accounts to prevent any potential alteration of data.

Cloud Service Provider staff trained in cloud forensics incidents, techniques and tools. Due to large volume of data CSP signed contracts with third parties (CSPs) to host its data. CSP authorizes its personnel to cooperate with organization stakeholder and LEA. CSP and agents are gathering information about the environment data is kept. Then they conduct third party where data is stored and ask for permission to gather potential evidence.

During the *Investigation* LEAs after getting the warrant and the permission to access the logs are defining the steps they are taking. Using the appropriate forensic tools agents together with the provider are collecting logs and relevant data and they are making an image of the system in a forensically sound manner. Confidentiality and privacy of other tenants is maintained. Without compromising evidence the image is handled to investigators and is transported securely to the laboratory for examination. Analysis of the image is conducted by the investigators in order to find and extract any evidence. Investigators focused on the activities took place near the date and time the incident occurred using the network time protocol (NTP). The log and data analysis revealed that the perpetrator accessed company's files and tracks of the stolen files were found.

As *solution* the legal officer followed the forensic procedures and once there was a problem with jurisdiction she called the law enforcement agents. On the other hand, agents obtained a warrant to proceed with the investigation. In order to overcome jurisdiction problem they communicated with attacker's country authorities and access was granted. The data analysis revealed evidence and the agents decided to run again the investigation process to gather more information about the perpetrator.

Appropriate *documents* are generated during the whole investigation. An incident manual has been created during the planning concept for all three parties (organization stakeholders, agents, providers) with guidelines and different case studies according to the incident. Administrator consults the manual and records all the steps are taking during the incident. The same applies to agents and providers. The steps followed to obtain the warrant, the method used to collect evidence and the persons involved in are documented. The mechanisms to ensure the confidentiality and privacy of other tenants and the integrity of evidence also are documented. During the investigation all the tools and methods used to acquire any evidence are documented together with any piece of digital evidence itself. The transportation of the evidence and the way they were kept are also recorded.

Finally, *Reports'* generation is necessary when the investigation and solution concepts conclude, in order to help the investigators to present their results to organization stakeholders. A report showing that the integrity of the evidence maintained and the procedures followed.

5   Conclusion

The aim of this paper was to design and present a conceptual model for cloud forensics. In order to do so, there was a detailed study on the challenges and methodologies proposed by the researchers on this area. The next step was to identify the different concepts that exist in a cloud forensic investigation, derived from the literature review. After identifying the concepts a description of each one of them and their relationships were presented. Finally, once all the information had been put together the conceptual model was produced. A case study was introduced to demonstrate how the different concepts and their categories apply to a fictional cloud forensic investigation.

References

1. Ruan, K., Carthy, J., Kechadi, T., Crosbie, M.: Cloud forensics. In: Peterson, G., Shenoi, S. (eds.) International Conference on Digital Forensics. LNCS, vol. 361, pp. 35–46. Springer, Heidelberg (2011)
2. NIST Cloud Computing Forensic Science Working Group, Information Technology Laboratory, NIST Cloud Computing Forensic Science Challenges (Draft NISTIR 8006). NIST Publication (2014)
3. Ben, M., Choo, K.K.R.: An integrated conceptual digital forensic framework for cloud computing. Digit. Invest. 9(2), 71–80 (2012)
4. Adams, R.: The emergence of cloud storage and the need for a new digital forensic process model. In: Ruan, K. (ed.) Cybercrime and Cloud Forensics: Applications for Investigation Processes, pp. 79–104 (2013)
5. Simou, S., Kalloniatis, C., Kavakli, E., Gritzalis, S.: Cloud forensics: identifying the major issues and challenges. In: Jarke, M., Mylopoulos, J., Quix, C., Rolland, C., Manolopoulos, Y., Mouratidis, H., Horkoff, J. (eds.) CAiSE 2014. LNCS, vol. 8484, pp. 271–284. Springer, Heidelberg (2014)
6. Simou, S., Kalloniatis, C., Kavakli, E., Gritzalis, S.: Cloud forensics solutions: a review. In: Iliadis, L., Papazoglou, M., Pohl, K. (eds.) CAiSE 2014 Workshops. LNBIP, vol. 178, pp. 299–309. Springer, Heidelberg (2014)
7. Pooe, A., Labuschagne, L.: A conceptual model for digital forensic readiness. In: Information Security for South Africa (ISSA). IEEE (2012)
8. Al-Fedaghi, S., Al-Babtain, B.: Modeling the forensics process. Int. J. Secur. Appl. 6(4), 97 (2012)
9. Ruan, K., Carthy, J.: Cloud computing reference architecture and its forensic implications: a preliminary analysis. In: Rogers, M., Seigfried-Spellar, K.C. (eds.) ICDF2C 2012. LNICST, vol. 114, pp. 1–21. Springer, Heidelberg (2013)
10. von Solms, S., Louwrens, C., Reekie, C., Grobler, T.: A control framework for digital forensics. In: Olivier, M.S., Shenoi, S. (eds.) IFIP international Conference on Digital Forensics, National Center for Forensic Science. IFIP, vol. 222, pp. 343–355. Springer, New York (2006)
11. Selamat, S.R., Yusof, R., Sahib, S.: Mapping process of digital forensic investigation framework. Int. J. Comput. Sci. Netw. Secur. 8(10), 163–169 (2008)
12. http://en.wikipedia.org/wiki/Evidence. Accessed December 2014)
13. Frederick Cohen, B.: Fundamentals of digital forensic evidence. In: Stavroulakis, P., Stamp, M. (eds.) Hand book of Information and Communication Security, pp. 789–808. Springer, Heidelberg (2010)
14. Brian, C., Spafford, Eugene H.: Getting physical with the digital investigation process. Int. J. Digit. Evid. 2(2), 1–23 (2003)
15. Ciardhuáin, S.Ó.: An extended model of cybercrime investigations. Int. J. Digit. Evid. 3(1), 1–22 (2004)
16. Beebe, N.L., Clark, J.G.: A hierarchical, objectives-based framework for the digital investigations process. Digit. Invest. 2(2), 147–167 (2005)
17. Sibiya, G., Venter, H.S., Fogwill, T.: Digital forensic framework for a cloud environment. In: Proceedings of IST-Africa 2012 Conference, pp. 1–8 (2012)

18. Aydin, M., Jacob, J.: A comparison of major issues for the development of forensics in cloud computing. In: 2013 International Conference on Information Science and Technology (ICIST). IEEE (2013)
19. Liu, F., et al.: NIST cloud computing reference architecture. NIST Special Publication 500: 292 (2011)
20. Zawoad, S., Hasan, R.: Cloud Forensics: A Meta-Study of Challenges, Approaches, and Open Problems. arXiv preprint arXiv:1302.6312 (2013)
21. Nurmi, D., et al.: The eucalyptus open-source cloud-computing system. In: 9th IEEE/ACM International Symposium on Cluster Computing and the Grid, CCGRID 2009. IEEE (2009)
22. Haeberlen, A.: A case for the accountable cloud. ACM SIGOPS Oper. Syst. Rev. **44**(2), 52–57 (2010)
23. Thorpe, S., et al.: Towards a forensic-based service oriented architecture framework for auditing of cloud logs. In: 203 IEEE Ninth World Congress on Services (SERVICES). IEEE (2013)
24. Wilkinson, S., Haagman, D.: Good practice guide for computer-based electronic evidence. Association of Chief Police Officers (2010)
25. Grispos, G., Storer, T., Glisson, W.B.: Calm before the storm: the challenges of cloud. In: Emerging Digital Forensics Applications for Crime Detection, Prevention, and Security, p. 211 (2013)
26. Kruse, I.I., Warren, G., Heiser, J.G.: Computer Forensics: Incident Response Essentials. Pearson Education, Boston (2001)
27. McKemmish, R.: What is Forensic Computing?. Australian Institute of Criminology, Canberra (1999)
28. Orton, I., Alva, A., Endicott-Popovsky, B.: Legal process and requirements for cloud forensic investigations. In: Ruan, K. (ed.) Cybercrime and Cloud Forensics. IGI Global, Hershey (2012)

Knowledge-Based Model to Represent Security Information and Reason About Multi-stage Attacks

Faeiz M. Alserhani[(⊠)]

Department of Computer Engineering and Networks, College of Computer
and Information Sciences, Sakaka Aljouf, Saudi Arabia
fmserhani@ju.edu.sa

Abstract. In an intrusion detection context, none of the main detection approaches (signature-based and anomaly-based) are fully satisfactory. False positives and false negatives are the major limitations of such systems. The generated alerts are elementary and in huge numbers. Hence, alert correlation techniques are used to provide a complementary analysis to link elementary alerts and provide a more global intrusion view. It has been widely recognised that real cyber attacks consist of phases that are temporally ordered and logically connected.

In this paper we present an improved knowledge-based causal alert correlation model. The correlation process is essentially modularized based on an extension of the properties and characteristics of the *"requires/provides"* model. The description of the knowledge base modeling is introduced consisting of attacks classes, vulnerabilities, and alerts generated by security tools. The proposed system is evaluated to detect simulated and real multi-stage attacks and it showes efficient capability to correlate the attacker behavior.

Keywords: Intrusion detection systems · Alert correlation · Multi-stage attack

1 Introduction

Malicious attacks by intruders and hackers exploit flaws and weaknesses in the deployed systems. This is done by several sophisticated techniques and cannot be prevented by traditional measures. Hackers are shifting their focus from looking for fame and advertised attacks to profit-oriented activities. The current trends in cyber attacks are hidden, slow-and-low, and coordinated. NIDS are considered to be important security tools to defend against such threats. The effectiveness of any NIDS depends on its ability to recognize different variations of cyber attacks. The current implementation of intrusion detection systems (commercial and open-source) is employing signature-based detection in addition to a few simple techniques for statistical analysis. The main task of signature-based systems is to inspect the network traffic and perform pattern matching to detect attacks and generate alerts. A huge number of alerts are generated every day stressing the administrator; this may oversight an actual threat. Quality of these alerts is debatable particularly if the majority is false positives. For this reason, high-level and real-time analysis techniques are needed. This can be achieved by discovering the logical connections between the isolated alerts. It has been practically identified that

© Springer International Publishing Switzerland 2015
A. Persson and J. Stirna (Eds.): CAiSE 2015 Workshops, LNBIP 215, pp. 482–494, 2015.
DOI: 10.1007/978-3-319-19243-7_44

most of attacker activities consist of multiple steps (attack scenario) and occur in a certain time (attack window). Identification of such strategy can lead to the recognition of attack intensions and also prediction of unknown attacks.

In this paper we have extended our previous work in [1, 2] to describe the details of the proposed model design. The underlying principle of the model based on *provides/ requires* model is defined precisely giving some clarification examples. The discussion has been supported by the evaluation using different metrics. The rest of this paper is organized as follows: Sect. 2 explains the concepts of the proposed model. In Sect. 3, we present a description of the knowledge-based modeling and its related components. Section 4 gives the experimental results and then we conclude in Sect. 5.

2 Model Design

The *requires/provides* model is a general attack model that has been proposed by [3] and is inspired from network management systems to deal with network faults. A cyber attack is described according to two components: (1) capabilities, and (2) concepts. The idea behind this model is that multi-stage intrusions consist of a sequence of steps performed by an attacker, and that the later steps are prepared by the early ones. The target system information collected from scanning or port mapping are advantages acquired and used in order to choose which exploit can be successful. Attacks are modelled in terms of abstract concepts and each concept requires certain capabilities (conditions) to occur and provides others to be used by another concept. Capabilities are defined as general descriptions of the conditions required or provided by each stage of the intrusion i.e. the system state that must be satisfied in order to launch an attack. For instance, a successful Trojan injection requires particular services to be running in the target system and the presence of certain vulnerabilities.

Formally, capabilities are a higher level of intrusion abstraction that specifies the system state after each attack attempt. The attacker uses the capabilities acquired through some of its early actions to generate certain new capabilities. The system state is incorporated in attack scenarios if instances of concepts have matched "*required*" and "*provided*" conditions.

The capability model proposed by [4] is also based on a *requires/provides* model for logical alert correlation, though the authors used different properties of capabilities. An attack model was presented to build blocks of capabilities in a multi-layer fashion and with more expressive definition. References [5, 6] have employed a *requires/ provides* model using the concept of predicates, which are similar to capabilities.

Both models mentioned above are reasoning models that aim to discover the causal relationships between elementary alerts. Attacker states are abstracted to describe the gained privileges and what level of access is obtained. Moreover, the system states are modelled into a higher level of abstraction to specify the impact of the attack. Relationships between these states are defined to generate rules that determine the dependency between alerts.

The *requires/provides* model has been selected because it fits our purpose to correlate alerts in the same intrusion. It has some advantages over other models:

i. Ability to uncover the causal relationships between alerts and it is not restricted to known attack scenarios.
ii. Ability to characterize complex scenarios or to generalize to unknown attacks.
iii. Attack is represented as a set of capabilities that provides support for the abstract attack concepts.
iv. Flexibility and extensibility as the abstract attack concepts are defined locally.
v. It does not require a priori knowledge of a particular scenario.
vi. Numerous attacks can be described implicitly and an unknown attack can be defined by generalisation.

Our approach is a variation of the *requires/provides* model, but differs in the following aspects:

- Different definitions for capabilities and concepts are employed to overcome the limitations expressed in other approaches. The work in [3] used a very detailed specification language called JIGSAW to describe attack scenarios. A complete satisfaction of "*required*" and "*provided*" conditions is necessary to correlate two alerts, which will fail in case of broken scenarios. However, the authors in [5] have adopted a partial satisfaction technique which is also implemented into our framework. The main concern with their approach is the high rate of false positives, and the possibility of a huge graph being created. We have managed to overcome this limitation by using certain techniques: hierarchical multi-layer capabilities, accumulated aggregation, alert verification and alert maintenance.
- A near real-time processing approach for correlation, aggregation and event generation. The security officer can monitor the attack progress which is displayed as an intrusion graph. An event is triggered once at the minimum of two alerts being correlated, and any additional related alert based on its attributes will join the same event.
- Online and offline graph reduction algorithms during the correlation process in addition to alert aggregation in order to provide a smaller manageable graph.
- We have modelled IDS signatures as abstracted attack concepts instead of defining new concepts locally. In *requires/provides* models, IDS signatures are considered complementary external concepts.
- Separation of the concepts and their capabilities from other dynamic information. Two different types of capabilities have been used: internal and external. The first type denotes abstract attack modeling consisting of IDS signatures and associated capabilities. The second type refers to dynamic details, including system configuration, services and vulnerabilities. This provides more flexibility to the model whilst at the same time allowing utilization of other knowledge resources.
- Capabilities' modeling has been made using a hierarchical methodology based on attack classes and inheritance between these classes.

Our approach is based on the assumption that the attack scenario consists of a sequence of related actions and that early stages can incorporate later ones. The link between these stages is determined using five factors:

   i. Temporal relationships (e.g. alert timestamps).
   ii. Spatial relationships (e.g. source IP addresses, destination IP addresses and port numbers).
  iii. Pre- and post-conditions of each attack.
  iv. Vulnerability assessment of the target system.
   v. Target system configuration.

Capabilities are formalized in terms of pre- and post-conditions by grouping conditions that share similar characteristics into a broad definition. Knowledge about elementary alerts is mapped to instantiate the attacker and the system states according to their temporal characteristics:

- *Pre-conditions:* are logical capabilities that characterize the system state to be satisfied in order to launch an attack. These capabilities are derived from the attack description. A hierarchical approach is adopted based on an attack classification to provide coarse-grained definitions of different alerts related to the same behaviour.
- *Post-conditions:* are logical capabilities that characterize the system state after the attack succeeds. In other words, specifications of the effects of intrusions on the system, such as the knowledge gained and the access level of the attacker. Moreover, attack classification incorporates the definitions of these capabilities in a hierarchical manner.

To formulize the capability sets as pre- and post-conditions of higher quality, certain requirements must be satisfied:

1- Capabilities must be expressive in order to achieve a true logical relationship.
2- Avoidance of ambiguity in defining capabilities.
3- Use of multi-layers of abstraction to achieve scalability.
4- Reduction of the number of elements in the capability sets without affecting attack coverage.
5- Inference rules should be separated from the capability set.
6- The set should also be constant and independent of variable information such as vulnerability and system-configuration knowledge.

Hence, capabilities are formulized based on two criteria:
(a) Level of abstraction

   i. Generic capabilities which illustrate a broad aspect of a certain attack, such as access, local access and remote access.
  ii. Capabilities which illustrate a lower level of attack abstraction, but not a specific one, such as server buffer overflow or client upload file.
  iii. Specific capabilities for each single alert in IDSs, such as TFTP Get.

(b) Properties of the system and the attacker state

   i. Access level of the attacker (remote, local, user or administrator).
  ii. Impact of the intrusion upon the victim machine, such as DOS and implementation of the system commands.
  iii. Knowledge gained by the attacker, such as disclosure of host or of service.

The elements in the two criteria above are mutually inclusive; for instance, *disclosure of host* is considered as a generic capability and at the same time is a system state description. In addition, attack classification, which will be presented in the next section, is also involved in defining capabilities.

Examples: generic capabilities are mainly a description of the intrusion's general objective, such as:

- Disclosure of host
- Disclosure of running service
- Disclosure of port number
- Access
- Read or write files

However, a *buffer overflow* attack is a general attack that can target the server, the Web server and the client, and the required and provided conditions are not the same for each category. The capability *client access attempt* is a specific capability for client attacks, because some attacks are client specific, such as ActiveX attacks. Snort [7] documentation contains a description for each signature, including the attack class type, the affected system, and the impact of the attack. This information is valuable in defining attack capabilities if other sources of intrusion analysis are considered.

3   Knowledge-Base Modeling

Two knowledge bases are used, one for attack concepts and the other for vulnerability details. In the attack knowledge base, IDS signatures (e.g. Snort) are modelled to the attack abstractions and their defined capabilities. The knowledge library specifies the relationship between low-level alerts and the attack abstraction. Thus, a knowledge base can be considered a broad template and each element can be instantiated to instances of specific conditions. A generalization mechanism has been used to specify a higher level of specification of attack concepts and capabilities.

The proposed model for the attack knowledge base consists of three sets:

(1) Capability C: This specifies a higher level of abstraction of the *"required"* and *"provided"* conditions of the intrusion model. Intrusion attempts are expressed in terms of a set of *"required"* or *"provided"* conditions, and vulnerability constraints of a given alert where:

- Required conditions R are a set of pre-conditions specified in the form of capabilities with variable arguments.
- Provided conditions P is a set of post-conditions specified in the form of capabilities with variable arguments.
- Vulnerability V is a description of the state of the target host or network with variable arguments.

(2) Attack concept AC specifies the constructor of a given attack and its related capabilities. *"required"* and *"provided"* conditions for each attack are coded in a language of capabilities.

(3) Arguments $[r_1, r_2, \ldots r_i] \rightarrow r$ are a set of associated attributes such as source IP addresses, destination IP addresses and port numbers.

Definition 1. Attack concept AC is an abstraction of elementary alerts generated by the IDS, defined by a set of arguments, required conditions and provided conditions.

Definition 2. *An* attack instance a_i is defined as a set of instances of attack concept AC by substituting the associated values in arguments tuple considering the time constraints (start-time and end-time).

Definition 3. Given an attack concept AC, the R(AC), P(AC) and V(AC) sets are the sets of all capabilities C. Given an attack instance a, the R(a), P(a) and V(a) sets are the capabilities by mapping the values to the corresponding arguments in AC considering the time constraints.

3.1   Attack Classification

Several attempts have been made to propose a different attack taxonomy or ontology; however, they are diverse and there is no common methodology for the categorization of security intrusions. The majority of the proposed classifications are entirely based on the analysis of published vulnerabilities. For instance, NIDS vendors such as Snort [7] use attack classes that describe the attacker's methods in exploiting these vulnerabilities. We have obtained our classification based on:

- Vulnerability analysis
- Generalized description of the target system (server, client, Web, etc.)

Elementary alerts generated by NIDS sensors are mapped to generalized descriptions of intrusion in a hierarchical representation. The classification is built in the form of a graph with nodes and edges. The nodes specify the attack class and the edges denote the inheritance relationship between attack classes. The classes are mutually exclusive and each alert belongs to only a single class horizontally, but to different classes vertically based on the inheritance relationship. This structural abstraction mechanism is to minimise redundancy and maximize diversity. Hence, even though some alerts are new and unknown, they can be predicted from the results of situation analyses. If an attack is in progress consisting of certain elementary alerts, these atomic alerts are mapped to a general attack description. For any suspicious or unknown actions not detected by the IDS, the probability of their being related to the detected attack is very high. The level of the abstraction progresses from general to specific in a top-down design of the classification hierarchy. For instance, the buffer overflow class can be classified under server, client or Web classes, as this type of attack can target different types of systems. However, some other classes are only categorized as specific system classes, such as DDoS client activity, which is a client-specific attack. Hence, each alert generated by the IDS will be categorized top-down in a hierarchical manner.

Figure 1 shows three examples of how sub-classes inherit attack features from upper classes and how alerts are classified based on these relationships. In Fig. 1(a), the lower class denotes the exact Snort signature *TFTP Get, id:1444*, while this signature is classified as *TFTP buffer overflow*. Similarly, in Fig. 1(b), any IDS signature of type of *ACTIVEX attack* can be classified under this class which is in turn classified as a *client buffer overflow*. Figure 1(c) shows that a *stored procedure attack* is described as a Web PHP injection attack. It should be noted that these are only abstract classes and do not denote instances of actual attacks.

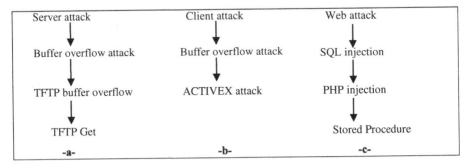

Fig. 1. Examples of attack class inheritance.

3.2   Knowledge-Base Representation

A capability set consists of all the derived elements of capabilities encoded to integer numbers. All alerts are represented in the form of three sections:

1- IDS signature ID to describe the attack by its elementary alert.
2- Pre-conditions set which consists of n capabilities where $n \geq 0$.
3- Post-conditions set which consists of n capabilities where $n \geq 0$.

The knowledge library of the alerts and their corresponding capabilities are defined into the form shown below:

$$\text{sid}:xxxx;\text{pre}:k_1(n);\text{pre}:k_2(n);\ldots\ldots\text{pre}:k_i(n);\ \text{pos}:l_1(n);\text{pos}:l_2(n);\ldots\ldots\text{pos}:l_j,$$

where $xxxx$ is the signature ID number, pre denotes pre-conditions, pos denotes post-conditions, k is the capability unique number, and n is a variable argument to specify the attack attributes as follow:

1: source IP address
2: source port
3: destination IP address
4: destination port

3.3   Alert Modeling

IDS alerts are the basic units that represent the occurrence of intrusion as a time series. Essential attack knowledge is derived from signature fields triggered by the IDS in case of any security violation. It should be noted that the alert generated by the IDS is not necessarily connected to a security attack, as sometimes a legitimate activity can cause some alarms. Moreover, the information in the signature does not contain any sign of whether the attack succeeded or not. However, the abstraction of these alerts to capabilities in respect to temporal and spatial details can give a true view of the security perspective.

Each received alert is mapped to its pre- and post-conditions. It is assumed that the alert is generated because some conditions have to be satisfied and that it will cause some impact on the target system. The relationship between different alerts is identified by matching these conditions. For example, the following alerts (Snort-generated signatures) are obtained from DARPA LLDDOS.1.0 [8] to clarify the correlation concept considering the following Snort signature:

RPC sadmind UDP PING

This signature is generated as result of attempts to test if the *sadmind* demon is running. A *sadmind RPC* service is used to perform administrative activities remotely. The impact of the signature includes disclosure of the running service and system access attempt:

RPC portmap sadmind request UDP

This signature is generated due to the use of a *portmap GETPORT* request to discover the port number of the RPC service, and consequently which port is used by the *sadmind* service.

RPC sadmind UDP NETMGT_PROC_SERVICE CLIENT_DOMAIN overflow attempt

This signature is generated as a result of an attempt to exploit a buffer overflow to obtain a root access.

RPC sadmind query with root credentials attempt UDP

This signature is generated due to the use of root credentials and is an indication of potential arbitrary command executions with root privilege.

RSERVICES rsh root

This signature is generated due to an attempt to login as a root user using *rsh*, and this is an indication of full control of the attacker.

From Table 1, it can be seen that the signatures have some pre- and post-conditions and if a match between these conditions is detected the two alerts are linked as a part of the attack scenario. If two signatures share at least one common capability for instance, *disclosure of running service*, hence they are correlated as a primary stage following by incorporating other factors from the rest of the model components.

3.4   Vulnerability Modeling

Several efforts have been made to correlate IDS signatures with vulnerability information. The aim is to reduce the false positives, which can be a major drawback of such systems. Moreover, these verification mechanisms are incorporated in the IDS to provide a higher quality of alerts, and hence more confidence. The origin of the problem of false positives is that IDSs have no information about the systems they

Table 1. Examples of pre- and post-conditions.

#	Signature	Pre-conditions	Post-conditions
1	RPC sadmind UDP PING	Disclosure of host	Disclosure of running service System access
2	RPC portmap sadmind request UDP	Disclosure of host	Disclosure of port number Disclosure of running service System access Remote Access
3	RPC sadmind UDP NETMGT_PROC_SERVICE CLIENT_DOMAIN overflow attempt	Disclosure of host Disclosure of port number Disclosure of running service	System access Remote access Admin access
4	RPC sadmind query with root credentials attempt UDP	Disclosure of host Disclosure of port number Disclosure of running service System access Remote access	Remote access Admin access

protect. Therefore they are not certain about the success of the attack, simply because the vulnerabilities of the target system are not available. Two trends have emerged in overcoming the false positives issue in IDS performance:

1- Tuning the IDS based on knowledge of the internal policy of the protected environment to operate with a lower number of signatures [9]. Knowledge of network configuration, running services and installed applications is used to disable all the unrelated signatures of the IDS. The advantage of this technique is that the IDS performance is improved significantly. However, some of the information on the activities of the attacker, which may be useful in tracking its behaviour, will be discarded. It should also be noted that real cyber attackers (persistent attackers) try to break into systems using different methods, and these attempts may be not in connection with a particular vulnerability. Moreover, some dangerous attacks in cyber crime do not require any system vulnerability, such as DDoS. In addition, this approach requires intensive and updated vulnerability assessment.

2- The other trend is not suppressing the IDS detection coverage, but instead aggregating, correlating and verifying the generated alerts in a systematic way [6, 10]. Summarized data of occurring events are displayed to the security manager according to their priorities and criticalness. If further details are required to support a specific situation, they can be retrieved by request. A repository of collected information is maintained to support the decision of the IDS management system. Vulnerability scanners are the main candidates to supply this type of data in a periodical manner.

In accordance with the nature of the developed correlation systems, which require full description of any activity in the protected environment, the second mechanism is adopted. The attacks are generalized to obtain a global view of the security situation. This generalization may increase the false positive rate; hence, a suppression technique is needed to reduce the false positive rate without losing any details. This suppression mechanism does not imply any reduction in the IDS coverage, but the consideration of only success attacks.

Snort signatures are supported by two useful fields:

- Vulnerability reference, referring to the major vulnerability standards such as CVE [11], bugtraq [12], and Nessus [13].
- Service to denote a list of the affected services, such as telnet, ftp and MSSQL.

A vulnerability knowledge base is maintained to store the vulnerability situation of each element of the protected network based on the collecting agent (e.g. Nessus). The scanner will also gather the network configuration details such as IP addresses of live hosts and running services, so manual configuration is not considered. In this respect, vulnerability information is considered as external capabilities.

The scope of vulnerability testing is only limited to investigating the presence of the vulnerability and the affected service. An extension can be carried out to consider the target host response; however, there are performance issues (e.g. communication overheads). Nessus is used to extract the following information, which can be used to support the vulnerability component:

- IP addresses of all hosts connected to the target network.
- Operating systems and their versions.
- Open ports and running services.
- Related vulnerability references (e.g. CVE).

When an alert is received from the IDS, its message contains the vulnerability reference and the affected system. Therefore, a logical formula is obtained by searching the vulnerability knowledge to find any matches, as follow:

- If the reference is found and the associated service is running, then the vulnerability is true with high priority.
- If the reference is found and the associated service is not running, then the vulnerability is true with low priority.
- If the reference is not found, then the vulnerability is unknown.

The complete algorithm of alert verification using vulnerability knowledge is shown in Fig. 2.

4 Experimental Results

DARPA 2000 datasets, including LLDDOS 1.0 and LLDDOS 2.0 [14], are often used to evaluate IDSs and alert correlation systems. They consist of two multi-stage attack scenarios to launch Distributed Denial of Service attacks (DDoS). The evaluation goal is to test the effectiveness of our approach to recognize attack scenarios, to correctly

Algorithm :Alert verification

Input: elementary alerts generated by IDS $A(IP,SV,VR)$

      Host vulnerability information generated by scanner $VN(IP,OS,SV,VR)$

Output: Vulnerable host $VH(IP,V,P)$

Methods:

     // IP: IP address, SV: service, VR: vulnerability, OS operating system

    for $i \leftarrow 0$ to $length[VN]$

      do

        if $A.IP = VN[i].IP$ **get** $VN(IP,OS,SV,VR)$

        in case of

             $A.VR = VN.VR$ **and** $A.SV = VN.SV$ **then** $VH.V \leftarrow true$, $VH.P \leftarrow high$

             $A.VR = VN.VR$ **and** $A.SV \neq VN.SV$ **then** $VH.V \leftarrow true$, $VH.P \leftarrow low$

             $A.VR \neq VN.VR$ **then** $VH.V \leftarrow false$, $VH.P \leftarrow unknown$

Fig. 2. Alert verification algorithm.

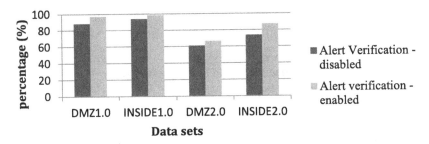

Fig. 3. Recall rate (%) of the DARPA dataset

correlate the alerts, and to minimize the false positives. This experiment is carried out mainly for functional testing to see how the system reconstructs attack stages. A reduction test is also studied in this respect; however, the background traffic in this dataset is limited. We have used these datasets for their available ground truth to assess our correlation approach and to compare our results with those of other researchers. These datasets do not contain the actual alerts from the IDS sensors, and hence we have generated them using a Snort sensor. The detected events evolve over time instead of by batch analysis.

Accuracy metrics are calculated to determine *recall, precision,* and *reduction rate.* Figures 3 to 5 illustrate the key results obtained from different scenarios. Our proposed system has achieved high levels of accuracy among the datasets in LLDDOS1.0, and acceptable levels in LLDDOS2.0. The only low accuracy rate recorded is from the analysis of the DMZ2.0 dataset, and of which we are aware because the actual attack was performed inside the network. The vulnerability model to verify the importance of alerts is also showing a considerable improvement. This is apparent from the number of

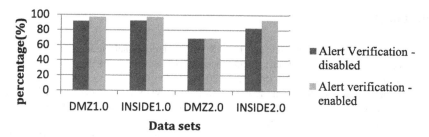

Fig. 4. Precision rate (%) of the DARPA dataset

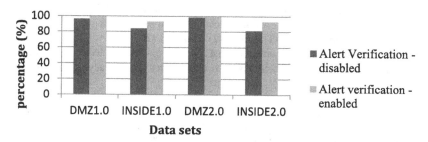

Fig. 5. Alert reduction rate (%) of DARPA dataset

detected events in each dataset. For instance, in DMZ1.0, the number of events has been reduced from 25 events to only 3 related events. The rates are higher if alert verification is used and satisfactory for other tests. In addition, the volume of alert information has been significantly reduced, achieving more than a 90 % reduction rate in most test cases.

5 Conclusion

We have presented the core concept of our knowledge-based reasoning model for alert correlation to address the problem of detection of coordinated attacks. A combined analysis of IDS's alerts and description of attack classes are used to derive the pre- and post- conditions of each received alert. A scheme to represent our knowledge base has been described using a hierarchal and a multilayer classification. Vulnerability modeling is used to support alert verification in order to reduce the generated attack graph.

The evaluation process is based on different metrics to identify the functionality, the reduction and the accuracy rates. An experimental platform has been developed to perform different tests. The obtained results have showed that the proposed system is capable to detect all attack instances with lesser false positive rates. We have confidence that our system has achieved an improvement in relation to identification of attack plans and reduction in graph complexity. False positives have been reduced comparing with other approaches using vulnerability knowledge base. In the next research stage, we will incorporate a statistical model to detect hidden relationships between different attack scenarios.

References

1. Alserhani, F., Akhlaq, M., et al.: MARS: multi-stage attack recognition system. In: Proceedings of the International Conference on Advanced Information Networking and Applications (AINA), pp. 753-759, Perth (2010)
2. Alserhnai, F., Akhlaq, M., et al.: Event-based correlation systems to detect SQLI activities. In: Proceedings Of the International Conference on Advanced Information Networking and Applications (AINA), Bioplis, Singapore (2011)
3. Templeton, S.J., Levitt, K.: A requires/provides model for computer attacks. In: Proceedings of the 2000 workshop on New security paradigms ACM (2000)
4. Zhou, J., Heckman, M., Reynolds, B., Carlson, A., Bishop, M.: Modeling network intrusion detection alerts for correlation. ACM Trans. Inf. Syst. Secur. (TISSEC) **10**(1), 1–31 (2007)
5. Ning, P., Cui, Y., Reeves, D.S., Xu, D.: Techniques and tools for analyzing intrusion alerts. ACM Trans. Inf. Syst. Secur. (TISSEC) **7**(2), 274–318 (2004)
6. Cuppens, F., Miege, A.: Alert correlation in a cooperative intrusion detection framework. In: Proceedings of the 2002 IEEE Symposium on Security and Privacy, 2002. pp. 202-215 (2002)
7. Snort; http://www.snort.org/
8. Haines, J.W., Lippmann, R.P., Fried, D.J., Tran, E., Boswell, S., Zissman, M.A.: DARPA intrusion detection system evaluation: Design and procedures, Technical report, Lincoln Laboratory, Massachusetts Institute of Technology (2000)
9. Valeur, F., Mutz, D., Vigna, G.: A learning-based approach to the detection of SQL attacks. In: Julisch, K., Kruegel, C. (eds.) DIMVA 2005. LNCS, vol. 3548, pp. 123–140. Springer, Heidelberg (2005)
10. Qin, X.: A probabilistic-based framework for infosec alert correlation," Ph.D., Georgia Institute of Technology (2005)
11. Common Vulnerabilities and Exposures (CVE). http://cve.mitre.org/cgi-bin/cvename.cgi?name=CVE-2010-0188
12. Security Focus - BugTraq. http://www.securityfocus.com
13. Nessus: Security Scanner. http://www.nessus.org
14. MIT Lincoln Laboratory; http://www.ll.mit.edu/

Towards the Integration of Security Transparency in the Modelling and Design of Cloud Based Systems

Moussa Ouedraogo[1(✉)] and Shareeful Islam[2]

[1] Luxembourg Institute of Science and Technology,
5 Avenue des hauts Fourneaux, L4362 Esch/Alzette, Luxembourg
Moussa.ouedraogo@list.lu
[2] The School of Architecture, Computing and Engineering,
University of East London, London, UK
shareeful@uel.ac.uk

Abstract. The lacks of security transparency and mutual auditability have recently been acknowledged by the industry and research community as one of the most salient security concerns inherent to the cloud model. This paper discusses the topic of security transparency and mutual auditability considering the cloud based services. In particular, the existing state of the art practice and initiatives for promoting more trust within the realm of cloud services are analysed throughout this paper. Finally, we highlight a number of avenues that can be further researched by the secure information system community to ensure the development of cloud systems that seamlessly blend concepts that help capture, not only the resource need of the future cloud service users, but also their need for further visibility on a security matter which responsibility somehow lies in the hand of a third party.

Keywords: Security transparency · Cloud services · Secure system · Mutual trust

1 Introduction

Commonly, Security transparency relates to the level of visibility into security policy and operations offered by the Cloud Service Provider (CSP) to the Cloud Service Consumer (CSC) [25]. Recent research has highlighted the need of security transparency and mutual auditability as salient factors for sustaining the current momentum of cloud services [1–4]. Such a narrative stems mainly from the very fact that, the data or processes used for storing or treating the CSC's information are geo-delocalized from the CSC's premises. A consequence of this, include the de facto devolution of security related responsibilities to the CSP whose capability to effectively safeguard data and processes may be feeble or simply mistrusted by the CSC. In the context of outsourced services such as the cloud, the due diligence of the CSP in promptly informing their clients in the event of a security compromise on their infrastructure can be decisive for the CSC to minimize its exposure to risk, by for instance stopping using it. However from a CSP perspective, reporting on security woes, is not always well perceived as their reputation can be tarnished. As a result, the fear of security shortcomings and the

© Springer International Publishing Switzerland 2015
A. Persson and J. Stirna (Eds.): CAiSE 2015 Workshops, LNBIP 215, pp. 495–506, 2015.
DOI: 10.1007/978-3-319-19243-7_45

lack of visibility on a salient security matter they no longer have full sights on, have been an hindrance for the broader adoption of cloud based services, especially by those companies involved with security critical data such as the banking a financial sector.

While researchers on service oriented architecture and network security along with certification bodies have been very active proposing a wide range of initiatives in response to the problem (including virtual machine monitoring [5–9]; service level agreement specification and monitoring [11–21]; certification and audits [1, 15, 17]), similar efforts remain to be seen from the software engineering community, the secure system engineering community in particular. This is a contrast to the leading role played by the community in the early 2000 on the salient issue of integrating security considerations earlier in the development stage of Software to ensure a smooth and efficient integration in the future software system [26–29]. The creation of cloud services, private and public alike, are mainly undertaken using cloud development and management software of the like of Openstack (https://www.openstack.org/) and Opennebula (http://opennebula.org/). Unfortunately, none of those tools support the integration of security transparency concepts. As such, most efforts that have been devised as a response to the issue have been ad hoc and primarily serve the purpose of the CSP. For instance, the terms of SLA clauses are often those the CSP is certain it can abide by and fail to comprehensively encompass all the specific expectations in terms of security transparency of the CSC. Demonstrating that a cloud service meets some security transparency requirements can play in the hand of both CSC and CSP, as it may serve as a way for the latter to demark itself from competitors while providing to the latter a baseline for an informed selection of a CSP for the handling of security critical data and processes. In that vein of idea, this paper argues that the cloud model could widen its appeal if concepts related to security transparency were integrated in the conceptualisation and development of cloud services. This would have the merit to help capture on the one hand, CSC's requirements in terms of security transparency while helping to provide a design solution as the means in which the CSP would be practically meeting such requirements. In another word, the engineering of cloud services that integrates security transparency have to be interactive, allowing each of prospective CSC to first specify its security transparency needs and for the CSP to then model the available capabilities to meet the CSC's expectations before it finally make a decision on whether to adopt the service. Alternatively, the method and resulting platform could be a tool in the hand of cloud broker who will be tasked with selecting the CSPs with the most adequate capability upon the specification of the requirements by the CSC.

This paper is organized as follows: Sect. 2 review existing efforts on security transparency and highlights their shortcomings as ad hoc rather than built-in initiatives. In Sect. 3 we provide some initial thoughts on a roadmap for fully integrating security transparency consideration in the engineering for cloud base services. Sect. 4 concludes the paper.

2 Enabling Security Transparency in the Cloud

There are several works in the literature that focus on enhancing the trust relationship in the cloud environment. These works have come mainly in the form of virtual machines monitoring; certification, audits and monitoring of Service Level Agreement (SLA).

We have performed a systematic literature review with these keywords along with audit and trusted cloud platform to identify the relevant literature, research project and industry practice. We use search engines from the following five sites: Google Scholar, Elsevier, IEEE Xplore, ACM Digital Library, EU projects, and Science Direct to extract the literature. The primary literatures were selected based on the keywords and by reviewing abstract and title. The initial selected literature further refined based two inclusion criteria, i.e., works that focus on transparency issues in cloud and studies that consider techniques, processes and tools for managing transparency and trusted cloud environment. Our findings are given below.

2.1 The Usage of Trusted Cloud Computing Platforms and Monitoring of Virtual Machines

A myriad of initiatives focusing on the usage of a trusted Cloud Computing Platform (TCCP) and the monitoring of Virtual Machines, have emerged as potential solutions for addressing the issue of security transparency in the cloud.

Santos et al. [5] proposed an architecture for a trusted platform called Trusted Cloud Computing Platform (TCCP) that purports to ensure the confidentiality and integrity of the data and computation undertaken by the provider. Using a program associated to TCCP, a customer may be able to detect whether the data or computation has been tampered with or been accessed even by the provider. Subsequently, the customer may decide on whether to terminate a Virtual Machine (VM) should they notice any abnormality. In particular, the TCCP needs to guarantee that the VM is launched on a trusted node and that the system administrator is unable to inspect or tamper with the initial VM state as it traverses the path between the user and the node hosting it. The TCCP approach builds upon a traditional trusted platform, such as TERRA [6], to ensure the integrity and confidentiality in the context of multiple hosts. Humberg et al. [30] propose a two –step based ontology driven approach to identify relevant regulation to support the compliance requirements for a trusted cloud based system. The regulator ontology is based on the rule, rule elements; situation and constraint, where constraint checked a specific situation using rule sets. The proposed process consists of three steps for identifying relevant rules, mapping business process with rules and finally verifies the rules. Finally a tool is presented to demonstrate the execution state of the process. Wenzel et al. [31] consider security and compliance analysis of outsourcing services in the cloud computing context and focuses on risk analysis and compliance issues of business processes that are planned to be outsourced.

Another initiative that uses the concept of trusted platform is the Private Virtual Infrastructure (PVI) proposed by Krautheim [7]. Krauthiem has suggested a means to allow monitoring in the cloud by combining the trusted platform module (TPM) and a Locator Bot that pre-measures the cloud for security properties, securely provisions the data-centre in the cloud, and provides situational awareness through continuous monitoring of the cloud security. In this approach, security appears as a shared responsibility between the provider and the consumer. Thus, the SLA between the client and the provider is critical to defining the roles and responsibilities of all parties involved in using and providing the cloud service.

The authors in [8] argued that the dependability of cloud services may be attained through the quantification of security for intensive compute workload clouds to facilitate provision of assurance for quality of service. They subsequently defined seven security requirements which include: Workload state integrity, Guest OS Integrity, zombie protection, Denial of Service attacks, malicious resource exhaustion, platform attacks and backdoor protection. Unfortunately the paper does not provide any evidence of effort towards quantification of security as it claimed. Moreover it remains unclear as to how information relating those security requirements may be conveyed to the provider and consumer alike.

De Chaves et al. proposed an initiative to private cloud management and monitoring called PCMONS [9]. The authors argued that despite the peculiarity of cloud services compared to traditional legacy systems, existing tools and methods for managing networks and distributed systems can be reused in cloud computing management. PCMONS is based on a centralised architecture with the following features [9]: (a) a Node Information Gatherer, which is responsible for gathering local information on a cloud node; (b) Cluster Data Integrator, an agent that gathers and prepares the data for the next layer (the monitoring data integrator); (c) a Monitoring Data Integrator that gathers and stores cloud data in the database for historical purposes, and provides such data to the Configuration Generator; (d) a Virtual Machine (VM) Monitor that sends useful data from the VM to the monitoring system; (e) a Configuration Generator for retrieving information from the database; (f) a monitoring Tool Server that receives monitoring data from different resources (e.g., the VM Monitor); and finally (g) a database where the data needed by the Configuration Generator and the Monitoring Data Integrator are stored. Given PCMONS was developed to respond to the needs of management in private cloud, the need of establishing mutual trust between the provider and the consumer does not arise.

Shao et al. have introduced a runtime monitoring approach for the Cloud, concentrating on QoS (Quality of Service) aspects [10]. Their model, RMCM (Runtime Model for Cloud Monitoring) uses multiple monitoring techniques to gather data from the cloud. However, their approach seems generic and security monitoring is not discussed in particular.

Overall, it can be said that the research community has moved from debating whether the cloud is a mere hype to devising some tangible initiatives for resolving one of its most salient issue that is security. Unfortunately the current efforts on trusted cloud computing platforms and monitoring of Virtual Machines have mainly been driven by the need to foster a better management of security for the CSP provider rather than addressing the complexities of multi-party trust considerations (particularly those related to security), and the ensuing need for mutual auditability. In fact monitoring of VMs is meant to be conducted by and for the CSP.

2.2 Security Transparency Through SLA Management

For Rak et al., the mutual trust between a provider and a customer should be considered only in context of an SLA management [11]. Using a cloud-oriented API derived from the mOSAIC project (http://www.mosaic-project.eu/), the authors built up an

SLA-oriented cloud application that enables the management of security features related to user authentication and authorization of an IaaS Cloud Provider. This gives the opportunity to the customer to select from amongst a number of security requirements templates, the one that may be appropriate for the nature of his/her application before the provider can set up the configuration of the concerned node accordingly. As noted by the authors, the consideration of SLA in the management of the cloud security provides the consumer with formal documentation about what he/she will effectively obtain from the service. Meanwhile, from the provider point of view, SLAs are a way to have a clear and formal definition of the requirements that the application must respect. However, the initiative by Rak et al. [11], does not go far enough to incorporate means for monitoring and reporting on the fulfilment of such SLA to the consumer. An extension of the work of Rak et al. in the context of the EU FP7 project Specs (http://specs-project.eu/) considered the provision of a platform for providing a security services based on SLA management.

The SLA@SOI project [12] also followed in the path of SLA management in service oriented architectures, which includes cloud technology. The monitoring of SLAs expressed in the SLA specification language of SLA@SOI requires the translation of these SLAs into operational monitoring specifications (i.e., specifications that can be checked by a low level monitor plugged into the SLA@SOI framework). The SLA monitoring in SLA@SOI relies on EVEREST+ [14], which is a general-purpose engine for monitoring the behavioural and quality properties of distributed systems based on events captured from them during the operation of these systems at runtime. The properties that can be monitored by EVEREST are expressed in a language based on Event Calculus [15], called EC-Assertion. Similarly, Chazalet discusses SLA (Service Level Agreements) compliance checking in cloud environments and uses JMX (Java Management Extensions) technology in the prototype implementation [16]. Their checking approach allows separating concerns related to the probes, information collection and monitoring and contract compliance checking.

The negotiation of SLA in the context of federated cloud has also been the focus of research initiatives. Such initiatives range from simulation frameworks purporting to help in selecting the optimal combination of cloud services which better meet SLA requirements [22] to the optimal negation of SLA using multi-objective genetic algorithms [23].

In a similar way, some recent work on accountability in the cloud has started to emerge through projects such as A4CLOUD (http://www.a4cloud.eu), whereby researchers are thriving to devise models that can help put in place the set of mechanisms that would ensure cloud providers are hold accountable should there be a breach of SLA or a security incident that can be traced back to a lax in their security. In the context of A4Cloud the concept of transparency in the broader sense is dealt with as an attribute of Accountability [17]. Readers interesting in further comprehending the scope and diversity of existing efforts on SLA based monitoring of cloud security can refer to the taxonomy of Petcu [21].

The major problem with the adoption of SLA management as a means to enhance security transparency is primarily on its practicality. Indeed the academic notion of SLA appears to be far more extensive than it is in reality. Form our own experience in approaching CSPs on the issue, most often, the content of such documents are restricted to the sole aspects of: allocated bandwidth, storage capacity, etc., while the only security aspects included often relate to service availability. Clearly, the items included in those specifications are those the companies were confident they could deliver on. Their argument on the most pressing and challenging issues such as security was that stringent and redundant mechanisms were in place for its guarantee, as witness by some of their security certification.

2.3 Security Certification and Audits

In their effort to reduce the fears of the CSCs and distinguish themselves from competitors by promoting their service as one that is secure, CSPs have often turned to certifications as a way of swaying CSCs. Reasons for this include the lack of metrics and sometimes resources from the CSC to adequately assess the cloud services. As such Certification from a third party organization has been hailed by proponents as the ultimate means of promoting trust and transparency in the cloud ecosystem, which is a key to its wider acceptance [1]. For instance, certification to ISO/IEC 27001 is valued in the industry, as it provides a holistic framework for appreciating how well a company manages its information security. The standard emphasizes the need for organisations to have clear means of understanding their security needs. Additionally it is meant to assist them in implementing controls to address risks facing their business and monitoring, reviewing and improving the performance and effectiveness of the Information Security Management Systems (ISMS). Importantly, the authors in [1] have also highlighted the need for certification scheme to be affordable to avoid smaller company having the carry those expenses in the price of their service delivery and thus become ultimately uncompetitive against their bigger rivals.

Following the argument that providers should rely more on a certification from a governing or standardized institution that stipulates the provider has established adequate internal security controls that are operating efficiently, the Cloud Security Alliance has made a number of effort towards the provision of clear guidelines towards controlling security risks in the cloud [15]. The CSA guidance is made up of 99 control specifications covering such area as: Compliance, Governance, Facility, human resource and Information security, Legal matters, Operations, Risk and Release management, Resiliency and the security architecture. The individual controls identified within the guideline emanate from well-established standards and guidelines pertinent in both the context of traditional Information Systems and the cloud, covering a wide range of domains including the IT Governance (COBIT, the banking and financial domain (PCI-DSS and BITS), Government (NIST SP800-53 and FedRAMP), Health care (HIPAA) and cross-domain standard for the management of information security systems (ISO/IEC27001). Recently, the CSA has put forwards the idea of a three-levelled certification scheme that would rely on the compliance to its set of security guidance and control objectives. According to the CSA each level will provide an incremental level of trust to CSP operations and a higher level of assurance to the CSC. The first of such levels (which it must be stressed is a mere self-assessment exercise) requires each CSP to submit a report on the CSA to assert its level of compliance to the advocated best practices. The second level, referred to as CSA STAR CERTIFICATION, is meant to provide a third-party independent assessment conducted by an approved certification body under the supervision of the CSA and BSI. The third level, will extend the STAR CERTIFICATION in view of providing a continuous monitoring based certification.

Similarly, the Certified Cloud Service of TÜV Rheinland, runs a certification scheme which is based on CSPs compliances on the most essential information security standards such as ISO 27001 basic protection standards issued by the German Federal Office for Information Technology and ITIL [17].

It is clear that standardization and certification bodies are rushing to make a foot print in the certification market related to cloud based services. Although the intention lies in helping to make an informed judgment about the quality of a given CSP, companies with interest in adopting the cloud could be swamped and confused by the sheer number of standards and their actual scope. In anticipation to this, a recent research conducted by the University of Cologne in Germany has suggested a taxonomy of cloud certification whereby commonly agreed structural characteristics of cloud service certifications could be adopted as a baseline for classifying certification schemes depending on their core purpose [20].

The adoption of certification as a way of making a statement about the reliance of the security of one's service has reinforced the importance of audits for the cloud model. Audits are meant to provide a third party independent assessment of the posture of the security. Until autumn 2011, the SAS70 was a standard audit approach for service companies to use with their customers instead of customers individually auditing the services companies [18]. The actual purpose of the standard was primarily aimed to assess the sufficiency and the effectiveness of the security controls of the CSP. The standard was superseded by SSAE16 (www.ssae16.com), which stands for Statement on Standards for Attestation Engagements No. 16. The rationale for such a change was to align the reporting standard of US based companies to that of the international standard ISAE3402 (http://isae3402.com/). One of the core difference between the two standards rests on the fact that the evaluated company is bound to provide a written statement about the accuracy of the description of their system and the corresponding time frame during which such an assessment has been made.

What becomes apparent after analyzing the different audits standard available is that they rely in a large part on the words and assessment of the CSP. Such information cannot be guaranteed to be immune from bias. For instance, the CloudAudit initiative from the CSA (http://cloudaudit.org/CloudAudit/Home.html) is seeking to provide a common API for CSPs to specify their assertion, assessment and assurance. Such information is meant to be made readily available to the CSCs and also allow the latter to make comparisons between potential providers based on their security. Given the CSP has often a greater control over the security in the cloud, with very little visibility (if any) for the CSC, the frequency and independence of such audits is paramount along with the appropriate reporting of the findings to the CSC. Thus automated and continuous audits will be more appropriate, especially when considering the evolving nature of the cloud infrastructure.

3   Requirements for Security Transparency Driven Cloud Service Engineering

As can be taken from the analysis above, addressing security transparency in the cloud as an afterthought raises a number of issues: first, the full extent of the CSC's requirements in terms of security transparency cannot be captured and accounted for. Secondly, most of the clauses that underpin the usage of existing initiatives are primarily in the terms of the CSP. Thirdly, they do not allow the CSC to formally appreciate if and how the CSP will meet their transparency need and help them make a consequent informed decision prior to adopting the service.

From the secure software engineering domain, a methodology such as Secure Tropos [24] appears to harbor some of the flavor of a methodology that could lend itself for the engineering of security transparency aware cloud systems. However this would first require some notable amendments. Such enhancement would have to account for the fact that any effort to devise methodologies and methods for the cloud that integrates security transparency concerns will have to consider at least two aspects: (i) bear some level of interactivity which will allow the security transparency requirement of the CSC to be captured and the strategy of the CSP to meet such requirements to be designed; (ii) be resource-oriented like the cloud paradigm. The rationale for putting emphasis on the resource rather than the goals of the consumer is primarily because consumers when considering the cloud, have a pretty good idea of what their needs are and their intention is known. What may elude them at this point are the specificities in terms of security (pros and cons) of the resource they would have to rent. After all the cloud is known to be an abstraction of a pool of computing resources made available upon request to the consumer. Consequently, it is therefore essential that the resource to be used is center-staged. Besides the potential adaptation of an existing methodology such as Secure Tropos, two main aspects have to be considered when considering a security transparency aware cloud engineering: the need of capabilities that allow the CSC to profile the resources she seeks to rent or Interactive Resource Profile modelling and for the CSPs to demonstrate the existing strategy in their midst to meet the expectation of the CSC or Strategic Assurance Modelling.

3.1   Interactive Resource Profile Modelling

By seeking to outsource to a third party, the future cloud user aspires to a number of requirements and non-functional requirements for its service. For each resource of interest to the consumer, security requirements should be specified. At this stage of the modelling, it must also be possible for the future CSC to select the set of security requirements that are the most critical to its activity and as such, would require some attention (through monitoring for instance) during the usage of the resource. Such security requirements are referred to as security transparency relevant or STA requirements. Unlike the other standard security requirements associated to a cloud resource, tagging a security requirement as STA would imply more analysis at a later stage of the methodology is needed and a clear strategy put in the place by the provider to: ensure their continuous fulfilment and inform the CSC should they be infringed. Once the whole security requirements for a resource are known, the profile of the prospective service as envisage by the CSC should be moved (made available to) the potential CSPs who will then associated to each security requirements, the set of security controls available in view of helping in their fulfilment. The exercise referred to as Coupling would determine the extent to which the listed security requirements can be met by the providers 'controls. A final validation from the consumer side for accepting or rejecting the capability of the provider's security resources to satisfactorily meet the underlining security requirements is possible at this stage. The whole process of resorting to a given provider's service may be brought to a halt in case of remaining STA security requirements without any association with the provider's security mechanisms or, when the proposed controls are considered not too satisfactory by the consumer.

3.2   Strategic Assurance Modelling

While the interactive resource profile modelling phase primarily purports to support the CSC in making an informed decision on the adequacy of a CSP to meet her security transparency needs, the strategic assurance modelling mainly aims at providing a framework for the CSP to effectively design her strategy around the efficient used of security resources in implementing security transparency needs of the CSC. Given that the need for security transparency will mainly translate into monitoring of and reporting on the status of the security resources and any potential security incident to the CSC, this step will mainly involve the elaboration of software agents tasked with continuously probing the security controls and other transparency relevant components. In order to achieve that, a decomposition of the security controls (provided by the provider) into finer key properties that underpin their functionalities will take place. This will have the benefit to enable the providers' security engineer to assign software components (agents for instance) responsible for the monitoring the correctness of such properties which is essential for the security resources to be effective. The actual decision on whether to assign individual agent for each property or for the monitoring of a group of properties across different security mechanisms is left to the discretion of the security engineer. In case of dependency between two security controls, a correlator agent may be created between the respective aggregator agents of those security controls. The role of the correlator agent will mainly consist in tuning in the status of the dependee security resource according to the status of the depender and the degree of the correlation parameter between the two. In another word, if a property of the security resource SR1 is known to be non-compliant with respect to the CSC security transparency need and, given that such property also play a role in the functionality of a secure resource SR2, the correlator will be the component downgrading the status level of SR2 based on the information on the non-complaint property. Unlike the correlator, an aggregator agent, is local for a given secure resource and is untrusted with the task to combine information gathered by all the probing agents associated to a secure resource.

4   Conclusion

This paper has provided an analysis of the set of initiatives seeking to address the salient issue of security transparency in the cloud. Our analysis of the proposed initiatives reveals that addressing security transparency as an afterthought bears three main shortcomings: (i) they fail to fully capture the security transparency need of the CSC; (ii) most of the clauses that underpin the usage of existing initiatives are primarily in the terms of the CSP; (iii) they do not allow the CSC to formally appreciate if and how the CSP will meet their transparency need and help the make a consequent informed decision prior to adopting the service. Consequently, the conclusion of our work was that both CSP and prospective SCC could benefit from the integration of security transparency concerns in the development cycle of cloud based services. We thus provide a number of desiderata and an initial direction for a security transparency driven cloud engineering. We believe such a roadmap can be a starting point for the secure system engineering community, which has so far overlooked the issue, to start investing some interest in the domain.

Acknowledgement. This work has been conducted in the context of the SAINTS project, financed by the national fund of research of the Grand Duchy of Luxembourg (FNR) under grant number C12/IS/3988336.

References

1. Sunyaev, A., Schneider, S.: Cloud services certification. Commun. ACM **56**(2), 33–36 (2013). ACM Digital Library
2. Chen, Y., Paxson, V., Katz R.H.: What's New about Cloud Computing Security? Report EECS Department, University of California, Berkeley (2010). http://www.eecs.berkeley.edu/Pubs/TechRpts/2010/EECS-2010–5.html. Accessed 13 September 2012
3. Nuñez, D., Fernandez-Gago, C., Pearson, S., Felici, M.: A metamodel for measuring accountability attributes in the cloud. In: Proceedings of the 2013 IEEE International Conference on Cloud Computing Technology and Science (CloudCom 2013). IEEE (2013)
4. Ouedraogo, M.: Mouratidis, M: Selecting a cloud service provider in the age of cybercrime. Comput. Secur. **38**, 3–13 (2013)
5. Santos, N., Gummadi, K.P., Rodrigues, R.: Towards trusted cloud computing. In: Proceedings of the 2009 conference on Hot topics in cloud computing (HotCloud). USENIX, San Diego (2009)
6. Garfinkel, T., Pfaff, B., Chow, J., Rosenblum, M., Boneh, D.: Terra: a virtual machine-based platform for trusted computing. In: Proceedings of SOSP 2003. ACM (2003)
7. Krautheim, F.J.: Private virtual infrastructure for cloud computing. In: Proceedings of the HotCloud Conference 2009. ACM (2009)
8. Arshad, J., Townend, P., Jie, X.: Quantification of security for compute intensive workloads in clouds. In: Proceedings of the 15th International Conference on Parallel and Distributed Systems. IEEE (2009)
9. De Chaves, S.A., Uriarte, R.B., Westphall, C.B.: Toward an architecture for monitoring private clouds. IEEE Commun. Mag. **49**(12), 130–137 (2011). IEEE
10. Shao, J., Wei, H., Wang, Q., Mei, H.: A runtime model based monitoring approach for cloud. In: Proceedings of IEEE 3rd International Conference on Cloud Computing. IEEE (2010)

11. Rak, M., Liccardo, L., Aversa, R.: A SLA-based interface for security management in cloud and GRID integrations. In: Proceedings of the 7th International Conference on Information Assurance and Security (IAS), pp. 378–383. IEEE (2011)

12. Wieder, P., Butler, J.M., Theilmann, W., Yahyapour, R. (eds.): Service Level Agreements for Cloud Computing. Springer, NewYork (2011)

13. Lorenzoli, D., Spanoudakis, G.: EVEREST+: runtime SLA violations prediction. In: Proceedings of the 5th Middleware for Service-Oriented Computing Workshop. ACM (2010)

14. Shanahan, M.: The event calculus explained. In: Veloso, M.M., Wooldridge, M.J. (eds.) Artificial Intelligence Today. LNCS (LNAI), vol. 1600, pp. 409–430. Springer, Heidelberg (1999)

15. Chazalet, A.: Service level checking in the cloud computing context. In: Proceedings of the Third International Conference on Cloud Computing, pp. 297–304. IEEE (2010)

16. Nuñez, D., Fernandez-Gago, C., Pearson, S., Felici, M.: A metamodel for measuring accountability attributes in the cloud. In: Proceedings of the 2013 IEEE International Conference on Cloud Computing Technology and Science (CloudCom 2013). IEEE (2013)

17. AICPA: Statement on Auditing Standards (SAS) n°70 (2012). http://sas70.com/sas70_overview.html. Accessed 20 October 2013

18. Rak, M., Luna, J., Petcu, D., Casola, V., Suri, N., Villano, U.: Security as a service using an sla-based approach via SPECS. In: Proceedings of IEEE 5th International Conference on Cloud Computing Technology and Science (CloudCom), pp. 1–6. IEEE (2013)

19. TÜV Rheinland's: Certification for cloud providers (2014). www.tuv.com/en/corporate/business_customers/information_scuriy_cw/strategic_information_security/cloud_security_certification/cloud_security_certification.html. Accessed 20 October 2014

20. Schneider, S., Lansing, J., Gao, F., Sunyaev, A.: A taxonomic perspective on certification schemes: development of a taxonomy for cloud service certification criteria. In: Proceedings of the 47th Hawaii International Conference on System Sciences (HICSS 2014). IEEE (2014)

21. Petcu, D.: A Taxonomy for SLA-based monitoring of cloud security. In: COMPSAC, pp. 640–641 (2014)

22. Kohne, A., Spohr, M., Nagel, L., Spinczyk, O.: FederatedCloudSim: a SLA-aware federated cloud simulation framework. In: Proceedings of the 2nd International Workshop on CrossCloud Systems. ACM, New York (2014)

23. Maity, S., Chaudhuri, A.: Optimal negotiation of SLA in federated cloud using multiobjective genetic algorithms, In: Proceedings of CLOUDNET, pp. 269–271. IEEExplore (2014)

24. Mouratidis, H., Paolo Giorgini, P.: Secure tropos: a security-oriented extension of the tropos methodology. Int. J. Softw. Eng. Knowl. Eng. 17(2), 285–309 (2007)

25. Winkler, V.: Securing the Cloud- Cloud Computer Security Techniques and Tactics. Syngress, Waltham (2011)

26. Devanbu, P.T., Stubblebine, S.G.: Software engineering for security: a roadmap. In: ICSE - Future of SE Track 2000, pp. 227–239 (2000)

27. Lodderstedt, T., Basin, D., Doser, J.: SecureUML: a UML-based modeling language for model-driven security. In: Jézéquel, J.-M., Hussmann, H., Cook, S. (eds.) UML 2002. LNCS, vol. 2460, pp. 426–441. Springer, Heidelberg (2002)

28. Mouratidis, H., Giorgini, P., Gordon, A., Manson, G.A.: Integrating security and systems engineering: towards the modelling of secure information systems. CAiSE 2003, 63–78 (2003)

29. Jürjens, J.: UMLsec: extending UML for secure systems development. In: Jézéquel, J.-M., Hussmann, H., Cook, S. (eds.) UML 2002. LNCS, vol. 2460, pp. 412–425. Springer, Heidelberg (2002)

30. Humberg, T., Wessel, C., Poggenpohl, D., Wenzel, S., Ruhroth, T., J¨urjens, j: Using ontologies to analyze compliance requirements of cloud-based processes. In: Helfert, M., Desprez, F., Ferguson, D., Leymann, F. (eds.) CLOSER 2013. CCIS, vol. 453, pp. 1–16. Springer, Heidelberg (2014)
31. Wenzel, S., Wessel, C., Humberg, T., Jürjens, J.: Securing processes for outsourcing into the cloud. In: 2nd International Conference on Cloud Computing and Services Science. SciTePress (2012)

A Framework for Secure Migration Processes of Legacy Systems to the Cloud

Luis Márquez[1(✉)], David G. Rosado[2], Haralambos Mouratidis[3],
Daniel Mellado[4], and Eduardo Fernández-Medina[2]

[1] Spanish National Authority for Markets and Competition (CNMC),
28004 Madrid, Spain
luis.marquez@cnmc.es

[2] GSyA Research Group, Department of Information Systems and Technologies,
University of Castilla-La Mancha, 13071 Ciudad Real, Spain
{david.grosado,eduardo.fdezmedina}@uclm.es

[3] Secure and Dependable Software Systems (SenSe),
University of Brighton, Brighton BN2 4GJ, UK
H.Mouratidis@brighton.ac.uk

[4] Spanish Tax Agency, 28046 Madrid, Spain
damefe@esdebian.org

Abstract. The emergence of cloud computing as a major trend in the IT industry signifies that corporate users of this paradigm are confronted with the challenge of securing their systems in this new environment. An important aspect of that, includes the secure migration of an organization's legacy systems, which run in data centers that are completely controlled by the organization, to a cloud infrastructure, which is managed outside the scope of the client's premises and may even be to-tally off-shore. This paper makes two important contributions. Firstly, it presents a process (SMiLe2Cloud) and a framework that supports secure migration of corporate legacy systems to the cloud. We propose a process based on a continuous improvement cycle that starts with a Knowledge Discovery Meta-Model (KDM) set of models from which a security model for legacy system migration to the cloud is derived. Secondly, it provides a set of clauses (derived from the models) for security cloud providers and custom security cloud controls.

Keywords: Cloud computing · Computer security · Legacy software migration · KDM · CSA

1 Introduction

One of the biggest challenges is defining cloud computing. Based on the Cloud Security Alliance (CSA) [1], cloud computing can be defined as: "Cloud computing is a model for enabling ubiquitous, convenient, on-demand network access to a shared pool of configurable computing resources (e.g. networks, servers, storage, applications, and services).

To really understand the level of expectation placed upon cloud computing, one only has to read the recent report published by the European Commission entitled "Unleashing the Potential of Cloud Computing in Europe" [2]. Within this report,

© Springer International Publishing Switzerland 2015
A. Persson and J. Stirna (Eds.): CAiSE 2015 Workshops, LNBIP 215, pp. 507–517, 2015.
DOI: 10.1007/978-3-319-19243-7_46

it anticipates the potential impact of cloud computing could result in "a net gain of 2.5 million new European jobs, and an annual boost of €160 billion to the European Union GDP (around 1 %), by 2020".

Cloud Computing claims to take enterprises search to a new level and allows them to further reduce costs through improved utilization, reduced administration and infrastructure cost and faster deployment cycles [3]. The essence of legacy system migration is to move an existing, operational system to a new platform, retaining the functionality of the legacy system while causing as little disruption to the existing operational and business environment as possible [4]. Legacy system migration is a very expensive procedure which carries a definite risk of failure. Consequently before any decision to migrate is taken, an intensive study should be undertaken to quantify the risk and benefits and fully justify the redevelopment of the legacy system involved [5, 6].

Security plays a recurring concern within multiple end-customer surveys regarding concerns/barriers toward cloud adoption, as do concerns about data privacy. Based on a survey of 489 "business leaders", the PwC report entitled "The Future of IT Outsourcing and Cloud Computing" [7] asked a series of questions to respondents across multiple geographies, industry verticals, and company sizes relating to cloud adoption. When asked about concerns regarding data security, respondents believed it represented the biggest risk to infrastructure in the public cloud. Indeed, 62 % of respondents believed data security as either a serious or an extremely serious risk.

Security consistently raises the most questions as consumers look to move their data and applications to the cloud. Cloud computing does not introduce any security issues that have not already been raised for general IT security. The concern in moving to the cloud is that implementing and enforcing security policies now involves a third party. This loss of control emphasizes the need for transparency from cloud providers [8]. In some cases the cloud will offer a better security posture than an organization could otherwise provide.

There are no initiatives where a migration process is proposed for security aspects [9]. There is an urgent need to provide methodologies, techniques and tools to provide a strategy that facilitate the migration process of security aspects.

Our aim in this paper is to propose a framework, to support secure migration in the cloud, in the form of a set of methods that address the issue of security and how security should be integrated with different kinds of processes in order to migrate legacy information systems to the cloud in [10].

This paper is structured in 2 more sections in addition to this introduction. Section 2 presents the framework and Sect. 3 provides some conclusions and an outline of our future work.

2 SMiLe2Cloud: Process for Security Migration of Legacy Systems to the Cloud

In this section, we propose a process (called as SMiLe2Cloud) for secure Legacy Information Systems (LIS) migration to the cloud model which is, on the one hand, based on the Software Engineering Institute (SEI) horseshoe model [11] and, on the other, on the Deming cycle of continuous improvement. Since we are interested in the security process itself, and not actually in the general reverse engineering efforts for functional specification, we have supposed that the engineers migrating the LIS have already developed a model that defines the functional specifications and architectural elements of the system (but not the security specifications and security architecture) and that they have documented these specifications and elements in a system that can be converted to a Knowledge Discovery Meta-Model (KDM) specification [12]. It is at this point that we take over and attempt to first to develop the security aspects of the reverse engineered design, and then continue with the rest of the process. We shall define the process by attempting to follow the Software & Systems Process Engineering Metamodel Specification (SPEM) notation as closely as possible.

2.1 Overview

As stated previously, the process starts at the highest point of the horseshoe model once a base security architecture has been obtained and just before the transformation. From there, it continues with the transformation and the refinement of the target system, focusing on specific cloud issues.

The SMiLe2Cloud process consists of five activities addressed by 16 security domains described in [1] and illustrated in Fig. 1. The extraction activity is focused on the use of reverse engineering to extract security issues from LIS to a security model (SMiLe model) defined for our migration process. The second activity is the analysis of the security requirements (SecR), which is based on the extension of the Secure Tropos methodology [13] for the cloud. The design activity is focused on selecting the service model, the deployment model and making the selection of the cloud provider based on CSA Security, Trust & Assurance Registry (STAR) [14]. The deployment activity is focused on developing the deployment specification based on a repository of cloud migration patterns and making the implementation of the system. The fifth activity is the evaluation when a verification and validation of the security model migrated is checked and captures the new security issues to be incorporated into a new cycle of the process and into an analysis of the improvements and changes proposed for our cloud system.

Since KDM lacked specific concerns regarding security issues, part of our process is in fact performed just before a complete reverse engineered specification of the system has been obtained. The extraction activity that is specifically addressed in our process deals with the last part of the reengineering phase of the horseshoe model. Nevertheless, it could be used separately with any security related method aimed at migrating LIS in a secure manner (no matter what the target architecture might be).

2.2 SMiLe2Cloud Activities

In this section we present an in-depth description of the set of activities in our SMiLe2Cloud process shown in Fig. 1. SMiLe2Cloud process has five activities: Extraction, Analysis, Design, Deployment and Evaluation, and a wide set of input and output artifacts for each of the activities that will be described as follows:

Activity 1: Extraction. The extraction is the activity in which the security model for the LIS is derived from the actual code and the technical documentation of the LIS. It is

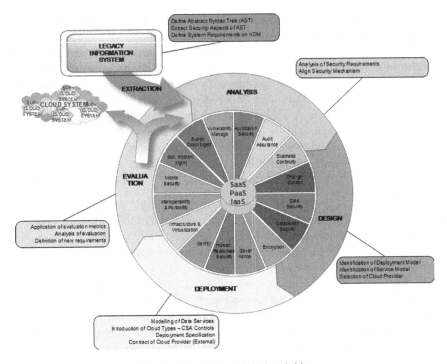

Fig. 1. The SMiLe2Cloud activities

a reverse engineering sub-process that is parallel to the sub-process of obtaining the general architectural model for the LIS. The process is assisted by reverse engineering tools in order to ease the tasks and steps that the analyst must perform to put the different requirements and controls in place.

The process is data oriented and is based on a formal specification of the sub-programs and data managed by each program unit in the LIS in the form of an abstract syntax tree (AST) that models each of the program units.

This activity produces internal artifacts which represent outputs for some tasks and inputs for others. Figure 2 shows a graphical representation of the extraction activity tasks using SPEM 2.0 diagrams.

A1.1 Extract Security Aspects

An abstract syntax tree is a tree representation of the syntactic structure of the program and data items of the LIS, and supports a 1-to-1 mapping of all the items included in the code in a tree like structure that is used as the basis to derive the security requirements of the system.

The task has two steps: the first step involves extracting all the information from the LIS by means of traditional reverse engineering techniques (static/dynamic analysis, slicing, etc.) and with the help of tools, while the second step involves defining the AST with the information extracted.

For each data element and each subprogram element that is present in the AST, the system analyst must extract the concrete security permissions that each of the different

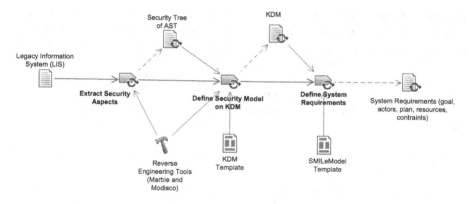

Fig. 2. Extraction activity

user profiles must have to be able to run the program normally (access, create, modify, delete, admin, audit).

A1.2 Define security model on KDM

As shown above, as a reengineering meta-model focused on functional specifications, KDM does not have security areas of concern built within the standard itself. Pérez-Castillo [15] state that there are some tools that use KDM to formalize machine-readable content prior to searching for vulnerability patterns and performing the static analysis of the representation of code, but the standard itself does not address the formalization of the security aspects of the LIS. It is true, however, that some of the domains, packages and models defined in the standard are bound to include security references (i.e., business rules domain, data domain, platform, source); but the security references have no single domain, package or model related to security and it is therefore easy for the LIS security requirements and artifacts to end up scattered around the entire collection of models and specifications.

We propose to avoid this situation by ensuring that every single artifact and security control in the LIS is instantiated in a business security rule and is included in the conceptual model during the analysis phase.

A1.3 Define system requirements

As described above the extraction activity is focused on the use of reverse engineering to extract security issues from LIS to a security model (SMiLe model) defined for our migration process.

We have at this point our KDM model with particular emphasis on security issues. Based on this model (KDM) we will define the system requirements (SMiLe model) defining the goals, actors, plans, resources and constraints.

The SMiLe model will be implemented as a XML file. This file will be the input for the next activity, the analysis activity.

Tools

In order to assist in this activity we are adapting the reverse engineering tool Marble [16] to support security aspects. We are developing a series of templates with which to identify and extract the security items in the model (i.e., business rules related to security goals and requirements and assets) from some of the different models defined in KDM (source, code, action, UI, data) and to define a set of business rules that encompass the security goals, policies and requirements for the LIS. We also intend to derive a set of items from most of the other domains of KDM (source, data, platform, UI) that will also be part of the security model.

Other reverse engineering tools that also obtain KDM models can be used to collect more information like Modisco [17].

Activity 2: Analysis. During this activity we define the actual security requirements (SecR), by extending the Secure Tropos methodology [13] for the cloud. We introduce some cloud-specific concepts, such as cloud specific threats, cloud specific security constraints and cloud service providers.

Figure 3 shows a graphical representation of the analysis activity tasks together with the input and output artifacts using SPEM 2.0 diagrams.

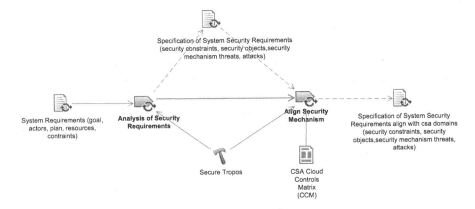

Fig. 3. Analysis activity

A2.1 Analysis of Security Requirements
The SMiLe model is used to derive a set of SecRS with which the system must comply in the new environment.

Two steps are defined in this task: analyze the LIS requirements that are no longer necessary and analyze the new cloud requirements that are applicable.

Some requirements of the original LIS may be no longer applicable to the target system, since the cloud ecosystem might simply have made them redundant or unnecessary. It is also necessary to bear in mind that not all the cloud controls may be applicable to the LIS; an analysis of the applicability of new cloud requirements is therefore necessary before we can proceed further.

A2.2 Align Security Mechanism
The CSA Cloud Control Matrix [18] provides a controls framework in 16 domains that are cross-mapped to other industry-accepted security standards, regulations, and controls frameworks. We have developed a catalogue of security mechanisms based in the

16 domains specified in the Cloud Control Matrix. The objective of this task is to map the security mechanism identified in the previous step (A2.1) with the 16 domains specified in the Cloud Control Matrix using the catalogue of security mechanisms.

Tools
Secure Tropos is a security requirements engineering methodology that considers security throughout the whole development process. SecTro is a tool which assists the security analysts in constructing the relevant Secure Tropos diagrams that are required in order to identify, model and analyze the security issues.

Activity 3: Design. The design activity is focused on selecting the service model, the deployment model and making the selection of the cloud provider based on CSA Security, Trust & Assurance Registry (STAR) [14].

Figure 4 shows a graphical representation of the design activity tasks together with the input and output artifacts using SPEM 2.0 specification.

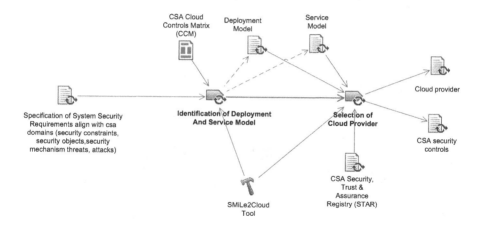

Fig. 4. Design activity

*A3.*1 Identification of Deployment Model
The National Institute of Standards and Technology (NIST) distinguishes between four cloud deployment models: public, private, hybrid and community.

In this task, based on the specification of system security requirements aligned with the CSA domains we will select the appropriate deployment model for our system.

*A3.*2 Identification of Service Model
The National Institute of Standards and Technology (NIST) distinguishes between three service models: software as a service (SAAS), platform as a service (PAAS) and infrastructure as a service (IAS).

During this task, based on the specification of system security requirements aligned with the CSA domains, the appropriate service model for our system is defined.

A3.3 Selection of cloud provider

Once we have selected the deployment model, the service model and we have our system security requirements aligned with the CSA domains we can select the cloud providers that fit with our security needs according to the CSA Security, Trust & Assurance Registry (STAR).

Tools

The SMiLe2Cloud Tool helps us throughout the migration process. In the early stages (extraction and analysis) is integrated with the above named tools (Marble, Modisco and SecTro). In the following phases (design, deployment and evaluation) uses its own interface.

Activity 4: Deployment. The deployment activity is focused on developing the deployment specification based on a repository of cloud migration patterns and the implementation of the system.

Figure 5 shows a graphical representation of the migration activity tasks together with the input and output artifacts using SPEM 2.0.

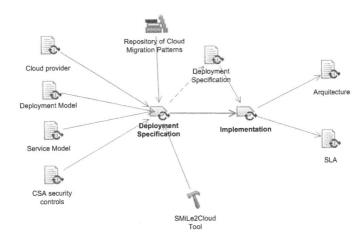

Fig. 5. Deployment activity

A4.1 Deployment Specification

Once we have selected the service model, the deployment model and the cloud provider the deployment specification takes place. This task focuses on the modelling of data services.

A4.2 Implementation

Finally, the implementation itself takes place. During the implementation task it could be necessary to contract the services and to sign the Service Level Agreement (SLA), develop the custom security elements or set all the security controls in working conditions.

Activity 5: Evaluation. Once the entire process has been moved to the cloud in a secure manner, it is time to verify and validate the security of the system. This activity is based on a repository of cloud migration metrics.

Figure 6 shows a graphical representation of the evaluation activity tasks together with the input and output artifacts using SPEM 2.0.

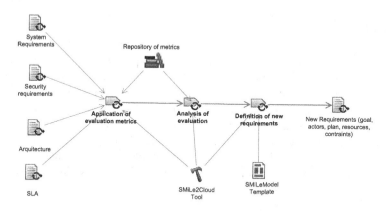

Fig. 6. Evaluation activity

A5.1 Application of evaluation metrics

Despite the obvious value of metrics in different scenarios to evaluate, a formal repository of security metrics in a changing environment like the Cloud is very helpful. In this task, the repository of metrics will be applied to our system.

A5.2 Analysis of evaluation

An analysis of the results obtained in the previous task is necessary. It is necessary to analyze if all the system requirements have been reached, all the security requirements are covered and the architecture is the complete.

A5.3 Definition of new requirements

The cloud is a changing environment. Some of the issues that most experts are now studying were still undetected only a couple of years ago. In two years' time, there might be completely new services that will help to strengthen the security of a LIS system migrated to the cloud. Furthermore, since we have delegated the responsibility for some controls, a continuous watch on the levels and metrics of security is advisable.

Even when the system is operating in working conditions, and as we have already seen, the verification of some parts needs a continuous effort to gather further evidence that the security is maintained at the levels agreed on and that security services are provided.

Activity 5.3 must therefore be periodically repeated, and the results must be analyzed within the limits of the specifications of the security architecture proposed.

But even if the security specifications are met as written, basing our process on a Deming cycle signifies some sort of continuous reevaluation of possible improvements to the system.

The improvements may come from technical advances in the field, from changes in the standard SLA or the services that the cloud provider offers, from legislative grounds, etc.

The new requirements will be implemented as an XML file based in the SMiLe model. This file will be the input for the activity 2, the analysis activity.

3   Conclusions

In this paper we have presented the main stages of a process that supports the secure migration of a legacy information system (LIS) to the cloud. We start at the point at which a system has been subjected to reverse engineering and a KDM set of models for the functional part of the LIS has been extracted. From this point, we propose a set of activities that will evolve that KDM into an LIS security architecture and from there to the target LIS migrated to the cloud; we are currently developing semiautomatic tools and templates in order to deliver a LIS security architecture and to map this security architecture onto a target architecture that specifically addresses cloud threats, cloud security requirements and cloud controls (either as SecaaS or customized controls) that meet cloud security standards such as CSA's controls matrix.

Our future work will focus on improving our process and demonstrate the applicability of the proposed framework. We are applying the proposed approach in a real-world case study based on the migration of the SICILIA system of the Spanish National Authority for Markets and Competition (CNMC) to the cloud. SICILIA manage the liquidation of the special regime installations (renewable and cogeneration). According to the latest report on the results of the provisional liquidation in November 2014 of the remuneration of the production facilities of renewable energy, cogeneration and waste has been cleared a total of 63,878 installations that were active in SICILIA and were entered in the Register of specific Remuneration system for the Ministry of Industry, Energy and Tourism.

Acknowledgments. This research is part of the following projects: SERENIDAD (PEII11-037-7035) financed by the "Viceconsejería de Ciencia y Tecnología de la Junta de Comunidades de Castilla- La Mancha" (Spain) and FEDER, and SIGMA-CC (TIN2012-36904) financed by the "Ministerio de Economía y Competitividad" (Spain).

References

1. Cloud Security Alliance, Security Guidance for Critical Areas of Focus in Cloud Computing V3.0 (2011)
2. European Commission, Unleashing the Potential of Cloud Computing in Europe. Communication from the commission to the European Parliament, the council, the European economic and social Committee and the Committee of the regions (2012)
3. Kushwah, V.S., Saxena, A.: A security approach for data migration in cloud computing. Int. J. Sci. Res. Publ. **3**(5) (2013)

4. Wu, B., et al.: Legacy system migration: a legacy data migration engine. In: 17th International Database Conference (DATASEM 1997), pp. 129–138. Czech Republic, Brno (1997)
5. Bisbal, J., et al.: Legacy information system migration: a brief review of problems. Solutions Res. Issues **16**(5), 103–111 (1999)
6. Bisbal, J., Lawless, D., Richardson, R.: A Survey of Research into Legacy System Migration. Computer Science Department, Trinity College Dublin (1997)
7. PwC, The Future of IT Outsourcing and Cloud Computing (2011)
8. Cloud Computing Use Case Discussion Group, Cloud Computing Use Cases White Paper version 4.0 (2010)
9. Alcañiz, L.M., et al.: Security in legacy systems migration to the cloud: a systematic mapping study. In: 11th International Workshop on Security in Information Systems, pp. 93–100. Lisbon, Portugal (2014)
10. Rosado, D.G., et al.: Security analysis in the migration to cloud environments. Future Internet **4**, 469–487 (2012)
11. Seacord, R., Plakosh, D., Lewis, G. (eds.): Modernizing Legacy Systems: Software Technologies, Engineering Processes, and Business Practices, Addison-Wesley Professional, p. 352 (2003)
12. OMG, Architecture-Driven Modernization. Knowledge Discovery Meta-Model (KDM), v1.3 (2011)
13. Mouratidis, H., Giorgini, P.: Secure tropos: a security-oriented extension of the tropos methodology. Int. J. Softw. Eng. Knowl. Eng. **17**(2), 285–309 (2007)
14. Cloud Security Alliance. CSA Security, Trust & Assurance Registry (STAR) (2014). https://cloudsecurityalliance.org/star/
15. Pérez-Castillo, R., García-Rodríguez de Guzmán, I., Piattini, M.: Knowledge discovery metamodel-ISO/IEC 19506: a standard to modernize legacy systems. Comput. Stand. Interfaces **33**, 519–532 (2011)
16. Pérez-Castillo, R., et al.: MARBLE: a modernization approach for recovering business processes from legacy systems. In: International Workshop on Reverse Engineering Models from Software Artifacts (REM 2009) (2009)
17. Bruneliere, H., et al.: Modisco: a model driven reverse engineering framework. Inf. Softw. Technol. **56**(8), 1012–1032 (2014)
18. Cloud Security Alliance. CLOUD CONTROLS MATRIX V3.0.1 (2014). https://cloudsecurityalliance.org/download/cloud-controls-matrix-v3-0-1/

An Experience Report on Scalable Implementation of DDoS Attack Detection

Sri Yogesh Dorbala, Kishore R., and Neminath Hubballi[✉]

Discipline of Computer Science and Engineering, Indian Institute of Technology Indore, Indore, India
{cs1100112,cs1100118,neminath}@iiti.ac.in

Abstract. Distributed Denial of Service (DDoS) attacks are increasingly becoming powerful and crippling many networks and services in Internet. Many methods have been proposed to mitigate and detect DDoS attacks in the literature. These techniques require processing large amount of network traffic in real time. In order to process this bulky network traffic, in this paper we report an experimental investigation of scalable implementation. In our experiments we used distributed computing framework of Apache Hadoop to achieve the scalability. We implemented clustering and classification algorithms for detecting DDoS attack. Several experiments on a DDoS dataset and normal dataset of sizes ranging from 1 GB to 80 GB resulted in performance improvements.

Keywords: Distributed Denial of Service · Scalable implementation · Attack detection

1 Introduction

Denial of Service (DoS) is a type of attack that aims to deny a legitimate user access to resource(s) for a prolonged time. These attacks have a huge impact depending on their intensity. In recent years these attacks have increased many fold and have crippled vital internet infrastructure. Attackers might have different intentions behind carrying out these attacks like financial gain and social protests.

To increase the intensity of DoS attacks, attackers use multiple sources with some of them across geographies. These multiple sources increase the complexity of attack detection. These attacks are known as **Distributed Denial of Service** (DDoS) attacks. The attacker initially takes control of many computers on internet by infecting those systems using different techniques. These infected systems are called botnets. Botnets are most commonly used sources for performing a DDoS attack. Bot master (usually attacker) sends commands to the botnets (slave machines) to launch attack against a particular target at a particular time.

According to a recent Verisign report on DDoS Trends [1], there is a 291 % increase in attacks in the first quarter of 2014 when compared to that of 2013. This is also shown in Fig. 1. This report also mention that the largest detected

© Springer International Publishing Switzerland 2015
A. Persson and J. Stirna (Eds.): CAiSE 2015 Workshops, LNBIP 215, pp. 518–529, 2015.
DOI: 10.1007/978-3-319-19243-7_47

DDoS attack was generating traffic at the rate of 300 Gbps against Spamhaus website. Another instance of a major DDoS attack is on Root DNS Servers. Root DNS Servers do the translation from domain name to IP Address. In 2007, 2 of 13 root DNS servers suffered due to DDoS attacks but the impact of the attack was very little thanks to the advanced measures like anycast and load balancing. If attacks on root DNS servers are successful, then access to many websites is forbidden as domain name to IP Address translation fails. If reliable and sufficient defenses are not in place to defend these attacks, the services and infrastructure under these attacks will be inaccessible [2].

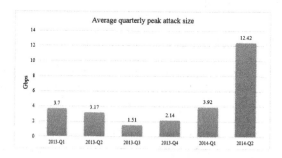

Fig. 1. DDoS Trends in 2014 [3]

Denial of Service (DoS) and Distributed Denial of Service (DDoS) attacks have been addressed by researchers in two main categories as preventive methods and detection methods. These techniques can work by monitoring traffic at the intermediate router level or individual host level. Techniques like Ingress filtering [4] and Egress filtering [5], MANAnet's Reverse Firewall [6] which is a reverse firewall limiting the rate of outbound traffic flow, excluding the acknowledgments (Ack's) to be sent to recently received packets, Unicast Reverse Path Forwarding [7] which discard IP packets that have been received on a different interface than the one used for sending a packet to that source and Traceroute work at the router level, while methods like Hop Count filtering [8], making initial sequence number of a TCP session a truly random number or a parameter of source and destination addresses [9] are deployed at the end host.

One of the challenge in detecting DDoS attacks is to collect and analyze large volume of network traffic in real time. This raises the question of scalability of detection methods. Recently few attempts are made [10,11] to address this issue. In this paper, we explore the scalability of DDoS detection techniques on Hadoop with two traffic pattern learning methods. First one is an unsupervised learning technique and second is a supervised learning method. In unsupervised learning method, only normal traffic is modeled and in the supervised learning method both normal and DDoS traffic is modeled. In both the cases a set of features extracted from the network traffic serve as feature vectors.

Rest of this paper is organized as follows. In Sect. 2 related work for detecting and mitigating DDoS attacks is elaborated. In Sect. 3 a very brief overview of Hadoop which is a distributed computing framework is given. In Sect. 4 two methods for DDoS detection namely unsupervised and supervised learning techniques are discussed. In Sect. 5 experiments done to evaluate the performance of the two methods is described. In Sect. 6 a discussion on lessons learnt are briefed. Finally, Sect. 7 concludes the paper.

2   Prior Work

There are number of methods proposed in literature to detect and mitigate DDoS attacks. Mainly these methods are of following types.

2.1   Methods Deployed at Source of Attack

D-WARD [12] is a source based preventive measure for DDoS attack. Here both inbound and outbound traffic is monitored and compared with already built models of normal traffic flows. If the current flows show huge difference with previously computed models they are identified as contributors to attack.

MUlti-Level Tree for Online Packet Statistics (MULTOPS) and Tabulated Online Packet Statistics (TOPS) MULTOPS [13] is a heuristic method to detect DDoS attacks. It uses a tree data-structure to capture rate statistics for various subnets in Internet. MULTOPS makes an assumption that at any time, traffic flow between two devices is proportional. Using this, if a flow between two hosts or subnets is not proportional then one of the host or subnet is either a source or a destination of an attack. The main disadvantage with this method is use of dynamic tree data structure. Attacker can leverage this to exhaust the memory resources at monitoring machine.

Proactive Surge Protection [14] is a filtering technique where packets originating from a source which is injecting more number of packets than previously seen are discarded by routers assuming they are contributing to DDoS attack. Backward Traffic Throttling [15] is a similar approach where traffic is prioritized based on historical rates observed rather than discarding.

Source-based methods make a poor choice in mitigating DDoS attacks because of following 3 reasons.

1. The attacker may employ different techniques to distribute the sources of attacks across geographies, making it impossible to know if one particular source is an attacker.
2. As the DDoS traffic is aggregated at the victim's end, the volume of traffic monitored/collected at a source might not be sufficient to draw any tangible conclusions.
3. Although source based methods are effective in mitigating DDoS attacks, they require cooperation from Internet Service Providers (ISPs). However these ISPs require huge investments and maintenance costs and in return find no incentive in implementing these methods.

2.2 Methods Deployed at the Destination of Attack

These methods are implemented at the receiver end or victim of an attack some-times called as destination. These methods have to be more sophisticated as they usually take into account all the traffic from multiple sources converging in on this destination unlike Source-based methods, where we have only one source.

Packet Marking [16–19]: In this method routers in the path from source to destination of a packet add their identity to the packet. This enables the recipeint to find the path which the packet has taken to reach destination. If there are any significant changes in the path compared to historic values those packets are suspected. One of the main challenge of this method is storing the entire path in the packet, as packet might take a longer path in which case whole path cannot be stored.

History-based IP filtering [20,21]: In this method statistics for various IP addresses is maintained. These statistics include rate of packets exchanged with the receiver. Any significant changes in these rates are detected as attack. This method can narrow down the access list to those IP addresses which were col-lected at an earlier time when there was no attack. A serious disadvantage of this method is some of the normal traffic is also denied access if those IP addresses were not seen earlier.

Hop-count filtering [8,22,23]: In this method, the source IP address and cor-responding hop-count of every arriving packet is logged. Subsequently, incoming packets with those source IP addresses are checked for their hop-count. Sig-nificant deviations in the originally logged and new hop-count is detected as suspicious and packets are identified as spoofed. Since spoofed packets are com-monly used in DDoS attacks, a significant percentage of spoofed packets are detected as DDoS attacks.

3 Hadoop

Apache Hadoop [24] is an open-source framework for distributed storage and processing of very large files. Hadoop cluster is a network of interconnected systems with Hadoop installed. Commodity computers can be configured to create a Hadoop cluster to run jobs in parallel.

Hadoop File System (HDFS) and MapReduce [25] are main components of Hadoop Framework. HDFS is the file storage system of Hadoop. Hadoop enables us to store data in multiple locations in the cluster by splitting files into blocks and also replicating file-blocks for data redundancy in case of system (node) failure. This has another advantage of data locality for computation, which plays a big role in distributed computing. MapReduce allows us to run jobs in parallel on different nodes in the cluster. This distributed computing achieves scale in computation.

4 Proposed Method

In this section we describe our methods for detecting DDoS attack. Here we use two learning techniques namely supervised and unsupervised learning techniques for detecting DDoS attacks. Learning is based on interval summary of network traffic. Each interval summary has the information of amount of network traffic flowing in and out of network. Both the techniques are based on interval summary calculated on per second basis. Each interval summary has the information as shown in Table 1.

Table 1. Interval summary

1 Number of Packets
2 Average Packet Length
3 Number of TCP packets
4 Number of UDP Packets
5 Number of ICMP Packets
6 Distinct Source IP Addresses Seen
7 Distinct Source ports
8 Distinct Destination IP Addresses Seen
9 Distinct Destination ports

An example interval summary is shown in Eq. 1. This interval summary constitute the input feature vectors for both supervised and unsupervised learning methods. As we can notice, the summary calculates few statistics from network traffic. A sample of traffic statistics of DARPA 99 and CAIDA 2007 dataset is shown in Table 2 indicating the difference between normal and DDoS traffic. We can notice that the difference is clearly visible in terms of values each feature takes.

$$Interval[t_1, t_2] : 173, 597.24, 171, 2, 0, 6, 6, 12, 12 \tag{1}$$

Table 2. Comparison between normal and DDoS traffic

Properties	Normal (1 min)	DDoS (1 min)
Distinct source IP's	22	7519
Distinct destination IP's	26	7522
Distinct source ports	826	65490
Distinct destination ports	670	234

4.1 Unsupervised Technique

Unsupervised learning is a method where hidden structure in the data is found from unlabeled dataset. This method summarizes the data and explains the essential characteristics of the dataset. As the data is unlabeled, there is no feedback provided to correct mistakes in learning. Data clustering is one such unsupervised learning method which we have used for DDoS attack detection. In this method DDoS attacks are detected as cases of outliers. Figure 2 shows a view of outliers in the dataset. In the figure there are two clusters and few points shown in red color constitute outliers.

Cluster is a group of objects with similar characteristics and Clustering is the method of forming these clusters from the set of unlabeled data. Any data object (vector) which does not fall into the clusters is termed as an outlier. Our approach is to form clusters of normal dataset and later detect whether a given input data object is within the cluster or an outlier, i.e., a normal one or DDoS attack instance.

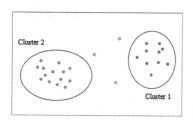

Fig. 2. Data clustering and outliers

(I) *Training*: The first stage of this method requires the formation of clusters. Hence in training phase normal instances are grouped into clusters. Clusters are represented by a cluster center and each cluster has a radius.

(II) *Detection:* In the detection phase a given input instance is to be detected as an outlier or not. In order to do this, calculated distance of the given input vector with respect to the center of the cluster is used. Those instances whose distances are within the radius of cluster are considered normal and those whose distance is outside the radius of the cluster is termed as outlier or DDoS attack instance.

In order to form clusters and find the distance of any input vector with cluster center a distance measure is used. In this case Manhattan distance given in Eq. 2 is used as a distance measure.

$$d(x, y) = \Sigma_{k=1}^{n} |x_k - y_k| \tag{2}$$

4.2 Supervised Technique

Supervised learning is a method where labeled training data is used to create a model in order to classify future data. The algorithm has to correctly label the unknown data in testing dataset by comparing it to the model created from the training dataset. Just like previous case this method also has a training phase and testing phase.

(I) *Training:* We use k-nearest neighbors classification algorithm, to classify testing data into normal or DDoS traffic, with the use of labeled training data. Since K-nearest neighbor classification requires identifying closest neighbors of a testing vector, training phase is trivial which is the training dataset itself.

(II) *Testing:* In this phase, each test vector's K nearest neighbors are found and a majority voting is done to label it. In order to calculate the nearest neighbors Manhattan distance metric is used. K closest neighbors in the training dataset are found for every interval in Testing dataset based on a distance measure. Distance of each testing data object (vector) to each training data object is computed using the Manhattan distance measure as in previous case.

5 Experiment Details

In our experiments we used two datasets for evaluation. First dataset is DARPA 99 week 1 and 3, outside traffic which is used as normal dataset and second one is CAIDA 2007 DDoS attack dataset. CAIDA 2007 dataset [26] is DDoS traffic of an hour collected from a real attack in internet.

Table 3. Dataset description

Properties	Normal	DDoS
Number of Packets	1,39,41,518	37,11,32,316
Number of Intervals	4,05,325	2,455

A summary of these two datasets is shown in Table 3. From these datasets we extracted packet header details using CLI version of Wireshark called tshark. This is a text file containing the header details of all packets. Text file of packet header details of DARPA 99 datset is around 1 GB where as similar file of the DDoS dataset is around 22 GB. We can notice that, there are 405325 intervals of one second each in the DARPA 99 dataset while CAIDA 2007 dataset has 2455 intervals. A java program is written to process this text file to generate interval summary per second. Although, DDoS dataset contains packets of only one hour network traffic it has many more packets compared to 5 days of normal traffic in DARPA 99 dataset.

5.1 Hadoop Configuration

We setup a Hadoop cluster with 4 nodes to study the scalability of network traffic processing. We used open source Apache Hadoop version 2.4.1 in our setup. Other configuration details of this cluster are below.

Hadoop Cluster Configuration:
Number of PC's: 4
Processor: Intel Core 2 Duo E8400 @ 3.00 GHz
RAM : 8 GB (Each node)
HDD : 500 GB (Each node)
Network : 100 Mbps DLink Switch connected using 1 Gbps Ethernet Cable.

5.2 Performance of Interval Summary

In order to assess the performance of Hadoop in processing these text files into interval summaries we conducted an experiment. In this experiment we used files of different sizes containing packet header details as input and generated interval summaries of one second each. Table 4 shows a comparison of processing time of a 4 node Hadoop cluster with a single node machine. We can notice that, the time taken for processing 1 GB file in a single node machine is faster in comparison to multinode Hadoop cluster. A similar analysis on a file of 20 GB (this is a DDoS dataset) brought down the difference between the two significantly with single node system still being the better of the two. We ran another experiment with a file size of 40 GB. This 40 GB file was generated by replicating DDoS dataset packets. In this case performance of Hadoop is found to be better than the single node machine. A similar experiment with 80 GB (generated similarly) data shows Hadoop's superiority over a single node machine. We can conclude from this experiment that Hadoop performance increases with increase in input dataset size.

5.3 Unsupervised Learning

Table 4. Processing time

	File Size			
	1 GB	20 GB	40 GB	80 GB
Single Node Machine	30 sec	7 min	25 min	52 min
4 Node Hadoop Cluster	90 sec	13 min	23 min	45 min

As discussed previously interval summaries are used as data vectors to detect DDoS attacks. In unsupervised learning method we used interval summaries of only normal data (for training) from DARPA 99 datset. We experimented by creating different number of clusters from this dataset and the performance is reported here. The dataset details used for unsupervised learning is shown in Table 5. In the first experiment we created only one cluster by taking the average of all vectors in the training set.

Table 5. Dataset used for unsupervised learning

Properties	Normal		DDoS	
	Training	Testing	Training	Testing
Number of intervals	2,02,662	2,02,663	0	2,455

Table 6 shows the performance of unsupervised learning method. Out of the 202663 intervals in the normal dataset 50 of them are incorrectly labeled as DDoS instances and the rest all are correctly labeled as normal instances. Likewise, 45 of the total 2455 intervals of the DDoS were wrongly labeled as normal intervals. We use *Recall* and *Precision* as the metrics to evaluate the performance of the system. These two are given in Eqs. 3 and 4 respectively. There is a *Recall* of 98.17 % and *Precision* of 97.97 %. in this method.

$$Recall = \frac{TP}{TP + FN} \tag{3}$$

$$Precision = \frac{TP}{TP + FP} \tag{4}$$

Table 6. Confusion matrix - complete

	Normal	DDoS
Normal	2,02,663	50
DDoS	45	2,410

Table 7. Confusion matrix-TCP

	Normal	DDoS
Normal	1,68,825	30
DDoS	56	2,376

In the second case we created one cluster for every protocol[1]. We report results for each of these protocols. Table 7 shows performance of TCP interval summaries. We used only TCP packets to generate interval summaries. Out of 337,650 intervals created, 50 % of the data i.e., 1,68,825 are used for training and remaining 50 % are used for testing. As we can see from the table 30 of them are incorrectly labeled as DDoS intervals. We can notice that 99.98 % of normal instances are correctly labeled. Similarly, 56 of the total 2432 TCP intervals are misinterpreted as normal intervals. *Recall* and *Precision* of this experiment are 97.69 % and 98.75 % respectively.

Table 8 shows the ICMP data vector detection performance. A cluster is generated by using 50 % of the 8059 ICMP intervals in the normal dataset. Out of 4029 normal testing instances all are correctly labeled as normal intervals thus giving a 100 % correct labeling. *Recall* and *Precision* in this case are 99.95 % and 100 %.

Table 8. Confusion matrix - ICMP

	Normal	DDoS
Normal	4,029	0
DDoS	1	2,454

5.4   Supervised Learning

As described earlier in supervised learning both normal and DDoS datset is used for training a classification algorithm. We used K-nearest neighbor classification algorithm for supervised learning. Since K-nearest classification is computationally very expensive we used a smaller representative dataset for this experiment. Table 9 shows dataset details. We have divided the entire data set into two sets as training and testing. Training phase had 1200 normal intervals from DARPA 99 and another 1200 DDoS intervals from CAIDA. The testing data set had 175,117 normal intervals and 1255 DDoS intervals.

Table 9. Dataset description

Properties	Normal		DDoS	
	Training	Testing	Training	Testing
Number of intervals	1,200	1,75,117	1,200	1,255

---

[1] Except UDP, whose number is very small in CAIDA 2007 datset.

Table 10. Confusion matrix - supervised

	Normal	DDoS
Normal	1,75,111	6
DDoS	0	1,255

With $K = 5$ we found nearest neighbors for each of the testing interval and labeled it with majority vote i.e., if 3 of its neighbors are labeled normal in training dataset the testing interval is also labeled as normal and otherwise. Table 10 shows the classification performance of this method. Table 11 shows the time taken to classify the testing dataset into normal or DDoS traffic. As we can see the time taken for performing the classification on a single node machine is slower than Hadoop cluster. We can notice that *Recall* is 100 % and *Precision* is 99.52 %.

6 Discussion

Table 11. Classification time

	Time (minutes)
Single Node	30
Hadoop	21

As we noticed from above results although Hadoop resulted in performance improvement in comparison to a single node processing, however the improvement is not substantial. There are several reasons for this including cluster configuration. Following are few insights gained from our experiments.

1. **Data Size:** For MapReduce to perform well, input data size should be larger. On smaller datasets the overhead in performing Map and Reduce operations will be the major contributors to the processing time. For our experiments we could not increase the dataset size further because of hardware constraints like memory size.
2. **Suitability of Algorithms for Parallel Processing:** Suitability of algorithm for parallel computation also contributes to the performance improvements. In our case the unsupervised learning method is not computationally involved where as K-nearest neighbor classification is not inherently parallelizable.
3. **Network Latency:** To use input data in sizes of few Giga Bytes, we need a very high speed network to transfer the portion of input files between nodes of cluster. Due to this network latency in transferring the file parts to slave nodes the total computation time is increased. In our experiments we used a low end 8 port switch which happened to be a bottleneck.
4. **Caching:** Hadoop has a feature to cache frequently accessed files to reduce the file-read time. By caching the data, a local copy of file is kept on all slave nodes. This reduces the time required for file access as compared to accessing the file from Master before the Map phase. We observed that, this feature reduces the network latency to a considerable extent and improve the performance in comparison with experiments without caching.

7   Conclusion

In this paper we described an experimental evaluation of DDoS attack detection with traffic interval summaries. We conducted scalability study of two detection methods namely unsupervised and supervised learning methods on Hadoop and compared its performance with a single node machine. An important observation is that although Hadoop improves performance there are several factors which affects its performance including size of data, suitability of algorithm for parallel computation, network latency, etc. In order to achieve the scale all of these need to be addressed.

Acknowledgement. The authors would like to acknowledge Center for Applied Internet Data Analysis (CAIDA) and MIT Lincoln Laboratory for providing access to their 2007 DDoS attack dataset and DARPA 99 dataset respectively.

References

1. Verisign. http://www.verisigninc.com/assets/report-ddos-trends-q22014.pdf
2. Geva, M., Herzberg, A., Gev, Y.: Bandwidth distributed denial of service: attacks and defenses. IEEE/ACM Trans. Network. **12**(1), 54–61 (2014)
3. Verisign, DDos attack stats (2014). http://www.stateoftheinternet.com/downloads/pdfs/resources-web-security-2014-q2-global-ddos-attack-report-infographic.pdf
4. Ferguson, P., Senie, D.: Network ingress filtering: defeating denial of service attacks which employ IP source address spoofing. RFC 2827, May 2000
5. Distler, D.: Performing Egress Filtering. SANS Institute Infosec Reading Room (2008)
6. MANANET: The reverse firewall: defeating DDOS attacks emanating from a local area network. http://www.cs3-inc.com/mananet.html
7. CISCO. http://www.cisco.com/web/about/security/intelligence/unicast-rpf.html
8. Wang, H., Jin, C., Shin, K.G.: Defense against spoofed IP traffic using hop-count filtering. IEEE/ACM Trans. Network. **15**(1), 40–53 (2007)
9. Gont, F., Bellovin, S.: Defending against sequence number attacks. RFC 6528, February 2012
10. Lee, Y., Kang, W., Lee, Y.: A hadoop-based packet trace processing tool. In: Domingo-Pascual, J., Shavitt, Y., Uhlig, S. (eds.) TMA 2011. LNCS, vol. 6613, pp. 51–63. Springer, Heidelberg (2011)
11. Lee, Y., Lee, Y.: Toward scalable internet traffic measurement and analysis with hadoop. SIGCOMM Comput. Commun. Rev. **43**(1), 5–13 (2012)
12. Mirkovic, J., Reiher, P.: D-ward: a source-end defense against flooding denial-of-service attacks. IEEE Trans. Dependable Secure Comput. **2**(3), 216–232 (2005)
13. Gil, T. M., Poletto, M.: MULTOPS: a datastructure for bandwidth attack detection. In: Proceedings of 10th Usenix Security Symposium, pp. 23–38 (2001)
14. Chou, J., Lin, B., Sen, S., Spatscheck, O.: Proactive surge protection: a defense mechanism for bandwidth-based attacks. IEEE/ACM Trans. Network. **17**(6), 1711–1723 (2009)
15. Gev, Y., Geva, M., Herzberg, A.: Backward traffic throttling to mitigate bandwidth floods. In: Proceedings of Global Communication Conference (GLOBECOME 2012), pp. 904–910 (2012)

16. Savage, S., Wetherall, D., Karlin, A., Anderson, T.: Practical network support for IP traceback. In: SIGCOMM 2000: Proceedings of the Conference on Applications, Technologies, Architectures, and Protocols for Computer Communication, pp. 295–306 (2000)

17. Peng, T., Leckie, C., Ramamohanarao, K.: Adjusted probabilistic packet marking for ip traceback. In: Gregori, E., Conti, M., Campbell, A.T., Omidyar, G., Zukerman, M. (eds.) NETWORKING 2002: Networking Technologies, Services, and Protocols; Performance of Computer and Communication Networks; Mobile and Wireless Communications. LNCS, vol. 2345, pp. 697–708. Springer, Heidelberg (2002)

18. Belenky, A., Ansari, N.: IP traceback with deterministic packet marking. IEEE Commun. Lett. **7**(4), 162–165 (2003)

19. Paruchuri, V., Durresi, A., Chellappan, S.: TTL based packet marking for IP traceback. In: GLOBECOM 2008: Proceedings of the GLOBCOM Conference, pp. 1–5 (2008)

20. Goldstein, M., Lampert, C., Reif, M., Stahl, A. Breuel, T.: Bayes optimal DDOS mitigation by adaptive history-based ip filtering. In: Proceedings of the Seventh International Conference on Networking, pp. 174–179 (2008)

21. Yi, F., Yu, S., Zhou, W., Hai, J., Bonti, A.: Source-based itering scheme against DDOS attacks. Int. J. Database Theory Appl. **1**(1), 9–20 (2008)

22. Jin, C., Wang, H., Shin, K.G.: Hop-count filtering: an effective defense against spoofed DDOS traffic. In: CCS 2003: Proceedings of the 10th ACM Conference on Computer and Communications Security, pp. 30–41 (2003)

23. Weinsberg, U., Shavitt, Y., Schwartz, Y.: Stability and symmetry of internet routing. In: IEEE International Conference on Computer Communications Workshops, pp. 407–408 (2010)

24. Apache. http://hadoop.apache.org/

25. Dean, J., Ghemawat, S.: Mapreduce: simplified data processing on large clusters. In: Proceedings of the 6th Conference on Symposium on Opearting Systems Design & Implementation, vol. 6, pp. 137–149 (2004)

26. T. C. U. D. A. Dataset. http://www.caida.org/data/passive/ddos-20070804_dataset.xml

Author Index